Social Work Administration:
A Resource Book

Edited by
HARRY A. SCHATZ

Council on Social Work Education
345 East 46th Street New York, N.Y. 10017

Preface

Social Work Administration: A Resource Book comes propitiously upon the scene at a time of great change in the social services and social work education. Competent social work leadership is needed, as never before, in administering and revitalizing existing programs and in planning new services. Schools of social work are recognizing their obligation to provide preparation for administrative practice as an essential option in the basic program of professional education for social work.

As a stimulus to curriculum development, the Council on Social Work Education, with a grant from the Edwin Gould Foundation for Children, took on the task of searching out materials for the teaching of social work administration. Through the talents of Dr. Harry A. Schatz, as editor, and with the guidance of a national advisory committee, this volume has been produced. A companion volume of case studies will also be published.

Traditionally, the social work administrator has slowly risen from practitioner ranks to executive responsibilities, with no special preparation for his new tasks. A few have sought special preparation in the doctoral programs offered by a small number of schools of social work. More have tried, through short-term workshops or institutes, to shore up their competence as administrators. But none of this has been enough and all of it has come too late in the educational experience to provide enough administrators for middle-level as well as top management positions in the social welfare field. This is particularly true in the current period when new patterns of interaction between the purveyors and consumers of service call for new approaches at many different levels of program operation to the exercise of leadership and decision making.

In this connection, it is interesting to note that for a number of years the Edwin Gould Foundation has sponsored an institute taught by Harvard Business School faculty at Andover, Massachusetts, for administrators of public and voluntary agencies. Through this experience, the need for increased effort in this area was recognized and the hope for greater cooperation between business schools and schools of social work was expressed.

This book and the volume of case studies that follows open up new possibilities for teaching and learning in the area of social work administration. The articles in this volume are presented within a frame of reference that is well suited but by no means limited to use in graduate schools of social work. The range and balance of the selected materials offer opportunities for a better introduction to social work administration at the undergraduate level. The theories and practice illustrated in the articles and, also, in the cases to be presented in the second volume should, indeed, have bearing on the tasks that face practitioners in all the human service occupations and, thus, be useful in their educational preparation. Both this source book and the companion case book can also be used by agencies for in-service training programs.

The Council on Social Work Education takes pleasure in acknowledging its debt and gratitude to the many people who participated in this project. Dr. Harry Schatz, a skilled practitioner and teacher of the art of administration, carried major responsibility for the conceptual framework and the screening and selection of materials. The excellent results of his work as editor are self-evident. To the Gould Foundation we express our thanks, not alone for the grant that made possible this project but also for the encouragement, advice, and participation of Mr. Schuyler M. Meyer, Jr., President, and Mr. Samuel B. Ross, Jr., Director of Program Planning Development.

Finally, the Council is deeply grateful to the Advisory Committee which constituted a great reservoir of experience, talent, and wisdom in the teaching and practice of social work administration. The participation of committee members in advisory meetings together with their individual contributions of materials and guidance in the course of the project enabled the editor and project director to move with confidence through a bewildering maze of theories and documents towards this final collection of materials.

To each of the members of the Committee, who of course bear no responsibility for any shortcomings of the volume, we express our thanks: Fred DelliQuadri, University of Wisconsin, Milwaukee, Chairman; C. Wilson Anderson, University of North Carolina; Mrs. Sarah Short Austin, Westinghouse Learning Corporation; Bertram H. Gould, American Jewish Committee; Laurin Hyde, Laurin Hyde Associates; Avis Kristenson, Columbia University; Arthur H. Kruse, Community Fund of Chicago; Schuyler M. Meyer, Jr., Edwin Gould Foundation; David Hawkins, Harvard University; Mrs. Beulah Rothman, Adelphi University; Rosemary C. Sarri, University of Michigan; Bernard Shiffman, Human Resources Administration, New York; Sue Spencer, University of Tennessee; Samuel Whitman, Case Western Reserve University.

The Resource Book is now ready for the test of use. It is the hope of the Council on Social Work Education and all who have been associated with it that it will adequately serve the purpose of stimulating more effective preparation of social workers for administrative responsibilities and practice.

Katherine A. Kendall
Project Director

V

VII

Introduction

NEED FOR EDUCATION IN SOCIAL WORK ADMINISTRATION

Social welfare services, including both governmental and voluntary agencies, constitute a major sector of our socio-economic life in America. In terms of the vast numbers of people served, the gigantic sums of money expended, the increasing numbers of people employed, it is comparable in size and complexity to our largest industries. Social welfare services are essential to the well-being of our American society.

The keystone for optimum efficiency and effectiveness in the achievement of social work goals in a changing society is the *administration* of social work programs. Such programs may be under public or voluntary auspices. Their scope may be broad or narrow. Their supporting or operating structures may be large or small in scale. Nevertheless, the quality and nature of their administration determine in large measure both the potential for and the realization of their success.[1]

Rapid expansion of programs within social work agencies and the formation of a multiplicity of new social welfare programs and services outside of the traditional framework contribute to the growing need for educationally prepared social work administrators who can make these programs effective instruments for the amelioration of social conditions and for the solution of social problems.

More and more graduates of social work schools and social work practitioners move rapidly into supervisory and administrative positions for which they require more adequate educational preparation.

The recognition of this vital need is evidenced by the growth of curriculum in social work administration in schools of social work and by the extensive executive development programs sponsored by leading national social welfare agencies in cooperation with a number of universities. There is also increased recognition of the need for sound orientation to social work administration on the part of professional social workers who provide direct service to individuals, groups, and communities.

KNOWLEDGE BASE OF SOCIAL WORK ADMINISTRATION

The knowledge base of social work administration draws from many disciplines and fields: the theory and practice of social work; behavioral science; eocnomic, political, and social science; and business and public administration.

The social work administrator must have knowledge of social work philosophy and concepts and practice, especially in those areas in which his agency operates. From the

---

[1] Council on Social Work Administration, "Social Work Administration — A Framework for Advancing Knowledge and Practice" (New York: National Association of Social Workers, 1967).

1

behavioral sciences he needs to know how and why individuals act and feel, especially in relation to their functioning in groups. Specific knowledge is required of role theory, small-group theory, the use of relationships, communication, and decision-making in an administrative setting. Political and social science provide knowledge of the cultural, social, economic, and political forces that constitute the local, national, and international communities out of which social problems evolve and from which must be drawn the human and economic resources for providing social services and solving social problems. Likewise, the requisite knowledge of organizational theory and the process of decision-making affecting institutional changes and agency operations are derived from the social sciences.

From public and business administration as well as from social work comes the knowledge concerning organization and processes that is especially essential for the social work administrator, whether he functions in a government or a voluntary agency. The social work administrator needs technical knowledge for effective internal management of the agency, including budgeting process, financial operations and control, purchasing and property management, personnel administration, service and financial records systems for reports, evaluation, and accountability.

Although the social work administrator need not be expert in all these areas, he must have an adequate working knowledge of them to know what data he requires to make intelligent decisions regarding their application to his agency and the personnel required for technical and professional services.[2]

OBJECTIVES OF *SOCIAL WORK ADMINISTRATION: A RESOURCE BOOK*

This resource book seeks to strengthen the teaching and learning of social work administration by selecting, assembling and making readily available pertinent ideas, concepts and experiences from the diverse but related fields of knowledge in social work, business and public administration, psychology, sociology and political science.

This volume is initially designed for use in the curriculum of graduate schools of social work. However, it can also be productively utilized at other levels of social work education: in undergraduate programs of administration orientation, in seminars and institutes for practicing administrators and in advanced executive development programs.

FORMAT AND SELECTION OF READINGS

The vast and growing literature related to the various aspects of administration presents a formidable challenge in selecting the most appropriate and useful material. Not only are the sources diverse, but they constitute different frames of reference with varying emphases and sometimes conflicting viewpoints.

The selection of materials from various "schools" of administration theory and practice is purposefully eclectic to indicate the various matrices from which administration knowledge has evolved and the multiple directions in which it is moving. This provides flexible use of the readings according to the teacher's own perspective and the educational needs of the students.

Many desirable writings which could not be encompassed within the limits of this volume have been included in the Selective Bibliography at the end of the book.

The readings have been assembled in several broad categories to facilitate their accessibility for use according to the reader's interest and needs. Some readings inevitably contain material related to two or more categories. The designation of each selection for a particular category is based on the arbitrary judgment of the editor.

---

[2] *Ibid.*

Section I: *Overview of Administration Theory* directs attention to broad perspectives of administration theory and concepts from the varying vantage points of social work, public administration, business management, and political and social science.

Section II: *Organizational Structure* is concerned primarily with the formal structure of organization and the problems of bureaucracy.

Section III: *Administration Processes* deals with administration as a series of processes and also focuses on some particular processes.

Section IV: *Man-In-Administration* moves into the human relations aspects of administration involving individuals and groups of people.

Section V: *Environment* reflects the growing awareness in recent years that the viability and effectiveness of an organization is determined in large measure by factors external to the organization. Rapidly changing social, economic, and political developments can render a social agency's services or methods outmoded or can alter direction and nature of its program to meet new needs or different priorities.

The multiplicity of interrelated social welfare organizations in both the public and private sectors with direct and indirect connection has created an interdependence in which changes in one agency influences the operation of others on local, regional and national levels. Thus administration requires a bi-focal perspective—internally within the organization and externally to the social, economic, and political environment.

Finally, Section VI: *Budget and Finance* deals with the economic aspects of social work administration and its relationship to planning, programming, and people.

IN APPRECIATION

Social Work Administration: A Resource Book is seen as a step forward in the development of instruments and programs that will advance the knowledge and practice of social work administration. The vital contributions to this endeavor by the authors whose writings are contained in this volume are self-evident. The wise guidance of Dr. Katherine Kendall, director of the CSWE Project on Social Work Administration, and the encouragement of Dr. Arnulf M. Pins, executive director of the Council on Social Work Education, were invaluable.

I. Overview

Social Work Administration

HERMAN STEIN

ADMINISTRATION

Definitions of administration abound, but central to those most accepted currently is the concept of administration as a process of defining and attaining the objectives of an organization through a system of coordinated and cooperative effort.

This concept stresses the administrative process, not just the responsibilities of management; defining objectives, which connotes the need to modify and reshape them, to be conscious of goals, and not to take them for granted; reaching these objectives, described as the central responsibility of management and the underlying raison d'etre of administrative process, the latter not then being an end in itself; involvement of people and their contributions in a planned pattern of cooperation, rather than administration being the activities of the executive group only.

While knowledge of administrative theory and practice has traditionally been seen as essential equipment of the executive or managerial group, practitioners in social work are now recognized to need an understanding of administrative principles in order to make the most effective use of their professional competence. Social work as it is carried on through organizations is not basically an entrepreneurial profession. How the social work organization is administered (whether the agency engages only in social work activity, or places social work as one department within a larger organization) makes it either more or less possible for social workers to render, and clients and community to receive, optimum service. Moreover, when administration is regarded as a system of cooperative effort, the stake of all staff members is considerable, not only in managerial competence but also in making their own appropriate contribution to administrative process.

The knowledge base of administration in social work, as elsewhere, is not confined to any one field of activity or to any one discipline. Efforts to systematize such knowledge are made by drawing on the social and behavioral sciences, on political science and public administration, and on the experience of industry, government, and non-social work voluntary organizations, as well as on the specific experience of social work agencies.

Orientations to Administrative Theory

Four major orientations may be differentiated in the history of administrative theory and research:

1. *Efficiency*. The emphasis on efficiency principles stems from a scientific, engineering approach to finding the most rational way to do whatever job has to be done, in terms of minimum cost, less time, and highest productivity. Concern for efficiency, incorporating those skills and techniques developed to achieve optimum efficiency and productivity, is an important principle in sound management, not only in industry but

Reprinted with permission of the National Association of Social Workers and the author, from Encyclopedia of Social Work, *Harry L. Lurie,* ed. *(New York: National Association of Social Workers, 1965), pp. 58-62.*

7

in all fields of management. This concern is being increasingly manifested in social work agencies with the growing appreciation of costs per interview hour or other definable units of service. Attention to efficiency concepts has contributed to the use of labor-saving machinery, routinization of mechanical operations, more effective use of trained and untrained manpower, and more economical arrangement of office equipment and flow of work.

A mechanistic approach to economy has, however, severe drawbacks when human factors are ignored. When an efficiency approach is magnified as an end in itself, serious consequences may ensue in the form of low staff morale, limited capacity of staff to develop, ebbing of organizational vitality and initiative, and deterioration of the very efficiency and productivity presumably sought. Concern with efficiency need not, however, conflict with concern for people in an organization or those served by it.

2. *Administrative management.* The administrative management theorists and planners have strongly influenced not only public administration but all large-scale organizations. It is they who have been concerned with such concepts as coordination, span of control, executive functions, decentralization, line and staff organization, and the organization chart itself. The major contributions in this orientation include rational blueprinting of organizational systems and objective analysis of administrative process. From the writings of these authorities and the wide experience based on their teachings one learns such principles as unity of direction and command, planning and coordination, defining roles and functions, and detecting, then reducing, communication gaps and overlapping responsibilities. Systematic and logical organization of both governmental and voluntary social agencies originates largely from the traditions that scientific management developed in this school.

The premise has become subject to question, however, that if all is rationally planned and conceived, then all will necessarily be well with an organization and its personnel. Additional approaches to administration have become necessary to take into account the complexities of relationship and motivation and the nonrational aspects of organizational behavior.

3. *Work groups.* The emphasis on interrelationships among work groups and supervisors and their consequences for productivity and morale has grown out of psychological and sociological research undertaken widely in industry and more recently in governmental agencies. Morale studies in industry have been considerably refined since those initiated by Elton Mayo and the ones pioneered by Western Electric. Such studies led to sharp emphasis on the "human relations" aspects of management, the significance of relationships among members of working groups, and the effects of such relationships on productivity. Some authorities have come to feel that the human relations concern itself became overdone, with too much reliance being put on job satisfaction as an end in itself. Nevertheless, the general approach and studies in this field have been most fruitful, and continue to enlarge the perspective of management and staff in the relationship between productivity and morale and in supervision work-group relationships. Such research—which has recently demonstrated that the relationship between employee satisfaction and productivity is more complicated than had originally been thought—has striking implications for social work administration, particularly in analyzing supervisor-staff roles and in defining and enhancing productivity in many areas of social work activity.

4. *Bureaucracy.* Bureaucratic theory, concerned with both formal and informal organization and nonrational aspects of administration, has become a major resource in understanding organizational problems. In the social sciences, the term bureaucracy has no invidious connotation. It refers to an organization characterized by relatively large size, departmentalization with special offices and functions, hierarchical arrangement of authority, and written or well-understood policies, regulations, and procedures. This

form of organization is considered indispensable to the large-scale production and distribution of goods and services, including social work services. All governmental agencies and large voluntary agencies in which social workers are employed are bureaucracies in this sense.

As a rational, consciously designed form of organization, bureaucracy depends for its most effective functioning upon planned coordination, clarity in its policies, specificity in the roles of all who are part of the organizational system, and objectivity and impersonality in the discharge of its functions. The potential assets particularly compatible with this form of organization are economy and efficiency, stability, role clarity, job security, fairness for staff and clientele in the execution of policies and procedures. At the same time there are inherent potential weaknesses: tendencies toward ritualism, where means become ends; overconformity; lack of adaptability to change; depersonalization of the client or consumer of service.

Implications of Organizational Theory

Understanding these potential weaknesses has led to a concern with mitigating or preventing them while maximizing the essential assets of large-scale formal organization; for these are not inevitable weaknesses, but the kind to which bureaucracies are most vulnerable. One central principle in applying countermeasures is that they should themselves be consistent with bureaucratic organization—that is, the countermeasures should be rational and official, help maintain specificity of roles, clarify procedures, and enhance impartiality. To prevent ritualism, for example, policies and procedures are being developed that make it possible for personnel to be well-oriented to the central objectives of the organization, to identify with these objectives, and to see how their functions relate to those of everyone else. Orientation of new staff, general meetings of staff, annual reports, and interdepartmental meetings are some of the more common devices. A well-administered agency should also encourage new ideas, individual initiative, and imagination. Above all, however, the supervisory chain of command is crucial in easing bureaucratic strains. Only through appropriate evaluation and supervisory process can nonritualistic behavior be rewarded and the channels provided for people to contribute initiative and ideas that will enhance service and organizational effectiveness.

Bureaucracy requires policies and regulations but also ways of individualizing when necessary. Provision should be made to centralize responsibility during exceptional situations or emergencies that lie outside existing policy and procedures. Large organizations do change and do adapt to different conditions. How much this adaptability is a passive response to external factors or how much it is planned as the organization attempts to control its own destiny depends heavily on the location of planning responsibility and the extent to which the agency can tap all its creative resources.

A "democratic" spirit in agency practice does not connote an equal voice in planning on the part of everybody who is in the agency. What is possible is to capitalize on the understanding, ideas, and motivations of all in an organization, according to their special competence and their special interests, through relevant participation. It thus becomes necessary to think of ways to build into the administrative process patterns of participation that would elicit whatever those in the agency have to contribute out of their legitimate functions, experience, and organizational interests. This can be true whether one is dealing with budget planning, locating new problems to be met by the agency, or devising approaches to meet existing conditions.

The concept of relevant participation is not the same as "giving people the feeling that they are participating." Specious involvement to give the illusion of participation leads to cynicism and is essentially self-defeating. The concept gaining acceptance is to maintain at all times appropriate channels for raising questions related to work problems of staff at any level of the organization. In effect, this approach seeks systematic evaluation of work tasks, procedures, and relationships and recognizes this process administratively as desired behavior without having the executive branch of the organization abdicate its authority for making managerial decisions.

By virtue of training and orientation, social workers are well aware of personality traits that enhance or diminish administrative competence. Social agencies are becoming increasingly conscious, however, of the importance of understanding the effects of different forms of agency organization and structure, not only in relation to staff performance but also to the service the agency performs. Whether in a child guidance clinic, a neighborhood center, a home for the aged, or a hospital social service department, the consequences of agency structure will be felt. With persistent attention an alert agency can adapt its structure as conditions change and can analyze administrative difficulties, not only in terms of personality attributes or shortcomings of given individuals, but also in terms of organizational arrangements—size of the agency, intake procedure, numbers of clientele, physical arrangements, organizational roles, supervisory systems, and the like.

Understanding different orientations in administrative theory suggests not only sources of principle and practice, but research needs in social agency administration (some of which have begun to be addressed), such as the following:

- To develop means for gauging the effectiveness of agency services, which in turn requires defining agency objectives in terms that can be objectively assessed.
- To develop means for determining acceptable standards of quality of service in relation to productivity, for those agencies rendering direct services.
- To develop comparative studies of agency organization in order to evaluate the consequences of different structures and administrative patterns.

Components of the Social Agency System Board. Whether under voluntary or government auspices, all social agencies have governing bodies that are ultimately responsible for policy. In the case of voluntary agencies, the governing body is a board of directors that recruits and elects its own members under its own system. Voluntary agencies, though chartered by governmental (usually state) authorities, operate under constitutions and bylaws of their own devising. The legal responsibility for the conduct of the agency rests with the board, which has the power to appoint or remove the executive, and is presumed to take responsibility for all major policies, including fiscal policy, personnel policy, and the general functions of the agency.

The governing bodies of social agencies are usually entrusted to represent the interests of the community being served. This may or (more frequently) may not mean that all major segments of the community are actually represented on the board, although many voluntary agencies have attempted to expand the base of board membership to include diverse economic and ethnic representation.

Executive. The executive of a social agency is responsible to the board or governing body for the execution of policies to which the agency, through the board, is committed. His essential functions are to represent the best interests of the agency and to take responsibility for the managerial processes of planning, organizing, staffing, coordinating, reporting, budgeting, and research. This of course does not mean that the executive has to accomplish all these tasks himself or give them technical supervision. The larger the organization, the more will specialized staff be involved in carrying on these functions. Ultimately, however, the executive is responsible for the character of all of these operations and for supervising them.

Personnel. Agency personnel are responsible to the executive, either directly or through a supervisory chain of command, where this exists. The larger the agency, the more will series of intervening supervisory and subexecutive levels pyramid toward the executive. In

10

some social agencies, personnel, including professional personnel, are organized; wages and hours, as well as other personnel practices, are subject to negotiations between the union and agency management. Those agency workers who are directly involved in rendering the service or services for which the agency is designed or who directly supervise such services are referred to as being in line positions. Those who are in positions that enable the line workers to get their jobs done but who are not directly involved in services (e.g., accounting departments, public relations departments) are termed to be in staff positions.

While the essential responsibilities of governing bodies, executives, and personnel of the social agencies may be thus briefly delineated, in the course of agency life many problems can arise in translating these responsibilities into practice. Executives may find themselves determining basic policy decisions, which should be the board's to make. Boards may encroach on professional terrain by becoming involved in technical matters that belong in the province of executive decision (e.g., in some institutions for the aged, board members themselves continue to do intake even when trained social workers are employed). In larger organizations, particularly in urban centers, staff may have little knowledge of board functions or of its composition. On the other hand, many executives view as part of their duties acquainting staff members as directly as possible with the board of the agency and helping both groups understand the function of the other. Conflicts may also arise between what professional personnel see as their professional interests and the interests of the agency itself. Part of the executive's task is to balance the agency's internal needs and the demands on personnel to be concerned with agency interests per se (a "local" orientation) with the needs of professional personnel for identification with the wider profession as well (a "cosmopolitan" orientation).

The total social agency system, however, is composed of more than a governing body, executive, and personnel. It encompasses clientele, other agencies, contributors, councils and chests of social agencies, social work professional groups, other professional bodies and disciplines, and governmental and non-governmental bodies directly or indirectly interacting with the agency.

Governmental social agencies, incorporated as they are within larger governmental organizations, are subject to decisions and influences over which they may have little control. Voluntary agencies through their relationships to central fund-raising and planning bodies, sources of financial support, and referrals are similarly limited in the range of decision open to them. It is the executive who is most centrally charged with being sensitive to the attitudes, needs, and wishes of these extra-agency components in the agency administrative system. The public relations policy for which the executive is responsible is designed to sustain the agency's interests and further its objectives in relation to these various publics.

The current trend is that executives of social work agencies should themselves be social workers, in order to be able to represent the best interests of the agency. Being a qualified social worker, however, does not of itself insure administrative competence; special training and experience are increasingly required to meet the demands of executive responsibilities. Since social work administration has become recognized as a field of practice, most schools of social work now include at least one course in this subject in the basic master's curriculum; advanced programs usually offer a major in this area.

While training in administrative management in social welfare should be part of the executive's preparation, all social workers who will eventually be working in organizations should be well-oriented to the administrative process. This will enhance their own capacity to contribute to the agency and to accept their responsibilities within the system of cooperative effort.

The Management Theory Jungle Revisited

DONALD AUSTIN WOOLF

WHAT IS A THEORY OF MANAGEMENT?

The term "theory" often seems to conjure up impressions of mystery and impracticality to managers and students of management alike. Indeed, in discussions of theory, one sometimes gets the impression tha people feel that a *theory* is impractical by definition. The phrase which frequently expresses this sentiment is, "Well, that may be all right in *theory*, but it will never work in *practice.*" One of the reasons for this common belief is that some of our previously held theories have been found unworkable; therefore, we are suspicious of the potential utility of present theory.

However, to generalize from prior unfortunate experience to the extent that *all* theory is rejected as a waste of time is to miss the point of having theory at all. A theory is an explanation of *why* something happens, and, sometimes, *how* something happens, as well as a statement of *what* happens. A good theory provides us with a reasonably reliable means of prediction. Because of this, there is by definition no such thing as a theory that is "all right" as a theory, but not "all right" in practice. If a theory is demonstrably unworkable in practice, then it ceases to have value as a theory.

* * *

We can propose a definition, viz., *organization refers to a group of people who have established patterns of authority, communication, and responsibility relating to the achievement of a common goal or goals.*

The determination of these assignments and relationships is not automatic. *The process of delineation of lines of authority, patterns of communication, and task assignment, as well as allocation of resources to achieve organizational goals is called management.* The central problem of constructing a theory of management and organization is to determine what authority is, how it ought to be distributed in the organization, the "best" patterns of communication, and the "best" allocation of resources to achieve organizational goals. In short, the purpose of management theory is not just to find a methodology that will work, but a method that will work better than any other.

* * *

TWO APPROACHES TO MANAGEMENT THEORY

Most theories of management found in recent textbooks and other writings in the field are eclectic, that is, their component parts are drawn from a variety of sources and points

Reprinted from Advanced Management Journal, *Vol. 30, No. 4 (October, 1965),pp. 6-15, by permission of the* Advanced Management Journal.

12

of view. However, it is possible to isolate and identify a number of "schools" of thought which have been incorporated into current composite theory. Although there are a number of different ways of classifying the contributions made by various authors dealing with the subject, the analysis here is going to be in terms of the following:

1. Is the theory (or subsystem) primarily directed toward identification and solution of mechanical problems of internal structure and operation or is it directed toward the human problems of organizational members and clientele?
2. Is the theory essentially descriptive, and is it developed primarily through deductive reasoning, or is it primarily analytical, incorporating inductive or experimental methodology?[1]

Generally speaking, most contemporary writers tend to use the dichotomy suggested by the first question, that is, is the theory organization-centered or is it person-centered? Organization-centered theory is sometimes identified as the "principles of management" school, while person-centered theory is summarized under the title of "human relations." However, it is noteworthy that both schools of thought include early theorists who relied primarily on description, deduction, and the assumption of a number of postulates, or axioms. Both schools also include theorists whose contributions are much more experimentally oriented, and tend to exclude untested principles or beliefs.

In the light of these considerations, we can construct a fourfold framework for the classification of theory, namely:

    I. Organization-Centered Theory
       A. Descriptive, deductive
       B. Analytical, inductive, experimental

   II. Person-Centered Theory
       A. Descriptive, deductive
       B. Analytical, inductive, experimental

THE ORGANIZATION-CENTERED APPROACH: DESCRIPTIVE THEORY

Most of the early attempts to define management were primarily concerned with the. . .activities of managers, and with attributes of organizational structure which would facilitate the achievement of organizational goals. This kind of theory is constructed via two means. One method is to observe one or more "successful" organizations, and try to describe and classify the apparent activities which lead to this success. The other is to attempt to deduce or hypothesize the appropriate logical solution to an organizational problem.

---

[1] This difference in approach may appear purely academic. Perhaps its importance may be illustrated by reference to the disparate findings, respectively, of Aristotle and Galileo about the behavior of falling bodies. Aristotle, relying on description and deduction, stated that heavier objects fall at a faster rate than comparatively lighter ones (they do not): Galileo, who experimented with this phenomenon, found that objects (in this case of the same density, in the atmosphere) fall at the same rate, regardless of weight.

Perhaps the most prominent of the early writers of this school is Henri Fayol.[2] In general, his theory is descriptive rather than analytical, and tends toward the use of deductive reasoning rather than experimental evidence. Fayol's writing is consistent with the general pattern of most of those who have written since his time. He proposed essential activities of goal setting (planning), determination of authority relationships and task assignment (organizing), and maintenance of communications (commanding, coordinating, and controlling) applied to functional areas of marketing, finance, controllership, technical problems (such as production), and security (safeguarding of property and persons).[3]

Although subsequent authors have proposed moderate variations in defining the activities and functions which are associated with the practice of management, the general approach has not been changed materially since Fayol's time.[4] After identifying the major activities and functions, the typical author utilizing this approach will propose "principles" for their proper execution, such principles being based on deductive logic and observation.[5]

This approach is usually referred to as the "principles of management" school, and less frequently, as the "management process"[6] or "administrative process" school.[7] The

---

[2] See, for example, Henri Fayol, *General and Industrial Management* (London: Sir Isaac Pitman & Sons, 1949). This pioneer in management conceived and practiced many of his ideas before the turn of the twentieth century; however, these ideas were not new by any means. Numerous examples of pre-Christian writings about management subjects may be found, such as Kautilya's *Arthasastra,* translated by T.N. Ramaswamy in *Essentials of Indian Statecraft* (London: Asia Publishing House, 1962), Plato's *Republic* (New York: Modern Library, 1941), and in the Old Testament. More recently, Gibbons' *Decline and Fall of the Roman Empire* (New York: Modern Library, n.d.) and Niccolo Machiavelli's *The Prince* (New York: Random House, 1937), all treat with familiar management topics such as the chain of command, the span of control, and the specialization of labor.

[3] See Fayol, *op. cit.,* pp. 3-6. In the Storrs translation, the term "activities" is used to refer to both management action *and* functional areas such as finance, etc. More recent authors tend to use the term "functions" to refer to both. Cf. Harld Koontz and Cyril O'Donnell, *op.cit.,* pp. 35-38, and Theo Haimann, *Professional Management* (Boston: Houghton-Mifflin, 1962). In the former work, management "Functions" of planning, organizing, staffing, etc., are defined on pp. 35-38, while "functions" of production, sales, finance, and merchandising are discussed on pp. 101-196 and 147-154. Similarly, Haimann uses the same term to describe the two different concepts on pp. 22-25, pp. 156-161, and 219ff. For purposes of clarity and internal consistency, the present author will use "activities" to denote planning, organizing, communicating, controlling, and related managerial actions, and the term "functions" to refer to finance, marketing, production, and similar operational reguirements.

[4] Most texts today use the familiar planning, organizing, staffing, directing, and controlling sequence of activities. See, for example, Theo Haimann, *op. cit.,* and Koontz and O'Donnell, *op. cit.*

[5] The comparison implied here is with the methodology of Taylor, or with that of the experimentally oriented behavioral scientists, some of whose works may be found in Dorwin Cartwright and Alvin Zander, eds., *Group Dynamics,* 2nd ed. (Evanston, Ill.: Row, Peterson, 1953).

[6] See William Newman, Charles Summer, and E. Kirby Warren, *The Process of Management,* 2nd ed. (Englewood Cliffs, N.J.: Prentice-Hall, Inc., 1967).

[7] Edward H. Litchfield, "Notes on a General Theory of Administration," *Administrative Science Quarterly,* Vol. I, No. 1 (June, 1956), pp. 3-29.

kinds of activities treated by the various authors utilizing this approach suggest that this theory is primarily directed toward the problems and practices of top management. However, managers also have the problem of making their plans operational, and need specific guides to action in addition to general principles. These specific guides have to be developed according to the needs of the particular individual enterprise. This kind of thinking resulted in the emergence of an analytical school of theory, sometimes called "scientific management."

THE ORGANIZATION-CENTERED APPROACH: ANALYTICAL METHODOLOGY

At about the same time that Fayol was attempting to generalize from his managerial experience in order to construct some sort of theory of management, Frederick Taylor and a number of his contemporaries and associates attempted to apply some of the experimental methodology derived from the physical sciences to problems of management. Taylor's attention and findings are directed primarily toward the problems of production management rather than top management, and his proposals pertaining to managerial activities and organizational structure constitute more of a byproduct of his work rather than the main object of it. However, a most important result of his work has been the inculcation of a healthy skepticism about the *status quo* on the part of many people in management positions, and the seeking of new uses for tools such as accounting, mathematics, and, especially, motion and time study.

The experimental approach to the logistical problems of management came to be known as "Scientific Management," and consisted primarily of systematically varying the physical factors in a given situation in order to find the "one best way" of achieving the organizational objective. The factors with which exponents of this methodology experimented were obtained by splitting any process into irreducible parts or actions. This resulted in rather minute specialization of labor and a splitting of authority giving rise to a need for careful coordination, as well as for improved methods of quality control.

*   *   *

AN OVERVIEW OF THE ORGANIZATION-CENTERED APPROACH

In attempting to place in perspective the schools known, respectively, as management process and scientific management,. . .we have found that the former is primarily directed toward considerations of *why* something is done, and *what* is done, while the latter is more concerned with *how* it should be done.

*   *   *

Implied or explicitly stated by the exponents of organization-centered theory is the proposition that people inherently are not prone to serve the goals of organizations, that is, that they are inclined to be lazy, and that subordinates are not intelligent enough to make substantial contributions even when their intentions are good. This is. . .why authority must be from the top down, in this frame of reference.

In summary, the organization-centered approach is primarily directed toward. . .the optimum utilization of all available resources to achieve organizational goals. In this context labor is treated as a commodity or factor of production, a circumstance which was distressing to some contemporaries of Taylor and Fayol as well as to some current observers.

15

THE PERSON-CENTERED APPROACH:
DESCRIPTIVE THEORY

Following a rather thorough Congressional investigation of the prevailing modes of management just prior to World War I, at least one able exponent suggested that organizations generally should be more concerned with people than they had been.[8] The reasons *why* we should be more concerned with people were (and are) twofold, and are both moral and practical in nature. Firstly, our methods of operating organizations should be consistent with national goals and beliefs concerning enhancement and development of the individual.

Secondly, it was proposed that people whose environment provided this enhancement and development would be happier, and happy people would make greater contributions to the organization. However, popular acknowledgment and some acceptance of this view do not appear to have occurred until after the publishing of *Management and the Worker* and *The Functions of the Executive* in the late 1930's.[9] Of these latter two works, Barnard suggested that the way people feel about what they do *should* affect their propensity to cooperate with management, and Roethlisberger and Dickson showed that it *did*. These two works are also illustrative of the description-analysis dichotomy proposed here as a tool for analysis of existing management theory. Barnard, and, for that matter, Follett, are illustrative of the descriptive approach, utilizing stated assumptions, and developing their argument primarily through deductive logic.

Although the methods utilized in the Hawthorne experiments by Roethlisberger and Dickson are now considered comparatively primitive, this series of studies is illustrative of the analytical or experimental school, discussed below.

Person-centered theory, whether of a descriptive or an analytical nature, is usually called "human relations." The full impact of this approach was not felt until after World War II, when courses relating to this subject began to appear in the catalogues of colleges of business and appropriate texts were published.

Descriptive person-centered theory provides a number of fairly radical departures from organization-centered theory, particularly in the area of authority. In general, early theorists—whether speaking from the perspective of government, the Roman church, the military, or business—postulated that the proper and *de facto* locus of authority is at the top of the organizational hierarchy.

However, as popular sovereignty gained favor as a theory of government and Protestantism challenged the position held by the Roman church, so Follett, Barnard, and more recent writers such as Simon and McGregor proposed that the proper and *de facto* of authority—and, indeed the origin, in a sense—was at the base of the organization rather than at the top.[10] Within this context of reasoning, leadership ultimately depends upon at least minimal acceptance of authority on the part of the led, and organizational goals must be mutually acceptable rather than imposed from the top. However, both Barnard and Simon readily agree that the level of acceptance may only consist of indifference to a particular action rather than fervent agreement with it. In other words, subordinates

---

[8] Henry C. Metcalf and Lyndall Urwick, eds. *Dynamic Administration: The Collected Papers of Mary Parker Follett* (New York: Harper & Row, Publishers, 1942).

[9] Fritz J. Roethlisberger and William J. Dickson, *Management and the Worker* (Cambridge: Harvard University Press, 1939); and Chester J. Barnard, *The Functions of the Executive* (Cambridge: Harvard University Press, 1938).

[10] Herbert A. Simon, *Administrative Behavior,* 2nd ed. (New York: The Macmillan Company, 1957); see also Douglas McGregor, *The Human Side of Enterprise* (New York: McGraw-Hill, 1960).

normally do what is asked of them because it is not objectionable, rather than doing what is asked of them because they enjoy it.[11]

A second departure from earlier theory is the disagreement of person-centered theorists with the concept of "economic man," that is, the dual concept of labor as a commodity or factor of production as well as the hypothesis that laborers are motivated primarily by personal economic gain. The dissenting view holds that the employer does *not* merely hire a hand; . . .a whole human being is attached to the part needed for the job. Moreover, the needs of this human being are considerably broader in scope than is suggested by the concept of economic man, and the entire environment—not merely the economic environment—must be considered by the organization requiring his services.[12]

Many of the writings which may be associated with this school of thought tend to use the vocabulary and are addressed to the problems associated with the organization-centered approach, and particularly the descriptive branch of that approach. For example, the writings of Simon and those of Argyris are directed toward and critical of such ideas as the span of control, the specialization of labor, and the chain of command.[13] By contrast, *experimentalists* using the person-centered approach tend not to use the postulates of more traditional theory as a point of departure.[14]

In summary, exponents of the descriptive variety of person-centered theory postulate an ethical position, viz., that organizations ought to demonstrate more interest in workers as people (rather than as factors of production), and hypothesize that such interest will result in happier workers as well as more production. Correlated with this position is the proposal that authority ought to— and does logically—originate at the base of the organization rather than at the top. These positions have been challenged not only by firm adherents to organization-centered theory, but also by some experimentally minded behavioral scientists.

THE PERSON-CENTERED APPROACH:
EXPERIMENTATION

Two central questions raised by the experimentalists may be summarized as follows:

1. Does the nature of the work environment, including supervision, composition of the work group, task assignment, method of compensation, and other working conditions result in measurable differences in employee attitudes?
2. Do differences in employee attitudes result in differences in productivity?

. . . For the most part, behavioral scientists engaged in these kinds of research have not utilized the vocabulary of the more traditional schools of thought, but have borrowed mainly from the fields of psychology, anthropology, sociology, and psychiatry. As a result, their findings often do not relate directly to the traditional "principles" of management and organization, but are supplementary to or different from these principles.

---

[11] Barnard, *op. cit.,* pp. 167-175; Simon, *op. cit.,* p. 116.

[12] For a summary of this point of view, see Temple Burling, *You Can't Hire a Hand and Other Essays,* Extension Bulletin No. 2 (Ithaca, N.Y.: New York State School of Industrial and Labor Relations, Cornell University, n.d.).

[13] Simon, *op. cit.,* Chapters 1 and 2; Chris Argyris, *Personality and Organization* (New York: Harper & Row, Publishers, 1957), Chapter 3.

[14] See Robert Tennenbaum, Irving R. Weschler and Fred Massarik, *Leadership and Organization* (New York: McGraw-Hill, 1961), particularly the Preface and Chapter 1.

Generally speaking, findings of those in this school indicate that the nature of the work environment has a definite effect on employee attitudes. However, the evidence concerning the relationship between attitudes and productivity has been inconclusive.[15] More precisely, only about half of the studies demonstrate a positive relationship between favorable job attitudes and productivity, while the balance shows either no correlation or a negative relationship.

Research tools employed in this kind of research range from observation of existing work groups to the creation of experimental groups and the utilization of instruments designed to measure social interaction, attitudes, aptitudes, and abilities of group members, as well as the nature and frequency of communications. In some respects, the overall point of view of the person-centered experimentalist is not substantially different from the organization-centered experimentalist. The major difference between these two schools is the object of research. In the case of the earlier school, represented by adherents to scientific management, the focus of attention is directed toward utilization of physical assets; the person-centered experimentalists are almost exclusively interested in the human problems of management.

* * *

Among the differences between these two approaches is the fact that the older, organization-centered approach is more-or-less self-prescribing, that is, it tells one in general or specific terms what to do and, sometimes, when and how to do it. Lacking this in some instances, it tells one how to find out what to do, when to do it, and how to do it. By contrast, the person-centered approach tends either to be primarily negative on the one hand, or fragmentary on the other. For this reason, the established community of organizations has not put into practice the "principles" of human relations, because the principles are either elusive or nonexistent.

Moreover, most of the research of the person-centered exponents has been directed toward either small groups or individuals, and may be of little immediate practical use to the organization of more than, say, 10,000 persons. In addition, this approach is comparatively silent about many of the problems of management. It was stated previously in this paper that a good theory should explain a phenomenon in terms of what happens, why it happens, and how it happens. The person-centered approach, by definition, fails to do this for many of the necessary functions and activities of management. In other words, it will not tell you how to set up an assembly line, nor how to organize a retail establishment.

---

[15] For a summary of research and findings on this point, see Frederick Herzbert *et al.*, *Job Attitudes* (Pittsburgh: Psychological Service of Pittsburgh, 1957), Chapters 3 and 4.

Some Views of the Study
of Social Welfare Administration

EDWARD E. SCHWARTZ

Studies of social welfare administration, such as investigations of the need for service, may be considered to be among the earliest forms of social work research.[1] Yet, considering historical priority and present potential, there has been remarkably little discussion in the literature of social work on research in administration. At present there is some interest in reviewing and developing this field of activity. The purpose of this paper is to provide an aid to discussion by setting down some of the ways of viewing the study of social welfare administration — considering study primarily as research but also as preparation for practice.

ADMINISTRATIVE SCIENCE
AND ADMINISTRATIVE MANAGEMENT

The term "administration" is generally used to refer both to an area of study and to an area of practice. As an area of study, says Waldo, administration is a science; as an area of practice, it is an art.[2] This is a useful distinction for our purposes. It will also be useful to open up the application of the term "study" by recognizing that administration is studied not only as a science, but also as an art or technology and, some say, as a profession.

In summarizing his survey of the study of administration since the eighteenth century, Malator concludes that a major feature is ". . . the impressive development of university teaching of administrative science in all parts of the world during the last 30 years or more. This progress is taking place as much in the European countries as in the African and Asian countries, as well as, of course, in America. It appears to be most developed in the United States."[3]

Administration as a respectable subject for academic study is of comparatively recent origin. In this country the study of administration emerged as the application of particular social sciences to management problems in particular fields of practice, namely, the application of economics to business administration, and of political science to public administration. Some expansion has taken place through subdivisions of these fields

[1] Mary E. Macdonald, *"Social Work Research: A Perspective,"* in *Social Work Research,* Norman Polansky, ed. (Chicago: University of Chicago Press, 1960).
[2] Dwight Waldo, *The Study of Administration* (Garden City: Doubleday & Company, 1955).
[3] Andre Malator, *The University Teaching of the Social Sciences: Public Administration* (Paris: UNESCO, 1959), p. 133.

Reprinted with permission of the National Association of Social Workers and the author, from *Research in Social Welfare Administration: Its Contributions and Problems*, David Fanshel, ed. (New York: National Association of Social Workers, 1962), pp. 33-43.

(*e.g.*, preparation for hotel administration, retailing, and the study of state and local government), but for our purposes a more important development has been the inclusion of the study of administration in the education of professional practitioners for such fields as health, education, and welfare. Specialties of these fields, too, have developed, such as hospital administration, library administration, and, now a-borning, university administration. The study and teaching of administration began in this country, then, as an effort to prepare practitioners for administration of specific types of enterprises. The organization of schools in this country for the teaching of administration has been characterized up to the present by increasing specialization by field of practice.

The development of the study of administrative method in a wider range of applications has been accompanied by a broadening of the scientific base. Important contributions to the study of administration are now being made by all the social and behavioral sciences — sociology, psychology, social psychology, anthropology — as well as by economics and political science plus such mathematically oriented techniques as statistics, game theory, and cybernetics. The study of administration in such forms as information and communication theory, group theory, decision theory, administrative behavior, and organization theory is now academically respectable indeed.

A recent move on the academic front, distinctly in contrast to the trend toward proliferation of specialized fields of administrative study, is toward the establishment of a unitary and autonomous discipline of administrative science. Litchfield writes:

> Only in recent years have we come to recognize that administration is a distinct and identifiable social process which occurs in all contemporary institutions and which becomes of increasing importance as those institutions and the environments in which they function become larger and more complex. With our recognition of the existence and importance of the process, administrative science has emerged as a distinctive field of inquiry. It is possible that it may develop ultimately into a separate discipline which will take its place beside the more traditional social and behavioral sciences.[4]

The study of administration as administrative science and the current study of administration as management method are to be distinguished chiefly by differences in focus and purpose and only secondarily by differences in subject-matter emphasis. Administrative science is focused on process and structure and on the relation of form to function, and its purpose, like that of all science, is to search for knowledge, understanding, and truth. The study of management method is concerned with applying administrative science to the control of administrative phenomena. As an art or technology the study of management method is interventional and instrumental in its approach Its immediate purpose is to improve practice and to prepare practitioners for administration.

As this paradigm suggests, administrative science is concerned both with administration in general and with administration in particular. The primary emphasis, however, is on generalization and formulation of theory. In pursuing its objectives this science, like others, will make use of the hypothetico-inductive method — the method of making observations of specific phenomena, generalizing from these, and then checking and amplifying through further observation. The specific fields of administrative practice are of chief interest to administrative science as the loci of observations and the primary sources of data.

---

[4] James D. Thompson *et al.*, eds., *Comparative Studies in Administration* (Pittsburgh: University of Pittsburgh Press, 1959). Foreword by Edward H. Litchfield. Litchfield also suggests that the founding of the journal, *Administrative Sciences Quarterly,* in 1956 by the Cornell Graduate School of Business and Public Administration is another evidence of the recognition of this area of study.

In the paradigm, the cell for the study of "Management Method" of the "General" field of administration suggests the question as to whether management can be effectively taught as a generic method as well as part of a substantive area of activity such as business or government. This question has been the subject of some pedagogical debate. Perhaps it is not necessary to resolve this issue before recognizing that there are some common elements in management methods, no matter where they are practiced, and that these elements can be a useful focus for both teaching and research. However, the study of management method has, in fact, tended to emphasize the specifics of operating situations in the various fields of practice.

Administrative science is largely an interest of social and behavioral scientists in the universities and specialized research institutions; the study of administrative method tends to be a shared activity between management and university faculty, especially, perhaps, those in the professional schools whose work is related to a field of practice. The view of administration as a method of social work will be discussed at a later point.

These two ways of viewing the study of administration are used as one axis of a framework or paradigm for discussing the place of social welfare in the study of administration, as follows:

Figure 1—Views of the Study of Administration and its Fields.

The Study of Administration Viewed as—	Field of Administration						
	General	Service (Not for Profit)					Other (For Profit)
		Social				Other Service	
		Welfare	Health	Education	Other Social		
Administrative Science							
Management Method							
Social Work Method							

THE FIELDS OF ADMINISTRATION

The literature of administration is, in large part, oriented to observations concerning political, governmental, military, church, and economic administration. A generally accepted modern classification of fields in administration is public administration and business administration, along with various classifications of each. This dichotomy includes only part of the field of our major interest, that is, the public sector of social welfare administration.

For purposes of the present discussion, a classification of fields of administration is presented, with our interest in the field of social welfare administration as the horizontal axis in the paradigm. The primary classification divides enterprises into those which have as their chief objective the making of profit, as in the case of business, and those which have as their chief objective the provision of services not for profit. Administration for "Service" is divided into "Social" and "Other Service." Finally subdivisions of "Social" are given.

For the present purpose, the term "social administration" is used to refer to the fields of welfare, health, and educational administration and to other fields which have certain important attributes in common with those named. One characteristic that these fields have in common is the key position which the professions offering direct personal help, such as social work, medicine, education, and psychology, occupy in the provision of their service. A second important common characteristic is that policy concerning their auspices and support, in respect to private or different levels of government control, is a matter of considerable current controversy.

In this country and at this juncture in history, the program interests and service objectives of the various fields of social administration are perceived by many as the battlegrounds in the fight for the Welfare State. This means that they share a common kind of administrative system and have common problems in relating to the community — gaining understanding and acceptance, obtaining financial support, and drawing on the community pool of manpower to staff their professional services.

The growing interdependence of professional workers and of administrative organizations is a phenomenon of major importance for the study of administration, both as administrative science and as management method. In the literature of administration the professional worker has traditionally been seen as a staff specialist. He was the man to be kept "on tap not on top" because, to use Veblen's phrase, of his "trained incapacity." However, in modern social administration the professional worker is also a line worker and may, in fact, be the principal and immediate operator at the point of delivery of service. He may also be the top administrator of a welfare, health, or educational establishment.

The important common characteristics of the different fields of social administration suggest the strategy of comparative study. Hammond *et al.* point out that "for reasons which are more accidental than logical, 'comparative public administration' has been synonymous with cross-cultural or cross-national studies of administration and 'comparative business administration' has referred to business outside of the United States or to the foreign operations of American firms."[5] They urge comparative studies of the different subject-matter fields of administration as part of the strategy for moving toward the development of administrative science.

The comparative study of social administration, if it exists at all, is in a very primitive stage. Yet the opportunity for such study presents itself in the fact that some structure in

---

[5] Peter B. Hammond, Robert W. Hawkes, Buford H. Junker, James D. Thompson, and Arthur Tuden, "On the Study of Administration," in James D. Thompson *et. al.*, eds., *Comparative Studies in Administration, op. cit.*, pp. 3-15.

both governmental and private fields exists for the making of comparative studies. Community chests and councils and the Department of Health, Education, and Welfare are outstanding examples of ready-made laboratories. Within the Department of Health, Education, and Welfare the office of Vocational Rehabilitation makes grants for the same type of programs to various branches of state governments, namely, departments of education and departments of welfare. The Children's Bureau makes grants for crippled children's programs both to state departments of health and to state departments of welfare. In local communities, school health and day care programs for children are administered under varying auspices, public and private. Type of auspice is but one variable that might be studied with profit through the comparative approach. Kurt Reichert's statement on the application of epidemiological or public health planning procedures to social welfare planning suggests some of the possibilities of the comparative approach to the study of methods of social administration.[6]

Past absorption with the analysis of internal organization in both its formal and informal aspects has resulted, according to Etzioni, in the neglect of the study of the interrelations among administrative organizations and other forms of human organization, such as the family, the community, and political entities.[7] This kind of study of administrative systems should be of particular interest in the study of the fields of social administration.

STUDY OF SOCIAL WELFARE ADMINISTRATION

Certainly the study of welfare administration would be impeded by too early and too exclusive an involvement in this field without reference to the broader area of social administration. Nevertheless, there is need for a focus on the field with which we are immediately concerned.

The formal objective or major purpose of social welfare administration can be defined as the enhancement of social functioning. The term "social functioning" is used as in Boehm's definition of the profession of social work.[8] Social welfare as a field of administration and social work as a profession may then be considered to have a shared objective. This is not to say that their objectives are in fact identical in all instances and in all respects. Using Banfield's formulation, organizational objectives can be seen as having both active and contextual elements.[9] Active elements are in the foreground, contextual elements are field conditions which have to be considered in seeking attainment of objectives. For example, the active element in the organizational objective of an Aid to Dependent Children program might be to improve the economic condition of needy children and their families. Contextual elements might be: (1) to avoid the charge that the program tended to increase the number of births out of wedlock, and (2) to protect the confidentiality of information provided to the agency by recipients of assistance.

The contextual elements of the professional objectives of social work may in fact be congruent with, or different from, the contextual bureaucratic objectives of given social welfare organizations. Some of the sources and characteristics of conflict between social

[6] Kurt Reichert, *In Program Planning, What Can Social Work Adapt from Public Health?* (Albany: New York State Department of Health, 1959). (Mimeographed.)

[7] Amitai Etzioni, "New Directions in the Study of Organization and Society," *Social Research*, Vol. 27, No. 2 (Summer, 1960), pp. 223-228.

[8] Werner Boehm, *Objectives of the Social Work Curriculum of the Future,* Vol. I, *Social Work Curriculum Study* (New York: Council on Social Work Education, 1959), p. 54.

[9] Edward C. Banfield, "Note on Conceptual Scheme," in Martin Meyerson and Edward C. Banfield, eds., *Politics, Planning and the Public Interest* (Glencoe, Ill.: The Free Press, 1955).

work and bureaucracy have been discussed by Wilensky and Lebeaux.[10] However, the supportive and, possibly, the neutral aspects of the differences also need exploration. The growth of both bureaucracy and professionalism can be interpreted, in part, as responses to the advantages of specialization. Hughes points out that the tendency of the professions to move from individual, entrepreneurial practice to organizationally administered service has utility to the professions by providing the opportunity for selective practice.[11]

One of the important characteristics of the profession of social work is that its claim for recognition as a profession arose, and has largely remained, as a practice within administrative organizations. Social work, unlike some of the other professions, has not passed through a private-practice stage of development. This seems to be regarded by a large sector of the profession as having generally positive values; in some quarters, current activity in the direction of the private practice of social work is regarded as atavistic or deviate professional behavior.

Dissatisfaction is expressed from time to time by social workers with some of the effects of bureaucratic forms and processes, and many show interest in the "team approach" and other collegial forms of organization which are hoped to emphasize professional over other hierarchical authority. On balance, the profession seems committed to the idea that administrative organization of social work is here to stay.

The purpose of teaching administration in schools of social work has been to prepare practitioners for their roles in welfare organizations. The emphasis in teaching administration to social work students seems to have varied with conceptions or anticipations — sometimes implicit — as to what part the students would play in the organization and administration of welfare services. If students are expected to be social reformers or "social actionists" most attention is likely to be given to description of the development of social welfare policies and programs and to analysis of their relationships to social work professional objectives, values, and ethics. However, most students at the master's level are preparing primarily for immediate practice as caseworkers or group workers. The emphasis in teaching is therefore on the role of the professional worker in a social welfare "setting and structure." A recent popular emphasis in post-master's work has been on the teaching of current or prospective supervisors, and especially that component of supervision concerned with in-service training for professional development. In only a few situations has social work education, at either the master's or doctoral level, been directed to the preparation of students for the administrative management function.

ADMINISTRATION AS A METHOD
OF SOCIAL WORK

The most recent and the most comprehensive discussion of the place of the study of administration in social work education is in *The Administration Method in Social Work Education* by Spencer.[12] A key statement in this report is:

[10] Harold L. Wilensky and Charles N. Lebeaux, *Industrialization and Social Welfare* (New York: Russell Sage Foundation, 1958), pp. 232-282. For a more general statement, see David N. Solomon, "Professional Persons in Bureaucratic Organizations," in *Symposium on Preventive and Social Psychiatry* (Washington, D.C.: Walter Reed Army Institute of Research, 1957).

[11] Everett C. Hughes, "The Professions in Society," *The Canadian Journal of Economic and Political Science,* Vol. 26, No. 1 (February, 1960), pp. 54-61.

[12] Sue Spencer, *The Administration Method in Social Work Education,* Vol. III, *(Social Work Curriculum Study).* (New York: Council on Social Work Education, 1959).

As the administration project progressed, it became more and more clear that what we were discussing in the preparation of social work students for executive level positions was social work in an administrative setting and *not* administration in a social work setting. It also became clear that if one sees the administrator's function as primarily that of enabling or helping all the people involved in the agency's program to make the maximum use of resources to produce the optimum program, then both theory and practice (field work or internships) courses in administration should give opportunity for the student to incorporate and implement his professional learning through a concentration of study in administration as appropriately as in any other major field of practice.[13]

In orienting the study of social welfare administration to the profession of social work, Spencer adopts the point of view that in the administration of social welfare the knowledge, skills, and attitudes of social work are more important than the knowledge and skills of general administrative method. It is, of course, not uncommon for social workers, like some other professional workers, to give higher rank to their values and competencies than to those of generic management. However, Spencer goes further, or possibly in a different direction, in suggesting that social work administration be recognized as a major field of social work study and practice in the same sense as casework, group work, and community organization. In the past, administration has been listed as one of the basic areas of social work education, but it has been considered, along with research, as an activity in support of the "direct treatment" methods of casework, group work, and most recently, community organization.

Figure I shows the view of administration as a method of social work as bounded by the field of social welfare — the field in which objectives of organizations are more closely related to social work than to any other profession. The recognition of administration as a method of social work is justified by Spencer on the basis of the importance of its component and distinctive social work knowledges, skills, and attitudes. Unlike some other methods of social work, such as casework and group work which can be and are practiced in other settings, the method of social work administration would logically seem to be specialized to the welfare field.

ADMINISTRATION AND OTHER METHODS
OF SOCIAL WORK

In his discussion of administration in the summary volume of the Curriculum Study, Boehm seems caught between the desire to accept Spencer's recommendation and the difficulty of fitting it into his conceptual scheme.[14] He lists administration, along with casework, group work, community organization, and research, as a major social work method. Then, following Lippitt, Watson, and Wesley,[15] he states, in effect, that the basic ingredients of social work method are: (1) a change-agent, (2) a client or client-system, and (3) an interaction between the two having the characteristics of a goal-directed, planned professional process. In Boehm's description of the various methods, using this framework, the identities of the change-agent and of the client emerge clearly in casework and group work, not so clearly in community organization, and not at all in administration or research.

---

[13] *Ibid.*, p. 9.

[14] Werner Boehm, *Objectives of the Social Work Curriculum of the Future,* Vol. I, *Social Work Curriculum Study,* (New York: Council on Social Work Education, 1959), Part III, Chapter 8, "The Methods Component."

[15] Ronald Lippitt, Jeanne Watson, and Bruce Wesley, *The Dynamics of Planned Change* (New York: Harcourt Brace & Company, 1958).

Lippitt *et al.* discuss planned change at the level of the personality, the group, the organization, and the community. Again at the organizational level, the change-agent and the client are seen only as rather shadowy and elusive figures. From the illustrative experiences cited, it may be inferred that the authors view the change-agent as a kind of management consultant and the client-system as the personnel of the organization. Even if one allows that the change-agent can be the executive himself, the question remains as to the identity of his social work client.

Hughes suggests the universality of this problem when he points out in another context:

> The problem of all professional codes has always been this: Whose agent is the professional? Turned around it is: Who is the client? The extreme ideology of the private practice of professions gives a simple answer. There is but one client, the person who applies for services and accepts them on the conditions dictated by the profession. This obviously cannot be the case when the application does not come in that way. [16]

The idea that professional method can be described in terms of the direct and immediate relationship of an individual practitioner to an individual may be adequate for some forms of the practice of some professions. In an organization-oriented profession such as social work a somewhat more complex model seems to be necessary. For example, Lippitt's expansion of the idea of client to client-system helps to cover not only the practice of the group worker and the community organization worker but also common aspects of casework practice. When the child welfare caseworker interacts with the foster mother he is not relating directly and immediately with the client, who is the child, but he is attempting to effect change in the client-system. The efforts of a medical social worker to help the family of a hospital patient is not direct treatment of the patient but it is treatment of the client-system in favor of the patient.

In the organizational context, expansion of the concept of agent to agent-system is also indicated, if the view of administration as a method of social work is to be defended. The individual client or the client-system frequently interacts with more than one change-agent in the organization. Furthermore, professional persons other than caseworkers immediately in contact with the client or client-system are involved in the interaction. The social work supervisor may interact with a caseworker and thus influence the treatment of the client. The supervisor's role in relation to the caseworker is that of teacher, consultant, or administrative officer. The caseworker may, functionally, be his consultee, but not his client. As a social worker, the supervisor relates to the agent's client system.

The social work executive similarly relates to agency personnel in a variety of roles. In one role, he relates indirectly to the agency's clients through the agency's social work system. His more direct leadership role may be not only in provisioning, supporting, and enabling caseworkers to do their jobs, but in influencing the determination of agency objectives and policy, marshalling resources, combining them in ways designed to aid the client system, coordinating staff effort to the end of offering a unified and appropriate approach to the client-system, evaluating, and influencing the improvement of performance standards.

The idea of the change-system as a structural component of the profession may possibly have some utility in investigating the relationship of professionalism to bureaucracy. The coordinating task of the social work executive who is a member of both systems would seem to be different, for example, than that of the administrator who is identified only with the bureaucratic component of the organization. Comparative studies of the

---

[16] Hughes, *op. cit.*, p. 60.

functions of physician-administrators, educator-administrators, and social work-administrators might test the extent to which the concept of change-system is helpful in analyzing their roles.

The professional change-system can be seen as extending into the organizational environment and as constituting an important part of the administrative system. This concept might be used, for example, in investigation of the impact of federal and other national standard-setting agencies on policy formulation in state and local operating agencies.

The expansion of the concept of change-agent to change-system in no way minimizes or blurs the distinctive differences among the several methods of social work. Using this concept, however, the methods are not distinguished on the basis of the client-system *for* which practitioners work or *to* whom services are directed. The differences become rather a matter of the level of human organization *with* which practitioners of the different methods are specialized to work and the process *within* which they are specialized to work. On this basis the methods of social work can then be aligned as follows:

METHOD OF CHANCE	LEVEL OF HUMAN ORGANI- ZATION WORKED WITH	PROCESS WORKED WITH
Casework	Individual	Individual growth and behavior
Group work	Small, informal group	Group process
Administrative management	Administrative organization	Administrative process
Community organization	Community	Community process

The practice of each method will sometimes involve working with the various levels of human organization and through a number of the processes, but with an integrated emphasis on a particular level and process. The client-system of each method will be defined by the policy of the agency or enterprise within which the method is employed. Practice of each method will be part of the change-system of an organization and of its administrative system.

Social work research can hardly be considered a method of social work within the framework which has been described here because it is not specialized to work with human organization along the continuum which has been suggested above. This is in substantial agreement with Greenwood's conclusion: "The research process and the social work process constitute two different orders of phenomena. The social work process is social-psychological in nature; the research process is logical in nature."[17]

Community organization has probably received more acceptance than administration as a method of social work, in part because of the apparent greater visibility or immediacy of the client-system to the change-agent. However, the level of human organization with which administrative management is specialized to work — the administrative organization — is at a somewhat lower order of abstraction than the community, and other things being equal should — at least in its internal aspects — lend itself somewhat more readily to available research techniques and resources.

---

[17] Ernest Greenwood, "Social Work Research: A Decade of Reappraisal," *Social Service Review,* Vol. 31, No. 3 (September, 1957), p. 311.

The suggestion has been made from time to time and most recently in the *Social Work Curriculum Study* that the common elements in social work administration and in community organization are so important a part of each method that the two can be considered together for purposes of practice and preparation for practice. That policy formulation is an important process common to both branches of organization is a point of agreement among a number of the writers contributing to the *Curriculum Study,* including Spencer, Weisman, and Burns. The theory of decision-making, for example, has assumed an important place in administrative science and applications are now being made to studies of community process.[18] This theory can provide one approach to integrated formulations for the methods of community organization and administration.

RELATIONSHIPS AMONG VIEWS OF ADMINISTRATION

Three views of the study of social welfare administration have been discussed, two as growing out of the orientation of social welfare to administration and one as the orientation of social work to administration.

Research points of view grow out of interest and purpose. The view of administrative science will be selected by one who believes that to know the truth is all that is needed — and that there is nothing as practical as a good theory. If one studies administration for the purpose of seeking improvement in administrative practice then one will probably adopt the view of administration as management method. The sharp focus of the view of administration as social work method may be attractive for research in social work education.

Research and educational programs will reflect combinations of various points of view. The relation of administrative science to research in administrative method is in the general relationship of basic to applied research. This is a two-way relationship with the applied field drawing upon the theoretical formulations, findings, and methods of the basic science and feeding back both related findings and the stimulation of formulated problems and other indications of interest in further basic research. The primary interest of research workers in the basic science is likely to be, with reference to our paradigm, in the "horizontal" relations across the different fields of administration — and even more broadly across the various social and behavioral disciplines which go to make up administrative science.

Research workers in management method in a particular field of administration such as social welfare will be interested in horizontal relationships or comparisons with allied fields of administration, but they will also be concerned with the vertical integration of the basic science with their field of application. The development of a discipline of administrative science which synthesizes the contributions of the underlying social and behavioral sciences will represent a powerful assist to research in social welfare administration as well as in the other applied fields. Social work research will be interested further in the explorations of the "vertical" relationships within the field of social welfare, from the points of view of administration as the general method of management and administration as a method of social work.

NOTE ON TERMINOLOGY

In view of the variations in the usage of the same terms in the literature of public, business, and social administration, and in the social and behavioral sciences, the sense in

---

[18] See Martin Meyerson and Edward G. Banfield, eds., *op. cit.* See also, Peter H. Rossi, "Community Decision-making," *Administrative Science Quarterly,* Vol. 1, No. 4 (March, 1957), pp. 415-443.

which key terms are used in this paper is as follows:

Administration is the process and the organization of people working toward objectives which entail the production of goods or the provision of services. The study of administration includes analysis of process and of organization and their interaction. Both process and organization include formal, that is, officially intended or publicly recognized aspects, and informal aspects. The term "administration" is used in this general sense unless modified expressly or by the context.

Administrative process is the activity of people in an organization working toward the formulation and achievement of shared objectives; also the operations of the organization itself. Activity of people includes individual behavior, rational and irrational – physical, affective, and cognitive; also behavior of people in small and large groups. The operation of the organization may be viewed as internal (*i.e.,* the interaction of personnel with each other and with the organization) and as external (*i.e.,* the interaction of the organization with its environment).

Administrative organization is: (1) the pattern or structure of the relationships of people engaged in the administrative process, and (2) the entity largely represented by the people included in a given administrative structure. The organization as an entity or enterprise includes not only its present personnel but also its charter, history, philosophy, and administrative process – internal and external.

Administrative system is the pattern of structure of relationships between an organization and its environment. The environment of an administrative organization includes not only the community from which it draws its personnel, clientele, and support, but also the full range of political, economic, and social institutions which influence or are influenced by its operation.

Bureaucracy is a model or type of administrative organization which may be characterized by such formal attributes as a hierarchy of authority, specialization of work, a system of rules, and impersonality. A specific organization may be seen as more or less bureaucratic depending on the extent to which it conforms to the model.

Administrative management is the formal and purposive process of creating an organization, designing its structure, and influencing the behavior of people in the organization and its administrative system in favor of organizational objectives. Management constitutes the method or intervention aspect of administrative process. Administrative process involves every person in the organization; administrative management is a specialized method employed by some. Such terms as "to administer" or "to organize" are used to denote intervention through the specialized method of management.

Policy is decision on administrative objectives. Decisions on objectives are made both outside the organization (*e.g.,* through legislation and by public opinion) and within (*e.g.,* through agency rules). Administrative management includes participation in the making of broad and controlling external policy decisions as well as in internal, implementing decisions.

Pittsburgh Committee Report on Common and Uncommon Elements in Administration

JAMES D. THOMPSON

The use of committees and debate over their merits are two universal facts of life in all large organizations. It is not unusual for a committee to begin in confusion and perhaps apprehension, as this one did. It is remarkable, however, for a committee to learn as much as we have, and for a group representing as many different experiences and points of view as ours to approach the consensus this one has.

Our conclusions stem from two primary sources. First, we drew on one another's experiences and observations gained from a wide variety of vantage points — including administrative positions in federal, state, and local government, in voluntary social welfare agencies, in research organizations, labor organizations, in education, and in consultation with various industrial firms. Second, we turned from time to time to selected academic sources,[2] which helped to crystallize our thinking and focus our deliberations. These sources were not simply swallowed, however. The report to follow makes use of them, but we have modified and elaborated them out of our collective experiences.

We are convinced that administration in whatever setting has more elements in common than traditional beliefs recognize, and that the importance of these common elements generally is underestimated. While we recognize variations, we feel that the significant differences are not necessarily at those points in the administrative process that tradition assumes them to be. We are convinced that *within* a "field," such as business or social welfare, organizations also vary in important ways. The traditional classifications of organizations as business, governmental, medical, of welfare are not very precise categories, and may hide as much truth as they help one discover. Our question, therefore, is not whether there are differences among organizations — however classified — but whether

---

[1] This report represents deliberations over a period of two years. We wish to acknowledge the wise consultation of Mrs. Ella W. Reed, Consultant on Special Projects for the National Conference on Social Welfare.

[2] E. H. Litchfield,"Notes on a General Theory of Administration," *Administrative Science Quarterly* (June, 1956); Sol Levine and Paul E. White, "Exchange as a Conceptual Framework for the Study of Interorganizational Relationships," *Administrative Science Quarterly* (March, 1961); Talcott Parsons, "Some Ingredients of a General Theory of Formal Organizations," in Parsons, *Structure and Process in Modern Society* (Glencoe, Ill.: 1959); J. D. Thompson and F. L. Bates,"Technology, Organization, and Administration," in Thompson, *et.al., Comparative Studies in Administration* (Pittsburgh: 1959), and Robert W. Hawkes, "The Role of the Psychiatric Administrator," *Administrative Science Quarterly* (June, 1961).

Reprinted with permission of the National Conference on Social Welfare, from *Common Elements in Administration*, Ella W. Reed, ed. (Columbus, Ohio: National Conference on Social Welfare, 1965).

and in what ways these differences are significant in the administration of the organization.

SOME MISLEADING DIFFERENCES

It is not uncommon to hear that, because business administration is profit-centered and all other varieties are oriented toward non-profit service, business administration cannot be compared with other types. We doubt that reality supports this notion as well as tradition implies. That results can be precisely measured is a myth, neither true nor confined to the business world, although it is more often accepted uncritically in the business-financial environment than in others.

Every organization develops systems of accounting — of computing accomplishments — whether these are expressed in dollar terms on profit and loss statements, or in terms of placements made relative to need. The fact that custom and preference lead to one type of accounting scheme or another is much less significant than the fact that administrators in every type of organization seek ways of evaluating the organization's accomplishments — and must use them sensibly, remembering that every such scheme yields only an approximation and depends on arbitrary and even fictitious units of measurements, and that the values related to overall results cannot be assigned to individual members or small units within the organization.

It is also commonplace to hear that, because business has the "profit-motive," it attains an efficiency which is not achieved in other types of organizations. In our opinion, this distinction is faulty on several grounds. If by "efficiency" is meant an optimum ratio of results from energy (or resources) expended under stated conditions and within time constraints, then clearly efficiency is a concern to organizations of all types.

Whether expressed as a ratio of (a) production to cost, (b) service to cost, (c) therapy achieved to effort expended, or more generally as (d) an excess of gains over losses, "efficiency" is a ratio of output to input recognizing time restrictions. The mechanics of computing efficiency certainly differ. The conditions certainly differ also; the public school system may have a fixed ceiling on resources and attempt to get the greatest output from those resources, whereas some other type of organization may have a fixed demand, and attempt to meet that target with the greatest economy of resources. But the quest for efficiency applies in equal measure to organizations of all types.

Again we are told that civil service regulations or tenure arrangements protect the incompetent in other types of organizations, but not in business firms. And again, we feel that the distinction is overdrawn. Sorting out and eliminating incompetence and mediocrity is a *universal* problem for organizations, and civil service-like practices and tenure assumptions grow up, *de facto* or by employment contract, in large business firms as well as in governmental or educational organizations.

The sharp distinctions between business and other enterprises probably had more validity in an earlier period, but we must be careful not to compare the corporation of yesterday with the public or social welfare agency of today. Fixation on short-term profit as the only significant goal of the corporation is less frequent today than it once was. The diffusion of ownership, and the impact of such external forces as governments, universities, unions, public opinion, and political necessity have blunted short-term profit as the major criterion for corporate decision making. Demands for corporate perpetuation, the necessity of forward planning, and the growing multi-disciplinary nature of the decisions of the corporation have made impractical concentration of authority in one or a very few persons. Stereotyped concepts of the business firm may sharply differentiate it from other types of organizations, but the complexities of reality make the firm comparable to other organizations.

31

SOME NECESSARY DISTINCTIONS

The sorts of trends just mentioned suggest a diffused type of control and administration in the business firm which is more like what one finds in government or institutional life than in the corporation of past years. As a consequence, differences in administrative characteristics tend to decline and common elements tend to increase. In seeking to identify elements of administration which are common to business, social welfare, government, education, and medicine, we quickly discovered that one of the least common elements is language usage. The same situation or occurence might signify to one of us "supervision" but imply "administration" to another, and "management" to still a third member of the committee. To overcome this barrier to effective exchange of experiences, we found it necessary to focus first on the *functions* of administration and then on the *behavior* of those holding major organizational responsibilities, and to ignore the terminology and labels diversely used in the field.

Even with this focus, it was necessary from time to time to give some labels to our topics, and to do this we had to adopt a few ground rules which will be employed in this report and explained as we go along.

At the outset we agreed to use a broad conception of "administration." If our report has a focal point it is on the "chief executive," but it became clear that in most instances the chief executive's role is one in a larger *administrative process,* and his role is in part defined by the other roles involved in that process. Even *within* a field — a single industry, for example — the chief executive's role varies considerably from one organization to another, or from time to time in the same organization, depending in part on how the administrative process is divided among a number of roles, and in part on the individual's conception or mental image of his role.

We believe, however, that if the *administrative process* is performed adequately, the *areas of decision* and the *functions performed* will be similar in all large organizations. We believe this also is true of the very small organization, where the total administrative process is the responsibility of one individual, but our deliberations have revolved around what we label as the diversified or "multi-disciplined" organization; that is, the type which includes two or more distinctly different professional or technical processes. An example may help at this point. A firm devoted solely to the manufacture of automobile batteries for one client would be a single-operation organization, whereas a firm devoted to the manufacture of several product lines, to research, and to sales would be a multi-disciplined organization. Similarly, the welfare agency concerned only with placing children in foster homes might be considered a single-purpose organization, whereas the agency which provides hospitalization, casework, and assistance programs would be a multi-disciplined or diversified organization.

The importance of this distinction will emerge later, but we want to make it clear now that we considered administration of the relatively large and relatively complex organizations in our several fields.

THE FUNCTIONS AND LEVELS OF ADMINISTRATION

We see three major functions performed by the administrative process, and we believe there usually is a close correspondence between these three functions and three general levels in the organizational hierarchy. We called one important function "organization-*directing*" in the sense of discovering opportunities for the organization to satisfy needs or demands of the environment, and in the sense of winning environmental support for organizational goals — not in the narrow sense of issuing orders to members of the organization. This function is concerned with what the organization, as a total entity, is now, is becoming, and should become, and with making sure that the organization continues to fit into the changing scheme of things.

Normally we think of this organization-*directing* function as the responsibility of a board – of trustees or directors – or of a commission or a legislative body, such as a city council. But we also know that often the chief executive is the key member of such a group and that when the board or council does effectively discharge organization-*directing* responsibilities this fact frequently reflects the chief executive's capacity to energize his board or council. We believe that for the administrative process to operate effectively the chief executive must play an important part in the organization-*directing* function, and that this also enables him to link the directing function to the second of our three – "the organization-*managing*" function.

The organization-*managing* function is concerned with the sustenance of the organization as a *total entity,* that is, with acquiring, assigning, and planning for the orderly and coherent utilization of resources, namely finances, personnel, physical facilities and materials, and authority. The organization-*managing* function of the administrative process does not accomplish the "ultimate" work of the organization, but it provides the ingredients, instructions, and climate essential to that ultimate work. It uses as one of its criteria the goals and objectives established in the organization-*directing* function, but it uses as another important criterion for decisions the realities of the technical and professional processes necessary to accomplish the "ultimate" work of the organization – operating the machinery which manufactures a product, calling on sales accounts, interviewing clients, treating patients, dispensing advice, etc. We do not conceive of these technologic behaviors as part of the administrative process as defined above; rather we believe the administrative process serves to give over all direction and meaning to technologic and professional processes, and to acquire and regulate the use of resources required by technologic and professional activity. We do believe, however, that technical and professional actions must interlink with the administrative process, and it is at this point that we find the third major function of administration, which we refer to as the "*supervisory*" function.

In our view the *supervisory* function of administration governs the utilization of the resources provided by the organization-*managing* aspect of administration, and orients their utilization in the way outlined by the organization-*directing* function of administration. The *supervisory* function results in the coordination of technical or professional activities, making sure that these are done at appropriate times and places, and in generally accepted fashion.

To recapitulate: we find administrative roles at three major levels of the organization. At each level administration performs a different function, and each level overlaps with and links those above and below it.

Now in order to identify common elements of administration, and to compare administrative roles in different organizations, we must first determine which function of administration is involved in the roles in question. We cannot do this simply by comparing similarly-labeled roles, for the word "foreman" may be applied to one kind of role in one industrial firm, and to a different kind of role by another industrial firm. Similarly, we cannot assume that "foundry foreman" is equivalent in the administrative process to "casework supervisor" – or that it is not. The personnel manager may have one kind of role in this organization, and a rather different one in that organization. And so on.

We must emphasize, then, that in the following remarks we will be comparing roles in terms of the kinds of responsibilities outlined above – irrespective of the variety of labels which organizations may attach to those roles.

We believe there are significant elements in the *supervisory* function of administration which are common to large organizations in all fields. Whatever the technical and professional processes, those at the *supervisory* level deal with people and therefore must give attention to interpersonal communications practices, to motivation, to teaching and

33

development, and to performance appraisal. More generally stated, concern with "human relations" is a common element of administration at the *supervisory* level, regardless of the field. A second important element at the *supervisory* level, common to all fields, is concerned with establishing work priorities, with shifting work loads as bottlenecks develop, with making sure that the activities of various technical specialists or professionals intermesh — in short, with coordination. A third common element at the *supervisory* level is in linking the technical and professional processes to the managerial function and managerial level of administration by anticipating future resource needs, negotiating with managers, and so on. These, we believe, are the three major components of *supervisory* roles, and are common to all types of large, complex organizations.

Jumping now over the managerial level to the organization – *directing* function and level of administration, we believe that some of the essential elements are common to all types of large organizations. Irrespective of the technological or professional bases of the organization, this function of administration identifies social, economic, and political trends which open new opportunities to the organization or pose new problems for it; it determines the elements of the environment to which the organization seeks to be related, and determines strategy for reacting to pressure groups or organized blocs in the environment. This is the broadest of the administrative functions, requiring consideration of the distant future.

Now we move back to the organization-*managing* function of administration. Here again the roles appear to us to be essentially the same in the several fields. Regardless of the technical or professional bases of administration, there are common needs for financial planning and management; personnel development; program planning, control and review; purchasing and property control, and so on. Even more important at the organization-managing level of the organization is the essential responsibility of meshing the several managerial activities into one cohesive whole which is both consistent with the overall direction and policy established for the organization and supportive of the technological or professional processes required by that overall direction. This problem of keeping the parts integrated into a whole is common, at the organization-managing level, to all types of large, complex organizations.

SOME MAJOR DIFFERENCES

There is no denying that organizations differ from one another in recognizable and significant ways. The offices of a social insurance agency contrast sharply with the floor of the industrial foundry, and the hospital appears to be quite different from the bank. Not only do the physical appearances differ, but the skills and behavior of employees, the responsibilitites, the tempo of the work, and the languages vary also.

Technologic/Professional Differences

To the casual observer the most striking differences stem from the technologic/professional activities of the organization, for at any given time these dictate whether, for example, the electronic computer, the steam turbine, the caseworker, or the medical team will be employed. That such differences also have consequences for the supervisory, managerial, and directing levels of administration cannot be disputed.

The technology appropriate to a particular goal or set of objectives governs the ratio of human to non-human resources needed by the organization. The automated production line, for example, calls for a heavy investment in capital equipment and relatively few human operators, whereas the casework agency relies largely on human abilities and relatively small investment in plant and equipment. In the first case, we would expect questions of long-range investment, depreciation, and preventive maintenance to lay large claims on administrative attention. In the other case, we should find matters of personnel recruitment, development, and motivation looming large.

Where the technology involves the standardized processing of non-human materials, we would expect the regulated flow of pre-sorted and pre-treated materials, and the stockpiling and warehousing of finished products, to be a second focus of attention. But where organizational "treatments" are applied directly to clientele, as in the school, the hospital, or the casework agency, we would expect more concern to be directed to questions of accurate diagnosis, flexibility in prescription, and an orderly and timely sequence of treatments.

Where a technology is addressed to standardized transformation of standardized, inert materials, elaborate standards and specifications can be developed, and close attention can be paid to control over quantity, quality, and cost. Where the technology rests on the judgment and ingenuity of professional personnel, quantitative controls over quality, quantity, and cost are more difficult, and standardization and routinization can easily block achievement of organizational objectives.

Differences in Client Relations

Every organization, if it is to persist, must have recipients for its services or products. The salesman must have customers, the teacher must have pupils, the prison guard must have prisoners, the caseworker must have clients, and the playground supervisor must have participants. But to say that each type of organization must have recipients must not hide the fact that the *relation* of the organization to its clientele or potential clientele may vary tremendously from one case to another.

We have already noted, in our consideration of technologic or professional differences, that the client to a professional organization "intrudes" into the production process through interaction with the professional. This is because, in the helping professions, "production" and "distribution" cannot be sharply divorced. But differences between "intrusion" and "separation" do not exhaust the significance of client relations.

Whether the organization must seek out and convince potential clients, on the one hand, or, on the other, respond to and meet the needs of claimants seems to us to be a significant variable. The potential customer in a highly competitive economic setting has not only several choices of firms but, perhaps, of salesmen within firms. He not only has a range of alternatives but may ignore any one of these without peril. Moreover, he may enter into a relationship but terminate it at any moment, before completion of a transaction. At the other extreme, the public school can exercise compulsion and usually need not be concerned with finding pupils, but rather with finding and allocating buildings, staff, and budget to meet the demand thrust upon it. At one extreme the volume of production is given and distribution effort is geared accordingly; at the other extreme, the demand is given and administrative energy is switched to problems of production.

Between these extremes various kinds of organizations vary widely. Significantly, the position of a particular organization can change in this respect. In the public health and social service fields, the notion of case-finding leads to a departure from earlier notions that the agency responds to demand. When it becomes clear that early treatment can prevent more serious problems, the role of the agency in creating demand and finding clients becomes significant. In certain communities this becomes a problem for public schools. With an influx of families from regions where school attendance norms are not well-developed, the public school system may find it necessary to search out those who belong in school, or to discourage high school drop-outs.

Whether client relations are fleeting or prolonged, anonymous or personal, are other important dimensions. The organization with a stable clientele can rely on goodwill to solve many of its problems; at the same time, if it abuses goodwill it may not only lose an individual transaction but all future transactions with the particular client. But the organization which can, under these conditions, guarantee satisfaction. But where the results of the organization's efforts are less tangible — as in education, personal counseling, or mental therapy — neither the organization nor the client can so measurably specify in advance what the end product will be or should be, nor can success or failure be reliably documented at the completion of treatment. This type of client relation, then, is fraught with doubts, and if the relationship is necessarily prolonged, problems of maintaining contact and rapport are likely to crop up again and again throughout the treatment process.

External Relations

Clients — customers, pupils, cases — are *part* of the external world to which an organization must relate, and satisfying or helping the client often is given as the *raison d'être* of the organization. But every organization operates in a network of relations with others and the patterns of these external relations are significant for administration.

Sources of financing constitute one of the important variables. Business firms usually can expect the customer to pay the full cost of the product or service — if he buys at all — so that costing and pricing become of central concern. The university and the hospital tend to collect only fractions of the cost of service from the client and to rely on private gifts or public tax money for the remainder. Still other organizations, such as the public school and some welfare agencies, recover none of their costs directly from the client and support themselves by public taxation or, via annual fund drives, by private taxation. Whether financial support comes from the investing public, the taxpaying public, the contributing public, or the fee-paying public, this support must be won and rewon on the basis of past performance and promise for the future. Financing is problematic in each case, even through the uncertainty connected with it takes a different form. The financial problem also can change significantly for particular organizations. When an agency provides services only for the indigent, client-fees as a source of income are inconceivable. But with the redefinition of clientele to include potentially the entire community, as in the case of family counseling or health clinics, client-fees can become important sources of revenue, and administrators face new problems in determining procedures for charging full or partial costs to the client.

The reputation or "public image" enjoyed by an organization is another significant variable, affecting the willingness of various elements of the social fabric to patronize the organization, to provide it with resources, and to cooperate with it. The problem is one of multiple images rather than a single reputation. These public images often are mediated by more or less organized bodies employing conflicting criteria. For the corporation, for example, the "decision" of the investing public may be formed by the action of institutional investing organizations whose "analysts" subject the corporation to irritating scrutiny, whereas the contributing public's "decision" with respect to a particular agency may be mediated by a United Fund Board or the taxpaying public's "decision" is formed by a legislature or budget committee. For each type of organization, its image among clientele or potential clientele may be formed on very different grounds, and its image as a place to work in still other ways. The management of its several reputations becomes particularly difficult when the organization is engaged primarily in professional activities, for the lay groups which mediate public opinion find it difficult to judge the organization on true merit and instead are likely to judge it on irrelevant or uncertainly evaluated factors.

The organization's recognized domain also is a significant variable. By this we refer to its role in a larger process, as recognized by other organizations involved in that process. The world looks very different, for example, to the business firm holding a prime contract than it does to the "satellite" firm which receives subcontracts. For the business firm, however, there usually is more freedom to renegotiate or change its domain than we find in other types of organizations. The firm dissatisfied with its associates in the larger process — those who supply it or receive its products — may search for new associates; and the firm unhappy about its role in the system may be able to change it by diversifying. For the governmental agency, however, the legislative mandate may spell out what classes of services are to be provided for which groups in the population, and getting a mandate revised often is a very difficult matter. The voluntary welfare agency must stake out and defend its claims in terms of diseases or problems covered, population served, and services rendered, and it must convince lay boards and other specialized agencies that such claims are legitimate. Because the governmental agency and the voluntary agency often are confined to a particular geographic territory, they are less free than the typical firm to search for new partners or sever an alliance. Instead, they must battle it out on the home grounds, get along in the alliance after the battle, and prepare always for new skirmishes ahead.

Thus we find three areas of important variations among organizations: (1) technologic or professional, (2) client relations, and (3) external relations. These, we feel, can affect the relative importance and difficulty of the common elements of administration.

Transferability of Administrative Know-How

One of the questions which persisted through all of our deliberations was the extent to which administrative ability is or can be transferred from one field to another. Are the differences more important than the common elements? In answering this, it helped to distinguish between the transfer of administrative techniques and the transfer of administrators. We are aware of instances of both, but it seems probable that the transfer of administrative techniques is the more frequent and easier.

Systems and procedures developed in one field frequently have been adopted and adapted by others, and we think it is likely that this kind of diffusion will increase in the future. It is generally true that for each field to discover by trial and error what has already been refined in another field is uneconomical; the belief that each field is entirely unique can be a major deterrent to the economy of borrowing. The fact does not discourage us, for *within* fields refinements are constantly being developed and systems modified to fit evolving technologies and changing circumstances.

With respect to the transferability of *individuals,* the picture is more complicated, for there are several kinds of transfers possible. At the level of organization-*directing,* the practice of appointing individuals from one field to responsibilities in quite a different kind of field is widespread. It is not unusual for an individual to be a "board member" in several distinctly different fields, and where individuals are selected for their competence — rather than for prestige or on the basis of occupational history — they can bring new insights and stimulation to the organization. At the *supervisory* and organization-*managing* levels of administration, one important factor in the question of transferability is the evolutionary stage of the fields involved.

Supervisory Level

Where the evolution of diversified or multi-disciplined organizations has been recent and rapid, *supervisory* roles may be built by adding to professional or technical roles, so that the supervisor is viewed merely as a super-technician or super-professional. When this is true, the supervisor in Department "A" is automatically disqualified from moving to Department "B" which uses another variety of professional skills. But when the evolution has progressed far enough to have clearly distinguished between *supervisory* roles and *professional* roles, the multi-disciplined organization frequently finds it desirable to transfer supervisors from one type of department to another, and indeed might be inefficient if it refused to consider the possibility.

Even where the supervisory role has been distinguished from the professional or technologic role, there are distinct limits to transferability. Where the appropriate technology calls for a low ratio of human to non-human resources, the supervisory concern may focus on relating personnel to machines and to work flows, and on care of machines. Where the technology is lodged mainly in human resources the protection and development of human capacities will be a dominant supervisory concern.

These, of course, are relative differences. In both cases personnel development and motivation are essential, just as consideration of work flows cannot be neglected. At the level of tactics, the supervisory jobs are very different; at the level of strategy, the differences seem less important. Similarly, when we consider the organization's problems of "distribution." The tactics of relating salesmen to customer appear very different from those of relating professionals to clients, but the strategy of supervision calls in both cases for supervising relationships with clientele.

This suggests to us that the tactical requirements of supervisory roles will limit the transfer of supervisors to roles where the technologies are closely related, but that strategic understanding and knowledge can be much more widely shared and exchanged.

Organization-Managing Level

The evolutionary stage of the organization is equally important here. In the rapidly evolving organization, organization-*managing* positions may be viewed as super-supervisory positions, with the responsibilities and activities of those in managerial positions reflecting the peculiarities of the technical bases of the organization. During this period of evolution the organization is likely to have difficulties, with managers giving too much attention to operational details, or too little attention to the acquisition and control of resources, or both. During this stage of evolution there are likely to be growing pains in the form of controversy over the importance of technical or professional expertness as a qualification for organization-managing roles. We believe this is a temporary issue, however, for the continued expansion and diversification of technical knowledge will cause greater size and complexity of organizations in all fields, and will make mandatory the recognition of managerial roles as distinct from expert roles.

We have said that the organization-*managing* function is concerned with the sustenance of the organization as a total entity, with acquiring, assigning, and planning for the orderly and coherent utilization of resources to achieve organizational objectives. Important differences in this function show up when we contrast organizations. The purchase of materials and the scheduling of their flow through a production process may loom large in the total managerial concerns of one organization, but require only occasional attention in another. Professional staffing and development may be a dominant managerial concern in one organization and of relatively less concern in another.

These differences are ones of emphasis, however. Despite the relative importance, no organization can neglect the acquisition of materials essential to its objectives, or the effective allocation and control over the use of those materials, nor can it escape considering manpower needs as those are defined by their particular goals and technologies. Knowledge and experience in the technologic or professional aspects of the organization's main work, then, are less important in the ability to cope with management problems, than is comprehension of the interrelationships of technical, clientele, and internal and external aspects of the organization.

The role of chief executive is particularly important in this respect. As organizations become multi-disciplined, and as they recognize the need for managerial specialists of various types, it becomes impossible for the chief executive to have *expert knowledge* of the several technical processes, client relations, or external relations. In these complicated organizations, then, the chief executive must be able to *comprehend* for administrative purposes a variety of things, and he must be able to fit them together. This is a "generalist" role, and indeed, the chief executive with expert knowledge in one of the organization's operations may be handicapped in behaving as a generalist — at least until his specialized technical knowledge has faded into memory or been subjected to self-control.

We believe that usually the chief executive first becomes one by transferring from *some* more specialized managerial role. In the early stages of an organization's evolution it frequently is the case that only those who at some point have been identified directly with the basic technology of the organization are considered qualified to step into the chief executive role. When the organization becomes multi-disciplined, any of several technical starting points may "qualify" an individual for consideration as a chief executive. When such organizations mature, however, it seems to us that the starting point and the route taken by the individual become of much less importance. Entering the organization by way of one of the managerial specialties, such as finance or personnel, may prepare the individual for executive responsibilities just as well as entering through one or another of the professions associated with the "ultimate work" of that organization.

We know that this view is not fully accepted in all quarters, but we believe it will become increasingly evident that the abilities of the individual, rather than arbitrary credentials, must be the basis of administrative selection — and that these abilities can be acquired in various ways.

The distinction is more clearly demonstrated at the organization-directing level where individuals may be quite effective without having had prior experience in the field. This is in spite of the fact that organizational differences in sources of financing, in public image, and in domain show up especially well at the organization-*directing* level.

All organizations potentially intrude into the domain of others, constantly competing and periodically negotiating for a "share of the market," or for jurisdiction, or for clientele. The aluminum industry now produces automobile components once preempted by the steel industry, and steel invades the furniture domain where wood formerly was unchallenged. Boys' Clubs, Boy Scouts, church clubs, "Ys," and school extra-curricular organizations compete for the time and energy of neighborhood boys, as well as for financial support by the community. The various armed services compete within the Pentagon for jurisdiction over new weapon systems and over outer space. Related disciplines compete with one another for the right to provide certain types of therapy or over the relative efficiencies of various therapeutic procedures.

All organizations thus constitute power and are potential misusers of power. All, therefore, face efforts by elements of the environment to guard against misuse, or otherwise limit the use of power. Whether this takes the form of governmental regulation of business, legislative investigation of executive agencies, "studies" by special consultants or accrediting groups, the effects on the administrative process are parallel. Considerations of external relations call in each case for consideration of the relatively distant future, for identification of broad trends, for strategy in reacting to pressures, and for maintaining organizational coherence and integrity in a heterogeneous environment whose diverse pressures would otherwise fragment the organization.

THE TRANSFERABILITY OF EXECUTIVES

It should be clear that we believe those who emphasize the differences in administration of various fields have failed to identify the fundamentals of the administrative process. We have also indicated our conviction that abilities rather than credentials — the true merit system — should govern the selection of administrators in any field. And we have sketched out the kinds of abilities, at each of three levels, which we believe are significant for administration.

We have indicated distinct limits to the transferability of supervisors and suggested that, while transfer poses difficulties at all levels, the limitations grow less severe as the individual moves to managing and finally to directing levels. This conclusion is based on a conviction that the knowledge component — what the administrator knows about the technologic or professional processes of the organization and about the context in which that organization operates — becomes relatively less important in the total requirement as we move from supervisory to managerial to directing levels.

We do not imply that every administrator is qualified to shift fields. We know of instances where the results have been disastrous, just as we know of examples where the results have been outstanding. We do suspect, however, that transfer among fields can profitably occur more often than it has in the past — with wider opportunities for organizations to recruit. The readiness of an individual for responsibilities in a new field, we suspect, depends on answers to two questions: What does the man need to bring to the job? And what does the field demand?

What does the man bring to the job? The administrator is a human being rather than a collection of skill or knowledge components, and there is a risk involved in the attempt to isolate certain kinds of abilities. The three to be suggested are not mutually exclusive; they overlap and they are difficult to identify and measure. They are discussed separately only to facilitate thinking about them.

What we have described as the functions of administration requires *ability to recognize and solve problems.* Establishment and modification of routines — or regular patterns of action — is a necessary facet of administration, but the individual who subordinates himself to routine is abdicating his responsibilities, and the "adaptability" mentioned earlier is missing. Nor is it sufficient to be able to solve problems. The able administrator must anticipate problems and be able to recognize and delineate problems before they grow to the point where he is forced to give them attention. This ability to recognize and solve problems is as important for the administrator who remains within a field as for the individual who transfers, and problem-solving ability is not unique to any of the fields under consideration here.

A second requirement might be termed *leadership*, by which we mean integrity and conviction as well as the ability to persuade and inspire respect and to be decisive when decisiveness is appropriate. The "operator" who views his organization as a platform for personal accomplishments will not consistently promote that organization or its mission. The unconvinced administrator will take the path of least resistance, responding opportunistically but inconsistently to various forces. But this is true whether the administrator remains with a field or switches. And we must emphasize our belief that leadership is not necessarily correlated with pre-eminence in a profession. It is as easy for the professionally certified administrator to subvert the organization's mission to the fads and doctrines of the profession as for the "outsider" to misunderstand the mission and opportunities.

The third requirement, we suggest, is *perceptiveness.* This includes the ability to recognize relationships, to think abstractly, to distinguish similarities and differences, and to sort important from irrelevant factors in a situation. Whether or not the individual moves from one field to another, he needs to be able to identify the underlying assumptions he has been able to make from his past experience and to recognize that these assumptions may — or may not — be appropriate in a new situation. This involves his understanding of the basic processes and responsibilities of administration, and his ability to distinguish and subordinate specific behavior patterns (both in himself and in others) from what we have referred to as fundamentals. Without such insight and perceptiveness it is doubtful that an administrator can successfully change fields — but it is equally doubtful that he can remain in a dynamic organization and perform effectively. No one field has a corner on perceptiveness, but there is some reason to believe that it is enhanced by transfer from one field to another, just as foreign travel or the study of primitive societies may help us better understand our own. Whether the executive transfers or not, the characteristic we have in mind is found only in those with catholic interests.

What does a field demand? The most important demand which an organization must place on its administrators, we believe, is one of *value commitment.* Unless the individual's personal convictions are consistent with the objectives or mission of the field, his leadership abilities will be wasted or, worse, exercised at cross-purposes to the organization. This requirement is problematic whether the field recruits from outside or internally, for the appropriate value commitment is not guaranteed by degrees or credentials. Not infrequently the certificated individual is committed to maintenance of the status quo or to traditional procedures, rather than to aggressive pursuit of new levels of achievement. Commitment to an out-dated version of a field's values can be disastrous.

A second requirement which may be levied by a field upon its administrators is the *knowledge component* referred to earlier. This requirement is more significant at lower administrative levels than at higher ones, more important in small single-operation organizations than in large, multi-discipline organizations, and more imperative during the early evolution of a field than when it becomes well-recognized. When an organization does not lie at either extreme of those considerations, we believe the transfer of executives from *nearby or adjacent* fields may be quite feasible, but that recruitment from highly different fields poses greater difficulties. For the diversified, well-established organization, administrative understanding as distinct from technical competence in the appropriate skills can be rather readily acquired by an alert administrator.

CONCLUSIONS

A serious impediment to the most effective allocation of administrative talent in our society is the parochialism which we see in each field. The traditions behind such parochialism are strong. We are told that the individual who has "never met a payroll" could not possibly administer a firm. It is said that he who has never taught classes certainly could not administer a school, and one who has not done casework could not possibly qualify as a social welfare administrator. Such traditions often are reinforced by formal or informal regulations which require professional certification.

We have indicated our conviction that the distinction between technical-professional activities and administrative activities has been inadequate, but that it is emerging gradually in our several fields. But where this distinction is not yet clear, the most dedicated and gifted administrator who lacks traditional credentials may fail. The emphasis on tradition is reinforced by the factor of vested interests — by the belief that the "limited opportunities" for the "top jobs" should be earmarked as a reward for those who start in the field and give it long, loyal service.

We believe there are several trends which will gradually bring about more effective utilization of administrative resources in our society, through increased transfer of administrators among fields:

A. The broadening and liberating educational base of our society is reducing the parochialism we have noted. Increasingly professional education is being preceded by liberal education, and the professional schools themselves are becoming less vocational under the impact of the basic academic disciplines.

B. The distinction between technologic or professional competence and administrative competence is emerging more clearly, as our organizations become more complex and activities are more clearly centered in specialized roles.

C. The vested interest in maintaining monopoly control over administrative positions will be offset, in part, by the development of prestigeful and rewarding opportunities in the technologic or professional field, so that administration is not the only way "to the top." Some experimentation with "scientific ladders" is underway in segments of industry, and we find signs of this sort of development in education and hospitals as well as in government.

D. Finally, the complexity of our times and the rapidity of change are gradually shifting attention from "limited opportunities" to a realization of the unlimited demand for competent, dedicated, insightful administrators.

In conclusion, we believe that the most effective allocation of administrative talents will come only with the development of administration itself as a recognized professional field, to be combined with other professional competencies.

Organization Theory:
Bureaucratic Influences and the Social Welfare Task

FRANK X. STEGGERT

As far as the general public is concerned, the terms bureaucracy and bureaucratic are normally used quite epithetically. In this popular sense, the terms connote such things as picayune red tape, unnecessary delay, coldly impersonal behavior and various forms of inefficiency — all of this, of course, viewed within the context of the authoritarian overly large public or corporate organization. To the social scientist, however, bureaucracy and bureaucratic are important technical terms lacking, for the most part, any such invidious implications. Bureaucracies are simply large-scale, complex, formal organizations empowered, under various systems of authority, and structured, on the basis of a number of rational principles and procedures, to achieve legitimate social objectives.

In Max Weber's initial and still seminal analysis of the bureaucratic form, his grand design for the modern, large-scale, technically complex organization provided for a system in which responsibilities would be assigned and authority relationships would be established most rationally and most efficiently. The bureaucratic structure, in his design, emphasized the office or the position rather than the individual, stressing the need for fully adequate job descriptions, clearly drawn jurisdictional boundaries, and specialists or experts fully qualified for their positions. The bureaucratic form is further characterized by notions of continuity and impersonality. In the ideal bureaucratized organization, officials are technically qualified, salaried careerists who base their administrative behavior on laws, rules, and standard operating procedures. Primarily a theory of structure which assumes a high degree of rationality on the part of organizational participants, classic bureaucratic theory posits a strict and well-defined hierarchy of authority functioning on the basis of clear-cut chain of command principles.[1]

If we conceive of Weber's pioneering achievements in constructing this ideal type organization as model building, then we should not be surprised, from our hindsight view, at the theory's omissions, inadequacies, and elements of artificiality or unreality. Model building involves using a variety of intellectual tools to try to understand "what's going on out there." It requires abstraction, and, given our limited ability to conceptualize, it results inevitably in simplifications of reality. Nevertheless, the frame of reference for organizational analysis established by Weber has provided one major foundation on which

---

[1] While Weber's theory of bureaucracy has been summarized in numerous secondary sources, Strother's analysis places the theory in a larger and most useful historical perspective. See George B. Strother, "Problems in the Development of a Social Science of Organization," in Harold J. Leavitt, ed., *The Social Science of Organizations* (Englewood Cliffs, N.J.: Prentice-Hall, 1963).

Reprinted with permission of the National Conference on Social Welfare, from Common Elements in Administration, *Ella W. Reed, ed. (Columbus, Ohio: National Conference on Social Welfare, 1965).*

43

a long line of sociologists have built theoretical refinements, and from which sociology and the various other disciplines of business and public administration, political science and economics have designed numerous research efforts.[2]

Bureaucratic theories, from which most of our traditional concepts of organization have been derived, have described organizations in mechanistic terms, viewing people primarily as a means of accomplishing work for certain organizational ends. Such traditional concepts of organization, to which the scientific management and administrative principle schools have also contributed, have been preoccupied with such problems as work assignments and the proper division of labor, and with budgeting, personnel, methods analysis, and related management technologies for direction and control. These traditionalist approaches have consistently emphasized the importance of formal structure. They have fixated, therefore, on processes of delegation of responsibility and authority, and on chain of command, span of control, and line-staff relationship concepts.

In a somewhat stereotypical sense, this traditional thinking has been exemplified in the fields of business administration and public administration and applied in both the business corporation and the government bureaucracy. As will be noted later, organizational thinking has changed very rapidly in the post-World War II era and there now exist numerous revisionist theories of administration and management.[3] Nevertheless, the bureaucratic theory which emerged from late nineteenth- and early twentieth-century notions about the proper practice of administration created an organizational tradition which is still very deeply rooted in practice. For administrative practitioners who assumed their organizational roles a generation or more ago, and who were therefore socialized accordingly, many of this tradition's assumptions may still be deeply ingrained.

What I have been identifying here, somewhat loosely, as the bureaucratic tradition, involves some basic interrelated assumptions. One is that the central, crucial, and important activities in organizations are conducted up and down the vertical hierarchy — that relevant information will flow up and that decisions and directives will, and should, flow down. This, according to traditional beliefs, is how formal organizations function. Traditionalists also tend to view organizations somewhat anthropomorphically—assuming that they have a kind of central nervous system (the chain of command) and a brain (top management) which acts as the principal steering device.

Since traditionalist modes of thought assume that an organization's business gets done in the vertical dimension, they further assume that vertical authority levels should (and do) roughly correspond to levels or gradations of talent and/or competence. It follows then that the superior-subordinate nexus constitutes the single most important type of organizational relationship. If this relationship is healthy and productive, organizational success follows naturally. While the description here is somewhat facetious, these are some of the assumptions which have contributed to the philosophic fabric of conventional organizational thought.

THE HUMAN RELATIONS MOVEMENT: PERSONALITY VERSUS ORGANIZATION

A few years ago, two spokesmen convening a special conference devoted to administra-

---

[2] For a cogent analysis of Weber's influence here, see Martin Landau, "Sociology and the Study of Formal Organization," paper presented at the 1965 Annual Meeting of the American Political Science Association, Washington, D.C., September 8-11, 1965.

[3] A partial range of some currently "competing" theories is summarized in Harold Koontz, "Making Sense of Management Theory," in Harold Koontz, ed., *Toward A Unified Theory of Management* (New York, McGraw-Hill, 1964).

tive problems argued that the style and practice of American management had undergone a silent revolution. In their opinion, ideas gradually emanating from psychiatry, psychology, and the behavioral sciences in general had radically revised basic administrative concepts about appropriate superior-subordinate relationships, the handling of employees, and the exercise of managerial authority.[4] In speaking in this vein, these gentlemen were accurately reflecting the "human relations" credo now prevalent, if not prevailing, in American management thought. At its worst, this school of thought tends to reduce organizational and administrative processes to the cliche that "the manager's job is to get things done through people." At its more sophisticated other extreme, it involves a pragmatic concern with human behavior phenomena as these clearly affect the structure and functioning of the organization and the principles on which it can be managed. This includes a concern for employee attitudes, expectations, value systems, tensions, and conflicts — particularly as these influence organizational productivity, adaptability, and cohesion.

Organizational thinking based on these newer human relations perspectives has created its own world of abstract maxims and its own stereotypes of what constitutes effective managerial behavior. In this regard it has repeated, at least to some extent, the often dogmatic theorizing characteristic of those applying the bureaucratic tradition.[5] Here too, it is not possible to assess the degree to which contemporary human relations theories have influenced administrative and managerial practices in what are still largely bureaucratized organizations.

It is quite clear, however, that some two decades of research around three interrelated aspects of organizational behavior — morale and employee productivity, satisfaction and motivation, and leadership and supervision — have crystallized in a new group of normative theories of management. The values implicit in these various human relations theories have indeed derived historically from convergent interests of social psychologists, social anthropologists, sociologists, and clinical psychologists in man-in-organization. While it is true that many students of administration had in the past considered people as an essential organizational resource, their main concerns had been with the formal system, its aims, and the principles on which it should be constituted to achieve its objectives. Most current human relations theorists argue instead that people constitute a special and significantly different organizational resource. In their view, people not only work for the organization — they *are* the organization.

Most human relations theories emphasize the dysfunctional behavioral consequences of traditional bureaucratic structures and, simultaneously, the need for more humane organizational environments compatible with the kinds of higher order human needs posited by a developmental psychology. As a principal PVO theorist,[6] the views of Argyris are illustrative. His thesis is simply that our traditional bureaucratized organizational structures require behavior that tends to frustrate, place in conflict, and create failure for psychologically healthy individuals.[7] If, as he contends, the natural pattern of

---

[4] Wallace Wohlking and Alan McLean, eds., "The Impact of Psychiatry on American Management," Reprint Series No. 129, New York State School of Industrial and Labor Relations, Cornell University, p.1.

[5] It is, of course, at the application level that both bureaucratic and human relations theories break down. In their enthusiasm to apply theoretical formulations to organizational situations and administrative practices, "Marketers" of a particular view frequently extrapolate far beyond what their model builders had in mind.

[6] I borrow the PVO term and the phrase personality versus organization from Professor Edward Gross of the University of Washington's Department of Sociology.

[7] Chris Argyris, *Personality and Organization* (New York: Harper, 1957).

human development in our society involves development toward mature activities along a number of behavioral continua, then bureaucratic structures seem designed to arrest this development. Bureaucratic structures and administrative processes which subordinate large numbers of organizational members — keeping them dependent and psychologically inactive, containing their task abilities, and requiring them to function within short time perspectives — are, from this particular human relations point of view, fostering immature attitudes and rewarding child-like behaviors.

As with bureaucratic theories, there are a number of interrelated philosophic assumptions at work here. For most human relations theorists, the organizational model is self-actualizing man. They assume, drawing largely from the work of Maslow, that man's needs are hierarchically arranged, ranging upward from basic physiological needs through affiliative needs to self-esteem, autonomy, and, finally, self-actualization or self-realization needs.[8] Beyond the assumption that bureaucracies largely ignore man's higher-order motives, theorists with strong human relations orientations seem to assume that formal organizations are more constraining and inhibiting than other social institutions. They rather clearly assume the need for widespread creative behavior within large, complex organizational structures. They do so, it would seem, because they assume the universality of the self-actualization drive and emphasize the importance of the job as a source of needs satisfaction in our society.

Managerial theories based on human relations perspectives have been criticized on the basis of these assumptions, as well as on a number of other grounds. Strauss, for example, contends that PVO hypotheses underemphasize the significance of economic rewards, while ignoring or misapplying organizational economics.[9] Most human relations theorists advocate power equalization approaches — deliberately reducing power and status differentials between superiors and subordinates — in approaching the problem of applied organizational change. There are, of course, certain costs as well as gains involved in applying power equalization notions in complex organizations. It should be noted here, however, that one measure of the strength of contemporary human relations theories is the generally qualified nature of the criticisms leveled agains them. Most critiques argue that there is some merit in the PVO position, but contend that the hypothesis tries to prove too much.

The psychological and sociological influences which have combined to create human relations management theories have, therefore, established new positions for evaluation of formal organizational structure and administrative behavior. These new sets of values have, in turn, resulted in a more eclectic perception of organizational objectives and consequent managerial practices, as well as an increasingly general recognition of formal organizations as conflict structures.[10] In this frame of reference, both organizations and individuals are seen as entitites striving for self-realization, with each constituent in each

---

[8] Abraham H. Maslow, *Motivation and Personality* (New York: Harper, 1954). Although Maslow has been only incidentally concerned with applying his motivational analyses to organizational situations, he is now so widely referred to in the general management and personnel management literatures that no single documentation of his significance would be meaningful.

[9] This is discussed in George Strauss, "Some Notes on Power Equalization," in Harold J. Leavitt, ed., *The Social Science of Organizations* (Englewood Cliffs, N.J.: Prentice-Hall, 1963).

[10] For a more extended analysis of these human relations results, see Frank X. Steggert, "The Contributions and Uses of Psychology in the Understanding of Administrative Behavior," paper presented at the 1965 Annual Meeting of the American Political Science Association, Washington, D.C., September 8-11, 1965.

organization-individual relationship attempting to influence the other. The organization seeks to shape its members in its image while each individual tries to express his personality by using the organization for his own ends.

How then does the manager in a bureaucratic structure resolve the conflict between his organization's legitimate needs for predictability (and thus for a variety of formal control and coordination procedures) and the human unpredictability resulting from allowing subordinates to function more autonomously (and thus engaging in more needs-satisfying behavior)? How does he simultaneously maintain that part of the organizational system for which he is responsible while satisfying, to use McGregor's term, the human side of his enterprise? The "solutions" to this particular "management dilemma" depend, in large part, on the particular conception of human behavior one holds.

There are some (theorists as well as practitioners) whose notions of management have been described as constituting a kind of theory of "benevolent autocracy." Adherents to this position believe that the average person is basically work-avoiding and that, as a result, he must be coerced, controlled, directed, and perhaps even threatened.[11] The "benevolence" involved stems from concurrent beliefs that the average person prefers direction, wants to avoid responsibility, has little ambition, and most wants security. This vestigial economic man model has been characterized by McGregor as a Theory X orientation.[12] At the other extreme (involving perhaps more theorists and fewer practitioners) is a much more optimistic perception of man-in-organization (McGregor's Theory Y orientations). PVO theorists, located here, see effort in work as natural. As a result, they assume that the average person will exercise self-direction and self-control toward objectives to which he is committed; that, under appropriate conditions, the average person learns to accept and even to seek responsibility. In terms of this more complex model of man, the capacity for imagination and creativity is widely distributed and the absence of creative behavior in organizations results from underutilization of human resources.

There are, therefore, two polar approaches suggested for resolution of the "management dilemma" cited above. In both instances, however, the resolution hinges upon denial of any fundamental conflict. The benevolent autocracy approach denies that there is any real need for people in large-scale organizations to be allowed much in the way of autonomous behavior, while PVO theory holds that organizations need not do very much in the way of establishing formal control and coordination mechanisms. As Roethlisberger has analyzed behavioral science contributions to management theory, these fundamental "doctrinal positions" determine differential attitudes toward organizational change. Human relations theorists are activist in their willingness to attempt modification of resistant-to-change organizational structures. Opposing schools of thought emphasize the impossibility of substantially altering bureaucratic forms designed as they are for very good functional reasons. To adherents to this position, "human relationists" who want to humanize bureaucracies are self-deluding, incurable romanticists.[13]

In closing this brief sketch of human relations impacts on bureaucratic theory, it should be made quite clear that many human relations positions are neither naive nor

---

[11] See, for example, Robert N. McMurry, "The Case for Benevolent Autocracy," *Harvard Business Review*, Vol. 36 No. 1 (January-February), 1958.

[12] For this and for contrasting Theory Y orientations, see Douglas McGregor, *The Human Side of Enterprise* (New York: McGraw-Hill, 1960).

[13] See Fritz J. Roethlisberger, "Contributions of the Behavioral Sciences to a General Theory of Management," in Harold Koontz, ed., *Toward A Unified Theory of Management* (New York: McGraw-Hill, 1964).

doctrinaire. Many theorists – particularly those whose professional work has involved major empirical studies and/or extended organizational consulting – are prepared to accept the reality of dilemma based on conflict elements in organization. The strategies (not solutions) they suggest have to do with the kinds of reciprocal accommodation behaviors which organizations can use to mediate organization-individual goal conflicts.[14] These more objective middle-ground positions recognize the large residue of mutual oppositions which remain even after reciprocal accommodations have been made, and they accept the need for continuous "fusion process" activities aimed at reconciling and harmonizing organizational, group, and individual motives.[15] They are not about to do away with budgets or other management control and improvement procedures.[16]

The human relations theorists who assume that man-in-organization is complex (not simply self-actualizing nor influenced solely by economic or social motives),[17] can discard the goal of a frustration-free work environment, while at the same time contending that bureaucratic control behavior can be modified without organizationally damaging consequences. The position they exemplify is that control can be exercised for both individual adjustment and organizational performance if intelligent utilization of human resources is recognized as an important criterion.[18] Operationally, therefore, organizational control procedures could recognize the diverse capabilities, temperaments, and attitudes of the people employed, could integrate personality predispositions with control patterns, and could seek consensus at the work group level.

SOME ADDITIONAL DIMENSIONS: TECHNOLOGICAL PROCESSES AND PROFESSIONAL PRACTICE

With the advent of human relations schools of thought, management theories became more eclectic and definitions of administration became more comprehensive. Most definitions of organizational and management objectives now include at least some kind of a human relations reference, and at least a secondary emphasis on the appropriate utilization of human resources. And yet there are quite a few theoreticians today who believe that such perceptions of organizational behavior are quite incomplete. For these critics, technical and technological factors in organization have been largely ignored. As Dubin has remarked in his recent study of supervision and productivity, this relative neglect of technology – the core feature of the modern industrial world – might be attributed to the current preoccupation with the psyche of man-in-organization.[19]

---

[14] For a useful non-technical analysis of such problems of accommodation, see Warren Bennis, "Beyond Bureaucracy," *Trans-action*, Vol. 2, No. 5 (July-August), 1965.

[15] For a more extended and more theoretical discussion of accommodation processes in organization, see E. Wight Bakke, *The Fusion Process* (New Haven: Yale University Press, 1953).

[16] The normative human relations theory discussed by Likert makes full use of such procedures. See Rensis Likert, *New Patterns of Management* (New York: McGraw-Hill, 1961).

[17] These various assumptions about men-in-organizations are well and succinctly discussed in Edgar H. Schein, *Organizational Psychology* (Englewood Cliffs, N.J.: Prentice-Hall, 1965).

[18] This position is outlined in Philip M. Marcus and Dora Cafagna, "Control in Modern Organizations," *Public Administration Review*, Vol. 25, No. 2 (June), 1965.

[19] Robert Dubin, "Supervision and Productivity: Empirical Findings and Theoretical Considerations," in Robert Dubin, ed., *Leadership and Productivity* (San Francisco: Chandler, 1965).

Dubin's study demonstrates that the technological characteristics of work settings may influence productivity significantly more than the supervisory behavior patterns of those in authority roles. Other earlier studies of supervision in industrial work settings have indicated that the primary and essential supervisory functions there may be basically technical.[20] In such settings, the system itself exercises the principal behavioral control and the supervisor is more the human monitor of a complex flow system. He is more a technical trouble-shooter, a facilitator, and a liaison between workers and their technical support activities than he is anything else.

Until very recently, relatively few organization theorists had paid much attention to the technical subsystem in bureaucracy.[21] Now more are developing a concern for such aspects of organizational behavior. Some recent contributions from British sociology have been particularly influential in developing this concern. The work of Burns and Stalker in studying the introduction of advanced technologies into established organizations indicated that the specific technical system which developed determined: the organization's communication patterns, its managerial activities, its superior-subordinate interactions, and the location and content of its authority relationships.[22] In pursuing a related line of inquiry, Woodward's research concluded that the level of technological development (from most simple through most complex production systems) significantly influences general patterns of organization as well as such specific features as authority levels, spans of control, clarity of role definitions, volume of written communication, and degree of functional specialization.[23]

These and related studies suggest that the essential behavior of organizations is becoming increasingly lateral or horizontal. Corporate structures as well as industrial production organizations are being affected,[24] and there is evidence that organizations of all kinds are feeling the pressures of increasing technical change and its consequences. The lateral or horizontal coordination of specialists is becoming a major problem in organizational functioning. This is particularly true as skilled experts and talented specialists are pulled out of the organizational mainstream and set aside in "staff" groupings — because they do not "fit" the typical chain of command structure. As new organizational technologies require well-integrated and well-coordinated flow process activities, in which various specialized functions are linked together, peer colleague interaction becomes the key human relationship. Good superior-subordinate relationships can not guarantee interfunctional effectiveness.

The fact that more management theorists no longer see technical and technological factors as peripheral should not be taken to mean that organizational structures are readily adapting to technical change pressures. As noted earlier, the essential elements of the bureaucratic tradition are deeply ingrained, and the vertical authority system (with all

---

[20] See C. R. Walker, R. H. Guest, and A. N. Turner, *The Foreman on the Assembly Line* (Cambridge: Harvard University Press, 1956); and R. L. Simpson, "Vertical and Horizontal Communication in Formal Organizations," *Administrative Science Quarterly*, Vol. 4, 1959.

[21] For an exception to this generalization, see Victor A. Thompson, *Modern Organization* (New York: Knopf, 1961).

[22] Tom Burns and G. M. Stalker, *The Management of Innovation* (London: Tavistock Publications, 1961).

[23] Joan Woodward, *Management and Technology* (London: Her Majesty's Stationery Office, 1958).

[24] For a discussion of these influences on the business organization, see F. J. Jasinski, "Adapting Organization to New Technology," *Harvard Business Review*, Vol. 37, No. 1 (January-February), 1959.

its efficiency and effectiveness assumptions) is still the dominant structural arrangement in large private and public organizations. At the same time, pressures for speed in operations is creating another kind of "management dilemma." How can the manager in a vertical authority structure effectively control and coordinate his subordinates, when they must constantly work with others in the lateral non-authority relations way required by the technical system?

A major deficiency in organizational analyses based on conventional bureaucratic theories and human relations perspectives has been the static nature of such critiques. The more recent concerns with problems and processes of technical change and technological influence have, if nothing else, created a much greater awareness of the open system character of large, complex, managed organizations.[25] Organizations are more and more being evaluated in terms of their ability to adapt to change forces in their internal and external environments. As one commentator has succinctly put the matter, our "once-reliable constants have now become galloping variables."[26] The kinds of bureaucratic structures eminently suited to fairly routinized tasks in a highly competitive, undifferentiated, and stable environment are, therefore, largely inappropriate in a technologically complex, socially interdependent, and cooperative milieu.

One can draw a number of object lessons, perhaps, by considering the rather extreme problems posed by providing technical assistance to nonindustrial developing nations in various sectors of the world. Among the problems currently frustrating governmental and academic development administrators is the problem of creating workable administrative structures in new emergent nations — in environments of extremely rapid economic, political and social change. Experience to date suggests that very little can be accomplished by exporting and transplanting western administrative practices derived from traditional control-oriented bureaucratic theories. In developmental bureaucracies in non-modern cultures, different administrative structures seem to be required. The structures which will likely emerge are those based on more adaptive administrative principles — principles which seek to maximize innovative atmospheres, free and open communication, shared planning and operational activities, fusing of planning and action functions, cosmopolitan professional values, recognition of technical influence, and toleration of organizational interdependencies.[27]

It should be emphasized here that professional practice and technical activity comprise the principal technological influences in bureaucratized organizations geared to the production of services. In such organizations, the professional capability and/or the technical skill involved is the basic technology. This is certainly so in highly professionalized organizations, regardless of the administrative superstructure or the mechanization of functions which are essential or incidental to basic work functions.

There are some theorists who believe that professional manpower utilization will constitute our most important and most difficult administrative problem during the decade or two to come. Generally speaking, **professionals** do not fit neatly into our traditional kinds of administrative structures. Another basic idea underlying conventional bureaucratic forms is the notion that differential decision-making and performance ratios must exist at different organizational levels. On the basis of this logic, lower levels in the vertical table of organization should be primarily concerned with performance **activities**

---

[25] This awareness is undoubtedly responsible for the current wave of interest in problems of innovation, creative behavior, and planned change in organizations — an interest apparent at the levels of both theory and practice.

[26] Bennis, *op. cit.*

[27] This enumeration is drawn from Victor A. Thompson, "Administrative Objectives for Development Administration," *Administrative Science Quarterly,* Vol. 9, 1964.

and minimally involved in decision processes. As one ascends in the organizational hierarchy, there should be less performance functions evident and more decision activities should be found. At the apex, organizational behavior should be almost exclusively non-performance in character.

One of the essential characteristics of truly professional activity is, of course, the fusion of decision-making and performance behaviors. The professional is by definition involved with a non-standardized product or service and the uniquely personal aspects of his skill are precisely those which can't be readily controlled or coordinated. His relation to his clients — in terms of both his own professional ethics and his clients' expectations — are such that the employing organization may again experience considerable difficulty in structuring these relationships. The professional is, in addition, not without power vis-a-vis his organization. Beyond the fact that his knowledge of specialized techniques makes him essential to the organization, he usually has the sanctions of professional colleague support and general social validation available to him. To complicate further this third type of "management dilemma," the evidence suggests that the "better" he is as a professional, the more he will be oriented to professional influences outside the organization and the less concerned will he be with organizational considerations and administrative processes.[28]

TOWARD AN EMERGING ORGANIZATION THEORY

There is, as yet, no general, comprehensive organization theory which encompasses all the parameters represented by traditional bureaucratic theory, human relations schools of thought, and the management science and other perspectives which emphasize technological and technical influences on organizational behavior. There has been, in addition, a pronounced tendency to use the term "organization theory" very loosely. The term is often used as a synonym for some traditional concerns of public administration (administrative theory), sociology (bureaucratic theory), economics (theories of choice), and social psychology (group dynamics).[29] It is also frequently employed to describe the esoteric new fields of study deriving from mathematics and the "hard sciences" — fields such as decision theory, information theory, game theory, systems theory, and operations research.[30]

It would be more accurate, therefore, to speak of organization theories since, at present, we have only sub-theories of various kinds which seek to describe and analyze different dimensions of organizational behavior. Study and research into organizational behavior are fairly recent phenomena (perhaps as new as space science) and, in this sense, the present volume and scope of available organizational knowledge is remarkable. What now exists is largely the result of a coming-together trend among social scientists who increasingly see the total organization (or at least larger pieces of it) as the basic unit for analysis in trying to resolve problems of administrative process and managerial behavior. Organization theory has thus become more multidisciplinary as theoreticians representing a number of different fields have approached the study of organizational behavior more precisely and more scientifically. As inquiries focusing on the essential properties of large, complex, managed systems continue and enlarge, an organization science applicable to

---

[28] This classic dilemma for the administrator is discussed in Alvin W. Gouldner, "Cosmopolitans and Locals," *Administrative Science Quarterly*, Vol. 2, 1957 and 1958.

[29] Landau, *op. cit.*

[30] See A. H. Rubenstein and C. J. Haberstroh, eds., *Some Theories of Organization* (Homewood, Illinois: Dorsey, 1960); and Mason Haire, *Modern Organization Theory* (New York: Wiley, 1961).

improving bureaucratic operations should develop. Somewhat conjecturally, bureaucratic organization may then be seen as involving an array of goal-seeking tasks which both influence and are influenced by decision processes, structural arrangements, technological factors, and human considerations. Although a primary emphasis on the internal aspects of organizational behavior is likely to continue, the organization's larger external task environment should be recognized as ultimately controlling. The effects of the technological milieu, the prevailing social philosophy, ethical frames of reference, public policies, public attitudes, public expectations, professional values and interorganizational dependencies will be much better understood. Bureaucratic behavior will then be evaluated in terms of responses to these external stimuli, as well as responses to internally generated relationships, pressures, tensions, conflicts and accommodations.[31]

This is, of course, a speculative view of a holistic organization theory which does not yet exist. There are, however, clear evidences that such enlarged frames of reference for analyzing organizational behavior are emerging. The present interest in general systems theory provides one illustration. General systems theory, or the "systems approach," represents a new scientific movement which seeks to break disciplinary knowledge barriers by providing a unified theory for both individual and group behavior. Originally generated by theoretical biologists, general systems theory has become one of the new umbrellas under which different social and behavioral scientists can approach common problems of organizational behavior.

The broader approach of systems theory involves looking at behavior from greater distances than has been the case with other theoretical points of vantage. At this greater distance, there is a better likelihood of seeing the many forces that influence behavior within a particular system, thus avoiding microscopic perceptions of the system's behavior. If a system is conceived of as including all the formal and informal processes that occur in a specific sector of life, then individuals, families, groups, formal organizations, and communities are all systems, with each functioning as an element within a still larger system.[32] For purposes of organizational analysis, the focal points of critical concern become the "interfaces," the points at which individual or group behaviors collide with bureaucratic systemic processes, and the points at which the organization or its various major parts interact with the community and other systems in its external task environment.

Traditional bureaucratic theories, human relations theories, and scientific management theories have all represented oversimplified unidimensional perceptions of organizational behavior. Bureaucratic theories have fixated on problems of formal structure, human relations theories have been preoccupied with behavioral issues, and scientific management theories have been almost exclusively concerned with technological process matters. Each position has tended to assume that its particular premises constituted a set of imperatives (structural, human or technical), and that other considerations should involve either natural or managed adaptations to its basic values. Contemporary organization theory reflects much less of these closed system approaches and is increasingly concerned with understanding and optimizing the interactions of structure-people-technology relationships. The centrality of organizational tasks is emphasized, and

---

[31] These definitional projections are, of course, personal interpretations. While they are shared in large part by colleagues at the University of Wisconsin's Center for Advanced Study in Organization Science, they may or may not be shared by others concerned with what is variously known as organization theory, organization behavior, organization studies, or organizational psychology.

[32] For an introductory discussion of the systems approach and for more detailed references, see R. A. Johnson, F. E. Kast, and J. E. Rosenzweig, *The Theory and Management of Systems* (New York: McGraw-Hill, 1963).

the influences of internal forces and external environmental factors on task definition and redefinition are more learly recognized and accepted.

Most of the more precise and more scientific interests of contemporary organization theorists have focused on internal dynamics of organizational behavior. According to a comprehensive review of recent studies of organizational behavior, analysis and research interests have clustered around four categories — decision processes and decision-making, technical change processes and the influence of technology on organizational functions and relationships, interpersonal relations within the organization, and a range of problems pertaining to the effectiveness of different organizational structures.[33] Within these categories, the greatest volume of research has occurred around interpersonal relationships within formal organizations, with, as might be expected, an emphasis on superior-subordinate interactions.

Research concerned with the varying ways in which supervisors adapt to situations in which their organizational role responsibilities conflict with the expectations of their subordinates is illustrative of the manner in which contemporary organization theory is producing more sophisticated insights into organizational behavior. In this instance, for example, eight different patterns of supervisory reaction to conflict situations have been identified as follows:

1. Some supervisors identify with superiors and their organizational demands, and evidence no overt concern for their subordinates. They reduce contacts with their subordinates to reduce guilt feelings over their lack of consideration. They may compromise by being friendly but only off the job.
2. Some supervisors identify with their subordinates to such a degree that they generally fail to carry out their organizational responsibilities.
3. Some successfully provide clear organizational guidance for their subordinates, at the same time maintaining an awareness of the needs of their subordinates.
4. Some acquiesce to the demands of their superiors and then rationalize their positions to their own subordinates.
5. Some are hypocritical and practice duplicity to avoid disapproval from above or below. In talking to their superiors, they blame their subordinates, and in talking to their subordinates they reverse the process.
6. Some develop blind spots, refusing to accept the existence of any conflict.
7. Some withdraw from conflict and develop a posture of apparent neutrality and objectivity.
8. Some employ other defense mechanisms, displacing aggression or introjecting.[34]

Research of this character, as well as related inquiries into supervisory styles and productivity, organizational climate and supervision, and structural constraints on supervisory behavior, have enlarged perceptions of the complexities of supervisory behavior far beyond earlier oversimplified discussions of the relative merits of authoritarian and democratic supervisory styles. New models for supervisory effectiveness in different task contexts continue to be developed as systemic factors in organizational behavior are better understood.[35]

Interest in supervisory behavior is part of a contemporary generalized interest on the part of organizational psychologists in the study of individuals in organizations. A number of sociological studies of role orientations — the end results of the interplay of

---

[33] Harold J. Leavitt and Bernard M. Bass, "Organizational Psychology," *Annual Review of Psychology*, Vol. 15 (1964).

[34] This analysis is summarized in Leavitt and Bass, *op. cit.*

[35] See, for example, Fred E. Fiedler, "Leader Attitudes, Group Climate, and Group Creativity," *Journal of Abnormal and Social Psychology*, Vol. 64, 1962.

individual (primarily psychological) factors and organizational (primarily sociological) forces — have established the notion that bureaucratic influences and bureaucratic experiences differentially affect organizational members. The degree to which individuals either accept or reject the organizational bargain will determine the range of acceptance of the organization's values and the manner in which their interests and aspirations will either be tied to the organization or directed to meaningful aspects of their non-organizational lives.[36] The idea that bureaucracies create mostly "organization men" is both a naive and an inaccurate concept.

Contemporary organization theory is also characterized by a more objective and more dispassionate interest in problems of organizational design. While traditional bureaucratic theories have tended to venerate a certain limited set of structural principles and while human relations theorists have generally viewed bureaucratic structures as dysfunctional obstacles to human fulfillment, today's organization theorists are far more likely to emphasize the situational determinants of appropriate structures. Reflecting the systems approach which now influences organizational analyses, they are concerned with the particular structural arrangement which is most relevant to a given organization's primary tasks, its available technology, and the character of its human resources.[37]

IMPLICATIONS FOR SOCIAL WELFARE ADMINISTRATION

As organizations which are bureaucratized, social welfare agencies and institutions are subject to all the ills which stem from failure to alter traditional administrative practices to fit new knowledge conditions and new environmental circumstances. As organizations which are also professionalized, they are subject to the tensions generated by attempts to reconcile administrative and professional values. Bureaucracies as organizational forms designed to coordinate large-scale, technically complex social enterprises are not going to disappear. There are no other appropriate organizational mechanisms available. If anything, bureaucratization of work will increase as it has ever since its introduction in the western culture. At the same time, scientific, professional, and technical influences in organization will accelerate, not diminish.

There may be a natural tendency under such circumstances to assume that bureaucratic structures must adapt to their professionalizing task environments and that more professional manpower must be acquired if the organization is to achieve its goals. The first of these assumptions is most certainly correct, but the second is, at best, conjectural. Organization theory — even in its still evolving state — can provide considerable information, insight, and knowledge about problems involved in bureaucratic adaptations to a wide range of change objectives. It cannot, however, provide any specific norms which would identify what these change objectives should be, nor can it specify what the character of professional practice should be in a given bureaucratic structure. These are normative considerations and a social science of organization is concerned not with ends but with means — with the implications, applications, and consequences of alternative patterns of administrative behavior.

As has been noted, the combined contributions of the contemporary social and behavioral sciences have not produced anything like a single comprehensive organization theory. They have, however, developed a variety of sub-theories with significant explan-

---

[36] For an interesting non-technical discussion of this matter, see Robert Presthus, *The Organizational Society* (New York: Knopf, 1962).

[37] The problem of bringing various system factors into congruence is discussed in Robert T. Golembiewski, "Authority as a Problem in Overlays," *Administrative Science Quarterly,* Vol. 9, No. 1 (June, 1964.)

atory power relative to specific aspects of organizational behavior. Organizational theories can explain why some bureaucrats (and some organizations) are so bureaucratic. They can also explain why some professionals in organizations are so professional and so non-organizational in their orientations. They can clarify the rationales of bureaucratic and professional processes and they can describe, quite objectively and analytically, significant conflict points in bureaucratic organizations. They can elaborate at length on human behavior phenomena within formal organizations, they can identify organizational structures most likely to result in efficiency or satisfaction or innovation outcomes, and they can suggest an array of methods and procedures designed to produce a variety of administrative results.

There is, therefore, a body of readily available knowledge of organizational behavior potentially available to the social welfare administrator — knowledge which is sufficiently well organized that it can be studied systematically. While it is neither simply nor neatly packaged, it can provide a more adequate preparation for administrative responsibility than the educational means now available — assuming, of course, that those responsible for professional preparation and staff development programs in social welfare are willing to utilize what is now available.

Professional organizations are usually very slow to recognize any potential utility in courses of study outside the normal boundaries of the particular professional disciplines on which they are based. It is not surprising, therefore, that most organizations which are significantly influenced by an established field of professional study are very tentative in appraising the educational relevance of "generalist" training for their administrative staffs. At the same time, the professional schools immediately concerned with the training of present or potential administrators tend to be both slow and cautious in incorporating other disciplinary perspectives within their own curricula.

As social welfare administrators become formally educated for their administrative roles and responsibilities — this will happen as soon as such preparation is recognized as an educational imperative — they should benefit from the now adequate knowledge and perspectives of contemporary organization theory. They are likely to be trained for an adaptive innovative kind of administrative behavior. Instead of being prepared for a control-oriented administrative process which assumes the stability of fixed conditions, goals and resources, they will be trained for a *change-oriented administrative process* which assumes ambiguity, open communication, group decision, and a general problem orientation as the most characteristic features of modern bureaucratic behavior. This latter focus is more likely since the thrust of organization theory is identifying behaviors such as these as more relevant to administrative effectiveness in contemporary bureaucracies.

It is important to reiterate that although contemporary organization theory is both analytical and increasingly research-based, it remains descriptive and not prescriptive. Reflecting as it does a focus on dynamic forces within bureaucratic organizations and within the social systems impinging on the organization's behavior, it is necessarily concerned with value premises of interacting systems. It could not, however, remain scientific if it were to prescribe specific alternatives for organizational behavior. The utility of organization theory will continue to be its ability to describe complexities and conflicts of organizational behavior. At the application level, it can suggest those interpersonal, structural, and technical arrangements which will maximize a particular organizational value or optimize a particular organizational process.

While organization theory can suggest enlarged parameters for the analysis of social welfare administration, only the social welfare field and the political community can examine the field's specific task environment — so that organizational tasks can be adequately redefined and understood and so that relevant professional technologies can be articulated. The movement from an income maintenance orientation to a service or case assistance focus in public welfare is illustrative here, creating as it did major structural inconsistencies within public welfare agencies. These structural strains and tensions should increase even further. Social welfare organizations of all kinds will become increasingly caught up in broader social action programs as society continues to recast its explanations of the causations of social pathologies.

It is already apparent that the psychoanalytic orientations and rehabilitative emphases of current social welfare theory and practice are being challenged by social science perspectives which view society as a differentially organized system and which emphasize the epidemiological and situational character of individual maladjustments. This ongoing shift with its transitional effects on social work education is bound to heighten professional tensions within social welfare organizations. Traditional perceptions of social welfare activities as involving a set of clinical tasks will not yield readily to new systems-oriented definitions.

A heightened emphasis on developmental concepts in welfare administration and the consequent need to design new systems for maximization of interorganizational relationships and interagency cooperation will require new divisions of labor and role and role relationship redefinitions within social welfare organizations. The need to cope with enlarged welfare tasks with staffs which are likely to be proportionately less professionalized than at present will require new organizational technologies geared to most effective utilization of available staff resources. This too will result in structural reorganization patterns and require, as a result, a more significant attention to problems of human relationships within social welfare bureaucracies. Some modern organizational theories are available to help with these readjustment processes.

Foundations of the Theory of Organization

PHILIP SELZNICK

Trades unions, governments, business corporations, political parties, and the like are formal structures in the sense that they represent rationally ordered instruments for the achievement of stated goals. "Organization," we are told, "is the arrangement of personnel for facilitating the accomplishment of some agreed purpose through the allocation of functions and responsibilities."[1] Or, defined more generally, formal organization is "a system of consciously coordinated activities or forces of two or more persons."[2] Viewed in this light, formal organization is the structural expression of rational action. The mobilization of technical and managerial skills requires a pattern of coordination, a systematic ordering of positions and duties which defines a chain of command and makes possible the administrative integration of specialized functions. In this context *delegation* is the primordial organizational act, a precarious venture which requires the continuous elaboration of formal mechanisms of coordination and control. The security of all participants, and of the system as a whole, generates a persistent pressure for the institutionalization of relationships, which are thus removed from the uncertainties of individual fealty or sentiment. Moreover, it is necessary for the relations within the structure to be determined in such a way that individuals will be interchangeable and the organization will thus be free of dependence upon personal qualities.[3] In this way, the formal structure becomes subject to calculable manipulation, an instrument of rational action.

But as we inspect these formal structures we begin to see that they never succeed in conquering the non-rational dimension of organizational behavior. The latter remain at once indispensable to the continued existence of the system of coordination and at the same time the source of friction, dilemma, doubt, and ruin. This fundamental paradox arises from the fact that rational action systems are inescapably imbedded in an institutional matrix, in two significant senses: (1) the action system—or the formal structure of delegation and control which is its organizational expression—is itself only an aspect of a concrete social structure made up of individuals who may interact as *wholes*, not simply in terms of their formal roles within the system; (2) the formal system, and the social structure within which it finds concrete existence, are alike subject to the pressure of an

---

[1] John M. Gaus, "A Theory of Organization in Public Administration," in *The Frontiers of Public Administration* (Chicago: University of Chicago Press, 1936), p. 66.

[2] Chester I. Barnard, *The Functions of the Executive* (Cambridge: Harvard University Press, 1938), p. 73.

[3] Cf. Talcott Parsons' generalization (after Max Weber) of the "law of the increasing rationality of action systems," in *The Structure of Social Action* (New York: McGraw-Hill, 1937), p. 752.

Reprinted from American Sociological Review, *Vol. 13 (Feb., 1948), pp. 25-35, with permission of the American Sociological Association and the author.*

institutional environment to which some over-all adjustment must be made. The formal administrative design can never adequately or fully reflect the concrete organization to which it refers, for the obvious reason that no abstract plan or pattern can—or may, if it is to be useful—exhaustively describe an empirical totality. At the same time, that which is not included in the abstract design (as reflected, for example, in a staff-and-line organization chart) is vitally relevant to the maintenance and development of the formal system itself.

Organization may be viewed from two standpoints which are analytically distinct but which are empirically united in a context of reciprocal consequences. On the one hand, any concrete organizational system is an *economy*; at the same time, it is an *adaptive social structure*. Considered as an economy, organization is a system of relationships which define the availability of scarce resources and which may be manipulated in terms of efficiency and effectiveness. It is the economic aspect of organization which commands the attention of management technicians and, for the most part, students of public as well as private administration.[4] Such problems as the span of executive control, the role of staff or auxiliary agencies, the relation of headquarters to field offices, and the relative merits of single or multiple executive boards are typical concerns of the science of administration. The coordinative scalar, and functional principles, as elements of the theory of organization, are products of the attempt to explicate the most general features of organization as a "technical problem" or, in our terms, as an economy.

Organization as an economy is, however, necessarily conditioned by the organic states of the concrete structure, outside of the systematics of delegation and control. This becomes especially evident as the attention of leadership is directed toward such problems as the legitimacy of authority and the dynamics of persuasion. It is recognized implicitly in action and explicitly in the work of a number of students that the possibility of manipulating the system of coordination depends on the extent to which that system is operating within an environment of effective inducement to individual participants and of conditions in which the stability of authority is assured. This is in a sense the fundamental thesis of Barnard's remarkable study, *The Functions of the Executive*. It is also the underlying hypothesis which makes it possible for Urwick to suggest that "proper" or formal channels in fact function to "confirm and record" decisions arrived at by more personal means.[5] We meet it again in the concept of administration as a process of education, in which the winning of consent and support is conceived to be a basic function of leadership.[6] In short, it is recognized that control and consent cannot be divorced even within formally authoritarian structures.

The indivisibility of control and consent makes it necessary to view formal organizations as *cooperative* systems, widening the frame of reference of those concerned with the manipulation of organizational resources. At the point of action, of executive decision, the economic aspect of organization provides inadequate tools for control over the concrete structure. This idea may be readily grasped if attention is directed to the role of the individual within the organizational economy. From the standpoint of organization as a formal system, persons are viewed functionally, in respect to their *roles*, as participants in

---

[4] See Luther Gulick and Lydall Urwick, eds., *Papers on the Science of Administration* (New York: Institute of Public Administration, Columbia University, 1937); Lydall Urwick, *The Elements of Administration* (New York: Harper, 1943); James D. Mooney and Alan C. Reiley, *The Principles of Organization* (New York: Harper, 1939); H. S. Dennison, *Organization Engineering* (New York: McGraw-Hill, 1931).

[5] Urwick, *The Elements of Administration, op. cit.,* p. 47.

[6] See Gaus, *op. cit.* Studies of the problem of morale are instances of the same orientation, having received considerable impetus in recent years from the work of the Harvard Business School group.

assigned segments of the cooperative system. But in fact individuals have a propensity to resist depersonalization, to spill over the boundaries of their segmentary roles, to participate as *wholes*. The formal systems (at an extreme, the disposition of "rifles" at a military perimeter) cannot take account of the deviations thus introduced, and consequently break down as instruments of control when relied upon alone. The whole individual raises new problems for the organization, partly because of the needs of his own personality, partly because he brings with him a set of established habits as well, perhaps, as commitments to special groups outside of the organization.

Unfortunately for the adequacy of formal systems of coordination, the needs of individuals do not permit a single-minded attention to the stated goals of the system within which they have been assigned. The hazard inherent in the act of delegation derives essentially from this fact. Delegation is an organizational act, having to do with formal assignments of functions and powers. Theoretically, these assignments are made to roles or official positions, not to individuals as such. In fact, however, delegation necessarily involves concrete individuals who have interests and goals which do not always coincide with the goals of the formal system. As a consequence, individual personalities may offer resistance to the demands made upon them by the official conditions of delegation. These resistances are not accounted for within the categories of coordination and delegation, so that when they occur they must be considered as unpredictable and accidental. Observations of this type of situation within formal structures are sufficiently commonplace. A familiar example is that of delegation to a subordinate who is also required to train his own replacement. The subordinate may resist this demand in order to maintain unique access to the "mysteries" of the job, and thus insure his indispensability to the organization.

In large organizations, deviations from the formal system tend to become institutionalized, so that "unwritten laws" and informal associations are established. Institutionalization removes such deviations from the realm of personality differences, transforming them into a persistent structural aspect of formal organizations.[7] These institutionalized rules and modes of informal cooperation are normally attempts by participants in the formal organization to control the group relations which form the environment of organizational decisions. The informal patterns (such as cliques) arise spontaneously, are based on personal relationships, and are usually directed to the control of some specific situation. They may be generated anywhere within a hierarchy, often with deleterious consequences for the formal goals of the organization, but they may also function to widen the available resources of executive control and thus contribute to rather than hinder the achievement of the stated objectives of the organization. The deviations tend to force a shift away from the purely formal system as the effective determinant of behavior to (1) a condition in which informal patterns buttress the formal, as through the manipulation of sentiment within the organization in favor of established authority; or (2) a condition wherein the informal controls affect a consistent modification of formal goals, as in the case of some bureaucratic patterns.[8] This trend will eventually result in the formalization of erstwhile informal activities, with the cycle of deviation and transformation beginning again on a new level.

---

[7] The creation of informal structures within various types of organizations has received explicit recognition in recent years. See F. J. Roethlisberger and W. J. Dickson, *Management and the Worker* (Cambridge: Harvard University Press, 1941), p. 524; also Barnard, *op. cit.,* c. ix; and Wilbert E. Moore, *Industrial Relations and the Social Order* (New York: Macmillan, 1946), chap. xv.

[8] For an analysis of the latter in these terms, see Philip Selznick, "An Approach to a Theory of Bureaucracy," *American Sociological Review,* Vol. VIII, No. 1 (February, 1943).

The relevance of informal structures to organizational analysis underlines the significance of conceiving of formal organizations as cooperative systems. When the totality of interacting groups and individuals becomes the object of inquiry, the latter is not restricted by formal, legal, or procedural dimensions. The *state of the system* emerges as a significant point of analysis, as when an internal situation charged with conflict qualifies and informs actions ostensibly determined by formal relations and objectives. A proper understanding of the organizational process must make it possible to interpret changes in the formal system—new appointments or rules or reorganizations—in their relation to the informal and unavowed ties of friendship, class loyalty, power cliques, or external commitment. This is what it means "to know the score."

The fact that the involvement of individuals as whole personalities tends to limit the adequacy of formal systems of coordination does not mean that organizational characteristics are those of individuals. The organic, emergent character of the formal organization considered as a cooperative system must be recognized. This means that the *organization* reaches decisions, takes action, and makes adjustments. Such a view raises the question of the relation between organizations and persons. The significance of theoretical emphasis upon the cooperative *system* as such is derived from the insight that certain actions and consequences are enjoined independently of the personality of the individuals involved. Thus, if reference is made to the "organization-paradox"—the tension created by the inhibitory consequences of certain types of informal structures within organizations—this does not mean that individuals themselves are in quandaries. It is the nature of the interacting consequences of divergent interests within the organization which creates the condition, a result which may obtain independently of the consciousness or the qualities of the individual participants. Similarly, it seems useful to insist that there are qualities and needs of leader*ship*, having to do with position and role, which are persistent despite variations in the character or personality of individual leaders themselves.

Rational action systems are characteristic of both individuals and organizations. The conscious attempt to mobilize available internal resources (e.g., self-discipline) for the achievement of a stated goal—referred to here as an economy or a formal system—is one aspect of individual psychology. But the personality considered as a dynamic system of interacting wishes, compulsions, and restraints defines a system which is at once essential and yet potentially deleterious to what may be thought of as the "economy of learning" or to individual rational action. At the same time, the individual personality is an adaptive structure, and this, too, requires a broader frame of reference for analysis than the categories of rationality. On a different level, although analogously, we have pointed to the need to consider organizations as cooperative systems and adaptive structures in order to explain the context of and deviations from the formal systems of delegation and coordination.

To recognize the sociological relevance of formal structures is not, however, to have constructed a theory of organization. It is important to set the framework of analysis, and much is accomplished along this line when, for example, the nature of authority in formal organizations is reinterpreted to emphasize the factors of cohesion and persuasion as against legal or coercive sources.[9] This redefinition is logically the same as that which introduced the conception of the self as social. The latter helps make possible, but does not of itself fulfill, the requirements for a dynamic theory of personality. In the same way, the definition of authority as conditioned by sociological factors of sentiment and cohesion—or more generally the definition of formal organizations as cooperative systems—only sets the stage, as an initial requirement, for the formulation of a theory of organization.

---

[9] Robert Michels, "Authority," *Encyclopedia of the Social Sciences* (New York: Macmillan, 1931), pp. 319ff.; also Barnard, *op. cit.*, c. xii.

Structural-Functional Analysis. Cooperative systems are constituted of individuals interacting as wholes in relation to a formal system of coordination. The concrete structure is therefore a resultant of the reciprocal influences of the formal and informal aspects of organization. Furthermore, this structure is itself a totality, an adaptive "organism" reacting to influences upon it from an external environment. These considerations help to define the objects of inquiry; but to progress to a system of predicates *about* these objects it is necessary to set forth an analytical method which seems to be fruitful and significant. The method must have a relevance to empirical materials, which is to say, it must be more specific in its reference than discussions of the logic or methodology of social science.

The organon which may be suggested as peculiarly helpful in the analysis of adaptive structures has been referred to as "structural-functional analysis."[10] This method may be characterized in a sentence: *Structural-functional analysis relates contemporary and variable behavior to a presumptively stable system of needs and mechanisms*. This means that a given empirical system is deemed to have basic needs, essentially related to self-maintenance; the system develops repetitive means of self-defense; and day-to-day activity is interpreted in terms of the function served by that activity for the maintenance and defense of the system. Put this generally, the approach is applicable on any level in which the determinate "states" of empirically isolable systems undergo self-impelled and repetitive transformations when impinged upon by external conditions. This self-impulsion suggests the relevance of the term "dynamic," which is often used in referring to physiological, psychological, or social systems to which this type of analysis has been applied.[11]

It is a postulate of the structural-functional approach that the basic need of all empirical systems is the maintenance of the integrity and continuity of the system itself. Of course, such a postulate is primarily useful in directing attention to a set of "derived imperatives" or needs which are sufficiently concrete to characterize the system at hand.[12] It is perhaps rash to attempt a catalogue of these imperatives for formal organizations, but some suggestive formulation is needed in the interests of setting forth the type of analysis under discussion. In formal organizations, the "maintenance of the system" as a generic need may be specified in terms of the following imperatives:

1. *The security of the organization as a whole in relation to social forces in its environment*. This imperative requires continuous attention to the possibilities of encroachment and to the forestalling of threatened aggressions or deleterious (though perhaps unintended) consequences from the actions of others.

---

[10] For a presentation of this approach having a more general reference than the study of formal organizations, see Talcott Parsons, "The Present Position and Prospects of Systematic Theory in Sociology," in Georges Gurvitch and Wilbert E. Moore, eds., *Twentieth Century Sociology* (New York: The Philosophical Library, 1945).

[11] "Structure" refers to both the relationships within the system (formal plus informal patterns in organization) and the set of needs and modes of satisfaction which characterize the given type of empirical system. As the utilization of this type of analysis proceeds, the concept of "need" will require further clarification. In particular, the imputation of a "stable set of needs" to organizational systems must not function as a new instinct theory. At the same time, we cannot avoid using these inductions as to generic needs, for they help us to stake out our area of inquiry. The author is indebted to Robert K. Merton who has, in correspondence, raised some important objections to the use of the term "need" in this context.

[12] For "derived imperative" see Bronislaw Malinowski, *The Dynamics of Culture Change* (New Haven: Yale University Press, 1945), pp. 44ff. For the use of "need" in place of "motive" see the same author's *A Scientific Theory of Culture* (Chapel Hill: University of North Carolina Press, 1944), pp. 89-90.

2. *The stability of the lines of authority and communication.* One of the persistent reference-points of administrative decision is the weighing of consequences for the continued capacity of leadership to control and to have access to the personnel or ranks.

3. *The stability of informal relations within the organization.* Ties of sentiment and self-interest are evolved as unacknowledged but effective mechanisms of adjustment of individuals and sub-groups to the conditions of life within the organization. These ties represent a cementing of relationships which sustains the formal authority in day-to-day operations and widens opportunities for effective communication.[13] Consequently, attempts to "upset" the informal structure, either frontally or as an indirect consequence of formal reorganization, will normally be met with considerable resistance.

4. *The continuity of policy and of the sources of its determination.* For each level within the organization, and for the organization as a whole, it is necessary that there be a sense that action taken in the light of a given policy will not be placed in continuous jeopardy. Arbitrary or unpredictable changes in policy undermine the significance of (and therefore the attention to) day-to-day action by injecting a note of capriciousness. At the same time, the organization will seek stable roots (or firm statutory authority or popular mandate) so that a sense of the permanency and legitimacy of its acts will be achieved.

5. *A homogeneity of outlook with respect to the meaning and role of the organization.* The minimization of disaffection requires a unity derived from a common understanding of what the character of the organization is meant to be. When this homogeneity breaks down, as in situations of internal conflict over basic issues, the continued existence of the organization is endangered. On the other hand, one of the signs of "healthy" organization is the ability to effectively orient new members and readily slough off those who cannot be adapted to the established outlook.

This catalogue of needs cannot be thought of as final, but it approximates the stable system generally characteristic of formal organizations. These imperatives are derived, in the sense that they represent the conditions for survival or self-maintenance of cooperative systems of organized action. An inspection of these needs suggests that organizational survival is intimately connected with the struggle for relative prestige, both for the organization and for elements and individuals within it. It may therefore be useful to refer to a *prestige-survival motif* in organizational behavior as a short-hand way of relating behavior to needs, especially when the exact nature of the needs remains in doubt. However, it must be emphasized that prestige-survival in organizations does not derive simply from like motives in individuals. Loyalty and self-sacrifice may be individual expressions of organizational or group egotism and self-consciousness.

The concept of organizational need directs analysis to the *internal relevance* of organizational behavior. This is especially pertinent with respect to discretionary action undertaken by agents manifestly in pursuit of formal goals. The question then becomes one of relating the specific act of discretion to some presumptively stable organizational need. In other words, it is not simply action plainly oriented internally (such as in-service training) but also action presumably oriented externally which must be inspected for its relevance to internal conditions. This is of prime importance for the understanding of bureaucratic behavior, for it is of the essence of the latter that action formally undertaken for substantive goals be weighed and transformed in terms of its consequences for the position of the officialdom.

Formal organizations as cooperative systems on the one hand, and individual personalities on the other, involve structural-functional homologies, a point which may help to clarify the nature of this type of analysis. If we say that the individual has a stable set of needs, most generally the need for maintaining and defending the integrity of his

---

[13] They may also *destroy* those relationships, as noted above, but the need remains, generating one of the persistent dilemmas of leadership.

personality or ego; that there are recognizable certain repetitive mechanisms which are utilized by the ego in its defense (rationalization, projection, regression, etc.); and that overt and variable behavior may be interpreted in terms of its relation to these needs and mechanisms—on the basis of this logic we may discern the typical pattern of structural-functional analysis as set forth above. In this sense, it is possible to speak of a "Freudian model" for organizational analysis. This does not mean that the substantive insights of individual psychology may be applied to organizations, as in vulgar extrapolations from the individual ego to whole nations or (by a no less vulgar inversion) from strikes to frustrated workers. It is the *logic*, the *type* of analysis which is pertinent.

This homology is also instructive in relation to the applicability of generalizations to concrete cases. The dynamic theory of personality states a set of possible predicates about the ego and its mechanisms of defense, which inform us concerning the propensities of individual personalities under certain general circumstances. But these predicates provide only tools for the analysis of particular individuals, and each concrete case must be examined to tell which operate and in what degree. They are not primarily organs of prediction. In the same way, the predicates within the theory of organization will provide tools for the analysis of particular cases. Each organization, like each personality, represents a resultant of complex forces, an empirical entity which no single relation or no simple formula can explain. The problem of analysis becomes that of selecting among the possible predicates set forth in the theory of organization those which illuminate our understanding of the materials at hand.

The setting of structural-functional analysis as applied to organizations requires some qualification, however. Let us entertain the suggestion that the interesting problem in social science is not so much why men act the way they do as why men in certain circumstances *must* act the way they do. This emphasis upon constraint, if accepted, releases us from an ubiquitous attention to behavior in general, and especially from any undue fixation upon statistics. On the other hand, it has what would seem to be the salutary consequence of focusing inquiry upon certain necessary relationships of the type "if . . . then," for example: If the cultural level of the rank and file members of a formally democratic organization is below that necessary for participation in the formulation of policy, then there will be pressure upon the leaders to use the tools of demagogy.

Is such a statement universal in its applicability? Surely not in the sense that one can predict without remainder the nature of all or even most political groups in a democracy. Concrete behavior is a resultant, a complex vector, shaped by the operation of a number of such general constraints. But there is a test of general applicability: it is that of noting whether the relation made explicit must be *taken into account* in action. This criterion represents an empirical test of the significance of social science generalizations. If a theory is significant it will state a relation which will either (1) be taken into account as an element of achieving control, or (2) be ignored only at the risk of losing control and will evidence itself in a ramification of objective or unintended consequences.[14] It is a corollary of this principle of significance that investigation must search out the underlying factors in organizational action, which requires a kind of intensive analysis of the same order as psychoanalytic probing.

---

[14] See R. M. MacIver's discussion of the "dynamic assessment" which "brings the external world selectively into the subjective realm, conferring on it subjective significance for the ends of action," in *Social Causation* (Boston: Ginn, 1942), Chapters 11, 12. The analysis of this assessment within the context of organized action yields the implicit knowlege which guides the choice among alternatives. See also Robert K. Merton, "The Unanticipated Consequences of Purposive Social Action," *American Sociological Review*, Vol. I, No. 6 (December, 1936).

A frame of reference which invites attention to the constraints upon behavior will tend to highlight tensions and dilemmas, the characteristic paradoxes generated in the course of action. The dilemma may be said to be the handmaiden of structural-functional analysis, for it introduces the concept of *commitment* or *involvement* as fundamental to organizational analysis. A dilemma in human behavior is represented by an inescapable commitment which cannot be reconciled with the needs of the organism or the social system. There are many spurious dilemmas which have to do with verbal contradictions, but inherent dilemmas to which we refer are of a more profound sort, for they reflect the basic nature of the empirical system in question. An economic order committed to profit as its sustaining incentive may, in Marxist terms, sow the seed of its own destruction. Again, the anguish of man, torn between finitude and pride is not a matter of arbitrary and replaceable assumptions but is a reflection of the psychological needs of the human organism, and is concretized in his commitment to the institutions which command his life; he is in the world and of it, inescapably involved in its goals and demands; at the same time, the needs of the spirit are compelling, proposing modes of salvation which have continuously disquieting consequences for worldly involvements. In still another context, the need of the human organism for affection and response necessitates a commitment to elements of the culture which can provide them; but the rule of the super-ego is uncertain since it cannot be completely reconciled with the need for libidinal satisfactions.

Applying this principle to organizations we may note that there is a general source of tension observable in the split between "the motion and the act." Plans and programs reflect the freedom of technical or ideal choice, but organized action cannot escape involvement, a commitment to personnel or institutions or procedures which effectively qualifies the initial plan. *Der Mensch denkt, Gott lenkt*. In organized action, this ultimate wisdom finds a temporal meaning in the recalcitrance of the tools of action. We are inescapably committed to the mediation of human structures which are at once indispensable to our goals and at the same time stand between them and ourselves. The selection of agents generates immediately a bifurcation of interest, expressed in new centers of need and power, placing effective constraints upon the arena of action, and resulting in tensions which are never completely resolved. This is part of what it means to say that there is a "logic" of action which impels us forward from one undesired position to another. Commitment to dynamic, self-activating tools is of the nature of organized action; at the same time, the need for continuity of authority, policy, and character are pressing, and require an unceasing effort to master the instruments generated in the course of action. This generic tension is specified within the terms of each cooperative system. But for all we find a persistent relationship between *need* and *commitment* in which the latter not only qualifies the former but unites with it to produce a continuous state of tension. In this way, the notion of constraint (as reflected in tension or paradox) at once widens and more closely specifies the frame of reference for organizational analysis.

For Malinowski, the core of functionalism was contained in the view that a cultural fact must be analyzed in its setting. Moreover, he apparently conceived of his method as pertinent to the analysis of all aspects of cultural systems. But there is a more specific problem, one involving a principle of selection which serves to guide inquiry along significant lines. Freud conceived of the human organism as an adaptive structure, but he was not concerned with all human needs, nor with all phases of adaptation. For his system, he selected those needs whose expression is blocked in some way, so that such terms as repression, inhibition, and frustration became crucial. All conduct may be thought of as derived from need, and all adjustment represents the reduction of need. But not all needs are relevant to the systematics of dynamic psychology; and it is not adjustment as such but reaction to frustration which generates the characteristic modes of defensive behavior.

Organizational analysis, too, must find its selective principle; otherwise the indiscriminate attempts to relate activity functionally to needs will produce little in the way of significant theory. Such a principle might read as follows: *Our frame of reference is to select out those needs which cannot be fulfilled within approved avenues of expression and thus must have recourse to such adaptive mechanisms as ideology and to the manipulation of formal processes and structures in terms of informal goals.* This formulation has many difficulties, and is not presented as conclusive, but it suggests the kind of principle which is likely to separate the quick and the dead, the meaningful and the trite, in the study of cooperative systems in organized action.[15]

The frame of reference outlined here for the theory of organization may now be identified as involving the following major ideas: (1) the concept of organizations as cooperative systems, adaptive social structures, made up of interacting individuals, sub-groups, and informal plus formal relationships; (2) structural-functional analysis, which relates variable aspects of organization (such as goals) to stable needs and self-defensive mechanisms; (3) the concept of recalcitrance as a quality of the tools of social action, involving a break in the continuum of adjustment and defining an environment of constraint, commitment, and tension. This frame of reference is suggested as providing a specifiable *area of relations* within which predicates in the theory of organization will be sought, and at the same time setting forth principles of selection and relevance in our approach to the data of organization.

It will be noted that we have set forth this frame of reference within the overall context of social action. The significance of events may be defined by their place and operational role in a means-end scheme. If functional analysis searches out the elements important for the maintenance of a given structure, and that structure is one of the materials to be manipulated in action, then that which is functional in respect to the structure is also functional in respect to the action system. This provides a ground for the significance of functionally derived theories. At the same time, relevance to control in action is the empirical test of their applicability or truth.

Cooptation as a Mechanism of Adjustment. The frame of reference stated above is in fact an amalgam of definition, resolution, and substantive theory. There is an element of *definition* in conceiving of formal organizations as cooperative systems, though of course the interaction of informal and formal patterns is a question of fact; in a sense, we are *resolving* to employ structural-functional analysis on the assumption that it will be fruitful to do so, though here, too, the specification of needs or derived imperatives is a matter for empirical inquiry; and our predication of recalcitrance as a quality of the tools of action is itself a *substantive theory*, perhaps fundamental to a general understanding of the nature of social action.

A theory of organization requires more than a general frame of reference, though the latter is indispensable to inform the approach of inquiry to any given set of materials. What is necessary is the construction of generalizations concerning transformations within and among cooperative systems. These generalizations represent, from the standpoint of particular cases, possible predicates which are relevant to the materials as we know them in general, but which are not necessarily controlling in all circumstances. A theory of transformations in organization would specify those states of the system which resulted typically in predictable, or at least understandable, changes in such aspects of organization as goals, leadership, doctrine, efficiency, effectiveness, and size. These empirical generalizations would be systematized as they were related to the stable needs of the cooperative system.

---

[15] This is not meant to deprecate the study of organizations as *economies* or formal systems. The latter represent an independent level, abstracted from organizational structures as cooperative or adaptive systems ("organisms").

Changes in the characteristics of organizations may occur as a result of many different conditions, not always or necessarily related to the processes of organization as such. But the theory of organization must be selective, so that explanations of transformations will be sought within its own assumptions or frame of reference. Consider the question of size. Organizations may expand for many reasons—the availability of markets, legislative delegations, the swing of opinion—which may be accidental from the point of view of the organizational process. To explore changes in size (as of, say, a trades union) as related to changes in nonorganizational conditions may be necessitated by the historical events to be described, but it will not of itself advance the frontiers of the theory of organization. However, if "the innate propensity of an organization to expand" is asserted as a function of "the inherent instability of incentives"[16] then transformations have been stated within the terms of the theory of organization itself. It is likely that in many cases the generalization in question may represent only a minor aspect of the empirical changes, but these organizational relations must be made explicit if the theory is to receive development.

In a frame of reference which specifies needs and anticipates the formulation of a set of self-defensive responses or mechanisms, the latter appear to constitute one kind of empirical generalization or "possible predicate" within the general theory. The needs of organizations (whatever investigation may determine them to be) are posited as attributes of all organizations, but the responses to disequilibrium will be varied. The mechanisms used by the system in fulfillment of its needs will be repetitive and thus may be described as a specifiable set of assertions within the theory of organization, but any given organization may or may not have recourse to the characteristic modes of response. Certainly no given organization will employ all of the possible mechanisms which are theoretically available. When Barnard speaks of an "innate propensity of organization to expand" he is in fact formulating one of the general mechanisms, namely, expansion, which is a characteristic mode of response available to an organization under pressure from within. These responses necessarily involve a transformation (in this case, size) of some structural aspect of the organization.

Other examples of the self-defensive mechanisms available to organizations may derive primarily from the response of these organizations to the institutional environments in which they live. The tendency to construct ideologies, reflecting the need to come to terms with major social forces, is one such mechanism. Less well understood as a mechanism of organizational adjustment is what we may term *cooptation*. Some statement of the meaning of this concept may aid in clarifying the foregoing analysis.

Cooptation is the process of absorbing new elements into the leadership or policy-determining structure of an organization as a means of averting threats to its stability or existence. This is a defensive mechanism, formulated as one of a number of possible predicates available for the interpretation of organizational behavior. Cooptation tells us something about the process by which an institutional environment impinges itself upon an organization and effects changes in its leadership and policy. Formal authority may resort to cooptation under the following general conditions:

1. When there exists a hiatus between consent and control, so that the legitimacy of the formal authority is called into question. The "indivisibility" of consent and control refers, of course, to an optimum situation. Where control lacks an adequate measure of consent, it may revert to coercive measures or attempt somehow to win the consent of the governed. One means of winning consent is to coopt elements into the leadership or organization, usually elements which in some way reflect the sentiment, or possess the confidence of the relevant public or mass. As a result, it is expected that the new elements will lend respectability or legitimacy to the organs of control and thus

---

[16] Barnard, *op. cit.*, pp. 158-9.

reestablish the stability of formal authority. This process is widely used, and in many different contexts. It is met in colonial countries, where the organs of alien control reaffirm their legitimacy by coopting native leaders into the colonial administration. We find it in the phenomenon of "crisis-patriotism" wherein normally disfranchised groups are temporarily given representation in the councils of government in order to win their solidarity in a time of national stress. Cooptation is presently being considered by the United States Army in its study of proposals to give enlisted personnel representation in the court-martial machinery—a clearly adaptive response to stresses made explicit during the war, the lack of confidence in the administration of army justice. The "unity" parties of totalitarian states are another form of cooptation; company unions or some employee representation plans in industry are still another. In each of these cases, the response of formal authority (private or public, in a large organization or a small one) is an attempt to correct a state of imbalance by *formal* measures. It will be noted, moreover, that what is shared is the *responsibility* for power rather than power itself. These conditions define what we shall refer to as *formal cooptation*.

2. Cooptation may be a response to the pressure of specific centers of power. This is not necessarily a matter of legitimacy or of a general and diffuse lack of confidence. These may be well established; and yet organized forces which are able to threaten the formal authority may effectively shape its structure and policy. The organization in respect to its institutional environment—or the leadership in respect to its ranks—must take these forces into account. As a consequence, the outside elements may be brought into the leadership or policy-determining structure, may be given a place as a recognition of and concession to the resources they can independently command. The representation of interests through administrative constituencies is a typical example of this process. Or, within an organization, individuals upon whom the group is dependent for funds or other resources may insist upon and receive a share in the determination of policy. This form of cooptation is typically expressed in informal terms, for the problem is not one of responding to a state of imbalance with respect to the "people as a whole" but rather one of meeting the pressure of specific individuals or interest-groups which are in a position to enforce demands. The latter are interested in the substance of power and not its forms. Moreoever, an open acknowledgement of capitulation to specific interests may itself undermine the sense of legitimacy of the formal authority within the community. Consequently, there is a positive pressure to refrain from explicit recognition of the relationship established. This form of the cooptative mechanism, having to do with the sharing of power as a response to specific pressures, may be termed *informal cooptation*.

Cooptation reflects a state of tension between formal authority and social power. The former is embodied in a particular structure and leadership, but the latter has to do with subjective and objective factors which control the loyalties and potential manipulability of the community. Where the formal authority is an expression of social power, its stability is assured. On the other hand, when it becomes divorced from the sources of social power its continued existence is threatened. This threat may arise from the sheer alienation of sentiment or from the fact that other leaderships have control over the sources of social power. Where a formal authority has been accustomed to the assumption that its constituents respond to it as individuals, there may be a rude awakening when organization of those constituents on a non-governmental basis creates nuclei of power which are able effectively to demand a sharing of power.[17]

[17] It is perhaps useful to restrict the concept of cooptation to formal organizations, but in fact it probably reflects a process characteristic of all group leaderships. This has received some recognition in the analysis of class structure, wherein the ruling class is interpreted as protecting its own stability by absorbing new elements. Thus Michels made the point that "an aristocracy cannot maintain an enduring stability by sealing itself off hermet-

The significance of cooptation for organizational analysis is not simply that there is a change in or a broadening of leadership, and that this is an adaptive response, but also that *this change is consequential for the character and role of the organization.* Cooptation involves commitment, so that the groups to which adaptation has been made constrain the field of choice available to the organization or leadership in question. The character of the coopted elements will necessarily shape (inhibit or broaden) the modes of action available to the leadership which has won adaptation and security at the price of commitment. The concept of cooptation thus implicitly sets forth the major points of the frame of reference outlined above: it is an adaptive response of a cooperative system to a stable need, generating transformations which reflect constraints enforced by the recalcitrant tools of action.

ically." See Robert Michels, *Umschichtungen in den herrschenden Klassen nach dem Kriege* (Stuttgart: Kohlhammer, 1934), p. 39; also Gaetano Mosca, *The Ruling Class* (New York: McGraw-Hill, 1939), pp. 413ff. The alliance or amalgamation of classes in the face of a common threat may be reflected in formal and informal cooptative responses among formal organizations sensitive to class pressures. In a forthcoming volume, *TVA and the Grass Roots,* the author has made extensive use of the concept of cooptation in analyzing some aspects of the organizational behavior of a government agency.

II Organizational Structure

Bureaucracy

MAX WEBER

CHARACTERISTICS OF BUREAUCRACY

Modern officialdom functions in the following specific manner:

I. There is the principle of fixed and official jurisdictional areas, which are generally ordered by rules, that is, by laws or administrative regulations.

A. The regular activities required for the purposes of the bureaucratically governed structure are distributed in a fixed way as official duties.

B. The authority to give the commands required for the discharge of these duties is distributed in a stable way and is strictly delimited by rules concerning the coercive means, physical, sacerdotal, or otherwise, which may be placed at the disposal of officials.

C. Methodical provision is made for the regular and continuous fulfilment of these duties and for the execution of the corresponding rights; only persons who have the generally regulated qualifications to serve are employed.

In public and lawful government these three elements constitute "bureaucratic authority." In private economic domination, they constitute bureaucratic "management." Bureaucracy, thus understood, is fully developed in political and ecclesiastical communities only in the modern state, and, in the private economy, only in the most advanced institutions of capitalism. Permanent and public office authority, with fixed jurisdiction, is not the historical rule but rather the exception. This is so even in large political structures such as those of the ancient Orient, the Germanic and Mongolian empires of conquest, or of many feudal structures of state. In all these cases, the ruler executes the most important measures through personal trustees, able-companions, or court-servants. Their commissions and authority are not precisely delimited and are temporarily called into being for each case.

II. The principles of office hierarchy and of levels of graded authority mean a firmly ordered system of super- and subordination in which there is a supervision of the lower offices by the higher ones. Such a system offers the governed the possibility of appealing the decision of a lower office to its higher authority, in a definitely regulated manner. With the full development of the bureaucratic type, the office hierarchy is monocratically organized. The principle of hierarchical office authority is found in all bureaucratic structures: in state and ecclesiastical structures as well as in large party organizations and private enterprises. It does not matter for the character of bureaucracy whether its authority is called "private" or "public."

When the principle of jurisdictional "competency" is fully carried through, hierarchical subordination—at least in public office—does not mean that the "higher" authority is simply authorized to take over the business of the "lower." Indeed, the opposite is the rule. Once established and having fulfilled its task, an office tends to continue in existence and be held by another incumbent.

III. The management of the modern office is based on written documents ("the files"), which are preserved in their original or draught form. There is, therefore, a staff of subaltern officials and scribes of all sorts. The body of officials actively engaged in a "public" office, along with the respective apparatus of material implements and the files, make up a "bureau." In private enterprise, "the bureau" is often called "the office."

In principle, the modern organization of the civil service separates the bureau from the private domicile of the offical, and, in general, bureaucracy segregates official activity as something distinct from the sphere of private life. Public monies and equipment are divorced from the private property of the official. This condition is everywhere the product of a long development. Nowadays, it is found in public as well as in private enterprises; in the latter, the principle extends even to the leading entrepreneur. In principle, the executive office is separated from the household, business from private correspondence, and business assets from private fortunes. The more consistently the modern type of business management has been carried through the more are these separations the case. The beginnings of this process are to be found as early as the Middle Ages.

It is the peculiarity of the modern entrepreneur that he conducts himself as the "first official" of his enterprise, in the very same way in which the ruler of a specifically modern bureaucratic state spoke of himself as "the first servant" of the state.[1] The idea that the bureau activities of the state are intrinsically different in character from the management of private economic offices is a continental European notion and, by way of contrast, is totally foreign to the American way.

IV. Office management, at least all specialized office management—and such management is distinctly modern—usually presupposes thorough and expert training. This increasingly holds for the modern executive and employee of private enterprises, in the same manner as it holds for the state official.

V. When the office is fully developed, official activity demands the full working capacity of the official, irrespective of the fact that his obligatory time in the bureau may be firmly delimited. In the normal case, this is only the product of a long development, in the public as well as in the private office. Formerly, in all cases, the normal state of affairs was reversed: official business was discharged as a secondary activity.

VI. The management of the office follows general rules, which are more or less stable, more or less exhaustive, and which can be learned. Knowledge of these rules represents a special technical learning which the officials possess. It involves jurisprudence, or administrative or business management.

The reduction of modern office management to rules is deeply embedded in its very nature. The theory of modern public administration, for instance, assumes that the authority to order certain matters by decree—which has been legally granted to public authorities—does not entitle the bureau to regulate the matter by commands given for each case, but only to regulate the matter abstractly. This stands in extreme contrast to the regulation of all relationships through individual privileges and bestowals of favor, which is absolutely dominant in patrimonialism, at least in so far as such relationships are not fixed by sacred tradition.

THE POSITION OF THE OFFICIAL

All this results in the following for the internal and external position of the official:

I. Office holding is a "vocation." This is shown, first, in the requirement of a firmly

---

[1] Frederick II of Prussia.

prescribed course of training, which demands the entire capacity for work for a long period of time, and in the generally prescribed and special examinations which are prerequisites of employment. Furthermore, the position of the official is in the nature of a duty. This determines the internal structure of his relations, in the following manner: Legally and actually, office holding is not considered a source to be exploited for rents or emoluments, as was normally the case during the Middle Ages and frequently up to the threshold of recent times. Nor is office holding considered a usual exchange of services for equivalents, as is the case with free labor contracts. Entrance into an office, including one in the private economy, is considered an acceptance of a specific obligation of faithful management in return for a secure existence. It is decisive for the specific nature of modern loyalty to an office that, in the pure type, it does not establish a relationship to a *person*, like the vassal's or disciple's faith in feudal or in patrimonial relationships of authority. Modern loyalty is devoted to impersonal and functional purposes. Behind the functional purposes, of course, "ideas of culture-values" usually stand. These are *ersatz* for the earthly or supra-mundane personal master: ideas such as "state," "church," "community," "party," or "enterprise" are thought of as being realized in a community; they provide an ideological halo for the master.

The political official—at least in the fully developed modern state— is not considered the personal servant of a ruler. Today, the bishop, the priest and the preacher are in fact no longer, as in early Christian times, holders of purely personal charisma. The supra-mundane and sacred values which they offer are given to everybody who seems to be worthy of them and who asks for them. In former times, such leaders acted upon the personal command of their master; in principle, they were responsible only to him. Nowadays, in spite of the partial survival of the old theory, such religious leaders are officials in the service of a functional purpose, which in the present-day "church" has become routinized and, in turn, ideologically hallowed.

II. The personal position of the official is patterned in the following way:

A. Whether he is in a private office or a public bureau, the modern official always strives and usually enjoys a distinct *social esteem* as compared with the governed. His social position is guaranteed by the prescriptive rules of rank order and, for the political official, by special definitions of the criminal code against "insults of officials" and "contempt" of state and church authorities.

The actual social position of the official is normally highest where, as in old civilized countries, the following conditions prevail: a strong demand for administration by trained experts; a strong and stable social differentiation, where the official predominantly derives from socially and economically privileged strata because of the social distribution of power; or where the costliness of the required training and status conventions are binding upon him. The possession of educational certificates—to be discussed elsewhere[2]—are usually linked with qualification for office. Naturally, such certificates or patents enhance the "status element" in the social position of the official. For the rest this status factor in individual cases is explicitly and impassively acknowledged; for example, in the prescription that the acceptance or rejection of an aspirant to an official career depends upon the consent ("election") of the members of the official body. This is the case in the German army with the officer corps. Similar phenomena, which promote this guild-like closure of officialdom, are typically found in patrimonial and, particularly, in prebendal officialdoms of the past. The desire to resurrect such phenomena in changed forms is by no means infrequent among modern bureaucrats. For instance, they have played a role among the demands of the quite proletarian and expert officials (the *tretyj* element) during the Russian revolution.

Usually the social esteem of the officials as such is especially low where the demand

---

[2] Cf. *Wirtschaft und Gesellschaft,* pp. 73ff. and part II [German editor's note].

for expert administration and the dominance of status conventions are weak. This is especially the case in the United States; it is often the case in new settlements by virtue of their wide fields for profit-making and the great instability of their social stratification.

B. The pure type of bureaucratic official is *appointed* by a superior authority. An official elected by the governed is not a purely bureaucratic figure. Of course, the formal existence of an election does not by itself mean that no appointment hides behind the election—in the state, especially, appointment by party chiefs. Whether or not this is the case does not depend upon legal statutes but upon the way in which the party mechanism functions. Once firmly organized, the parties can turn a formally free election into the mere acclamation of a candidate designated by the party chief. As a rule, however, a formally free election is turned into a fight, conducted according to definite rules, for votes in favor of one of two designated candidates.

In all circumstances, the designation of officials by means of an election among the governed modifies the strictness of hierarchical subordination. In principle, an official who is so elected has an autonomous position opposite the superordinate official. The elected official does not derive his position "from above" but "from below," or at least not from a superior authority of the official hierarchy but from powerful party men ("bosses"), who also determine his further career. The career of the elected official is not, or at least not primarily, dependent upon his chief in the administration. The official who is not elected but appointed by a chief normally functions more exactly, from a technical point of view, because, all other circumstances being equal, it is more likely that purely functional points of consideration and qualities will determine his selection and career. As laymen, the governed can become acquainted with the extent to which a candidate is expertly qualified for office only in terms of experience, and hence only after his service. Moreover, in every sort of selection of officials by election, parties quite naturally give decisive weight not to expert considerations but to the services a follower renders to the party boss. This holds for all kinds of procurement of officials by elections, for the designation of formally free, elected officials by party bosses when they determine the slate of candidates, or the free appointment by a chief who has himself been elected. The contrast, however, is relative: substantially similar conditions hold where legitimate monarchs and their subordinates appoint officials, except that the influence of the followings are then less controllable.

Where the demand for administration by trained experts is considerable, and the party followings have to recognize an intellectually developed, educated, and freely moving "public opinion," the use of unqualified officials falls back upon the party in power at the next election. Naturally, this is more likely to happen when the officials are appointed by the chief. The demand for a trained administration now exists in the United States, but in the large cities, where immigrant votes are "corralled," there is, of course, no educated public opinion. Therefore, popular elections of the administrative chief and also of his subordinate officials usually endanger the expert qualification of the official as well as the precise functioning of the bureaucratic mechanism. It also weakens the dependence of the officials upon the hierarchy. This holds at least for the large administrative bodies that are difficult to supervise. The superior qualification and integrity of federal judges, appointed by the President, as over against elected judges in the United States is well known, although both types of officials have been selected primarily in terms of party considerations. The great changes in American metropolitan administrations demanded by reformers have proceeded essentially from elected mayors working with an apparatus of officials who were appointed by them. These reforms have thus come about in a "Caesarist" fashion. Viewed technically, as an organized form of authority, the efficiency of "Caesarism," which often grows out of democracy, rests in general upon the position of the "Caesar" as a free trustee of the masses (of the army or of the citizenry), who is unfettered by tradition. The "Caesar" is thus the unrestrained master of a body of highly qualified military officers and officials whom he selects freely and personally without regard to tradition or to any other considerations. This "rule of the personal genius," however, stands in contradiction to the formally "democratic" principle of a universally elected officialdom.

C. Normally, the position of the official is held for life, at least in public bureaucracies; and this is increasingly the case for all similar structures. As a factual rule, *tenure for life* is presupposed, even where the giving of notice or periodic reappointment occurs. In contrast to the worker in a private enterprise, the official normally holds tenure. Legal or actual life-tenure, however, is not recognized as the official's right to the possession of office, as was the case with many structures of authority in the past. Where legal guarantees against arbitrary dismissal or transfer are developed, they merely serve to guarantee a strictly objective discharge of specific office duties free from all personal considerations. In Germany, this is the case for all juridical and, increasingly, for all administrative officials.

Within the bureaucracy, therefore, the measure of "independence," legally guaranteed by tenure, is not always a source of increased status for the official whose position is thus secured. Indeed, often the reverse holds, especially in old cultures and communities that are highly differentiated. In such communities, the stricter the subordination under the arbitrary rule of the master, the more it guarantees the maintenance of the conventional seigneurial style of living for the official. Because of the very absence of these legal guarantees of tenure, the conventional esteem for the official may rise in the same way as, during the Middle Ages, the esteem of the nobility of office[3] rose at the expense of esteem for the freemen, and as the king's judge surpassed that of the people's judge. In Germany, the military officer or the administrative official can be removed from office at any time, or at least far more readily than the "independent judge," who never pays with loss of his office for even the grossest offense against the "code of honor" or against social conventions of the salon. For this very reason, if other things are equal, in the eyes of the master stratum the judge is considered less qualified for social intercourse than are officers and administrative officials, whose greater dependence on the master is a greater guarantee of their conformity with status conventions. Of course, the average official strives for a civil-service law, which would materially secure his old age and provide increased guarantees against his arbitrary removal from office. This striving, however, has its limits. A very strong development of the "right to the office" naturally makes it more difficult to staff them with regard to technical efficiency, for such a development decreases the career-opportunities of ambitious candidates for office. This makes for the fact that officials, on the whole, do not feel their dependency upon those at the top. This lack of a feeling of dependency, however, rests primarily upon the inclination to depend upon one's equals rather than upon the socially inferior and governed strata. The present conservative movement among the Badenia clergy, occasioned by the anxiety of a presumably threatening separation of church and state, has been expressly determined by the desire not to be turned "from a master into a servant of the parish."[4]

D. The official receives the regular *pecuniary* compensation of a normally fixed *salary* and the old age security provided by a pension. The salary is not measured like a wage in terms of work done, but according to "status," that is, according to the kind of function (the "rank") and, in addition, possibly, according to the length of service. The relatively great security of the official's income, as well as the rewards of social esteem make the office a sought-after position, especially in countries which no longer provide opportunities for colonial profits. In such countries, this situation permits relatively low salaries for officials.

---

[3] *Ministerialen.*

[4] Written before 1914 [German editor's note].

E. The official is set for a *"career"* within the hierarchical order of the public service. He moves from the lower, less important, and lower paid to the higher positions. The average official naturally desires a mechanical fixing of the conditions of promotion; if not of the offices, at least of the salary levels. He wants these conditions fixed in terms of "seniority," or possibly according to grades achieved in a developed system of expert examinations. Here and there, such examinations actually form a character *indelebilis* of the official and have lifelong effects on his career. To this is joined desire to qualify the right to office and the increasing tendency toward status group closure and economic security. All of this makes for a tendency to consider the offices as "prebends" of those who are qualified by educational certificates. The necessity of taking general personal and intellectual qualifications into consideration, irrespective of the often subaltern character of the educational certificate, has led to a condition in which the highest political offices, especially the positions of "ministers," are principally filled without reference to such certificates. . . .

TECHNICAL ADVANTAGES OF BUREAUCRATIC ORGANIZATION

The decisive reason for the advance of bureaucratic organization has always been its purely technical superiority over any other form of organization. The fully developed bureaucratic mechanism compares with other organizations exactly as does the machine with the non-mechanical modes of production.

Precision, speed, unambiguity, knowledge of the files, continuity, discretion, unity, strict subordination, reduction of friction and of material and personal costs—these are raised to the optimum point in the strictly bureaucratic administration, and especially in its monocratic form. As compared with all collegiate, honorific, and avocational forms of administration, trained bureaucracy is superior on all these points. And as far as complicated tasks are concerned, paid bureaucratic work is not only more precise but, in the last analysis, it is often cheaper than even formally unremunerated honorific service.

Honorific arrangements make administrative work an avocation and, for this reason alone, honorific service normally functions more slowly; being less bound to schemata and being more formless. Hence it is less precise and less unified than bureaucratic work because it is less dependent upon superiors and because the establishment and exploitation of the apparatus of subordinate officials and filing services are almost unavoidably less economical. Honorific service is less continuous than bureaucratic and frequently quite expensive. This is especially the case if one thinks not only of the money costs to the public treasury—costs which bureaucratic administration, in comparison with administration by notables, usually substantially increases—but also of the frequent economic losses of the governed caused by delays and lack of precision. The possibility of administration by notables normally and permanently exists only where official management can be satisfactorily discharged as an avocation. With the qualitative increase of tasks the administration has to face, administration by notables reaches its limits—today, even in England. Work organized by collegiate bodies causes friction and delay and requires compromises between colliding interests and views. The administration, therefore, runs less precisely and is more independent of superiors; hence, it is less unified and slower. All advances of the Prussian administrative organization have been and will in the future be advances of the bureaucratic, and especially of the monocratic, principle.

Today, it is primarily the capitalist market economy which demands that the official business of the administration be discharged precisely, unambiguously, continuously, and with as much speed as possible. Normally, the very large, modern capitalist enterprises are themselves unequalled models of strict bureaucratic organization. Business management throughout rests on increasing precision, steadiness, and, above all, the speed of operations. This, in turn, is determined by the peculiar nature of the modern means of communication, including, among other things, the news service of the press. The extraordinary increase in the speed by which public announcements, as well as economic and political facts, are transmitted exerts a steady and sharp pressure in the direction of speeding up the tempo of administrative reaction towards various situations. The optimum of such reaction time is normally attained only by a strictly bureaucratic organization.[5]

Bureaucratization offers above all the optimum possibility for carrying through the principle of specializing administrative functions according to purely objective consider-ations. Individual performances are allocated to functionaries who have specialized training and who by constant practice learn more and more. The "objective" discharge of business primarily means a discharge of business according to *calculable rules* and "without regard for persons."

"Without regard for persons" is also the watchword of the "market" and, in general, of all pursuits of naked economic interests. A consistent execution of bureaucratic domination means the leveling of status "honor." Hence, if the principle of the free-market is not at the same time restricted, it means the universal domination of the "class situation." That this consequence of bureaucratic domination has not set in everywhere, parallel to the extent of bureaucratization, is due to the differences among possible principles by which polities may meet their demands.

The second element mentioned, "calculable rules," also is of paramount importance for modern bureaucracy. The peculiarity of modern culture, and specifically of its technical and economic basis, demands this very "calculability" of results. When fully developed, bureaucracy also stands, in a specific sense, under the principle of *sine ira ac studio*. Its specific nature, which is welcomed by capitalism, develops the more perfectly the more the bureaucracy is "dehumanized," the more completely it succeeds in elimin-ating from official business love, hatred, and all purely personal, irrational, and emotional elements which escape calculation. This is the specific nature of bureaucracy and it is appraised as its special virtue.

The more complicated and specialized modern culture becomes, the more its external supporting apparatus demands the personally detached and strictly "objective" *expert*, in lieu of the master of older social structures, who was moved by personal sympathy and favor, by grace and gratitude. Bureaucracy offers the attitudes demanded by the external apparatus of modern culture in the most favorable combination. As a rule, only bureau-cracy has established the foundation for the administration of a rational law conceptually systematized on the basis of such enactments as the latter Roman imperial period first created with a high degree of technical perfection. During the Middle Ages, this law was received along with the bureaucratization of legal administration, that is to say, with the displacement of the old trial procedure which was bound to tradition or to irrational presuppositions, by the rationally trained and specialized expert. . . .

THE CONCENTRATION OF THE MEANS OF ADMINISTRATION

The bureaucratic structure goes hand in hand with the concentration of the material means of management in the hands of the master. This concentration occurs, for instance, in a well-known and typical fashion, in the development of big capitalist enterprises, which find their essential characteristics in this process. A corresponding process occurs in public organizations.

The bureaucratically led army of the Pharaohs, the army during the later period of the

---

[5] Here we cannot discuss in detail how the bureaucratic apparatus may, and actually does, produce definite obstacles to the discharge of business in a manner suitable for the single case.

Roman republic and the principate, and, above all, the army of the modern military state are characterized by the fact that their equipment and provisions are supplied from the magazines of the war lord. This is in contrast to the folk armies of agricultural tribes, the armed citizenry of ancient cities, the militias of early medieval cities, and all feudal armies; for these, the self-equipment and the self-provisioning of those obliged to fight was normal.

War in our time is a war of machines. And this makes magazines technically necessary, just as the dominance of the machine in industry promotes the concentration of the means of production and management. In the main, however, the bureaucratic armies of the past, equipped and provisioned by the lord, have risen when social and economic development has absolutely or relatively diminished the stratum of citizens who were economically able to equip themselves, so that their number was no longer sufficient for putting the required armies in the field. They were reduced at least relatively, that is, in relation to the range of power claimed for the polity. Only the bureaucratic army structure allowed for the development of the professional standing armies which are necessary for the constant pacification of large states of the plains, as well as for warfare against far-distant enemies, especially enemies overseas. Specifically, military discipline and technical training can be normally and fully developed, at least to its modern high level, only in the bureaucratic army.

Historically, the bureaucratization of the army has everywhere been realized along with the transfer of army service from the propertied to the propertyless. Until this transfer occurs, military service is an honorific privilege of propertied men. Such a transfer was made to the native-born unpropertied, for instance, in the armies of the generals of the late Roman republic and the empire, as well as in modern armies up to the nineteenth century. The burden of service has also been transferred to strangers, as in the mercenary armies of all ages. This process typically goes hand in hand with the general increase in material and intellectual culture. The following reason has also played its part everywhere: the increasing density of population, and therewith the intensity and strain of economic work, makes for an increasing "indispensability" of the acquisitive strata[6] for purposes of war. Leaving aside periods of strong ideological fervor, the propertied strata of sophisticated and especially of urban culture as a rule are little fitted and also little inclined to do the coarse war work of the common soldier. Other circumstances being equal, the propertied strata of the open country are at least usually better qualified and more strongly inclined to become professional officers. This difference between the urban and the rural propertied is balanced only where the increasing possibility of mechanized warfare requires the leaders to qualify as "technicians."

The bureaucratization of organized warfare may be carried through in the form of private capitalist enterprise, just like any other business. Indeed, the procurement of armies and their administration by private capitalists has been the rule in mercenary armies, especially those of the Occident up to the turn of the eighteenth century. During the Thirty Years' War, in Brandenburg the soldier was still the predominant owner of the material implements of his business. He owned his weapons, horses, and dress, although the state, in the role, as it were, of the merchant of the "putting-out system," did supply him to some extent. Later on, in the standing army of Prussia, the chief of the company owned the material means of warfare, and only since the peace of Tilsit has the concentration of the means of warfare in the hands of the state definitely come about. Only with this concentration was the introduction of uniforms generally carried through. Before then, the introduction of uniforms had been left to a great extent to the arbitrary discretion of the regimental officer, with the exception of individual categories of troops to whom the king had "bestowed" certain uniforms, first, in 1620, to the royal body-

---

[6] *Erwerbende Schichten*

78

guard, then, under Frederick II, repeatedly.

Such terms as "regiment" and "battalion" usually had quite different meanings in the eighteenth century from the meanings they have today. Only the battalion was a tactical unit (today both are); the "regiment" was then a managerial unit of an economic organization established by the colonel's position as an "entrepreneur." "Official" maritime ventures (like the Genoese *maonae*) and army procurement belong to private capitalism's first giant enterprises of far-going bureaucratic character. In this respect, the "nationalization" of these enterprises by the state has its modern parallel in the nationalization of the railroads, which have been controlled by the state from their beginnings.

In the same way as with army organizations, the bureaucratization of administration goes hand in hand with the concentration of the means of organization in other spheres. The old administration by satraps and regents, as well as administration by farmers of office, purchasers of office, and, most of all, administration by feudal vassals, decentralize the material means of administration. The local demand of the province and the cost of the army and of subaltern officials are regularly paid for in advance from local income, and only the surplus reaches the central treasure. The enfeoffed official administers entirely by payment out of his own pocket. The bureaucratic state, however, puts its whole administrative expense on the budget and equips the lower authorities with the current means of expenditure, the use of which the state regulates and controls. This has the same meaning for the "economics" of the administration as for the large centralized capitalist enterprise.

In the field of scientific research and instruction, the bureaucratization of the always existing research institutes of the universities is a function of the increasing demand for material means of management. Liebig's laboratory at Giessen University was the first example of big enterprise in this field. Through the concentration of such means in the hands of the privileged head of the institute, the mass of researchers and docents are separated from their "means of production," in the same way as capitalist enterprise has separated the workers from theirs.

In spite of its indubitable technical superiority, bureaucracy has everywhere been a relatively late development. A number of obstacles have contributed to this, and only under certain social and political conditions have they definitely receded into the background. . . .

THE PERMANENT CHARACTER OF THE BUREAUCRATIC MACHINE

Once it is fully established, bureaucracy is among those social structures which are the hardest to destroy. Bureaucracy is *the* means of carrying "community action" over into rationally ordered "societal action." Therefore, as an instrument for "societalizing" relations of power, bureaucracy has been and is a power instrument of the first order—for the one who controls the bureaucratic apparatus.

Under otherwise equal conditions, a "societal action," which is methodically ordered and led, is superior to every resistance of "mass" or even of "communal action." And where the bureaucratization of administration has been completely carried through, a form of power relation is established that is practically unshatterable.

The individual bureaucrat cannot squirm out of the apparatus in which he is harnessed. In contrast to the honorific or avocational "notable," the professional bureaucrat is chained to his activity by his entire material and ideal existence. In the great majority of cases, he is only a single cog in an ever-moving mechanism which prescribes to him an essentially fixed route of march. The official is entrusted with specialized tasks and normally the mechanism cannot be put into motion or arrested by him, but only from the very top. The individual bureaucrat is thus forged to the community of all the functionaries who are integrated into the mechanism. They have a common interest in seeing that the mechanism continues its functions and that the societally exercised authority carries on.

The ruled, for their part, cannot dispense with or replace the bureaucratic apparatus of authority once it exists. For this bureaucracy rests upon expert training, a functional specialization of work, and an attitude set for habitual and virtuoso-like mastery of single yet methodically integrated functions. If the official stops working, or if his work is forcefully interrupted, chaos results, and it is difficult to improvise replacements from among the governed who are fit to master such chaos. This holds for public administration as well as for private economic management. More and more the material fate of the masses depends upon the steady and correct functioning of the increasingly bureaucratic organizations of private capitalism. The idea of eliminating these organizations becomes more and more utopian.

The discipline of officialdom refers to the attitude-set of the official for precise obedience within his *habitual* activity, in public as well as in private organizations. This discipline increasingly becomes the basis of all order, however great the practical importance of administration on the basis of the filed documents may be. The naive idea of Bakuninism of destroying the basis of "acquired rights" and "domination" by destroying public documents overlooks the settled orientation of *man* for keeping to the habitual rules and regulations that continue to exist independently of the documents. Every reorganization of beaten or dissolved troops, as well as the restoration of administrative orders destroyed by revolt, panic, or other catastrophes, is realized by appealing to the trained orientation of obedient compliance to such orders. Such compliance has been conditioned into the officials, on the one hand, and, on the other hand, into the governed. If such an appeal is successful it brings, as it were, the disturbed mechanism into gear again.

The objective indispensability of the once-existing apparatus, with its peculiar, "impersonal" character, means that the mechanism—in contrast to feudal orders based upon personal piety—is easily made to work for anybody who knows how to gain control over it. A rationally ordered system of officials continues to function smoothly after the enemy has occupied the area; he merely needs to change the top officials. This body of officials continues to operate because it is to the vital interest of everyone concerned, including above all the enemy.

During the course of his long years in power, Bismarck brought his ministerial colleagues into unconditional bureaucratic dependence by eliminating all independent statesmen. Upon his retirement, he saw to his surprise that they continued to manage their offices unconcerned and undismayed, as if he had not been the master mind and creator of these creatures, but rather as if some single figure had been exchanged for some other figure in the bureaucratic machine. With all the changes of masters in France since the time of the First Empire, the power machine has remained essentially the same. Such a machine makes "revolution," in the sense of the forceful creation of entirely new formations of authority, technically more and more impossible, especially when the apparatus controls the modern means of communication (telegraph, et cetera) and also by virtue of its internal rationalized structure. In classic fashion, France has demonstrated how this process has substituted *coups d'état* for "revolutions": all successful transformations in France have amounted to *coups d'état*....

THE POWER POSITION OF BUREAUCRACY

Everywhere the modern state is undergoing bureaucratization. But whether the *power* of bureaucracy within the polity is universally increasing must here remain an open question.

The fact that bureaucratic organization is technically the most highly developed means of power in the hands of the man who controls it does not determine the weight that bureaucracy as such is capable of having in a particular social structure. The ever-increasing "indispensability" of the officialdom, swollen to millions, is no more decisive for this question than is the view of some representatives of the proletarian movement that the economic indispensability of the proletarians is decisive for the measure of their social and political power position. If "indispensability" were decisive, then where slave labor prevailed and where freemen usually abhor work as a dishonor, the "indispensable" slaves ought to have held the positions of power, for they were at least as indispensable as officials and proletarians are today. Whether the power of bureaucracy as such increases cannot be decided *a priori* from such reasons. The drawing in of economic interest groups or other non-official experts, or the drawing in of non-expert lay representatives, the establishment of local, inter-local, or central parliamentary or other representative bodies, or of occupational associations—these *seem* to run directly against the bureaucratic tendency. How far this appearance is the truth must be discussed in another chapter rather than in this purely formal and typological discussion. In general, only the following can be said here:

Under normal conditions, the power position of a fully developed bureaucracy is always overtowering. The "political master" finds himself in the position of the "dilet-tante" who stands opposite the "expert," facing the trained official who stands within the management of administration. This holds whether the "master" whom the bureaucracy serves is a "people," equipped with the weapons of "legislative initiative," the "referendum," and the right to remove officials, or a parliament, elected on a more aristocratic or more "democratic" basis and equipped with the right to vote a lack of confidence, or with the actual authority to vote it. It holds whether the master is an aristocratic, collegiate body, legally or actually based on self-recruitment, or whether he is a popularly elected president, a hereditary and "absolute" or a "constitutional" monarch.

Every bureaucracy seeks to increase the superiority of the professionally informed by keeping their knowledge and intentions secret. Bureaucratic administration always tends to be an administration of "secret sessions"; in so far as it can, it hides its knowledge and action from criticism. Prussian church authorities now threaten to use disciplinary measures against pastors who make reprimands or other admonitory measures in any way accessible to third parties. They do this because the pastor, in making such criticism available, is "guilty" of facilitating a possible criticism of the church authorities. The treasury officials of the Persian shah have made a secret document of their budgetary art and even use secret script. The official statistics of Prussia, in general, make public only what cannot do any harm to the intentions of the power-wielding bureaucracy. The tendency toward secrecy in certain administrative fields follows their material nature: everywhere that the power interests of the domination structure toward *the outside* are at stake, whether it is an economic competitor of a private enterprise, or a foreign, potentially hostile polity, we find secrecy. If it is to be successful, the management of diplomacy can only be publicly controlled to a very limited extent. The military administration must insist on the concealment of its most important measures; with the increasing significance of purely technical aspects, this is all the more the case. Political parties do not proceed differently, in spite of all the ostensible publicity of Catholic congresses and party conventions. With the increasing bureaucratization of party organizations, this secrecy will prevail even more. Commercial policy, in Germany, for instance, brings about a concealment of production statistics. Every fighting posture of a social structure toward the outside tends to buttress the position of the group in power.

The pure interest of the bureaucracy in power, however, is efficacious far beyond those areas where purely functional interests make for secrecy. The concept of the "official secret" is the specific invention of bureaucracy, and nothing is so fanatically defended by the bureaucracy as this attitude, which cannot be substantially justified beyond these specifically qualified areas. In facing a parliament, the bureaucracy, out of a sure power instinct, fights every attempt of the parliament to gain knowledge by means of its own experts or from interest groups. The so-called right of parliamentary investigation is one of the means by which parliament seeks such knowledge. Bureaucracy naturally welcomes a poorly informed and hence a powerless parliament — at least in so far as ignorance somehow agrees with the bureaucracy's interests. . . .

Notes on a Non-Weberian Model of Bureaucracy: The Case of Developmental Bureaucracy

BERTON H. KAPLAN

In examining the problem of the management of social change, that is, the modernization process, it is questionable whether the usual Weberian model, directed toward organizational efficiency and effectiveness, is appropriate for many problems of organizational design; such as, the poverty program, population programs, the Alliance for Progress, and other attempts at massive change. In this paper, an attempt is made to clarify these doubts and the related puzzles of how best to understand organizational structures designed to solve problems of social development and modernization.[1]

As a tentative definition, a development bureaucracy is assumed to involve the following elements: (1) the management of change, that is, the direction of efforts to alter the basic pattern(s) of a way of life; (2) the *design* of structures to plan change, that is, the specification of workable criteria of organizational structure to effect and direct a change process; and (3) the focus on the goal of altering the whole "way of life" or parts of it, so as to increase the adaptive capacities of individuals and groups.

THE PROBLEM

The fundamental problem can be stated as follows: What are the organizational requirements for a development bureaucracy? This raises three related questions: (1) What are the basic values and structural features of development bureaucracies? (2) What is the range of types of such structures? (3) What are the transactions between development bureaucracies and their environment, such as input-output systems? The focus in this paper is on the first question, in hopes of stimulating fresh views on the problem of organizational design (better yet, a range of designs) for managing development processes in the context of the limits and possibilities of various socio-cultural matrices.

[1] I wish to express my gratitude to Thomas M. Lodahl, Alexander H. Leighton, Robert N. Wilson, and Robin Williams for their encouragement in the development of this paper. They are not, of course, responsible for its shortcomings.
Robert K. Merton, "Notes on Problem-Finding in Sociology," in Robert K. Merton, Leonard Broom, and Leonard S. Cottrell, Jr., eds., *Sociology Today* (New York: Basic Books, 1959), pp. ix-xxiv, especially, xiii.

Reprinted with permission of the Administrative Science Quarterly, *and the author, from* Administrative Science Quarterly, *Vol. 13, No. 3 (December, 1968), pp. 471-483.*

The questions raised can be readily shown to be both practical and to pose interesting theoretical problems.[2] Indeed, from the practical side, recognizing some dilemmas in development efforts, Alexander Leighton observed: "When someone writes the history of efforts by great nations to aid in the development of smaller nations, he will be tempted to call it 'How to Back Wrong Horses.' " Leighton goes on to observe that: "Such a title would not be a reflection on the purposes or philosophy of aid, but on the difficulty that has been encountered in selecting the procedures that will insure success."[3]

The questions are also significant because development is one of the major social processes today, and requires more creative organizational models in how to think imaginatively about development bureaucracies and their *design.*[4] Design here is seen in the light of Triandis' criteria. He observes:

> If we consider this [design] analogy and attempt to apply it to the problem of the design of organizations, it is obvious that we must answer a number of questions: (a) What are the dimensions that define the environments of organizations? (b) What are the dimensions that define the characteristics of organizations? (c) What are the criteria of organizational effectiveness? The first question calls on us to identify the constraints of our problem, the second to identify the different designs that are possible, and the third to evaluate the cost and utility of a solution.[5]

Review of Literature

It is important to locate our approach in relation to classical organizational theory. The sociological study of complex organizations originated with Max Weber. A bureaucracy, according to Weber, was an organization characterized by rationality, expertise, task orientation, established positions, hierarchical arrangements, and explicit rules for procedure, all directed toward specific organizational goals, such as, the manufacturing of automobiles, organizational efficiency, and so on. Fred Katz recently observed: "It is probably fair to say that recent sociological theories of complex organizations are a series of footnotes to Weber."[6]

---

[2] See W. G. Bennis, K. D. Benne, and Robert Chin, eds., *The Planning of Change* (New York: Holt, Rinehart and Winston, 1961); H. G. Barnett, *Innovation,* (New York: McGraw-Hill, 1953); Howard Freeman and Robert Sherwood, "Research and Large Scale Intervention Programs," *Journal of Social Issues,* Vol. 21 (January, 1965), pp. 11-28; Arthur R. Cohen, *Attitude Change and Social Influence* (New York: Basic Books, 1964); Alexander H. Leighton and Jane Murphy, "Concluding Note," in their *Approaches to Cross-Cultural Psychiatry* (Ithaca: Cornell University, 1965), pp. 393-397; Ronald Lippitt, Jane Watson, and Bruce Westley, *Planned Change* (New York: Harcourt, Brace, 1958).

[3] Preface in Ward H. Goodenough, *Cooperation in Change* (New York: Russell Sage Foundation, 1963), p. 7.

[4] Goodenough, *op. cit.* The entire work is relevant to this point. See also Everett E. Hagen, *On the Theory of Social Change* (Homewood: Dorsey Press, 1962). The literature on social change pays little attention to the problem of bureaucratic design for the management of socioeconomic change. It is this gap which has led to the discussion in this paper.

[5] Harry C. Triandis, "Notes on the Design of Organizations," in James D. Thompson, ed., *Approaches to Organizational Design* (Pittsburgh: University of Pittsburgh, 1966), p. 59.

[6] Fred Katz, "The School as a Complex Social Organization," *Harvard Educational Review,* Vol. 34 (Fall, 1964), p. 431.

In a recent review of the correlates of bureaucracy, Hall and Tittle[7] analyzed bureaucratization along the dimensions of impersonality, hierarchy, division of labor, specificity, complexity of rules, and technical competence. Examining the dimensions of Weber's theory, Stanley Udy emphasizes the rationality dimension of bureaucracy.[8] In a review of theories of organizational structure, Hickson points out that, from Weber to the present, most of organizational theory reduces to a basic concern with role expectations, particularly the degree of role specificity and the range of role discretion. He also points. out that such a preoccupation might inhibit the development of new ideas.[9]

Many of the concerns deriving from the classic work of Weber have been related to means of making organizations more effective and more efficient so they can achieve particular ends, for example, efficient government, higher efficiency in production, and so on. Thus, one might say that much of what has been done in the spirit of Weber's interests in beaucracies reflects an outgrowth of the way in which one makes organizations more efficient. Therefore, much of this work is devoted to an analysis of the structural patterns related to efficiency and rationality. In fact, much of the theory for planned change is in support of increasing Weberian type efficiency. Bennis, summarizing, defines planned change as "a deliberate and collaborative process involving a change agent and client system. These systems are brought together to solve a problem or, more generally, to plan and attain an improved state of functioning in the client system by utilizing and applying valid knowledge."[10] The focus of this point of view, as Bennis sees it, is on effecting organizational change in order to improve organizational effectiveness, and three models are proposed by which change is induced: (1) equilibrium: concerned with excessive work tension;[11] (2) organic: concerned with structures, and especially cognitive adequacy;[12] and (3) developmental: concerned with transforming organizational values to greater output efficiency.[13] The planned change approach is thus preoccupied, according to Bennis, with making organizations more viable and effective, with eliminating interferences with problem solving. Although the concern here is related to Bennis', the focus is on the design of organizations that function to develop another system, in this case, a cultural one.

There are many development structures, organizations set up to manage change, which do not entirely fit classical organizational theory, such as: the Cornell Vicos project, the Stirling County efforts in the improvement of mental health, a population program, the Alliance for Progress, AID, or the community action part of the Poverty Program. This variety of development structures makes it of interest to attempt some theoretical ordering of the diversity of development bureaucracies. For theoretical continuity, the problem of organization-environment transactions can be considered as a way of refining the

[7] Richard H. Hall and Charles R. Tittle, "A Note on Bureaucracy and its Correlates," *American Journal of Sociology*, Vol. 72 (November, 1966), pp. 267-272.

[8] Stanley H. Udy, Jr., "Bureaucracy and the Rationality in Weber's Organizational Theory: An Empirical Study," *American Sociological Review*, Vol. 24 (December, 1959), pp. 491-495.

[9] D. J. Hickson, "A Convergence in Organizational Theory," *Administrative Science Quarterly*, Vol. 11 (September, 1966), pp. 224-237.

[10] Warren G. Bennis, "New Role for Behavioral Science," *Administrative Science Quarterly*, Vol. 8 (September, 1963), pp. 125-165, especially p. 139.

[11] *Ibid.*, p. 140.

[12] *Ibid.*, p. 148.

[13] *Ibid.*, p. 154.

problem and trying out a very general model, our next task.

In relating Weber's work to the present problem, it is well to be more specific as to what kind of subtraditions have been generated by his model. In a review by Blau and Scott of typologies of formal organizations, classification is proposed on the basis of *cui bono*; that is, on the criteria of who benefits:[14]

1. Mutual benefit — the members are the primary beneficiary, as in clubs and political parties;
2. Business organizations — the owners are the primary beneficiary, as in industrial firms;
3. Service organizations — public users of services are the primary beneficiary, as in public health agencies;
4. Commonweal organizations — the public-at-large is the primary beneficiary, as in a food and drug agency.[15]

Where does the development bureaucracy, the management of change, fit in this typology? To some extent a development structure involves issues common to service and commonweal organizations. But when one is interested in the design of development organizations to manage the development processes of an entire social system, the problems of organization and environment may not be adequately classified by a *cui bono* set of criteria.

With an interest in organization-environment transactions, Litwak and Meyer[16] pointed out four models of bureaucratic organizations:

1. Rationalistic — described by Weber, e.g., impersonal, detailed rules, hierarchy, specialization, expertise, etc.;
2. Human relations — focusing on such issues as general policies, human relations, colleagueships, and merit evaluations;
3. Professional — includes both rationalistic and human relations dimensions with the focus on professional settings, e.g., school systems, hospitals;
4. Nonmerit — focuses on friendship, discrimination, and on personal rather than organizational goals.

Litwak and Meyer were primarily interested in a better conceptualization of organization-client relationships and they suggest a balance-theory approach to client control.[17] Indeed, the area of organization-environment transaction is crucial to the present problem.[18] A discussion by Lefton and Rosengren is closer to the present problem; that is,

[14] Peter M. Blau and W. Richard Scott *Formal Organizations* (San Francisco: Chandler, 1962), p. 42.

[15] *Ibid.,* pp. 45-54.

[16] Eugene Litwak and Henry F. Meyer, "A Balanced Theory of Coordination Between Bureaucratic Organizations and Community Primary Groups," *Administrative Science Quarterly,* Vol. 11 (June, 1966), pp. 48-49.

[17] *Ibid.,* p. 31.

[18] The area of organization and environment transaction is relatively underdeveloped. This point is strongly made by Amitai Etzioni in *Complex Organizations* (New York: Holt, Rinehart, Winston, 1961). There is indeed a growing and *highly diverse* literature on this subject: see, for example, Richard L. Simpson and William H. Gully, "Goals, Environmental Pressures, and Organizational Characteristics," *American Sociological Review,* Vol. 27 (June, 1962); James D. Thompson and William J. McEwen, "Organizational Goals and Environment: Goal Setting and Interaction Process," *American Sociological Review,* Vol. 23 (February, 1958); William R. Dill, "The Impact of Environment on Organizational Development," in Sidney Mailick and E. H. Van Ness, eds., *Concepts and Issues in Administrative Behavior* (Englewood, N.J.: Prentice-Hall, 1962); Sol Levine and Paul E. White, "Exchange as a Conceptual Framework for the Study of Interorganizational Relationships," *Administrative Science Quarterly,* Vol. 5 (March, 1961); William M. Evan,

the transaction between organization and environment when the major purpose of the organization is development, not necessarily efficiency.[19] With a focus on an organizational analysis of a service goal, and the linkage between clients and formal organizations, Lefton and Rosengren point out four distinct traditions of research: (1) Weber's concern with bureaucracy and legitimate authority;[20] (2) studies examining the impact of demographic and ecological characteristics on the structure and functioning of such organizations;[21] (3) social-system perspective emphasizing structural linkages between the formal organization and the larger social order;[22] and (4) the study of symbolic interaction in organizational settings.[23] They emphasize that, "In so far as they do not explicitly deal with the clients of organizations, the major traditions in organizational analysis remain conceptionally divergent instead of substantively distinct."[24]

Lefton and Rosengren develop a model of organization and clients focusing on the problem of a service ethic; e.g., on the biographical interests an organization has in their clients and the compliance problems posed because of the kind of organizational-client interest involved. The present position, however, is toward a more generalized interest in the nature of development bureaucracies, and Lefton and Rosengren's focus on a service function and on the impact of the kind of client interest on the subsequent organization would be but one type of interest.

In the light of the preceding review, and in the tradition of Weber, a preliminary typology of a development bureaucracy model is now suggested, with the focus on some of the critical structural patterns and some major constraints acting on such an organization.

PRELIMINARY TYPOLOGY OF DEVELOPMENT BUREAUCRACIES

In a summary of a recent paper on development bureaucracy, Thompson observed:

"The Organizational-Set: Toward a Theory of Interorganizational Relations," in James Thompson, ed., *Approaches to Organizational Design* (Pittsburgh: University of Pittsburgh, 1966).

[19] Mark Lefton and William R. Rosengren, "Organization and Clients: Lateral and Longitudinal Dimensions," *American Sociological Review,* Vol. 31 (December, 1966), pp. 802-810.

[20] Amitai Etzioni, *A Comparative Analysis of Complex Organizations* (New York: Free Press, 1961); for other examples of this point of view, see: Alvin Gouldner, *Patterns of Industrial Bureaucracy* (Glencoe: Free Press, 1954); Robert K. Merton, ed., *Reader in Bureaucracy* (Glencoe: Free Press, 1959); Peter M. Blau *The Dynamics of Bureaucracy* (Chicago: University of Chicago, 1955).

[21] Elliot Freidson, ed., *The Hospital in Modern Society* (Glencoe: Free Press 1963); see also for other illustrations: Ivan Belknap and J. Stienle, *The Community and Its Hospital* (Syracuse: Syracuse University, 1963); Delbert Miller, "Industry and Community Power Structure: Comparative Study of an American and English City," *American Sociological Review,* Vol. 23 (February, 1958), pp. 9-15.

[22] Philip Selznick, "Foundations of the Theory of Organization," *American Sociological Review,* Vol. 13 (February, 1948), pp. 25-35; also his *T.V.A. and the Grass Roots* (Berkeley: University of California, 1953); Talcott Parsons, "Suggestions for a Sociological Approach to the Theory of Organization," *Administrative Science Quarterly,* Vol. 1 (June, 1956), pp. 63-85.

[23] Erving Goffman, *The Presentation of Self and Everyday Life* (Edinburgh: University of Edinburgh, 1956), and Julius Roth, *Timetables* (Indianapolis, Ind.: Bobbs-Merrill, 1963).

[24] Lefton and Rosengren, *op. cit.,* p. 804.

Administrative practice and principles of the West have derived from preoccupation with control and therefore have little value for development administration in undeveloped countries where the need is for an adaptive administration, one that can incorporate constant change. However, adaptive administrative principles can be derived from the researches and theories of the behavioral sciences, and these should become the administrative objectives of development administrators. Illustrative of such objectives are the following: an innovative atmosphere; the operationalizing and sharing of goals; the combining of planning (thinking) and acting (doing); the minimization of parochialism; the diffusion of influence; the increasing of toleration of interdependence; and the avoidance of bureaupathology.[25]

On the question of the contributions of public administration to economic development, Thompson further observes that: "On the face of it the answer would seem to be 'not very much,' "[26] but also, "I believe such a contribution can be made, but it most definitely will not come from the doctrines of management or administration most prevalent in the West."[27] La Palombara[28] has observed that managerial doctrines have not always worked well in the U.S. and that we may be exporting our management mythology. Thompson also observed that: "Development administration is in the crisis period; it desperately needs ideas."[29]

Now, with development bureaucracy defined as having to do with the management of change, and in the spirit of Weber's *ideal* typological approach[30] to the structural characteristics of bureaucracy, some of the major *ideal* structural patterns of a development bureaucracy are suggested:

1. The organization is theoretically oriented.[31] If one wants to change or develop something, one needs a theory about the process of development. This theory then determines organizational strategies and alternatives. For example, much of the community-focused poverty program can be considered relevant to a theory of socialization or resocialization.

2. Since the process of change or development involves processes over time, the organizational structure must be adapted to shifting its priorities and strategies with time, e.g., possible organizational equivalents to the psychoanalytic process in which reactions and inputs are related to the change process.[32] The organizational structure must be

[25] Victor A. Thompson, "Administrative Objectives for Development Administration," *Administrative Science Quarterly,* Vol. 9 (June, 1964), p. 91.

[26] *Ibid.,* p. 91.

[27] *Ibid.,* p. 93.

[28] Joseph La Palombara, *Bureaucracy and Political Development* (Princeton: Princeton University, 1963).

[29] Thompson, *op. cit.,* p. 108.

[30] Max Weber, *The Theory of Social and Economic Organization* (New York: Oxford University, 1947).

[31] For example: William F. Whyte, "Models for Building and Changing Organization," unpublished paper; Berton H. Kaplan, "Social Issues and Poverty Research," *Journal of Social Issues,* Vol. 21 (January, 1965), pp. 1-10; administration model proposed in Fred Riggs, *Administration in Developing Countries* (Boston: Houghton Mifflin, 1964), illustrates a theory that deals both with organizations for development and with the cultural matrix of limits and possibilities.

[32] See for example: Leighton and Murphy, *op. cit.,* pp. 393-397; Peter Savage, "Of Time and Change," in *Comparative Administration Group Occasional Papers,* (Bloomington: Comparative Administration Group, 1968).

flexible and include numerous latent structures which become manifest as required.

3. This type of organization is client-centered and normally would focus on the larger system of the client's life styles;[33] therefore, it is related to the working of an entire social system as its significant object of orientation. Riggs' impressive model would illustrate this approach.

4. A major normative characteristic of these organizations is their having development or socialization as a primary goal. Such organizations function as an acculturative system, with possible parallels to the individual stages of development. For example, an early organizational conflict could focus around analogous parent-child issues. Functioning is this way, the bureaucracy would soon have to resolve the issues of "parental" legitimacy.

5. A major organizational focus will be on an *experimental approach* — whether there are actual experiments or not. The organization must show significant results. Many of the successful population programs reflect this organizational pattern[34] of programs carried out as experiments.

6. Community development efforts will be influenced by the particular alternatives for action available to the development organization,[35] therefore, these alternatives must be assessed. This might be called the norm of defined limited possibilities.[36] It could also be pointed out that the development effort will not only be influenced by its own alternatives for action, but also that these alternatives are very much affected by the kinds of constraints imposed by most development efforts.

This set of ideal structural patterns is by no means definitive. Also, through research and continuing synthesis of findings, this model will be drastically revised. And there is surely a range of types of development bureaucracies. The aim here is merely to suggest general and *ideal* patterns.

ENVIRONMENTAL CONSTRAINTS

In a meaningful typology, it is important to begin to consider some of the environ-

---

[33] There is probably a diversity of types represented here. See, for the Stirling Experiment, Alexander H. Leighton, "Poverty and Social Change," *Scientific American,* Vol. 212 (May, 1965), pp. 21-27; and Laura Thompson, *Toward a General Theory of Behavior* (New York: McGraw-Hill, 1959), whose approach is ecological. William F. Whyte and Lawrence K. Williams, *Toward an Integrated Theory of Development* (Ithaca, N.Y.: School of Industrial and Labor Relations, 1968); Riggs, *op. cit.*

See, for one kind of illustration: Morley Beiser, "Poverty, Social Disintegration, and Personality," *Journal of Social Issues,* Vol. 21 (January, 1965), pp. 56-78, whose model is essentially from Erickson. See also Riggs, *op. cit.,* especially pp. 2, 99-240.

[34] Bernard Berelson and Ronald Freedman, "A Study of Fertility Control," *Scientific American,* Vol. 210 (May, 1964), pp. 29-37; Reuben Hill, J. Mayone Stycos, and Kurt Back, *The Family and Population Control: A Puerto Rican Experiment in Social Change* (Chapel Hill: University of North Carolina, 1959).

[35] Betty Cogswell, *The Influence of Social Organization on Socialization,* unpublished manuscript.

[36] This is obviously a use of Goldenweiser's "principle of limited possibilities." See Robert K. Merton, *Social Theory and Social Structure,* 2nd ed., (Glencoe: Free Press, 1957), pp. 52-53, for a discussion of this idea.

mental constraints[37] operating on development bureaucracies. The constraints that follow clarify some of the basic structural dimensions of such organizations; they are basic and too often neglected environmental constraints, which influence the kind of development bureaucracy designed and the possibilities of such bureaucracies:

1. Social disintegration is a widespread phenomena.[38] That social disorganization is often associated with poverty and rapid urbanization is well known.
2. Impaired mental health is often a widespread phenomena[39] among those in the lower social class or where there is social disintegration. Impaired mental health is likely to interfere seriously with development efforts.
3. Social disintegration and impaired mental health tend to be associated. Leighton, for example, found that if community effectiveness is improved, mental health ratings improved,[40] and vice versa.
4. Social or community development activities have not been as successful as expected, especially considering the resources expended.[41]
5. Other types of constraints are: enduring child rearing frustrations, motivational problems, learning problems, problem-solving inadequacies, etc.
6. The lack of success in social and community development activities may often be associated with the lack of effective and relevant organizational models for community integration or development.[42]

In view of these constraints, and there are surely others, how does one design more effective bureaucratic models for development and arrive at a better understanding of constraints in the modernization process?

CONCLUSION

Classical organizational theory has been reviewed with the aim of suggesting a very general model of development bureaucracies, that is, organizations whose basic function is the management of change. With an organization-environment transaction focus, a number of environmental constraints were suggested, which greatly affect the success and design of development structures (for example, social disintegration and correlated mental illness). The utility of these *ideal type* proposals will no doubt lead to refinements.

---

[37] *Ibid.,* pp. 52-53. See also Vernon E. Buck, "Model for Viewing an Organization as System of Constraints," in James D. Thompson, ed., *Approach to Organizational Design* (Pittsburgh: University of Pittsburgh, 1966), pp. 105-172.

[38] Alexander H. Leighton, *op. cit.,* pp. 1-19.

[39] Leo Srole, Thomas S. Langner, Stanley T. Michael, Marvin K. Opler, Thomas A. C. Rennis, *Mental Health in the Metropolis: The Midtown Study* (New York: McGraw-Hill, 1962), pp. 157-324; Thomas S. Langner and Stanley T. Michael, *Life Stress and Mental Health* (Glencoe: Free Press, 1963); Dorothea C. Leighton, John Harding, David B. Macklin, Allister N. MacMillan, and Alexander H. Leighton, *et al., The Yoruba Study* (Ithaca, N.Y.: Cornell University, 1965).

[40] Leighton, *op. cit.,* pp. 1-19.

[41] Goodenough, *op. cit.,* p. 7.

[42] See Goodenough, *op. cit.;* Leighton, *op. cit.,* pp. 1-19; Hagen, *op. cit.* The large family size of the poor and the socially disintegrated is another type of interference.

Thus, this paper is written in the spirit of Abraham Kaplan's observation that:

Every taxonomy is a provisional and implicit theory (or family of theories). As knowledge of a particular subject-matter grows, our conception of that subject-matter changes; as our concepts become more fitting, we learn more and more. Like all existential dilemmas in science, of which this is an instance, the paradox is resolved by a process of approximation: the better our concepts, the better the theory we can formulate with them, and in turn, the better the concepts available for the next, improved theory. V. F. Lenzen has spoken explicitly of 'successive definition.' It is only through such successions that the scientist can hope ultimately to achieve success.[43]

---

[43] Abraham Kaplan, *The Conduct of Inquiry* (San Francisco: Chandler, 1964), pp. 53-54.

Formal Organizations

CHESTER I. BARNARD

An organization comes into being when (1) there are persons able to communicate with each other (2) who are willing to contribute action (3) to accomplish a common purpose. The elements of an organisation are therefore (1) communication, (2) willingness to serve, and (3) common purpose. These elements are necessary and sufficient conditions initially, and they are found in all such organizations. The third element, purpose, is implicit in the definition. Willingness to serve, and communication, and the interdependence of the three elements in general, and their mutual dependence in specific cooperative systems, are matters of experience and observation.

For the continued existence of an organization either *effectiveness* or *efficiency* is necessary;[1] and the longer the life, the more necessary both are. The vitality of organizations lies in the willingness of individuals to contribute forces to the cooperative system. This willingness requires the belief that the purpose can be carried out, a faith that diminishes to the vanishing point as it appears that it is not in fact in process of being attained. Hence, when effectiveness ceases, willingness to contribute disappears. The continuance of willingness also depends upon the satisfactions that are secured by individual contributors in the process of carrying out the purpose. If the satisfactions do not exceed the sacrifices required, willingness disappears, and the condition is one of organization inefficiency. If the satisfactions exceed the sacrifices, willingness persists, and the condition is one of efficiency of organization.

In summary, then, the initial existence of an organization depends upon a combination of these elements appropriate to the external conditions at the moment. Its survival depends upon the maintenance of an equilibrium of the system. This equilibrium is primarily internal, a matter of proportions between the elements, but it is ultimately and basically an equilibrium between the system and the total situation external to it. This external equilibrium has two terms in it: first, the effectiveness of the organization, which comprises the relevance of its purpose to the environmental situation; and, second, its efficiency, which comprises the interchange between the organization and individuals. Thus the elements stated will each vary with external factors, and they are at the same time interdependent; when one is varied compensating variations must occur in the other if the system of which they are components is to remain in equilibrium, that is, is to persist or survive.

---

[1] See definitions in *The Functions of the Executive,* Chapters II and V, pp. 19 and 55 ff., also Chapter XVI.

Reprinted with permission of Harvard University Press, from Chester I. Barnard, The Functions of the Executive *(Cambridge, Mass.: Harvard University Press, copyright, 1938, by the President and Fellows of Harvard College), pp. 82-95, 104-113.*

We may now appropriately consider these elements and their interrelations in some detail, having in mind the system as a whole. In later chapters we shall consider each element in greater detail with reference to its variability in dependence upon external factors, and the interrelations of the elements as determining the character of the executive functions.

Willingness to Cooperate. By definition there can be no organization without persons. However, as we have urged that it is not persons, but the services or acts or action or influences of persons, which should be treated as constituting organizations,[2] it is clear that *willingness* of persons to contribute efforts to the cooperative system is indispensable.

There are a number of words and phrases in common use with reference to organization that reach back to the factor of individual willingness. "Loyalty," "solidarity," "*esprit de corps*," "strength" of organization, are the chief. Although they are indefinite, they relate to intensity of attachment to the "cause," and are commonly understood to refer to something different from effectiveness, ability, or value of personal contributions. Thus "loyalty" is regarded as not necessarily related either to position, rank, fame, remuneration, or ability. It is vaguely recognized as an essential condition of organization.

Willingness, in the present connection, means self-abnegation, the surrender of control of personal conduct, the depersonalization of personal action. Its effect is cohesion of effort, a sticking together. Its immediate cause is the disposition necessary to "sticking together." Without this there can be no sustained personal effort as a contribution to cooperation. Activities cannot be coordinated unless there is first the disposition to make a personal act a contribution to an impersonal system of acts, one in which the individual gives up personal control of what he does.

The outstanding fact regarding willingness to contribute to a given specific formal organization is the indefinitely large range of variation in its intensity among individuals. If all those who may be considered potential contributors to an organization are arranged in order of willingness to serve it, the scale gradually descends from possibly intense willingness through neutral or zero willingness to intense unwillingness or opposition or hatred. The *preponderance of persons in a modern society always lies on the negative side* with reference to any particular existing or potential organization. Thus of the possible contributors only a small minority actually have a positive willingness. This is true of the largest and most comprehensive formal organizations, such as the large nations, the Catholic Church, etc. Most of the persons in existing society are either indifferent to or positively opposed to any single one of them; and if the smaller organizations subordinate to these major organizations are under consideration the minority becomes of course a much smaller proportion, and usually a nearly negligible proportion, of the conceivable total.

A second fact of almost equal importance is that the willingness of any individual cannot be constant in degree. It is necessarily intermittent and fluctuating. It can scarcely be said to exist during sleep, and is obviously diminished or exhausted by weariness, discomfort, etc., a conception that was well expressed by the saying,"The spirit is willing, but the flesh is weak."

A corollary of the two propositions just stated is that for any given formal organization the number of persons of positive willingness to serve, but near the neutral or zero point, is always fluctuating. It follows that the aggregate willingness of potential contributors to any formal cooperative system is unstable — a fact that is evident from the history of all formal organizations.

Willingness to cooperate, positive or negative, is the expression of the net satisfactions or dissatisfactions experienced or anticipated by each individual in comparison with those

---

[2] Page 72 [of *The Functions of the Executive*].

experienced or anticipated through alternative opportunities. These alternative opportunities may be either personal and individualistic or those afforded by other organizations. That is, willingness to cooperate is the net effect, first, of the inducements to do so in conjunction with the sacrifices involved, and then in comparison with the practically available net satisfactions afforded by alternatives. The questions to be determined, if they were matters of logical reasoning, would be, first, whether the opportunity to cooperate grants any advantage to the individual as compared with independent action; and then, if so, whether that advantage is more or less than the advantage obtainable from some other cooperative opportunity. Thus, from the viewpoint of the individual, willingness is the joint effect of personal desires and reluctances; from the viewpoint of organization it is the joint effect of objective inducements offered and burdens imposed. The measure of this net result, however, is entirely individual, personal, and subjective. Hence, organizations depend upon the motives of individuals and the inducements that satisfy them.

Purpose. Willingness to cooperate, except as a vague feeling or desire for association with others, cannot develop without an objective of cooperation. Unless there is such an objective it cannot be known or anticipated what specific efforts will be required of individuals, nor in many cases what satisfactions to them can be in prospect. Such an objective we denominate the "purpose" of an organization. The necessity of having a purpose is axiomatic, implicit in the words "system," "coordination," "cooperation." It is something that is clearly evident in many observed systems of cooperation, although it is often not formulated in words, and sometimes cannot be so formulated. In such cases what is observed is the direction or effect of the activities, from which purpose may be inferred.

A purpose does not incite cooperative activity unless it is accepted by those whose efforts will constitute the organization. Hence there is initially something like simultaneity in the acceptance of a purpose and willingness to cooperate.

It is important at this point to make clear that every cooperative purpose has in the view of each cooperating person two aspects which we call (1) the cooperative and (2) the subjective aspect, respectively.

1. When the viewing of the purpose is an *act of cooperation*, it approximates that of detached observers from a special position of observation; this position is that of the interests of the organization; it is largely determined by organization knowledge, but is personally interpreted. For example, if five men are cooperating to move a stone from A to B, the moving of the stone is a different thing in the organization view of each of the five men involved. Note, however, that what moving the stone means to each man personally is not here in question, but what he thinks it means to the organization *as a whole.* This includes the significance of his own effort as an element in cooperation, and that of all others, in his view; but it is not at all a matter of satisfying a personal motive.

When the purpose is a physical result of simple character, the difference between the purpose as objectively viewed by a detached observer and the purpose as viewed by each person cooperating *as an act of cooperation* is ordinarily not large or important, and the different cooperative views of the persons cooperating are correspondingly similar. Even in such cases the attentive observer will detect differences that result in disputes, errors of action, etc., even though no *personal* interest is implicated. But when the purpose is less tangible — for example, in religious cooperation — the difference between objective purpose and purpose as cooperatively viewed by each person is often seen ultimately to result in disruption.

We may say, then, that a purpose can serve as an element of a cooperative system only so long as the participants do not recognize that there are serious divergences of their understanding of that purpose as the object of cooperation. If in fact there is important difference between the aspects of the purpose as objectively and as cooperatively viewed, the divergencies become quickly evident when the purpose is concrete, tangible, physical; but when the purpose is general, intangible, and of sentimental character, the divergencies can be very wide yet not be recognized. Hence, an objective purpose that can serve as the basis for a cooperative system is one that is *believed* by the contributors (or potential contributors) to it to be the determined purpose of the organization. The inculcation of belief in the real existence of a common purpose is an essential executive function. It explains much educational and so-called morale work in political, industrial, and religious organizations that is so often otherwise inexplicable.[3]

2. Going back to the illustration of five men moving a stone, we have noted "that what moving the stone means to each man personally is not here in question, but what he thinks it means to the *organization as a whole.*" The distinction emphasized is of first importance. It suggests the fact that every participant in an organization may be regarded as having a dual personality — an organization personality and an individual personality. Strictly speaking, an organization purpose has directly no meaning for the individual. What has meaning for him is the organization's relation to him — what burdens it imposes, what benefits it confers. In referring to the aspects of purpose as cooperatively viewed, we are alluding to the *organization* personality of individuals. In many cases the two personalities are so clearly developed that they are quite apparent. In military action individual conduct may be so dominated by organization personality that it is utterly contradictory of what personal motivation would require. It has been observed of many men that their private conduct is entirely inconsistent with official conduct, although they seem completely unaware of the fact. Often it will be observed that participants in political, patriotic, or religious organizations will accept derogatory treatment of their personal conduct, including the assertion that it is inconsistent with their organization obligations, while they will become incensed at the slightest derogation of the tenets or doctrines of their organization, even though they profess not to understand them. There are innumerable other cases, however, in which almost no organization personality may be said to exist. These are cases in which personal relationship with the cooperative system is momentary or at the margin of willingness to participate.

In other words, we have clearly to distinguish between organization purpose and individual motive. It is frequently assumed in reasoning about organizations that common purpose and individual motive are or should be identical. With the exception noted below, this is never the case; and under modern conditions it rarely even appears to be the case. Individual motive is necessarily an internal, personal, subjective thing; common purpose is necessarily an external, impersonal, objective thing even though the individual interpretation of it is subjective. The one exception to this general rule, an important one, is that the accomplishment of an organization purpose becomes itself a source of personal satisfaction and a motive for many individuals in many organizations. It is rare, however, if ever, and then I think only in connection with family, patriotic, and religious organizations under special conditions, that organization purpose becomes or can become the *only* or even the major individual motive.

Finally it should be noted that, once established, organizations change their unifying purposes. They tend to perpetuate themselves; and in the effort to survive may change the reasons for existence. I shall later make clearer that in this lies an important aspect of executive functions.[4]

Communication. The possibility of accomplishing a common purpose and the existence of persons whose desires might constitute motives for contributing toward such a common purpose are the opposite poles of the system of cooperative effort. The process

---

[3] This is expanded in Chapter XVII [of *The Functions of the Executive*].

[4] See also Chapters II and III [of *The Function of the Executive*].

95

by which these potentialities become dynamic is that of communication. Obviously a common purpose must be commonly known, and to be known must be in some way communicated. With some exceptions, verbal communication between men is the method by which this is accomplished. Similarly, though under crude and obvious conditions not to the same extent, inducements to persons depend upon communication to them.

The method of communication centers in language, oral and written. On its crudest side, motions or actions that are of obvious meaning when observed are sufficient for communication without deliberate attempt to communicate; and signaling by various methods is an important method in much cooperative activity. On the other side, both in primitive and in highly complex civilization "observational feeling" is likewise an important aspect of communication.[5] I do not think it is generally so recognized. It is necessary because of the limitations of language and the differences in the linguistic capacities of those who use language. A very large element in special experience and training and in continuity of individual association is the ability to understand without words, not merely the situation or conditions, but the *intention*.

The techniques of communication are an important part of any organization and are the preeminent problems of many. The absence of a suitable technique of communication would eliminate the possibility of adopting some purposes as a basis for organization. Communication technique shapes the form and the internal economy of organization. This will be evident at once if one visualizes the attempt to do many things now accomplished by small organizations if each "member" spoke a different language. Similarly, many technical functions could hardly be carried on without special codes; for example, engineering or chemical work. In an exhaustive theory of organization, communication would occupy a central place, because the structure, extensiveness, and scope of organization are almost entirely determined by communication techniques. To this aspect of communication much of the material in subsequent chapters will be devoted.[6] Moreover, much specialization in organization originates and is maintained essentially because of communication requirements.

Effectiveness of Cooperation. The continuance of an organization depends upon its ability to carry out its purpose. This clearly depends jointly upon the appropriateness of its action and upon the conditions of its environment. In other words, effectiveness is primarily a matter of technological[7] processes. This is quite obvious in ordinary cases of

---

[5] The phrase "observational feeling" is of my coining. The point is not sufficiently developed, and probably has not been adequately studied by anyone. I take it to be at least in part involved in group action not incited by any "overt" or verbal communication. The cases known to me from the primitive field are those reported by W. H. R. Rivers on pages 94-97 of his *Instinct and the Unconscious* (2nd edition; Cambridge University Press, 1924), with reference to Polynesia and Melanesia. One case is summarized by F. C. Bartlett, in *Remembering* (Cambridge University Press, 1932), at p. 297. Rivers states in substance that in some of the relatively small groups decisions are often arrived at and acted upon without having ever been formulated by anybody.

I have observed on innumerable occasions apparent unanimity of decision of equals in conferences to quit discussion without a word to that effect being spoken. Often the action is initiated apparently by someone's rising; but as this frequently occurs in such groups *without* the termination of the meeting, more than mere rising is involved. "Observational feeling," I think, avoids the notion of anything "occult."

[6] Especially in Chapter XII, latter half [of *The Functions of the Executive*].

[7] Using "technological" in the broad sense emphasized in Chapter III [of *The Functions of the Executive*].

purpose to accomplish a physical objective, such as building a bridge. When the objective is nonphysical, as is the case with religious and social organizations, it is not so obvious.

It should be noted that a paradox is involved in this matter. An organization must disintegrate if it cannot accomplish its purpose. It also destroys itself by accomplishing its purpose. A very large number of successful organizations come into being and then disappear for this reason. Hence most continuous organizations require repeated adoption of new purposes. This is concealed from everyday recognition by the practice of generalizing a complex series of specific purposes under one term, stated to be "*the* purpose" of this organization. This is strikingly true in the case of governmental and public utility organizations when the purpose is stated to be a particular kind of service through a period of years. It is apparent that their real purposes are not abstractions called "service" but specific acts of service. A manufacturing organization is said to exist to make, say, shoes; this is its "purpose." But it is evident that not making shoes in general but making specific shoes from day to day is its series of purposes. This process of generalization, however, provides in advance for the approximate definition of new purposes automatically — so automatically that the generalization is normally substituted in our minds for the concrete performances that are the real purposes. Failure to be effective is, then, a real cause of disintegration; but failure to provide for the decisions resulting in the adoption of new purposes would have the same result. Hence the generalization of purpose which can only be defined concretely by day-to-day events is a vital aspect of permanent organization.

Organization Efficiency. It has already been stated that "efficiency" as conceived in this treatise is not used in the specialized and limited sense of ordinary industrial practice or in the restricted sense applicable to technological processes. So-called "practical" efficiency has little meaning, for example, as applied to many organizations such as religious organizations.

Efficiency of effort in the fundamental sense with which we are here concerned is efficiency relative to the securing of necessary personal contributions to the cooperative system. The life of an organization depends upon its ability to secure and maintain the personal contributions of energy (including the transfer of control of materials or money equivalent) necessary to effect its purposes. This ability is a composite of perhaps many efficiencies and inefficiencies in the narrow senses of these words, and it is often the case that inefficiency in some respect can be treated as the cause of total failure, in the sense that if corrected success would then be possible. But certainly in most organization — social, political, national, religious — nothing but the absolute test of survival is significant objectively; there is no basis for comparison of the efficiencies of separate aspects. . . . The emphasis now is on the view that efficiency of organization is its capacity to offer effective inducements in sufficient quantity to maintain the equilibrium of the system. It is efficiency in this sense and not the efficiency of material productiveness which maintains the vitality of organizations. There are many organizations of great power and permanency in which the idea of productive efficiency is utterly meaningless because there is no material production. Churches, patriotic societies, scientific societies, theatrical and musical organizations, are cases where the original flow of *material* inducements is toward the organization, not from it — a flow necessary to provide resources with which to supply material inducements to the small minority who require them in such organizations.

In those cases where the primary purpose of organization is the production of material things, insufficiency with respect to the nonmaterial inducements leads to the attempt to substitute material inducements for the nonmaterial. Under favorable circumstances, to a limited degree, and for a limited time, this substitution may be effective. But to me, at least, it appears utterly contrary to the nature of men to be sufficiently induced by material or monetary considerations to contribute enough effort to a cooperative system to enable it to be productively efficient to the degree necessary for persistence over an extended period.

If these things are true, then even in purely economic enterprises efficiency in the offering of non-economic inducements may be as vital as productive efficiency. Perhaps the word efficiency as applied to such non-economic inducements as I have given for illustration will seem strange and forced. This, I think, can only be because we are accustomed to use the word in a specialized sense.

The non-economic inducements are as difficult to offer as others under many circumstances. To establish conditions under which individual pride of craft and of accomplishment can be secured without destroying the material economy of standardized production in cooperative operation is a problem in real efficiency. To maintain a character of personnel that is in attractive condition of employment involves a delicate art and much insight in the selection (and rejection) of personal services offered, whether the standard of quality be high or low. To have an organization that lends prestige and secures the loyalty of desirable persons is a complex and difficult task in efficiency — in all-round efficiency, not one-sided efficiency. It is for these reasons that good organizations — commercial, governmental, military, academic, and others — will be observed to devote great attention and sometimes great expense of money to the non-economic inducements, because they are indispensable to fundamental efficiency, as well as to effectiveness in many cases.[8]

The theory of organization set forth in this chapter is derived from the study of organizations which are exceedingly complex, although it is stated in terms of ideal simple organizations. The temptation is to assume that, in the more complex organizations which we meet in our actual social life, the effect of complexity is to modify or qualify the theory. This appears not to be the case. Organization, simple or complex, is always *an impersonal system of coordinated human efforts;* always there is purpose as the coordinating and unifying principle; always there is the indispensable ability to communicate, always the necessity for personal willingness, and for effectiveness and efficiency in maintaining the integrity of purpose and the continuity of contributions. Complexity appears to modify the quality and form of these elements and of the balance between them; but fundamentally the same principles that govern simple organizations may be conceived as governing the structure of complex organizations, which are composite systems. . . .

THE GROWTH OF ORGANIZATIONS

It will be noted that when the origin of organization is spontaneous, or is the result of the initiative of one man, or is the deliberate creation of a parent organization, the beginning is small. The organization comes into being when two or more persons begin to cooperate to a common end. Where there is division by schism, rebellion, this is likewise true, but is usually not so recognized because attention is given to the final breakup of a large complex organization. What takes place beforehand is the growth of a new counter organization or independent organization supported by the efforts of individuals who may in part still continue to support the older organization. So far as I have learned, this beginning is always small; that is, it results from the spontaneous acceptation of a new purpose, independent of and perhaps definitely conflicting with the older purpose, by a small group; or it is prompted by one individual who associates others with himself.

[8] The economics of cooperative systems and their relation to organizations is presented in Chapter XVI [of *The Functions of the Executive*].

Hence, all organizations of complex character grow out of small, simple organizations.[9] It is impossible for formal organizations to grow except by the process of combining unit organizations already existing, or the creation of new units of organization to be added to those in an existing complex.

It may, therefore, be said that all large formal organizations are constituted of numbers of small organizations[10] It is impossible to create a large organization except by combining small organizations.[11]

The basic organization, if measured by the number of persons simultaneously contributing to it, is usually quite small — from two to fifteen or twenty persons, and probably not having an average of more than ten. Certain special types of simple organization, however, are very large, just as in biology some cells, such as birds' eggs, are very large. The largest of such organizations which I have observed are a full orchestra or orchestra and chorus; and a public speaker and his audience, which under radio technique reaches enormous size.[12]

The clue to the structural requirements of large complex organizations lies in the reason for the limitations of the size of simple organizations. The limitations are inherent in the necessities of intercommunication.[13] In Chapter VII we discussed communication

---

[9] Perhaps this will be clearer if the process is visualized of trying to organize a group of one hundred or five hundred men. Under the most favorable circumstances, i.e., when they are willing to be organized because there has come about some consensus of opinion as to purpose or objective, the mass must be broken up into small groups with group leaders. Only when by this process unit organizations have been created is it possible to combine these units into a complex organization that can manage itself.

In this connection, I should regard a mob not as a formal organization, simple or complex, but a special type of informal organization, until it has formal leaders.

[10] I exclude the very extreme and special case of large audiences as being of limited pertinence to a discussion of the functions of the executive.

[11] The origins of the major organizations being historically so remote, and the processes of reorganization being apparently often directed from central points or by central authority, we are much under the delusion that large mass organizations are subdivided as a secondary process, the mass having first been created. This is the order in which intellectually we approach the understanding of most large complex organizations; it is the method of analysis, of breaking down a whole into parts. Thus, if we wish to study a government organization or a large telephone system, we may often effectively begin with the constitution, the major departments, the parent company, etc. But this procedure is as if we subdivided a trunk of a tree or a piece of flesh into fibres and membranes and finally into cells, being misled into thinking that these subdivisions developed after the existence of an undifferentiated protoplasm of the same mass.

Many theoretical and practical errors arise from employing this analytical approach except for immediate limited purposes. For it is, I think, as true of organization as it is of all living things that they grow by the multiplication of cells and begin with single cells. It is true that quite often a fusion of two existing simple or complex organizations into one complex organization takes place; but fundamentally the growth is from single-cell organizations.

[12] A descriptive catalogue and classification of organizations from the standpoint of unit size would be of interest in a more exhaustive treatment. For example, clubs furnish an illustration of rather units which are partly structured by "working" units (staff, officers, committees and official meetings of members), and temporary "playing" or "social" units.

[13] These limitations, therefore, arise out of the joint effect of physical, biological, and social factors. See Chapter V [of *The Functions of the Executive*].

between persons as an essential element of cooperative systems; it is also the limiting factor in the size of simple organizations and, therefore, a dominant factor in the structure of complex organizations. We must now consider why this is true.

Under most ordinary conditions, even with simple purposes, not many men can see what each is doing or the whole situation; nor can many communicate essential information regarding or governing specific action without a central channel or leader. But a leader likewise is limited in time (and capacity) in communicating with many persons contemporaneously, especially if they are widely separated so that he must move about. In practice a limit of usually less than fifteen persons obtains, and for many types of cooperation five or six persons is the practicable limit.

These limits are widely exceeded in certain special cases, chiefly those where the action involved is that of extreme habitual practice within narrow limits, as in military drill and orchestral performance, where there are both individual and collective habituation and a precise special system of language or some other special means of communication; and those where the action is limited substantially to one person, the others being relatively passive, as in an audience. In this case the organization is practically limited (at least for the time being) to communication in one direction only.[14] Moreover, in the case of audiences and speakers, this communication is an end in itself.

Fundamentally, communication is necessary to translate purpose into terms of the concrete action required to effect it — what to do and when and where to do it. This necessitates knowledge of the conditions of the environment, and of the action under way. Under very simple and usually temporary conditions and with small numbers of persons the communication problem often appears simple, but under many conditions, even with small numbers, a special channel of communication is required. For if all talk at once there is confusion; and there is indecision particularly as to timing of actions. This creates the necessity for a leader. The size of the unit, therefore, usually is determined by the limitations of effective leadership. These limitations depend upon (1) the complexity of purpose and technological conditions, (2) the difficulty of the communication process, (3) the extent to which communication is necessary, and (4) the complexity of the personal relationships involved, that is, of the social conditions.

1. It is clear that when the purpose is not simple — that is, when its requirements are complex and not obvious, or the conditions require precision of coordinated movements, or the nature of the individual action necessary is difficult to grasp by the actor (or by the leader) — much more communication is necessary than under the contrary conditions.

2. It is also evident that the difficulty of the communication process has an important bearing on the size of the organization unit. There are many things that are difficult to communicate by words — in some matters it is impossible. When the difficulty is great it is evident that the time required may limit the number between whom communication may be effectively had; for example, communication perhaps must be accomplished by demonstration.

3. It is apparent that if each actor can see what the other is doing and can see the situation as a whole, the amount of positive communication is reduced. Thus, if five men are working together on a simple task (say pulling a boat into the water) little communication is required; but if five men are coordinating efforts under conditions such that they cannot see each other and the whole situation, constant communication is often necessary. Moreover, if men know what to do from previous experience and can work on the basis of habit and acquired skill, a minimum of communication is required; or if they are accustomed to working together, a special language which they evolve cuts down the time of communication.

---

[14] Where not limited to one direction, a leader — moderator, chairman, i.e., an executive is required.

4. The complexity of the relationships in any group increases with great rapidity as the number of persons in the group increases. If the simplest possible relationship between two persons is that of "knowing" each other as accomplished by a mutual introduction, then the relational complexity at the very least increases as follows:

NUMBER IN GROUP	NUMBER OF RELATIONSHIPS	INCREASE IN RELATIONSHIPS WITH EACH ADDITION TO GROUP
2	1	—
3	3	2
4	6	3
5	10	4
6	15	5
7	21	6
8	28	7
9	36	8
10	45	9
15	105	—
20	190	—
50	1225	—

The relationships between persons in a group will be "active" in a great variety of subgroupings which may constantly change. If A, B, C, D, and E constitute a group of five, then subgroups may be made as follows: ten pairs, ten triplets, five groups of four, one of five. If only one person be added to the group of five, the possible subgroups become: fifteen pairs, twenty triplets, fifteen groups of four, six groups of five, and one of six.

A person has relationships not only with others individually and with groups, but groups are related to groups. As the number of possible groups increases, the complexity of group relationship increases in greater ratio.[15]

The complexity of relationships within groups is important in two aspects: technologically and socially. Technologically, the burden of coordination, that is, the communication function of a leader, will increase in the proportion that the relationships increase; and the ability of individuals and groups without leadership to coordinate is also quickly outrun with increase in the size of groups. The same is true of the social or informal organization relationships. The capacity of persons to maintain social relationships is obviously limited. If the technological group is larger than is adapted to social limitations, the social organization groupings cannot correspond to the technological requirements. Since a large part of the communication of organizations is informal, the burden on

---

[15] A suggestive exposition of this subject in quantitative terms is given by V. A. Graicunas' "Relationship in Organization," reprinted in *Papers on the Science of Administration,* edited by Gulick and Urwick (New York: Institute of Public Administration, 1937).

formal channels is thereby increased.[16]

These factors, and probably others also, limit the size of the fundamental organization cell. I shall call the simple basic organization form a "unit" organization. It differs from the ideal organization of Chapter VII in that it is never found isolated from other organizations and is always subordinate to some other formal organization directly or indirectly, being ultimately subordinate to and dependent upon either a church or a state or both.

The size of a unit organization being usually restricted very narrowly by the necessities of communication, it follows that growth of organization beyond the limits so imposed can only be accomplished by the creation of new unit organizations, or by grouping together two or more unit organizations already existing. When an organization grows by the addition of the services of more persons it is compelled, if it reaches the limit of size, to establish a second unit; and henceforward, it is a complex of two unit organizations. All organizations except unit organizations are a group of two or more unit organizations. Hence, a large organization of complex character consists not of the services of individuals directly but of those of subsidiary unit organizations. Nowhere in the world, I think, can there be found a large organization that is not composed of small units. We think of them as having descended from the mass, whereas the mass can only be created from the units.[17]

Usually when two and always when several unit organizations are combined in one complex organization, the necessities of communication impose a super-leader who becomes, usually with assistants, an "overhead" unit of organization. Similarly, groups of groups are combined into larger wholes. The most obvious case of complex structure of this type is an army. The fact that these large organizations are built up of small unit organizations is neglected in the spectacular size that ensues, and we often pass from the whole or major divisions to "men." The resulting dismissal from the mind of the inescapable practice of unit organization often leads to utterly unrealistic attitudes regarding organization problems.

THE EXECUTIVE ORGANIZATION

In a unit organization there are executive functions to be performed, but not necessarily by a single individual continuously. They may be performed alternately by the

---

[16] See also discussion on p. 225 [of *The Functions of the Executive*]. I have strongly the opinion that there may be substantial variations in social satisfactions related to disparities between the size of organizations as determined technologically by organization purpose and the size of "natural" social groups. "Natural" would be affected by the personalitites involved.

[17] A group of two or more unit organizations may cooperate as a whole without a formal superior organization or leader. Under many conditions this is observed, especially where two small organizations (or a large and a small) work together under contract for specified purposes. The method of communication is primarily that of conference. Because of our habit of considering an organization as a group of persons rather than as systems of cooperative services of persons, the usually temporary combinations that are made as a result of contracts or agreements are not recognized as organizations, since they have no name or common officials. Most large building operations are so organized, however; and it will be readily seen that a very large part of the organized activities of today are carried on by temporary limited combinations under contracts without a general coordinating "authority." The state, through the law of contracts and the provisions of courts, is a general formal executive in these cases in limited degree; but the real general executive is custom, etc.

several persons who contributed to the organization. In complex organizations, on the other hand, the necessities of communication result almost invariably in the localization of the executive functions of the subordinate unit organizations normally in one person. This is necessary for reasons of formal communication; but it is also necessary to establish executive organizations, that is, those units specializing in the executive functions. The executives of several unit organizations as a group, usually with at least one other person as a superior, form an executive organization. Accordingly, persons specializing in the executive functions in most cases are "members" of, or contributors to, two units of organization in one complex organization—first, the so-called "working" unit, and second, the executive unit. This is clearly seen in practice, it being customary to recognize a foreman, or a superintendent of a shop section, or a captain, at one time or from one point of view as a "member" of his gang, shop crew, or company, at another time or from another point of view as a member of a "district management group," or the "shop executives' group," or the "regimental organization." Under such conditions a single concrete action of decision is an activity of two different unit organizations. This simultaneous contribution to two organizations by a single act appears to be the critical fact in all complex organization; that is, the complex is made an organic whole by it. Here again, it will be noted that the definition of formal organization as an impersonal system of efforts and influences is supported by the facts more closely in accord with concrete phenomena than the "group membership" idea. One person often functions in or contributes services to several different units of the same complex organization, as well as to different external organizations. For payroll, and many other formal purposes, it is convenient to regard every person as being "in" only one unit organization; but this is merely a matter of convenience for certain purposes, and is misleading as to the actual operation of organizations even for many other practical purposes.

The size of executive units of organization is limited generally by the same conditions that govern the size of unit organizations of other kinds. When there are many basic working units, therefore, there must be several primary executive unit organizations, from the heads of which will be secured the personnel of superior executive units. And so on, in extensive pyramids of executive units in very large complex organizations.[18]

In summary, we may say that historically and functionally all complex organizations are built up from units of organization, and consist of many units of "working" or "basic" organizations, overlaid with units of executive organizations; and that the essential structural characteristics of complex organizations are determined by the effect of the necessity for communication upon the size of a unit organization.

---

[18] Professor Philip Cabot, in a published address, once quoted my opinion that organizations are best regarded as circular or spherical, with the chief executive positions in the center. This was based on discussions with him and an unpublished manuscript which he was kind enough to examine. I have, however, followed the conventional figures here, because they are well established, and because there appears to be no practicable way to diagram the system of authoritative communication that does not result in a "pyramid" (usually in two-dimensional perspectives, however) which put the chief executive positions at the top. They also are frequently located on top floors. Probably all spatial figures for organization are seriously misleading; but if they are used to cover the functioning of organizations as distinguished from its structural aspects, either the center of a circle or of a sphere better suggests the relationships. The nearest approach to this, I think, is the practice of regarding the location of G.H.Q. in field armies as *behind* the lines centrally.

Organizational Requisites
for a Socio-Behavioral Technology

ROSEMARY C. SARRI and
ROBERT D. VINTER

Social influence methodologies of central concern to social work are conducted in and through agencies and other service organizations. Each methodology poses its own demands for agency arrangements, and each presents a distinctive configuration of requirements for effective implementation. It is no less true that service agencies, as organizations, shape and constrain the various technologies they embody, and that the functional requirements of an organization are never simply those defined by one or another technology. Aspects of this reciprocal relation will be examined here and the particular demands posed for organizations by socio-behavioral technology will be considered. In doing so, concentration will be on direct-service agencies that are primarily concerned with individual clients, but much said also has relevance to community practice and other organizations. Analysis is necessarily limited both by the extent to which those reporting socio-behavioral practice have discussed its organizational aspects, and because such practice is very much in an emerging phase.

THE HUMAN SERVICE ORGANIZATION

The perspective of this paper on social agencies as "human service" organizations initiates the discussion. Such organizations consist of community agencies for welfare, education, and social control that are mandated by society, some for the socialization of individuals so that they will be prepared to perform social roles adequately, and others for the treatment and resocialization of persons who are not adequately performing conventional social roles.[1] These units process individuals into new statuses, and utilize human relations technologies to reduce deviant behavior and to assist individuals in the acquisition of acceptable modes of behavior. Included in this range of organizations are mental hospitals and clinics, prisons, public welfare agencies, juvenile courts, family service and children's agencies, public schools, and agencies for the physically handicapped and retarded.

Social welfare agencies must be viewed both as administrative bureaucracies and as

[1] For a discussion of the distinctive characteristics of human service organizations, see Robert D. Vinter, "The Analysis of Treatment Organizations," *Social Work*, Vol. 8, No. 3 (July, 1963), pp. 2-15; and for an analysis of the qualities and practices of these organizations as they relate to differential outcomes, see Stanton Wheeler, "The Structure of Formally Organized Socialization Settings," in Orville Brim and Stanton Wheeler, *Socialization After Childhood* (New York: Wiley, 1966), pp. 51-107.

Reprinted from The Socio-Behavioral Approach and Applications to Social Work, *Edwin J. Thomas, ed. (New York: Council on Social Work Education, 1967), pp. 87-99.*

social systems.[2] They are administrative bureaucracies in that they are established to attain specific goals, and their internal structures, technologies, and procedures are designed to implement these goals. The particular nature of an agency's goals serves to define relationships between itself and its social environment; they influence the choice of technologies and staff personnel; and they guide the coordination of organizational members. Agencies are thus rationally planned collectivities, with formal structures and explicit policies and rules governing significant segments of their behavior.

But rationality and formalism should not be overstressed since agencies are also social systems that adaptively respond to external and internal pressures, and that generate informal patterns that may both facilitate and hamper goal attainment. The dynamic interrelations among parts of an agency and between it and units in its environment cannot be fully understood by reference to formal arrangements, administrative provisions, and professed goals. The implementation of any technology and the introduction of new procedures generate and are shaped by forces that are partially beyond administrative control and rational planning.

Keeping these general perspectives in mind, several case examples involving socio-behavioral practice will first be reviewed. Points at which organizational issues are readily apparent in the reports of these developments will be noted, and an attempt will then be made to derive a series of organizational requisites essential for use of socio-behavioral technology.

CASE EXAMPLES

The first example to be considered is a report by Wetzel of behavioral treatment of a ten-year-old boy in a residential institution for children.[3] The boy was in and out of this institution and of courts, schools, and foster homes for a period of more than five years for severe compulsive stealing, enuresis, tantrums, and other acting-out behavior. It is not necessary to present here the assessment and treatment protocol, but compulsive stealing and enuresis were the problematic behaviors selected, with the former receiving primary attention. This study was undertaken in a typical children's institution where opportunities for behavioral control were far from unlimited. The children lived in the institution but attended a community school during the day. Wetzel was particularly interested in evaluating what could be done in such a setting where the majority of staff were untrained cottage parents, recreation aides, cooks, and so forth. He was able to design and implement a treatment plan by which the problematic behaviors were eliminated within a three and one-half month period. An essential part of the plan involved the choice of one staff member who would function as an effective reinforcer. Reinforcement was then made contingent upon not stealing. The cook was selected as the reinforcing person, and she and other members of the staff were instructed in a specified set of procedures. Wetzel points out that the client was not anxious to change his behavior; in fact, there were intrinsic satisfactions and environmental contingencies that maintained the stealing. Therefore, the environment had to be re-ordered so that the stealing behavior was no longer gratifying.

---

[2] For a discussion of approaches to organizational analysis, see Alvin Gouldner, "Organizational Analysis," in Robert Merton, Leonard Bloom, and Leonard Cottrell, eds., *Sociology Today* (New York: Basic Books, 1959), pp. 400-428; also see Amitai Etzioni, *Modern Organizations* (Englewood Cliffs, New Jersey: Prentice-Hall, 1964), pp. 10-50; and James Thompson, *Organizations in Action* (New York: McGraw-Hill, 1967).

[3] Ralph Wetzel, "Use of Behavioral Techniques in a Case of Compulsive Stealing," Peter J. Lang, "The Transfer of Treatment," and James A. Dinsmoor, all in *Journal of Consulting Psychology*, Vol. 30, No. 5 (October, 1966), pp. 367-380.

A number of procedures were employed that involved organizational considerations. The staff had to be trained in behavior modification principles, in specific recording procedures, and in particular techniques for this case. Experience later showed that the content had to be communicated to staff frequently, and that pre-treatment training was insufficient.

Baseline performance data were required about the client's stealing behavior, visits with the cook, bedwetting, and so forth. Staff were often inconsistent in their recording and in controlling visits with the cook. This became particularly problematic as the plan started to become effective. Staff then modified their standards informally and inconsistently, necessitating close monitoring. The feasibility of monitoring and controlling staff behaviors is an important criterion against which to judge any behavior modification plan. For example, staff observed, and were concerned about, other inappropriate behavior of this client and other clients in the unit.

There were many staff members in direct or indirect contact with the boy in this agency, greatly aggravating control problems. Three shifts of cottage staff were assigned each day and, in addition, the employment turnover rate was fairly high in this institution. As a result, mechanisms had to be developed for continual training and supervision of staff. Special communication procedures were needed between shifts of staff workers. Despite efforts to accomplish these plans, there continued to be inconsistencies that impinged on the client's treatment plan. Staff were helped to become aware of inconsistent behavior and to devise procedures for handling problematic situations. Guiding and controlling the behavior of staff groups, as well as individuals, then, involves a high level of coordinative effort to maintain the consistency required by this technology.

Generalization of non-stealing behavior to the boy's usual social environment posed a number of problems. Although his stealing stopped in the institution, the staff did not know whether it would reappear in other social settings, except in the school attended while he was in the institution. Opportunities for observations outside the institution, at home, and in other social situations needed to be provided. Positive reinforcement of non-stealing behavior after departure from the institution seems essential to maintain the modifications achieved within the program.

The Wetzel report reveals several organizational requisites that must be satisfied and indicates that a socio-behavioral technology can be implemented even in an on-going institutional program. It also suggests a number of areas that could have been planned more carefully to achieve greater environmental control.

Our second case example illustrates the application of socio-behavioral theory, and particularly of operant procedures, in a cottage at the National Training School for Boys in Washington, D.C.[4] The CASE II project was initiated by Harold Cohen and his colleagues to stimulate the educational achievement of delinquent boys and to evaluate the utility of operant procedures with this type of clientele. Originally, the project was entirely focused on education and spanned only a three-hour period each day. Recently, it was extended to a 24-hour program for a cottage of 28 boys, representative of all youth in the institution.

Cohen utilizes a system of external reinforcers (points that are earned and exchanged only by the earner for money or services) and has tried to simulate a "real-world" economy to improve academic, vocational, and social behavior. This project is especially noteworthy in the socio-behavioral literature because of its attempts to link the institutional program directly to the future social environment of the clients. In addition, the

---

[4] Harold Cohen, James A. Filipiczak, and John S. Bis, "Contingencies Applicable to Special Education of Delinquents: Establishing 24-hour Control in an Experimental Cottage" (Silver Spring, Maryland: Institute for Behavioral Research, Inc., 1966, mimeographed).

behavior upon which the points are contingent is that which may be objectively measured with reference to modification goals; examples are test scores, completion of programmed courses; and demonstrated ability to work for specified periods of time. An elaborate design has been developed for both the formal and the informal program of the cottage. This project has been under way for only a short period, but preliminary results show very positive outcomes with reference to institutional and post-institutional behavior. Anti-social behavior within the cottage is reported to be almost non-existent, and behavior, such as truancy, is less than half the rate for the rest of the institution.

The CASE II project report makes clear that many aspects of organizational behavior must be controlled for an effective behavior modification program. In order to implement the regimen, the physical and social environment had to be explicitly designed in a manner and with equipment different from that found in the usual training school for delinquent boys. The education program, for example, included 89 programmed or auto-instructional courses, each of which had particular resource requirements in materials and staff. Socio-behavioral technology, like any other treatment approach, poses its own requirements for essential artifacts, material and even architecture. The agency must be able to supply these and to make the re-arrangements required by the plan.

Introduction of a token economy throughout the cottage (work, leisure, education, cottage living were all included) required considerable ingenuity and innovation in organizational arrangements. Special provisions were required for private study, for availability of facilities throughout the day and evening, and for accurate and consistent monitoring. Choices had to be made about which behavior was to be controlled under the point system, since it was not feasible to include every possible activity. Cohen deliverately chose activities that were linked most directly to the extra-institutional environment such as education, work, and parole status.

Professional and non-professional staff had to be trained in the use of the behavior modification procedures. CASE II used many non-professional staff who had been in the institution for a number of years. It was found that they could be successfully retrained, but ingenuity was important in the conduct of this in-service training. The project is now being engineered for the total institution. Cohen and his staff have observed that variables such as size and organizational complexity require particular consideration, because preconditions sufficient for one cottage or unit may be inadequate when implemented for the entire organization.

A third example is the Hartwig project described by Rose.[5] The organizational features of this effort will be examined without restating its details. The Hartwig project differs from those reported by Cohen and Wetzel, because it was developed in an open community-based agency rather than in a closed institution. Because of this, variations can be expected in the organizational requisites. Rose's account of the Hartwig project touches on several requisites. First of all, means had to be developed for routinized assessment and referral of potential clients by such referring agents as teachers, and staff of the police youth bureau. Instruments were needed to present information about who defined the unacceptable behavior, about conditions preceding and accompanying this behavior, as well as about the environmental consequences of the behavior. Next, baseline performance criteria were necessary for each client, and in the case of group treatment approaches, for behavior at the group as well as at the individual level. Information had to be obtained from school teachers, parents, and staff members in other agencies. It was observed that other agencies had different goals and employed contrasting technologies. Thus, it was difficult to obtain sufficient comparable information unless some controls were instituted.

---

[5] Sheldon Rose, "A Behavioral Approach to Group Treatment of Children," Edwin J. Thomas, ed., in *The Socio-Behavioral Approach and Applications to Social Work* (New York: Council on Social Work Education, 1967), pp. 39-55.

Mechanisms for monitoring behavior pose additional requirements once the baseline criteria have been established. Rose noted that workers' observations were inadequate for this purpose and that systematic procedures had to be developed for monitoring intra-group and extra-group behavior. The school and the home were chosen in this project as the sites for periodic monitoring, and precise information from these sources was required at particular points.

It was reported that frequent problems were encountered in the development of systematic assessment and reporting procedures. Information had to be obtained in brief periods of time and had to be analyzed continuously so that the findings could be used in modifying or stabilizing treatment plans. Attention also was directed to procedures of "feed-back" to teachers and parents so that the information communicated would have the desired effect rather than an unanticipated and undesirable consequence.

Staff without professional training were employed in the Hartwig project and, like Wetzel, Rose found that they could be successfully trained in the use of socio-behavioral theory. In fact, Rose implies that non-professionals may be trained to implement much of the direct service to clients, with professional staff responsible for design and overall supervision of the program.[6]

DISCUSSION OF REQUISITES

The three reports illustrate a number of important organizational requisites for effective use of a socio-behavioral technology.[7] Let us restate the issues derived from examination of these cases and consider their more general implications. Attention will be focused on the distinctive requirements posed by the use of socio-behavioral technologies and on those requirements that are essential for goal attainment and survival of viable human service organizations. Inevitably, the examination of prerequisites will be incomplete and tentative, and the discussion of rationale for choice of certain preconditions rather than others will not be completely specific. The utilization of socio-behavioral practice in these organizations is very new; much more research and extensive application under variable conditions is necessary before prerequistes can be unambiguously specified.

Information Requirements

The information requirements of this technology are far more demanding in several areas than those of other treatment approaches. Concrete and specific information about client malperformance must be obtained from problem-defining agents outside the agency (e.g., referral sources) as well as within. In the absence of this knowledge, it is impossible to formulate behavior modification objectives and to note changes. Procedures for obtaining baseline performance data for individual clients and groups of clients must be organizationally routinized, as both the Wetzel and Rose reports indicate. Some work has been done in this area and preliminary findings indicate that procedures can be successfully

---

[6] Albert Bandura and Richard Walters, *Social Learning and Personality Development* (New York: Holt, Rinehart and Winston, 1063), pp. 224-259. They also suggest similar roles for professionally trained staff.

[7] It was not possible to identify in this paper the organizational precondition for the example of casework treatment reported by Richard Stuart. His attention was directed primarily to client-worker interaction and only indirectly to the agency. There is no reason to believe, however, that the preconditions identified in this paper would not be equally applicable in casework treatment.

operationalized and engineered.[8] These results also suggest that instruments and procedures can be established not only for practitioners in their programming for clients but also for agency administrators who need systematic information for planning and evaluative purposes.

When change procedures have been initiated, additional types of information are needed on a continuing basis. There must be observational assessment and feedback of information about client behavior relevant to the foci of treatment. The availability today of automated information systems makes it possible to plan for rapid feedback of needed information to the appropriate staff. The application of these systems in most social agencies, however, will require substantial changes in information collection and processing.

Staff activities must be monitored in order to maintain adherence to the modification program and consistency among personnel. There must be continuing ways to determine the degree to which changed behavior is sustained in diverse situations during and subsequent to the modification program. Far too often, today, practitioners rely on highly impressionistic information, directly contrary to the requirements of a socio-behavioral technology. Taken together, these demands call for markedly improved systems for the collection, analysis, and feedback of specific kinds of information throughout the agency. The Wetzel and Cohen cases document the problems of fulfilling these requirements in the context of multi-staff institutional programs, while the Rose case points to the problems of crossing agency boundaries in obtaining information essential to the technology.

Staff Selection and Training

The introduction of a socio-behavioral technology is likely to require new staff or, at least, the retraining of existing personnel. Both professional staff and other echelons will be affected by the different performance requirements. The case examples all illustrate that non-professional staff can be trained to apply successfully behavior modification procedures. In each situation, explicit instruction was necessary and, furthermore, continuing training was required because of staff turnover and tendencies to drift back to former practices.

Coordination and Control

Much more than in-service training is required to implement a socio-behavioral technology. Conduct of each modification program calls for respecification of responsibilities among certain staff members, and, equally important, for arrangements to articulate the behaviors of all others in a unified, consistent plan of service. Authority and control structures in agencies must insure the performance of the required behavior by all members and yet not provoke responses of resistance or apathy. Existing authority structures in many social agencies permit bifurcation in the management and treatment of clients, with the frequent outcome that rehabilitative goals are displaced by custodial or manage-

---

[8] For a discussion of one approach in the development of systematic recording procedures in a social agency, see James Seaberg, "Case Recording by Code," *Social Work*, Vol. 10, No. 1 (October, 1965), pp. 92-99. Also see Robert D. Vinter, Rosemary C. Sarri, Darrel Vorwaller, and Walter E. Schafer, *Pupil Behavior Inventory* (Ann Arbor: Campus Publishers, 1966); Edgar F. Borgatta and David Fanshel, *Behavioral Characteristics of Children* (New York: Child Welfare League of America, 1965); Eugene Litwak, *et al.* "A Design of Utilization of Special Services in Detroit Public Schools" (Ann Arbor: The University of Michigan, 1965, unpublished manuscript).

rial goals.[9] Management and treatment functions must be integrated as these impinge on the client(s). Engineering problems are often enormous, particularly in the large complex agencies that provide twenty-four-hour care for clients—prisons, hospitals, nursing homes, and so forth. The utilization of socio-behavioral technologies will not prevent bifurcation or goal displacement. Therefore, special procedures must be instituted. For example, closed institutions may utilize an approach in which treatment is decentralized and integrated with management tasks at the living unit level.

Agencies in which there are large numbers of staff who represent different professions may have additional problems of coordination, because each of these groups may resist bureaucratic controls. Some mechanisms have been developed whereby the basis and criteria for allocating authority complement professional roles and structures, and still meet technical requirements for control. Goss has described a number of mechanisms employed in general hospitals whereby certain areas of physicians' roles are controlled by formal bureaucratic mechanisms and, in other areas, high degrees of informality and individual autonomy are allowed to prevail.[10]

Relatively high levels of specialization in staff roles can be expected if widely varied socio-behavioral technologies are utilized to attain the desired change goals for clients. Here, again, decentralization of decision-making about treatment planning and implementation is one strategy for resolution of control problems. However, this may be insufficient if a client is exposed to several different and, perhaps, unrelated technologies in different departments of the agency.

The importance of coordination is obvious if rational organizational behavior is to be enhanced. Nonetheless, as was pointed out earlier, the agency is also to be viewed as a social system that adaptively responds to external and internal pressures. These pressures may generate informal patterns that may hamper treatment objectives, and yet they are often ignored when considering coordinative mechanisms. If socio-behavioral technologies are to be successfully employed, social system requirements must be served. The Essexfield project, described by Thomas, is an example of an attempt to create a new type of social system within the agency as the primary treatment strategy.[11] To serve these requirements minimally, the agency would need to provide mechanisms for coping with or responding to informal client systems behavior, unanticipated consequences, or side effects of rationally planned interventions.

Redesign of Agency Environments

Introduction of new technologies based on socio-behavioral theory is likely to call for extensive alterations in the design of services, and, not infrequently, of physical facilities. It poses its own requirements for essential artifacts, material, and even, perhaps, architecture. The need for such changes in the examples given here was more apparent in the CASE II project that centered on a complete residential unit. Considerable effort and imagination went into the design of new types of "hardware," particularly in the educational program. Greater use of electronic and physical hardware, heretofore mainly nonexistent in social agencies, can be safely predicted. There are obvious parallels in the new

[9] David Street, Robert D. Vinter and Charles Perrow, *Organization for Treatment* (New York: Free Press Division of Macmillan, 1966), pp. 93-137.

[10] Mary Goss, "Patterns of Bureaucracy Among Hospital Staff Physicians," in Eliot Friedson, ed., *The Hospital in Modern Society* (New York: Free Press Division of Macmillan, 1963), pp. 170-194.

[11] Edwin J. Thomas, "The Socio-Behavioral Approach: Illustrations and Analysis," in Thomas, *op. cit.*, pp. 4-5, 8ff.

developments that are taking place today in education where computers, electronic consoles, and teaching machines are increasingly employed.

Much more than alterations are involved in the technical or service arrangements directly relevant to a behavior modification program. The case examples given point to the manifold ways in which a broad range of physical and social agency patterns serve as controlling conditions and reinforcing contingencies (positive and negative) with respect to behavior modification programs. These reinforcing contingencies must be assessed and utilized planfully if socio-behavioral approaches are to be employed successfully. Many social agencies today provide extensive physical and social deprivations and punishments, and very few gratifications.[12] In assessing positive and negative reinforcers in the agency, attention is to be given to individual, group, and community variations in perceptions of what is or may be reinforcing or punishing. Having accomplished this, a balanced economy of gratifications must be provided and controlled, with mechanisms for allocations of rewards throughout the system by clients as well as staff. The findings from studies of the systems for distribution of rewards and sanctions in human service organization provide additional specification of these requirements.[13]

New models for closed institutions will clearly be required if simulation of crucial features of the external environment is to be achieved, as required by many behavior modification procedures. The Wetzel and Cohen reports both deal with the redesign of aspects of the agency environment, and there are other extensive plans reported in the literature.[14] Blum and Polansky, for example, observed that the organizational structure of staff roles played a significant part in children's behavior patterns in a residential setting.[15] Worker interactions with clients were governed more by the organizational structure than by individual attributes. In community agencies, such as that in which the Hartwig project is located, services are provided outside the usual building-centered program and the eight-to-five office schedule. This requires modification of many contemporary agency arrangements if provision is to be made for continuing innovation, adaptation, and flexibility. Some agencies have been able to implement programs of this type, but problems and strains inevitably emerge unless agencies provide mechanisms for routinized problem-solving to handle the continuing need for adaptation and change. Routinized problem-solving procedures will also stimulate staff to conceptualize more alternatives to existing operational patterns and to predict probable consequences from alternative courses of action. Thus, forecasting and planning for the future will be enhanced. Discussion earlier in the paper about informational requirements is also pertinent here

[12] For penetrating descriptions of these conditions in human service organizations, see Erving Goffman, "On the Characteristics of Total Institutions: The Inmate World and Staff-Inmate Relations," in Donald Cressey, ed., *The Prison: Studies in Institutional Organization and Change* (New York: Holt, Rinehart and Winston, 1961), pp. 15-106; Lloyd M. McKorkle and Richard Korn, "Resocialization Within the Walls," *The Annals*, 293 (May, 1954), pp. 88-98; Julius Roth, *Timetables* (Indianapolis: Bobbs-Merrill, 1963); and Brim and Wheeler, *op cit.*, pp. 83-89.

[13] See Street *et al.*, *op cit.*, pp. 224-227 and 279-285.

[14] Teodoro Ayllon and Nicholas H. Azrin, "The Measurement and Reinforcement of Behavior of Psychotics," *Journal of the Experimental Analysis of Behavior*, Vol. 8, No. 6 (November, 1965), pp. 357-385; Teodoro Ayllon and Jack Michael, "The Psychiatric Nurse as a Behavioral Engineer," in Arthur Staats, ed., *Human Learning* (New York: Holt, Rinehart and Winston, 1964), pp. 445-448; Sidney Bijou, "Experimental Studies of Child Behavior, Normal and Deviant," in Leonard Krasner and Leonard Ullmann, eds., *Research in Behavior Modification* (New York: Holt, Rinehart and Winston, 1965), pp. 56-82.

[15] Arthur Blum and Norman A. Polansky, "Effect of Staff Role on Children's Verbal Accessibility," *Social Work*, Vol. 6, No. 1 (January, 1961), pp. 29-34.

since rationalized problem-solving by all levels of staff require the feed-back of information about cases and case management, about programs, and about outcomes.[16] Despite the difficulties, identification and deliberate control or redesign of intra-agency environments is necessary in order not to negate behavioral treatment plans.

External Linkages

Important connections between intra-agency procedures and external processes were cited at several points in the prior case examples and discussion. These involved (1) the obtaining of client malperformance information and definitions from outside sources, (2) the establishment of behavior modification criteria having direct relevance to conventional roles and standards, (3) the creation of intra-mural situations and experiences directly analogous to externally significant behavioral areas, and (4) the problem of sustaining behavioral change through reinforcement procedures and monitoring performance after departure from the agency. The first three of these are essential to insure that treatment plans focus directly on behavioral patterns at issue in the client's "real world" environment, while the fourth addresses generalization of changes into post-treatment situations. Also implicated is the notion that the client's experience is appropriately viewed as a career into, through, and out of the agency. This perspective requires that continuing attention be directed to the linkages between the external environment and intra-agency phenomena.[18] The spanning or surmounting of agency boundaries is a special problem where it becomes necessary to effect controls on the client's external social system. Where the target of change is a group or neighborhood rather than individual clients, still other approaches may be required to cope with environmental linkages. Some strategies of the latter type were suggested in the paper that considered application of socio-behavioral theory to community practice.[19] Unless effective external linkages are developed, behavioral modification programs risk being irrelevant as well as impotent.

CONCLUSIONS

This analysis of the organizational requisites clearly indicates that a number of essentials can be identified. Furthermore, preliminary evidence suggests that many of these can be met at least partially. Introduction of this technology can be expected to have both direct and indirect benefits for social agencies. At the interpersonal and community levels of intervention, problems have frequently arisen in the past because external forces exerted considerable pressure on human service organizations to concretize and specify both goals and means. The latter task was particularly difficult because of the ambiguity and indeterminancy of many human relations technologies. Socio-behavioral theory provides a marked contrast to theories that underlie many of these other interpersonal change technologies. It is based on empirically validated knowledge and is specific, pre-

---

[16] John K. Harris has suggested that administrative planning and decision-making would be markedly enhanced by the use of more systematic information processing. See John K. Harris, "System Designs for Welfare Programs: The Role of EDP," *Public Welfare*, Vol. 24, No. 2 (April, 1966), pp. 112-117.

[17] Eugene Litwak and Henry J. Meyer, "A Balance Theory of Coordination Between Organizations and Community Primary Groups," *Administrative Science Quarterly,* Vol. 11, No. 1 (June, 1966), pp. 31-58.

[18] Robert Rapaport, *The Community as Doctor* (Springfield, Illinois: C. C. Thomas and Co., 1960).

[19] Philip A. Fellin, Jack Rothman, and Henry J. Meyer, "Implications of Socio-Behavioral Theory for Community Organization Practice," in Thomas, *op. cit., pp. 119-135.*

scriptive and adaptable. It also demands that linkages be established between the problematic behavior that brought the client to the agency, treatment plans and outcomes, and agency goals. Far greater attention is paid to the design and engineering of service technologies directly related to behavior desired in the larger social system. What distinguishes the socio-behavioral technology is the extent to which its particular requirements are explicit through and integral to its procedures, rather than suggested by its ideology or action orientations.

For the agency, utilization of this approach is potentially valuable, because its behaviorally specific objectives and prescriptions for action facilitate comparisons across levels, subsystems, and organizations. The focus on specificity of change goals is congruent with the need to achieve greater demonstrability of service effectiveness. Rising pressures are being exerted today on social agencies to specify their goals and validate their accomplishments.

Although limits on rationality are recognized, a socio-behavioral approach suggests that the agency can be conceived as an instrument for behavior modification at individual, group and larger social system levels. It is, perhaps, too early to determine if there are unique requirements posed by the utilization of this technology. There is little doubt that as the tenets of this technology are accepted and its procedures introduced in a broader range of organizations, marked changees can be expected in the physical and social design of agencies, in the deployment of staff, in procedures for information collection and processing, in mechanisms for monitoring staff and client behavior and evaluating outcomes, and in the explicit linking of treatment technologies to clients' usual social environments.

Program Change and Organizational Properties: A Comparative Analysis [1]

JERALD HAGE AND MICHAEL AIKEN

A major problem in the study of organizations is the analysis of organizational change. One of the difficulties in studying change is the determination of an adequate definition of organizational change.[2] Etzioni has suggested that most organizational studies implicitly, if not explicitly, involve the study of change of some variable or property.[3] This difficulty has been labeled by Parsons as the problem of change within a system as opposed to change of the system.[4] The difficulty lies in determining which kind of change results in a change of the organizational system. New techniques may be adopted, new models may be tried, and new rules and policies may be formulated; yet these are changes that do not necessarily imply fundamental changes in the organizational system. We shall offer a tentative solution to this problem by limiting our analysis to one kind of change within the system—the adoption of new programs or services. This kind of change appears to be an important one albeit not the only kind because it can imply changes in techniques, rules, or even goals. We are interested in studying the relationship between different organizational properties and the rate of program change, and we assume that the rate of program change, as well as other organizational properties, can be conceived most advantageously as variables in a system. We assume that a change in one variable leads to a change in other variables. If different rates of program change are related to different configurations on other organizational properties, then we can speak of differ-

[1] This investigation was supported, in part, by a research grant from the Vocational Rehabilitation Administration, Department of Health, Education, and Welfare, Washington, D.C. We are deeply indebted to Professor Harry Sharp and the Wisconsin Survey Laboratory for their helpful suggestions and assistance in the preparation and execution of the interviewing involved in this study and to the University of Wisconsin Computing Center and the National Science Foundation for their research support. We are also grateful to Keith Warner for his insightful comments on an earlier version of this paper. A special note of thanks is given to M. Garcon for his assistance in the final revision of this paper.

[2] See Jerald Hage, "Organizational Response to Innovation" (unpublished Ph.D. thesis, Columbia University, 1963), Chap. III, for a discussion of several different kinds of change .

[3] Amitai Etzioni, ed., in Introduction to section on "Organizational Change," *Complex Organizations: A Sociological Reader* (New York: Holt, Rinehart & Winston, 1961), pp. 341-343.

[4] Talcott Parsons, *The Social System* (Glencoe, Ill.: Free Press, 1951), Chap. XII.

ent systems. This is our approach to the problem of studying organizational change.

In our study, we have measured the rate of program change in sixteen organizations over a five-year period.[5] This rate is then related to other organizational properties, for example, job satisfaction, codification of rules, decision making, which are measured cross-sectionally, not longitudinally. While this prevents our making any statements about cause and effect, it does allow us to examine how different rates of program change are associated with various organizational properties.

To this end, we studied sixteen social welfare organizations staffed largely by professionally trained personnel. These organizations provide a particularly interesting testing ground for hypotheses relating rate of program change to other organizational properties, since the organizations provide services for the physically handicaped, emotionally disturbed, or mentally retarded. It might be assumed that each agency would attempt to add as many new programs as resources allow, but this was not the case. Some welfare organizations were primarily concerned with the quantity of client service. Given additional financial resources, these organizations would probably either reduce the case load of staff members or increase the number of clients serviced. For example, a county children's welfare department had added only one new program in the previous five years and had no plans for future changes. This agency was primarily concerned with reducing the case loads of its social workers. The rationale was not to improve the quality of service but, rather, to reduce turnover among its social workers, since the case load was unusually high in this agency, well beyond typical limits. Similarly, the head of a private home for emotionally disturbed children reported that no new programs had been added in his agency in the previous five years. In contrast, some welfare organizations were primarily concerned with the quality of client service. These organizations would probably use additional financial resources to add new programs or techniques. A county mental hospital, the organization in our study with the highest rate of program change, had added eight new programs in the past five years, including a sheltered workshop, a training program in group therapy for the attendants, and a placement service. In addition, there were already plans afoot for future changes. Similarly, a private home for emotionally disturbed boys had added six new programs in the last five years and had plans for still more. One of the greatest concerns in this organization was that the case load might increase, since the agency head felt that the major emphasis should be placed on improving the quality rather than the quantity of client service. The contrasting policies of these organizations cut across the different kinds of goals and are reflected in the varying rates of program change among the sixteen organizations. The rate of program change by type of organization is shown in Table 1. While rehabilitation centers have the greatest incidence of program change, and social casework agencies the least, there are still considerable variations among these categories of organizations that ostensibly have similar goals. Furthermore, the crucial question is whether a rehabilitation center with a low rate of program change has organizational characteristics that are similar to a social casework agency with a low rate of program change.

The assumption of an organization as a system implies that certain organizational configurations are most likely to be associated with a high rate of program change. This also implies that if a high rate of program change occurs in an organization, it is likely to

---

[5] Executive directors were asked: "How many new programs or services have you added in the last five years?" In many cases the new programs did not involve the addition of new personnel or new funds but, instead, represented reallocation of existing resources. The question used a standard interval of time so that the rate could be expressed as a number. It might also be noted that the choice of an interval of time is not an easy one. We selected an interval of five years as a minimum because any shorter period is too likely to be subjected to random or episodic fluctuations.

bring about changes in the working conditions of the organization.[6] Our data are not longitudinal, and thus it becomes impossible to stipulate any cause or effect relationships.[7] That is, we are unable to stipulate if program change brings about alternatives in other organizational properties or if new programs are introduced because of the presence of some other organizational characteristics. While our study is framed in the latter sense, this is simply for the convenience of the presentation of our findings. We would like to know organizational scores at both the beginning and end of the five-year period to unravel this problem, but unfortunately we only know organizational characteristics at the *end* of the five-year period.

Our purpose in this paper, then, is to relate the organizational characteristics of complexity, centralization, formalization, and job satisfaction to the rate of program change. We hypothesize that the rate of program change is positively related to the degree of complexity and job satisfaction and negatively related to the degree of centralization and formalization.[8] The rationale for each hypothesis is discussed below as the data are examined.

TABLE 1

Average Number of Program Changes by Type of Organization

Type of Organization	Number of Organizations	Average Number of Program Changes	Range
Rehabilitation centers	3	4.67	3-6
Hospitals	3	4.67	3-8
Special education department — public schools	1	4.00	4
Homes for emotionally disturbed	3	2.67	0-6
Social casework agencies	6	1.33	0-3

STUDY DESIGN AND METHODOLOGY

The data upon which this study is based were gathered in sixteen social welfare agencies located in large midwest metropolis in 1964. Ten agencies were private; six were either public or branches of public agencies. These agencies were all the larger welfare organizations that provide rehabilitation, psychiatric services, and services for the mentally retarded as defined by the directory of the Community Chest. The agencies vary in size from twelve to several hundred. Interviews were conducted with 314 staff members of these sixteen organizations. Respondents within each organization were selected by the following criteria: (a) all executive directors and department heads; (b) in departments of less than ten members, one-half of the staff was selected randomly; (c) in departments of

---

[6] In other words, all hypotheses are reversible; see Hans Zetterberg, *On Theory and Verification in Sociology* (rev. ed.; Totowa, N.J.: Bedminster Press, 1963), p. 11.

[7] We are presently engaged in the second logical step of research, namely, the attempt to predict the future rate of program change on the basis of organizational properties measured prior in time.

[8] For a discussion of why these properties should be related as hypothesized, see Jerald Hage, "An Axiomatic Theory of Organization," *Administrative Science Quarterly*, Vol. X (December, 1965), pp. 289-321.

more than ten members, one-third of the staff was selected randomly. Non-supervisory administrative and maintenance personnel were not interviewed.

This sampling procedure divides the organization into levels and departments. Job occupants in the upper levels were selected because they are most likely to be key decision makers and to determine organizational policy, whereas job occupants in the lower levels were selected randomly. The different ratios within departments insured that smaller departments were adequately represented. Professionals, such as psychiatrists, social workers, rehabilitation counselors, etc., are included because they are intimately involved in the achievement of organizational goals and are likely to have organizational power. Non-professionals, such as attendants, janitors, and secretaries, are excluded because they are less directly involved in the achievement of organizational goals and are likely to have organizational power. The number of interviews varied from seven in the smallest to forty-one in one of the larger agencies.

It should be stressed that in this study the units of analysis are organizations, not individuals in the organizations. Information obtained from respondents was pooled to reflect properties of the sixteen organizations, and these properties are then related to one another.[9] Aggregating individual data in this way presents methodological problems for which there are yet no satisfactory solutions. For example, if all respondents are equally weighted, undue weight is given to respondents lower in the hierarchy. Yet those higher in the chain of command, not those lower in the chain of command, are most likely to make the decisions which give an agency its ethos.[10]

We attempt to compensate for this by computing an organizational score from the means of social position within the agency. A social position is defined by the level or stratum in the organization and the department or type of professional activity. For example, if an agency's professional staff consists of psychiatrists and social workers, each divided into two hierarchal levels, the agency has four social positions: supervisory psychiatrists, psychiatrists, supervisory social workers, and social workers. A mean was then computed for each social position in the agency. The organizational score for a given variable was determined by computing the average of all social position means in the agency.[11]

The procedure for computing organizational scores parallels the method utilized in selecting respondents. It attempts to represent organizational life more accurately by not giving disproportionate weight to those social positions that have little power and that are

---

[9] A very common error in statistical analysis is the failure to realize that assumptions must be made not only about the unit of analysis, usually the individual, but also about the time and place. Few studies systematically examine these three factors together, yet each is important. Most studies should be qualified with reference to a specific time and place.

[10] For a discussion of some of the basic differences between individual and collective properties, see Paul Lazarsfeld and Herbert Menzel, "On Individual and Collective Properties," in Etzioni, *op. cit.*, pp. 422-440; and James S. Coleman, "Research Chronicle: The Adolescent Society," in Phillip E. Hammond, ed. *Sociologists at Work (New York: Basic Books, 1964).*

[11] One advantage of this procedure is that it allows for the cancellation of individual errors made by the job occupants of a particular position. It also allows for the elimination of certain idiosyncratic elements that result from the special privileges a particular occupant might have received as a consequence.

An alternative procedure for computing organizational means is to weigh all respondents equally. These two procedures yield strikingly similar results for the variables reported in this paper. The product moment correlation coefficients between the scores based on these two computational procedures were as follows for the variables indicated:

little involved in the achievement of organizational goals.

Computation of means for each social position has the advantage of avoiding the potential problem created by the use of different sampling ratios. In effect, responses are standardized by organizational location — level and department — and then combined into an organizational score. Computation of means of social position also has a major theoretical advantage in that it focuses on the sociological perspective or organizational reality. We consider an organization to be a collection of social positions which we call jobs, not simply an aggregate of individuals. Ideally, sociological properties are more than a summation of psychological properties. We feel that our computation procedures are, hopefully, more consistent with a "sociological imagination."

ORGANIZATIONAL PROPERTIES AND RATE OF PROGRAM CHANGE

Following the work of Pugh *et al.*, we find it useful to make a distinction between structural variables and performance variables as two special kinds of organizational properties.[12] The former refers to the arrangements of positions or jobs within the organization, for example, the utilization of different professional specialties or the degree of complexity, the distribution of power or the degree of centralization, the utilization of rules or the degree of formalization. The latter refers to the outcomes of the arrangements of positions, for example, the rate of program change, the degree of job satisfaction, the volume of production. In addition we examine a personality characteristic of the individuals who work in the organization, namely, their attitudes toward change. Since we are interested in rates of program change, it is entirely possible that this is affected not only by the structural and performance characteristics of the organization but also by the general orientations of the individual members. Admittedly these are not the only distinctions that can be made, but they provide a useful framework for distinguishing among major kinds of variables, helping to isolate the characteristics that are part of the system.

STRUCTURAL VARIABLES: THE DEGREE OF COMPLEXITY

Since the publication of the English translation of Durkheim's *The Division of Labor*, the degree of complexity, or specialization, has been a key concept in the organizational literature.[13] Yet, this variable has seldom been systematically related to other organiza-

---

Hierarchy of authority 70
Actual participation in decision making 90
Job codification 68
Rule observation 88
Job satisfaction 89
Satisfaction with expressive relations 88
Professional training 90
Professional activity 87
Index of self-interest and non-change 87
Index of values and pro-change 74

[12] D. S. Pugh *et al.*, "A Scheme for Organizational Analysis," *Administrative Science Quarterly*, Vol. VIII (1963), pp. 289-316.

[13] Emile Durkheim, *The Division of Labor in Society* (New York: Macmillan Co., 1933), Part I; also Preface to 2d ed.

tional properties. For our purposes, we define organizational complexity with three alternative empirical indicators: occupational specialties, the length of training required by each occupation, and the degree of professional activity associated with each occupation. The greater the number of specialties, the greater the length of training required by each occupation; and the greater the degree of professional activity, the more complex the organizational structure. The term "specialization" has frequently been used to describe both this phenomenon and the minute parceling of work such as that of an assembly line where training of job occupants is minimized. From our perspective, the latter is the opposite of complexity. In order to avoid terminological confusion, we prefer to use the word "complexity" to refer to the former phenomenon, since we feel that this is more consistent with Durkheim's usage of the term.[14]

A recently published axiomatic theory hypothesizes a direct relationship between complexity and the rate of program change.[15] There are several reasons why these two properties should be related in this way. The addition of new programs frequently necessitates the addition of new occupations. Job occupants of such occupational specialties often have a particular organizational perspective which leads to the introduction of still other new programs. Further, the professional activities of job staff members function as communications links between the organization and its competitors, providing a source of information about new ideas and techniques. In addition, conflicts among the different occupational specialties in an organization act as a further dynamic force for the creation of new programs. The more professionalized the occupations, the greater the struggle to prove the need for expansion.[16]

In our interviews with staff members of organizations, each respondent was asked to describe the nature of his duties, the extent of his training, and the amount of his professional activity. Just as the number of jobs reflects the complexity of the organization, it was our belief that the more the training required, the more the probable complexity of the job itself, so that this needed to be considered as well. Furthermore, the more the professional activity of the job occupants, the more likely there would be continued increases in the complexity of the job. On the basis of the respondents' answers to our questions, three indicators of organizational complexity were computed. The first indicator is the number of occupational specialties, which was measured by counting the numbers of different kinds of work that exist in an agency. There is a correlation of .48 between the number of occupational specialties and the rate of program change. A variety of occupational perspectives is associated with a higher rate of change.

We have already stated that we are unable to determine causation because our data are taken at one point of time. Since occupational specialties more than any of our other variables can be closely linked to the programs that are added, we reconstructed the number of occupational specialties that existed in each organization prior to 1959, the beginning of the five-year period we used for measuring the rate of program change. While the number of occupational specialties was altered in several organizations, the correlation between these two properties remained virtually unchanged $(r = .45)$.[17]

---

[14] See Victor Thompson, *Modern Organization* (New York: Alfred A. Knopf, Inc., 1964), Chap. III.

[15] See Hage, "An Axiomatic Theory," *op. cit.*, p. 303.

[16] Durkheim, *op. cit.*, pp. 267-270.

[17] It should be noted that our count of occupational specialties is not based on the number of specific job titles. Instead, each respondent was asked what he did and then this was coded according to the kind of professional activity and whether it was a specialty. This procedure was used for two reasons. First, it allows for comparability across organizations. Second, it avoids the problem of task specialization where one activity might be divided into many specific and separate tasks (see Thompson, *op. cit.*).

The amount of professional training is another indicator of the complexity of organizations. This was measured by computing an index reflecting the degree of formal training and other professional training for each social position in the organization.[18] As can be seen from Table 1, there is a weak but positive correlation between the organization score of professional training and the rate of program change ($r = .14$). Thus the amount of professional training in an organization is positively associated with the rate of program change.

To measure the extent of the extra-organizational professional activity of members of each organization, the respondents were asked to report the number of professional associations to which they belonged, the proportion of meetings attended, the number of papers given, and offices held, all of which represent professional involvement.[19] The higher this score, that is, the greater the extra-organizational professional activities of members of the organization, the more likely it was to have a high rate of program change, as shown in Table 2 ($r = .37$). It should be noted that the amount of professional involvement is more highly related to program change than the amount of professional training.

Involvement in extra-organizational professional activities evidently heightens awareness of programmatic and technological developments within a profession.[20] Professionally active job occupants introduce new ideas into the organization, and the outcome is a high rate of program change. Similarly, new programs require the addition of new job occupants who are highly trained. A plausible line of reasoning is that greater extra-organizational professional activity implies a greater emphasis on the improvement of the quality of client service, whether the clients are emotionally disturbed or mentally retarded. Such an emphasis requires a continual application of new knowledge, whether reflected in new programs or in new techniques. The number of occupational specialties and the amount of extra-organizational professional activity were themselves related; the correlation coefficient was .29. The sheer presence of different occupational perspectives, implying the idea of occupational conflict, appears to heighten professional involvement, as was suggested by Durkheim.[21]

STRUCTURAL VARIABLES: THE DEGREE
OF CENTRALIZATION

There are many debates in the organizational literature about the relative merits of

---

[18] The index was scored as follows: (a) An absence of training beyond a college degree and the absence of other professional training received a score of 0; (b) an absence of training beyond college degree and the presence of other professional training received a score of 1; (c) a presence of training beyond a college degree and the absence of other professional training received a score of 2; (d) a presence of training beyond a college degree and the presence of other professional training received a score of 3.

[19] The index of professional activity, which ranged from 0 to 3 points, was computed as follows: (a) 1 point for belonging to a professional organization; (b) 1 point for attending at least two-thirds of the previous six meetings of any professional organization; (c) 1 point for the presentation of a paper or holding an office in any professional organization.

[20] See Victor Thompson, "Bureaucracy and Innovation," Administrative Science Quarterly, Vol. X (June, 1965), pp. 10-13.

[21] Durkheim, op. cit.; although he was discussing the characteristics of city life, the argument is that much more compelling in the context of an organization where interaction is facilitated.

TABLE 2

RATE OF PROGRAM CHANGE AND OTHER ORGANIZATIONAL PROPERTIES

	Pearson Product-Moment Correlation Coefficients of Each Organizational Characteristic with Rate of Program Change*

Structural variables:

1. Degree of complexity:
   a) Measure of the number of occupational specialties . . . . .48 +
   b) Measure of the amount of extra-organizational professional
      activity . . . . .37 +
   c) Measure of the amount of professional training . . . . .14 −

2. Degree of centralization:
   a) Measure of the degree of participation in organizational decision
      making 49
   b) Measure of hierarchy of authority . . . . −.09

3. Degree of formalization:
   a) Measure of the degree of job codification . . . . −.47
   b) Measure of the degree of rule observation 13
Performance variables:
   1. Degree of satisfaction:
   a) Measure of job satisfaction 38
   b) Measure of expressive satisfaction . . . . −.17
Personality variables:
   1. Motive of self-interest and negative attitude toward change . . . . −.04
   2. Motive of values and positive attitudes toward change . . . . −.15

*The measures of association reported here are Pearson product-moment correlation coefficients. The units of analysis in this report are the sixteen organizations in our study, not our 314 individual respondents. Product-moment correlation coefficients are highly sensitive to even slight modifications of numerical scores with so few cases. We rejected the use of non-parametric measures of association because our scales are lineal and not ordinal; non-parametric statistics necessitate our "throwing away" some of the magnitude of variations in our data. Since these sixteen organizations represent a universe of organization, tests of statistical significance are inappropriate.

121

centralization as opposed to decentralization of decision making. On the one hand, Weber argued that strict hierarchy of authority increased both the volume of production and the efficiency of an organization.[22] On the other hand, the human relations specialists have argued that decentralization increases job satisfaction and reduces resistance to change.[23] Both arguments are probably correct.

In our study the staff members were asked how often they participated in organizational decisions regarding the hiring of personnel, the promotions of personnel, the adoption of new organizational policies, and the adoption of new programs or services.[24] The organizational score was based on the average degree of participation in these four areas of decision making. As can be seen from Table 2, the greater the participation in agency-wide decisions, the greater the rate of program change in the organization ($r = .49$). Decentralization allows for the interplay of a variety of occupational perspectives. As Thompson has suggested, a centralized organization is one in which change can be, and frequently is, easily vetoed.[25]

Agency-wide decisions are not the only kind that are made. Other decisions are those concerning the performance of a specific job. Agency-wide decisions are basically decisions about the control of resources, while job decisions are basically decisions about the control of work. It is at least logically possible that the centralization of the former kind of decision making can be associated with the decentralization of the latter kind of decision making. We measure the degree of decision making about work with a scale called the "Hierarchy of authority."[26] This scale was found to have little relationship

---

[22] Max Weber, *The Theory of Social and Economic Organization*, trans. Henderson and Parsons (Glencoe, Ill.: Free Press, 1947), pp. 334-340.

[23] The classic study is, of course, Lester Coch and John French, Jr., "Overcoming Resistance to Change," *Human Relations*, Vol. I (1948), pp. 512-532. For a review of the literature and organizational experiments reflecting this dilemma between satisfaction and production, see Nancy Morse and Everett Reimer, "The Experimental Change of a Major Organizational Variable," *Journal of Abnormal and Social Psychology*, Vol. LII (1955), pp. 120-129.

[24] The index of actual participation in decision making was based on the following four questions: (1) How frequently do you usually participate in the decision to hire new staff: (2) How frequently do you usually participate in the decisions on the promotion of any of the professional staff? (3) How frequently do you participate in decisions on the adoption of new policies? (4) How frequently do you participate in the decisions on the adoption of new programs? Respondents were assigned numerical scores from 1 (low participation) to 5 (high participation), depending on whether they answered "never," "seldom," "sometimes," "often," or "always," respectively, to these questions. An average score on these questions was computed for each respondent, and then the data were aggregated into organizational scores as described above.

[25] Thompson, "Bureaucracy and Innovation," *op. cit.*, pp. 13-18.

[26] The empirical indicators of these concepts were derived from two scales developed by Richard Hall, namely, hierarchy of authority and rules (see his "The Concept of Bureaucracy: An Empirical Assessment," *American Journal of Sociology*, LXIX [July, 1963], 32-40). The index of hierarchy of authority was computed by first averaging the replies of individual respondents to each of the following five statements: (1) There can be little action taken here until a supervisor approves a decision. (2) A person who wants to make his own decisions would be quickly discouraged here. (3) Even small matters have to be referred to someone higher up for a final answer. (4) I have to ask my boss before I do almost anything. (5) Any decision I make has to have my boss's approval. Responses could vary from 1 (definitely false) to 4 (definitely true). The individual scores were then combined into an organizational score as described above.

with the rate of program change, although it was in the predicted direction ($r = - .09$). It is the centralization of decisions about organizational resources, not the centralization of work control, that is highly related to low rates of this kind of organizational change.

STRUCTURAL VARIABLES: THE DEGREE
OF FORMALIZATION

Rules or regulations are important organizational mechanisms that may be used to insure the predictability of performance. There are two aspects of the use of rules as a mechanism of social control; one is the number of regulations specifying who is to do what, where, and when; we call this the degree of job codification. Another is the diligency in enforcing these rules that specify who is doing what, where, and when; this we call rule observation. The latter is important because many organizations may not enforce all regulations. The degree of formalization is defined as both the degree of job codification as well as the degree of rule observation.

While it has been commonplace to argue that bureaucracies retard change, there have been few studies that have examined this proposition in a comparative framework. One of the essential elements of bureaucracy is its emphasis on formalization. Our hypothesis is that the two aspects of formalization outlined above retard the adoption of new programs because they discourage individual initiative.[27] Clearly codified jobs that are closely supervised to insure conformity also reduce the search for better ways of doing work. Such a use of rules encourages ritualistic and unimaginative behavior.

The two indexes of formalization were constructed on the basis of a factor analysis of scales developed by Hall.[28] At best these scales are only rough indicators of the degree of formalization in an organization. As indicated by Table 2, job codification is inversely related to the rate of organizational change ($r = - .47$). The relationship between the degree of rule observation and the rate of program change is much weaker and is in a direction opposite from our prediction ($r = .13$).

In order to determine whether each of the observed relationships between each of our indicators of various structural properties and the rate of program change are spurious, multiple and partial correlation analyses are introduced.

As shown in Table 3, only two of these variables have strong and independent relationships with the rate of program change: the degree of job codification ($rp = - .47$) and the degree of participation in decision making ($rp = .39$). It should be noted that the β weights for participation in decision making are greater (.555), however, than the β

[27] Robert K. Merton, "Bureaucratic Structure and Personality," in Etizioni, *op. cit.*, pp. 48-61.

[28] Hall, *op. cit.* The index of job codification was based on the following five questions: (1) I feel that I am my boss in most matters. (2) A person can make his own decisions without checking with anybody else. (3) How things are done here is left up to the person doing the work. (4) People here are allowed to do almost as they please. (5) Most people here make their own rules on the job. Replies to these questions were scored from 1 (definitely true) to 4 (definitely false), and then each of the respondent's answers was averaged. Thus, a high score on this index means high job codification.

The index of rule observation was computed by averaging the responses to each of the following two statements: (1) The employees are constantly being checked on for rule violations. (2) People there feel as though they are constantly being watched, to see that they obey all the rules. Respondents' answers were coded from 1 (definitely false) to 4 (definitely true), and then the average score of each respondent on these items was computed. Organizational scores were computed as previously described. On this index, a high score means a high degree of rule observation.

weights for job codification (− .379).

The number of occupational specialties and the degree of hierarchy have moderate but independent relationships with the number of program innovations, although the latter variable is related in the opposite direction when the other six variables are controlled. The degree of extra-organizational activity, the degree of professional training, and the degree of rule observation have little relationship with the number of program innovations after controlling for the other factors, although rule observation remains virtually unchanged.

TABLE 3

MULTIPLE AND PARTIAL CORRELATION ANALYSIS OF THE NUMBER OF PROGRAM CHANGES AND OTHER ORGANIZATIONAL PROPERTIES

Organizational Properties	Partial Correlation Coefficient*	β Coefficients in Standard Form†
1. Degree of complexity:		
a) Measure of the number of occupational speccialties††	+.24	+.202
b) Measure of the amount of extra-organizational professional activity	+.08	+.104
c) Measure of professional training	−.10	−.137
2. Degree of centralization:		
a) Measure of the degree of participation in organizational decision making	+.39	+.555
b) Measure of hierarchy of authority	+.23	+.231
3. Degree of formalization:		
a) Measure of degree of job codification	−.47	−.379
b) Measure of degree of rule observation	+.15	+.134
Coefficient of determination		.558
Multiple correlation coefficient		.75

* These are the partial correlation coefficients between each variable and the rate of program change, controlling for the other six structural variables. Thus, each is a sixth-order partial correlation coefficient.

† These are β coefficients in standard form, i.e., β weights.

†† This is the number of occupational specialties as of 1959, before the program changes discussed in this paper were introduced.

124

PERFORMANCE VARIABLES: THE DEGREE
OF SATISFACTION

Since the famous French and Coch experiment, the advocates of the human relations approach to organizational analysis have emphasized the importance of morale as a factor in understanding differential acceptance of change and, therefore, implicitly differential rates of program change.[29] We developed two different measures of morale — an index of job satisfaction and an index of satisfaction with expressive relations.[30] There is a correlation of .38 between job satisfaction and rate of program change. On the other hand, satisfaction with expressive relations is negatively correlated, albeit the size of the correlation is small ($r = -.17$). This suggests a plausible explanation for several contradictory viewpoints in the literature concerning morale and organizational change. The work of Coch and French suggests a positive relationship between morale and change, but a series of studies by Mann, Hoffman, and others at the University of Michigan have noted that change creates social strain in the organization.[31] One may infer, not necessarily from our data, that job satisfaction may be a necessary precondition for the introduction of changes, but after this change has been introduced it may have disruptive and negative effects on social relationships among members in an organization. It is also plausible to argue that the organizational conditions that facilitate the introduction of change, namely, occupational diversity and decentralization, reduce satisfaction with expressive relationships because of the conflicts they engender.

---

[29] Coch and French, *op. cit.*

[30] We used a satisfaction scale developed by Neal Gross, Ward Mason, and Alexander McEachern, *Explorations in Role Analysis* (New York: John Wiley & Sons, 1958), Appendix B. When factor analyzed, this battery provided the following scales: job satis-. faction, satisfaction with expressive relations, satisfaction with salary, and satisfaction with time. The index of job satisfaction was computed on the basis of responses to the following six questions: (1) How satisfied are you that you have been given enough authority by your board of directors to do your job well? (2) How satisfied are you with your present job when you compare it to similar positions in the state? (3) How satisfied are you with the progress you are making toward the goals which you set for yourself in your present position? (4) On the whole, how satisfied are you that (your superior) accepts you as a professional expert, to the degree to which you are entitled by reason of position, training, and experience? (5) On the whole, how satisfied are you with your present job when you consider the expectations you had when you took the job? (6) How satisfied are you with your present job in light of career expectations?

The index of expressive satisfaction was computed from responses to the following two questions: (1) How satisfied are you with your supervisor? (2) How satisfied are you with your fellow workers?

[31] See Floyd C. Mann and Lawrence Williams, "Observations on the Dynamics of a Change to Electronic Data-processing Equipment," *Administrative Science Quarterly*, Vol. V (September, 1960), pp. 217-57; and Floyd Mann and T. Hoffman, *Automation and the Worker* (New York: Henry Holt, 1960). The same point is made in several other studies of organizational change; see, for example, Harriet Ronken and Paul Lawrence, *Administering Changes* (Cambridge, Mass.: Harvard Graduate Business School, 1952); and Charles Walker, *Toward the Automatic Factory* (New Haven, Conn.: Yale University Press, 1957).

PERSONALITY VARIABLES: GENERAL
ORIENTATION TO CHANGE

It is argued by some social psychologists and psychologists that all collective properties of organization, such as the degree of centralization, the degree of formalization, or the degree of complexity, are ultimately reducible to psychological factors. Since this is a common argument, we attempted to measure several personality variables that might account for differences in organizational rates of program change. It could be argued that change occurs in organizations because the organization has a high proportion of individuals who are favorably oriented to social change. Selznik has suggested the idea of selective recruitment of certain personality types; that is, when an organization needs new job occupants, the attempt is made to recruit individuals who have personality attributes consistent with organizational needs.[32] Mann and Hoffman have hypothesized the obverse of this process, namely, that individuals who cannot tolerate change will leave changing organizations and seek work in more stable ones.[33] Finally, Homans and others have argued that sociological variables are fundamentally reducible to psychological variables.[34] While we do not except this argument, we included measures of individual orientations toward change developed by Sister Marie Augusta Neal in an attempt to test the validity of such assertions.[35]

The Neal batteries of self-interest motives, value motives, pro-change motives, and anti-change motives were factor analyzed and yielded two clear factors; one factor contains items representing attitudes of self-interest and a negative attitude toward change, while the second factor contains items representing attitudes of ideals and a positive orientation toward change. We would expect the former to be *negatively* associated with rate of program change and the latter to be *positively* associated with program change. We found only a modest relationship between these measures of attitudes toward change and the amount of organizational program change.

The measure of self-interest and anti-change was virtually unrelated to program change ($r = -.04$), while the measure of ideals and pro-change was related to program change opposite from the expected direction ($r = -.15$).

An organization can have a high proportion of job occupants who are favorably disposed toward change in their personal orientations, and yet the organization does not necessarily adopt new programs. The reverse pattern is equally true.

What this suggests is that the personality attributes included in our study add little to our understanding of organizational change as we have measured it. On the other hand, there is the possibility that there are other personality variables that are appropriate for the understanding of organizational change.

It would be desirable to know the relative importance of performance variables, such as job satisfaction and the structural properties, but the limited size of our universe of organizations ($n = 16$), makes a multiple correlational and partial correlational analysis (reported in Table 3) for all the variables that we have measured inappropriate. It should

---

[32] Philip Selznick, "Critical Decisions in Organizational Development," in Etzioni, *op. cit.*, pp. 355-62.

[33] See Mann and Hoffman, *op. cit.*

[34] George Homans, "Bringing Men Back In," *American Sociological Review*, Vol. XXIX (December, 1964), pp. 809-819.

[35] Four scales that purport to measure attitudes toward change developed by Sister Marie Augusta Neal, *Values and Interests in Social Change* (Englewood Cliffs, N.J.: Prentice-Hall, Inc., 1965), were used.

be understood that there is a very strong relationship between the degree of centralization and job satisfaction in particular.[36] At the same time, the concept of a system assumes that there is this high degree of interdependence. The precise importance of each of these variables must be determined with a much larger number of organizations and preferably with longitudinal measurements.

CONTEXTUAL VARIABLES, ORGANIZATIONAL PROPERTIES, AND RATE OF PROGRAM CHANGE

The fact that there are varying rates of program for our different kinds of agencies, as indicated in Table 1, suggests that there may be disparate situations faced by each of our organizations. The rate of technological change may be faster in rehabilitation than in social casework agencies.

In particular, the organizations in our study vary considerably in their ease of access to resources, whether personnel or finances. They differ considerably in their age and autonomy. These and other indicators of their environmental situation can have an impact on the organization and its ability to adopt new programs. By studying the impact of such variables as auspices, size, and function, it becomes possible to view the process by which organizations are likely to develop one or another system. It also allows us some insight into the generalizability of our findings. If one of these variables accounts for most of the observed relationship between the rate of program change and the organizational properties, then we are aware of a significant limitation on our findings.

In a recent review of the organizational literature, Pugh and his associates suggest a number of contextual variables that can be used either as controls or as independent variables when examining the relationships among organizational properties. The variables that they discuss are: origin and history, ownership and control, size, charter, technology, location, resources, and interdependence.[37] Presumably, each of these factors could have an impact on the characteristics of the organization, including the rate of program change. In particular, there is always the possibility that any of the relationships reported in Table 2 are simply a function of some of these contextual variables. For example, there is a standard organizational hypothesis that increasing size means more centralization and formalization, and, therefore, one might expect large organizations to have low rates of program change as a consequence. Another standard hypothesis is that older organizations are likely to be more bureaucratic and therefore to have lower rates of change.

To explore the relative importance of these environmental factors for the relationships discussed above, we employed partial correlations. A fourth-order partial correlation was computed between each of the organizational properties and rate of program change, controlling for *size*, auspices, age of organization, and major function.

Size represents the rank order of organizations by number of employees in the organization; it is the same as the contextual concept discussed by Pugh *et al.*

Auspices, that is, whether the organization is public or private, is similar to their concept of ownership and control. Since none of our organizations is a business, most of the analytical distinctions that they discussed do not apply. It should be noted that "auspices" not only includes the idea of the nature of the accountability of the chief executive, but it suggests the sources of revenue, an idea contained in the concept of

---

[36] See Michael Aiken and Jerald Hage, "Organizational Alienation,"*American Sociological Review* Vol. XXXI (August, 1966), pp. 497-507, for a discussion of this relationship.

[37] D. S. Pugh *et al., op. cit.* See Hage, "An Axiomatic Theory," *op. cit.*, pp. 304-306, for hypotheses concerning these contextural variables.

resources. The public agencies are largely tax supported, while the private agencies rely upon donations, grants, and fees. In other words, the distinction between public and private carries many implications; therefore, the word "auspices" appears to be a more appropriate one than either ownership or resources.

The age of the organization is only one aspect of the organization's origin and history, but it is an attempt to measure some of the ideas discussed by Pugh *et al*.

Finally, function is our attempt to divide a relatively homogeneous universe of organizations into at least two kinds of goals and technologies. We separated our organizations into those that deal with their clients for a relatively short period of time, the typical casework situation found in the social welfare agencies, and into those that deal with their clients for a relatively long period of time, the sheltered workshop, the school, and hospital situations. The one-hour interview and the total institution reflect different kinds of technology, at least in terms of the intensiveness, even though all of our agencies are concerned with providing rehabilitative and psychiatric services.[38]

Location and interdependence are two contextual variables discussed by Pugh *et al*. that are not included in our analysis. Location is impossible to include because all of our agencies are in the same metropolitan area. We feel that interdependence is an exceedingly important contextual variable, but we are still in the process of collecting data on it. A separate analysis of this contextual variable and its impact will be made at a later date.

Not all of the four contextual variables are related to the rate of program change. Both age ($r = -.03$) and auspices ($r = -.06$) were unrelated to this kind of organizational change as we have measured it. But size ($r = -.61$) and function ($r = .58$) were highly related to the rate of program change. The larger the size of the organization and the more time the client spends in the organization, the higher the rate of program change. Since these contextual factors are themselves interrelated (larger organizations were much more likely to be total institutions) and since these factors do have an impact on rate of program change, the question remains whether the relationships between our dependent variable and the other organizational properties will be maintained if we simultaneously control for all four of the contextual variables. To put it another way, we want to know if our results are a consequence of organizational arrangements or a consequence of the environmental situations.

The partial correlation analysis is reported in Table 4. If this table is compared with Table 1, it will be noted that the correlations remain approximately the same when size, age, auspices, and function are controlled, except for two measures: the number of occupational specialities and the hierarchy of authority. Function has a very high correlation with the number of occupational specialities, while size and auspices have moderately high correlations. The more time the client spends in the organization, the greater the number of occupational specialties ($r = .67$). If the organization is public, there are likely to be more occupational specialties than if it is private, suggesting different availability of funds ($r = .39$). Similarly, larger organizations have more occupational specialties

---

[38] Size was based on a rank order of all salaried employees. Rank ordering was used because we had an extremely skewed distribution. Auspices is a natural dichotomy between tax supported and non-tax supported. Age was treated as a trichotomy because all the organizations were founded either prior to 1900, between 1919 and 1923, or after the Great Depression period. Function was measured by creating a dummy variable based on the amount of contact per week between the agency and the client. An hour or less per week, the typical casework interview, was treated as low client involvement. The sheltered workshops, the rehabilitation agencies, and the total institutions were categorized as high-involvement agencies. Ideally more distinctions would be desirable, but with only sixteen organizations additional refinement becomes impossible.

128

(r = .41). When function, size, and auspices are held constant, the relationship between number of occupational specialties and rate of change disappears. This suggests a process when the time ordering of these variables is considered.

The function of the organization, its size, and its auspices affect the number of specialties it has; this in turn is associated with the rate of program change. The partial correlation analysis makes clear, however, that the number of occupational specialties has little independent effect in explaining the variation in rate of program change once auspices, size, age, and function are held constant.

In contrast, the partial correlation between rate of program change and hierarchy of authority, holding constant the four contextual factors, has the predicted negative relationship with rate of program change. In fact, the relationship is stronger after controlling for these contextual factors.

In general, the observed relationships between rate of program change and the organizational properties remain, even after simultaneously controlling for these contextual factors. That is, even though the context or environment affects the organization, most of the organizational properties examined are still related to the rate of program change.

TABLE 4

RATE OF PROGRAM CHANGE AND OTHER ORGANIZATIONAL PROPERTIES WHEN SIZE, AUSPICES, AGE OF ORGANIZATION, AND FUNCTION ARE CONTROLLED

	Partial Correlations with Rate of Program Change*
Structural variables:	
1. Degree of complexity:	
a) Measure of the amount of occupational specialties†	.00
b) Measure of the amount of professional activity	.11
c) Measure of the amount of professional training	.14
2. Degree of centralization:	
a) Measure of the degree of participation in decision making	.46
b) Measure of hierarchy of authority	−.37
3. Degree of formalization:	
a) Measure of the degree of job codification	−.33
b) Measure of the degree of rule observation	−.02
Performance variable:	
Degree of satisfaction:	
a) Measure of job satisfaction	.27
b) Measure of expressive satisfaction	−.19

* There are fourth order partial correlations, i.e., the partial correlation coefficients between each factor listed and the rate of program change, controlling for size, auspices, age of organization, and function.

† This is the number of occupational specialties as of 1959, before the program changes discussed in this paper were introduced.

Another way of determining the generalizability of these findings is the examination of other studies of organizations to see if they found similar results. In a study of large business firms in the United States, Chandler suggests that increases in complexity as measured by product diversification led to the decentralization of decision making.[39] This was especially likely to occur after the introduction of professional managers. These firms were also more likely to allocate a much larger proportion of their budget to research, indicating a higher rate of program change. Woodward's study of some ninety industrial firms in South Essex, England, suggests that those firms that made small batches of products or custom models were more likely than the assembly-line manufacturers to have professional managers, skilled labor, decentralized decision making, higher job satisfaction, and less routinization of procedures.[40] While this study does not have a direct measure of the rate of program change, both of these studies are at least supportive of the findings reported here.

CONCLUSIONS AND DISCUSSION

Our findings suggest the following two stories about the rate of program change. One line of reasoning is as follows: Given that there is a high rate of program change, there is likely to be relatively decentralized decision making because of the necessity for discussions about the problems of change. There is a variety of decisions involving the allocation of personnel and funds attendant to the addition of new programs. In addition, the implementation of programs inevitably indicates contingencies not considered and engenders conflicts that must be resolved. Similarly, the high rate of program change will necessitate the relaxation of rules in order to solve the problems of implementation. There will be conflicts between the demands of the new program and previous regulations that will make rule observation difficult. The addition of new programs is likely to attract better-trained and active professional personnel who will like the challenge of change. And new programs can require, in many cases, new skills or areas of expertise relative to the organization. The high rate of job satisfaction can flow from the satisfaction of being a member of a dynamic organization. But the high rate of change creates strain in interpersonal relationships.

Another line of reasoning is as follows: If an organization is relatively decentralized, it is likely to have a variety of information channels which allow the consideration of both the need for new programs and their appropriateness. The sheer number of occupational specialties also increases the diversity of informal channels of communication. This is likely to lead to conflict among competing ideas for organizational resources. In contrast, the amount of job codification reduces the diversity of informal channels of information by circumscribing the occupants' perspectives, including the recognition of needs and the choice of remedies. Given that an organization is complex, decentralized, and non-formalized, then it is likely to be high in rate of program change. Such an organization is also likely to have high job satisfaction but low satisfaction with expressive relations. High job satisfaction evidently facilitates the introduction of changes, but the changes themselves are evidently disruptive of interpersonal relationships. The structural arrangements that facilitate change seem to generate conflicts among staff members. The diversity of occupational specialties, the power struggles in a decentralized arrangement of decision making, and the lack of clear work boundaries — consequences of the lack of formalization — are all conducive to organizational conflicts that are manifested in dissatisfaction with expressive relationships.

[39]A.D. Chandler, Jr., *Strategy and Structure* (Cambridge, Mass.: M.I.T. Press, 1962).

[40]Joan Woodward, *Industrial Organization: Theory and Practice* (London: Oxford Press, 1965), Chap. II, pp. 23-25.

The nature of our data does not allow us to choose between these two lines of reasoning. It is our belief that both are correct and reflect again the system nature of organizations. However, future research should be directed to verifying which line of reasoning is more pervasive, but this will require longitudinal studies. Our analysis indicates that rate of program change is associated with configurations on other organizational properties, supporting the basic assumption that an organization is best viewed as a system of variables. While program change is only one kind of change within the system, future research should be directed to the question of whether other changes within the system, such as changes in rules as opposed to changes in degree of job codification, changes in who makes decisions as opposed to changes in emphasis on hierarchy, changes in techniques as opposed to changes in technology, can be analyzed in the same way. We feel that this study provides an illustration of how change within the system and change of the system can be differentiated.

Our analysis indicated that different empirical indicators of the three structural properties of organizations, that is, centralization, complexity, and formalization, are related differently to the rate of change in new programs, at least among the sixteen organizations in this study. The number of occupational specialties in the organization, an indicator of complexity, is a better predictor of program change than professional training or professional activity. Participation in agency-wide decision making is a more powerful predictor of organizational change than the degree of hierarchy of authority. Finally, the degree of job codification, an indicator of formalization, is a more powerful predictor of program change than the rule observation.

A partial correlation analysis simultaneously controlling for size, auspices, age of organization, and function demonstrated that most of the organizational properties have associations with rate of program change which are independent of variations in these contextual factors. However, function and auspices, to a lesser extent, were so strongly related to the number of occupational specialties that the relationship between number of occupational specialties — one indicator of complexity — and rate of program change disappears. Future research should attempt to consider additioal contextual variables besides the ones included here.

A major theme contained in this paper is that it is important to view organizations from a sociological viewpoint. Our method for drawing the sample and the procedure for computing scores for organizational properties conceive of organizations as a collection of social positions (or jobs), not simply as an aggregate of individuals. Several different collective properties of organizations were found to be related to the rate of change. When individual orientations toward change were measured, they were found to be relatively unrelated to the rate of organizational change, at least as we have defined it. Our findings are supportive of Durkheim's famous phrase that "social facts must be explained by other social facts." That is, we were able to explain the rate of organizational change better with other organizational properties, such as degree of centralization, degree of complexity, or degree of formalization, than with measures of attitudes of organizational members toward change. Certainly this does not constitute definitive proof, but it does suggest that emphasis on structural and performance variables in organizations may be a more fruitful way to study organizational change.

131

III Administration Processes

The Administrative Process
in a Social Welfare Agency

SUE W. SPENCER

Lester Robb, executive of the Nashville United Givers Fund, shocked our students considerably when he said:

> Social welfare is the only noncompetitive operation which our society allows to survive. We protect and keep alive poor, insignificant, inefficient, obsolete operations when we really should be going all out to support the good, healthy, contemporary services so that they can serve community need at an optimum level.[1]

Though we may not agree that the social welfare services operate on a noncompetitive basis, Mr. Robb's statement suggests the major tests for social welfare administration:

1. Can agency administration bring together, and mold into an effective instrument, the conflicting community values, the professional knowledge and skill, and the community resources to provide a high level of service to a designated area?

2. Can administration not only provide an efficient and economically sound service to a designated segment of the community, but also contribute consistently to the community-wide assessment of community needs and the projection of plans for meeting community needs effectively?

The administrative process is essentially the same in all human enterprises, profit-making as well as nonprofit. It includes: determination of goals; acquisition of the resources; determination of policies and standards of service; allocation of resources in accordance with a work plan; maintenance of operations so as to produce the desired kind and amount of service; evaluation; and accounting for the use of resources. It begins at the point at which a service is still only in embryonic form in the minds of a group of people — when goals are being formulated and methods of achieving these goals are being weighed and estimates made of costs of program services — not after charters have been secured, boards established, or legislation passed providing for the new agency.

There are certain propositions concerning administration which have particular significance for the social welfare field. The first of these is that the administrative process is not limited to the intra-agency management of resources, nor to the fulfillment of an assignment made to the agency by an outside body. Instead it is seen as a continuous, circular process which involves securing resources and transforming them into a pattern of community service in accordance with expressed community will.

This definition of social welfare agency administration is in keeping with current administration theory which makes no sharp dichotomy between proprietorship as the

---

[1] Lester Robb, in an informal address delivered at the University of Tennessee School of Social Work, 1958.

Reprinted with permission of Columbia University Press, from Social Welfare Administration, *Ella W. Reed, ed. (New York: Columbia University Press, 1961), pp. 30-49.*

135

policy-making body and management as the agent which uses the resources according to policies prescribed by proprietorship.[2] It is also in line with the general theory of systems and subsystems which sees any community enterprise (profit or nonprofit) as a subsystem of the community, acting, interacting with, and being kept in a state of equilibrium by, community forces to which it also contributes.[3]

There is general agreement that administration is the conscious direction of the internal relationships and activities of the enterprise toward the achievement of goals. In the view presented here, administration is also the conscious intervention in the interacting forces operating between the agency and the larger community of which it is a part.

If one accepts these propositions as setting the boundaries for the administrative process in social welfare, it follows that the agency has the primary right and responsibility, through its administrative process, to set its own objectives, policies, and program rather than merely to implement the plans which are made for it by a community-wide planning body. Certainly its selection of objectives, the rate at which it is able to achieve these objectives, and the ways in which its services mesh with other community services, should fit into a design developed and maintained at the community-wide level. Nevertheless, the administrative process within the agency should make the agency a participant in the development of the community-wide design, and it should provide for the continual reassessment and refocusing of goals, resources, and services of the agency.

A second proposition, and one which is essential to this approach to administration, is that the locus of the agency is the community and everything which the agency does should be focused on community needs and directed toward the intermeshing of its program with other agency programs to provide optimum service on a community-wide basis. Although our services have grown up agency by agency, and each has the legal right to raise its own funds and carry out its activities autonomously (within certain broad legal limits), everything which we are learning about agency behavior indicates that the community should exercise the controlling function in terms of the community good.

The problem is whether or not we can build into the agency administrative process on the part of every participant – board, staff, and clientele – an awareness of community needs so that agency behavior can be patterned accordingly. When this is achieved voluntarily, as a part of agency administration rather than through dictation from a community-wide or governmental body, and when it is achieved by the majority of agencies in any community, the result should be agency administration at a high level; it also should make possible the best type of community planning and coordination.

An interesting example of this focus of agency concern on a community-wide basis was observed in the spring of 1959 in the sixth-quarter course in administration and community organization at the University of Tennessee. This is the third in the sequence of required courses, and William Moynihan, Executive of the Nashville Family and Children's Service, had been asked to present for student discussion the major administrative problem or problems which his agency was facing. The following is a direct quotation of his phrasing of the problem against a brief background statement of the agency's history, resources, and present program:

1. Should an agency plan and budget and request funds from United Givers Fund for new services needed by the community even though UGF goal-setting barely permits maintenance of present program:
2. What portion of the cost of private agency services should be borne by

[2] Francis X. Sutton, *The American Business Creed* (Cambridge, Mass.: Harvard University Press, 1955).

[3] Chester I. Barnard, *The Functions of the Executive* (Cambridge, Mass.: Harvard University Press, 1938, pp. 77-80.

clients? And by other or all non-UGF sources?

3. Should an agency proceed with plans for annual review and revision of salary scales, board-rates, etc., when expected income will not be adequate to cover the increases and both staff and volume of service would have to be reduced in order to make implementation of the increases possible?

4. To what extent is a private agency responsible to the community for volume versus quality of service?

5. How does an agency reconcile its need to finance its own program adequately with its conviction about the importance of other, newer agencies which are beginning to "compete" for the contributor's dollar?[4]

Note that his concern was expressed for the interrelatedness of this agency's service area to broad community needs.

Take another and much more complex example. At the present time, according to authoritative statements concerning the needs of the aging, the Federal governmental departments and bureaus must choose what to recommend to the President and to the Congress. Shall it be enough billions to raise the level of old age assistance and old age insurance plus an assurance of adequate medical care for the aging? Shall it be a crash program of research and education to discover ways of conquering the major chronic diseases? Shall it be a program to make possible and to encourage employment for large numbers of people beyond the age limits which the present labor market sets? If such staggering sums are taken out of our production economy through taxation, what will be the effect on the economy generally? How much of this particular type of welfare program can the country afford? How much should it be asked to afford? What is the best strategy for securing the goal which is eventually agreed upon?

This example and the earlier one concerning the local family and children's agency support the thesis that the administrative process should be concerned with all areas of community need and with increasing recognition of need and allocation of resources to meet community needs. Administration attempts to set priorities and to make decisions governing agency service in the context both of community need and of claims upon community resources.

If one accepts the propositions that agency administration involves more than the intra-agency management of resources according to an assignment made by an outside body and that the locus of the agency is the community, it is perhaps unnecessary to point out that administration is responsible for "provisioning" the agency, and that this, too, will be done in the community-wide contest. However, because much of the fund-raising, both for voluntary and tax-supported services, appears to be done by an organization or an activity outside the agency, it may be well to note that in the final analysis the responsibility for securing the necessary resources rests with agency administration.

The importance of this phase of administration needs no underscoring. For unless the administrative process can assure to the agency that it will have essential money, manpower, and other resources, when and in such quantity as they are needed, all other aspects of administration fall short and the agency's general productiveness and efficiency are reduced. The means of securing the resources may be as direct as a financial campaign or a rummage sale. They may be as intangible as making sure that a staff member does not alienate a member of the community power structure or run counter to local cultural patterns in handling a particular type of request for service – in other words, maintaining good relations with the public and rendering good service. If the funds are not raised by

---

[4] William Moynihan, Executive, Family and Children's Service, Nashville, Tenn., discussion materials prepared for Course 566, University of Tennessee School of Social Work, spring, 1959.

137

the agency directly, it is the function of administration to provide sufficiently convincing evidence to the fund-raising and fund-allocating body to secure an appropriate share of the community's resources.[5]

Finally, administration is responsible for optimum use of resources, and this requires the creation of an appropriate organizational structure, the maintenance of channels of communication, and the facilitation of sound and productive human relationships within the agency. It is the function of administration to maintain equilibrium within the agency, taking into account informal as well as formal groupings, and to enable the agency to maintain an effective relationship with the other agencies and with the community.

To summarize, three ideas have been suggested:

1. The administrative process is the same for all types of human enterprise and it involves the selection of goals and the formulation of policy, and the procuring of resources as well as their proper utilization in agency operation.

2. The locus of the agency is the community, and the agency administrative process should be concerned with community-level needs, resources, and services.

3. The setting of agency goals and priorities should, therefore, be done in the context of what furthers the community's ability to deal with its own social welfare needs as a totality rather than in the narrower framework of what furthers the agency's status and special interests.

What differentiates the social welfare enterprise from other types of enterprise (and hence directly affects the administrative process) is the fact that the social welfare agency is socially sponsored, socially focused, and socially accountable rather than privately sponsored, profit-focused, and privately accountable. In its simplest form the social welfare agency comes into being because several people see an unmet need, want to meet that need, get community permission to meet that need, and accept legal responsibility for seeing that the resources secured, or made available, are used for the specific purpose for which they were given rather than for some other purpose.[6]

Reference has already been made to the network of interrelated services which are to be found in any community, and these may be termed the "community welfare system." The current effort in any community to relieve conditions of involuntary dependency, to provide a particular level of subsistence, and to enhance individual, group, and community life may be referred to as the "social welfare function" of the community.

In the typical community, gaps exist between services, and there is often a wide variation between the degree to which services of the same quality are available to different groups that have the same needs. Nevertheless, it is possible in any community at a given time to observe a lower level below which the community will not tolerate lack of service or poor quality of service, and an upper limit beyond which it will not consistently support services. Although the lower and upper limits generally present uneven rather than straight or level lines of demarcation, this range can be charted. Borrowing a phrase used by William H. Whyte, Jr., in a somewhat different sense, this set of prevailing values may be termed "the community social ethic";[7] that is, whatever the majority of the people in a community accept as fitting and right in respect to what an individual may claim in the way of protection or relief, or of services which will enable the individ-

---

[5] Jesse Burkhead, *Government Budgeting* (New York: John Wiley and Sons, Inc., 1956), pp. 45-50.

[6] Peter F. Drucker, *The Practice of Management* (New York: Harper and Brothers, 1954), p. 21.

[7] William H. Whyte, Jr., *The Organization Man* (New York: Doubleday Anchor Books, 1957), pp. 7-11.

ual to fulfill his potentialities.[8]

Over a period of time, and in an expanding economy, the community social ethic will tend to allow an increase in the range and quality of the community welfare services. Speaking of the health services, for example, Max Lerner points out that "what once had been deemed the province of the rich, following World War II, became a necessity for all classes"[9] and that within another generation we may well see in this country "a gridiron intermeshing" of public and voluntary health services which will offer complete protection for all groups.[10]

Two aspects of this concept of the community social ethic are worth noting. First, agency administration may contribute to the change in the level of the community social ethic. What certain agencies do in the way of community service, and what they tell the public about why they do what they do in the particular way in which they do it, may have a direct effect on the community's value system and, eventually, on what the community will support or demand in quality and quantity of service. This is in keeping with the thesis that the locus of the agency is the community. If this is accepted, then social welfare administration may appropriately be concerned with improving, or raising, the community social ethic.

Such an assumption recognizes the validity of social welfare's affirmation of certain values as being more desirable than other values and of consciously seeking to modify the community's attitudes in these areas in order to facilitate the achievement of social welfare objectives. This is similar to what is done by administration in other types of enterprise and is not unique to the social welfare field.

If the agency is to engage consciously in the attempt to bring about such changes in the community value system, the current findings of social scientists are pertinent. Their studies reveal that resistance to change derives not so much from unwillingness to try new ideas as from the threat which the proposals make to the continuity of functioning (or role fulfillment) of the people who would be directly affected by the change.[11] We in the social welfare field know that you do not bring about real change by simply battering down people's resistances or "sweet talking" them into taking something they do not want. Rather, people must believe that the proposed roles, attitudes, or behavior will give greater satisfactions than those which are being given up.

The second aspect of this concept of the community social ethic, as we are using it here, is that social welfare programs frequently are caught squarely in the middle of conflicting values or appear to run counter to values which have a particularly high emotional affect for large groups of people in the community. Robin Williams describes value as a continuum rather than an all-or-none matter, shading from "those intense and rigid moral values that are true matters of conscience" which when violated subject the individual to strong guilt and strong group censure, into "those evoking less intense guilt and less severe social sanctions."[12] These latter he identifies as "aesthetic standards, conventional proprieties, and simple norms of expedience or technical efficiency."[13]

---

[8] Paul Deutschberger and Sue W. Spencer, "Social Work Administration" (unpublished manuscript), Chap. 5.

[9] Max Lerner, *America as a Civilization* (New York: Simon and Schuster, 1957), p. 124.

[10] *Ibid.*, p. 126.

[11] Ronald Lippitt, Jeanne Watson, and Bruce Westley, *The Dynamics of Planned Change* (New York: Harcourt, Brace and Co., 1958).

[12] Robin M. Williams, Jr., *American Society: A Sociological Interpretation* (New York: Alfred A. Knopf, 1951), pp. 375-376.

[13] *Ibid.*, p. 376.

Some of the aspects of human life with which social agencies deal have great emotional affect, so far as community values are concerned. For example, society feels compelled to protect itself in such areas as the proper rearing of children, the care of the sick or helpless members of the family by the family rather than at public expense, the necessity for people to be economically productive rather than dependent, and the protection of life and property against attack or loss. The social welfare agencies, by and large, have the same long-range goals as those which are generally held by the public: the provision of good home life and rearing of children; the fulfillment of personal and financial responsibility to one's dependents; the development of one's capacities for useful living; the humane care of the sick and helpless; and the curbing of crime and delinquency. There is little, if any, difference between the long-range goals of society and those of the social welfare services. The difference or gap occurs primarily through lack of understanding of the methods being used or of confidence in these methods to achieve their ultimate objectives.

When the social welfare services not only appear to be ineffective means of safeguarding society's welfare but may actually appear to stand in the way of society's achievement of its goals, the social welfare agency may deflect the community's disapproval from the individual or community group on to itself. Examples of areas in which the social welfare agency's program may operate in violation of accepted community values, and thus draw upon itself the community's displeasure, may be observed in child welfare when Aid to Dependent Children grants are continued in homes which the community considers grossly unsuitable, or in the area of corrections when medical and psychological services take precedence over punishment. In both situations the community wishes to protect itself from damage or loss which will result unless the individual's behavior is brought into line with community standards. Only as social welfare programs can be proved to produce the desired results will the community support the program.

The task of social welfare administration, then, is to utilize the best knowledge and skill available to help the community achieve its own goals in the agency's designated sphere of activity and to help the community raise its sights in relation to what the community recognizes as affecting its own social welfare. This requires an understanding of community values as well as skill in determining community will and in projecting the agency's program at as high a level as possible in view of the community social ethic. In this context social welfare administration would also include the constant search for more effective methods of service and would give more attention to improving community understanding of its goals and services.

As already indicated, the social welfare agency is the product of community desire to meet a community need. Though the structural relationship between a community and its social welfare agency staff varies somewhat, in every formally organized service there is a body of citizen-representatives who take responsibility for establishing the specific compass of the service, for securing and transmitting funds, and for accounting to the community for the agency's use of its resources. In voluntary agencies this is the board of directors. In governmental agencies this may be a commission, though frequently these functions are actually carried by the legislative branch of government and by the chief executive and his "cabinet." In addition, the various aspects of the public's concern may be further represented by pressure groups or lobbies.

Much has been written about the community power structure and the fact that, in the final analysis, many important and far-reaching decisions concerning the community's services are made by a relatively small group of individuals whose power comes primarily from their success in the business or political sphere.[14] The vesting of such authority in the hands of so few people in a democratic society may appear to be an anachronism.

Yet two factors operate in our society to provide broader channels for the expression of public will. The first is the general practice of selecting to membership on boards and commissions a somewhat broader and more diversified citizen group than the power elite to represent the public interest in the management of our health, education, and welfare services. The second factor is the spontaneous development and national scope of many special-interest groups composed of persons with a direct and vital interest in a particular problem. Typical of such groups are the organizations of parents of blind or mentally retarded children.

If we add to these such groups as the veterans' organizations and the labor unions, the sphere of citizen participation in shaping our welfare services is still further enlarged. The concern of the taxpayer, and the voluntary contributor, for the use which is made of his dollar affects at least indirectly the projection and maintenance of the social welfare services.

Decision-making on welfare matters by all four levels or types of groups (the power elite, the administrative boards, the special-interest organizations, and the total citizenry who provide the resources) will reflect trends in popular attitudes and opinions. Some of these conflict with each other and have to be reconciled; some are at variance with those held by the agency's professional staff. Among those which reflect popular concepts and values are:

1. The wish to do for needy people and expecting them to appreciate the help.

2. The wish to help only the "worthy" and to punish the "unworthy."

3. The high value set on certain methods of controlling or changing human behavior.

4. The maximum emphasis on internal efficiency of agency operation rather than on concern with the way in which the agency is serving the community.

5. A lack of confidence in the professional expert in the field of social adjustment and community welfare.

The very fact that such opinions and attitudes still have considerable popular support highlights the value of citizen participation in policy-making, either as members of boards or as members of governmental legislative bodies, if for no other reason than to assure that the agency will stay in close touch with its public. However, conflicts do arise, either between individuals or groups within the board or between board and staff. Prolonged and unresolved conflict can seriously impede the agency's development and service. Sharp breaks within the leadership can set the agency back and can actually lead to its destruction.

The executive in all types of enterprise is expected to be skilled in the decision-making process itself. Various authorities in the field of administrative theory give a variety of labels to this skill. In educational administration, for example, and in business administration also, this is often referred to as the "problem-solving" approach to administration. In social work the term "enabling" has been used to identify its similarities to social casework or social group work methods.

Reduced to its simplest terms, executive function when faced with a problem of conflict within the board: (a) sees that the full range of opinions is brought out against a background of fact, including the explicit objectives of the agency; (b) provides the grounds for reaching an agreement through a process of clarification; (c) sees that consensus is reached, if possible; (d) points out the consequences of any action based on the decision which has been reached; and (e) motivates the group to take action which is responsible. This means that the executive function makes explicit, as the grounds for administrative action, what was formerly implicit and unchanneled. (It should not be necessary to point out that throughout this process the activity of the administrator is a

---

[14] Floyd Hunter, *The Community Power Structure* (Chapel Hill, N.C.: University of North Carolina Press, 1953); also C. Wright Mills, *The Power Elite* (London: Oxford University Press, 1956), p. 277.

facilitating or enabling one in which he works with the chairman and members of the group to secure appropriate consideration and decision.)

Urwick has pointed out that true leadership is the ability to reconcile differences at the point of action.[15] A crucial test of leadership occurs when it is not possible for the board to reach a decision to which all can subscribe. In such instances, an individual or a group may actually not be willing to continue to participate on the board. Executive function has the responsibility for seeing that the consequences of such action are understood by all the parties concerned and for facilitating a reconsideration, if this is appropriate. (An annotated bibliography on the decision-making process has been published.[16])

In regard to the degree to which boards do represent community opinion, Rossi has pointed out that when an individual is asked to take the role of community representative and to be a decision-maker for the community, he tends to take a rather broad view of the community and its problems rather than to speak exclusively either from narrow personal interests or from limited class identifications.[17]

Of particular interest to the social welfare field are the vision and effective action of certain recent Congressional committees, particularly in the matter of programs of research and training in the health field in recent years. Such reports as that of the Senate committee on the appropriations requests of the National Institutes of Health illustrate this point. The following is picked almost at random from the Committee report:

> In view of progress in medical research, leading to gains in humanitarian and economic terms that far outweigh the cost in money, the committee must again reiterate that it will continue to insure that lack of money will not be permitted to impede the advancement of medical research in this country. Moreover, the committee will continue to recommend funds ample for the training of scientists and for the construction of research facilities so that the Nation can have a well balanced and progressively stronger medical research effort.[18]

Since the great bulk of social welfare services is carried on under public auspices, the patterns of citizen-professional collaboration in government are of primary importance. Appleby's delineation of decision-making at the Federal level is particularly useful:

> The process of democratic public administration is one of group judgment at each hierarchal level, judgment of groups of levels, group judgment subject to review, modification, revocation, and punitive action in any one of the many higher levels as consequences of the judgment's having come to bear upon citizens and having become subject to the reaction of citizens. It is a process in which facilities of appeal and levels of review are more numerous, various, and open than in any other action-laden process yet devised. It is a process carried on in an environment more critical and more politically active and potent than the environment of any other administrative process. It is a process in which the pattern of responsibility runs to public representativeness of many kinds and roles, to subordinates, to

[15] Lyndall F. Urwick, "The Obstetrics of Leadership," *British Management Review*, XIII (1955), pp. 75-89.

[16] Paul Wasserman and Fred S. Silander, *Decision-making: an Annotated Bibliography* (Ithaca, N.Y.: Graduate School of Business, Cornell University, 1958).

[17] Peter H. Rossi, "Community Decision Making," *Administrative Science Quarterly*, Vol. I (1959), pp. 415-43.

[18] Senate Committee on DHEW Labor Appropriations Report on Requests of National Institutes of Health for 1958-59, dated June 17, 1958 (Bethesda, Md.: National Institutes of Health, 1958).

associates in the same unit, to contiguous and related units with somewhat different responsibilities, to higher executive levels where repose broader responsibilities; it runs outward to special publics, outward from higher levels to other and larger publics, outward and upward from executive agencies to the Chief Executive, to the Congress, and to the general public.[19]

In summary, we have noted that the social welfare agency structure offers many opportunities for the community representative, be he board member, elected public official, or special-interest representative, to share with professional staff in policy-making and programming for the agency. The melding of citizen and professional values, knowledge, and skill in the policy-making process requires rigorous self-discipline on the part of all participants. It is perhaps the most challenging and demanding aspect of social welfare administration. When achieved to a high degree, it is valuable to the agency and is a satisfying and rewarding experience for the participants.

Fifteen years ago, Arlien Johnson pointed out that the social welfare field could and should make greater use of the technical knowledge of management which was being developed by both business and public administration, while continuing to recognize the importance of human relations within both the structure and the process of agency administration.[20]

In my view, the social welfare field has improved its administration along the lines suggested. It is interesting to note, however, that the major additions and enlargements in general administration theory in the past 15 years have been in the areas which are central to the concerns and understanding of the social welfare field. I refer to the literature of administration on the theory of systems, on executive leadership, on the decision-making process, and on the whole area of human relations. All of these are areas in which our knowledge should serve us in good stead — knowledge of the complexity of individual and group behavior, of motivations, of the freeing of individuals to operate with as much autonomy as possible within the agency structure, and of how social change comes about. To put the matter quite simply, this side of administration is one with which we feel right at home and which at the same time is sufficiently advanced to offer to most of us the excitement of having to reach for its meaning and significance for our practice.

Perhaps I too should caution against our being carried away, at this time in our history, with what is fascinating and illuminating in this aspect of current administration literature. Fritz Morstein Marx has proposed the idea that administration must meet four essentials: rationality, responsibility, competence, and continuity.[21] Administration is said to be rational when it involves the conscious use of means to achieve explicit objectives. It is the attempt to substitute choice for chance on every level of agency operation. Administration is said to be responsible when it develops policy in the light of a well-based and accurate knowledge of the technical issues involved and exposes its operations to existing preferences in the community. Administration is said to be competent when it meets five requirements: technical proficiency, equity, explicitness, appropriateness, and efficiency. Administration meets the criterion of continuity when it provides at least a minimal standard of service despite any contingency and under any

---

[19] Paul H. Appleby, *Morality and Administration* (Baton Rouge, La.: Louisiana State University Press, 1952), p. 251.

[20] Arlien Johnson, "The Administrative Process in Social Work," in *Proceedings of the National Conference of Social Work, 1946* (New York: Columbia University Press, 1947), pp. 249-258.

[21] Fritz Morstein Marx, *The Administrative State* (Chicago: University of Chicago Press, 1957), pp. 34-53.

circumstances.

Skill in executive function is measured by the degree to which the administrator can exercise rational control over his own participation in the intra-agency process and in community level activities. Brooks Adams describes administration (or executive function) as:

> the capacity of coordinating many, and often conflicting, social energies in a single social organism, so adroitly that they shall operate as a unity. This presupposes the power of reorganizing a series of relations between numerous special social interests, with all of which no single man can be intimately acquainted.[22]

Thus, executive function requires the ability to stimulate and free those who participate in the agency to use their abilities to the fullest, to reduce tensions and unproductive conflicts, and to provide for all groups involved a seeing of the project as a whole and a seeing of it in its proper relationship to other forces, past, present, and future.

It is a common concern within our contemporary society that we will be overwhelmed as individuals by the very magnitude of our administrative organizations. And yet it is only by means of these organizations that contemporary society can bring to each one of us, as individuals and in our small groups, the satisfaction of our basic needs. It is in this process that the quality of social welfare administration can make a major difference. It can be the deciding factor in whether or not we preserve human values in attempting to meet human needs.

---

[22] Brooks Adams, *The Theory of Social Revolutions* (New York: Macmillan, 1913), pp. 207-208.

General Principles of Management

HENRI FAYOL

The managerial function finds its only outlet through the members of the organization (body corporate). Whilst the other functions bring into play material and machines the managerial function operates only on the personnel. The soundness and good working order of the body corporate depend on a certain number of conditions termed indiscriminately principles, laws, rules. For preference I shall adopt the term principles whilst dissociating it from any suggestion of rigidity, for there is nothing rigid or absolute in management affairs, it is all a question of proportion. Seldom do we have to apply the same principle twice in identical conditions; allowance must be made for different changing circumstances, for men just as different and changing and for many other variable elements.

Therefore principles are flexible and capable of adaptation to every need; it is a matter of knowing how to make use of them, which is a difficult art requiring intelligence, experience, decision and proportion. Compounded of tact and experience, proportion is one of the foremost attributes of the manager. There is no limit to the number of principles of management, every rule or managerial procedure which strengthens the body corporate or facilitates its functioning has a place among the principles so long, at least, as experience confirms its worthiness. A change in the state of affairs can be responsible for a change of rules which had been engendered by that state.

I am going to review some of the principles of management which I have most frequently had to apply; viz. —

1. Division of work.
2. Authority.
3. Discipline.
4. Unity of command.
5. Unity of direction.
6. Subordination of individual interests to the general interest.
7. Remuneration.
8. Centralization.
9. Scalar chain (line of authority).
10. Order.
11. Equity.
12. Stability of tenure of personnel.
13. Initiative.
14. Esprit de corps.

Reprinted with permission of Sir Isaac Pitman & Sons, Ltd. from General and Industrial Management, *by Henri Fayol, Chapter IV, pages 19-42. Translated from the French by Constance Storr. (London: 1949.)*

1. DIVISION OF WORK

Specialization belongs to the natural order; it is observable in the animal world, where the more highly developed the creature the more highly differentiated its organs; it is observable in human societies, where the more important the body corporate[1] the closer is the relationship between structure and function. As society grows, so new organs develop destined to replace the single one performing all functions in the primitive state.

The object of division of work is to produce more and better work with the same effort. The worker always on the same part, the manager concerned always with the same matters, acquire an ability, sureness, and accuracy which increase their output. Each change of work brings in its train an adaptation which reduces output. Division of work permits of reduction in the number of objects to which attention and effort must be directed and has been recognized as the best means of making use of individuals and groups of people. It is not merely applicable to technical work, but without exception to all work involving a more or less considerable number of people and demanding abilities of various types, and it results in specialization of functions and separation of powers. Although its advantages are universally recognized and although possibility of progress is inconceivable without the specialized work of learned men and artists, yet division of work has its limits which experience and a sense of proportion teach us may not be exceeded.

2. AUTHORITY AND RESPONSIBILITY

Authority is the right to give orders and the power to exact obedience. Distinction must be made between a manager's official authority deriving from office and personal authority, compounded of intelligence, experience, moral worth, ability to lead, past services, etc. In the make-up of a good head personal authority is the indispensable complement of official authority. Authority is not to be conceived of apart from responsibility, that is apart from sanction — reward or penalty — which goes with the exercise of power. Responsibility is a corollary of authority, it is its natural consequence and essential counterpart, and wheresoever authority is exercised responsibility arises.

The need for sanction, which has its origin in a sense of justice, is strengthened and increased by this consideration, that in the general interest useful actions have to be encouraged and their opposite discouraged. Application of sanction to acts of authority forms part of the conditions essential for good management, but it is generally difficult to effect, especially in large concerns. First, the degree of responsibility must be established and then the weight of the sanction. Now, it is relatively easy to establish a workman's responsibility for his acts and a scale of corresponding sanctions; in the case of a foreman it is somewhat difficult, and proportionately as one goes up the scalar chain of businesses, as work grows more complex, as the number of workers involved increases, as the final result is more remote, it is increasingly difficult to isolate the share of the initial act of authority in the ultimate result and to establish the degree of responsibility of the manager. The measurement of this responsibility and its equivalent in material terms elude all calculation.

---

[1] *"Body corporate."* Fayol's term "corps social," meaning all those engaged in a given corporate activity in any sphere, is best rendered by this somewhat unusual term because (a) it retains his implied biological metaphor; (b) it represents the structure as distinct from the process of organization. The term will be retained in all contexts where these two requirements have to be met. *(Translator's note.)*

146

Sanction, then, is a question of kind, custom and convention, and judging it one must take into account the action itself, the attendant circumstances, and potential repercussions. Judgment demands high moral character, impartiality, and firmness. If all these conditions are not fulfilled there is a danger that the sense of responsibility may disappear from the concern.

Responsibility valiantly undertaken and borne merits some consideration; it is a kind of courage everywhere much appreciated. Tangible proof of this exists in the salary level of some industrial leaders, which is much higher than that of civil servants of comparable rank but carrying no responsibility. Nevertheless, generally speaking, responsibility is feared as much as authority is sought after, and fear of responsibility paralyses much initiative and destroys many good qualities. A good leader should possess and infuse into those around him courage to accept responsibility.

The best safeguard against abuse of authority and against weakness on the part of a higher manager is personal integrity and particularly high moral character of such a manager, and this integrity, it is well known, is conferred neither by election nor ownership.

3. DISCIPLINE

Discipline is in essence obedience, application, energy, behaviour, and outward marks of respect observed in accordance with the standing agreements between the firm and its employees; whether these agreements have been freely debated or accepted without prior discussion, whether they be written or implicit, whether they derive from the wish of the parties to them or from rules and customs, it is these agreements which determine the formalities of discipline.

Discipline, being the outcome of different varying agreements, naturally appears under the most diverse forms; obligations of obedience, application, energy, behaviour, vary, in effect, from one firm to another, from one group of employees to another, from one time to another. Nevertheless, general opinion is deeply convinced that discipline is absolutely essential for the smooth running of business and that without discipline no enterprise could prosper.

This sentiment is very forcibly expressed in military handbooks, where it runs that "Discipline constitutes the chief strength of armies." I would approve unreservedly of this aphorism were it followed by this other, "Discipline is what leaders make it." The first one inspires respect for discipline, which is a good thing, but it tends to eclipse from view the responsibility of leaders, which is undesirable, for the state of discipline of any group of people depends essentially on the worthiness of its leaders.

When a defect in discipline is apparent or when relations between superiors and subordinates leave much to be desired, responsibility for this must not be cast heedlessly, and without going further afield, on the poor state of the team, because the ill mostly results from the ineptitude of the leaders. That, at all events, is what I have noted in various parts of France, for I have always found French workmen obedient and loyal provided they are ably led.

In the matter of influence upon discipline, agreements must be set side by side with command. It is important that they be clear and, as far as is possible, afford satisfaction to both sides. This is not easy. Proof of that exists in the great strikes of miners, railwaymen, and civil servants which, in these latter years, have jeopardized national life at home and elsewhere and which arose out of agreements in dispute or inadequate legislation.

For half a century a considerable change has been effected in the mode of agreements between a concern and its employees. The agreements of former days fixed by the employer alone are being replaced, in ever increasing measure, by understandings arrived

147

at by discussion between an owner or group of owners and workers' associations. Thus each individual owner's responsibility has been reduced and is further diminished by increasingly frequent State intervention in labour problems. Nevertheless, the setting up of agreements binding a firm and its employees from which disciplinary formalities emanate, should remain one of the chief preoccupations of industrial heads.

The well-being of the concern does not permit, in cases of offence against discipline, of the neglect of certain sanctions capable of preventing or minimizing their recurrence. Experience and tact on the part of a manager are put to the proof in the choice and degree of sanctions to be used, such as remonstrances, warnings, fines, suspensions, demotion, dismissal. Individual people and attendant circumstances must be taken into account. In fine, discipline is respect for agreements which are directed at achieving obedience, application, energy, and the outward marks of respect. It is incumbent upon managers at high levels as much as upon humble employees, and the best means of establishing and maintaining it are —

1. Good superiors at all levels.
2. Agreements as clear and fair as possible.
3. Sanctions (penalties) judiciously applied.

4. UNITY OF COMMAND

For any action whatsoever, an employee should receive orders from one superior only. Such is the rule of unity of command, arising from general and ever-present necessity and wielding an influence on the conduct of affairs, which to my way of thinking is at least equal to any other principle whatsoever. Should it be violated, authority is undermined, discipline is in jeopardy, order disturbed, and stability threatened. This rule seems fundamental to me and so I have given it the rank of principle. As soon as two superiors wield their authority over the same person or department, uneasiness makes itself felt and should the cause persist, the disorder increases, the malady takes on the appearance of an animal organism troubled by a foreign body, and the following consequences are to be observed: either the dual command ends in disappearance or elimination of one of the superiors and organic well-being is restored, or else the organism continues to wither away. In no case is there adaptation of the social organism to dual command.

Now dual command is extremely common and wreaks havoc in all concerns, large or small, in home and in State. The evil is all the more to be feared in that it worms its way into the social organism on the most plausible pretexts. For instance —

(a) In the hope of being better understood or gaining time or to put a stop forthwith to an undesirable practice, a superior S^2 may give orders directly to an employee E without going via the superior S^1. If this mistake is repeated there is dual command with its consequences, viz., hesitation on the part of the subordinate, irritation and dissatisfaction on the part of the superior set aside, and disorder in the work. It will be seen later that it is possible to by-pass the scalar chain when necessary, whilst avoiding the drawbacks of dual command.

(b) The desire to get away from the immediate necessity of dividing up authority as between two colleagues, two friends, two members of one family, results at times in dual command reigning at the top of a concern right from the outset. Exercising the same powers and having the same authority over the same men, the two colleagues end up inevitably with dual command and its consequences. Despite harsh lessons, instances of this sort are still numerous. New colleagues count on their mutual regard, common interest, and good sense to save them from every conflict, every serious disagreement and, save for rare exceptions, the illusion is short-lived. First an awkwardness makes itself felt, then a certain irritation, and, in time, if dual command exists, even hatred. Men cannot

148

bear dual command. A judicious assignment of duties would have reduced the danger without entirely banishing it, for between two superiors on the same footing there must always be some question ill-defined. But it is riding for a fall to set up a business organization with two superiors on equal footing without assigning duties and demarcating authority.

(*c*) Imperfect demarcation of departments also leads to dual command: two superiors issuing orders in a sphere which each thinks his own, constitutes dual command.

(*d*) Constant linking up as between different departments, natural intermeshing of functions, duties often badly defined, create an ever-present danger of dual command. If a knowledgeable superior does not put it in order, footholds are established which later upset and compromise the conduct of affairs.

In all human associations, in industry, commerce, army, home, State, dual command is a perpetual source of conflicts, very grave sometimes, which have special claim on the attention of superiors of all ranks.

5. UNITY OF DIRECTION

This principle is expressed as: one head and one plan for a group of activities having the same objective. It is the condition essential to unity of action, coordination of strength and focusing of effort. A body with two heads is in the social as in the animal sphere a monster, and has difficulty in surviving. Unity of direction (one head, one plan) must not be confused with unity of command (one employee to have orders from one superior only). Unity of direction is provided for by sound organization of the body corporate, unity of command turns on the functioning of the personnel. Unity of command cannot exist without unity of direction, but does not flow from it.

6. SUBORDINATION OF INDIVIDUAL INTEREST TO GENERAL INTEREST

This principle calls to mind the fact that in a business the interest of one employee or group of employees should not prevail over that of the concern, that the interest of the home should come before that of its members and that the interest of the State should have pride over that of one citizen or group of citizens.

It seems that such an admonition should not need calling to mind. But ignorance, ambition, selfishness, laziness, weakness, and all human passions tend to cause the general interest to be lost sight of in favour of individual interest and a perpetual struggle has to be waged against them. Two interests of a different order, but claiming equal respect, confront each other and means must be found to reconcile them. That represents one of the great difficulties of management. Means of effecting it are —

1. Firmness and good example on the part of superiors.
2. Agreements as fair as possible.
3. Constant supervision.

7. REMUNERATION OF PERSONNEL

Remuneration of personnel is the price of services rendered. It should be fair and, as far as is possible, afford satisfaction both to personnel and firm (employee and employer). The rate of remuneration depends, firstly, on circumstances independent of the employer's will and employee's worth, viz. cost of living, abundance or shortage of personnel, general business conditions, the economic position of the business, and after that it depends on the value of the employee and mode of payment adopted. Appreciation of the factors dependent on the employer's will and on the value of employees demands a fairly good knowledge of business, judgment, and impartiality. Later on in connection with selecting personnel we shall deal with assessing the value of employees; here only the mode of payment is under consideration as a factor operating on remuneration. The method of payment can exercise considerable influence on business progress, so the choice of this method is an important problem. It is also a thorny problem which in practice has been solved in widely different ways, of which so far none has proved satisfactory. What is generally looked for in the method of payment is that —

1. It shall assure fair remuneration.
2. It shall encourage keenness by rewarding well-directed effort.
3. It shall not lead to over-payment going beyond reasonable limits.

I am going to examine briefly the modes of payment in use for workers, junior managers, and higher managers.

Workers

The various modes of payment in use for workers are —

1. Time rates.
2. Job rates.
3. Piece rates.

These three modes of payment may be combined and give rise to important variations by the introduction of bonuses, profit-sharing schemes, payment in kind, and non-financial incentives.

1. *Time Rates.* Under this system the workman sells the employer, in return for a pre-determined sum, a day's work under definite conditions. This system has the disadvantage of conducing to negligence and of demanding constant supervision. It is inevitable where the work done is not susceptible to measurement and in effect it is very common.

2. *Job Rates.* Here payment made turns upon the execution of a definite job set in advance and may be independent of the length of the job. When payment is due only on condition that the job be completed during the normal work spell, this method merges into time rate. Payment by daily job does not require as close a supervision as payment by the day, but it has the drawback of levelling the output of good workers down to that of mediocre ones. The good ones are not satisfied, because they feel that they could earn more; the mediocre ones find the task set too heavy.

3. *Piece Rates.* Here payment is related to work done and there is no limit. This system is often used in workshops where a large number of similar articles have to be made, and is found where the product can be measured by weight, length, or cubic capacity, and in general is used wherever possible. It is criticized on the grounds of emphasizing quantity at the expense of quality and of provoking disagreements when rates have to be revised in the light of manufacturing improvements. Piece-work becomes contract work when applied to an important unit of work. To reduce the contractor's risk, sometimes there is added to the contract price a payment for each day's work done.

Generally, piece rates give rise to increased earnings which act for some time as a stimulus, then finally a system prevails in which this mode of payment gradually approximates to time rates for a pre-arranged sum.

The above three modes of payment are found in all large concerns; sometimes time rates prevail, sometimes one of the other two. In a workshop the same workman may be seen working now on piece rates, now on time rates. Each one of these methods has its advantages and drawbacks, and their effectiveness depends on circumstances and the

150

ability of superiors. Neither method nor rate of payment absolves management from competence and tact, and keenness of workers and peaceful atmosphere of the workshop depend largely upon it.

Bonuses

To arouse the worker's interest in the smooth running of the business, sometimes an increment in the nature of a bonus is added to the time-, job-, or piece-rate: for good time keeping, hard work, freedom from machine breakdown, output, cleanliness, etc. The relative importance, nature, and qualifying conditions of these bonuses are very varied. There are to be found the small daily supplement, the monthly sum, the annual award, shares, or portions of shares distributed to the most meritorious, and also even profit-sharing schemes such as, for example, certain monetary allocations distributed annually among workers in some large firms. Several French collieries started some years back the granting of a bonus proportional to profits distributed or to extra profits. No contract is required from the workers save that the earning of the bonus is subject to certain conditions, for instance, that there shall have been no strike during the year, or that absenteeism shall not have exceeded a given number of days. This type of bonus introduced an element of profit-sharing into miners' wages without any prior discussion as between workers and employer. The workman did not refuse a gift, largely gratuitous, on the part of the employer; that is, the contract was a unilateral one. Thanks to a successful trading period the yearly wages have been appreciably increased by the operation of the bonus. But what is to happen in lean times? This interesting procedure is as yet too new to be judged, but obviously it is no general solution of the problem.

In the mining industry there is another type of bonus, dependent upon the selling price of coal. The sliding scale of wages depending on a basic rate plus a bonus proportionate to the local selling price, which had long flourished in Wales, but was discontinued when minimum wages legislation came into force, is to-day the principle regulating the payment of miners in the Nord and Pas de Calais *départements,* and has also been adopted in the Loire region. This system established a certain fixed relationship between the prosperity of the colliery and the miner's wage. It is criticized on the grounds that it conduces to limitation of production in order to raise selling price. So we see it is necessary to have recourse to a variety of methods in order to settle wages questions. The problem is far from being settled to everyone's satisfaction and all solutions are hazardous.

Profit-Sharing

Workers. The idea of making workers share in profits is a very attractive one, and it would seem that it is from there that harmony as between Capital and Labour should come. But the practical formula for such sharing has not yet been found. Workers' profit-sharing has hitherto come up against insurmountable difficulties of application in the case of large concerns. Firstly, let us note that it cannot exist in enterprises having no monetary objective (State services, religions, philanthropic, or scientific societies) and also that it is not possible in the case of businesses running at a loss. Thus profit-sharing is excluded from a great number of concerns. There remain the prosperous business concerns, and of these latter the desire to reconcile and harmonize workers' and employers' interests is nowhere so great as in French mining and metallurgical industries. Now, in these industries I know of no clear application of workers' profit-sharing, whence it may be concluded forthwith that the matter is difficult, if not impossible. It is very difficult indeed. Whether a business is making a profit or not the worker must have an immediate wage assured him, and a system which would make workers' payment depend entirely on eventual future profit is unworkable. But perhaps a part of wages might come from business profits. Let us see. Viewing all contingent factors, the worker's greater or lesser share of activity or ability in the final outcome of a large concern is impossible to assess and is, moreover, quite insignificant. The portion accruing to him of distributed dividend would at the most be a few centimes on a wage of five francs for instance, that is to say the smallest extra effort, the stroke of a pick or of a file operating directly on his wage, would prove of greater advantage to him. Hence the worker has no interest in being rewarded by a share in profits proportionate to the effect he has upon profits. It is worthy of note that in most large concerns, wages increases, operative now for some twenty years, represent a total sum greater than the amount of capital shared out. In effect, unmodified real profit-sharing by workers of large concerns has not yet entered the sphere of practical business politics.

Junior Managers. Profit-sharing for foremen, superintendents, engineers, is scarcely more advanced than for workers. Nevertheless, the influence of these employees on the results of a business is quite considerable, and if they are not consistently interested in profits the only reason is that the basis for participation is difficult to establish. Doubtless managers have no need of monetary incentive to carry out their duties, but they are not indifferent to material satisfactions and it must be acknowledged that the hope of extra profit is capable of arousing their enthusiasm. So employees at middle levels should, where possible, be induced to have an interest in profits. It is relatively easy in businesses which are starting out or on trial, where exceptional effort can yield outstanding results. Sharing may then be applied to overall business profits or merely to the running of the particular department of the employee in question. When the business is of long standing and well run the zeal of a junior manager is scarcely apparent in the general outcome, and it is very hard to establish a useful basis on which he may participate. In fact, profit-sharing among junior managers in France is very rare in large concerns. Production or workshop output bonuses — not to be confused with profit-sharing — are much more common.

Higher Managers. It is necessary to go right up to top management to find a class of employee with frequent interest in the profits of large-scale French concerns. The head of the business, in view of his knowledge, ideas, and actions, exerts considerable influence on general results, so it is quite natural to try to provide him with an interest in them. Sometimes it is possible to establish a close connection between his personal activity and its effects. Nevertheless, generally speaking, there exist other influences quite independent of the personal capability of the manager which can influence results to a greater extent than can his personal activity. If the manager's salary were exclusively dependent upon profits, it might at times be reduced to nothing. There are, besides, businesses being built up, wound up, or merely passing through temporary crisis, wherein management depends no less on talent than in the case of prosperous ones, and wherein profit-sharing cannot be a basis for remuneration for the manager. In fine, senior civil servants cannot be paid on a profit-sharing basis. Profit-sharing, then, for either managers or workers is not a general rule of remuneration. To sum up, then: profit-sharing is a mode of payment capable of giving excellent results in certain cases, but is not a general rule. It does not seem to be possible, at least for the present, to count on this mode of payment for appeasing conflict between Capital and Labour. Fortunately, there are other means which hitherto have been sufficient to maintain relative social quiet. Such methods have not lost their power and it is up to managers to study them, apply them, and make them work well.

Payment in Kind, Welfare Work, Non-financial Incentives

Whether wages are made up of money only or whether they include various additions such as heating, light, housing, food, is of little consequence provided that the employee be satisfied.

From another point of view, there is no doubt that a business will be better served in proportion as its employees are more energetic, better educated, more conscientious and more permanent. The employer should have regard, if merely in the interests of the business, for the health, strength, education, morale, and stability of his personnel. These elements of smooth running are not acquired in the workshop alone, they are formed and developed as well, and particularly, outside it, in the home and school, in civil and religious life. Therefore, the employer comes to be concerned with his employees outside the works and here the question of proportion comes up again. Opinion is greatly divided on this point. Certain unfortunate experiments have resulted in some employers stopping short their interest, at the works gate and at the regulation of wages. The majority consider that the employer's activity may be used to good purpose outside the factory confines provided that there be discretion and prudence, that it be sought after rather than imposed, be in keeping with the general level of education and taste of those concerned and that it have absolute respect for their liberty. It must be benevolent collaboration, not tyrannical stewardship, and therein lies an indispensable condition of success.

The employer's welfare activities may be of various kinds. In the works they bear on matters of hygiene and comfort: ventilation, lighting, cleanliness, canteen facilities. Outside the works they bear on housing accomodation, feeding, education, and training. Provident schemes come under this head.

Non-financial incentives only come in the case of large-scale concerns and may be said to be almost exclusively in the realm of government work. Every mode of payment likely to make the personnel more valuable and improve its lot in life, and also to inspire keenness on the part of employees at all levels, should be a matter for managers' constant attention.

8. CENTRALIZATION

Like division of work, centralization belongs to the natural order; this turns on the fact that in every organism, animal or social, sensations converge towards the brain or directive part, and from the brain or directive part orders are sent out which set all parts of the organism in movement. Centralization is not a system of management good or bad of itself, capable of being adopted or discarded at the whim of managers or of circumstances; it is always present to a greater or less extent. The question of centralization or decentralization is a simple question of proportion, it is a matter of finding the optimum degree for the particular concern. In small firms, where the manager's orders go directly to subordinates, there is absolute centralization; in large concerns, where a long scalar chain is interposed between manager and lower grades, orders and counter-information too have to go through a series of intermediaries. Each employee, intentionally or unintentionally, puts something of himself into the transmission and execution of orders and of information received too. He does not operate merely as a cog in a machine. What appropriate share of initiative may be left to intermediaries depends on the personal character of the manager, on his moral worth, on the reliability of his subordinates, and also on the condition of the business. The degree of centralization must vary according to different cases. The objective to pursue is the optimum utilization of all faculties of the personnel.

If the moral worth of the manager, his strength, intelligence, experience and swiftness of thought allow him to have a wide span of activities he will be able to carry centralization quite far and reduce his seconds in command to mere executive agents. If, conversely, he prefers to have greater recourse to the experience, opinions, and counsel of his colleagues whilst reserving to himself the privilege of giving general directives, he can effect considerable decentralization.

Seeing that both absolute and relative value of manager and employees are constantly changing, it is understandable that the degree of centralization or decentralization may itself vary constantly. It is a problem to be solved according to circumstances, to the best satisfaction of the interests involved. It arises, not only in the case of higher authority, but for superiors at all levels; and not one but can extend or confine, to some extent, his subordinates' initiative.

The finding of the measure which shall give the best overall yield: that is the problem of centralization or decentralization. Everything which goes to increase the importance of the subordinate's rôle is decentralization, everything which goes to reduce it is centralization.

9. SCALAR CHAIN

The scalar chain is the chain of superiors ranging from the ultimate authority to the lowest ranks. The line of authority is the route followed — via every link in the chain — by all communications which start from or go to the ultimate authority. This path is dictated both by the need for some transmission and by the principle of unity of command, but it is not always the swiftest. It is even at times disastrously lengthy in large concerns, notably in governmental ones. Now, there are many activities whose success turns on speedy execution, hence respect for the line of authority must be reconciled with the need for swift action.

Let us imagine that section F has to be put into contact with section P in a business whose scalar chain is represented by the double ladder $G-A-Q$ thus —

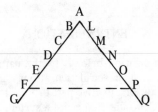

By following the line of authority the ladder must be climbed from F to A and then descended from A to P, stopping at each rung, then ascended again from P to A, and descended once more from A to F, in order to get back to the starting point. Evidently it is much simpler and quicker to go directly from F to P by making use of FP as a "gang plank" and that is what is most often done. The scalar principle will be safeguarded if managers E and O have authorized their respective subordinates F and P to treat directly, and the position will be fully regularized if F and P inform their respective superiors forthwith of what they have agreed upon. So long as F and P remain in agreement, and so long as their actions are approved by their immediate superiors, direct contact may be maintained, but from the instant that agreement ceases or there is no approval from the superiors direct contact comes to an end, and the scalar chain is straightway resumed. Such is the actual procedure to be observed in the great majority of businesses. It provides for the usual exercise of some measure of initiative at all levels of authority. In the small concern, the general interest, viz. that of the concern proper, is easy to grasp, and the employer is present to recall this interest to those tempted to lose sight of it. In government enterprise the general interest is such a complex, vast, remote thing, that it is not easy to get a clear idea of it, and for the majority of civil servants the employer is somewhat mythical and unless the sentiment of general interest be constantly revived by higher authority, it becomes blurred and weakened and each section tends to regard itself as its own aim and end and forgets that it is only a cog in a big machine, all of whose parts must work in concert. It becomes isolated, cloistered, aware only of the line of authority.

The use of the "gang plank" is simple, swift, sure. It allows the two employees F and P to deal at one sitting, and in a few hours, with some question or other which via the scalar chain would pass through twenty transmissions, inconvenience many people, involve masses of paper, lose weeks or months to get to a conclusion less satisfactory generally than the one which could have been obtained via direct contact as between F and P.

Is it possible that such practices, as ridiculous as they are devastating, could be in current use? Unfortunately there can be little doubt of it in government department affairs. It is usually acknowledged that the chief cause is fear of responsibility. I am rather of the opinion that it is insufficient executive capacity on the part of those in charge. If supreme authority A insisted that his assistants B and L made use of the "gang plank" themselves and made its use incumbent upon their subordinates C and M, the habit and courage of taking responsibility would be established and at the same time the custom of using the shortest path.

It is an error to depart needlessly from the line of authority, but it is an even greater one to keep to it when detriment to the business ensues. The latter may attain extreme gravity in certain conditions. When an employee is obliged to choose between the two practices, and it is impossible for him to take advice from his superior, he should be courageous enough and feel free enough to adopt the line dictated by the general interest. But for him to be in this frame of mind there must have been previous precedent, and his superiors must have set him the example — for example must always come from above.

10. ORDER

The formula is known in the case of material things, "A place for everything and everything in its place." The formula is the same for human order: "A place for everyone and everyone in his place."

Material Order. In accordance with the preceding definition, so that material order shall prevail, there must be a place appointed for each thing and each thing must be in its appointed place. Is that enough? Is it not also necessary that the place shall have been well chosen? The object of order must be avoidance of loss of material, and for this object to be completely realized not only must things be in their place suitably arranged but also the place must have been chosen so as to facilitate all activities as much as possible. If this last condition be unfulfilled, there is merely the appearance of order. Appearance of order may cover over real disorder. I have seen a works yard used as a store for steel ingots in which the material was well stacked, evenly arranged and clean and which gave a pleasing impression of orderliness. On close inspection it could be noted that the same heap included five or six types of steel intended for different manufacture all mixed up together. Whence useless handling, lost time, risk of mistakes because each thing was not in its place. It happens, on the other hand, that the appearance of disorder may actually be true order. Such is the case with papers scattered about at a master's whim which a well-meaning but incompetent servant re-arranges and stacks in neat piles. The master can no longer find his way about them. Perfect order presupposes a judiciously chosen place and the appearance of order is merely a false or imperfect image of real order. Cleanliness is a corollary of orderliness, there is no appointed place for dirt. A diagram representing the entire premises divided up into as many sections as there are employees responsible facilitates considerably the establishing and control of order.

155

Social Order. For social order to prevail in a concern there must, in accordance with the definition, be an appointed place for every employee and every employee be in his appointed place. Perfect order requires, further, that the place be suitable for the employee and the employee for the place — in English idiom, "The right man in the right place."

Thus understood, social order presupposes the successful execution of the two most difficult managerial activities: good organization and good selection. Once the posts essential to the smooth running of the business have been decided upon and those to fill such posts have been selected, each employee occupies that post wherein he can render most service. Such is perfect social order, "A place for each one and each one in his place." That appears simple, and naturally we are so anxious for it to be so that when we hear for the twentieth time a government departmental head assert this principle, we conjure up straightway a concept of perfect administration. This is a mirage.

Social order demands precise knowledge of the human requirements and resources of the concern and a constant balance between these requirements and resources. Now this balance is most difficult to establish and maintain and all the more difficult the bigger the business, and when it has been upset and individual interests resulted in neglect or sacrifice of the general interest, when ambition, nepotism, favouritism or merely ignorance has multiplied position without good reason or filled them with incompetent employees, much talent and strength of will, and more persistence than current instability of ministerial appointments presupposes, are required in order to sweep away abuses and restore order.

As applied to government enterprise the principle of order, "A place for each one and each one in his place," takes on an astounding breadth. It means national responsibility towards each and all, everyone's destiny mapped out, national solidarity, the whole problem of society. I will stay no longer over this disturbing extension of the principle of order. In private businesses and especially in those of restricted scope it is easier to maintain proportion as between selection and requirements. As in the case of orderly material arrangement, a chart or plan makes the establishment and control of human arrangement much more easy. This represents the personnel in entirety, and all sections of the concern together with the people occupying them.

11. EQUITY

Why equity and not justice? Justice is putting into execution established conventions, but conventions cannot foresee everything, they need to be interpreted or their inadequacy supplemented. For the personnel to be encouraged to carry out its duties with all the devotion and loyalty of which it is capable it must be treated with kindliness, and equity results from the combination of kindliness and justice. Equity excludes neither forcefulness nor sterness and the application of it requires much good sense, experience and good nature.

Desire for equity and equality of treatment are aspirations to be taken into account in dealing with employees. In order to satisfy these requirements as much as possible without neglecting any principle or losing sight of the general interest, the head of the business must frequently summon up his highest faculties. He should strive to instill a sense of equity throughout all levels of the scalar chain.

12. STABILITY OF TENURE OF PERSONNEL

Time is required for an employee to get used to new work and succeed in doing it well, always assuming that he possesses the requisite abilities. If when he has got used to it, or before then, he is moved, he will not have had time to render worthwhile service. If this be repeated indefinitely the work will never be properly done. The undesirable consequences of such insecurity of tenure are especially to be feared in large concerns, where the settling in of managers is generally a lengthy matter. Much time is needed indeed to get to know men and things in a large concern in order to be in a position to decide on a plan of action, to gain confidence in oneself, and inspire it in others. Hence it has often been recorded that a mediocre manager who stays is infinitely preferable to outstanding managers who merely come and go.

Generally the managerial personnel of prosperous concerns is stable, that of unsuccessful ones is unstable. Instability of tenure is at one and the same time cause and effect of bad running. The apprenticeship of a higher manager is generally a costly matter. Nevertheless, changes of personnel are inevitable; age, illness, retirement, death, disturb the human make-up of the firm; certain employees are no longer capable of carrying out their duties, whilst others become fit to assume greater responsibilities. In common with all the other principles, therefore, stability of tenure of personnel is also a question of proportion.

13. INITIATIVE

Thinking out a plan and ensuring its success is one of the keenest satisfactions for an intelligent man to experience. It is also one of the most powerful stimulants of human endeavour. This power of thinking out and executing is what is called initiative, and freedom to propose and to execute belongs too, each in its way, to initiative. At all levels of the organizational ladder zeal and energy on the part of employees are augmented by initiative. The initiative of all, added to that of the manager, and supplementing it if need be, represents a great source of strength for businesses. This is particularly apparent at different times; hence it is essential to encourage and develop this capacity to the full.

Much tact and some integrity are required to inspire and maintain everyone's initiative, within the limits imposed, by respect for authority and for discipline. The manager must be able to sacrifice some personal vanity in order to grant this sort of satisfaction to subordinates. Other things being equal, moreover, a manager able to permit the exercise of initiative on the part of subordinates is infinitely superior to one who cannot do so.

14. ESPRIT DE CORPS

"Union is strength." Business heads would do well to ponder on this proverb. Harmony, union among the personnel of a concern, is great strength in that concern. Effort, then, should be made to establish it. Among the countless methods in use I will single out specially one principle to be observed and two pitfalls to be avoided. The principle to be observed is unity of command; the dangers to be avoided are (a) a misguided interpretation of the motto "divide and rule," (b) the abuse of written communications.

(a) *Personnel must not be split up.* Dividing enemy forces to weaken them is clever, but dividing one's own team is a grave sin against the business. Whether this error results from inadequate managerial capacity or imperfect grasp of things, or from egoism which sacrifices general interest to personal interest, it is always reprehensible because harmful to the business. There is no merit in sowing dissension among subordinates; any beginner can do it. On the contrary, real talent is needed to coordinate effort, encourage keenness, use each man's abilities, and reward each one's merit without arousing possible jealousies and disturbing harmonious relations.

(b) *Abuse of written communications.* In dealing with a business matter or giving an order which requires explanation to complete it, usually it is simpler and quicker to do so verbally than in writing. Besides, it is well known that differences and misunderstandings which a conversation could clear up grow more bitter in writing. Thence it follows that, wherever possible, contacts should be verbal; there is a gain in speed, clarity, and harmony. Nevertheless, it happens in some firms that employees of neighbouring departments with numerous points of contact, or even employees within a department, who could quite easily meet, only communicate with each other in writing. Hence arise increased work and complications and delays harmful to the business. At the same time, there is to be observed a certain animosity prevailing between different departments or different employees within a department. The system of written communications usually brings this result. There is a way of putting an end to this deplorable system and that is to forbid all communications in writing which could easily and advantageously be replaced by verbal ones. There again, we come up against a question of proportion.

It is not merely by the satisfactory results of harmony obtaining as between employees of the same department that the power of unity is shown: commercial agreements, unions, associations of every kind, play an important part in business management.

The part played by association has increased remarkably in half a century. I remember, in 1968, workers of primary industries without cohesion, without common bond, a veritable cloud of individual dust particles; and out of that the union has produced collective associations, meeting employers on equal terms. At that same time, bitter rivalry prevailed between large firms, closely similar, which has given place gradually to friendly relations, permitting of the settlement of most common interests by joint agreement. It is the beginning of a new era which already has profoundly modified both habits and ideas, and industrial heads should take this development into account.

* * *

There I bring to an end this review of principles, not because the list is exhausted — this list has no precise limits — but because to me it seems at the moment especially useful to endow management theory with a dozen or so well-established principles, on which it is appropriate to concentrate general discussion. The foregoing principles are those to which I have most often had recourse. I have simply expressed my personal opinion in connection with them. Are they to have a place in the management code which is to be built up? General discussion will show.

This code is indispensable. Be it a case of commerce, industry, politics, religion, war, or philanthropy, in every concern there is a management function to be performed, and for its performance there must be principles, that is to say acknowledged truths regarded as proven on which to rely. And it is the code which represents the sum total of these truths at any given moment.

Surprise might be expressed at the outset that the eternal moral principles, the laws of the Decalogue and Commandments of the Church are not sufficient guide for the manager, and that a special code is needed. The explanation is this: the higher laws of religious or moral order envisage the individual only, or else interests which are not of this world, whereas management principles aim at the success of associations of individuals and at the satisfying of economic interests. Given that the aim is different, it is not surprising that the means are not the same. There is no identity, so there is no contradiction. Without principles one is in darkness and chaos; interest, experience, and proportion are still very handicapped, even with the best principles. The principle is the lighthouse fixing the bearings but it can only serve those who already know the way into port.

The Management Process

WILLIAM H. NEWMAN, CHARLES E. SUMMER, and
E. KIRBY WARREN

A manager is a man who get things done by working with people and other resources; in order to reach an objective, *he coordinates the activities of others rather than perform operations himself.* This definition helps us identify a manager, but it tells us little about *how* he manages. What is the nature of the process? How can we divide it up for study?

Managing is a social process. It is a *process* because it comprises a series of actions that led to the accomplishment of objectives. It is a *social* process, because these actions are principally concerned with relations between people.

We have many social processes in civilized society: We worship together, play games, stand in queues waiting for buses, negotiate contracts, and try men for murder. In each case, by having an established pattern of what we should do, and what we expect others to do, we can achieve an end result that would not otherwise be feasible. The particulars of a process may, of course, be changed from time to time: An Army and Navy football game has quite different rituals for spectators and players from those of the old-fashioned jousting match, and a modern murder trial has changed considerably from legal procedures in the days of Henry VIII. But to understand what is happening in any social activity – including the management of an enterprise – and, especially, to insure that what we want to happen happens, we need a keen appreciation of the social process involved. The aim of this article is to help develop such an understanding about the process of managing.

Business management, like education or government is a *continuing* process. There are always new mouths to feed, fresh minds to stimulate, and more people to govern. And the satisfaction of needs today invites higher aspirations for tomorrow. Thus, new problems crop up before old ones are solved. For purposes of analysis, of course, we may focus on a single problem – on just one series of actions that lead to a specific end; but in practice, a manager must learn to deal with a wide range of problems, each in a different stage of resolution. This continuing flow of problems underscores the need to comprehend the management process, for we will be able to give discriminating guidance about this variety of problems only if we understand what is taking place in a large conglomeration of actions.

Managing is so complex that our minds cannot consider all its facets at the same moment. We need to divide up the whole activity into parts in order to grasp the full significance of each – just as we get a clear picture of a company by looking separately at its financial statements, its key personnel, its reputation, its facilities, its policies and organization, its traditions and social structure. Then we can fit the different aspects into a total picture.

Reprinted from William H. Newman, Charles E. Summer, and E. Kirby Warren, The Process of Management: Concepts, Behavior, *and* Practice *(Second Edition; copyright 1967), pp. 9-14. Reprinted by permission of Prentice-Hall, Inc., Englewood Cliffs, N.J.*

A highly useful way of dividing up the total task of management is in terms of organizing, planning, leading, and controlling. Although all are closely interrelated, each of these elements of managing can be analyzed as a subprocess. Each is vital to the success of managers at all levels — from first-line supervisors to presidents. And these four elements are present in the managing of every kind of enterprise: small and large, manufacturing and selling, partnership and corporation, profit and non-profit. Let's take a brief look at these four processes.

ORGANIZING

Once the work of an enterprise grows beyond what a single craftsman can do, organization becomes necessary. We have to assign the various tasks to different people and to coordinate their efforts. As the enterprise expands, this process leads to departments and divisions, each of which has its particualr mission. One way to think about the resulting organization is as a complex machine — say, an airplane designed for transatlantic passenger service. Each part of a plane performs a necessary function — supplying power, pressure, heat, steering, communication, and so forth; *and* the different parts are so carefully balanced and fitted together that changing any one of them often calls for an adjustment in several others.

But a manager must also view organization as a social arrangement, because it is composed of people rather than physical objects. The men who are assigned tasks are independent, self-respecting individuals with a variety of motives; informal groups influence the way men respond to managerial action; and the attitudes of all these people are continually shifting and evolving. In organizing, then, we have to seek ways of getting the necessary work done at the same time we build a social structure that helps meet the needs of people doing the work.

PLANNING

A key activity of all managers is planning the work under their direction. Working with each other and with the people who will carry out the plans, they clarify objectives and set goals for each subdivision; they establish policies and standard methods to guide those who do the work; and they develop programs, strategies, and schedules to keep the work moving toward the objectives. Most of these plans they will have to readjust periodically in the light of new information and changes in operating conditions. And time and again managers will face questions about how detailed the plans should be, who should participate in formulating them, and how much freedom of action should be given to subordinates.

The process of planning can be best understood if we first examine the basic stages in making a specific decision. These stages are: diagnosing the problem, finding good alternative solutions, projecting the results of each alternative, and finally, selecting the one course of action to be followed.

Decision-making, however, is not the act of an isolated individual; it takes places in the organization we have established. In fact, many different persons may contribute to the formulation and final selection of a major plan. Consequently, it is necessary to know how the organization can be used most effectively in this decision-making (or planning) process.

LEADING

Clear plans and sound organization set the stage, but a manager must also provide leadership if the people in his organization are to work together to achieve its goals.

Leadership involves the way a manager behaves in his man-to-man relationships with his subordinates. In leading, a manager strives to integrate the needs of people with the welfare of his company or department. He recognizes that people have their own desires, but at the same time he knows that cooperation and efficiency are necessary for the survival and growth of the firm. In short, a leader tries to act so as to maintain a good balance between individual motivation *and* cooperative efficiency.

Such behavior is not always easy. But establishing two-way communication, assisting subordinates to perform their duties, and helping them achieve their personal aspirations are activities that lay a basis for voluntary cooperation. This kind of behavior by a leader also fosters an atmosphere of trust, respect, and confidence between himself and his subordinates.

At the same time, a manager must provide guidance toward a system of order and cooperation. In no complex social system — whether it be national society or a company society — can an individual do as he pleases, without regard for the activities of others. Clear direction, coupled with a spirit of cooperation, typically achieves the necessary coordinated effort. But there are times when a leader must be tough, hold people to high standards of performance, discipline wisely,and, occasionally, use power.

MEASURING AND CONTROLLING

For a ship to reach its destination without sailing far off course, the captain regularly "takes his bearings." A manager, likewise, has to measure his progress if he is to obtain his objectives. And when he discovers that operations are not proceeding according to plan, he takes corrective action to get back on course or, if this is not feasible, he readjusts his plans. This process of measuring progress, comparing it with plans, and taking corrective action, we call control. In practice, control is not so simple as it sounds. Measuring intangibles such as customer good will or executive morale poses difficulties, and devising corrective action that both overcomes an immediate difficulty and creates a favorable climate for future performance often calls for ingenuity. Moreover, the dispersal of activities that result from organization creates problems of just who should control what.

FRAMEWORK RATHER THAN PROCEDURE

We shall examine each of these four elements — organizing, planning, leading, and controlling — in some detail, and we shall divide these major aspects of the over-all management process into even narrower subprocesses. Our analysis, we hope, will reveal the structure of the important elements in managing. Such a systematic view of management provides a convenient device (a) for diagnosing complex management problems and (b) for working on improvements at one stage without losing sight of other stages.

But a framework that helps us think in an orderly fashion is not necessarily a step-by-step procedure that we must follow. Actually, when we deal with a concrete management problem, the available information is not neatly classified and labeled; instead, a great array of facts hits us at once, while some data remain stubbornly hidden. In response to such confusion our thoughts tend to flit first to one subject and then to another. So the chief purpose of a conceptual framework, such as the systematic examination of the management process, is to help us quickly to place diverse ideas in a useful order. The framework is more than a series of pigeonholes to tuck ideas in, however, for among the pigeonholes there is a rational relation that we know in advance. Thus, when we mentally classify a new bit of information as bearing on, say, the long-range objectives of department X, we can immediately relate it to a host of other ideas we have stored in our mind, and, in this relation, the piece of information takes on meaning because it contributes to our comprehension of the total situation. Mankind has advanced from a primitive state largely by developing orderly ways of thinking about problems; in proposing a systematic approach to management, then, we are simply following this time-proven method.

There are, of course, many ways to think about as complicated a subject as management, and one way may provide useful insights that another approach glosses over. But if we are to make progress in understanding management, we must follow some kind of orderly thinking. The approach presented here has proven to be very useful for both practical and theoretical analyses of a wide variety of management situations. So while we should be alert for improvements, we can proceed with confidence that this approach does have practical value for anyone in a managerial or staff position — or for the researcher who is trying to understand how managers get things done.

162

Coordination as a Task of Management: A Review

ROBERT C. HEIDE

Organizations and management are dynamic viable creations and must continue to be so if they are to keep pace with changing social needs and new programs. The challenge is a formidable one to meet. Old programs are being retreaded and new innovative services launched each day. The multiplication of numbers of organizational relationships, further complicated by increased specialization of staff and departmentalization of services, already taxes the structure and threatens to overwhelm the administrator. Informational systems, data processing, and functional forms of organization rise to meet some of the challenge. However, the administrator will still need to rely to a large extent on tested traditional principles of management to fulfill his role in the organization. Such principles and techniques should receive repeated review, adaptation, and reinforcement if they are to continue to be workable tools of the administrator.

One such element of management warranting review is that of coordination, a task which may take on ever-increasing dimensions for the middle manager of a public welfare program. Although much writing has been devoted to the importance and need for coordination at all levels of management, a review of the literature leaves the neophyte hanging somewhere between "so what else is new?" and "exactly what is coordination?"

Popular belief in the importance of coordination almost takes on the aura and dedication awarded to motherhood and the flag. Yet, we use "coordinate" and "coordination" so loosely that in this day of rapid communication the meaning to the listener is fuzzy, and the true essence is all but lost. In addition, "coordination" is applied to almost any human endeavor, whether of a physical, social, or scientific basis, making it almost impossible to apply a universal definition. For purposes of clarification, and because coordination is presumed to be a task of considerable importance to the manager, it would seem appropriate to examine its usage and variety of meanings, and to review techniques for its use.

One of the earliest recorded uses of the word "coordinate" (c. 1641) was in its application to church organization, indicating equal rank among churches.[1] Its use in modern grammar suggests members of equal rank, such as coordinate clauses in a compound sentence. In mathematics it may be used to determine position by the use of points in common on a plane. The use of "coordinate" in military operations adds the essential element of appropriate timing to the usual interrelationships. The juxtaposition of the parts, the synchronization of their functioning, and a common goal are the ingredients of the meaning of the word in its general use today.

---

[1] Cf. *"The Oxford Universal Dictionary on Historical Principles* (London: Oxford University Press, Amen House).

Reprinted with permission of the American Public Welfare Administration and the author, from Public Welfare, *Vol. 27, No. 3 (July, 1969), pp. 279-283.*

In addition to its use in terms of equal (balanced) and spatial relationships and timing, "coordination" should be perceived in two other dimensions, namely, as an action, and as a condition of being.

A cursory review of recent history of governmental operations discloses that the concept and use of coordination was seen first as "an action," and applied earliest to the function of control, specifically in the area of budgeting for a multidepartmental organization. Interdepartmental coordination "arose as an essential factor from the demand for strengthened executive responsibility. . . ."[2] Coordination was applied in an attempt to centralize expenditure control by delegating appropriate authority to an agency attached to a central public office. On a Federal level this took place in the early 1920's, following a similar innovation at the state level by the Illinois Legislature in 1917.

Coordination assumed increasing importance in the Federal government operations during World War II, specifically in the assignment of this task to the Office of War Mobilization. This office was charged with the duties to "unify the activities" and "resolve or determine controversies . . ." and "issue directives on policy. . . ."[3] In addition, this assignment appeared designed to relieve the Executive Office of handling details and avoid becoming involved with problems directly. An earlier attempt at coordination during the 1920's and the early 1930's involved a number of interdepartmental committees which were "collected" under the Federal Coordinating Service for the purpose of promoting good management practice, and to achieve high level production. As might be expected in an era reflecting but emerging from the classical theory of organization, the answer to the lack of functional coordination was to devise reporting systems and central planning bodies.

In more recent times, "coordination" has become a byword, and, in the thinking of at least one expert, the essence of management. Gulick described the functions of management as "Planning . . . Organizing . . . Staffing . . . Directing . . . Coordinating (that is the all important duty of interrelating the various parts of the work), Reporting . . . Budgeting."[4] Other authorities have proposed that coordination is included in each of the parts described by Gulick and others, insisting that none of these tasks by management is without coordination as an essential element in its functioning. The importance of this element has grown so that few job descriptions or program plans are written today without emphasis being placed on coordination as a major task of the manager, director, or coordinator. It is difficult to preceive how and where further importance can be attached to it. This may explain in part why in very recent years there have been suggestions to see coordination in a different perspective, as a "condition of being," that has a nature or properties. It is suggested that coordination may be seen as something that exists and is built of substance, as well as an action that can be taken. It might be superfluous to note that one without the other portends only limited success for the organization. Nor does the presence of one ensure the natural inception and promotion of the other. It may be posited that both need to be worked on, consciously and deliberately by management, if high level achievement is to be realized throughout the organization.

[2] Fritz M. Marx, *Elements of Public Administration* (Englewood Cliffs, N.J.: Prentice-Hall, Inc., 1963), p. 177.

[3] *Ibid*, p. 179.

[4] Luther Gulick, as quoted by Bertram M. Gross, *The Managing Of Organizations* (New York: Free Press of Glencoe, 1964), Vol. I, p. 144.

Considering first the aspect of coordination as a condition of being, one might ask "what makes for its existence?" "what properties lend themselves to identification, examination, and planning?"

Likert emphasizes the importance of human resources and relationships. In a recent publication he devotes an entire chapter to recognizing problems and suggesting solutions for the development of coordination in a highly functionalized organization.[5] The framework and concepts of traditional organizational theory, such as manifested in large governmental agencies and industry, compound problems in the promotion of coordination. Solutions appear to lie in promoting coordination and formulating channels for decision-making along more than one line in the operation, as well as in a departure from the usually conceived hierarchal table of organization.

One of the bases of Likert's thesis stresses the importance of the relationship between the superior and the subordinate, concerning which he urges the use by the manager of the principle of supportive relationships. The definition of this term closely follows that applied in social work, and parallels the ends sought for a client by his caseworker. As such, it is not new to the manager of a social service agency. Yet, its significance may often escape one in the everyday operation and the professional interactions of the staff. It would seem obvious that meaningful relationships are key indicators of and contribute much to the nature of the organization and its functioning. Staff relationships are built upon interactions, vertically and horizontally, between people, albeit they may usually be seen as positions. People inside as well as outside of formal organizations have personal needs which respond to ego-building relationships and satisfying experiences.

A second contributor to a "condition of being" is the existence of defined and understood goals of the organization that are needed to provide the framework within which the employee can seek realization of personal objectives.[6] Clear purpose, aided by defined staff patterns and specific objectives, is basic to organizational planning and functioning. It is just as basic to another organism, man. Without these important guideposts for the individual to relate to and identify with, activity would tend to become random, relatively dysfunctional and productive of anxiety.

The third substance, and closely interrelated with the first two, is the potential and means for free-flowing, candid, and multidirectional communication. Obviously, interdependence of personal and organizational goals, and assurance that would come from supportive relationships would have little value and *raison d'etre* without means for communication. Together, *supportive relationships, shared purpose, and communication* make for the substance or essence that builds coordination.

Let us turn then to examine techniques for coordination through action by administration. One of the first questions posed in literature has to do with the proper degree of central authority in effecting coordination. Does management coordinate employees? Most if not all authorities agree that coordination cannot be accomplished *ad dictum*, but rather, only facilitated by administration. Coordination more often ,occurs, one might

---

[5] Rensis Likert, *The Human Organization: Its Management and Values* (New York: McGraw-Hill, Inc., 1967), Chapter 10, pp. 156-188.

[6] Definitions of organizational goals vary from what may be otherwise thought of as missions, or projected levels of program effectiveness, or work plan objectives. Is the purpose of the goal statement to impress, inspire, give direction, or provide bases for measurement? If the employee is a high priority target for involvement, he might relate even more meaningfully to statements that include or are supplemented by the administrator's individualized professional philosophy as well.

conclude, as a result of administratively promoted and directed interaction among staff, whose goals are compatible with the climate and purpose of the organization.

ACTION BY ADMINISTRATION

In describing principles of collective planning or coordination of industry on a national scale, Follett contributes a unique viewpoint of coordination, which may be applicable at any level within any one hierarchy, as well as in the relationships of superior-subordinate organizations. Follett contrasts coercion — the imposition of arbitrary planning, with coordination — the voluntary adjusting or the reciprocal relating of all factors to each other within a situation. "But the process of adjusting is not one which can be imposed from outside — it is essentially, basically, by its very nature, a process of auto-controlled activity. No one can issue a fiat by which I am adjusted, I can only be helped to adjust myself."[7]

As a test to evaluate national planning as well as to assist the process of coordination, Follett suggested four principles of organization:
1. co-ordination by direct contact of the responsible people concerned;
2. co-ordination in the early stages;
3. co-ordination as the reciprocal relating of all the factors in a situation;
4. co-ordination as a continuing process.[8]

Follett continues on to make the point that coordination is more than placing components in proper and harmonious relationship to each other, but that "interpenetration" of its parts must also occur. If the individual elements have not changed because of their reciprocal relationships, then coordination has not taken place.

In addition to the application of the principles stated above, how otherwise can coordination, hopefully with interpenetration, be promoted by management? Some of the following methods illustrate a variety of impositions by administrative direction.

METHODS

Long distance action by a central authority to bring about coordination in a field office may be attempted through definition and design in a number of ways: "Increased uniformity in . . . boundaries and . . . offices; incidental coordinating responsibilities of service and control agencies; reliance on informal coordination; appointment of regional coordinators; and the use of committees and commissions."[9]

Each of the five carries with it a different degree of "coordination by order." No one method may have higher hopes for success than the others. "Informal coordination" and "committees and commissions" depend much upon personal factors, e.g., common concerns and interrelated problems, mutual accessibility, authority and compensation level and status, so the "sitting down together" may have varied results.

Common boundaries and shared office buildings are obvious and direct methods to employ, and an appointed coordinator at least provides some definition of the need and degree of local authority to promote efforts. The degree of authority delegated to the local coordinator may vary widely, from one empowered to act as an agent of top administration to one who merely encourages harmony and cooperation. One advantage of a local coordinator is that the task is fixed at the local level, which should promote consonance with the uniqueness of that office and level of operation.

---

[7] Mary Parker Follett, *Dynamic Administration*, H. C. Metcalf, and L. Urwick, eds. (New York: Harper and Brothers, 1940), p. 296.

[8] *Ibid*, p. 297.

[9] Fritz M. Marx, *op. cit.*, p. 266.

Another means for coordination through long distance direction, and something basic to all functioning at the local level, is the structure of the organization itself. Built into the framework, hopefully, is the grouping together of efforts seen as being necessary to accomplish the organization's purposes. The very proximity of the elements enhances their integrated functioning, and the authority necessary to ensure the success of the operation carries the means to develop relationships through which would flow coordination.

Coordination may be promoted at short range within any organization through a variety of means used for a variety of purposes. A common method is that manifested in the role of supervisors, who may not be explicitly coordinating several staff members, but nevertheless " . . . employ directional devices, teach principles of coordination, illustrate their application, and apply tests to determine the quality of synchronized effort."[10] Common directional devices and means to teach and illustrate principles may include any type of written communication, as well as the use of the individual conference and group staff meeting. Successfully administered, the group process in such conferences and meetings epitomizes the purpose of the functioning of the whole organization, which came into existence, in part at least, as an expression of collective needs for social relationships.

A long-range goal of the efforts for coordination by management is the sensitization of each element to the potential of meaning of particular things and interdependency with another. All of the devices, techniques, and structures will have failed if the individual does not become a link in a reciprocating, interpenetrating chain of relationship and reaction. He will not perceive this role in the process until he senses the significance and interdependence of himself with others and within the organization.[11]

The essence of coordination as part of the role of the administrator was aptly expressed many years past by Reynolds in writing about the group aspect of administration. "Organization to administer any enterprise or service calls for a group of people working together, with their individual functions coordinated into a smoothly working whole. Since they are human, they will require help at times in relating themselves to the whole, and seeing themselves as important but not isolated, significant only as others are significant too. Skill in administration consists not only in building organizational machinery which is adapted to the work to be done, but also in so dealing with the human parts of the machine that they all work at their individual and collective best."[12]

Coordination will not just happen, but can result from conscious appreciation of the needs of man, and efforts by administration to provide a climate that encourages harmony, interdependence and teamwork, through supportive relationships, understood goals, and freedom of communication. Directed interaction will best come about with a clear definition of roles, an integrated organizational structure, and face-to-face and supporting directional devices. Within such a climate and with these aids of administrative direction, man has the opportunity to fulfill his social needs and personal achievement goals. In providing such a climate, administration is manifesting a major achievement commensurate with its assumed lofty station in a hierarchy.

---

[10] Harold Koontz and Cyril O'Donnell, *Principles of Management* (New York: McGraw-Hill Book Company, 1964), p. 43.

[11] Another reminder may be in order to emphasize that as in the case of staff relationships, coordination may take place vertically as well as horizontally. Perhaps the concept of a grid would be more apt than the illustration of a chain in describing a circuitry for organizational interaction.

[12] Bertha C. Reynolds, as quoted by Gertrude Wilson and Gladys Ryland, *Social Group Work Practice* (Cambridge, Massachussetts: The Riverside Press, 1949), p. 618.

Conflict Resolution – A Modern Approach

DANIEL E. GRIFFITHS

The resolution of conflicts within the school, as well as between the school and the community, consumes a large part of any administrator's time. Other articles have dealt with this problem to some extent, particularly by referring to studies of role conflict, but in this article we will discuss one of the latest and most powerful management tools, game theory. The theory was first published in 1944 by Von Neumann and Morgenstern, but it was so highly mathematical and, therefore, abstract that few understood or appreciated its usefulness.[1] Since that time numerous social scientists and mathematicians have refined the theory and its use has become more and more obvious. The University Council for Educational Administration has published two games together with an excellent manual by Ohm which relates game theory directly to educational administration.[2] Here, we shall make reference to the work of Ohm, as well as to articles by Harsanyi[3] and Schelling.[4]

THE USE OF GAME THEORY

There are two major uses of game theory:

1. Classifying conflict situations in a way that helps to clarify the kind of action that should be taken.

2. Suggesting specific solutions to conflict situations.

In order to use game theory the administrator has to retreat from the situation sufficiently to reflect upon what is happening. He has to adopt an analytical, reasoning approach and cannot allow himself to become as emotionally involved as the others in the conflict. Game theory, as we shall shortly see, provides the concepts with which to work. Once a situation is analyzed, game theory provides guides to the strategy and tactics that might be employed together with some indication of outcomes. In the modern vernacular, it provides feedback.

[1] John von Neumann and Oskar Morgenstern, *Theory of Games and Economic Behavior* (Princeton: *Princeton University Press*, 1944).

[2] Robert E. Ohm, *Leadership Game – Secondary Principalship Instructor's Manual* (Columbus: University Council for Educational Administration, 1968).

[3] John C. Harsanyi, "Rationality Postulates for Bargaining Solutions in Cooperative and in Non-cooperative Games," *Management Science*, Vol. 9, No. 1 (October, 1962), pp. 141-153.

[4] Thomas C. Schelling, "The Strategy of Conflict," *Journal of Conflict Resolution*, Vol. 2, No. 3, pp. 203-264.

Reprinted with permission of the publisher, Croft Educational Services, Inc., New London, Conn., and the author, from the Executive Action Letter, *Vol. 8, No. 7, February, 1969.*

All conflict situations can be classified as "game" and "non-game". Taking the latter first, a "non-game" conflict situation is one to which a rule applies. Whenever a conflict occurs the administrator should first employ a rule-searching behavior. He should look at the personnel policies and rules, school board policies and administrative rules, or even the state code, should there be one. If there is a rule, he should then apply it as judiciously as possible. The rule-searching behavior might not uncover an appropriate rule, but the situation might be one which obviously requires a rule. For example, a conflict might arise over a newly adopted sick leave policy and the administrator knows that this type of situation will arise continuously. He may have to resort to game theory to solve the problem, but he should also immediately invoke the school district's rule-making apparatus so that there will be a rule to apply when the situation recurs.

On occasion, when there is an appropriate rule, conflict may arise over the nature or origin of the rule. In that case, the rule should be applied, but there should be a grievance or appeal system in operation so that the rule might be changed, if it is indeed a poor one.

If the conflict situation is one that cannot be solved by applying a rule, it is most likely one that has "game" characteristics. As Ohm states,

> If the [situation] involves a conflict of interest, no decision rule exists, and/or a discretionary decision is required within the framework of a general rule or policy, the [situation] may be classified as an . . . event to which game models of interaction can be applied. Such situations may have one or more of the characteristics of games, namely, opposing sets of interest, a set of choices of strategies, interdependence, change, imperfect information, and a preferred ordering of outcomes.[5]

Once it is determined that a situation is a game, it can be further classified as to type of game. There are four categories of games: two-person, zero sum; two-person, non-zero sum; n-person, zero sum; and n-person, non-zero sum.

Two-person, zero sum. In this type of game there are two opposing interests and one of the interests wins and the other losses to the same extent, i.e., the gains of player X equal the losses of player Y.

Two-person, non-zero sum. This is a somewhat more common administrative situation than the above in that the sum of gains and losses does not equal zero; in other words, one side does not win or lose everything. The losing party may be allowed to "save face" by having the winner grant a small concession. Some teacher-board collective negotiations fights fit this category, especially those in which the superintendent is completely on the board's side.

N-person, zero sum. (The n-person concept in this type means more than two sets of interests.) This category probably does not exist in real life since the n-sides generally form coalitions and so become a number of two-person, zero sum games.

N-person, non-zero sum. This is by far the most common type of game in organizations. The administrative conflict situations generally involves the administrator as the third person and generally winning or losing is not complete and cannot be considered as zero-sum.

GAME THEORY STRATEGY

Since most of the conflict situations the administrator deals with are n-person, non-zero sum, let us deal with this class in some depth. Some of the situations covered by this category are strikes, arguments between two or more teachers which must be resolved by

---

[5] Ohm, *op. cit.*, p. 12.

an administrator, disputes between a teacher and a parent involving a child, conflict between departments over the use of certain facilities or equipment, and on and on. There is no end to the n-person, non-zero sum conflict situations in a school.

The most important strategy for the administrator to adopt in this type of conflict is that of mediation. As Ohm states so succinctly,

> The perception of and capacity to mediate conflicts or discontinuities has become a primary administrative task. Balancing, mediating, or relating individual needs and organizational demands or rationalizing [conflicts in] organizational structure are crucial administrative functions.[5]

When confronted with an n-person, non-zero sum situation, the administrator should know that the players will attempt to form a coalition with the administrator and to move the conflict to a two-person, zero sum game. This will resound to the advantage of one set of players, and to the disadvantage of the other set or sets of players. However, it will generally be to the disadvantage of the administrator over the long term to be forced to side with one or the other sets of players. His fundamental strategy must be to mediate, that is, to see that all sides win to some extent and lose to some extent. In terms of game theory, he must keep an n-person, non-zero sum game going as an n-person, non-zero sum game.

A second approach to resolving conflict through game theory is to employ appropriate postulates or guidelines developed by Harsanyi.[7] Since these are quite numerous, only one postulate will be discussed as an illustration.

> *Symmetry* in a bargaining game indicates that a bargainer facing a rational opponent cannot rationally expect his opponent to make a concession in a situation in which he himself, following his own criteria of rational behavior, would refuse to make a concession.[8]

The last suggestion from game theory to be discussed here is from Schelling and is the concept of convergence.[9] When two or more sets of persons are engaged in a game in which they must agree on a division of gains or lose them all, their expectations for themselves and of the others have a tendency to converge. Schelling argues that what brings them together is an "intrinsic magnetism." In simple language it would appear that what Schelling is saying is that what looks good to one party is apt to look good to the others. Most likely, this is the rationale on which the arbiter or mediator functions. His role, and the role of the administrator, is to create a range of alternatives and to select those which should have appeal to one, in the hope it will appeal to the others also. Technically, the new alternatives are called new boundaries or extensions of the problem.

Ohm summarizes the strategy an administrator should follow in an n-person, non-zero sum in the following way:

> Maintaining an n-person game through action to determine the boundaries of the conflict could be rationally expected to lead to a solution to the conflict, a solution which, desirably, would be perceived as at least a partial win by both parties in conflict.[10]

---

[6] Ohm, *op. cit.*, p. 17.

[7] Harsanyi, *op. cit.*

[8] By Harsanyi, quoted from Ohm, *op. cit.*, p. 16.

[9] Schelling, *op. cit.*

[10] Ohm, *op. cit.*, p. 22.

This is a brief introduction to game theory, the latest tool for administrators. Game theory enables administrators to sort out their problems into useful categories and then suggests solutions to these problems. This is much more than most theories offer.

The Theory of Communication:
Its Application to Public Administration

CHARLES E. REDFIELD

Communication is, in the first instance, by its very nature the process of transferring a selected bit of information from an information source to a destination. This process is depicted diagrammatically in Figure 1. There are many examples of information sources: A radio studio is one; the brain of a lecturer, or writer, or painter is another. The selected messages may be transmitted as spoken or written words, as pictures, or in some other form. In oral communication, the transmitter is the voice box; in telegraphy, it is the telegraph key, which codes the message into dots and dashes. As the message moves toward its destination, it is decoded by a receiver into a form understandable to the information destination. The receiver may be the mechanism of the ear, which converts sound waves to a form recognizable to the brain. The television receiver in any living room performs the same function when it decodes electromagnetic waves into recognizable audio-visual representations.

Speaking of television, another element of the communication process appears in Figure 1. This element, of course, is called "noise." Noise is a generic term for the distortions, additions and errors which adversely affect the message en route from transmitter to receiver. Noise, in this concept, is not necessarily something that is heard although static is an excellent example of noise. Noise can be the snow on the television screen, it can be the movement of a train when you are trying to read. It can be, conceivably, an attitude of distrust or disbelief on the part of the receiver which interferes with his reception of the message as transmitted.

Figure 1

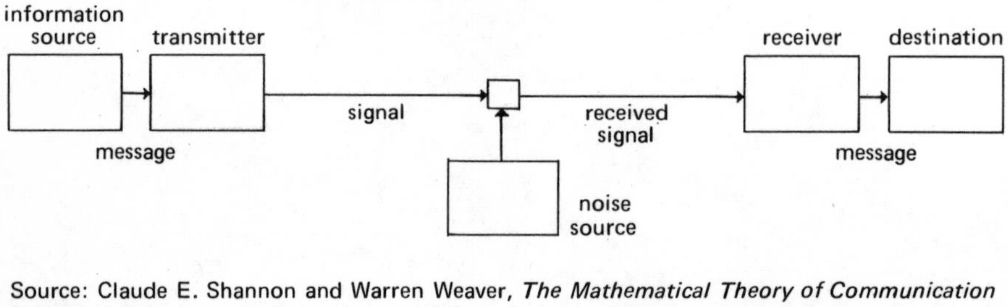

Source: Claude E. Shannon and Warren Weaver, *The Mathematical Theory of Communication* (Urbana: University of Illinois Press, 1949), p. 5. Reproduced by permission of the publisher.

Reprinted with permission of the Bureau of Public Administration, University of Alabama, from The Theory of Communication: Its Application to Public Administration, *Robert B. Highsaw and Don L. Bowen, eds. (University, Alabama: Bureau of Public Administration, University of Alabama, 1965), pp. 11-25.*

The schematic representation of the communication process shown in Figure 1 was developed originally by and for physicists and mathematicians. It is an excellent model of the communication process as seen by an engineer. It is also readily applicable to the processes of mass communication, of which commercial radio, television, motion pictures, and other mass media are examples. The emphasis will be on getting information out to people. This is the process of informing, and public relations and advertising are concerned primarily with informing.

Figure 2

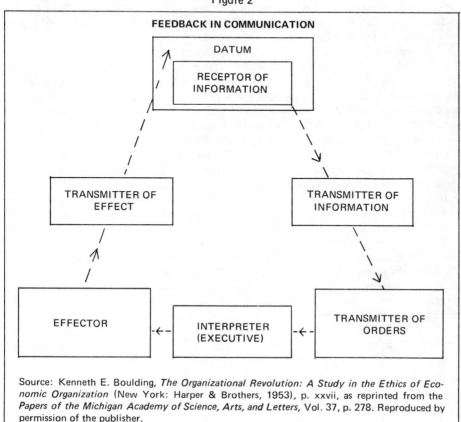

FEEDBACK IN COMMUNICATION

Source: Kenneth E. Boulding, *The Organizational Revolution: A Study in the Ethics of Economic Organization* (New York: Harper & Brothers, 1953), p. xxvii, as reprinted from the *Papers of the Michigan Academy of Science, Arts, and Letters*, Vol. 37, p. 278. Reproduced by permission of the publisher.

To a certain extent, information returns. That is to say, there is some response. This response or information return is referred to as "feedback." The feedback process is shown in Figure 2. It is interesting to note parenthetically that this diagram, to the biologist, is a model of the process of homeostasis as well as an excellent model of the process of two-way communication. (It is only natural that Kenneth Boulding, who developed the diagram, is not a biologist, is not an engineer, and is not actively engaged in the field of communication. Instead, he is an economist first and a student of business organization second.)

The nature of the feedback process is illustrated if, in looking at the diagram, one thinks of the datum as the temperature in a living room, and the receptor of information as being the thermostat which has been pre-set to 70 degrees. If the temperature falls below 70 degrees, the thermocouple in the thermostat tells the furnace control switch (the interpreter or executive in the diagram) to turn on the furnace. The furnace, which is the effector in the diagram, starts up and, through the pipes or ducts, sends additional

173

heat into the room, changing the body of datum to match that requested by the receptor of information, that is, the thermostat. The thermocouple in the thermostat now notifies the furnace control switch to turn off the furnace, and that condition obtains until the heat again falls below 70 degrees.

The model is easily applied to communication in administration. An executive has certain standards, like the 70-degree setting on a thermostat. When the conditions in his community or in his organization markedly diverge from those standards, an action cycle is initiated through the vehicle of communication. The divergence, or divergences, are signaled to the executive, perhaps by dots or lines on a chart or graph. The executive orders certain remedial action. For example, a city manager schedules additional garbage pickups, or additional safety patrols. These actions presumably affect the body of datum in a manner which bring conditions back into line with the standards.

Feedback is a term which has come into fashion to characterize the closed cycle as we see it here. Feedback is the element of response. In mass communication — advertising or public relations — the element of response is often absent and it is generally elusive. An advertiser measures his response in terms of sales, but he is seldom certain just to which advertisement the public has responded. The response element — the element of feedback — is never absent when we are dealing with administrative communication. By administrative communication, I mean, basically, that communication which goes on within the organization. I mean the communication between superior and subordinate, or between a subordinate and a superior, or between and among people within a department or an agency — what we often call "horizontal" communication. In conventional public opinion polling, as conducted by Gallup, Roper, or someone else, members of the public furnish a pollster with answers to the polling questions, and that concludes the relationship between the pollster and the respondents. In employee opinion polling, however, management cannot avoid responding to the respondents. When there is a notification in the house organ, or a positive response in terms of action such as installation of a water cooler, employees will recognize these as being responses to the polling results. And if you do nothing, if you don't notify them, and if you don't install the water cooler, those actions, too, are meaningful responses.

Figure 3

ELEMENTS OF THE COMMUNICATION PROCESS

A **Communicator** (a speaker, sender, issuer)
  who

Transmits (says, sends, issues)

  Messages (orders, reports, suggestions)
    to a

      Communicatee (addressee, respondent,
        audience)
        to influence the behavior of the
        communicatee, as seen in his

      Response (reply, reaction)

Source: Charles E. Redfield, *Communication in Management: A Guide to Administrative Communication* (Chicago: University of Chicago Press, 1953), p. 4. Copyright 1953 by the University of Chicago. Reproduced by permission of the publisher.

Principal factors in the communication process as applied to management are summarized in Figure 3. A *communicator* (a speaker, a sender, an issuer — right now I am the communicator) *transmits* (sends or issues) *messages* (which can be orders, reports, or suggestions) to a *communicatee* (the communicatee is the addressee, the respondent, the audience). And the communicator transmits these messages to the communicatee to influence the behavior of the communicatee as seen in his *response* (his reply or reaction). Now, the communicatee's response, or reply, or reaction feeds back to the communicator, that is, to the original communicator. In the feedback process, the original communicatee becomes the communicator, and the original communicator now becomes the communicatee. The person who issued the order now reads the report. Let me point out that that communicator is not necessarily a superior and the communicatee a subordinate, although we naturally think of this arrangement first. When a subordinate drops a suggestion into the suggestion box, he is the communicator; the superior is the communicatee.

The communication process can be analyzed in terms of any of these five elements, although ultimately all of them are involved. A person's role as a communicator, whether a superior or a subordinate, depends on who he is, what he is, and where he is. Individuals at work are total personalities, but their work — their positions and the kinds of work they do in those positions — involves only segments of their personalities. Here we get into the problem of positional communication.

A look at the communicatee (the listener, the reader, or the viewer) leads us into many problems of perception and cognition: What does one hear when he listens? What does he see when he looks? What does he remember when he reads? And what does he believe? Questions such as these about the communicator and the communicatee, and similar questions applying to the processes of transmission, to messages, and to the element of response or feedback are the concern of people working in the field of communication. Much of the material presented in this volume revolves about these questions and leads into discussions of other subjects which bear on communication — such subjects as semantics, sociology, anthropology, psychology, education, and above all, administration.

THE ORGANIZATIONAL SETTING

Every organization, no matter how large or how small, abounds with communication. Some of the communication is overt — you can hear it, you can see it, and you can read it. But much of the communication that goes on is not verbalized; it is conveyed by gestures, by imitation, and in other nonverbal ways. One can communicate by a nod or a glance, by a frown or a smile, or simply by being present or absent. In 1956, a book was published by the University of California Press, under the title *Nonverbal Communication*. Jurgen Ruesch, one of the authors, is a psychiatrist. Weldon Kees, the other author, is a photographer. Reading this book, and looking at the pictures in it, one is constantly reminded of the meaningfulness of many nonverbal expressions. There are several that I remember particularly well: when a person cups his hands behind his ear; another, when one person lays a reassuring hand on another person's shoulder; and yet another, when two characters are loafing in a doorway on Third Avenue.[1] Their stance and their expressions will tell you whether they are sharing the doorway as two friends, or whether they are each occupying his half of the doorway as two nonfriends.

Within any organization, there is more than one system of communication at work. There is the formal system of which you in your position are a member, but there may be one or more other formal systems. For example, the communication system of the labor

---

[1] Jurgen Ruesch and Weldon Rees, *Nonverbal Communication* (Berkeley: University of California Press, 1956), pp. 68, 77, and 84.

union, if you have one, for the labor union is a formal organization, too, and subordinates in any organization, who are also members of a labor union, are communicators and communicatees in two systems of communication. These two systems may be compatible and mutually supportive, or they may be incompatible and competitive.

Besides the formal organizations with their formal systems of communication, there are a host of informal organizations with informal systems of communication. There are social cliques, work groups, supervisory groups, groups of oldtimers, bridge playing groups, and what have you. A classic example of informal communication is the so-called grapevine, which can be thought of as the "rumor network." This network is not firmly structured and follows different directions in different situations. Thus, there are several or many grapevines rather than just one in every organization. Just as a second, or possibly a third, system of communication of co-existing formal organizations may be helpful or unhelpful, in like manner, the various systems of informal communication can be helpful or unhelpful. Some executives pride themselves on their use of the grapevine on the basis that it helps their formal systems of communication. The difficulty is that the grapevine is a most undependable means of communication. The sociologists Allport and Postman, leading authorities on rumors, have made a number of studies of the subject. On the basis of these studies, it can be asserted here that no one can predict with assurance the direction, speed, or final substance of a message transmitted by grapevine.[2] The process of leveling, sharpening, and assimilation impinges on a rumored message to abbreviate it, to magnify what remains of it, and to restructure it to the needs and interests of the individual rumorers. Thus, no extensive, complex, or vital instruction or report can be entrusted to the grapevine. It is so difficult to get full and accurate information to the right person in the right position at the right time through formal mechanisms, that I can only wonder why people even attempt to use informal mechanisms.

POSITIONAL COMMUNICATION

Every formal organization, whether it be a federal agency, or a city department, starts with a broad purpose or objective. The purpose or objective is subdivided into activities and the activities are assigned to positions and to groups of positions. Organizational relationships are established between position "A" and position "B," not between Mr. Smith and Miss Jones. Since communication is the vehicle for carrying on relationships between positions, we find in many organizations a phenomenon which can be designated as positional communication. The entire organization, as it appears on an organization chart, can be referred to as a positional communications network. The nature of positional communication is shown diagrammatically in Figure 4.

Positional communication is upset in practice, however, because positions are staffed with human beings. These human beings have total personalities. The relationship between position "A" and position "B" does not exist apart from the relationship between Joe and Gertrude and the other folks in the office. Yet, although it is impossible completely to insulate the position from the incumbent's personality, communication depends most of the time on positional behavior, including positional communication. People in positions are required to communicate in accordance with their positional roles to a certain extent and, in connection with some matters, they do communicate to a surprisingly great extent. For instance, an employee "Joe" asks his office manager for an

[2] Gordon Allport and Leon Postman, "The Basic Psychology of Rumor," *The Process and Effects of Mass Communication,* ed. Wilbut Schramm (University of Illinois Press, 1955), pp. 146-153.

Figure 4

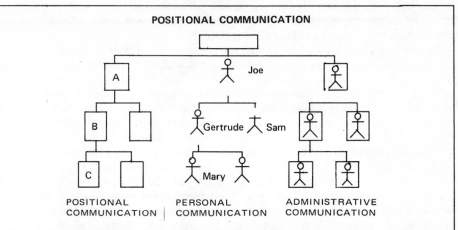

POSITIONAL COMMUNICATION

POSITIONAL COMMUNICATION | PERSONAL COMMUNICATION | ADMINISTRATIVE COMMUNICATION

Source: Charles E. Redfield, *Communication in Management: A Guide to Administrative Communication* (Chicago: University of Chicago Press, 1953), p. 12. Copyright 1953 by the University of Chicago. Reproduced by permission of the publisher.

afternoon off. But his manager, remindful of his being in position "A," says, "If this were just a matter between you and me, Joe, I would tell you to go ahead. But it would set a bad example. So, as office manager, I must say 'no.' "

Just as his position may affect the way a person communicates, so an individual can, and often does, affect pure positional communication. Take the case of the first sergeant who posts his K.P. list for the next morning. The first four names on the list are Anderson, Bennett, Costello, and Dennison, all of them privates whose names appear on the company roster in that order. Despite the fact that names are used, this is clearly an example of positional communication from a first sergeant to four privates. But the fifth and final name on the K. P. list is Zilch. Obviously, something outside the scope of positional communication has caused the first sergeant to put Private Zilch's name next on the list.

COMMUNICATION, MORALE, AND EFFICIENCY

The subject of communication first appeared on the managerial horizon during and immediately after World War II. At that time, the thinking went something like this: "The efficiency of our operation can be increased if we can only improve the morale of our employees. We can do this by improving communication with them. So let's communicate."

This line of reasoning — that we need to communicate to improve morale, which, in turn, will increase efficiency — held sway for about ten years. Today it is seldom encountered at all. At least three lines of inquiry and thinking have caused the picture to change.

First, it was found that morale was a much more complex phenomenon than had been believed theretofore. Morale was not something that you could measure very easily, nor was it, speaking crudely, something that you could turn on and off like a faucet. Morale, it was decided, was a very delicate, fragile, and unpredictable property, something like the changing moods of a child, which are so hard for adults to understand. There had been too many instances in which men with so-called poor morale were doing a competent day's work. It was found, too, that many of the roots of poor morale lay outside the office, where management could not be very effective. The whole subject became so tenuous that the very word "morale" tended to retreat in favor of the term "job satisfaction," which has a much more limited connotation.

Another development was the appearance of experimental evidence questioning, if not negating, the assumed relationship between communication and morale. Bavelas and Barrett, two researchers at the Massachusetts Institute of Technology, building on the earlier work of Levitt and other experimental psychologists, found that communication is a variable that can affect both morale and efficiency but not necessarily in the same direction.[3] Essence of the Bavelas and Barrett findings is shown schematically in Figure 5. Experimental groups are arranged in three different kinds of networks: The first (on the left) a circle, and the other two conventional hierarchies, the one with two levels and the other with three. The results were found to be that the group with everyone on a par reported the best morale; that is, the participants felt best about their work situation, in the circle arrangement, but in the circle arrangement, the work was the least efficient. In the other two arrangements, the morale score was not as good, but efficiency was considerably better. These findings do not suggest that anyone needs to add a little bad morale in his organization to increase its efficiency.

Figure 5

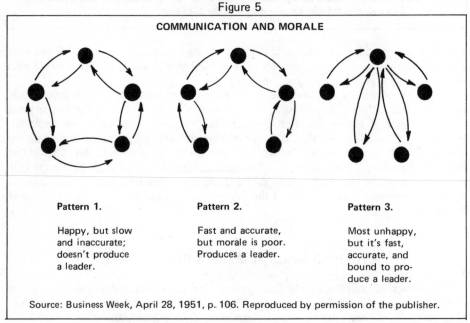

COMMUNICATION AND MORALE

Pattern 1.

Happy, but slow
and inaccurate;
doesn't produce
a leader.

Pattern 2.

Fast and accurate,
but morale is poor.
Produces a leader.

Pattern 3.

Most unhappy,
but it's fast,
accurate, and
bound to pro-
duce a leader.

Source: Business Week, April 28, 1951, p. 106. Reproduced by permission of the publisher.

A group at the University of Minnesota's Industrial Relations Center tested the relationship between communication and morale in five firms. Their hypothesis was that there is a relationship between communication and morale, that is, a positive relationship. But their conclusions after their research were to the contrary. They found no significant relationship whatsoever between employees' attitudes toward the company and their knowledge about the company. Strangely, and interestingly, they found consistent, though not statistically significant, negative correlations between information and attitude for supervisory groups in all five firms. Among these supervisory groups, the more infor-

---

[3] Alex Bavelas and Dermot Barrett, "An Experimental Approach to Organizational Communication,"*Personnel,* Vol. 27 (March, 1951), pp. 366-371.

mation they had about the company, the poorer their attitude was toward the company.[4] These findings were not statistically significant, but that does not make them less interesting.

Other blows to the assumed relationship between morale and communication came from theorists in the field. P. H. Cooke, in Australia, suggested that the efforts to improve morale through communication were entirely misdirected. Morale, he said, does not depend on communication. Instead, communication depends on morale.[5] In other words, there has to be an atmosphere favoring rather than interfering with successful communication. Recently, T. M. Higham, an English psychologist, came out in support of Cooke's position. Higham says that: "The pathetic notion that you can improve communication by giving more and better information should surely be allowed to die a natural death; you will not get any reception if you are not trusted; but if relations are good, then there is a good chance that what you say will be received, and that you will get cooperation in return."[6]

MORALE AND COMMUNICATION: A SUMMARY VIEW

These developments have forced us to retreat to a more conservative position. As I have said, we very seldom talk any longer about communication and morale. We talk instead about an "atmosphere" for communication. A good atmosphere for communication is evidenced by a feeling of mutual trust and respect. The parties to a communicative act need to understand and share a common concern for the success of their joint endeavors. This relationship is illustrated in Figure 6. "A" is any communicative act or system of communication — an order would be an example, a report would be another, manuals of policies or procedures would be yet others. Recollect that earlier (see Figure 2) the element of response or feedback was emphasized. Response is triggered and supported by interest and acceptance and I show, as element "C" at the base of the diagram, what I call 'interest and acceptance leading to response." Atmosphere for communication is shown as element "B" in the upper right portion of the diagram.

Figure 6

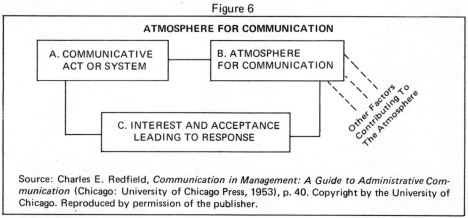

ATMOSPHERE FOR COMMUNICATION

A. COMMUNICATIVE ACT OR SYSTEM

B. ATMOSPHERE FOR COMMUNICATION

C. INTEREST AND ACCEPTANCE LEADING TO RESPONSE

Other Factors Contributing To The Atmosphere

Source: Charles E. Redfield, *Communication in Management: A Guide to Administrative Communication* (Chicago: University of Chicago Press, 1953), p. 40. Copyright by the University of Chicago. Reproduced by permission of the publisher.

[4] Dallis Perry and Thomas A. Mahoney, "In-Plant Communications and Employee Morale," *Personnel Psychology,* Vol. 8 (Autumn, 1955), pp. 339-346.

[5] P. H. Cook, "An Examination of the Notion of Communication in Industry," *Occupational Psychology,* Vol. 25 (January, 1951), pp. 1-14.

[6] T. M. Higham, "Basic Psychological Factors in Communication," *Occupational Psychology,* Vol. 31 (January, 1957), pp. 4-5.

The challenging thing about this three-part relationship is that it works in several directions. "C" is an element of "B"; that is to say, interest and acceptance improve the atmosphere for communication. "C" is also an element of "A"; that is, interest and acceptance improve the technical efficiency of a communicative act or system. A subordinate submits a report, "A," to which the superior responds, "C," which improves the atmosphere for communication between him and the subordinate "B." This improvement in "B," the atmosphere, improves the efficiency of "A" (whether it is an existing communication, or a subsequent communicative act).

It should be noted, though it is quite evident, that I do not suggest for a minute that the atmosphere for communication depends entirely on communicative behavior. There are other factors contributing to the atmosphere, but I personally draw the line here at saying what those factors are. Let us return now to Figure 6 and take an adverse situation: A superior has issued a number of instructions "A" which were unadaptable or were only for the record, and not to be enforced. The atmosphere for communication "B" has been adversely affected, which pretty well precludes any wholehearted interest and acceptance "C" preliminary to response.

There are serious barriers in many situations that limit the degree to which the atmosphere for communication can be improved and the degree to which interest and acceptance can be secured. These barriers form the subject matter of another chapter in this volume. Others discuss media and techniques of communication, subjects that fall in the area of "A." The atmosphere, no matter how good, is not enough. The media and the methods of transmission, no matter how efficient, are not enough. It is a combination of an efficient communicative act or system with a good atmosphere for communication that will assuredly elicit wholehearted interest and acceptance leading to response, and without interest, and without acceptance, and without response, you may as well talk to yourselves.

The Nature and Use of Committees

ESTILL I. GREEN

Never before have committees had it so good. Now that the psychologists, the social scientists, and the managerial mentors have led business safely away from that horrendous thing they refer to as monolithic organization; now that all the blessings of conjoint decision and consultative supervision have been showered upon us; now that we have reached the promised land of milk and honey and group-mindedness, the committee has become a widely used instrument of organization. No longer is the suggestion to appoint a committee greeted with sarcasm, suspicion or distrust. Everybody knows that management committees have made Jersey Standard and DuPont what they are today. Obviously, what's good at the top is good at all levels. So committeeism is rampant. In the vernacular, business has gone whole hog for committees.

To be sure, you do find an occasional skeptic. Herrymon Mauer, for example, tosses in this paragraph in *Fortune*,[1]

> When the chairman declares the meeting adjourned, the discussion has already gone on for an hour beyond schedule. One member has expressed opposition to the project at hand because he is in the habit of expressing opposition. A second has discussed extraneous issues in detail until finally ruled out of order. A third has asked the chairman to explain the project more fully. A fourth has repeated what the chairman has just said. And two members have fallen into an acrimonious dispute, using the project under discussion for display of personal rivalry. In the course of the meeting, one member dozed off; two others lost themselves in doodling; another began writing a memo on a different topic; and the chairman – uncertain at the beginning of the meeting as to the merits of the project – finds himself addled and exhausted at the end of it.

Then, too, you can find an occasional oldtimer who recalls the Kettering innuendo about committees. It appears that Mrs. Kettering was reading the newspaper account of Lindbergh's historic flight to LeBourget. "Isn't it wonderful!" she exclaimed. "And to think he did it all alone!" "Well," remarked the Boss, "it would have been still more wonderful if he had done it with a committee."

But who nowadays would take such detractors seriously? The old saw that a committee keeps minutes and squanders hours is clearly an exaggeration. The fact is that many estimable committees don't keep any minutes. Besides all this, committees have been

---

[1] H. Maurer, "Management by Committee," *Fortune*, April, 1953, p. 145.

Reprinted with permission of the Society for the Advancement of Management, from Advanced Management – Office Executive, *July, 1959,* pp. 24-28.

researched at Harvard. The Laboratory of Social Relations up there, in a bold departure from the mathematical theory of decision-making, has conducted an experimental investigation of the functioning of committees.[2] The result is nothing less than a set of working formulas for the successful conduct of committees.

The Harvard experts have determined the optimum number of members for a committee. And it isn't 7/10 of a man, that delightful if somewhat illusory figure deduced by Bruce Old in his classic treatise, *On the Mathematics of Committees, Boards and Panels*.[3] Not so, say the Cantabrigians. The optimum number of members is five, and the half-efficiency points lie in the vicinity of 3.8 and 6.9 members, respectively. As to that so-called Old's Law, perhaps better referred to as Old's Hypothesis — which asserts that the work output of a committee is inversely proportional to the organizational level of its members — recent results suggest that the Pentagon environment may have vitiated Old's researches. There appears to be some correlation, but the proportionality factor is not a unity.

Neglecting more esoteric details, the conditions prescribed by the Harvard sociologists for most effective committee performance are these: The committee members should be so chosen that their index of participation falls along a gradient — a multistep function ranging, presumably, from proficient members to drones. Fifty percent of the meeting time should be devoted to information and questions, and 50 percent to answers and reactions. The reactions are particularly important. There should be precisely two positive reactions for each negative one. A ratio lower than this indicates a divisive and emotional situation, while a higher one indicates inhibition, restraint, and domination by the chairman.

Thus an old art is by way of becoming an exact science. Among the instrumentalities of this new technology we find: high-level committees, low-level committees, technical committees, task forces, working groups, one-man committees, program committees, community fund committees and eleemosynary committees generally, anniversary luncheon committees, committees *ad hoc* and committees *ad infinitum*.

In view of the growing elaboration of committeeism, it appeared that a survey of certain committees existing in the organization with which the author is identified might yield interesting conclusions. Most of these committees were created for the purpose of exercising joint responsibilities where liaison between the staff and the technical departments is essential.

Figure 1 is a smokestack chart showing the density of committees by numbers of members. Except for the four committees out on the right-hand tail, we find a compact universe ranging in size from three to ten members, with a median, not at five, but at seven, and with two large peaks at six and eight. This might indicate either that committee efficiency falls below the optimum, or that, in the particular circumstances involved, people have learned to work together so harmoniously that the optimum number of members is larger than the Harvard figure.

Another interesting fact is that two-thirds of the committees have an even number of members. This seems to fly in the face of the tradition that the number of members should be odd. It would appear either that deadlocks are not frequent enough to generate a large demand for odd numbers, or that chairmen are quite adept at resolving tense situations.

The next chart (Fig. 2) shows the cumulative distribution curve of committees as a function of number of members. For comparison, a cumulative Poisson distribution curve

[2] R. F. Bales, "In Conference," *Harvard Business Review*, March-April, 1954, p. 44.

[3] Bruce Old, "On the Mathematics of Committees, Boards and Panels," *Scientific Monthly*, August, 1946, p. 129.

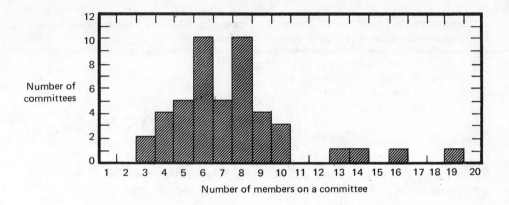

Figure 1—Density Distribution of Committees.

is shown. The close fit suggests that the committees under consideration are characterized by a high degree of randomness. All this is a long way from fulfilling Lord Kelvin's dictum that you haven't much of a science until you can put numbers on things, but at least there is progress in that direction. So much for quantitative analysis. From here on we shall not need to concern ourselves with anything so tightly disciplined as numbers or facts.

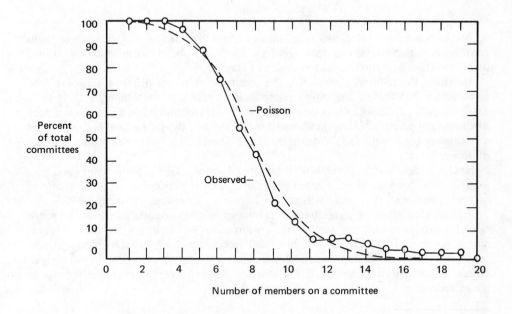

Figure 2—Cumulative Distribution Curve for Committees

Considering the prevalence of committees, we might, in all seriousness, ask ourselves a few questions about them. Here are some rather obvious ones:

1. What are the advantages of committees?
2. What are their disadvantages?
3. How should they be used?
4. How can successful operation be achieved?

ADVANTAGES

To start with, let's look at advantages. A lot has been written about this. Following is a list of some of the merits of committees, both published and unpublished.

Merits of Committees

1. Excellence of Decisions
   (a) Group solution
   (b) Combined judgment
   (c) Continuity
2. Strength of Decisions
   (a) Conjoint decision
   (b) Prestige of committee
3. Development of Personnel
   (a) Broadening
   (b) Teamwork
   (c) Leadership (chairman)
4. Supplement to Line Organization
   (a) Liaison
   (b) Communication

At the top of the list comes excellence of committee decisions. A number of heads contribute to the solution of each problem. There is a pooling of information. Mutual discussion stimulates the flow and interplay of ideas.

Moreover, the solution is objective. The combined judgment of many heads is bound to be better than that of one. Any weak spots in an individual suggestion are likely to be detected. As C. J. Berwitz has pointed out, the final answer should be a realistic synthesis of theory and practice.[4] Also, the committee has a sort of flywheel effect. It can be made a continuing body, with sufficient overlap of personnel assignments to provide continuity of policy.

Next, perhaps, comes strength of committee decisions. Group participation and conjoint decision conduce to good acceptance throughout the organization. Achievement of deserved prestige by the committee can be a further factor toward the same end.

Still another merit of committees is development of personnel. The members profit from friendships in different parts of the organization. The problems that confront them are different from the day-to-day grist, and frequently much broader. Moreover, the committee members develop a spirit of teamwork and a sense of respect for the ideas of others. And not least important is the practical training that the chairman receives in group leadership.

---

[4] C. J. Berwitz, "The Work Committee – An Administrative Technique," *Harvard Business Review*, January-February, 1952, p. 110.

Finally, a committee which includes in its makeup broad representation from different parts of the organization can be a useful supplement to the line organization. Almost of necessity the committee provides liaison between parts of the organization. Moreover, it can be made a valuable instrument for communication, both communication of its decisions and of the reasoning that underlies them, and also communication of general informational matter.

Some people say that one of the merits of a committee is that it counteracts organizational deficiencies. Another way of saying it might be that crosslinkages of elements make for strength and flexibility in organizations of people just as with molecules.

This is indeed an imposing array of advantages. Clearly committees are not used nearly enough. But before jumping to conclusions, we might inquire whether by chance there may be anything wrong with committees. Drawing in part upon published material, and in part upon experience, another list, this time of shortcomings of committees, has been compiled.

Shortcomings of Committees

1. Inferiority of Decisions
   (a) Compromise
   (b) Domination
   (c) Unqualified members
   (d) Lack of continuity
   (e) Inadequate motivation
   (f) Haste
2. Impotency of Decisions
   (a) Intermittency
   (b) Executive instrumentalities lacking
3. Wastefulness
4. Depreciation of Line Organization

SHORTCOMINGS

In the first place, committee decisions are notoriously inferior. The reasons for this are not far to seek. Committees must operate on an essentially unanimous basis. The members, drawn from different parts of the organization, will have conflicting interests. The net result is a wishy-washy compromise. Unanimity spells mediocrity.

Furthermore, the committee is subject to domination by the chairman. Discussion is therefore denied, creativity is stifled and the members are inhibited. In addition, committee decisions of any importance are subject to political influence. The members are chosen, not for their qualifications, but merely to represent departments.

Because of personnel turnover, committees lack continuity, so that their policies are likely to be erratic. Moreover, committees lack motivation. They are apt to be irresponsible and indifferent. The members can't be held to account for their mistakes. Someone has observed that a committee, like a corporation, "has neither a soul to be damned nor a body to be kicked."

Even worse is haste. As a rule the committee meets very seldom. Hence it has to rush through a crowded agenda, with no time for adequate consideration of anything. Awkward issues are usually placed in cold storage. No wonder the decisions are less than perfect!

185

Committee decisions likewise lack authority. This is explained in part by factors already mentioned. Furthermore, the committee is by its nature a spasmodic phenomenon, a discontinuous function. Its existence is necessarily limited to the time when it is in session. In between times it is a disembodied spirit. As such it possesses no power to carry out its decisions, and cannot handle subsidiary problems as they arise.

To go on with the list, committee operation is wasteful. Travel to and fro, tardiness, and outside interruptions during meetings, these are all spendthrifts of time. The committee operates at the speed of the least informed member. Hours are consumed in coming to grips with a problem. High-priced time is frittered away on irrelevancies and non-essential details. Moreover, old committees never die. After all, you can't expect them to commit hara-kiri. The best you can hope for is that an astute committee, when it has accomplished what it set out to do, will enter into a state of suspended animation. All in all, committees are an expensive luxury. As a final drawback, any committee setup detracts from the effectiveness of the line organization, and obscures the chain of command.

So now where are we? Just a short while ago we seemed to have found the foot of the rainbow. Now the sun's gone dim and the moon's turned black. We begin to suspect that the truth lies somewhere in between. But just where? Perhaps we can best get the answer by asking when and for what purposes a committee is useful.

USES OF COMMITTEES

The next chart (Fig. 3) lists some of the purposes more commonly served by committees, and over on the side a characterization of the effectiveness of each. To some extent these characterizations stem from published sources,[5] but in all cases they represent the opinions of the author.

Figure 3—Uses of Committees

Function	Value
For operational decisions	Special situations only
For facilitating acceptance	Fair
For implementing decisions	Poor
For advising management	Excellent
For creative technology	Fair to Poor
For unifying points of view	Good
As educational agency	Fair
As training agency	Fair

For handling regular administrative decisions, a committee is not very effective. For the most part such use should be limited to special situations. In facilitating acceptance of decisions, a well-chosen committee can play a useful part. It would, however, be inadvisable to place exclusive reliance on a committee to exercise this function. When it comes to implementing decisions, it is extremely difficult to clothe a committee with adequate authority. In general, such use of committees should be avoided like the plague.

---

[5] W. R. Spriegel and J. K. Bailey, "Functions of the Committee," *Advanced Management*, December, 1953, p. 12.

On the other hand, committees can be of extremely high utility in the area of advice to management. For such purposes as defining policies, formulating objectives and recommending plans, they are often nearly indispensable. Even in matters of less importance, the power of a committee in reflecting different points of view should not be underestimated. And consensuses, though seldom soul-stirring, are none the less valuable.

As to the question of whether a committee can contribute effectively to creative solution of technical problems, this is merely one phase of the broad questions of group creativity, which has been the subject of extensive discussion and limited investigation. To some extent the answer depends on semantics. Obviously neither a committee nor any other group can, as an entity, create ideas. Only individuals can do this. Individuals meeting as a group may, however, stimulate one another to create ideas, as in the rather overadvertised technique of "brain-storming." In most situations, a committee is likely to be less original and less efficient in producing ideas than its members acting separately. On the other hand, a committee confronted with the type of problem that requires a combination of creativity and judgment can usually reach a better solution than any one member could achieve.

Not only can committees reflect different points of view; they can on occasion go a long way toward reconciling differences. More broadly, a committee sometimes can be used to advantage as an educational agency. If this is a serious aim, then the committee members should have adequate individual time to devote to it.

Finally, the broadening and development that members and chairman receive through service on a committee is a real and valuable by-product. We should not forget, however, that the curve of individual benefit vs. time flattens off quite rapidly.

MANAGEMENT RESPONSIBILITIES

Comes now the fourth question: how can successful committee operation be achieved? Anything that can be said about this will sound obvious. Even so, a few things may be worth saying. After all, neglect of the obvious probably causes more trouble in this world than failure to fathom the obscure.

Suppose now for simplification we phrase the question this way: How can management, members and chairman contribute to committee success? Management, being the creator of committees, naturally comes first.

A few suggestions as to the usual obligations of management toward its committee offspring are ventured below. It needs no sage to tell us that management should start the committee off with a sound charter. More specifically, management should assign real problems, make the objectives clear and clothe the committee with adequate authority. In most cases the purpose and composition of the committee should be announced in writing.

Obligations of Management Toward Committees

1. Sound Charter
2. Qualified Members
3. Right Size
4. Turnover
5. Reports
6. Follow up Decisions
7. Discharge

Next, management has the responsibility of choosing qualified members. Actually, the desired characteristics are not too different from those we look for in the usual team approach to creative technology. Committee members should have broad vision, should be well-informed, creative, analytical, objective, and cooperative. They should be good workers, good listeners and so forth. Rarely is it possible to find all the desired qualities in a single person. The members should therefore be chosen so that their characteristics supplement one another. Also, the members should usually be representative of different parts of the organization, with good balance as to points of view. At most there should be only one peculiar member, or so-called "odd ball."

Of course, the magic figure of five committee members is not mandatory. However, the matter of committee size deserves careful attention.

There seems to be general agreement that for any continuing committee there are advantages to be had through turnover of membership. If left to the chairman or members this can lead to embarrassment. Accordingly, management should make definite arrangements for planned rotation or staggered terms.

Management has still other obligations. If a committee is worth having, it is worth at least occasional recognition. Management should know what its progeny are doing. Periodic reports, either oral or written, should be required. Any decisions reached by the committee should, to whatever extent necessary, be followed up by management. When at last the committee has fulfilled its purpose, it should not be left to linger on the vine. Let it be discharged with grateful appreciation.

RESPONSIBILITIES OF MEMBERS

Now what about the responsibilities of committee members? A few are noted below. First is advance preparation. The members have an obligation to familiarize themselves with any material circulated before the meeting. If they are assigned specific tasks to be done between meetings, they are obligated to complete these on time, or to inform the chairman that they cannot do so. In attendance the members should be regular and punctual.

Responsibilities of Committee Members

1. Advance Preparation
2. Regularity and Punctuality
3. Intelligent Participation

But most important, the members should participate intelligently in the proceedings. This means that they should be willing to work, that they should apply to the committee problems as much of scientific analysis and ingenuity as possible, that they should submerge bias, respect the integrity of other members, avoid irrelevant discussion, and contribute to the collective decision.

THE CHAIRMAN

Now we come to the key figure in the whole business — the committee chairman. It's easy enough to write a set of specifications. The chairman must be able to encourage, cajole, soothe, or inhibit. He must be calm, alert, agressive. He must at once use and restrain the genius. He must embolden the timid, stimulate the indifferent, convince the stubborn, make the superficial think.

Such demigods are hard to come by. Fortunately, an inexperienced chairman does not have to learn solely in the rugged school of experience. He can find a lot of published material to help him do his job. Enough has been written about successful committee operation to establish certain essentials. Some that should concern the chairman are listed here:

Responsibilities of Committee Chairman

1. Advance Planning
2. Business-like Procedure
3. High Participation
4. Familiarity with Published Material

Few things are more important to committee success than advance planning. A prepared agenda, normally circulated in advance, is a great help toward economy of committee time. A good secretary can relieve the chairman of a lot of work of this kind between meetings.

No one but the chairman can hold the committee to business-like procedure. He should first state and define each problem. Next he should solicit discussion, usually be asking questions. Only then should he invite solutions. The chairman should talk to the whole group, and show interest in the reactions of each member. In difficult situations, he should discover and exploit all areas of agreement. The meeting should proceed with neither undue haste nor waste time.

One key to success is a high rate of participation by the members. On any important matter, the chairman should obtain at least some verbal comment from each member. A high rate of suggestion, if it can be had, is even more valuable. In most cases, the accomplishments of the committee can be greatly enhanced by assigning in-between-meeting tasks to different members.

As already suggested, the chairman should make it his business to get acquainted with some of the available literature on committee or conference leadership, committee operation, group decision-making and the like. True, some of the socio-psychological studies go beyond the limits of practical application. Anyone who wades in very deep should be politely skeptical. Nevertheless, there is in the published material a good deal of direct value to any practitioner in the field of committee operation.

CONCLUSION

In summary, committees are here to stay. We can't do without them, and we can't do with them all that we might wish. Let us make the best of them. For advising management on how to do this, recourse might be had to a Committee on Committees.

Traditional Decision-Making Methods

HERBERT A. SIMON

Let us examine the western half of our map of decision-making techniques (Fig. I). This half represents methods that have been widely understood and applied in human organizations at least from the time of the building of the pyramids. In painting with a broad brush, I may convey the impression that there was no progress in organizational matters during the course of three millennia. I do not believe this to be true, and I do not intend to imply it. But the progress that was made did not enlarge the repertory of basic mechanisms to which I shall refer.

We shall consider, in turn, techniques for making programmed decisions and techniques for making nonprogrammed decisions.

Figure 1. Traditional and Modern Techniques of Decision Making

TYPES OF DECISIONS	DECISION-MAKING TECHNIQUES	
	Traditional	Modern

Programmed:
 	
Routine, repetitive decisions
Organization develops specific
    processes for handling them
	1. Habit
	2. Clerical routine:
	    Standard operating
	    procedures
	3. Organization structure:
	    Common expectations
	    A system of subgoals
	    Well-defined informa-
	    tional channels
		1. Operations Research:
		    Mathematical analysis
		    Models
		    Computer simulation
		2. Electronics data processing

Nonprogrammed:
 	
One-shot, ill-structured, novel,
    policy decisions
Handled by general problem-
    solving processes
	1. Judgment, intuition, and
	    creativity
	2. Rules of thumb
	3. Selection and training of
	    executives
		Heuristic problem-solving tech-
		niques applied to:
		    (a) training human decision-
		        makers
		    (b) constructing heuristic
		        computer programs

From The New Science of Management Decision *by Herbert A. Simon (New York: Harper & Row, 1960), pp. 8-13. Copyright © 1960 by School of Commerce, Accounts, and Finance. Reprinted by permission of Harper & Row, Publishers.*

has emerged over the years has been called facetiously "Gresham's Law of Planning." It states that programmed activity tends to drive out nonprogrammed activity. If an executive has a job that involves a mixture of programmed and nonprogrammed decision-making responsibilities, the former will come to be emphasized at the expense of the latter. The organizational implication of Gresham's Law is that special provision must be made for nonprogrammed decision making by creating specific organizational responsibilities and organizational units to take care of it. The various kinds of staff units that are so characteristic of large-scale modern organizations are mostly units specialized in particular aspects of the more complex nonprogrammed decision-making tasks. Market research units and research departments, to cite some examples, specialize in the intelligence phase of decision making; planning departments and product development departments specialize in the design phase. The creation of organizational units to carry on these activities allocates brain-power to nonprogrammed thought, and provides some minimal assurance that such thought will occur in the organization.

In summary, we have not had, in the past, adequate knowledge of the processes that are involved in decision making in complex situations. Human thinking, problem solving, and learning have been mysterious processes which we have labeled but not explained. Lacking an understanding of these processes, we have had to resort to gross techniques for improving nonprogrammed decision making: selection of men who have demonstrated their capacity for it; further development of their powers through professional training and planned experience; protection of nonprogrammed activity from the pressure of repetitive activity by establishing specialized organizational units to carry it on. We cannot say that these traditional techniques have failed — decisions do get made daily in organizations. Neither can we say that we might not do very much better in the future as our knowledge of the decision-making process grows.

New Techniques for
Programmed Decision Making

HERBERT A. SIMON

World War II brought large numbers of scientists trained in the use of mathematical tools into contact for the first time with operational and managerial problems. Designers of military aircraft could not plan aircraft armament without making assumptions about the formations in which the planes would be flown and the strategy of their commitment to action. Mathematical economists responsible for material allocation had to come to grips with complex logistics systems. The need for solving these problems, coupled with the tools of quantitative analysis that the scientists and econometricians brought with them, have produced some new approaches to management decision making that are of fundamental importance.

OPERATIONS RESEARCH

Many people — notably some of the pioneer operations researchers themselves — have tried to define operations research. The net result is usually to identify it with scientific method or straight thinking applied to management problems, and to imply that it is something that can be done only by natural scientists. Definitions of this kind, unintentionally imperialistic, raise the hackles of those identified with the earlier phrase "scientific management," who had thought that clear, scientific thinking is what they had always been doing. Except in matters of degree (e.g., the operations researchers tend to use rather high-powered mathematics), it is not clear that operations research embodies any philosophy different from that of scientific management. Charles Babbage and Frederick Taylor will have to be made, retroactively, charter members of the operations research societies.

A more understandable and defensible definition of operations research is a sociological one. Operations research is a movement that, emerging out of the military needs of World War II, has brought the decision-making problems of management within the range of interests of large numbers of natural scientists and, particularly, of mathematicians and statisticians.[1] The operations researchers soon joined forces with mathematical economists who had come into the same area — to the mutual benefit of both groups. And by

[1] Some standard works on operations research by leading members of the group are C. West Churchman, Russell L. Ackoff, and E. Leonard Arnoff, *Introduction to Operations Research* (New York: John Wiley & Sons, Inc., 1957); and Philip M. Morse and George E. Kimball, *Methods of Operations Research* (New York: John Wiley & Sons, Inc., 1951). The Operations Research Society of America publishes the journal *Operations Research*.

From The New Science of Management Decision *by Herbert A. Simon (New York: Harper & Row, 1960), pp. 14-20. Copyright © 1960 by School of Commerce, Accounts, and Finance. Reprinted by permission of Harper & Row, Publishers.*

now there has been widespread fraternization between these exponents of the "new" scientific management and men trained in the earlier traditions of scientific management and industrial engineering. No meaningful line can be drawn any more to demarcate operations research from scientific management or scientific management from management science.[2]

Along with some mathematical tools, which I shall discuss presently, operations research brought into management decision making a point of view called the systems approach. The systems approach is no easier to define than operations research for it is a set of attitudes and a frame of mind rather than a definite and explicit theory. At its vaguest, it means looking at the whole problem — again, hardly a novel idea, and not always a very helpful one. Somewhat more concretely, it means designing the components of a system and making individual decisions within it in the light of the implication of these decisions for the system as a whole.[3] We now know a *little* about how this might be done:

1. Economic analysis has something to say about rational behavior in complex systems of interacting elements, and particularly about the conditions under which the choices that are optimal for subsystems will or will not be optimal for a system as a whole. Economic analysis also has a great deal to say about the price system as a possible mechanism for decentralizing decision making.[4]

2. Mathematical techniques have been developed and adapted by engineers and economists for analysing the dynamic behavior of complex systems. Under the labels of servomechanism theory and cybernetics, such techniques underwent rapid development at about the time of World War II. They have considerable usefulness in the design of dynamic systems.[5]

Systems design is such a modish, if not faddish, word at the moment that I don't want to exaggerate the amount of well-understood technique that stands behind it. Nevertheless, it is fair to say that we can approach the design and analysis of large dynamic systems today with a good deal more sophistication than we could ten years ago.

THE MATHEMATICAL TOOLS

Operations research progressed from the talking to the action stage by finding tools with which to solve concrete managerial problems. Among the tools, some of them relatively new, some of them already known to statisticians, mathematicians, or economists, were linear programming, dynamic programming, game theory, and probability theory. Behind each of these formidable terms lies a mathematical model for a range of management problems. Linear programming, for example, can be used to provide a mathematical model for the operations of a gasoline refinery, or a commercial cattle-feed manufacturing operation. Dynamic programming can be used as a model for many inventory and production planning situations. Game theory models have been used to repre-

---

[2] The term "management science" was the trademark invented by the quantitatively oriented social scientists, primarily econometricians, who entered the area and who initially distinguished themselves from the operations researchers. The Institute of Management Sciences was organized in 1954. Its journal is the quarterly *Management Science*.

[3] See Churchman *et. al., op. cit.,* pp. 109-111.

[4] See Tjalling C. Koopmans, ed., *Activity Analysis of Production and Allocation* (New York: John Wiley & Sons, Inc., 1951).

[5] The word cybernetics was first used by Norbert Wiener in *Cybernetics* (New York: John Wiley & Sons, Inc., 1948), p. 19. A good exposition of these techniques may be found in Arnold Tustin, *The Mechanism of Economic Systems* (Cambridge: Harvard University Press, 1953).

sent marketing problems. Probability models have been used in a wide variety of contexts — they have been, perhaps, the most versatile of all.

Whatever the specific mathematical tool, the general recipe for using it in management decision making is something like this:[6]

1. Construct a *mathematical model* that satisfies the conditions of the tool to be used and which, at the same time, mirrors the important factors in the management situation to be analysed.

2. Define the *criterion function*, the measure that is to be used for comparing the relative merits of various possible courses of action.

3. Obtain *empirical estimates* of the numerical parameters in the model that specify the particular, concrete situation to which it is to be applied.

4. Carry through the mathematical process of finding the course of action which, for the specified parameter values, maximizes the criterion function.

In any decision-making situation where we apply this recipe successfully, we have, in fact, constructed a *program* for the organization's decisions. We have either annexed some decisions that had been judgmental to the area of programmed decision making,[7] or we have replaced a rule-of-thumb program with a more sophisticated program that guarantees us optimal decisions — optimal, that is, within the framework of the mathematical model.

But certain conditions must be satisfied in order to apply this recipe to a class of decision problems. First, it must be possible to define mathematical variables that represent the important aspects of the situation. In particular, a quantitative criterion function must be defined. If the problem area is so hopelessly qualitative that it cannot be described even approximately in terms of such variables, the approach fails. Second, the model will call for certain parameters of its structure to be estimated before it can be applied in a particular situation. Hence, it is necessary that there be ways of making actual numerical estimates of these parameters — of sufficient accuracy for the practical task at hand. Third, the specification of the model must fit the mathematical tools to be used. If certain kinds of nonlinearities are absolutely crucial to an accurate description of the situation, linear programming simply won't work — it is a tool adapted to mathematical systems that are, in a certain sense, linear. Fourth, the problem must be small enough that the calculations can be carried out in reasonable time and at a reasonable cost.

Some relatively simple management problems — for example, many problems of factory scheduling — turn out to be far too large for even such a powerful tool as linear programming. It is easy for the operations research enthusiast to underestimate the stringency of these conditions. This leads to an ailment that might be called mathematician's aphasia. The victim abstracts the original problem until the mathematical intractabilities have been removed (and all semblance to reality lost), solves the new simplified problem, and then pretends that this was the problem he wanted to solve all along. He expects the manager to be so dazzled by the beauty of the mathematical results that he will not remember that his practical operating problem has not been handled.

It is just as easy for the traditionalist to overestimate the stringency of the conditions. For the operations research approach to work, nothing has to be exact — it just has to be close enough to give better results than could be obtained by common sense without the mathematics. Furthermore, it is dangerous to assume that something is essentially qualitative and not reducible to mathematical form until an applied mathematician has had a try at it. For example, I have often been told that "you can't place a dollar value on a lost order from inventory runout." But why, the answer goes, can't you estimate the penalty cost of taking emergency action to *avoid* losing the order — shipping, for example, by air

---

[6] See Churchman *et al., op. cit.*, chap. V.

[7] Thus, operations research, in addition to providing techniques for programmed decisions, also expands their boundaries.

express? Thus, many things that seem intangible can be reduced, for management decision-making purposes, to dollars and cents.

But we need not spin out these generalities. Mathematical techniques are now being applied in a large number of situations. In many of these situations, when mathematical techniques were first proposed there was much head shaking and muttering about judgment. The area of application is large. It is growing. But there is no indication that it will cover the whole of management decision making.

ENTER THE COMPUTER

It was an historical accident with large consequences that the same war which spawned operations research saw also the birth of the modern digital computer as a practical device.[8] The computer was conceived as a device for exploring by numerical analysis the properties of mathematical systems too large or too complex to be treated by known analytic methods. The systems of differential equations that were arising in aerodynamics, meteorology, and the design of nuclear reactors were obvious candidates for this treatment. It was soon realized that even larger problems were generated by the linear programming and dynamic programming models of management decision problems. Whatever the conceptual power of the mathematical models that have been used in operations research, their actual use in practical schemes for decision making hinged on the fortuitous arrival on the scene of the computer.

While computers were initially conceived as devices for doing arithmetic on problems that had first been cast in a mathematical form having known solution procedures, it gradually became clear that there were other ways of using them. If a model or simulation of a situation could be programmed for a computer, the behavior of the system could then be studied simply by having the computer imitate it and without solving, in the traditional sense, the mathematical equations themselves. In putting it this way, I make simulation sound like a simpler and more powerful technique than it really is. In general, we would need to simulate the behavior of the system not under a single set of conditions but over a whole range of conditions. Having simulated it, we would need some procedure for evaluating the results — for deciding whether the system behavior was satisfactory or not. Finally, before we could simulate the behavior, we would have to estimate accurately enough the structure of the system — simulation techniques do not at all reduce the burden of providing numerical estimates.

In spite of these limitations and difficulties, simulation has enabled an airline to determine how many reserve aircraft it should keep on hand, has been used to study highway congestion, has led to improvement in inventory control procedures for a huge warehousing operation, and has accomplished many other difficult tasks.

Of course, the bread-and-butter applications of computers to business decision making have had little to do with either mathematical models or simulation. They have had to do with automating a whole host of routine and repetitive data-processing activities that had for many years been highly programmed but not nearly so completely automated. Through this development, large-scale data processing is becoming a factory operation, an operation that exceeds in degree of automation all but a few manufacturing processes.

THE REVOLUTION IN PROGRAMMED DECISION MAKING

The revolution in programmed decision making has by no means reached its limits, but

---

[8] A general book on the history of the development of computers and on their use by management is John A. Postley, *Computers and People* (New York: McGraw-Hill Book Company, Inc., 1960).

we can now see its shape. The rapidity of change stems partly from the fact that there has been not a single innovation but several related innovations, all of which contribute to it.

1. The electronic computer is bringing about, with unexpected speed, a high level of automation in the routine, programmed decision making and data processing that was formerly the province of clerks.

2. The area of programmed decision making is being rapidly extended as we find ways to apply the tools of operations research to types of decisions that have up to now been regarded as judgmental — particularly, but not exclusively, middle-management decisions in the area of manufacturing and warehousing.

3. The computer has extended the capability of the mathematical techniques to problems far too large to be handled by less automatic computing devices, and has further extended the range of programmable decisions by contributing the new technique of simulation.

4. Companies are just beginning to discover ways of bringing together the first two of these developments: of combining the mathematical techniques for making decisions about aggregative middle-management variables with the data-processing techniques for implementing these decisions in detail at clerical levels.

Out of the combination of these four developments there is emerging the new picture of the data-processing factory for manufacturing, in a highly mechanized way, the organization's programmed decisions — just as the physical processing factory manufactures its products in a manner that becomes increasingly mechanized. The automated factory of the future will operate on the basis of programmed decisions produced in the automated office beside it.

Systems Analysis in Public Welfare

ARTHUR SPINDLER

Describing systems analysis in public welfare today is no different than predicting the adult vocation of a child when he has just passed his first birthday. It represents future expectations, not present accomplishment. The thrust of systems analysis has been in the physical sciences, with, of course, major emphasis given to our defense and space establishments and defense and space industries. It has been only during the past few years that the social sciences have emerged as the arena for systems analysis, with the same professional groups of operations research, mathematicians and computer programmers leading the way in a small, but decisive effort.

We could take a poll and ask how many of you have been involved in, or have read of, a bonafide systems analysis in public welfare. I am sure few would respond affirmatively. This should not surprise us. Very little has yet been done to apply systems analysis in public welfare. At the national level we occasionally have received reports of this. Recently, we were apprised of the use of the PERT technique to evaluate several programs of the Virginia State Department of Welfare and Institutions in Richmond. The District of Columbia Department of Public Welfare last year completed an analysis of several of its new family-assistance programs. The Title V work experience program has been given its fair share of analysis.

SPANNING ALL HUMAN BEHAVIOR

Because public welfare deals with social and economic problems spanning all human behavior, its program goals which become the heart of systems analysis can be defined in varying degrees of specificity. At one extreme, we can cite the explicit goal of public assistance income maintenance to meet the basic needs of individuals and families. We may disagree on the definition of basic needs, but I believe we can all agree that this program goal is readily identifiable and universally acknowledged.

At the other extreme, a program goal which is amorphous, is the provision of social services to improve the social functioning of the child and family to remove dependency and achieve self-support. We recognize this goal to be a significant one in public welfare. But because we cannot reach agreement readily on its definition to permit any meaningful dialogue on the subject, it becomes essential to spell out its components and make these subgoals the common ground of understanding, discussion and evaluation. In DHEW we identify three separate subgoals to improve the social functioning of the child and family: to prevent and alleviate social and economic handicaps which face the child and family; to protect dependent children; and to develop the basic and employment

Reprinted with permission of the American Public Welfare Association and the author, from Public Welfare, *Vol. 28, No. 3 (July, 1968,) ,pp. 227-230.*

199

skills of the older child and the family head. These subgoals are an integral part of the DHEW planning, programming, budget system.

The state of the art of public welfare today needs all the talent, resources, and technique it can muster. A quick review of the agenda of this conference and those of recent years confirms the fact that we have more questions which need answering than we have of money, facilities, and staff. We can all agree this condition will continue into the foreseeable future.

Systems analysis offers us a tool which combines method with imagination. It is obviously not the only one we can turn to, but is one which opens an avenue for looking at our problems differently and provides us with a number of alternatives supported by facts and figures presented in a new and different way. True, the alternatives may be those we have considered before and the data may also be familiar, but their presentation has never been more vivid. Systems analysis does not give us an automatic solution to the problems we face, but does offer to bring them into clearer focus so that, if we choose to make decisions objectively and rationally, we will more likely make them through systems analysis. One of the certainties we must emphasize, however, is the fact that public welfare policy and program decisions are always so politically, socially, and economically sensitive that the choice is rarely one which can be made solely on the basis of objective, rational thought.

IT DOES SHED LIGHT

This does not mean that the scientific method which systems analysis represents does not have an important place in public welfare, because it does shed light where there is more than a full measure of emotion and bias. Somehow we must find a way to change the environment of public welfare to fulfill the promise expressed in our public welfare goals. I am reminded of the National Advisory Council on Public Welfare Report of June, 1966, which I keep on my desk and refer to frequently. It enunciates public welfare goals more clearly than any other document I have ever read, and the program plans which we are responsible for developing on the national scene to meet the objectives in that report must be formulated rationally and objectively.

The example of the value of systems analysis in public welfare which I have chosen deals with the all-important program of AFDC. The program goal which national, state, and local welfare agencies aspire to alike, is to improve the capability of AFDC parents who can and want to work to be properly trained and employed, thus to become economically self-supporting. The Social Security Amendments of 1967 recently passed by the Congress make this one of its most important objectives. Three closely related programs are to become a means for achieving this general objective: the community work and training program, the day care program, and a program to provide wage subsidies in jobs for which trainees could be qualified.

One of my colleagues, Dr. Worth Bateman of the DHEW Office of the Assistant Secretary for Program Coordination, devoted several months of inquiry to this subject encompassing not only Health, Education, and Welfare programs, but those of the Office of Economic Opportunity, the Department of Labor, Department of Housing and Urban Development, other Federal agencies, and the experiences of state and local governments. Nor did he constrain himself to acceptance of the features of programs which are now in operation, as you will observe.

SOUGHT ANSWERS

He sought the answers to the following questions:

1. What is the universe of AFDC parents who are employable?
2. What are the handicaps which prevent their employment?
3. What governmental measures can be taken to eliminate or reduce the effect of these handicaps to permit them to undergo education and training to become fully employed?
4. What programs are now authorized or which can be devised to have them become employed and self-supporting?
5. What is the most economical and effective mix of programs which can achieve these goals for the maximum number of this group?
6. What are the costs of the alternative program mixes?
7. What expectations can be reasonably forecast to the success of these programs?
8. What impact will these programs have upon the reduction in AFDC caseloads?
9. How will this affect the Federal program of grants to states for public assistance and state and local public welfare agencies for the next five years?

I do not plan to give you the specifics of Dr. Bateman's findings or his analysis at this time. This is a subject which should be dealt with separately with enough time for fuller treatment. I believe it more valuable here to review the logical steps in the systems analysis he performed which make this tool so effective and which helped convince the Secretary of the Department to reach the conclusion to support it.

First, the basis for analysis was a continuing increase in AFDC caseloads throughout the nation. The DHEW staff predicted no end to this trend in the foreseeable future, assuming no change in present social and economic conditions.

Second, the decision was made following staff discussions of alternatives for a systems workup to undertake a massive effort to train AFDC mothers and fathers for employment and job placement.

Third, a model was created which characterized the total problem and the effects upon it of different program approaches. These included various combinations of arrangements for day care services, community work and training and employment services and support.

Fourth, cost effectiveness measures were applied using historic cost factors of similar or related programs and forecasts of cost trends for a five-year period. In every instance cost factors were selected on a conservative basis so that economic conclusions would be understated rather than overstated. The mix of programs were measured using these cost factors and the resultant offsets or cost reductions computed from the anticipated reduction in payments to AFDC families.

Fifth, each of the program elements of day care, community work and training, and employment was analyzed in the search for the most practical and most economical groupings. Among those considered to be immediately significant for day care in light of present-day experience were the employment of AFDC mothers to provide neighborhood family day care services for children of parents to free them for training and employment, the employment of other poor but non-recipient mothers to provide such day care services; and the purchase of group day care for children of AFDC families. Other alternatives were also considered as worthy of more intensive review once the overall program was adopted and its implementation became a reality. Among these were : the expansion of full or preschool programs modeled on the OEO full year Headstart Program to be administered under Title I of the Elementary and Secondary School Act; expansion in the use of commercial group care facilities, use of baby-sitters, expansion of child care services as part of the Child Welfare Services Program of the Children's Bureau (introduced in the bill sponsored by Senator Abraham Ribicoff); expansion of OEO day care services through child and parent centers; and an expansion of day care services provided in multiservice centers sponsored by neighborhood facilities grants of HUD.

To reveal the comprehensiveness of this analysis further, a number of different approaches was applied to the model in regard to the employment of AFDC parents. One approach, mentioned above, was their employment in the provision of neighborhood family day care to "kill two birds with one stone." A second approach was the supplementation of income of AFDC parents who become employed with an inadequate income to meet their basic needs. A third approach, and, of course, the most successful, was to envision employment of former AFDC parents with income adequate to maintain themselves independently. The fourth approach was to foresee the expectation of fully trained AFDC parents who are unable to obtain employment. Provision was made in the model to support this latter group through Federal financial participation in the creation of jobs with public agencies.

A selection was made among the various combinations of alternatives to provide for significantly enlarged community work and training programs in all states, with Federal financial participation consistent with the provision of the Social Security Amendments of 1967 at the rate of 75-25 percent matching. In addition, the day care program was selected with a mix of equal numbers of children in neighborhood family day care and group care. To assure successful employment of trained AFDC mothers and fathers, conservative estimates were drawn of the expectation of those who would find immediate employment at favorable income levels, those who would succeed in employment with incomes which would require supplementation through public assistance, and finally, those who want, but cannot find, suitable employment. This latter group would become employed through a program of subsidized wages in Federal, state and local public agencies and, perhaps, in the private sector. The specifics of this have not yet been developed, although there is full realization that it is a deeply sensitive area of public policy.

This systems analysis was made part of a program memorandum to support the DHEW five-year program and financial plan 1969-1973. Needless to say, if adopted, the plan will have major ramifications throughout public welfare at Federal, state, and local levels for years to come. The steps required to implement it are now being worked on by staff of the Social and Rehabilitation Service of the Department.

Here then is a living example of the value of systems analysis in public welfare. There is every good reason to surmise that as we advance in the use of this technological resource, we will have other reports of systems analysis initiated throughout the public welfare system.

Putting Action into Planning

ROBERT H. SCHAFFER

Corporate planning — that collection of methods, departments, functions, tools, and activities which companies buy or create to help assure their future — has acquired an enviable reputation in books, articles, management seminar programs, and business courses. But this reputation or "image," like the visible part of an iceberg, is only part of the story. Very little attention has been paid to the submerged part of the iceberg — the increasingly widespread reports of disappointment and frustration among those companies which have tried formal long-range planning. Furthermore, there still remain great numbers of companies which, for all the glowing reports, cannot or will not undertake formal corporate planning as a tool for their own development.

The trouble is that as corporate planning has become increasingly popular and sophisticated, its methods have become increasingly divergent from corporate reality.

The essential purpose of corporate planning should be to enable managers to act today with increased skill, speed, and confidence to produce desired results tomorrow. In practice, however, planning consists of activities and programs designed to produce written plans and blueprints. And even though planning technologists have devised powerful tools for analysis and prediction, the procedures for producing written corporate plans frequently fail to expand management's capacity to take the actions that will achieve its goals.

Let us first examine the reasons planning so often fails to achieve its purposes, and then turn to a more promising approach.

TRADITIONAL STARTING POINTS

Over the years, a fairly uniform pattern for corporate planning has taken shape under the leadership of specialists in business forecasting, economic analysis, market research, financial planning, and related disciplines. The classic steps are these:

1. *Research* — to analyze corporate strengths, weaknesses, and other factors, and to determine the opportunities and risks created by external trends.

2. *Formulation of objectives* — to define what the company should become in the long-term future.

3. *Strategic planning* — to develop an overall framework outlining how the corporation will move to its ultimate objectives.

4. *Operational planning* — to create steps that each department and function should take in order to carry out the strategic plans.

The procedure seems perfectly logical. But what actually happens when companies follow it? Here are some typical examples:

□ One company, dependent on a few large customers who distributed through supermarkets, made a thorough analysis of its business and competition as a basis for long-range planning. Most of the findings were promising, but there was some evidence that one competitor might be testing a material which could threaten the future of this enterprise. Top management rationalized, saying, "There's been talk about using that material ever since we've been in the industry. It will never happen."

Accordingly, the company undertook a major expansion program which, as it turned out, trapped it into obsolescence.

□ A large company conducted some thorough studies of future technology and markets which highlighted important opportunities for the firm and exposed some major risks. At the time, however, the company was engaged in a major profit-improvement program, the absorption of several acquisitions, and some critical negotiations with government agencies. The planning studies seemed remote from these projects. The vice president responsible for planning could never get his associates to devote the thought and time necessary to analyze and act on his studies, and as a result their potential was never realized.

□ In the course of setting possible objectives for a successful consumer products company, its top managers decided it could broaden its limited product line or push into new market areas, or both. Two senior executives, however, took exactly opposite positions on this question. The president could not see how to resolve the dispute. Since this management believed that further planning depended on its ability to set long-range objectives, it failed to take any more steps (which undoubtedly would have showed that the conflict of opinion oversimplified the real choices open to management).

Unanticipated Hazards

These cases illustrate that no matter how logical it may seem to start planning with objective research, a company's past can easily trap it into doing the wrong research or prevent it from accepting or coping with the results of the right research. The cases also illustrate that even greater hazards loom in attempts to formulate long-range objectives at the beginning of the planning process. If the objectives are either mere extrapolations into the future of current trends, or vague expressions of high aspirations, they are worthless. If, on the other hand, they call for a major change in direction, management may well lack the know-how, confidence, and commitment necessary to translate them into real achievement.

The fact is that the ability to define future objectives in terms that crystallize the needs for new, effective action today is one of the most subtle and consummate skills of the manager. It requires extensive experience and wisdom. Yet in the conventional plan-making process it comes at the beginning; it is the step on which all other steps are based, not the product of those steps.

A similar discrepancy between logic and reality is encountered at the next step. Having defined objectives, management must now create strategic plans which are further refined into specific operating plans. In theory, when the "whistle is blown," the plans should become infused into the mainstream of the enterprise as dynamic, coordinated actions. In practice, however, the actions required to carry out the plans may not be consistent with the actions required to meet immediate operating goals. They may even conflict with the steps necessary to increase sales, introduce a new product line, settle a labor contract, or improve operating efficiency. It is not hard to guess which plans give way.

In short, no matter how impeccable the logic of plan making or how powerful its tools, it is not surprising to hear with increasing frequency of:

- Companies that have developed new objectives and plans but continue operating much as before.
- Staff planners who produce brilliant studies and blueprints which end up in file drawers.
- Managers of departments or divisions who are required to set one- and five-year goals but regard this as a dreary chore and cannot wait to deliver their "plans" to headquarters in order to get back to the real work of running their divisions.
- Companies that create ambitious plans only to discover they lack the resources, know-how, or drive to carry them out; or, equally as bad, companies that design long-term plans in terms of present performance levels and thus guarantee that today's inadequacies will become tomorrow's standards of performance.
- Companies that formulate bold, long-term plans when they do not know how to achieve the short-term results that are essential to remaining in business.

To these must be added the countless medium-size and smaller companies which are afraid to tackle corporate planning — or try it and give it up quickly — because the formal plan-making procedures, which are universally equated with corporate planning, are too expensive, too diversionary, and are focused on issues remote in time and foreign in concept.

Placing the Blame

These corporate planning failures — and the failure to plan at all — are almost always ascribed to top management. "They spend too much time on today's crises and not enough time thinking about tomorrow," say the critics, or, "They are not really committed to long-range planning." From these oversimplified diagnoses follow equally oversimplified cures, such as "top management must get behind planning," or "the people who will implement the plans should be involved in making them," or "management must devote more time to planning."

These diagnoses and cures are all based on the same faulty assumption; namely, that the formal plan-making processes constitute the essence of what corporate planning ought to be. It is ignored that these intellectual/technical processes provide only a few of the elements a management needs in order to increase control over the direction of an enterprise. These processes do not teach managers how to translate remote objectives into workable step-by-step plans, nor how to translate plans into tangible immediate actions. They do not help top management mesh the work of departments and groups in new ways to produce new results. They do not help managers become more skilled in gaining consensus about and commitment to new directions.

Nor do traditional plan-making procedures teach managers how to think about old problems in new ways, how to get new performance from the same people, or how to use current successes and frustrations as the basis for constantly recreating longer term objectives and plans. In fact, such procedures do just the opposite. They often impose the requirements for tomorrow's success as *additional* demands competing for the time and attention of already overloaded managers.

In short, the procedures of research and analysis, objective-formulation, and plan making simply do not accelerate progress in many areas where progress is necessary to gain control over where the enterprise is going.

If corporate planning is to make its full contribution to management, it will have to be redesigned so that it not only expands the capacity of executives to analyze and conceptualize, but also increases their ability to shift corporate directions and to accomplish new objectives with the same resources. It must become an overall strategic framework for moving forward on many fronts toward the goal of increased managerial control. Of especial importance, it must help management to gain *practical, successful experiences in setting a goal, creating a plan to reach it, and making the plan succeed*.

The need is for what might be described as a "development approach" to mesh corporate planning and corporate action. Managers begin by using planning disciplines to accomplish immediate and urgent but relatively simple goals; then they exploit the skills and abilities developed by these early projects to tackle more complex, and more far-reaching goals. Thus corporate planning begins not with the remote, but with the immediate. Top management focuses on a few urgent issues and sets about to deal with them in a new way. For example:

☐ In one company the process began with a plant move which was hopelessly behind schedule even though each of the vice-presidents and functional managers was doing the best he could to facilitate it. The president sent a letter to each of his executives saying that (a) the move had to accelerate and (b) an all-day conference was scheduled in two weeks to decide how to do so. Each man was to come with his thoughts on how the original schedule could be met.

After the day's session, the group drafted work assignments outlining what had to be done on each critical question. These were issued to several task groups. It was agreed that within one week each group would prepare a specific plan for accomplishing its part of the job.

The groups produced the plans. Eventually they were able to improve the schedule. But they accomplished much more than that. They had seen and grasped in a new way the relationship between a company-wide objective, an interrelated set of plans to achieve it, and the actions necessary to make the plans work. They could now begin to apply this pattern to other knotty questions confronting the company.

Key Principles

At the heart of the development approach to planning are two strategic principles:

1. The first planning projects should be focused on goals that are urgent but achievable, so that success can be realized in a relatively short time. It should be possible to get the "feel" of the complete cycle from objective-setting to planning, action, and accomplishment within a matter of weeks or months.

2. These initial projects should be designed and carried out in ways that help managers to develop new competence and confidence in using planning tools and disciplines. For instance, each project's goals should be carefully spelled out. The steps to reach a goal should be thought through to the point where they can be stated in the form of rigorous, disciplined, written plans, including managerial responsibilities, timing, subprojects, and related information. Methods for measuring and for reviewing progress should also be incorporated in the plan.

In effect, therefore, each project parallels, in miniature, the ponderous steps of the master-plan-making procedure. Instead of taking years to get around the cycle for the first time (as with a master plan), however, each task is done in weeks or months. Instead of making each step of the planning process a monumental undertaking, which requires time, energy, perseverance, and commitment well beyond what management can realistically invest, the aim is: to move from the identification of a goal to its accomplishment in a short time, using more disciplined and rigorous approaches, and then to move to more ambitious planning cycles.

Let us see how two companies used the development approach to gain a new grasp of their futures:

☐ A manufacturing company whose product line was becoming obsolete began planning with what appeared to be a logical step; it employed a consulting firm to create a long-term product-development program. In collaboration with the company's managers, the firm produced a sound and comprehensive plan which was to begin with a detailed study of the company's present markets and then move to a careful identification of the new markets that might be served and an analysis of each. But the company had neither the time nor the resources for such an elaborate long-term plan.

Then an alternative approach was tried. The company managers selected one new product idea in which they all had some faith. A group of key managers was assigned to translate this idea into a profitable product. They were to treat the project as an experiment. Success would be measured not just by results on this product idea, but also by the quality of plans that could be developed from this "pilot project" for testing and exploiting other product ideas. This was an exciting assignment that could bear fruit within a year.

☐ A large service company whose planning department had developed some very far-reaching corporate plans discovered these would be only "castles in Spain" unless the company could overcome some fairly immediate hazards to survival. Top management undertook a major operations-improvement effort aimed both at rejuvenating immediate profits and at developing managerial competence to adjust operations more rapidly in response to changing market conditions. Considerable stress was placed on developing new tools and methods of management as well as on achieving immediate profit results. As the operating managers progressed on this program, they began to see that planning was part of their jobs. And for the first time a meaningful bridge was built between shorter range operational planning and longer range corporate development.

Extending the Scope

Once some tangible results have been produced in the initial projects, managers are in position to move to a more sophisticated level of planning and action. Now that they have been through the entire cycle, they have more confidence and sureness as to how to select and define objectives, lay out plans to reach them, generate action to fulfill the plans, and coordinate different elements of a complex action program. They are in a position to take further steps, to broaden and extend the process which I have described:

☐ An aggressive young executive from the headquarters of a diversified corporation was appointed general manager of the appliance division, the original business of the company. Recognizing that the division was drifting, he decided that he had to generate a new sense of direction. He brought his executives together to consider what the division's objectives should be. He issued imaginative assignments to study long-term growth opportunities. But no matter what they studied, and no matter how they went about it, the answers all seemed to suggest that they continue doing more or less what they had been doing.

Months drifted by. Realizing that his associates were not ready to think about future objectives in bold, creative terms, the general manager tried a new tack. He held some conversations with his subordinates, not to persuade them of the importance of planning, but to learn about the things *they* felt needed to be done. Almost all of them offered suggestions for improving relationships between the plants and sales offices. In addition, there was widespread dissatisfaction over the service that technical departments were giving to operating people. Also, they all were concerned with the complexities of the product line and what might be done to simplify it.

The general manager organized some relatively modest projects to achieve immediate progress on these issues. The projects were designed to get people from different plants and different functions collaborating on careful studies and finding alternative solutions. Though the assignments were modest, the general manager outlined precise directions. He required each group to define its goals carefully, to support assumptions with data, and to be explicit about the purposes of each project. In the case of action programs, plans were to be written and they were to specify steps, dates, responsibilities, and measures of progress.

The managers began to make headway on the long-standing problems and roadblocks they were investigating. Of course, they were still focusing on what were, to the general manager, tactical operating matters, not on the division's business strategy. But they were working effectively on organized, planned change; they were making progress, succeeding, and developing new skill and confidence.

Gradually, as this happened, the general manager began to issue more far-reaching assignments. These new projects called for technical know-how which his colleagues did not have, and they began to consult the corporation's staff experts, whom they had formerly regarded as intruders. Their horizons gradually broadened, their sophistication in planning methodology improved. The general manager still hit some roadblocks when he tried to push his people too fast, but he found no other limits to the progress he could generate.

FRAMEWORK FOR PROGRESS

What role should specialists have in planning? This question has often perplexed businessmen, and justifiably so. Too often, staff specialists, outside consultants, and other "experts" in planning are cast in the role of missionaries. They "sell" new techniques, urge management to spend more time on planning, or push for acceptance of plans which they have developed. The results are often discouraging.

In the developmental approach to planning, things work the other way. Under the spur of having to program their way toward increasingly tough goals, operating managers come to staff people for help — help in carrying out studies and in using planning techniques, information systems, mathematical modeling, market research, and so forth. Line managers develop skill in defining their own needs, and thus become better customers for staff and consulting experts. Staff contributions are designed to support line management's progress in increasing its grasp and control. The staff work never develops a "life of its own."

Similar progress occurs in the sphere of executive development. Instead of "training" managers in the hope that they will become more skilled in setting objectives and organizing people to accomplish them, the development approach encourages learning by doing. Managers take part in projects which require the use of new techniques and disciplines to produce new results. In other words, growth and development of managers is a natural product of successful experience, not a prerequisite.

What about the "human relations" aspects of planning? Many top managers have become convinced that their companies cannot progress rapidly toward new goals until management conflicts are "confronted" and resolved, resistance to change is overcome, and people are committed to planning. But all this takes vast investments of time and energy and, even when apparently successful, can leave top management still wondering how to set and achieve new goals. Success in reaching even one new goal and in mastering new disciplines, on the other hand, can produce better understanding among managers and commitment to further action.

The same logic applies to shifts in organizational structure. In the initial planning projects, managers may experiment with temporary committees, changed alignments of executives, or new methods of collaboration. This gives them fresh perspective on questions of how to group people in order to get work done. Then, as they tackle increasingly complex and far-reaching objectives, they are more certain about organization changes which will support the desired progress.

Goals Match Capability

As the foregoing suggests, the developmental approach means that the scope of corporate goals expands in close relationship to growth in management's ability to achieve difficult goals. By contrast, in the traditional approach to corporate planning, objectives almost always outreach the steps that can be programmed with real confidence, thus tending to produce a perpetual sense of frustration and inadequacy. To highlight the difference between the traditional and the developmental approaches, let us consider a case example of planning as it evolved in a company making paper products:

☐ The manager of corporate marketing and the head of R&D agreed that even though their company was enjoying unprecedented growth and profitability, its product line was getting too complex, its markets were shifting too rapidly, and its technology was presenting it with too many choices. They further agreed that management could not deal with these problems using an informal approach, as had traditionally been done. The two executives strongly recommended that a planning department be established to help the company set objectives and develop plans to achieve them.

The president was adamant. "We already have too many plans," he said; "we need to learn how to carry them out." He pointed out how successful the company had been, and he inquired how some young "academic types" could possibly contribute to the acceleration of this progress.

The two executives were depressed. They almost convinced themselves that unless the president could be reformed, there was little hope for the future. Fortunately they realized in time there was an alternative course of action. The turning point came when they reluctantly decided to do the best planning they could with whatever resources they themselves could muster. They began by responding to an obvious need for better control over the work of the R&D function itself — for such steps as internal coordination and supervision of projects, schedules, and budgets. Some managers in the department were invited to help draft their own assignments for restructuring activities where the need for better control was most obvious and urgent. These managers drew up action plans and began making progress within a few weeks.

Heartened by this initial success, the marketing and R&D heads went further. To guide their efforts in product development, they began with some very rough corporate growth goals which the president had once outlined. They asked the sales department to help them estimate the gap between projected sales of company products and the growth objectives. A series of informal discussions began. For the first time, the sales, marketing, and R&D departments collated all their data on the future of current products; also, some marketing studies were carried out to supplement these data. A small group began to meet regularly to put the pieces of the puzzle together. The information developed by the group was periodically discussed with the entire top management team.

209

Next, a series of work-planning conferences was organized for the marketing, sales, and R & D departments. Other departments willingly agreed to help prepare for these conferences and to participate in them.

Thus an important change in the company came about. Top management began to collect, look at, and act on the right data. It began to ask the right kinds of questions about the data. It began to formulate tentative study projects and action plans, thus laying the foundations for longer term strategic control. Effective planning was becoming a reality.

Creating Momentum

Sometimes it makes sense to begin developmental planning in one department or one function; sometimes it makes sense to begin with a corporate-wide goal; and often the process can begin in several places at once. The initial undertaking may be rather modest or it can be very ambitious. There is considerable discretion over questions like these. What *does* matter is that the company has what it takes to move with confidence and certainty, under disciplined control, and in a reasonably short time from the definition of the objective to the creation of a plan and the generation of action to accomplish the objective.

Once under way, the challenge is to keep the process moving, accelerating, and expanding. The goals must be revised and extended as the enterprise expands its capacity or else the work will drift into a succession of improvement programs or drives.

There is never a time when the planning is completed. Each new definition of objectives generates new programs of action. Similarly, as the enterprise moves successfully into new areas and achieves new gains, it can set increasingly difficult and demanding objectives. Constant, controlled change becomes the ordinary way of life for the enterprise and its people.

CONCLUSION

It is time to change our perspective on what corporate planning ought to be. It has become equated with the formal steps of research, formulation of objectives, and creation of written plans. To view planning in this way, making it distinct from and even remote from the managing process, is to limit severely the help it can provide managers in gaining control over the destiny of their companies.

Moreover, the traditional, formal approach to planning imposes competing demands on managers rather than helping them respond to demands and requirements which may be currently overwhelming them. Such an approach may require top executives to delegate work they now regard as important and "take time to plan." They may have to get rid of managers who are "resistant to planning." They may have to reorganize the company in order to make planning feasible. They may have to commit themselves, even with little confidence, to five- or ten-year objectives. They may have to hire teams of planning technicians whose prolific output they will then have to cope with. The net result of all this is the production of plans and programs which may have little relationship to what the enterprise is ready, able, or willing to do right now — or to what it needs to do right now.

It is necessary to see planning in a new way, as a total strategy for increasing the control which managers have over the performance and direction of their enterprises — particularly as action today affects results tomorrow. Exciting and dynamic possibilities open up if planning is viewed in this way. And these opportunities exist not only for the president, but for every manager in a position of responsibility.

Whatever the level of sophistication of a company, and whatever a manager's level of responsibility, there are some important and urgent objectives that he can select now. Further, he can see to it that disciplined plans are created for reaching the goals he chooses with the resources currently available to him. He can make these plans succeed, and in doing so he will have advanced his company's planning process. As he progresses, he will be able to extend the range and scope of the objectives he attacks. He will become more skilled in using the help of planning specialists. He will be able to use more sophisticated and powerful planning tools. And by these steps he will help to make planning an accelerating, self-sustaining, and ever more effective process for his company.

Dynamic Administration of the Jewish Community Center

WILLIAM H. NEWMAN and HARRY A. SCHATZ

As Jewish Community Centers grow rapidly in size and complexity, their successful operation depends increasingly upon skillful and dynamic administration. Yet Center workers are trained professionally as social group workers, not as administrators. Many men move rapidly from the functions of practitioner to those of administration — serving as department heads, as assistant directors in large agencies or as directors in small agencies — without benefit of special training or of adequate years of administrative "apprenticeship."

While a few men may be regarded as "born administrators," most of the able administrators have become so by conscious use of sound administrative principles and methods.

All executives can become more skillful and creative by identifying the basic processes of administration and applying them to everyday Center operation. This is true of the veteran executive as well as of the novice. In passing, it should be noted that the Center executive has primary but not the exclusive administrative responsibility. Each department head, supervisor, and worker has administrative responsibilities in varying degrees.

There are five basic processes in the administration of business, industry, and government which are equally applicable to Jewish Community Centers. They are:

1. *Planning* — determining in advance what is to be done.

2. *Organizing* — grouping the activities necessary to carry out the plans into administrative units and defining their relationships.

3. *Assembling Resources* — obtaining personnel, facilities, budget, equipment, supplies, and other things necessary to execute plans.

4. *Directing* — issuing instructions.

5. *Controlling* — seeing that operating results conform as nearly as possible to the plans.

These five processes are a useful framework for understanding and improving Center administration. While in reality these processes are dynamically interrelated, let us look at them separately for the purpose of analysis.

PLANNING

A plan is a projected course of action. Planning covers a wide range of decisions including the clarification of Center objectives, establishment of program and administra-

Reprinted with permission of the National Jewish Welfare Board and the authors from Jewish Center Program Aids, *Vol. XV, No. 1 (1954), pp. 1-4.*

tive policies, projecting program activities, mapping out membership campaigns, determining specific operational methods and procedures and fixing day-to-day schedules.

Planning normally involves at least the following steps:

1. *Recognition of the need for action.* This may arise from demands for new programs and services, from a significant statement showing financial operations at considerable variance from the projected budget, from a report of various membership dropouts or of membership increases beyond the service capacity of the Center. For a variety of reasons, it is recognized that matters cannot be permitted to simply drift with a "do nothing" attitude. Some kind of action is called for.

2. *Investigation and analysis.* Here the facts of the present situation are studied so that possible alternative plans may be identified and information gathered as to the benefits and the difficulties in applying them.

3. *Proposal for action.* On the fasis of the investigation, the executive develops one or more proposed courses of action. He "initiates" a plan.

4. *Decision.* A plan does not really exist unless a clear decision is made as to a course of action. There are usually two steps, namely, tentative decisions and final approval.

Plans may be divided into three broad groups — goals, single-use plans, and standing plans.

1. *Goals.* Sound administration starts with a statement or at least a clear recognition of goals to be achieved. It is useful to express plans in terms of the results to be accomplished — for example, a balanced Center program serving all members of the family. "A clear statement of purpose universally understood is the outstanding guarantee of effective administration," says Luther Gulick in "Administrative Reflections from World War II."

2. *Single-use plans* lay out a course of action to fit a specific situation and are "used up" when the goal is achieved, i.e., a building campaign, a season workplan for a department or individual.

3. *Standing plans* are designed to be used over and over again. For example, a standard procedure for the requisition and purchase of supplies may be used in all departments for a wide variety of needs. A policy is a standing plan. It is a general plan of action that guides the staff of a Center in the conduct of its operation. Standing plans greatly simplify the task of the administrator. They establish a pattern of action that the planner assumes as "normal" and he can then concentrate his attention on abnormal circumstances.

ORGANIZING

Organizing is grouping the activities necessary to carry out the plans into administrative units and defining their relationship. Plans call for a variety of activities. If these are to be administered effectively, some form of organization is essential. The following principles can be helpful.

1. It is necessary to have an understanding as to "who does what." Duties need to be combined together into jobs so as to promote the most effective results. Jobs should be clearly defined, preferably in writing and should be encompassable — that is reasonably achievable within the limitations of time and resources.

2. Administrative organization, by its very nature, creates executive-subordinate relationships. It also creates a variety of departments which are intimately related. It is vital to good administration that these relationships be wisely defined and clearly understood.

3. Organization is primarily concerned with the obligation of operational responsibility and authority. A subordinate can be held accountable for an operation only to the extent that it is subject to his authority and control.

4. Authority and responsibility shouls be co-extensive. Yet the executive should retain overall responsibility and authority. Accountability does not end with delegating responsibility.

A common problem to be avoided in organization is dual supervision, such as is occasioned when clerical workers are assigned to professional staff and are at the same time supervised by office manager; or when special interest workers are responsible to an age-division supervisor and also to the Arts Department head. It is necessary to distinguish clearly specific responsibility and authority.

Staff committees are an administrative device often regarded as an important aspect of democratic administration. However, there is much confusion regarding the proper use of committees. It may be helpful to consider the conditions favorable and unfavorable to the use of committees.

1. *Favorable:*

   a. When a wide divergence of information is necessary to reach a sound conclusion.

   b. When the decision is of such importance that the judgment of several qualified individuals is desired.

   c. When successful execution of decisions depends upon full understanding of their ramifications by committee members.

   d. When activity of three or more divisions need to be adjusted frequently to secure coordination.

2. *Unfavorable:*

   a. When speed is vital.

   b. When the decision is not particularly important.

   c. When qualified personnel is not available.

   d. When the problem is one of execution rather than decision.

Span of supervision is an increasing problem in the Center. As an operation increases in size, the question arises as to how many can be adequately supervised by a single person. This is no new problem. In Exodus 18: 13-26 there is an account of how Moses set up an administrative organization.

The skillful organizer will analyze at least the following points in arriving at an optimum span for an individual supervisor:

1. Variety and importance of activities supervised

2. Other duties the supervisor is expected to perform

3. Stability of operations

4. Capacity of subordinates and their degree of delegations

214

Organization charts and manuals are useful tools in clarifying relationships. Greatest benefits often come during their preparation by providing an occasion to think objectively and critically about existing organization. They are also useful as training devices.

ASSEMBLING RESOURCES

Assembling resources – is the obtaining of personnel, facilities, budget, equipment and supplies and other things necessary to executive plans. The practicability of any plan is determined by the availability of the necessary resources. It is at this point that plans frequently need to be revised in the light of limitations and that greatest demands are placed upon administrative creativity and skill. In fact, a sound plan will specify the necessary personnel, facilities, budget, supplies, and equipment. These will, in turn, be used as bases for administrative control of the implementation of the plan.

All too frequently, good ideas and programs are acted upon without careful appraisal as to the availability of resources to carry through the plan. If additional personnel and other resources are not available, it is advisable to review the Center's program and operation and to establish a new set of priorities consistent with the current situation. These will, in turn, be used as bases for administrative control.

DIRECTING

Directing is issuing instructions. Direction is the vital step between preparation and actual operation. This includes indicating plans to those who are responsible for carrying them out and also the day-to-day personal relations between the executive and his subordinates.

Every instruction should possess these basic features:

1. Compliance should be reasonable.
2. It should be complete as to what is to be done and when.
3. It should be clear to the person receiving it.

If the instruction is complex, detailed, or of major importance, it should be in writing. Explaining why an instruction is being issued contributes to understanding, motivation, and good morale.

Coordination is concerned with harmonious and unified action directed toward a common objective. It is not a separate activity but a condition that permeates all phases of administration. It depends upon clear-cut organization and procedures with good communication and consistency in plans. Easy and frequent informal contact between workers goes a long way to expedite coordination.

CONTROLLING

Controlling – is seeing that operating results conform as nearly as possible to the plans. This involves the establishment of standards and criteria, motivation of people to achieve these standards, comparison of actual results against the standard and necessary corrective action when performance deviates from the plan.

There are three essential steps in any control process:

1. Setting standards at strategic points
2. Checking and reporting on performance
3. Taking corrective action.

215

Standards — for purposes of control — are the goals and objectives of the Center as a whole and as broken down into objectives for individual departments and sections.

These objectives are stated periodically in terms of projected program plans, membership goals, participation levels, amount of income anticipated from various sources, amount of expenditures anticipated for the several budget items, extent of active participation of board and committee members, projected improvements in facilities and equipment, recruitment and training of professional and volunteer workers.

Control begins with the process of checking actual results against such stated objectives. If the control is to have an effective influence on performance, the administrator should make sure that the goals are identified with individual responsibility.

For example, budget controls are most effective when department heads participate in drawing up departmental budgets to conform with program and operational plans and are held responsible for expenditures over which they have authority. Periodic departmental budget reviews are essential.

Another example: participation records by department or activity should be kept on a comparative basis — that is, compared numerically with previous years or other statistical periods or stated in terms of the ratio of attendance to membership.

Thus department heads will have objective bases for evaluating their own work and for the scope of accountability to which they may be held by the executive.

Another strategic point of control is the cost per person served in a particular program. While minimum cost per person is not a valid criteria by itself, yet it should be weighed against the benefits to be derived from the activity. These benefits are to be considered both in terms of the quality of the experience as well as of the number of persons served — in contrast to other comparable programs. For example, the evaluation of a varsity basketball team as against inter-club teams.

Some situations cannot be readily measured in numerical results. Control is then placed on the process. For example, a parents' discussion series in which the parents themselves are primarily involved in developing and carrying out programs with the guidance of professional staff may be considered a more beneficial experience than a program exclusively arranged for by staff. The degree of participation of parents in planning and evaluating the series thus becomes a criteria and basis of control.

This is also true in the involvement of lay committee members in program planning for larger projects and for entire departments.

Corrective action is the decisive factor in control. Comparison of actual results with projected objectives and standards often show discrepancies. As soon as this is discovered steps must be taken to correct past action or to bring similar action in the future closer to the desired goal. This may require revision of the operation or a modification of the goal.

The control process either completes the task of the executive or, more likely, shows the need for further action.

DYNAMIC ADMINISTRATION

Administration is a continuing cycle of planning, organizing, assembling resources, directing and controlling, all of which are intimately tied in together toward achieving the stated objectives. The conscious application of these processes makes for skillful and dynamic administration of the Center.

IV Man-In-Administration

The Human Aspects of Administration

L. J. GANSER

There is probably reason to believe that we in mental health and welfare agencies have less knowledge of the general emotional welfare of our organizations in their relationship to our programs than we have of those of the people who receive our services. Having only recently entered the ranks of administrators, I have found it of interest to look into administrative customs, procedures, and methods in an effort to define for myself the basic task of administration.

It has been a startling experience for me to become aware of the human and personal nature of administration and its function.

People in psychiatry are concerned about the present effectiveness of the large organizations that have traditionally taken care of the mentally ill in this country. The concerns as to the unwieldy and unyielding nature of those agencies would also seem appropriate to our large welfare agencies and any large organization. We have all at times been uncomfortably aware that, although we have higher standards of training, employ more highly trained and usually more highly paid people, our mental health and welfare agencies seem to have developed a kind of lethargy. Our first concern is how this lethargy influences the effectiveness of an agency in carrying out its program responsibility. An important part of that same concern is how the persons who work for such an agency are involved in, and affected by, that lethargy.

People have been involved in interpersonal relationships and in management for a long time, but efforts to organize the techniques of psychiatry and administration into a systematized body of knowledge for the purpose of a planned course of action are relatively recent for both fields. These sciences have developed as efforts have been made to organize, into a sensible form, the methods by which things have been and are being done by the practitioner. Because of this, there is a danger that they will be sciences which unwittingly set significant limits to their own development.

Administration, as a science, is an interest of the late nineteenth and early twentieth centuries. Its development has followed the closing of the frontier and the accumulation of large numbers of people in small areas. As a natural result of such changes, planned cooperation and managed activity became necessary, since the problems of large populations were quite different from those of the frontiersmen.

In public administration, there has been an impetus to systematize in order to avoid the vagaries of politics and to obtain more effective program results and in private administration to increase production or profits. Wars have always required organizational and administrative skill. The depression along with the philosophy of this country, which resulted in the assumption of responsibility for the provision of needed services to large

Reprinted with permission of the Columbia University Press, from Social Welfare Administration, *Ella W. Reed, ed. (New York: Columbia University Press, 1961), pp. 75-90.*

numbers of people, also resulted in further development of public administration as an important part of our culture.

Efforts to study the science of administration have placed emphasis on those aspects which conveniently lend themselves to present methods of evaluation and measurement. The human elements are not so conveniently evaluated and are frequently left until later. As a result of this inclination, those aspects of administration which are presumed to lead to rational action are stressed. There still remains a large unmanageable area of administration dealing with human values which is not sufficiently understood to be used effectively.

Management is the most simple definition of administration; although ordinarily thought of in reference to large government operations or private firms, it is not a stranger to any of us. Each of us integrates an enormous number of factors into some kind of a whole which represents the affairs of our life. These administrative functions are carried out with an unlimited amount of individual variation. Some carry out these functions by intuition entirely; others may make an occasional major decision which has been thought through in detail; others carry them out in a consistently rational manner which allows for regular, well-planned progress and accomplishment. Still others perform these functions by way of such a welter of self-determined rules, procedures, and precautions that any change in the status quo is effectively nipped in the bud. Personal management responsibilities are given official recognition at the time of death or incompetence when an administrator is designated to care for certain aspects of an individual's affairs. Each of us can be thought of as the administrator of a complex total operation which requires management skill and is different from management by an appointed administrator because our total goals in life, our motivations, and our self-concept are a part of it.

The individual involved in his own private enterprise, in addition, integrates his business, with its immediate and long-term goals, into the already complex management of his personal affairs. He must coordinate an ongoing complex of immediate actions into a planned effort to achieve long-term goals. Thus, he formulates policy, establishes procedure, determines the results, and profits from them.

Since administration as a science has developed since the closing of the American frontier, it may be valid to think of the pioneer as an example of the entrepreneur who manages the combined affairs of his family and his occupation in such a way as to achieve a degree of fulfillment of total purpose in his efforts or in his life. It is a common idea that such an entrepreneur exerts large amounts of energy and works with unusual effectiveness despite poor tools which make it necessary for him to improvise. It is also a traditional idea that such a person achieves unusual satisfaction as the result of his efforts and has greater personal dignity presumably because, even though he undergoes hardships, he is working toward a kind of fulfillment which coincides with his internal concept of himself.

Administration and management have as their purpose the production of something or the carrying out of a program. Whereas the entrepreneur of our example participates in each step and sees the end result. If he were to be placed in an organization of any size, he would most likely carry out only one aspect of a program. It would become difficult for him under such circumstances to relate himself to the final goal of the organization. He would continue to have the same need for self-fulfillment but would now find it more difficult to attain that self-fulfillment.

The purpose of mental health and welfare administration present some special problems. In private industry, efficiency and economy can be stressed in an understandable way since output can usually be measured. Consideration of the human needs of the employee, as an effort to maintain positive feelings about employment, is accepted as part of an effort to get efficient economical operation. Such a superficial efficiency-economy orientation would be a grotesque oversimplification of the purpose of welfare administration except in the case of dire emergency when rapid, immediate action with temporary goals is indicated. Administration in welfare is especially complex because the programs deal with other human beings and their needs. In the administration of programs involving these human needs there are more areas for problem development than in some other less complex administrative structures. There is also a greater need for initiative on the part of the staff person.

While it is apparent that the purposes of programs which are being administered and managed vary widely, the goals within the organization are somewhat more standard. Administration must somehow provide for conversion of the employee's energies, motivations, and drive to self-fulfillment into effective total action aimed at the accomplishment of the program purpose. Effectiveness and economy are related to the skill with which the qualities that characterize the approach of the entrepreneur to his own project can be maintained in the employee of a large organization or can be encouraged if they have not already developed.

Despite efforts to train and develop executives in the science of administration, the manner in which they actually function continues to be a highly individual matter. The techniques used by the expert administrator can be evaluated and taught, but it is more difficult to evaluate the unique personal qualities which he uses in carrying out his responsibilities. Thus, the specific management techniques used by an administrator may be given credit for his success, but it may be that this success is more related to how he deals with some of the more unmanageable aspects of his job.

The executive, despite some efforts to interpret otherwise, without question does manage and does direct. Ordinarily he has freedom to interpret the purposes of a program to the people working in it. As a matter of fact, a major part of his responsibility is to do this in such a way that staff members identify themselves with the broad purposes of the total program.

The administrator must be a person who gets some satisfaction out of influencing others to do what he thinks is worth while. Some administrators seem to thrive on situations which are ordinarily anxiety-provoking, and there is reason to believe they may well gain satisfaction from such situations. It is important that the administrator have an adventuresome and optimistic view of the future yet that he retain sufficient freedom of action so that he can use good judgment in making stable decisions. Such qualities might seem difficult to find, yet they are a great deal like those of the entrepreneur of our example who is able to work with short-term and long-term goals and unfinished plans, partially on the basis that he is at the same time experiencing a sufficient degree of self-fulfillment. The administrator usually represents in a very real way the responsibility of the total organization.

The employee can be thought of as a reasonably healthy person who is in the position of managing or administering the affairs of himself or his family. If he has been reared in this country, he has been saturated with our philosophy that education, knowledge, and wisdom result in freedom, independence, and the opportunity to do the things that are necessary to achieve success. He has a high regard for self-determination.

In his own personal development and growth from childhood he has to a degree progressed from an early state of total dependency to relative independence. To do this, he has had to break away from people upon whom he was formerly dependent. As he has become independent and has assumed responsibilities, he frequently then has become the dominant member of a family or may have developed strong assertiveness in his own self-identity. He would ordinarily possess or have the potential to develop the attitudes of the entrepreneur whom we have referred to previously as an effective workman.

Motivation is difficult to evaluate on a superficial basis, partially because it is easy to romanticize motivation on the basis of results. The frontiersman is usually thought of as a stalwart pioneer who carried civilization forward, and certainly he is thus interpreted in our textbooks. The successful public administrator also may be considered to be a person who has strong primary motivation to build up a social welfare program of an advanced nature. In each of these examples, although there may be a lively interest in the broad aspects of the project or program that the individual is involved with, the basic motivation for the person being where he is is much more closely related to fundamental factors in his personality which are largely outside his awareness.

Each person in his living activities is making continuous adaptations directed at maintaining a reasonable degree of balance or equilibrium between himself and his total environment. Both the executive and the employee, when faced with a variety of choices in making a decision, choose that which will lead to the creation of a situation in which they feel most comfortable. A series of these choices must take place before they are established in a job. It has been apparent also in past times that the entrepreneur has an inclination to assume responsibility even in the face of hardship as part of his effort to self-fulfillment. His motivation for doing this is because his self-concept includes a picture of himself as an independent, assertive person who takes care of his own affairs unhampered by dependency on others. For purposes of discussion here, we will assume that the average person in our culture either has already developed, or has the potential for development of, an inclination to assume responsibility of this type as part of his effort to self-fulfillment. He should then have motivation in that direction in his adaptive maneuvers, and if he is successful in these maneuvers he will be aware of a reasonable equilibrium and balance as a result.

The task of administration appears to be oversimplified in ordinary consideration of the scientific aspects of administrative techniques. Researchers are interested in developing methods of working with personnel in such a way that they can depend on highly responsible performance from them. This is the same kind of performance which people are willing to produce without specific outside stimulation when they are working in the general direction of self-fulfillment. At present, despite greater training and active efforts to work with administration problems, there is a general impression that personal performance continues to show a gradual decline in quality. At the same time, the personnel involved continue to put greater monetary value on their work and seek increased pay. The nature of administration itself may be a major factor in causing this.

As an agency becomes more complex, it requires a more concrete organizational pattern of responsibility. With more employees it is difficult to provide understandable interpretation of over-all purpose; and, thus, more superficial types of leadership are depended upon. Having less knowledge of each individual on the payroll, the administrator feels the need to set more limits for the staff in an effort to retain control and to be sure that the program is going in the direction that he wishes it to go. As more active management techniques are evolved, there is less opportunity for the individual employee to use his own initiative. It is interesting that management also, in an effort to impress employees with its benevolence, institues benefits, such as retirement plans, health insurance, life insurance, medical care and, under certain circumstances, may even supply clothing, laundry or similar services. As a result, administration gradually assumes responsibilities which the adult employee has been motivated to assume are his own. These are some of the responsibilities which, when carried by the person himself, result in a greater degree of self-fulfillment and a more comfortable equilibrium with his surroundings. It is important to remember that the employee has developed his desire for independence and responsibility as a part of a normal maturation process — a process during which he has actively defined his concept of himself by gradually changing from a totally dependent infant to an independent adult. During that maturation process, the person often finds it necessary to struggle with the people who are taking care of him in order to attain this

222

independence, and thus it has a high value for him. When the highly valued prerogatives which have been obtained by this process are threatened, the person's picture of himself is threatened and he becomes anxious or out of balance with his environment.

The administrator, on the other hand, is in a position where his sense of responsibility can develop with full flourish. As he assumes responsibilities — and it must be remembered that he is in his position because his motivations are strong in that direction — he enhances his degree of self-fulfillment. It may even be that in some people there is a resultant decrease in ability to be sufficiently free to make rational or reasonable decisions. If that is the case, there may be a strong inclination for him to remove all responsibility from people who work with him in order to increase his own comfort. Whether that happens or not, the administrator actually is in a position where he can remove all the responsibility from the employee or staff person. Just by being in such a position, he presents a threat to the person under him. There is evidence of this in the common observation that an administrator is usually initially thought of as being dictatorial and authoritative until that opinion is corrected by further knowledge of the individual administrator himself.

The employee in an organization is placed in a conflictive situation. To retain the responsibilities that have been highly prized, he must struggle, and if he does this his source of income is placed in jeopardy and he faces an even further loss of self-fulfillment. In the face of this, he can become anxious and uncomfortable and then must develop a supplementary method of maintaining or returning to his state of equilibrium. In general, he might do one of the following things:

1. He can get out and be independent.

2. He can compete within the organization in the hope of joining the administrative forces himself.

3. He can give in. To do so, means that he must deny the value to him of assuming any responsibility at all and return to a dependent position in reference to the administration, thus making himself less productive and again raising problems that were difficult for him to solve at an earlier stage in his development.

4. Develop a strong personal goal within his own limited area of the organization which, because there is added drive to self-fulfillment, may be pushed to the detriment of the total purpose of the organization.

Alternative number one may not be feasible for economic reasons. Number two is a choice that only a few people can gain comfort from because only a few advance to higher executive positions. Number three and number four are likely to be the most popular choices. Although alternative number four is open, there is less premium on this one within an organization since that person is more likely then to become isolated, his destructive influence on the total goal becomes more apparent, and he may lose favor. The person who chooses number three, denies the value to himself of assuming responsibility and thus returns to a dependent position, places himself in jeopardy, since under those circumstances it is almost necessary that he develop angry feelings toward the organization. Yet, he has given in and cannot actively express those feelings. This may result in active suppression of initiative and potentially is surreptitiously destructive since it is an added weight to the inertia of the organization.

We have been talking about a reasonably average person. Someone with greater than average neurotic inclinations may present a different problem if he is sensitive in this area of responsibility. He may conclude without rational reason but as a result of his own immaturity that the administrator or supervisor is going to act as an unreasonable authority. He then behaves in such a way that the supervisor is pulled into assuming just such an unreasonably authoritative position following which the victim can relax in dependency and unconsciously feel that he is justified in not asserting himself or using his initiative.

The personal motivations and personality characteristics of the administrator may be equally disturbing to an organization. Perhaps the most obvious source of problem would be the administrator who has an unreasonable need to retain the total responsibility within his own active function, and, in a sense, by doing so deprives people in his organization of an opportunity for self-fulfillment. Such an executive is in the most vulnerable position in so far as developing an organization which has as its major goal the procedures that it carries out rather than the total program aims. By withdrawing from the interpersonal aspects of his administrative job, the administrator can direct his organization into that special preoccupation with procedure. This may lead to the development of what some people consider typical of bureaucracy, that is, an agency whose major function becomes the maintenance and continuation of the agency.

Professional people who work for public agencies present some unique problems. Since they have had more training, they frequently are people who have been influenced by a desire for independence and self-determination to a more than average extent. The specialized professional worker is likely strongly to insist that he wants no administrative responsibility and cannot tolerate it. Because we have accepted his statement, we have frequently made every effort to arrange for working conditions that make it possible for that professional to work at his specialty and we protect him from administrative responsibilities. Despite this, we have difficulty in retaining those specialists in public work. This is probably especially true of the physician. In public employment the physician complains about limitations that are put on his initiative; he complains of the amount of administration that he must do; he then goes into private practice, where he feels much more satisfied. He feels more satisfied despite the fact that there are gross limitations imposed upon him by patients' ability to pay or by his inability to serve the number of patients who come to him for help. He probably spends almost as much time on administration in private practice, and perhaps in some situations even more, than he would in his public job. Yet, because he has become an entrepreneur and everything that he does has a share in the attainment of some degree of self-fulfillment, he is more comfortable.

Recently, we attempted to obtain higher salaries for physicians in our agency. Our local mental health association was interested in helping us with this project and tried to get some opinion from private practitioners in the community. Responses to these efforts seemed to indicate that the private practitioner saw his work in a different way than he did the work of the public hospital staff member. Part of this was a feeling that he had to be more responsible, took more risk, and invested more in his own work. One might then be led to wonder whether we do not force our professional staff members to deny their normal interests in total responsibility by "depriving" them of the administrative responsibility which they consider a symbol of complete and total responsibility. If this were true, then they are being deprived of opportunity for self-fulfillment in terms of their own concept of themselves as independent professional persons.

It is also interesting to speculate upon the effect of introducing more rigid administrative techniques in a large public agency or in a group of public agencies. Frequently this is done as an effort to achieve economy. If the factors that have been discussed are important, it may explain why such efforts so seldom result in economy.

Skill in dealing with, and knowledge of, these human aspects of administration are important for the administrator. All too frequently he has little opportunity to learn these skills in a systematized way as he does administrative techniques, and his own unique personality qualities become the most important factors in how effectively he functions. Skill of this sort once developed is difficult to teach or pass on because it is so closely related to the personal qualities and the personal motivations of the individual administrator.

The real task of administration is to convert the individual's potential for responsible performance into that kind of performance within a large organization.

The internal motivation of both the executive and the staff person represents a large area of management which is in reality quite unmanageable. Ignoring or denying this area of unmanageability results in considerable oversimplification of the task of administration.

There are tendencies in a large organization for administration to assume increasing organization responsibility and at times even personal responsibility for the employee, depriving the employee of self-fulfillment experience. Such deprivation may result in denial of the need to assume responsibility at work and in other areas with loss of initiative and concomitant addition to a body of lethargy within an agency.

The matter of responsibility may be a special problem with professional personnel. Although they state a strong desire to practice their specialty only, their need for other executive responsibility as a source of self-fulfillment experience may also be great.

Our methods of administration in large agencies with echelons of supervisors and protection of the specialist may well be an indication or our failure to recognize a relatively ordinary human need and may result in such agencies forcing themselves into more massive lethargy.

We are left with a final question. Because of these human aspects, current administration techniques may well be uneconomical. Standard methods to achieve economy by greater control may well only increase the problem and add to the accumulating drag. In view of this, how can the executive or supervisor continue to provide an increasingly responsible performance and at the same time avoid depriving the staff member or employee of his right to management responsibility of a significant nature? It would appear to be a part of the public executive's responsibility to be aware of these issues and how they may be impairing the effectiveness of his agency or how they can be used to increase the effectiveness of an agency.

The effectiveness of how an agency furnishes the "product" of their organization to their clients is closely related to the mental health of the organization. This mental health may well be a function of how much self-fulfillment is possible for the staff people.

The Human Dilemmas of Leadership

ABRAHAM ZALEZNIK

Not too long ago, the citizens of the United States and of the world became witnesses to a political drama that had all the ingredients of a first-class Greek tragedy. Were it not for the fact that the episode revealed some sense of the nature of power conflicts among influential men, one could safely have stopped reflections on the event at the point where its human interest ended and its deeper significance for leadership began. I am referring, of course, to the Adlai Stevenson episode that exploded on the public scene with an article in the *Saturday Evening Post* by Stewart Alsop and Charles Bartlett.[1]

I do not intend to go into a commentary on this article but, rather, I want to use this episode to launch my reflections on the human dilemmas of leadership as they affect every person who works in a position of authority and responsibility. In the course of the Stevenson affair, we became privy to backstage rivalry among subordinates close to the President. We saw attempts at political homicide and character assassination through the use of the "the leak" of so-called secret positions in the deliberations of high councils of government. We saw the President of the United States drop his guard, if only momentarily, to show us how difficult it is to make or hold friends while in the Presidency. And throughout the revelations, charges, and countercharges, we learned just what the medium of exchange can be in power conflicts; namely, prestige, personal integrity, friendship and loyalty, jealousy and egotism — all typical human sentiments likely to be found in any human encounter where people care about what they are doing.

In the professional literature on the job of the executive one seldom finds much reference to or intelligent discussion of the dilemmas posed by the exercise of power and authority. The dramatists, novelists, biographers, and journalists attempt to portray these struggles in their works, but much is left to the sensitivity and intiution of the audience. And least of all are we ever invited to consider the underlying dynamics of leadership dilemmas and the different forms open to us for their resolution.

I should like to try to lift the veil somewhat on the nature of conflicts in exercising leadership. The two points I want to develop are:

(1) The main source for the dilemmas leaders face can be found within themselves, in their own inner conflicts.

(2) Dealing more intelligently with knotty decisions and the inevitable conflicts of interest existing among men in organizations presupposes that executives, at least the successful ones, are able to get their own house in order. It presupposes that the executive is able to resolve or manage his inner conflicts so that his actions are strongly grounded in

---

[1] Stewart Alsop and Charles Bartlett, "In Time of Crisis," December 8, 1962, p. 15.

Reprinted from the Harvard Business Review, *July-August, 1963, pp. 49-55.* © *1963 by the President and Fellows of Harvard College; all rights reserved. Reprinted with permission.*

reality, so that he does not find himself constantly making and then undoing decisions to the service of his own mixed feelings and to the disservice and confusion of his subordinates.

TENDENCY TO PROJECT

Most of us are accustomed by virtue of our training and inclinations to externalize conflicts and dilemmas. If an executive finds himself immobilized in the face of a difficult problem, he is apt to look to the outside for an explanation. He might perhaps say to himself that he is unable to act because he has inadequate authority delegated to him. Or he might hesitate because he feels subordinates are holding out on him by providing too little information, confused positions, and mixed signals. In this case, he is likely to vent his frustrations on their incompetence.

This generalized tendency to place conflicts in the outside world is part and parcel of a well-known mechanism of the mind called *projection*. A person projects when, unknown to himself, he takes an attitude of his own and attributes it to someone else. In the example just cited, the executive who despairs because his subordinates are confused and who charges them with holding back and with indecision may well be reading his own state of mind and attributing it to others.

It is just not within us to be able consistently to separate those issues which arise from our own concerns from those issues that reside in the realities of a situation. Let me cite another example:

> The president of a large company became concerned with the possibility that his organization had failed to develop executive talent. This concern of his arose in connection with his own retirement. He organized a committee composed of assistants to vice presidents to study this problem and to report to him with recommendations.
>
> The president's forthcoming retirement was well known, and there was private speculation as to who among the vice presidents would be named as his successor. This succession obviously implied that several persons among the assistant vice presidents would be promoted. The task force met several times, but its discussions were not too productive or interesting. The group spent most of its time attempting to define what the president wanted the committee to do, instead of dealing with the issues the organization faced in attracting and developing executive talent.
>
> In other words, they projected their own concerns and anxiety onto the president and attributed to him confused motives in undertaking the assessment of the company's needs in executive development. In reality the individuals themselves shared confused motivations. They were in intensive rivalry with one another over who among their immediate superiors would become president and how this change would affect their fate in the organization.

By centering attention on the inner conflicts of the executive, I do not mean to imply that conflicts are not based in the relations among individuals at work. The illustrations presented so far clearly indicate how vicious these relations may become. The point I am suggesting is that external conflicts in the form of power struggles and rivalry become more easily understood and subject to rational control under those conditions where the executive is able to separate the conditions within himself from those existing on the outside.

This process of separation is more easily said than done. Nevertheless it is crucial for the exercise of leadership, and sometimes the separation is the very condition for survival.

227

One wonders, for example, whether the failure to maintain this separation lay at the basis of the breakdown and subsequent suicide of such a brilliant man as James Forrestal. At the very least, by attending to the conditions within himself, the executive can expect to be dealing with those situations most susceptible to his rational control. It is in the long run a lot easier to control and change the world in which we live.

Forms of Inner Conflict

But before we examine some of the ways in which a man can learn to deal more competently with his inner life, we need to know something more about the nature of inner conflicts. Let us take two types that are quite prevalent among executives in organizations:

1. *Status anxiety* – This refers to those dilemmas frequently experienced by individuals at or near the top in their organizational world.

2. *Competition anxiety* – This refers to the feelings generated while climbing to the top.

These two prevalent types of anxiety, while resembling each other in a number of respects, are worth keeping separate for purposes of furthering understanding.

STATUS ANXIETY

When an individual begins to achieve some success and recognition in his work, he may suddenly realize that a change has occurred within himself and in his relations with associates. From a position of being the bright young man who receives much encouragement and support he, almost overnight, finds himself viewed as a contender by those who formerly acted as mentors. A similar change takes place in his relations with persons who were his peers. They appear cautious with him, somewhat distant, and constrained in their approach, where once he may have enjoyed the easy give-and-take of their friendship. The individual in question is then ripe for status anxiety. He becomes torn between the responsibilities of a newly acquired authority and the strong need to be liked.

There is a well-established maxim in the study of human behavior that describes this situation tersely and even poetically; namely, that "love flees authority." Where one individual has the capacity to control and affect the actions of another, either by virtue of differences in their positions, knowledge, or experience, then the feeling governing the relationship tends to be one of distance and (hopefully) respect, but not one ultimately of warmth and friendliness.

I do not believe that this basic dichotomy between respect or esteem and liking is easily changed. The executive who confuses the two is bound to get into trouble. Yet in our culture today we see all too much evidence of people seeking to obscure the difference. Much of the current ethos of success equates popularity and being liked with competence and achievement. In Arthur Miller's *Death of a Salesman*, Willie Loman in effect was speaking for our culture when he measured a person's achievement in the gradations of being liked, well liked, or very well liked.

Reaction & Recognition

In what ways do executives react when they are caught in the conflict between exercising authority and being liked?

Sometimes they seek to play down their authority and play up their likability by acting out the role of the "nice guy." This is sometimes called status stripping, where the individual tries in a variety of ways to discard all the symbols of his status and authority.

228

This ranges from proclaiming the open-door policy, where everyone is free to visit the executive any time he wants, to the more subtle and less ritualistic means such as democratizing work by proclaiming equality of knowledge, experience, and position. And yet these attempts at status stripping fail sooner or later. The executive may discover that his subordinates join in gleefully by stripping his status and authority to the point where he becomes immobilized; is prevented from making decisions; is faced with the prospect of every issue from the most trivial to the most significant being dealt with in the same serious vein. In short, problem solving and work become terrorized in the acting out of status stripping.

The executive soon becomes aware of another aspect of his dilemma. Much to his horror, he finds that attempts to remove social disease in the interests of likability have not only reduced work effectiveness, but have resulted in an abortion of the intent to which his behavior has been addressed. He discovers that his subordinates gradually come to harbor deep and unspoken feelings of contempt toward him, because he inadvertently has provided them with a negative picture of what rewards await them for achievement — a picture unpleasant to behold. In effect, the process of status stripping helps to destroy the incentives for achievement and in the extreme can produce feelings of helplessness and rage.

There is yet another side to the dilemma of status anxiety which is well worth examining. This side has to do with the hidden desire to "touch the peak." Executives frequently want to be near the source of power and to be accepted and understood by their bosses. Such motivations lead to excessive and inappropriate dependency bids, and to feelings of lack of autonomy on the part of the subordinate and of being leaned on too hard on the part of the superior. Under such conditions, communication between superior and subordinate tends to break down.

So far I have discussed the problem of status anxiety as an aspect of seeking friendship, warmth, and approval from subordinates and bosses. Status anxiety is also frequently generated by the fear of aggression and retaliation on the part of persons who hold positions of authority. Executives sometimes report feeling lonely and detached in their position. A closer look at the sense of loneliness reveals a feeling that one is a target for the aggression of others. This feeling occurs because the executive is called upon to take a position on a controversial issue and to support the stand he assumes. He must be able to take aggression with a reasonably detached view, or the anxiety can become intolerable.

If in your experience you have encountered an executive who seemed unable to take a stand on a problem, who seemed to equivocate or talk out of two sides of his mouth at once, then the chances are reasonably good that you have come upon a man in the throes of status anxiety. Sometimes this will appear in the form of hyperactivity — the case of the executive who flits from problem to problem or from work project to work project without really seeing an activity through to completion. In this case, the executive is utilizing the tactic of providing a shifting target so that other persons have difficulty in taking aim at him.

Constructive Approach

Now, in referring to aggression and the avoidance of aggression as aspects of status anxiety, I do not mean to imply hostile aggression. I mean to suggest instead that all work involves the release of aggressive energy. Solving problems and reaching decisions demand a kind of give-and-take where positions are at stake and where it is impossible for everyone concerned to be equally right all the time. But having to give way or to alter a position in the face of compelling argument is no loss. The executive who can develop a position, believe in it, support it to its fullest, and then back down, is a strong person.

It is just this type of person who does not suffer from status anxiety. He may love to provide a target because he knows this may be a very effective catalyst for first-class work accomplishment. He is secure enough to know that he has nothing to lose in reality, but much to gain in the verve and excitement of interesting work. This type of executive is able to take aggression, and in fact encourage it, because he probably has abandoned the magical thinking that seems to equate his position of authority with omnipotence. No one has the power to make everyone else conform to his wishes, so it is no loss to learn that one has been wrong in the face of the arguments aggressively put forth by others. In fact, such ability to retract a stand results in heightened respect from others.

I am suggesting, in other words, that we should not be misled into equating the virtue of humility with executive behavior that appears modest, uncertain of a stand, and acquiescent toward others — behavior which frequently is feigned modesty to avoid becoming a target. True humility, in my opinion, is marked by the person who thinks his way through problems, is willing to be assertive, is realistic enough to encourage assertiveness from others, and is willing to acknowledge the superiority of ideas presented by others.

COMPETITION ANXIETY

The second main pattern of inner conflict that badly needs attention is what I have termed competition anxiety, a close kin of status anxiety. It goes without saying that the world of work is essentially a competitive one. Competition exists in the give-and-take of solving problems and making decisions. It also exists in the desire to advance into the more select and fewer positions at the top of a hierarchy. An executive who has difficulty in coming to terms with a competitive environment will be relatively ineffective.

From my observations of executives — and would-be executives — I have found two distinct patterns of competition anxiety: (1) the fear of failure and (2) the fear of success. Let us examine each in turn.

Fear of Failure

You have perhaps seen the fear of failure operate in the activities of the child, where this type of problem generally originates:

> The child may seem to become quite passive and unwilling to undertake work in school or to engage in sports with children his age. No amount of prodding by parents or teachers seems to activate his interests; in fact, prodding seems to aggravate the situation and induce even greater reluctance to become engaged in an activity. When this child progresses in school, he may be found to have considerable native talent, and sooner or later becomes tabbed as an "underachiever." He gets as far as he does thanks in large measure to the high quality of his native intelligence, but he does not live up to the promise which others observe in him.
>
> When this child grows up and enters a career, we may see the continuation of underachievement, marked by relative passivity and undistinguished performance. Where he may cast his lot is in the relative obscurity of group activity. Here he can bring his talents to bear in anonymous work. As soon as he becomes differentiated, bring his talents to bear in anonymous work. As soon as he becomes differentiated, he feels anxious and may seek to become immersed once again in group activity.

An important aspect of this pattern of response is the ingrained feeling that whatever the person undertakes is bound to fail. He does not feel quite whole and lacks a strong sense of identity. He is short on self-esteem and tends to quit before he starts in order to avoid confrontation with the fear that he might fail. Instead of risking failure he is willing to assume anonymity, hence the sense of resignation and sometimes fatigue which he

230

communicates to those near to him.

A closer study of the dilemma surrounding the fear of failure indicates that the person has not resolved the concerns he has with competing. It may be that he has adopted or "internalized" unrealistic standards of performance or that he is competing internally with unreachable objects. Therefore he resolves to avoid the game because it is lost before it starts.

If you recall James Thurber's characterization of Walter Mitty, you may get a clearer indication of the problem I am describing. Walter was a meek, shy man who seemed to have difficulty in mobilizing himself for even the simplest tasks. Yet in his inner world of fantasy, as Thurber portrays so humorously and touchingly, Walter Mitty is the grand captain of his destiny and the destiny of those who depend on him. He populates his inner world with images of himself as the pilot of an eight-engine bomber or the cool, skillful, nerveless surgeon who holds the life of his patient in his hands. Who could ever work in the world of mortals under standards that one had best leave to the gods!

You can observe from this description that fear of failure can be resolved only when the person is able to examine his inner competitive world, to judge its basis in reality, and to modify this structure in accordance with sensible standards.

Fear of Success

The fear of failure can be matched with its opposite, the fear of success. This latter pattern might be called the "Macbeth complex," since we have a ready illustration available in Shakespeare's *Macbeth*. The play can be viewed symbolically for our purposes:

Macbeth was an ambitious man. It is interesting to note that the demon ambition is projected out in the form of the three witches and Macbeth's wife, who, Macbeth would lead us to believe, put the idea into his head to become king. But we do not believe for a minute that the ambition to become number one existed anywhere but within Macbeth himself. You remember that to become king, Macbeth killed Duncan, a nice old man who had nothing but feelings of admiration and gratitude for Macbeth.

As the story unfolds, we find the crown resting uneasily on a tormented head. Macbeth is wracked with feelings of guilt for the misdeed he has committed and then with uneasy suspicion. The guilt is easy enough for us to understand, but the suspicion is a bit more subtle. Macbeth presents himself to us as a character who committed a foul deed to attain an ambition and is then suspicious that others are envious of him and seek to displace him in the number one position. So, there are few lieutenants to trust. And, paradoxically, the strongest subordinates become the ones least trusted and most threatening.

The play portrays in action the morbid cycle of the hostile-aggressive act followed by guilt and retribution. In addition, if we view the play symbolically, we can say that the individual, like Macbeth, may experience in fantasy the idea that one achieves position only through displacing someone else. Success, therefore, brings with it feelings of guilt and the urge to undo or to reverse the behavior that led to the success. If such concerns are strong enough — and they exist in all of us to some degree — then we may see implemented the fear of success.

The form of this implementation will vary. One prominent pattern it takes is in striving hard to achieve a goal, but just when the goal is in sight or within reach, the person sabotages himself. The self-sabotage can be viewed as a process of undoing — to avoid the success that may generate guilt. This process of self-sabotage is sometimes called snatching defeat out of the jaws of victory.

231

I am not certain just what Theodore H. White had in mind in his book, *The Making of the President — 1960*, portraying Nixon's defeat in the 1960 Presidential election, but he certainly conveys the impression that Nixon may have been going through a cycle such as the one described here — the fear of success. There were just too many errors of commission and omission that prevent us from passing off the election simply in terms of external events and forces, as important as these were.

MANAGING INNER CONFLICTS

To summarize the discussion thus far, I have called attention to the not easily accepted notion that conflicts of interest can and do exist within individuals and are not restricted to the relations among men in the ordinary conduct of affairs. I have said that the inner conflicts rooted in the emotional development of the individual are at the core of the leadership dilemma. It is misleading, in other words, to seek for causes of conflict exclusively in external forces.

Then, touching on a few of the inner conflicts of executives, I grouped them into two main types: (1) status anxiety and (2) competition anxiety. Both of these forms of inner conflict are rooted in the very process of human development in the strivings of individuals for some measure of autonomy and control over their environment. The forms happen to be especially crucial in the executive's world simply because he acts in the center of a network of authority and influence that at any point in time is subject to alteration. In fact, one can think of decision making and action in organizations as a continuing flow of influence interchanges where the sources of the power to influence are many. But whatever the external source through which any one person achieves power to influence, its final manifestations will reflect the inner emotional condition of the man.

Let us now see what guidelines exist for resolving and managing inner conflicts. There are six ideas I would like to suggest.

1. The necessity of acknowledging and accepting the diversity of motivations.

The control of one's own responses and actions presupposes some accurate understanding of one's motivations. Everyone would like to believe that his inner world is populated only by the socially nice drives and wishes. But this is not the case. It is fruitless to attempt to deny awareness of the less nice, but equally human, feelings that we all experience such as rivalry, dislike, rebelliousness, anger, and contempt. I am not urging executives to express these feelings impulsively. I am not of the school of thought that believes the catharsis of feelings in everyday relationships at work and at home is a good thing. But the awareness of how one is reacting in a situation is beneficial and permits more flexibility in thinking and action. Unless an executive establishes a close connection between his realms of thought and feeling, the two can exist in relative isolation from one another to the detriment of his effectiveness as a manager. At the very least, such self-estrangement involves considerable costs in the waste of energy.

2. The necessity of establishing a firm sense of identity.

The exercise of leadership requires a strong sense of identity — knowing who one is and who one is not. The myth of the value of being an "all-around guy" is damaging to the strivings of an individual to locate himself from within and then to place himself in relation to others. This active location and placement of one's self prevents the individual from being defined by others in uncongenial terms. It prevents him also from being buffeted around the sea of opinions he must live within. A sense of autonomy, separateness, or identity permits a freedom of action and thinking so necessary for leadership.

232

Not the least significant part of achieving a sense of identity is the creative integration of one's past. There is no tailor who can convert a hayseed into a big-city boy — any more than a dude can become a cowboy for all the hours he spends on the range. Coming to terms with being a hayseed or a dude permits the development of a unique person who goes beyond the stereotypes offered to him as models.

3. The necessity of maintaining constancy and continuity in response.

Closely related to the need for a sense of identity is a constancy in how one represents and presents himself to others. Constant alterations of oneself are confusing to work associates. These shifts are particularly damaging to subordinates who are entitled to the sense of security that comes from a feeling of reasonable continuity in the responses of their boss. For instance:

> I knew of one group of executives, many of whom had the practice of taking tranquilizers before a meeting with the president of the company. They claimed that they needed the tranquilizers to help them withstand the angry reactions the president demonstrated when people acted as though they had not thought through the ideas they were presenting. I think they were mistaken. They used the tranquilizers because they were very unsure as to just what he would get angry about or when. If they had had some sense of the standards of performance to which he reacted kindly or harshly, they would have been able to spend less time worrying and more time working.

4. The necessity of becoming selective in activities and relationships.

Most executives believe that gregariousness and participation in many activities at work and in the community are of great value in their life. In a sense this belief is true. But I would urge that greater attention needs to be paid to selectivity. Without carefully selecting the matters he gets involved in, the executive faces a drain on his emotional energy that can become quite costly. Selectivity implies the capacity to say "no" without the sense that one has lost esteem. The capacity to say "no" also implies that one is so constituted that he does not need esteem from diffuse persons and activities to enhance his self-worth.

5. The necessity of learning to communicate.

Conflict resolution, both inner and external, depends on the capacities of men to communicate. Communication is a complex process and one that requires careful thought and attention. Here are two suggestions for improving communication:

1. Try to develop a keen awareness of your own reactions (a point I referred to previously).

2. Try to make your opinions and attitudes known without wasteful delays. (An unexpressed reaction that simmers and then boils within is apt to explode at inappropriate times; this may lead to increased confusion and concern in the minds of listeners, to the detriment of information interchange.)

6. The necessity of living within a cyclical life pattern.

The effective utilization of energy seems to involve a rhythmic pattern of alternating between quite different modes or cycles of response. The prototype of alternating modes

233

is probably best found in the comparison of wakefulness and sleep. Wakefulness suggests activity, conscious attention to problems, and the tension of concentration and action. Sleep is the epitome of passivity in the adult as well as in the child; here concerns are withdrawn from the outside world to a state of inner bliss. In this passive state the organism is rejuvenated and made ready for a new cycle of activity.

This prototype can be applied to a wide range of events in the daily life of the executive. Building oneself into a rhythmic pattern, whether it be around work or play, talking or listening, being at work alone or in association with others, may be essential for dealing with the strains of a difficult role.

SUMMING UP

Training oneself to act and react in the ways just discussed may sound like a formidable task. Formidable it is, but perhaps the basic necessity is to overcome the sense of inertia to which we are all susceptible from time to time. While it sounds puritanical, the most elementary step necessary for achieving a mature orientation as an executive is to assume responsibility for one's own development. Basic to this responsibility is the experiencing of one's self in the active mode. (The sense of inertia referred to before is just the opposite; here life and events appear to occur apart from one's own intentions.) As soon as an executive is able to assume responsibility for his own experience and in the course of doing so overcomes the sense of inertia, he is on the road toward experiencing leadership as an adventure in learning.

Fortunately, increasing recognition by executives of the importance of their continuing development has made it possible for them, in conjunction with universities and institutes, to examine the dilemmas of leadership and to experiment with new approaches for their resolution.

Interpersonal Barriers to Decision Making

By CHRIS ARGYRIS

- The actual behavior of top executives during decision-making meetings often does not jibe with their attitudes and prescriptions about effective executive action.
- The gap that often exists between what executives say and how they behave helps create barriers to openness and trust, to the effective search for alternatives, to innovation, and to flexibility in the organization.
- These barriers are more destructive in important decision-making meetings than in routine meetings, and they upset effective managers more than ineffective ones.
- The barriers cannot be broken down simply by intellectual exercises. Rather, executives need feedback concerning their behavior and opportunities to develop self-awareness in action. To this end, certain kinds of questioning are valuable; playing back and analyzing tape recordings of meetings has proved to be a helpful step; and laboratory education programs are valuable.

These are a few of the major findings of a study of executive decision making in six representative companies. The findings have vital implications for management groups everywhere; for while some organizations are less subject to the weaknesses described than are others, *all* groups have them in some degree. In this article I shall discuss the findings in detail and examine the implications for executives up and down the line. (For information on the company sample and research methods used in the study, see below.)

NATURE OF THE STUDY

The six companies studied include: (1) an electronics firm with 40,000 employees, (2) a manufacturer and marketer of a new innovative product with 4,000 employees, (3) a large research and development company with 3,000 employees, (4) a small research and development organization with 150 employees, (5) a consulting-research firm with 400 employees, and (6) a producer of heavy equipment with 4,000 employees.

The main focus of the investigation reported here was on the behavior of 165 top executives in these companies. The executives were board members, executive committee members, upper-level managers, and (in a few cases) middle-level managers.

Approximately 265 decision-making meetings were studied and nearly 10,000 units of behavior analyzed. The topics of the meetings ranged widely, covering investment decisions, new products, manufacturing problems, marketing strategies, new pricing policies, administrative changes, and personnel issues. An observer took notes during all but ten of the meetings; for research purposes, these ten were analyzed "blind" from tapes (i.e., without ever meeting the executives). All other meetings were taped also, but analyzed at a later time.

The major device for analyzing the tapes was a new system of categories for scoring decision-making meetings.* Briefly, the executives' behavior was scored according to how often they:

1. Owned up to and accepted responsibility for their ideas or feelings;
2. Opened up to receive others' ideas or feelings;
3. Experimented and took risks with ideas or feelings;
4. Helped others to own up, be open, and take risks;
5. Did not own up; were not open; did not take risks; and did not help others in any of these activities.

A second scoring system was developed to produce a quantitative index of the *norms* of the executive culture. There were both positive and negative norms. The positive norms were:

1. *Individuality*, especially rewarding behavior that focused on and valued the uniqueness of each individual's ideas and feelings.
2. *Concern* for others' ideas and feelings.
3. *Trust* in others' ideas and feelings.

The negative norms were:

1. *Conformity* to others' ideas and feelings.
2. *Antagonism* toward these ideas and feelings.
3. *Mistrust* of these ideas and feelings.

In addition to our observations of the men at work, at least one semistructured interview was conducted with each executive. All of these interviews were likewise taped, and the typewritten protocols served as the basis for further analysis.

WORDS VS. ACTIONS

According to top management, the effectiveness of decision-making activities depends on the degree of innovation, risk taking, flexibility, and trust in the executive system. (Risk taking is defined here as any act where the executive risks his self-esteem. This could be a moment, for example, when he goes against the group view; when he tells someone, especially the person with the highest power, something negative about his impact on the organization; or when he seeks to put millions of dollars in a new investment.)

Nearly 95 percent of the executives in our study emphasize that an organization is only as good as its top people. They constantly repeat the importance of their responsibility to help themselves and others to develop their abilities. Almost as often they report that the qualities just mentioned — motivation, risk taking, and so on — are key characteristics of any successful executive system. "People problems" head the list as the most difficult, perplexing, and crucial.

In short, the executives vote overwhelmingly for executive systems where the contributions of each executive can be maximized and where innovation, risk taking, flexibility, and trust reign supreme. Nevertheless, the *behavior* of these same executives tends to create decision-making processes that are *not* very effective. Their behavior can be fitted

---

*For a detailed discussion of the system of categories and other aspects of methodology, see my book, *Organization and Innovation* (Homewood, Illinois, Richard D. Irwin, Inc., 1965).

into two basic patterns:

Pattern A – *thoughtful, rational, and mildly competitive.* This is the behavior most frequently observed during the decision-making meetings. Executives following this pattern own up to their ideas in a style that emphasizes a serious concern for ideas. As they constantly battle for scarce resources and "sell" their views, their openness to others' ideas is relatively high, not because of a sincere interest in learning about the point of view of others, but so they can engage in a form of "one-upmanship" – that is, gain information about the others' points of view in order to politely discredit them.

Pattern B – *competitve first, thoughtful and rational second.* In this pattern, conformity to ideas replaces concern for ideas as the strongest norm. Also, antagonism to ideas is higher – in many cases higher than openness to ideas. The relatively high antagonism scores usually indicate, in addition to high competitiveness, a high degree of conflict and pent-up feelings.

Chart I summarizes data for four illustrative groups of managers – two groups with Pattern A characteristics and two with Pattern B characteristics.

Chart 1—Management Groups With Pattern A and Pattern B Characteristics

	PATTERN A				PATTERN B			
TOTAL NUMBER OF UNITS ANALYZED*	GROUP 1 198		GROUP 2 143		GROUP 3 201		GROUP 4 131	
UNITS CHARACTERIZED BY:								
OWNING UP TO OWN IDEAS AND FEELINGS	146	74	105	74	156	78	102	78
CONCERN FOR OTHERS' IDEAS AND FEELINGS	122	62	89	62	52	26	56	43
CONFORMITY TO OTHERS' IDEAS AND FEELINGS	54	27	38	26	87	43	62	47
OPENNESS TO OTHERS' IDEAS AND FEELINGS	46	23	34	24	31	15	25	19
INDIVIDUALITY	4	2	12	8	30	15	8	6
ANTAGONISM TO OTHERS' IDEAS AND FEELINGS	18	9	4	3	32	16	5	4
UNWILLINGNESS TO HELP OTHERS OWN UP TO THEIR IDEAS	5	2	3	2	14	7	4	3

Practical Consequences

In both patterns executives are rarely observed:

- Taking risks or experimenting with new ideas or feelings;
- Helping others to own up, be open, and take risks;
- Using a style of behavior that supports the norm of individuality and trust as well as mistrust;
- Expressing feelings, positive or negative.

These results should not be interpreted as implying that the executives do not have feelings. We know from the interviews that many of the executives have strong feelings indeed. However, the overwhelming majority (84%) feel that it is a sign of immaturity to express feelings openly *during decision-making meetings*. Nor should the results be interpreted to mean that the executives do not enjoy risk taking. The data permit us to conclude only that few risk-taking actions were *observed* during the meetings. (Also, we have to keep in mind that the executives were always observed in groups; it may be that their behavior in groups varies significantly from their behavior as individuals.)

Before I attempt to give my views about the reasons for the discrepancy between executives' words and actions, I should like to point out that these results are not unique to business organizations. I have obtained similar behavior patterns from leaders in education, research, the ministry, trade unions, and government. Indeed, one of the fascinating questions for me is why so many different people in so many different kinds of organizations tend to manifest similar problems.

WHY THE DISCREPANCY?

The more I observe such problems in different organizations possessing different technologies and varying greatly in size, the more I become impressed with the importance of the role played by the values or assumptions top people hold on the nature of effective human relationships and the best ways to run an organization.

Basic Values

In the studies so far I have isolated three basic values that seem to be very important:

1. *The significant human relationships are the ones which have to do with achieving the organization's objective.* My studies of over 265 different types and sizes of meetings indicate that executives almost always tend to focus their behavior on "getting the job done." In literally thousands of units of behavior, almost none are observed where the men spend some time in analyzing and maintaining their group's effectiveness. This is true even though in many meetings the group's effectiveness "bogged down" and the objectives were not being reached because of interpersonal factors. When the executives are interviewed and asked why they did not spend some time in examining the group operations or processes, they reply that they were there to get a job done. They add: "If the group isn't effective, it is up to the leader to get it back on the track by directing it."

2. *Cognitive rationality is to be empahsized; feelings and emotions are to be played down.* This value influences executives to see cognitive, intellectual discussions as "relevant," "good," "work," and so on. Emotional and interpersonal discussions tend to be viewed as "irrelevant," "immature," "not work," and so on.

As a result, when emotions and interpersonal variables become blocks to group effectiveness, all the executives report feeling that they should *not* deal with them.

238

For example, in the event of an emotional disagreement, they would tell the members to "get back to facts" or "keep personalities out of this."

3. *Human relationships are most effectively influenced through unilateral direction, coercion, and control, as well as by rewards and penalties that sanction all three values.* This third value of direction and control is implicit in the chain of command and also in the elaborate managerial controls that have been developed within organizations.

Influence on Operations

The impact of these values can be considerable. For example, to the extent that individuals dedicate themselves to the value of intellectual rationality and "getting the job done," they will tend to be aware of and emphasize the intellectual aspects of issues in an organization and (consciously or unconsciously) to suppress the interpersonal and emotional aspects, especially those which do not seem relevant to achieving the task.

As the interpersonal and emotional aspects of behavior become suppressed, organizational norms that coerce individuals to hide their feelings or to disguise them and bring them up as technical, intellectual problems will tend to arise.

Under these conditions the individual may tend to find it very difficult to develop competence in dealing with feelings and interpersonal relationships. Also, in a world where the expression of feelings is not valued, individuals may build personal and organizational defenses to help them suppress their own feelings or inhibit others in such expression. Or they may refuse to consider ideas which, if explored, could expose suppressed feelings.

Such a defensive reaction in an organization could eventually inhibit creativity and innovation during decision making. The participants might learn to limit themselves to those ideas and values that were not threatening. They might also decrease their openness to new ideas and values. And as the degree of openness decreased, the capacity to experiment would also decrease, and fear of taking risks would increase. This would reduce the *probability* of experimentation, thus decreasing openness to new ideas still further and constricting risk taking even more than formerly. We would thereby have a closed circuit which could become an important cause of loss of vitality in an organization.

SOME CONSEQUENCES

Aside from the impact of values on vitality, what are some other consequences of the executive behavior patterns earlier described on top management decision making and on the effective functioning of the organization? For the sake of brevity, I shall include only examples of those consequences that were found to exist in one form or another in all organizations studied.

Restricted Commitment

One of the most frequent findings is that in major decisions that are introduced by the president, there tends to be less than open discussion of the issues, and the commitment of the officers tends to be less than complete (although they may assure the president to the contrary). For instance, consider what happened on one organization where a major administrative decision made during the period of the research was the establishment of several top management committees to explore basic long-range problems:

As is customary with major decisions, the president discussed it in advance at a meeting of the executive committee. He began the meeting by circulating, as a basis for discussion, a draft of the announcement of the committees. Most of the members' discussion was concerned with raising questions about the wording of the proposal:

- "Is the word *action* too strong?"
- "I recommend that we change 'steps can be taken' to 'recommendations can be made.' "
- "We'd better change the word 'lead' to 'maintain.' "

As the discussion seemed to come to an end, one executive said he was worried that the announcement of the committees might be interpreted by the people below as an implication "that the executive committee believes the organization is in trouble. Let's get the idea in that all is well."

There was spontaneous agreement by all executives: "Hear, hear!"

A brief silence was broken by another executive who apparently was not satisfied with the concept of the committees. He raised a series of questions. The manner in which it was done was interesting. As he raised each issue, he kept assuring the president and the group that he was not against the concept. He just wanted to be certain that the executive committee was clear on what it was doing. For example, he assured them:

- "I'm not clear. Just asking."
- "I'm trying to get a better picture."
- "I'm just trying to get clarification."
- "Just so that we understand what the words mean."

The president nodded in agreement, but he seemed to become slightly impatient. He remarked that many of these problems would not arise if the members of these new committees took an overall company point of view. An executive commented (laughingly), "Oh, I'm for motherhood too!"

The proposal was tabled in order for the written statement to be revised and discussed further during the next meeting. It appeared that the proposal was the president's personal "baby," and the executive committee members would naturally go along with it. The most responsibility some felt was that they should raise questions so the president would be clear about *his* (not *their*) decision.

At the next meeting the decision-making process was the same as at the first. The president circulated copies of the revised proposal. During this session a smaller number of executives asked questions. Two pushed (with appropriate care) the notion that the duties of one of the committees were defined too broadly.

The president began to defend his proposal by citing an extremely long list of examples, indicating that in his mind "reasonable" people should find the duties clear. This comment and the long list of examples may have communicated to others a feeling that the president was becoming impatient. When he finished, there was a lengthy silence. The president then turned to one of the executives and asked directly, "Why are you worried about this?" The executive explained, then quickly added that as far as he could see the differences were not major ones and his point of view could be integrated with the president's by "changing some words."

The president agreed to the changes, looked up, and asked, "I take it now there is common agreement?" All executives replied "yes" or nodded their heads affirmatively.

As I listened, I had begun to wonder about the commitment of the executive committee members to the idea. In subsequent interviews I asked each about his view of the
proposal. Half felt that it was a good proposal. The other half had reservations ranging
from moderate to serious. However, being loyal members, they would certainly do their
best to make it work, they said.

Subordinate Gamesmanship

I can best illustrate the second consequence by citing from a study of the effectiveness
of product planning and program review activities in another of the organizations studied:

It was company policy that peers at any given level should make the decisions.
Whenever they could not agree or whenever a decision went beyond their authority,
the problem was supposed to be sent to the next higher level. The buck passing
stopped at the highest level. A meeting with the president became a great event.
Beforehand a group would "dry run" its presentation until all were satisfied that they
could present their view effectively.

Few difficulties were observed when the meeting was held to present a recommendation agreed to by all at the lower levels. The difficulties arose when "negative"
information had to be fed upward. For example, a major error in the program, a major
delay, or a major disagreement among the members was likely to cause such trouble.

The dynamics of these meetings was very interesting. In one case the problem to
present was a major delay in a development project. In the dry run the subordinates
planned to begin the session with information that "updated" the president. The
information was usually presented in such a way that slowly and carefully the president was alerted to the fact that a major problem was about to be announced. One
could hear such key phrases as:

- "We are a bit later than expected."
- "We're not on plan."
- "We have had greater difficulties than expected."
- "It is now clear that no one should have promised what we did."

These phrases were usually followed by some reassuring statement such as:

- "However, we're on top of this."
- "Things are really looking better now."
- "Although we are late, we have advanced the state of the art."
- "If you give us another three months, we are certain that we can solve this prob-
  lem."

To the observer's eyes, it is difficult to see how the president could deny the
request. Apparently he felt the same way because he granted it. However, he took
nearly 20 minutes to say that this shocked him; he was wondering if everyone was
really doing everything they could; this was a serious program; this was not the way he
wanted to see things run; he was sure they would agree with him; and he wanted their
assurances that this would be the final delay.

A careful listening to the tape after the meeting brought out the fact that no subordinate gave such assurances. They simply kept saying that they were doing their best; they
had poured a lot into this; or they had the best technical know-how working on it.

241

Another interesting observation is that most subordinates in this company, especially in presentations to the president, tended to go along with certain unwritten rules:

1. Before you give any bad news, give good news. Especially emphasize the capacity of the department to work hard and to rebound from a failure.

2. Play down the impact of a failure by emphasizing how close you came to achieving the target or how soon the target can be reached. If neither seems reasonable, emphasize how difficult it is to define such targets, and point out that because the state of the art is so primitive, the original commitment was not a wise one.

3. In a meeting with the president it is unfair to take advantage of another department that is in trouble, even if it is a "natural enemy." The sporting thing to do is say something nice about the other department and offer to help it in any way possible. (The offer is usually not made in concrete form, nor does the department in difficulty respond with the famous phrase, "What do you have in mind?").

The subordinates also were in agreement that too much time was spent in long presentations in order to make the president happy. The president, however, confided to the researcher that he did not enjoy listening to long and, at times, dry presentations (especially when he had seen most of the key data anyway). However, he felt that it was important to go through this because it might give the subordinates a greater sense of commitment to the problem!

Lack Of Awareness

One of our most common observations in company studies is that executives lack awareness of their own behavioral patterns as well as of the negative impact of their behavior on others. This is not to imply that they are completely unaware; each individual usually senses some aspects of a problem. However, we rarely find an individual or group of individuals who is aware of enough of the scope and depth of a problem so that the need for effective action can be fully understood.

For example, during the study of the decision-making processes of the president and the nine vice presidents of a firm with nearly 3,000 employees, I concluded that the members unknowingly behaved in such a way as *not* to encourage risk taking, openness, expression of feelings, and cohesive, trusting relationships. But subsequent interviews with the ten top executives showed that they held a completely different point of view from mine. They admitted that negative feelings were not expressed, but said the reason was that "we trust each other and respect each other." According to six of the men, individuality was high and conformity low; where conformity was agreed to be high, the reason given was the necessity of agreeing with the man who is boss. According to eight of the men, "We help each other all the time." Issues loaded with conflict were not handled during meetings, it was reported, for these reasons:

- "We should not discuss emotional disagreement before the executive committee because when people are emotional, they are not rational."
- "We should not air out dirty linen in front of the people who may come in to make a presentation."
- "Why take up people's time with subjective debates?"
- "Most members are not acquainted with all the details. Under our system the person who presents the issues has really thought them through."
- "Pre-discussion of issues helps to prevent anyone from sandbagging the executive committee."

- "Rarely emotional; when it does happen, you can pardon it."

The executive committee climate or emotional tone was characterized by such words as:

- "Friendly."
- "Not critical of each other."
- "Not tense."
- "Frank and no tensions because we've known each other for years."

How was I to fit the executives' views with mine? I went back and listened to all the interviews again. As I analyzed the tapes, I began to realize that an interesting set of contradictions arose during many of the interviews. In the early stages of the interviews the executives tended to say things that they contradicted later; Chart II contains examples of contradictions repeated by six or more of the ten top executives.

Chart II—Contradictory Statements

DURING ONE PART OF THE INTERVIEW AN EXECUTIVE SAID:	YET LATER IN THE SAME INTERVIEW HE SAID:
The relationship among the executive committee members is "close," "friendly," and based on ye years of working together.	I do not know how [my peers] feel about me. That's a tough question to answer.
The strength of this company lies in its top people. They are a dedicated, friendly group. We never have the kinds of disagreements and fights that I hear others do.	Yes, the more I think of it, the more I feel this is a major weakness of the company. Management is afraid to hold someone accountable, to say, "You said you would do it. What happened?
I have an open relation ship with my supreior.	I have no direct idea how my superior evaluates my work and feels about me.
The group discussions are warm, friendly, not critical.	We trust each other not to upset one another.
We say pretty much what we think.	We are careful not to say anything that will antagonize anyone.
We respect and have faith in each other.	People do not knowingly upset each other, so they are careful in what they say.
The executive committee tackles all issues.	The executive committee tends to spenc to much time talking about relatively unimportant issues.
The executive committee makes decisions quickly and effectively.	A big problem of the executive committee is that it takes forever and a day to make important decisions.
The members trust each other.	The members are careful not to say something that may make another member look bad. It may be misinterpreted.
The executive committee makes the major policy decisions.	On many major issues, decisions are really made outside the executive committee meetings. The executive committee convenes to approve a decision and have "holy water" placed on it.

243

What accounts for these contradictions? My explanation is that over time the executives had come to mirror, in their behavior, the values of their culture (e.g., be rational, nonemotional, diplomatically open, and so on). They had created a culture that reinforced their own leadership styles. If an executive wanted to behave differently, he probably ran the risk of being considered a deviant. In most of the cases the executives decided to forgo this risk, and they behaved like the majority. These men, in order to live with themselves, probably had to develop various defenses and blinders about their acquiescence to an executive culture that may not have been the one they personally preferred and valued.

Incidentally, in this group there were two men who had decided to take the other route. Both men were viewed by the others as "a bit rough at the edges" or "a little too aggressive."

To check the validity of some of the findings reported, we interviewed the top 25 executives below the executive committee. If our analysis was correct, we knew, then they should tend to report that the members of the executive committee were low in openness to uncomfortable information, risk taking, trust, and capacity to deal with conflicts openly, and high in conformity. The results were as predicted (see Chart III).

Chart III—How The Executive Committee Was Rated By 25 Executives Below It.

Number of Managers Rating the Committee As:

CHARACTERISTIC RATED	LOW	MODERATE	HIGH
OPENNESS TO UNCOMFORTABLE INFORMATION*	12	6	4
RISK TAKING	20	4	1
TRUST	14	9	2
CONFORMITY	0	2	23
ABILITY TO DEAL WITH CONFLICTS	19	6	0

*Three executives gave a "don't know" response.

Blind Spots

Another result found in all organizations studied is the tendency for executives to be unaware of the negative feelings that their subordinates have about them. This finding is not startling in view of the fact that the executive problem-solving processes do not tend to reward the upward communication of information about interpersonal issues that is emotionally laden and risky to communicate. To illustrate:

In one organization, all but one of the top executive committee members reported that their relationships with their subordinates were "relatively good to excellent." When asked how they judged their relationships, most of the executives responded with such statements as: "They do everything that I ask for willingly," and "We talk together frequently and openly."

The picture from the middle management men who were the immediate subordinates was different. Apparently, top management was unaware that:

- 71 percent of the middle managers did not know where they stood with their superiors; they considered their relationships as ambiguous, and they were not aware of such important facts as how they were being evaluated.
- 65 percent of the middle managers did not know what qualities led to success in their organizations.
- 87 percent felt that conflicts were very seldom coped with; and that when they were, the attempts tended to be inadequate.
- 65 percent thought that the most important unsolved problem of the organization was that the top management was unable to help them overcome the intergroup rivalries, lack of cooperation, and poor communications; 53 percent said that if they could alter one aspect of their superior's behavior, it would be to help him see the "dog eat dog" communication problems that existed in middle management.
- 59 percent evaluated top management effectiveness as not too good or about average; and 62 percent reported that the development of a cohesive management team was the second most important unsolved problem.
- 82 percent of the middle managers wished that the status of their function and job could be increased but doubted if they could communicate this openly to the top management.

Interestingly, in all the cases that I have observed where the president asked for a discussion of any problems that the top and middle management men present thought important, the problems mentioned above were never raised.

Rather, the most frequently mentioned problem (74 percent of the cases) was the overload problem. The executives and managers reported that they were overloaded and that the situation was getting worse. The president's usual reply was that he appreciated their predicament, but "that is life." The few times he asked if the men had any suggestions, he received such replies as "more help," "fewer meetings," "fewer reports," "delay of schedules," and so on. As we will see, few of these suggestions made sense, since the men were asking either for increases in costs or for a decrease in the very controls that the top management used to administer the organization.

Distrust And Antagonism

Another result of the behavior patterns earlier described is that management tends to keep promotions semisecret and most of the actual reasons for executive changes completely secret. Here is an example from an organization whose board we studied in some detail over a period of two years:

The executives complained of three practices of the board about which the board members were apparently unaware: (1) the constant alteration of organizational positions and charts, and keeping the most up-to-date versions semiconfidential; (2) shifting top executives without adequate discussion with all executives involved and without clearly communicating the real reasons for the move; and (3) developing new departments with product goals that overlapped and competed with the goals of already existing departments.

The board members admitted these practices but tended not to see them as being incompatible with the interests of the organization. For example, to take the first complaint, they defended their practice with such statements as: "If you tell them everything, all they do is worry, and we get a flood of rumors"; "The changes do not *really* affect them"; and "It will only cut in on their busy schedule and interrupt their productivity."

The void of clear-cut information from the board was, however, filled in by the executives. Their explanations ranged from such statements as "They must be changing things because they are not happy with the way things are going" to "The unhappiness is so strong they do not tell us." Even the executives who profited from some of these moves reported some concern and bewilderment. For example, three reported instances where they had been promoted over some "old-timers." In all cases they were told to "soft-pedal the promotion aspect" until the old-timers were diplomatically informed. Unfortunately, it took months to inform the latter men, and in some cases it was never done.

There was another practice of the board that produced difficulties in the organization:

Department heads cited the board's increasing intervention into the detailed administration of a department when its profit picture looked shaky. This practice was, from these subordinates' view, in violation of the stated philosophy of decentralization.

When asked, board members tended to explain this practice by saying that it was done only when they had doubts about the department head's competence, and then it was always in the interests of efficiency. When they were alerted about a department that was not doing well, they believed that the best reaction was to tighten controls, "take a closer and more frequent look," and "make sure the department head is on top of things." They quickly added that they did not tell the man in question they were beginning to doubt his competence for fear of upsetting him. Thus, again we see how the values of de-emphasizing the expression of negative feelings and the emphasizing of controls influenced the board's behavior.

The department heads, on the other hand, reported different reactions. "Why are they bothered with details? Don't they trust me? If not, why don't they say so?" Such reactions tended to produce more conformity, antagonism, mistrust, and fear of experimenting.

Still another board practice was the "diplomatic" rejection of an executive's idea that was, in the eyes of the board, offbeat, a bit too wild, or not in keeping with the corporate mission. The reasons given by the board for not being open about the evaluation again reflected adherence to the pyramidal values. For example, a board member would say, "We do not want to embarrass them." or "If you really tell them, you might restrict creativity."

This practice tended to have precisely the impact that the superiors wished to *avoid*. The subordinates reacted by asking, "Why don't they give me an opportunity to really explain it?" or "What do they mean when they suggest that the 'timing is not right' or 'funds are not currently available'?"

Processes Damaged

It is significant that defensive activities like those described are rarely observed during group meetings dealing with minor or relatively routine decisions. These activities become most noticeable when the decision is an important one in terms of dollars or in terms of the impact on the various departments in the organization. *The forces toward ineffectiveness operate most strongly during the important decision-making meetings*. The group and organizational defenses operate most frequently when they can do the most harm to decision-making effectiveness.

Another interesting finding is that the more effective and more committed executives tend to be upset about these facts, whereas the less effective, less committed people tend simply to lament them. They also tend to take on an "I told them so" attitude — one of resignation and noninvolvement in correcting the situation. In short, it is the better executives who are negatively affected.

WHAT CAN BE DONE?

What can the executive do to change this situation?

I wish that I could answer this question as fully as I should like to. Unfortunately, I cannot. Nevertheless, there are some suggestions I can make.

Blind Alleys

First, let me state what I believe will *not* work.

Learning about these problems by listening to lectures, reading about them, or exploring them through cases is not adequate; an article or book can pose some issues and get thinking started, but — in this area, at least — it cannot change behavior. Thus, in one study with 60 top executives:

> Lectures were given and cases discussed on this subject for nearly a week. A test at the end of the week showed that the executives rated the lecturers very high, liked the cases, and accepted the diagnosis. Yet when they attempted to apply their new-found knowledge outside the learning situation, most were unable to do so. The major problem was that they had not learned how to make these new ideas come to life in their behavior.
>
> As one executive stated, pointing to his head: "I know up here what I should do, but when it comes to a real meeting, I behave in the same old way. It sure is frustrating."[1]

Learning about these problems through a detailed diagnosis of executives' behavior is also not enough. For example:

> I studied a top management group for nearly four months through interviews and tape recordings of their decision-making meetings. Eventually, I fed back the analysis. The executives agreed with the diagnosis as well as with the statement by one executive that he found it depressing. Another executive, however, said he now felt that he had a clearer and more coherent picture of some of the causes of their problems, and he was going to change his behavior. I predicted that he would probably find that he would be unable to change his behavior — and even if he did change, his subordinates, peers, and superiors might resist dealing with him in the new way.
>
> The executive asked, "How can you be so sure that we can't change?" I responded that I knew of no case where managers were able to alter successfully their behavior, their group dynamics, and so forth by simply realizing intellectually that such a change was necessary. The key to success was for them to be able to show these new strategies in their behavior. To my knowledge, behavior of this type, groups with these dynamics, and organizational cultures endowed with these characteristics were very difficult to change. What kind of thin-skinned individuals would they be, how brittle would their groups and their organizations be if they could be altered that easily?
>
> Three of the exectuves decided that they were going to prove the prediction to be incorrect. They took my report and studied it carefully. In one case the executive asked his subordinates to do the same. Then they tried to alter their behavior. According to their own accounts, they were unable to do so. The only changes they reported were: (*1*) a softening of the selling activities, (*2*) a reduction of their aggressive persuasion, and (*3*) a genuine increase in their asking for the subordinates' views.
>
> My subsequent observations and interviews uncovered the fact that the first two changes were mistrusted by the subordinates, who had by now adapted to the old

---

[1] See my article, "Explorations in Interpersonal Competence II," *Applied Behavioral Science*, Vol. I, No. 3 (1965), p. 255.

behavior of their superiors. They tended to play it carefully and to be guarded. This hesitation aggravated the executives, who felt that their subordinates were not responding to their new behavior with the enthusiasm that they (the superiors) had expected.

However, *the executives did not deal with this issue openly*. They kept working at trying to be rational, patient, and rewarding. The more irritated they became and the more they showed this irriation in their behavior, the more the subordinates felt that the superiors "new" behavior was a gimmick.

Eventually, the process of influencing subordinates slowed down so much that the senior men returned to their more controlling styles. The irony was that in most cases the top executives interpreted the subordinates' behavior as proof that they needed to be needled and pushed, while the subordinates interpreted the top managers' behavior as proof that they did not trust their assistants and would never change.

The reason I doubt that these approaches will provide anything but temporary cures is that they do not go far enough. If changes are going to be made in the behavior of an executive, if trust is to be developed, if risk taking is to flourish, he must be placed in a different situation. He should be helped to (a) expose his leadership style so that he and others can take a look at its true impact; (b) deepen his awareness of himself and the dynamics of effective leadership; (c) strive for these goals under conditions where he is in control of the amount, pace and depth of learning.

These conditions for learning are difficult to achieve. Ideally, they require the help of a professional consultant. Also, it would be important to get away from the organization — its interruptions, pressures, and daily administrative tensions.

Value Of Questions

The executive can strive to be aware that he is probably programmed with a set of values which cause him to behave in ways that are not always helpful to others and which his subordinates will not discuss frankly even when they believe he is not being helpful. He can also strive to find time to uncover, through careful questioning, his impact on others. Once in a while a session that is focused on the "How am I doing?" question can enlighten the executive and make his colleagues more flexible in dealing with him.

One simple question I have heard several presidents ask their vice presidents with success is: "Tell me what, if anything, I do that tends to prevent (or help) your being the kind of vice president you wish to be?" These presidents are careful to ask these questions during a time when they seem natural (e.g., performance review sessions), or they work hard ahead of time to create a climate so that such a discussion will not take the subordinate by surprise.

Some presidents feel uncomfortable in raising these questions, and others point out that the vice presidents are also uncomfortable. I can see how both would have such feelings. A chief executive officer may feel that he is showing weakness by asking his subordinates about his impact. The subordinate may or may not feel this way, but he may sense that his chief does, and that is enough to make him uncomfortable.

Yet in two companies I have studied where such questions were asked, superiors and subordinates soon learned that authority which gained strength by a lack of openness was weak and brittle, whereas authority resting on open feedback from below was truly strong and viable.

Working With The Group

Another step that an executive can take is to vow not to accept group ineffectiveness as part of life. Often I have heard people say, "Groups are no damned good; strong leadership is what is necessary." I agree that many groups are ineffective. I doubt, however, if either of the two leadership patterns described earlier will help the situation. As we have seen, both patterns tend to make the executive group increasingly less effective.

If my data are valid, the search process in executive decision making has become so complicated that group participation is essential. No one man seems to be able to have all the knowledge necessary to make an effective decision. If individual contributions are necessary in group meetings, it is important that a climate be created that does not discourage innovation, risk taking, and honest leveling between managers in their conversations with one another. The value of a group is to maximize individual contributions.

Interestingly, the chief executive officers in these studies are rarely observed making policy decisions in the classic sense, viz., critical selections from several alternatives and determination of future directions to be taken. This does not mean that they shy away from taking responsibility. Quite the contrary. Many report that they enjoy making decisions by themselves. Their big frustration comes from realizing that most of the major decisions they face are extremely complex and require the coordinated, honest inputs of many different executives. They are impatient at the slowness of meetings, the increasingly quantitative nature of the inputs, and, in many cases, their ignorance of what the staff groups did to the decision inputs long before they received them.

The more management deals with complexity by the use of computers and quantitative approaches, the more it will be forced to work with inputs of many different people, and the more important will be the group dynamics of decision-making meetings. If anyone doubts this, let him observe the dry runs subordinates go through to get a presentation ready for the top. He will observe, I believe, that much data are included and excluded by subordinates on the basis of what they believe those at the top can hear.

In short, *one of the main tasks of the chief executive is to build and maintain an effective decision-making network*. I doubt that he has much choice *except* to spend time in exploring how well his group functions.

Such explorations could occur during the regular workday. For example:

> In one organization the president began by periodically asking members of his top group, immediately after a decision was made, to think back during the meeting and describe when they felt that the group was not being as effective as they wished. How could these conditions be altered?
>
> As trust and openness increased, the members began to level with each other as to when they were inhibited, irritated, suppressed, confused, and withholding information. The president tried to be as encouraging as he could, and he especially rewarded people who truly leveled. Soon the executives began to think of mechanisms they could build into their group functioning so they would be alerted to these group problems and correct them early. As one man said, "We have not eliminated all our problems, but we are building a competence in our group to deal effectively if and when they arise."

Utilizing Feedback

Another useful exercise is for the superior and his group members to tape-record a decision-making meeting, especially one which is expected to be difficult. At a later date, the group members can gather and listen to the tape. I believe it is safe to say that simply listening to the tape is an education in itself. If one can draw from skilled company or outside help, then useful analyses can be made of group or individual behavior.

Recently, I experimented with this procedure with an "inside" board of directors of a company. The directors met once a month and listened to tape recordings of their monthly board meetings. With my help they analyzed their behavior, trying to find how they could improve their individual and group effectiveness. Listening to tapes became a very involving experience for them. They spent nearly four hours in the first meeting discussing less than ten minutes of the tape.

'Binds' Created. One of the major gains of these sessions was that the board members became aware of the "binds" they were creating for each other and of the impact they each had on the group's functioning. Thus:

Executive A was frequently heard antagonizing Executive B by saying something that B perceived as "needling." For example, A might seem to be questioning B's competence. "Look here," he would say, "anyone who can do simple arithmetic should realize that. . . . "

Executive B responded by fighting. B's way of fighting back was to utilize his extremely high capacity to verbalize and intellectualize. B's favorite tactic was to show A where he missed five important points and where his logic was faulty.

Executive A became increasingly upset as the "barrage of logic" found its mark. He tended to counteract by (a) remaining silent but manifesting a sense of being flustered and becoming red-faced; and/or (b) insisting that his logic *was* sound even though he did not express it in "highfalutin language" as did B.

Executive B pushed harder (presumably to make A admit he was wrong) by continuing his "barrage of logic" or implying that A could not see his errors because he was upset.

Executive A would respond to this by insisting that he was not upset. "The point you are making is so simple, why, anyone can see it. Why should I be upset?"

Executive B responded by pushing harder and doing more intellectualizing. Executive A eventually reached his breaking point, he too began to shout and fight.

At this point, Executives C, D, and E could be observed withdrawing until A and B wore each other out.

Progress Achieved. As a result of the meetings, the executives reported in interviews, board members experienced fewer binds, less hostility, less frustration, and more constructive work. One member wondered if the group had lost some of its "zip," but the others disagreed. Here is an excerpt from the transcript of one discussion on this point:

EXECUTIVE A: My feeling is, as I have said, that we have just opened this thing up, and I for one feel that we have benefited a great deal from it. I think I have improved; maybe I am merely reflecting the fact that you [Executive B] have improved. But at least I think there has been improvement in our relationship. I also see signs of not as good a relationship in other places as there might be.

I think on the whole we are much better off today than we were a year ago. I think there is a whole lot less friction today than there was a year ago, but there's still enough of it.

Now we have a much clearer organization setup; if we were to sit down here and name the people, we would probably all name exactly the same people. I don't think there is much question about who should be included and who should not be included; we've got a pretty clean organization.

EXECUTIVE B: You're talking now about asking the consultant about going on with this week's session?

EXECUTIVE A: It would be very nice to have the consultant if he can do it; then we should see how we can do it without him, but it'd be better with him.

EXECUTIVE B: But that's the step, as I understand it, that should be taken at this stage. Is that right?

EXECUTIVE A: Well, I would certainly favor doing something; I don't know what. I'm not making a specific recommendation: I just don't like to let go of it.

EXECUTIVE C: What do you think?

EXECUTIVE D: I'm not as optimistic as A. I wonder if anybody here agrees with me that maybe we haven't made as much progress as we think. I've personally enjoyed these experiences, and I'd like to see them continued.

EXECUTIVE A: Would you like to venture to say why I think we have made progress and why I might be fooled?

EXECUTIVE D: Well, I think maybe you are in the worst position to evaluate progress because if the worst possible thing that can happen is for people to no longer fight and struggle, but to say, "yes, sir," you might call that progress. That might be the worst thing that could happen, and I sort of sense some degree of resignation — I don't think it's progress. I don't know. I might be all alone in this. What do you think?

EXECUTIVE C: On one level it is progress. Whether it is institutional progress and whether it produces commensurate institutional benefits is a debatable question. It may in fact do so. I think it's very clear that there is in our meetings and in individual contact less heat, less overt friction, petulance, tension, than certainly was consistently the case. Do you agree?

EXECUTIVE D: Yes, I think so.

EXECUTIVE C: It has made us a great deal more aware of the extent and nature of the friction and clearly has made all of us intent on fighting less. There's some benefit to it; but there are some drawbacks.

EXECUTIVE A: Well, if you and D are right, I would say for that reason we need more of the program.

Laboratory Training

Another possibility is for the executive to attend a program designed to help increase competence in this area, such as laboratory education and its various off-shoots ("T-groups," the "managerial grid," "conflict management labs," and so on). These learning experiences are available at various university and National Training Laboratory executive programs. They can also be tailor-madefor the individual organization.

I believe outside programs offer the better way of becoming acquainted with this type of learning. Bear in mind, though, that since typically only one or two executives attend from the same organization, the biggest payoff is for the individual. The inside program provides greater possibilities for payoff to the organization.

At the same time, however, it should also be kept in mine that in-house programs *can* be dangerous to the organization. I would recommend that a thorough study be made ahead of time to ascertain whether or not a laboratory educational experience would be helpful to company executives individually and to the organization.

251

I have never observed a group whose members wanted it to decay. I have never studied a group or an organization that was decaying where there were not some members who were aware that decay was occurring. Accordingly, one key to group and organizational effectiveness is to get this knowledge out into the open and to discuss it thoroughly. The human "motors" of the group and the organization have to be checked periodically, just as does the motor of an automobile. Without proper maintenance, all will fail.

Resistance to Change–
Its Analysis and Prevention

ALVIN ZANDER

In order to derive the benefit from research in industrial relations, someone must plan a program of action to apply them. When one begins implementing, he must change the social system in some way. The creation of this change can cause the development of resistance in those influenced by the change.

First, we shall look at what resistance is; second, the conditions that appear to be associated with its development; and third, some means whereby resistance may be prevented or decreased.

NATURE OF RESISTANCE

Let us look at some examples of resistance growing out of administrative changes.

A large number of foremen in a company were given training in how to treat their men like human beings. They liked the course and were eager to apply their learnings on the job. The company found, however, that relatively few of the foremen are really behaving any differently on the job. They know their stuff but do not use it.

In one of the paper-shuffling government agencies a new data form was developed which all admitted was briefer, more logical, and easier to use. Yet, this department found that the employees often omitted much of the data needed on this form, their speed of work decreased, and they objected to it on many insignificant grounds.

Our favorite example of resistance was furnished by a farmer in the TVA area. He assured us that he knew all about contour plowing, the rotation of crops, and the use of what he called "phosaphate" for improving the soil. He allowed as how these were good ideas, "But," he said, "I don't do it that way."

These examples have one common denominator which might serve here as a definition of resistance. They describe behavior which is intended to protect an individual from the effects of real or imagined change. This reaction might be to either real or imagined change since the resister might be reacting to things that were really not changed but he thinks were, or fears that they might be. If a person believes a change has been made, or fears potential change, it makes no difference whether or not it is true in fact. He will act as though there has been a change.

How can one recognize when resistance is working? Unfortunately, there is no list of typical behavior which can be described as the symptoms of resistance, which, if present, indicate that one is dealing with this phenomenon. It is the protective function which the behavior is providing which determines whether or not a person is resisting, rather than the kind of thing he does. By the same token, all behavior which opposes change is not

Reprinted with permission of the Society for the Advancement of Management, from "Resistance to Change: Its Analysis and Prevention," Advanced Management, Vols. 15-16 (January, 1950), pp. 9-11.

necessarily resistance. Some opposition to change may be perfectly logical and grounded on well supported reasons. The behavior must be attempting to protect the person against the consequences of the change in order for it to be resistance. This may be clearer if we look at the origin of the concept.

THE HOSTILITY PATTERN

The term and the concept we are using here has been borrowed from psychotherapy. When a therapist is attempting to change the behavior of the patient, he expects resistance from him. The therapist takes the position that the pattern of behavior used by the patient (which makes him a "sick" person) is a means to some satisfaction for him even though it also may make him ineffective or unhappy. Resistance occurs in the patient when the process of change (therapy here) comes close to being successful. When faced with the unpleasant necessity of giving up the behavior he does not like, but somehow needs, he begins to balk. He becomes silent, blushes, changes the subject, tells fibs, comes late to appointments, becomes angry with the therapist, or any of a number of similar things. The therapist watches for the context in which these signs of resistance occur since these indicate the crucial problems in the way the patient sees and deals with his world.

For the administrator, resistance may occur under fairly similar conditions. When he attempts to create a change the administrator may develop, unintentionally, many threats to the person or groups with whom he works. The behavior used by the resister may take many forms.

It may take the form of hostility either openly expressed or obliquely implied. The aggression may be directed against the change itself or against the administrator. What is done depends on how the person can safely resist without further endangering himself in that situation. Other symptoms of resistance may be sloppy effort after the change has been made, or fawning submissiveness which is a hybrid of apple polishing and apathy. It can occur by lowering the level of aspiration to an inefficient degree, discouragement, or the development of unhappy cliques and outspoken factions. It is important, however, to remind ourselves, that it is the function which such actions are performing for the person that makes them resistance rather than what they look like.

WHERE RESISTANCE STARTS

It will be helpful if we look at a few conditions conducive to resistance.

1. Resistance can be expected if the nature of the change is not made clear to the people who are going to be influenced by the change. In one of the largest government agencies, a change required one department which originally had the responsibility of processing papers involved in contacts with certain industries to share this task with another office. Announcement of the change was issued in a brief statement. The immediate reaction was violent objection, even though some of the workers privately admitted that it was a wise and necessary move. They were reacting to incomplete information. Many people fear incomplete information about changes which influence them. It is more comfortable to know exactly where one stands.

There is some evidence to support the hypothesis that those persons who dislike their jobs, will most dislike ambiguity in a proposed change. They want to know exactly what they must do in order to be sure to avoid the unpleasant aspects of their jobs. Some administrators may attach too much importance to the value of information itself. Apparently they reason that people "ought not" to resist the way they do, because the administrator has told them everything he thinks is important for them to know about the impending change.

2. Different people will see different meanings in the proposed change. Some of the resistant reaction described above came about because some workers saw the change as an indication that they had been doing a poor job, others assumed it meant their office would soon be abolished, still others were troubled since they were losing some of the power they had formerly controlled. We tend to see in our world the things that we expect to see. Complete information can just as readily be distorted as incomplete information, especially so if the workers have found discomfort and threats in their past work situation.

3. Resistance can be expected when those influenced are caught in a jam between strong forces pushing them to make the change and strong forces deterring them against making the change.

4. Resistance may be expected to the degree that the persons influenced by the change have pressure put upon them to make it, and will be decreased to the degree that these same persons are able to have some "say" in the nature or direction of the change. In a garment factory a change was required. The switch meant that workers would be asked to change their jobs and, in many cases, to develop working relationships with new people. An experiment was made in which three different styles of introducing this change were tried out. One group of workers were simply informed about the change and were allowed to ask questions. They developed the most resistance as measured by turnover, absenteeism, and slowness in learning the job. Resistance was *less* in those groups who sent representatives to a meeting in which the nature of the change was discussed and all persons present made plans to carry out the change.

Resistance was *least* in the groups in which those to be affected discussed the nature of the change, laid plans for making it, and as a total group made decisions which were satisfactory to the entire group. In this latter group everyone participated. They had an opportunity to develop their own motivation instead of making the change only on the basis of orders from the boss. The fact that they were able to develop their own understanding of the need for the change and their own decisions about how to do it, reduced resistance most effectively.

5. Resistance may be expected if the change is made on personal grounds rather than impersonal requirements or sanctions. A supervisor posted the following notice:

> I have always felt that promptness is an important indicator of an employee's interest in his job. I will feel much better if you are at your desk at the proper time.

Employees responded to this notice by appointing a committee to get information which would justify their late arrival at the office. Many administrators can expect trouble in establishing a change if it is requested in terms of what "I think is necessary"; rather than making the request in the light of "our objectives," the rules, the present state of affairs, or some other impersonal requirement.

6. Resistance may be expected if the change ignores the already established institutions in the group. Every work situation develops certain customs in doing the work or in the relations among the workers. The administrator who ignores institutionalized patterns of work and abruptly attempts to create a new state of affairs which demands that these customs be abolished without further consideration will surely run into resistance.

These are a few of the conditions in which resistance might be expected to occur. There probably are many others.

DECREASING RESISTANCE

Some procedures on the part of the administrator might be useful in preventing or decreasing the resistance which arises in a changed situation. Let us look at a major principle in preventing resistance and some of its basic implications:

> Resistance will be prevented to the degree that the changer helps the changees to develop their own understanding of the need for the change, and an explicit awareness of how they feel about it, and what can be done about those feelings.

This principle implies that the administrator can use resistance as an important symptom. Specifically, he can use the nature of the resistance as an indicator of the cause of resistance. It will be most helpful to him as a symptom, if he diagnoses the causes for it when it occurs rather than inhibiting it at once. The same resistant behavior, for example, may indicate that one person feels that he has lost prestige by the change, to another it may mean that he has lost power over an area of influence which he formerly controlled, and to still another it may mean that he fears that his friends will think less well of him. An administrator must know what the resistance means in order that he may effectively lessen it by working on the causes instead of the symptom.

There has been a good deal of experience in recent years in staff meetings and in work conferences like the National Training Laboratory for Group Development with the use of a group observer. This observer gives to the group, and the leaders, information about the group and the nature of any resistance. In these cases, the data about itself is made common group property for all members to discuss and to use in planning better work relations.

This communication must go in both directions. If two-way communication is not maintained, negative attitudes created during resistance will tend to persist.

RESTORING UNDERSTANDING

In a utility company a new office was formed with a new set of supervisors. The entire staff of supervisors called the workers together and scolded them for shortcomings in their performance. The tone used by the supervisors was so aggressive that the employees found it difficult thereafter to discuss anything with them except those topics directly related to the effectiveness of production. The workers kept themsleves at a distance from the supervisors and the supervisors made no move to close the gap. The result was that distance between these two groups made it impossible for them to come to any new understanding of each other. This mounting hostility was lessened only when the personnel department advised a number of "gripe-sessions" with small groups of workers in which the two levels developed a new understanding of each other.

Another implication in the above principle is that there is value in blowing off steam. The psychologists call this a "catharsis." There is good evidence that new attitudes can be accepted by a person only if he has a chance to thoroughly air his original attitude. Resistance to accepting the rigid, and often apparently meaningless, rules of military life, showed itself in flagrant violation of the rules, often in a most aggressive manner. Punishment only increased the resistance. Relief was provided by group sessions in which men were able to thoroughly gripe. After this relief of tension, they were able to turn to a reasonable discussion about what they could do to learn to live in terms of these requirements. It is as though new air can be put in the tire only after the old air is released.

A third implication of the earlier expressed principle is that resistance may be less likely to occur if the group participates in making the decisions about how the change should be implemented, what the change should be like, how people might perform in the changed situation, or any other problems that are within their area of freedom to decide. The experiment in which three ways of introducing a change were tried out showed that the workers, who had a chance to make a group decision about the ways in which the change should be made, developed much less resistance than did those who were simply called together to be told about the change and have all of their questions answered. What is important here is that the workers feel that they have a chance to discuss the major factors involved in the change, a chance to understand the nature of the fears they have in facing this change, and a chance to plan what they will do to calm their fears.

SELF-DIAGNOSIS GETS ACTION

Still another implication is that resistance will be less likely to develop if facts which point to the need for change are gathered by the persons who must make the change. A number of high level supervisors in a utility industry came to feel that the workers had many negative attitudes about their jobs which were due to poor supervisory practices. Each supervisor, quite naturally, felt that other supervisors were at fault. Top management set up a number of study groups in which the supervisors first learned how they could diagnose the causes of these negative attitudes. Each supervisor then returned to his own work place and gathered facts that would be necessary for him to analyze the causes of negative attitudes he could spot among his workers. Later the supervisors came together to report their findings. At this meeting their enthusiasm for change in their own practices was high because they had participated in gathering the facts which best described their problems. People will be more likely to act in terms of information they gather themselves than in terms of information gathered by others and delivered to them. If it is clear that a change is indicated in a given state of affairs, but the people who must abide by the change are resisting the shift, they can come to see it themselves by obtaining the facts which properly "case" the situation.

To summarize, we have said that resistance is a problem which any person who is responsible for social change must face. Even though it is strange and unexpected behavior, there are causes for the development of this phenomenon. These causes may be understood, and resistance may be prevented, if the administrator will help the changees develop their own understanding of the need for change and explicit awareness of how they feel about it, and what can be done about those feelings.

What's Not on the Organizational Chart

HAROLD STIEGLITZ

Organization charts come in various sizes, colors, and even textures. Most are black and white and printed on paper. Some are affixed to office walls — and made of materials that are easily changed. Some charts are highly detailed; some are very sketchy. Some are stamped *confidential* and secreted in the desks of a chosen few; others are broadly distributed and easily available. Despite these and other variations that might be noted, all organization charts have at least one thing in common: they don't show how the organization works. Or, as some people say, they don't show the *real* organization.

Such a statement, which usually emerges as a criticism of organization charts, goes beyond the fact that the organization chart, like milk, may be dated but not fresh. For it is increasingly understood that no organization chart is 100% current. Rather, the criticism is that even the most current chart is utterly inadequate as a diagram of the organization.

Few organization planners, even those whose major preoccupation is drawing charts, argue too vehemently against this criticism. They just go on drawing their charts. Most often, the charts they draw are of the conventional type made up of boxes and lines. These usually end up in a pyramidal shape with a box (generally larger) at the top to represent the chief executive.

However, behind the preparation and issuance of the chart, there is, presumably, this basic understanding: An organization chart is not an organization. And there is far more to an organization — even in the limited sense of an organization structure — than can ever be put on a chart.

But while the chartist himself may be aware of it, this knowledge is seldom pervasive. Some companies recognize this and attempt to underscore the fact that a chart is just a two-dimensional representation by placing the following caution at the bottom of the chart:

> Level of boxes shows reporting relationships and has no significance with regard to importance of position or status.

Such a caution or demurrer is seldom sufficient to quiet the critics or unruffle ruffled feathers, and is quite often taken with a large grain of salt — sometimes because the chart does show some of the very things that the demurrer may say it doesn't. If nothing else, for example, the head of a unit that doesn't appear on an organization chart can be reasonably sure that his unit is not rated important enough to merit inclusion.

Reprinted with permission from The Conference Board Record, *September, 1964, pp. 372-376. Copyright 1964 by National Industrial Conference Board.*

Actually, the conventional organization chart (see Fig. 1) shows very little. It implies a little more than it shows. But the inferences that are drawn from it are limited only by the experience, imagination and biases of the beholder — in or outside of the company. In other words, one of the troubles with charts seems to be the people who read them.

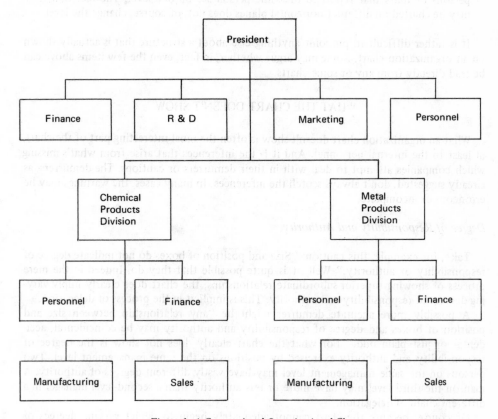

Figure 1. A Conventional Organizational Chart.

WHAT IT SHOWS

The organization chart of most companies shows — indeed is designed to show — just two things:

1. Division of work into components. These components may be divisions or departments or they may be individuals. Boxes on the conventional chart represent these units of work.
2. Who is (supposed to be) whose boss — the solid lines on the chart show this superior-subordinate relationship with its implied flow of delegated responsibility, authority and attendant accountability.

Implicit in these two are several other things that the chart is designed to show:

3. Nature of the work performed by the component. Depending upon the descriptive

title placed in the box, what this shows may be specific (Facilities Engineering), speculative (Planning) or spurious (Special Projects).

4. Grouping of components on a functional, regional or product basis. This is also conveyed to some extent by the labels in the boxes.
5. Levels of management in terms of successive layers of superiors and subordinates. All persons or units that report to the same person are on one level. The fact that they may be charted on different horizontal planes does not, of course, change the level.

It is rather difficult to pinpoint anything else about a structure that is actually shown on an organization chart. Some may argue whether, in fact, even the few items above can be read directly from any or some charts.

WHAT THE CHART DOESN'T SHOW

What an organization chart doesn't show is often the most interesting part of the chart, at least to the internal personnel. And it is the inferences that arise from what's missing which companies attempt to deal with in their demurrers or cautions. The demurrers, as already suggested, don't always scotch the inferences. In many cases, the warnings may be erroneous or incomplete.

Degree of Responsibility and Authority

Take, for example, this caution: "Size and position of boxes do not indicate degree of responsibility or authority." Well, it is quite possible that they do. Indeed in the mere process of showing superior-subordinate relationships, the chart does clearly imply varying degrees of responsibility and authority. This is implicit in the process of delegation.

A possibly more accurate demurrer might be "any relationship between size and position of boxes and degree of responsibility and authority may be coincidental, accidental or just plain odd." For what the chart clearly does not show is the degree of responsibility and authority exercised by positions on the same management level. Two persons on the same management level may have vastly different degrees of authority. A man on the third level may have more or less authority than a second-level manager in a different chain of delegation.

Of course, because the chart cannot adequately begin to depict varying degrees of authority, it cannot show the degree of decentralization. Decentralization, organizationally speaking, has relevance only in terms of delegation of decision-making authority. Almost by definition, it refers to the level at which decisions are made.

Inferences about decentralization are often drawn from charts; the company chart that shows activities grouped into product divisions or regional divisions as opposed to a purely functional grouping is often referred to as decentralized. That may or may not be the case. The view from the top may be of a highly decentralized company; the view from the bottom or intermediate layers may be quite the opposite. And a functionally organized company can be as highly decentralized as a divisionally organized company. It all depends on the level at which decisions are being made. The chart cannot depict that, nor can it depict the extent of the restrictions — in the form of policies, budgets, procedures, reports, audits — that make for more or less decentralization.

Staff and Line

Distinguishing between staff and line is an arduous, hazardous, and so far as some organization planners are concerned, an academic chore. Attempting to determine line

260

and staff from an organization chart presents similar hazards. Titles or functional labels alone won't do it. What one company considers line may be staff to another. Again, it depends on the responsibility and authority delegated to the units.

Of course, the nature of the company's business may have clues to what is staff or line. In a manufacturing company, for example, certain functions are traditionally viewed as staff: personnel administration, public relations, legal and secretarial, and finance are examples. In a services company the arrangement may be quite different. But reliance on the nature of the business can be misleading. In manufacturing, for example, divisionalization has brought into being staff units with labels such as manufacturing and marketing, labels that typically would belong to line components in a functionally organized firm.

In some companies, charting methods are used to attempt to distinguish what these firms consider to be line and staff (or service and operating) units. Sometimes the so-called staff units are charted on one horizontal plane, line on another. Other companies use skinny little lines to connect staff, healthier looking lines to connect line or operating units. Still others add labels to underscore this visual aid.

With all these visual distinctions, a chart reader might readily infer what is obviously being implied: there is a difference between the two types of units. To try to interpret these differences in terms of line-staff responsibilities, authorities, and relationships presents the same difficulties as reading the degree of decentralization from the chart.

Status or Importance

To some people, inclusion on the organization chart is, in itself, a status symbol. The physical location on the chart — the linear distance from the chief executive — is viewed as a measure of importance. And there's the rub. Given the limitations of a piece of paper, not everyone can be charted equidistant from the chief executive. Reassurances like "size and position of boxes do not reflect importance or status" are seldom reassuring enough. The incumbent charted in a particular spot may realize the truth of this statement; but he may fear that the "other fellows may not," or vice versa.

There is little question but that position on an organization chart, in some companies, does imply relative importance and status. But it has the same limitations in implying (or covering up lack of) importance as do size of office, titles, parking lot space, etc. Most people still rely on the pay envelope as a more accurate reflection of relative importance. And the organization chart just isn't designed to reflect the pay structure of the company.

In short, the organization chart may imply relative importance or status, but, to re-phrase a caution that might appear on a chart, "Any inferences drawn from this chart regarding relative importance or status may or may not be correct."

Lines of Communication

Another caution that shows up is "This chart does not indicate channels of contact." Actually it does. What it doesn't show is *all* the channels of contact or communication. Possibly a more appropriate warning might be: "This chart indicates a few of the major channels of contact — but if the organization sticks to only these, nothing will get done." For it is a truism of organization that no one unit or individual operates in isolation from all the others. All are linked by an intricate network of communication. (Maze may be a more apt term than network.) Proper organization performance relies on this network and on each unit and individual becoming party to it. To chart the total network is practically impossible. To attempt to chart it — and thus introduce certain rigidities into it — might easily frustrate its workings.

Relationships

In a real sense, lines of communication are really relationships. "You can't have one without the other" — and the picture of either that shows, up on the chart is that of only a few key links in the total network.

Any organization is a hotbed of relationships. Not all of them, of course, necessarily grow out of the nature of the work of the company. Even those that do, however, do not show up on the conventional or even unconventional organization chart.

On occasion a company has noted: "This chart shows relationships only and does not represent levels of management." The caution may have been on the wrong chart, for on the chart in question the opposite seemed true.

More frequently the company notes: "This chart shows reporting relationships only . . . ." Even this seems questionable — it is accurate only if the phrase reporting relationships is understood to mean superior-subordinate reporting relationships.

Organizational relationships — as opposed to social, etc. relationships within a company — grow out of the division of work and delegation of responsibility and authority. A number of functional relationships, authority relationships, staff-line relationships, and just plain work relationships may come into play in reaching any decision or in completing any given piece of work. Most companies long ago gave up any attempt to even begin to show all of these relationships on a chart.

The "Informal" Organization

To some people, that mystical entity known as the "informal" organization is the *real* organization. It is how things really get done.

The *it* referred to, however, may be any number of things, depending upon the point of view. To narrow it to just two types — there is the "informal" organization and the *informal* organization.

The "informal" organization, in this makeshift dichotomy, encompasses all relationships and channels of communication that mature, reasonable people are expected to develop and use in order to meet organizational objectives. As mature, reasonable people, they are expected, of course, to also respect their superior's need to be kept informed of matters affecting his area of accountability. This "informal" organization is viewed as a logical and necessary extension of the formal organization. It is informal only in the sense that nobody has found it necessary to inundate the organization with memorabilia that fully spell out its workings.

The *informal* organization, on the other hand, encompasses all the relationships, communication channels, and influences or power centers that mature, reasonable people develop because a lot of other people in the organization are not mature and reasonable — "especially the bosses who needn't be informed because they'll only say 'no.'" Rather than being a logical extension of the formal organization, it comes into being because the formal organization is viewed as being illogical or inflexible or inefficient or just plain inconsistent with the personal and possibly organizational objectives being worked toward. This *informal* organization, according to "informal" organization specialists, gets work done in spite of the formal organization.

Neither shows up on the organization chart: the "informal" because it's too complex to be reduced to a two-dimensional chart; the *informal* because that would make it formal — a heresy that would immediately give rise to another *informal* organization.

For those not fully satisfied with this dichotomy, there may be a third type — the INFORMAL organization. It includes parts of the "informal" and *informal*. By definition, it covers everything not shown on the organization chart; by definition, it can't be charted.

262

Attempts to revamp the conventional organization chart in order to overcome these and other limitations have produced many examples of modern, nonobjective art (Alexander Calder's mobiles have been mistaken for organization charts.) There is the circular chart (and its variants) designed to better convey internal relationships and to better camouflage "status." There is the chart with the vertical lines between boxes stretched to reflect similar levels of responsibility or similar levels of pay (scrapped after first attempt — required too long a sheet of paper). There is the chart with the pyramid upended to reflect the true flow of authority — from subordinates to superiors (scrapped after first attempt — "That's rubbing it in").

Despite all its limitations, the conventional chart is increasingly used to depict the skeletal structure of the organization. For more complete documentation of what this chart means, companies rely on position guides, linear responsibility charts, statements of general responsibilities and relationships — indeed, the whole organization manual.

The essential value of the chart seems to lie in the fact that it does strip the organization to the skeletal framework. In so doing, it serves a useful purpose both as a tool of organizational analysis and a means of communication.[1] As a complete picture of the organization, it is recognized as being completely inadequate. But it evidently is less inadequate than most substitutes.

---

[1] See "Charting the Company Organization Structure," *Studies in Personnel Policy*, No. 168, for detailed description of charts and their uses.

Conflicts in Human Values

ROBERT N. McMURRY

One of man's most prized possessions is his intellect. Of all his attributes, it is probably his *reason* in which he takes the greatest pride. He even describes himself as "Homo sapiens," the thinking man. Yet much of his behavior, if observed impartially by a visitor from Mars, might better be characterized as "unreasoned," rather than "reasoned."

In the realm of business and industry alone, he provides ample evidence that logic and reason are far from the sole determinants of his actions. For example:

- Management — like the Bourbon kings — often fails to learn from its errors and perpetuates practices which successfully alienate if from the workers.
- The workers, in turn, not infrequently limit their output, even though this diminishes their earnings, and engage in other practices that endanger the security of the jobs on which they depend for a livelihood.
- Superiors and subordinates as well as principal divisions and departments within a business are often unable to work in harmony with each other even though it is clearly in their interest to do so.
- Nor are management and the workers always able to communicate effectively with each other even though their messages may be exquisitely logical and beautifully reasoned.
- Intellectuals and politicians are constantly launching attacks on the businessman designed to denigrate and disparage him. Yet the businessman, through his gifts and taxes, is a principal supporter of both.

Since this behavior is costly and sometimes self-destructive, the question may be asked: Why is there so much "unreason" in interpersonal relations in industry? The tendency these days seems to be to blame the failure on poor communications, conflicts of interest, lack of knowledge, or inadequate management control. I readily agree that such matters are frequently factors in the picture — but not always the most important ones. In case after case with which I am familiar the real cause of breakdown is conflicting *values*. This diagnosis throws many key management problems in an entirely different light and suggests radically different prescriptions for action.

Before proceeding with the discussion, let me comment briefly on the terms to be used:

A value, according to Webster, has, among other meanings, "the quality or fact of being excellent, useful or desirable; worth in a thing." As a verb it means "to place in a scale of values; as to value honor above riches." An ideology, according to Webster, is the

Reprinted from the Harvard Business Review, *May-June, 1963, pp. 130-145.* © *1963 by the President and Fellows of Harvard College; all rights reserved. Reprinted with permission.*

"manner or content of thinking characteristic of an individual or class; as, bourgeois ideology." A belief, by contrast, is "a conviction or persuasion of truth." Typical management values are the sanctity of property and the desirability of the free enterprise system. Values more commonly held by all Americans include the worthwhileness of the idea that virtue tends inevitably to be rewarded in the end and that motherhood is sacred.

"PEOPLE PROBLEMS"

Everyone has opinions and attitudes, many of which, being highly toned emotionally, are coeval in influence with the intelligence that people use in determining what they think and how they act.

Because of these emotional influences, despite mankind's pretensions to the contrary few persons are wholly reasonable in a strict sense of the word; they do not go from fact to fact to form conclusions or revise opinions in the light of new observations.

Many of industry's most costly, frustrating, and chronic dilemmas arise from aberrant opinions and attitudes on the part of management, supervisors, and workers. These, in turn, often lead to behavior which is eccentric, unrealistic, and self-defeating, when not inescapably irrational and deviant. This is why many of management's greatest difficulties have their roots in "people problems."

Significantly, these peculiarities of thinking, acting, and behaving are in no sense the products of mental deficit. They are not limited to the mentally handicapped and ignorant. Nor are they limited to the emotionally disturbed. They appear with equal frequency among experienced, highly trained, happy, and intelligent executives; among intellectuals, scientists, and engineers; among labor leaders and union officials at all levels; and among faithful plant and office employees of long service. The aberrant thinking of these people, too, contributes to management problems. Witness, for instance:

- The usually "rational" owner who will liquidate his business rather than be forced to negotiate with a union.
- The scientist who, perhaps because he happens to be a misguided idealist, becomes a poor security risk.
- The labor leader who foments a long and costly strike simply to demonstrate his "muscle."
- The hourly rated worker who welds pop bottles inside the body of the automobile he is assembling simply for "kicks."
- The intellectuals and politicians who advocate confiscatory taxes on the grounds that profits are unwarranted.

The fact that the motives of an individual or group are indisputably exalted does not mean that the people are realistic. This was dramatically demonstrated by the "noble experiment" of national prohibition of alcoholic beverages.

How Values Alter Behavior

The common denominator of nearly all of these people problems is to be found in the area of *values*. While it is commonly recognized that values differ widely from person to person and from culture to culture, their influence on people's thinking, acting, and behavior tends to be seriously underestimated. Their influence on the individual is powerful because:

1. They principally determine what he regards as right, good, worthy, beautiful, ethical, and so forth (thus establishing his vocation and life goals and many of his motivations, for it may be assumed that he will seek that which he deems desirable).

2. They also provide the standards and norms by which he guides his day-to-day behavior. (In this sense they constitute an integral part of his conscience.)

3. They chiefly determine his attitudes toward the causes and issues (political, economic, social, and industrial) with which he comes into contact daily.

4. They exert a powerful influence on the kinds and types of persons with whom he can be personally compatible and the kinds of social activities in which he can engage.

5. They largely determine which ideas, principles, and concepts he can accept, assimilate, remember, and transmit without distortion.

6. They provide him with an almost unlimited number and variety of moral principles which can be employed to rationalize and justify any action he has taken or is contemplating. (If his stand is totally unrealistic, ludicrous, or even harmful, he can still defend it "on principle.")

Conflicts and Inconsistencies

Human values would be of only minor concern to industry were it not for the fact that they are often extremely unreliable guides to thinking and acting. They tend to create internal and external conflict, to show internal inconsistency, and to deny reality. Few, if any, of a person's values are the products of ratiocination. Instead, they reflect faithfully the mores and ideologies of the cultures in which the individual has lived. The principal sources of his values are:

• The heroes he has worshiped in the course of his development (the parental, school, athletic, theatrical, political, and other authority figures with whom he has identified himself) and whose values, beliefs, and standards he has introjected — usually quite uncritically.

• His associates and peers whose acceptance and esteem are vital to him. (Many people feel they must conform absolutely and blindly to the beliefs, standards, and values of their groups on penalty of ostracism. This is why the behavior of young people is frequently so bizarre and unrealistic.)

Everyone's values have had a wide variety of sources and have been acquired over a long period of time; hence, in the aggregate a person's value system may be riddled with inconsistencies. He may have spent his childhood in a religiously orthodox environment and acquired a corresponding system of values. Later in life, he may have attended a very liberal university, come under the influence of instructors and associates who were atheists, and acquired values that are the polar opposites of his earlier ones.

These internalized value conflicts are often both painful and anxiety-provoking. Not knowing which set of values to use as a guide, the individual resolves the problem as he does others by repressing (putting out of consciousness, i.e., locking away in logic-tight compartments of his mind) those values which are in conflict.[1] In consequence, he is no longer aware of the conflict between and among his values. Thus, he can be opposed to integration with the Negro but employ him (or her) for the most intimate personal services: cooking, laundry, as a wet nurse, even as a mistress. Normally he is conscious of only one set of values at at time — those that are appropriate to the circumstances which happen fortuitously to prevail. At the same time, he also has a wide variety of values from which to draw in rationalizing and defending his beliefs and actions. Hence, in terms of values he is comparable to the churchgoer who can justify an act or opinion by an apt

---

[1] For a fuller explanation of the theory behind various aspects of psychology, see Harry Levinson, "What Killed Bob Lyons?" *Harvard Business Review*, January-February, 1963, p. 127.

quotation from the Bible, paying little attention to the apparent inconsistencies in his interpretation.

EFFECT ON BEHAVIOR

Some values help us build productive human relationships; some do not. But in any case there is one outstanding characteristic of the effect of values on behavior. The more important a value to us, the more likely we are to believe that it is indisputably the *right* one. Commonly, in my observation, people are neither open-minded nor tolerant in the field of values. More often than not the manager, worker, union official, or public official whom I see believes that all values which are inconsistent or in conflict with his are *wrong*. Their possessors are misinformed, ignorant, stupid, or wilfully benighted and evil, in his judgment. He tends thus to be wholly unreceptive to others' values. Many things are seen by him as either black or white; there are no grays. (Attitudes favoring or against Communism are typical.) Moreover, attempts by others to convince him that his values are faulty are rarely effective and often provoke violent outbursts of hostility. This is because to question *his* values is to undermine the foundations of his way of life. He must be sure that his values are the right ones, or he will be at sea with neither chart nor compass.

In extreme cases, the person believes that anyone who possesses values other than his must be set right, using persuasion or logic; failing in this, through imposition by force. In both the radical right and radical left, this missionary zeal easily becomes fanaticism.

No Testing

How often do we wish to subject our values to careful, controlled reality testing? *We are afraid that they might be proved false*. It is safer to assume that the "authorities" or other sources of the values are infallible. In consequence, many superficially plausible but clinically questionable assumptions relative to human nature are regularly made in industry without ever being tested. To illustrate:

▼ Many people who value hard work, self-improvement, the Horatio Alger tradition, group participation, and democratic progress believe that the typical employee sincerely desires a high degree of job autonomy and is eager to accept responsibility for guiding his own and his group's activities. On this premise, it has been argued that decision making should be pushed to the lowest possible rank in the organization, ideally to the machine-tender level. (This is the philosophy of so-called "bottom-up management.") It is believed that this exercise will not only strengthen and develop the employees, but will improve their morale as well.

▲ On the other hand, there are people with more authoritarian (and perhaps more cynical) values who are led to feel that most employees, because of their acute need for certainty, security, and structure, wish to participate in an absolute minimum of decision-making activities. They point to evidence that employees want a high degree of relatively authoritarian supervision. Decisions entail risks which may threaten their security, they argue. Hence, there is a constant tendency for problems and questions to be "bucked upward" to the top levels of the enterprise for adjudication. (This is why President Truman characterized his office as "the level at which the buck stopped.")

Are there not possibilities for objectively testing such values and beliefs? To be sure, the intangible, evanescent, and idealistic nature of many values does render them difficult to subject to controlled experiment, but this is not true of all values all the time. For example, part of the value of democratic progress and group participation is the idea that people are perfectible and that everyone sincerely desires to learn of his limitations in order to take constructive action to overcome them. The validity of these assumptions is not difficult to test empirically. For instance:

All that is necessary is to study two groups of "problem" employees in an identical setting. One group, perhaps 50 in number, is intensively counseled; its members' shortcomings are clearly defined for them, and opportunities are provided for them to correct the conditions causing them to be unsatisfactory as employees. The second matched group of like size, serving as a control, receives only conventional supervisory guidance. At the end of one year, the status of the members of the two groups is compared. If the hypothetical assumption is valid, the first group will show a marked degree of improvement, the second none.

Such a test might be conducted at various levels of responsibility under different conditions. It might be found that both democratic and authoritarian values are vulnerable; i.e., that the assumptions about people on which they are based hold up only part of the time or under limited circumstances.

Cult of Masculinity

Certain traits, such as masculinity, boldness, aggressiveness, self-reliance, and decisiveness — the concept of the "winner," the person who invariably triumphs — have come to be widely overvalued in the prevailing business and industrial culture. While these traits are certainly helpful, if not always essential, to success in management, sales, and related occupations, there are many vocations in which they are neither required nor particularly advantageous. Such vocations are often unfairly patronized and depreciated; and those who tend to be rather passive, submissive, and dependent are characterized by many as "weak," a term of disparagement in the prevailing value systems of business.

In consequence, many persons are driven to attempt to exhibit masculinity, aggressiveness, and decisiveness, and to seek positions which call for these qualities when they do not have them. As a result, such people often find themselves in jobs for which they are totally unsuited. In their efforts to exhibit the esteemed qualities or to fill positions which demand such qualities, they often subject themselves to pressures and tensions which, because they are in excess of their ability to tolerate them, often induce such psychogenic symptoms as ulcers and allergies, and such flight manifestations as obesity, excessive smoking, alcoholism, frantic random activity, or overpreoccupation with detail. These effects figure prominently in some of the company problems we shall look at later.

Identifying Situations

If management is to cope successfully with its people problems, it must take into greater account than it usually does the roles played by values, with all of their inconsistencies, conflicts, and unrealities. And it should attack the problems discriminately, without attaching value labels to whole groups.

In view of the number and variety of values involved in most "people problem" situations, and because of the complexity of their interrelationships, each must be considered on its own merits. In the following pages I shall focus on six situations that top executives find particularly troublesome:

1. Labor-management strife.
2. Poor employee morale, especially if resulting from ultra-authoritarian management.
3. Declines in performance standards.
4. Failures in superior-subordinate relations.

268

5. Communication problems.
6. Attacks on business by intellectuals and politicians.

LABOR-MANAGEMENT STRIFE

Conflicts of values between labor and management cause strife more often than is usually recognized. Economic factors are often of lesser importance than are value conflicts. Each party naturally regards its goals, standards, and shibboleths — especially insofar as these can be identified with values — as indisputably the right ones; each side is intolerant of the values of the other. Each contestant supports his position by appeals to logic, by moral arguments, and by reference to the principles on which he stands; but the basic problem lies in conflicts of values. Typical was the Studebaker-United Auto Workers strike of 1962:

Its cause was management's desire to become more competitive with Detroit by reducing its men's wash-up time from 39 to 24 minutes per day. This, it was estimated, would save $600,000 per year in production costs with no corresponding reduction in wages.

The union, in response, charged that to reduce the wash-up allowance by 15 minutes per day was an evidence of management's desire to exploit the workers. It stated emphatically that it "would not bow the head and bend the knee to management greed and exploitation," and went on a six-week strike marked by some violence.

The strike cost the workers $750,000 in lost pay and the company $21,000,000 in lost production. (It was ultimately settled by a compromise — a reduction in wash-up time by 5 minutes, effective at model-change time in 1963.)

Steps to Improvement

There is no simple, inexpensive, sovereign remedy for conflicts of this nature. Improved communication for instance, is no answer. The roots of conflict are too deep and complex, and the values of both parties are too bitterly opposed. The important thing to face is the fact that when the causes of strife are primarily value-oriented, the arguments are more emotional than rational. They are not only manifestations of unreason, frequently by both parties, but, by the same token, largely proof against logic. In fact, the application of logic often succeeds only in *exacerbating* the difficulty.

However, it is realistic to try to lessen the bitterness of the strife. To that end, the following principles and steps are available:

Initiative. Management must realize that it must take the initiative in seeking remedial action. It usually has greater freedom and latitude in which to act than the union has, and is less compelled to follow a rigid course shaped primarily by the ideologies of its members.

Recognition of Union's Role. Management must also recognize the fact that the typical union member's value system is so constituted that he *must* prove to his employer, to the world, and to himself that he fears no one; and that he is a wholly autonomous, independent individual who should have as influential a voice in what he does on the job as does the company. This he must do to deny his passive, dependent needs and to compensate for his deeply rooted feelings of helplessness, of inadequacy. Since the union is both the instrument by which he can express his defiance with impunity and his only protection against mistreatment by the company, he is doubly dependent on it. (This is a condition which the union exploits for its own ends.) This emotional need to prove his "manhood" frequently leads to the eruption of violence.

269

Self-Review. Management should openly, honestly, and candidly review its own values, particularly as they impinge on the lives, duties, and responsibilities of its employees. It must define its own goals vis-à-vis its people, establish what it wants from them, and, at the same time, decide what it proposes to contribute to their welfare.

Evaluation of Situation. Executives should ascertain by means of a joint analysis of (a) union policies and demands and (b) the results of employee information and opinion polls, the content and goals of prevailing worker ideologies. In conducting the polls, particular effort must be made to ascertain the precise conditions which not only give the workers legitimate grounds for complaint but also justify existing antimanagement sentiments — conditions such as poor working facilities, low pay, and weak or incompetent supervision. It is also essential to discover the "facts" about the enterprise which are believed by the employees but do not happen to be true. For example, it may be believed that the company nets 25% profit after taxes.

Executives who have not been close to the blue-collar scene may be surprised at the results of a probing survey. Such convictions as the following are likely to emerge:

• A worker acquires a property right to his job which grows greater the longer he holds it.

• He has a right to a share of the profits he helps to produce.

• He should have a voice in determining the conditions under which he works; work rules are a fit subject of negotiations.

• In some instances he may even feel that it is all right for him to keep his production at the level of the least competent to protect the latter's job security.

• Likewise, he may even go so far as to believe that any profit made by the employer is at his expense; accordingly, it is all right for him to steal from the employer or at least to soldier on the job.

Value Comparison. Management must compare, as objectively as possible, *its* values with those of its employees, within the broad frame of reference of conditions which prevail within the company, its industry, and the economy. The aim of this study is to find *common goals and values,* i.e., to seek to integrate conflicting desires. For instance, it may be possible to find a solution, such as profit sharing or the Scanlon Plan, which will offer a common goal and minimize conflicts of interest.

Where great psychological and cultural distances separate top management and members of the bargaining unit, it will never be possible to integrate their ideologies completely. The key to the minimization of conflict lies, therefore, in a willingness by management to take an impartial, objective, and tolerant view of opposed values and ideologies. Management must accept the fact that since most worker values cannot be significantly modified, the only thing left for it to do is to accept them as unchangeable facts of life and plan its communications and labor relations programs accordingly.

A direct, frontal attack on an opposed ideology accomplishes nothing other than the stimulation of greater intolerance and, often, of violence. Bitter as this pill may be to some intransigent members of management, a desire for understanding and a search for a common ground with labor may be much more productive of labor peace and cooperation than will a more direct and aggressive anti-union campaign.

POOR MORALE

Poor employee morale with consequent excessive labor turnover, substandard productivity, and "poor attitudes" often arises from the arbitrary implementation of authoritarian, sometimes ultrarightist management values. The values in these cases often tend not only to be unnecessarily rigid and restrictive but to constitute an affront to the employee's image of himself as an intelligent, autonomous human being. Thus the time clock is commonly regarded as a symbol of worker bondage.

Moreover, many managements are not content simply to promulgate their values; actively, sometimes brutally, they seek to *impose* their values on their employees. Their thinking is solely in "blacks and whites," and in their minds their values are always the right ones. Some of them attempt to build good morale by force, by disciplining or discharging all nonconformists and damning them as "troublemakers" or "communists." Other managements reportedly have even attempted to dominate the private lives of their personnel and to exercise thought control over those who were tenants in company housing projects (e.g., those developed by Henry Ford, the elder, and by the Kohler Company).

Problems of Remedial Action

The outlook for remedial action in such cases is poor, in my opinion. Most executives I have seen in authoritarian organizations have the "John Birch society mentality," i.e., they have a compulsive, obsessive drive to impose their values on everyone else, particularly their subordinates. With this mentality, they are completely impervious to reason and are aggressively hostile to all values which conflict even in the slightest with theirs; to question their values is, of course, to exacerbate their underlying insecurities.

Furthermore, they cannot tolerate strong subordinates. Hence it is to be expected that the law of diminishing competence will come into play, resulting in considerable weakness at the first, second, and third levels of supervision. And since such executives tend to select subordinates in their own image, it is to be expected that those managers, superintendents, and foremen will not only be weak but also autocratic, and will subscribe to the same rigid values as their superiors. Thus, they too become petty tyrants.

Only the replacement, retirement, or death of the more autocratic members of such a management offers any lasting solution to the problem. For then there is the possibility that the successors will be more secure. Hence, they would be capable of assessing their own values with reasonable objectivity and of ascertaining the appropriateness, validity, and acceptability of these to employees. This would mean they could adopt a tolerant, understanding, and openminded attitude toward their employees' ideologies. Only under these circumstances can management initiate the necessary remedial steps to ensure that company values, policies, and practices are reasonably consistent with worker needs and ideologies.

Probably the executives' greatest difficulty will lie in assessing objectively the qualifications of supervisors. Since these men and women will be technically competent, of long service, and loyal, their superiors may see no reason why any of them should be replaced. After all, "They think right." Authoritarian executives tend to be quite insensitive to evidences of weaknesses such as their own in subordinates. Because many of these subordinates will be loud, dictatorial, "bulls of the woods," they will be regarded by their superiors as strong and decisive.

In the meantime, if not already organized, companies with such managements will be exceptionally vulnerable to unionization. When the employees join a labor organization to provide themselves with some defense against management and supervision, and to find a group sympathetic to their ideologies, company executives will fail to understand why the workers are "disloyal" to them after they have "done everything possible for their welfare." Unable to comprehend the role that they themselves have played in creating disaffection among their people, they will seek scapegoats elsewhere. They may even charge union organizers and sympathizers with being "communists" and "traitors to the

271

American (their) way of life." The chances are good that they will succeed not only in winning sympathy for the union but in "proving" to employees that management is indeed the villain it is often pictured to be.

DECLINE OF WORK STANDARDS

Charles H. Brower, president of Batten, Barton, Durstine & Osborne, Inc., a leading advertising agency, stated some time ago in a widely publicized talk before the Sales Executives Club of America:

> Here in America we have reached the high tide of mediocrity, the era of the great goof-off, the age of the half-done job. The land from coast to coast has been enjoying a stampede away from responsibility. It is populated with laundry men who won't iron shirts, with waiters who won't serve, with carpenters who will come around someday maybe, with executives whose mind is on the golf course, with teachers who demand a single salary schedule so that achievement cannot be rewarded, nor poor work punished, with students who take cinch courses because the hard ones make them think, with the spiritual delinquents of all kinds who have been triumphantly determined to enjoy what was known until the present crises as 'the new leisure.'[2]

These persons' consciences do not trouble them because in the mores of the prevailing welfare state, as they see it, craftsmanship and excellence of performance in general have ceased to be as widely accepted values as they may have been in the past. How many employees, short of those in the topmost echelons (and not even some of these), can be characterized today as "dedicated"? The motto of many is: "I only work here." In large corporations, it is not unusual for a number of the employees to regard the company as many people think of the government: as having unlimited resources. Hence they feel no obligation to consider the economic welfare of their employer.

As a result of this and other influences, the prevailing worker ideology in a company may contain such sentiments as:

• The employee has little obligation to his employer; after all, the latter is making an excessive profit on each worker's efforts.

• No employer has any right to deny a spirited boy the privilege of engaging in some good clean fun, e.g., welding pop bottles in a gasoline tank, even though this may necessitate the subsequent disassembly of the entire car in order to locate the source of the noise.

Perhaps the greatest paradox is the fact that the same employee who soldiers on the job may be extremely industrious off it, building an addition to his home or making a hi-fi set.

Steps to Improvement

Attempts to change the attitudes and consequent productivity of such employees by reason or admonition are rarely fruitful, because:

---

[2] Address before the National Sales Executives Convention, May 20, 1958, published in Speeches and Articles by BBDOers, Gen. 1202.

— Their ideologies and value systems are very resistant to change, especially where there is little identity with or respect for the author of the proposed change.

— They have little or no incentive to change their individual values or way of life; they are quite content with themselves as they are.

— Most of their associates and personal heroes subscribe to the same values as their own; an employee would be a nonconformist in his group were he to change, possibly an outcast.

— The motives of management are distrusted; the employer is seen as grasping and greedy, seeking only to make a profit at the workers' expense.

Since, with many employees, little or no improvement can be expected to occur spontaneously, it must be understood that improvement has to be induced *from without and above* by the provision of comprehensive job structuring and the application of fair but firm discipline. This entails:

- A clear definition of company rules and policies as they relate to the employee.
- A clear definition of each employee's job duties, responsibilities, and authority.
- A clear definition of the expectations of each employee's supervisor as to his job performance.
- An understanding by all personnel that management does not believe in appeasement; that offenders will be disciplined at once, union or no union.
- The provision of first-, second-, and third-line supervision of sufficient competence and strength to win and hold employee respect, to implement company policies, and to ensure that reasonable discipline is maintained.

Management must recognize that no business organization which intends to remain solvent can afford to function continually as a rehabilitation center for the delinquent and a home for the indigent. It cannot afford the luxury of being "democratic" or practicing "human relations" at the cost of order and discipline. Over the long pull, management must —

. . . assess it own values objectively and try to ensure that its policies are sound;

. . . make clear its expectations to its marginal "problem" cases, with the understanding that they are being warned to improve the quality of their performance;

. . . act decisively if, after due warning, the employee does not show improvement (all new hourly rated employees should, ideally, be on probation for at least 90 days);

. . . establish comprehensive selection techniques to ensure the exclusion of potential "problem employees" (those whose previous records, test results, and interview findings indicate that they are chronic troublemakers, irresponsible, emotionally immature, psychopathic personalities, or borderline psychotics);

. . . recognize those, even among the well-adjusted, whose values do not preclude their joining in antimanagement activities (these may include some brilliant technicians, but they must always be regarded as questionable security risks).

INDIVIDUAL RELATIONSHIPS

Values also play an important (although not all-inclusive) role in personal relationships. Both incompatibility and excessive compatibility are troublesome.

Four factors are critical if the character of any superior-subordinate relationship, particularly when those involved work close to each other, is to be a good one:

273

1. The superior's technical expectations and standards must be met by the subordinate.

2. The superior's personal values must be relatively similar to those of his subordinate.

3. The subordinate's competence must not be so great as to make him a threat to his superior's job security.

4. As far as possible, the superior must meet his subordinate's expectations technically and personally, so that he is respected by him.

In cases of either overcompatibility or undercompatibility, the true causes are rarely enunciated because often the parties themselves are unaware of their nature. For example, the anxious (and correspondingly incompatible) superior is rarely able to face the fact that it is his subordinate's competence which frightens him. All he knows consciously is that he somehow does not like his subordinate, as in the old bit of doggerel about Dr. Fell: "I do not love thee, Dr. Fell/The reason why I cannot tell/But this alone I know full well/I do not love thee, Dr. Fell." Under such circumstances, the superior often finds a value-oriented rationalization for his attitude, such as that his subordinate has execrable taste in clothes.

Realistic Approach

In coping with cases of incompatibility, little is to be gained by any attempt to influence the relationship by a straightforward, logical approach.. This is because the primary determinant of any such relationship is the congruence or dissonance of the parties' values (with overtones of anxiety where the superior fears his subordinate). Where incompatibility exists, corrective or preventive action must include the determination of the kind of person who *is* compatible with the superior, particularly by observing those of the superior's present subordinates who are clearly compatible with him. What kinds of persons (technically, value-wise, and in terms of competence) can he tolerate comfortably? And to what values must the subordinates subscribe in order for them to be acceptable to him?

Where overcompatibility exists, a study must be made to determine what needs (for support, reassurance, or flattery) current favorites satisfy in the superior. On the basis of these findings, standards can be established for use in evaluating candidates for the position of subordinate to a particular executive. An intensive appraisal of the candidate can then be made, using very thorough interviewing techniques to ascertain the extent to which his technical qualities will meet his superior's expectations, the extent to which the pattern of his values is consonant with those of his prospective boss, and the extent to which he is or is not a potential threat to his superior.

Since neither supervisory values nor the capacity in the superior to tolerate a strong subordinate is susceptible to significant change in a few months or years, where actual overcompatibility or undercompatibility is encountered corrective actions usually consist of:

• Separating *over*compatible superiors and subordinates. (In many such instances, the subordinate is so weak and pliable that he is little more than a clerk regardless of his title. To keep him there will simply be to perpetuate a bad situation. The superior will rarely part with him voluntarily. Hence the initiative for change must come from management.)

• Studying each case of incompatibility to ascertain whether the roots of the difficulty lie principally in a conflict of basic values or in a threat to the superior from the junior, or because both these elements are involved in the situation.

• Recognizing that where the difficulty lies in a conflict of basic values, the two men had best be separated and teamed up with more compatible associates.

- Recognizing that where the cause of the problem lies in the fact that the superior fears his junior, *they should be left together.* (Otherwise the law of diminishing competence will almost certainly come into play, and a weaker man will be selected by the superior to take his junior's place. The weak senior will resent a strong, competent subordinate and constantly emphasize his faults, but if management is aware of the situation, it can be on guard against being misled by the superior to the subordinate's disadvantage.)
- Using care in initial employment, transfers, or promotions to match prospective superiors and subordinates. (This attention should ensure that their technical and personal values are reasonably in agreement and that a condition of overcompatibility will not develop in which the junior is too little a threat to his superior.)

No business can expect to have a completely harmonious staff; a reasonable degree of dissonance and conflict is, in most instances, healthy. Successful management faces the fact that some discord is inevitable, and it attempts only to maintain a balance between harmony and conflict. Its goal, in view of this, is to discourage open internecine warfare, and at the same time to ensure that no subordinates are discriminated against unfairly by incompatible or frightened superiors.

BARRIERS TO COMMUNICATION

Many companies are constantly plagued with failure of their internal communication systems, both horizontally (between departments and divisions) and vertically (between top management and the hourly rated employees). In such cases messages often fail to get through to their intended recipients or become distorted and garbled in transmission. Most critical, the effects of intensive educational, morale-building, and attitude-changing campaigns are often negligible.

One of the primary reasons for these failures of communication is a conflict of values. The breakdown can occur where (as in the Studebaker case) the standards of management are not only unacceptable to the workers but may create violent hostilities; intermediate supervision is unable to transmit the message effectively because many of its members are, say, ex-machine tenders and hence have retained the values of their men; the recipients are unable to accept, assimilate, and remember the message without distortion (as was the case with the members of the Studebaker bargaining unit). In office groups, interdepartmental rivalries may exist (i.e., each unit — sales, production, engineering, and so on — may have its own unique constellation of values) so that what is acceptable to one division will not necessarily be so to another.

Building Rapport

Management or interdepartmental communications must, of course, be clear, concise, and unambiguous. But this is only the first step. *It is still essential that the content of communications be oriented to take into account existing union, worker, or departmental ideologies.* These can be ascertained by an analysis of union demands, by information and opinion polls, and by studying employee complaints, grievances, or other expressions of departmental attitudes.

Communications must express only those values of management or the department which are reasonably consonant with the recipients' ideologies. They must not reinforce convictions prevalent in worker ideologies. Thus, direct pleas for greater productivity reinforce the belief that the company is greedy and seeks to exploit its employees. Nor should a communication conflict with prevailing divisional ideologies. It is also imperative that the message contain no sentiments derogatory to worker self-images. For example, it

275

should not imply that they, the employees, are unimportant (faceless automatons or clock numbers), that their attitudes are wrong, or that their leaders have betrayed them. Likewise, there must be no implication that the contributions of one group in the business are more important than those of another.

The more egregiously erroneous beliefs revealed by information polls, e.g., that company profits are 25% after taxes, should be corrected where unassailable factual information can be offered in refutation. Opportunities can also be provided for personal contacts with top executives, permitting personal discussions with a direct "feedback" from the workers. These can be of great help in dispelling misunderstandings. Finally, wherever possible, all intracompany communications should be limited to matters of fact. Care must be employed to exclude value-oriented statements such as those often expressed in monthly letters from the president which stress the merits of the free enterprise system, and so on. All communications should be designed to emphasize common values — for instance, the merits of the company profit-sharing plan, if there is one. This is suitable because it represents an integration of the values of both management and the workers.

To ensure clear channels of *upward* communication, management must make clear, by its responses to employee opinions, that it will tolerate expressions of values which conflict with its own. This means that it will not be necessary for employees to tell management only "what it wants to hear." Management must demonstrate that it is open-minded toward values which conflict with its own and will do its best to integrate them with its own.

In the final analysis, however, company executives must face the fact that there will be failures of communication whenever a message must be filtered through the minds of one or more persons. What is possible is to keep the number and gravity of failures down so that operations are not needlessly disrupted.

ATTACKS ON BUSINESS

Business often is subjected to scathing attacks by intellectuals and politicians. It is charged with degrading the public taste, seducing people by promotional campaigns into making purchases which they neither need nor can afford, setting prices that are too high, and foisting shoddy and even deleterious merchandise upon the public. For example:

• Bertrand de Jouvenal, the French economist and political theorist, says that the hostility of the intellectuals toward the businessman is the result of a clash between their value systems. The businessman's philosophy is: give the public what it wants. The intellectual's is: give the public what it ought to have.[3]

• According to Joseph Schumpeter, noted Harvard economist, intellectuals do not have direct responsibility for practical affairs; they stand outside the circle, as it were, and can only gain recognition by making a nuisance of themselves.[4]

Thus, the intellectuals' attacks often consist of plausible, value-oriented rationalizations designed to gratify a profound underlying envy and hostility. This is why their attacks are sometimes violent and vitriolic to the point of unreason.

Similarly, many politicians who are opportunists of the first order are not above the cynical use of such an issue as the high price of certain ethical pharmaceutical products to dramatize themselves colorfully. To publicize themselves as defenders of the public weal, they will charge that businessmen are greedy and make excessive profits.

---

[3] As quoted in LeBaron R. Foster, "The Businessman — Through the Eyes of the Intellectual," *Encore*, Spring, 1962, p. 13.
[4] *Ibid.*, p. 12.

To attempt to meet charges of this character head-on (whether leveled by intellectuals or by politicians) and to try to demolish them by force of logic is usually futile, because most of these accusations lie in the realm of values. They are, therefore, often evanescent, elusive, and extremely difficult to pin down and counter factually and categorically. Furthermore, there is a constant danger that in attempting to disprove charges of this nature, the businessman may find himself taking a position or making allegations which will conflict with prevailing ideologies in business, social, and political circles. Antagonisms can be created which will be as damaging to the businessman as the original charges against which he is attempting to defend himself. Where the issues are vague, nebulous, and cloudy, or the charges difficult to refute, it is easy for the businessman to become involved in endless, specious argument.

In view of this, the most expeditious course for the businessman is as follows:

1. He should disdain to answer the irresponsible charges directly, implying that they are not worthy of his serious attention. (This is the same tactic commonly used by both intellectuals and politicians when faced with rebuttals and counter-charges.) The businessman should learn to simply shrug them off.

2. Immediately upon learning of any grave charges — regardless of their source management should attempt to ascertain by market research studies in depth, employing the techniques of motivational research, the exact character of the public's prevailing ideologies relating to business in the area in question.

3. Using these research findings as a basis, management can then conduct a positive, value-oriented campaign to stress the *positive* contributions of business to the public welfare. These statements must, of course, be designed to confirm, never to conflict with, prevailing public ideologies. Under no circumstances should the statements directly refute existing beliefs, even blatantly erroneous beliefs such as that anything left in a tin can will spoil and become poisonous. Instead, the campaign should emphasize what the business or industry has already done in the public interest (e.g., the misery and suffering that the new antibiotics have prevented) and what it will offer in the future. If this story is properly dramatized and is consistent with the values of the audience to whom it is directed, it will tend to erase the memory of the original charges and substitute a more favorable public image.

It is well to remember that, in the final analysis, the net effect of the intellectuals' and politicians' attacks, even when they are not answered, is usually negligible. They are rarely a cause for great concern, no matter how flamboyant. This is because many of the issues are only of incidental concern to the public. Also, neither the intellectual nor the average politician is usually a heroic figure to the man in the street. Therefore, he has little incentive to identify himself with them, and their pronouncements ordinarily have little impact or influence on his thinking. His interest in the charges is only a passing one and rarely leads him to take action of any sort, at the polls or elsewhere. In short, most of these harangues where the businessman and his works are viewed with alarm by intellectuals and politicians are actually of little significance.

LIVING WITH VALUES

Despite the fact that many human values are inconsistent, conflicting, and unrealistic, and so are dubious guides to beliefs, attitudes, and actions, they are a fact of life. They are here to stay. Everyone must have his quota of values; without them, he is a ship without a rudder. If management is to build and maintain an effective, well-integrated

277

work force, it must constantly test its own values and the policies which result from them to make certain that they are:

- Reasonably consistent internally.
- Not too acutely in conflict with the values of other members of the management group, with those of company employees, and with those of the public.
- Reasonably consistent with reality.
- Not arbitrarily imposed on the company personnel.
- Recognized not to be infallibly correct but at least subject to debate.

Values are not only ubiquitous but indispensable in every culture. However, if their limitations and proneness to error are not recognized by management, they may do great harm. Heretofore, their role has not been adequately understood and evaluated, particularly in the fields of employee, labor, and public relations. In consequence, much unnecessary friction, strife, and even violence have occurred. Production has often been held to unnecessarily low levels. Superior and subordinate relations have not been as compatible and productive as they should be. Individuals and businesses have pursued courses of action which were less than fully productive, sometimes even deleterious to the enterprise. Intracompany communications have often been ineffective, and businessmen have sometimes been unnecessarily terrified by the attacks of intellectuals and politicians.

The best approach to the problem of dealing with inconsistent, conflicting, or unrealistic values is a relatively simple one. It is based on the recognition that, as already stated, *nearly everyone has more than one set of values which relate to a given topic.* Often these values are of a totally opposed character. Instead of questioning expressed values, the individual or the group must either be researched thoroughly, using sophisticated interviewing techniques, or encouraged to "talk the problem out" at length. By this means, alternative and, hopefully, more appropriate values which are already a part of their ideological systems (though not always clearly appreciated) may often be discovered. These can then be seized on by management and strongly advocated. Since they already were held by the persons or groups whom it is desired to influence, their advocacy by management will constitute no affront to the employees' self-respect and create few resentments.

Obviously, most such solutions are in the nature of compromises; hence few are perfect. Nevertheless, their consequences are often far superior to the results obtained by direct, frontal attacks on aberrant values.

Of all problems in the entire field of value judgments in industry, the greatest one probably is to convince top management of some simple truths. Its members are often accustomed to believing that their standards are infallible and should prevail. Great progress can be made if they can be led to see that:

1. Their points of view are not the only ones.
2. Most issues are not absolutely black or white but do have some gray areas.
3. They personally do not enjoy a monopoly of the truth.
4. Because someone espouses a system of values which differs from theirs, he is not necessarily ignorant, stupid, or disloyal.

Staff Involvement in Agency Administration

HARRY A. SCHATZ

INTRODUCTION

"In what ways and to what extent does staff — other than the executive director participate in the administration of a social agency?" This seemingly simple question evokes complex and varied responses, beginning with "It all depends:

1. On what you mean by *administration*.
2. On *whom* you ask — board member, executive, supervisor, or worker.
3. On the *kind* of agency or setting in which social services are rendered — family case work agency, community center, group work agency, public welfare department, hospital social service department, parole and probation department.
4. On the *size* of the particular agency — large, intermediate, small.

WHAT DOES ADMINISTRATION MEAN?

Administration means different things to different people and different things to the same person at different times. Here are some of the responses from various persons when asked "What does the term *administration* with reference to your agency mean to you?"

"Administration means to me the formulation and determination of agency purposes and policies primarily by the board, assisted by the executive. The staff carries out the policy and provides the services or program designed to fulfill the agency's purposes."

"Administration is the primary function of the executive in giving direction to the board and staff and coordinating their efforts towards the achievement of agency goals."

"Administration is the function of providing money, facilities, equipment, clerical services and all the other services which make it possible for us social workers to carry out our primary professional function of providing social service."

"Administration is all those non-professional tasks — filling out forms, keeping

Reprinted with permission of the National Association of Social Workers, from Trends in Social Work Practice and Knowledge: NASW Tenth Anniversary Symposium *(New York: NASW, 1966), pp. 237-238.*

statistics, preparing budgets, writing special reports, etc., which social workers are expected to do which can be done better by other people who have been trained for clerical and managerial skills."

"Administration is the major obstacle to developing qualitative social services."

"Administration is the bane of my professional life."

In a class on social work administration the instructor, in his effort to portray graphically the complexity of administration, to reveal the tendency of people to view administration from their own particular vantage point, and to stress the need to understand administration in its multi-faceted totality, related the Indian fable of the elephant and the five blind men. It turned out, however, that the use of this parable had surprising results when, in a subsequent examination, one of the students wrote,"Administration is an elephant" and drew a reasonable likeness of this fabulous creature.

FURTHER DEFINITIONS OF ADMINISTRATION

The wide diversity as to what is meant by administration is also reflected in the literature, as is evident by the following:

... nature of Administration is twofold — the provision of services to people by people. The total process of formulating social policy, developing a program, and providing the services is bound up in a circular fashion in the administration of social programs.

Social Administration is the utilization of staff competency and the securing of cooperative behavior which enables the organization to develop social policy and provide the social services needed by the people and the community — a process that involves the integrated use of social work concepts and methods with appropriate methods drawn from public and business administration. [1]

Administration has been described and defined . . . as a process, as a method, as a set of relationships with and between people working toward common objectives. It has been called the process of transforming social policy into social action.

Stated simply, administration is the process of setting objectives and establishing policies, creating and maintaining an organization, making plans and carrying them out, evaluating the results. [2]

Administration is the guidance, leadership and control of the efforts of a group of individuals toward some common goal. Basic processes are:

1. *Planning* — that is, determining what shall be done. Planning covers a wide range of decisions including the clarification of objectives, establishment of policies, mapping of programs determining specific methods and procedures, and fixing day-to-day schedules.

2. *Organizing* — that is, grouping the activities necessary to carry out the plans

---

[1] Corinne H. Wolfe, "Basic Components In Supervision," *The Social Welfare Forum, 1958* (New York: Columbia University Press, 1959), pp. 172-189.

[2] Ray Johns, *Executive Responsibility* (New York: Association Press, 1954).

into administrative units, and defining relationships among executives workers in such units.

3. *Assembling resources* – that is, obtaining for the use of the enterprise the executive personnel, finances, facilities and other things necessary to carry out the plans.

4. *Directing* – that is, issuing instructions. This includes the vital matter of indicating plans to those who are responsible for carrying them out, and also the day-to-day personal relationship between the "boss" and his subordinates.

5. *Controlling* – that is, seeing that the operating results conform as nearly as possible to the plans. This involves the extablishment of standards, motivation of people to achieve these standards, comparison of actual results against the standards, and necessary corrective action when performance deviates from the plan. [3]

Administration includes –

a. *Policy formation*

b. *Planning and setting up of the organization*

c. *Running of the organization.* [4]

The functions of administration may be summarized as follows:

1. *To determine the goals to be achieved and the tasks to be performed (expressed in terms of such things as policy statements, procedures, practices, inter-agency agreements, public legislation, and constitutions and by-laws).*

2. *To find the necessary resources to perform the required tasks and to achieve the stated goals (resources include finances, personnel and property).*

3. *To manage the resources in such a manner that efficient and effective services are performed (this involves such aspects of administration as leadership, organizational structure, staff development, communication and coordination, and assurances of the quality and quantity of staff performance).* [5]

Definitions of administration abound, but central to those most accepted currently is the concept of administration as a process of defining and attaining the objectives of an organization through a system of co-ordinated and co-operative effort.

This concept stresses the administrative process, not just the responsibilities of management; defining objectives, which connotes the need to modify and reshape them, to be conscious of goals, and not to take them for granted; reaching these objectives, described as the central responsibility of management and the underlying raison d'etre of administrative process, the latter not then being an end in itself; involvement of people and their contributions in a planned pattern of cooperation, rather than administration being the activities of the executive group only . . .

---

[3] William H. Newman, *Administrative Action* (New York: Prentice Hall, 1953), p. 4.

[4] Leon C. Marshall, *Administration* (Lepawsky, New York: Knopf, 1955), p. 38.

[5] Arthur Kruse, *Social Work Year Book, 1960* (New York: Columbia University Press, 1960), p. 79.

How the social work organization is administered (whether the agency engages only in social work activity, or places social work as one department within a larger organization) makes it either more or less possible for social workers to render, and clients and community to receive, optimum service. Moreover, when administration is regarded as a system of co-operative effort, the stake of all staff members is considerable, not only in managerial competence but also in making their own appropriate contribution to administrative process.[6]

People tend to think of administration either in broad terms of policy formulation, sometimes distantly removed from the daily rendering of professional service, or in terms of the business and technical operations of the supporting services — clerical, financial, maintenance, etc. This dichotomy is frequently strengthened by a caste system feeling, differentiating between professional and non-professional employees in the agency. It is further strengthened by the formality and rigidity of rank order in the hierarchical structure, particularly in the bureaucracy of a large agency.

THE TASK-CENTERED VS. HIERARCHICAL CONCEPT
OF ADMINISTRATIVE ORGANIZATION

The hierarchical administrative organization characteristic of bureaucracy, as defined by Max Weber[7] and others, identifies succeeding levels of authority with power emanating or delegated from the top downward. Responsibility is also delegated in a similar fashion downward, echelon by echelon. This classical, formal structure tends toward rigidity and minimizes the opportunity for staff participation in any area beyond their immediately circumscribed area of responsibility.

The task-centered concept of administrative organization does not abandon hierarchical distribution of authority and responsibility but minimizes this aspect. It focuses concern on the problem or task at hand and involves all persons who may have a contribution to make, thus cutting across professional and hierarchical lines. This approach maximizes the opportunity for staff members with diverse competencies and with responsibilities at all levels to work together in reaching a common objective.

Perhaps this can best be clarified by two contrasting examples of the process of agency budget formulation and control. In some agencies the fiscal authority which frequently is far removed from the actual providing of social services, makes the determination as to how much money is to be spent for the operation of the social services. Most frequently the decisions are related to fiscal, political and public relations value systems rather than primarily to the value system of social service. The budget may be further circumscribed by a line-by-line designation as to how the funds are to be expended. Sometimes a total sum allocation is indicated with the well-meaning good wishes of "Do the best you can with what is available."

In other agencies the process of budget formulation begins with the staff and board committees on the program or service level who evaluate the program of the past year, project the program of the coming year and translate services into administrative requirements, including budget. In this process, priorities are also indicated so that in the event that the total amount requested cannot be fully met, there is a built-in accommodation to deal with the fiscal realities. One of the important by-products of this budget process

---

[6] Herman D. Stein, "Administration," *Encyclopedia of Social Work* (New York: National Association of Social Workers, 1965), p. 58.

[7] H. H. Gerth and C. Wright Mills, *From Max Weber: Essays in Sociology* (New York: Oxford University Press, 1958), Chapter VIII.

is that the budget is formulated by the persons most knowledgeable of daily operations and urgent priorities. It also relates program more closely to administration and administration to program. Program staff develop an understanding and appreciation of administrative realities which enables them to interpret program and budget realistically and persuasively.

The budget is usually thought of as an instrument for fiscal control and for program planning. It also can serve as an administrative x-ray which to the discerning eye reveals the agency's prevailing value system.

An analysis of the income items will reveal the extent of dependence for sources of income outside the agency. The degree of self-support will reveal the extent of autonomy.

An analysis of the distribution of expenditures will reveal what programs and services are deemed more important than others, how much emphasis is placed on continuing staff development, to what extent is there an interest in research and experimentation. A comparison of budget items with those of comparable agencies is much more revealing than news releases or interpretive speeches.

INTERDEPENDENCE OF PROFESSIONAL AND SUPPORTING SERVICES

When the social work staff gathers to discuss agency services, they tend to think exclusively of services to be rendered by professional staff. Yet professional service is in large measure dependent on supporting services. Any significant change or improvement in professional services necessarily involves other staff, including administration, clerical, maintenance, etc. This is exemplified by the following experience:

In a large city the Department of Public Welfare obtained executive approval from the Mayor's office to improve the quality of professional social services by reducing the case load through the employment of more social workers. This approval was endorsed by the Budget Bureau and the Personnel Bureau. The social workers felt that this long sought--after goal had finally been achieved. However, several months elapsed in which there was no appreciable evidence of change. This led to mutterings on the inefficiency of the administrative staff. When feelings found expression in a crescendo of overt criticism, a meeting was called. The administrative staff pointed out to the professional staff the following obstacles which had to be overcome and which were inevitably time-consuming in spite of the diligence of the administrative staff:

1. The city's Personnel Bureau, with its own full schedule and priority pressures, had to advertise, recruit, accept and review applications, arrange for examinations and grade the results, make up an eligibility list and arrange for placement. At that point the training staff of the Department of Public Welfare would have to orient the new worker to her job and begin the process of orientation and in-service training.

2. Each new worker required a desk, a chair, a telephone, a lamp, and other furnishings, and equipment which had to be obtained from the city Property Department, which in turn had its full schedule of work load and priorities.

3. Where to put all these new desks and new workers? This required additional office space. It involved the city's Real Estate Department which had its own work load and pressure of priorities.

4. In increasing the number of case workers, it became necessary to increase the number of supervisors. This again involved Personnel Bureau, this time in arranging for supervisor's exams, grading the results, and establishing an eligibility list. Here

again arose the matter of orienting new staff to supervisory responsibilities and finding appropriate facilities and space for them. It was also observed that since supervisors are recruited primarily from the more experienced workers, this increased the recruitment and assignment burden of the Personnel Bureau in addition to the ever-present 40% annual turnover of workers.

5. With an enlarged staff of workers and supervisors, it became necessary to enlarge the staff of clerical workers. Here again is repeated the same problems of recruiting and engaging clerical staff, orienting them to their jobs, finding appropriate space, furnishings, and equipment.

For the first time the social workers became acutely aware of the immensity and complexity of the task of the administrative staff in implementing that which had been legally and formally approved, namely the improvement of the quality of professional services by reducing case loads through increasing the number of case workers to the staff.

The social workers' criticism of the administrative staff was appreciably reduced. New and profound respect was evidenced for the administrative staff who, though not professional in terms of social work, were people of professional competence in their respective fields. This illustrated the importance of involving staff members on various levels and with different competencies to focus on mutual problems and to strive towards mutual goals. The reduction of professional stratification and caste system attitudes through continuing dialogue between professional and administrative staff in a task force makes possible the achievement of professional goals.

It is interesting to note that during one of the early discussions one of the social workers remarked: "After all, we social workers deal with people and you administrators only deal with things." One of the administrative staff responded, "It may be true that typewriters have no feelings, but typists do."

STAFF INVOLVEMENT IN POLICY MAKING

It is true that staff members in a social agency, particularly on the worker level, have little if any involvement or influence in the formulation of agency policy. Workers in large agencies, particularly governmental agencies, tend to feel impotent with regard to shaping or amending policy. Among government workers there frequently is the notion that influencing policy is not only beyond their scope but is contrary to law.

The separation of the making of policy from the implementation of policy is deeply rooted in American government. It was expressed in a classical essay by Woodrow Wilson in 1887 when he was professor of government at Princeton.[8] "Politics is the formulation or policy. Administration is the carrying out of policy." The essay points out that these two functions are and should be discretely separate.

Reference is sometimes made to the Hatch Act as evidence of the prohibition of government workers from participating in policy or political matters. In reality the Hatch Act defines the rights of government workers in exercising their citizenship rights, including the influencing of policy Paul Appleby[9] in *The Big Democracy* points out that the separation of policy and administration is an illusion and that administrative personnel are actually very much involved in formulating and influencing policy. In fact, government employees are utilized by members and committees of Congress in providing

---

[8] Woodrow Wilson, "The Study of Administration," *Political Science Quarterly* (June 1887), reprinted in Vol. 56 (December, 1941).

[9] Paul Appleby, *The Big Democracy* (New York: Knopf, 1945).

the background material supporting proposed legislation and in drawing up legislation.

In both governmental and voluntary agencies the extent to which staff is involved in influencing or formulating policy depends upon many factors, including the kind and size of the agency, the nature of the problem or issue and not least of all, the personality of the chief executive and of the agency board or commission. Along with all these variables is the important factor of administrative philosophy or organization concept. As indicated earlier, if the rigid lines of the bureaucratic hierarchy are strictly adhered to, staff will have little opportunity for influencing policy until the build-up of frustrations leads to an explosion in the form of a strike or other violent expression. The task-centered administrative concept will enhance the opportunities for staff to participate in policy formulation.

It should be made clear that the involvement of staff members from different echelons and different competencies in a common task force does not relieve the ranking staff member from his personal accountability. In the final analysis he is held responsible for the decision and for the action taken. He cannot delegate this accountability or disassociate himself from responsibility on the basis that it was a group decision.

This brings to mind an experience in which an agency executive had, in his characteristic manner, solicited the opinions and recommendations of his staff. This led to a group consensus and recommendation for a particular action. At the conclusion of the discussion the executive expressed his appreciation to the staff but announced that he was going to take a contrary action. This arbitrary statement astounded the staff since it was not consistent with the usually democratic administrative philosophy of the executive. The looks and sounds of surprise, disbelief, and disapproval moved the executive to explain that their recommendation was based on a judgment which could not be fully corroborated by fact. Since he was held responsible for the consequences of any decision and action — with all due respect to the staff — he felt impelled to proceed on the basis of his own judgment, which he hoped would prove to be correct.

A wise and competent administrator continually turns to his staff members at all levels and in various areas areas of competency for information and for various viewpoints. He places facts and opinions before him, weighing one factor against another, and ultimately makes a decision which is partially based on fact and partially based on a value system. The observation is made that the value system of the professional may not always be consistent with the value system of the agency. The executive frequently finds himself in a position of contradiction and conflict. Sometimes staff members also find themselves in a similar position.

ADMINISTRATIVE RESEARCH IN STAFF
RESPONSIBILITY FOR ADMINISTRATIVE FUNCTIONS

It was noted earlier that the ways and the extent to which staff participate in the administration of the agency depend on whom you ask and also on the size and kind of agency.

In a recent study of 110 Jewish Community Centers, 30 administrative functions were identified. The presidents, executive directors, program directors, and health and physical education directors of these Centers were asked to indicate who carried primary responsibility in their agency for each of these administrative functions — the board, the executive, or the staff.

Board Members' Views

The greatest number of presidents ascribed *no* administrative functions as being primarily carried out by staff (as distinguished from board and executive). However, an analysis of the presidents' responses by size of community revealed a difference between large, intermediate, and small agencies. Out of 30 defined functions, four were perceived as primarily the responsibility of staff in large Centers, two in intermediate Centers, and none in small Centers.

The Executives' Views

The greatest number of executives in the same 110 Jewish Community Centers ascribed five administrative functions as being primarily carried out by staff. The responses of the executives as analyzed by size of community followed the pattern of diminishing staff responsibility by size of community from large to small, although more responsibility was perceived as being carried out by the staff than was perceived by the presidents: nine functions in large Centers, six functions in intermediate Centers, and one function in small Centers.

Program Directors' Views

The greatest number of program directors ascribed eight administrative functions as being primarily carried out by staff. Analyzed by size of agency, there were nine functions in large Centers, nine in intermediate Centers, and six in small Centers.

Health and Physical Education Directors' Views

The greatest number of health and physical education directors ascribed eight functions to the staff. By size of community, there were variations: eleven in large Centers, nine in intermediate Centers, and five in small Centers.

Observations and Commentary

We note the following observations:

1. Staff members do carry primary responsibility for certain administrative functions.

2. The number of functional responsibilities carried by staff members tends to be greater in the large agency than in the small agency.

3. If we make a distinction between "what is" and "what should be" we need to make a further distinction in terms of "who" is perceiving "what is."

4. From this study we find that the perceptions differ according to the role of the perceiver. The closer the perceiver is to the staff, the more administrative functions he ascribes to the staff.

Do these findings and observations have any implications for other kinds of agencies? Are there significant differences between voluntary and public social agencies, between case work and group work and community organization agencies? What are the diagnostic implications for the health of an agency when there is great divergence as to the perception of who carries primary responsibility for administrative functions?

STAFF TIME USED FOR NON-PROFESSIONAL TASKS

Thus far we have been discussing the under-use of professional staff in policy formula-

286

tion. The other side of the coin is the over-use of professional staff in non-professional tasks. An analysis of the daily tasks of a professional social worker frequently reveals that many of the tasks performed are of a clerical or administrative nature that could be performed as well or sometimes even better by a non-professionally trained person whose competency and skill has been developed in the clerical or administrative field. In fact, one way of meeting the shortage of professional staff is not necessarily by adding professional staff, but by adding clerical and administrative staff to take over that part of the job load which does not require professional social work skill. This is a practical solution or alleviation of the problem for many agencies where salaries are budgeted for positions that are vacant. Appropriate interpretation needs to be made in transferring funds from professional to clerical salaries, making it clear that the clerical staff are not being engaged to substitute for professional staff but only for clerical and administrative tasks. For example, an administrative assistant can serve one or more professional workers in scheduling and arranging for meetings and conferences, providing general information, maintaining statistical records and routine reports, filling out requisitions and other procedural forms, and assembling records and materials related to conferences or meetings.

The analysis of daily tasks actually performed requires the keeping of a task and time record for a specific period. Staff is frequently reluctant to maintain such a record. The given reason is lack of time. The real reason is an underlying distrust and rejection of the efficiency expert. "We don't have enough time to do our job, so how can we waste time on keeping task-time records" is the usual complaint. However, such an analysis usually reveals surprising findings that serve as a basis for more productive professional service.

Apart from the poor economics of paying professional salaries for clerical tasks, there is also the matter of staff morale. Social workers naturally feel that the years and money invested in professional training should be applied to the performance of social work tasks in attaining social work objectives. The draining off of time and energy for non-professional tasks frustrates and demoralizes social workers and affects adversely their total performance.

IN SUMMARY

Administration involves both the formation of policy and the implementation of policy. While the board of directors, commission or legislature formally decides policy, staff at various levels and in varying degrees can and should participate in the preparation and formulation of policy. The task-centered concept of administrative organization provides greater opportunity for staff to participate in policy formulation than does the classical bureaucratic hierarchy.

The formation and implementation of sound, realistic policy depends on the cooperative efforts of both the professional and supporting services. Cooperation between services is more likely to take place in a task-centered operation cutting across departmental lines than in an agency adhering to the caste-system of hierarchical echelons.

In carrying out policy, professional staff is all too frequently occupied with clerical and administrative tasks which can be carried out more economically and even more efficiently by non-social workers who are trained and skilled in clerical and administrative disciplines.

Finally, there is the plea for more research based on the analysis of tasks actually performed by professional staff and of relationships between professional staff with the board or commission on one hand, and the supporting services on the other.

Administrative Leadership in Complex Service Organizations

HERMAN D. STEIN

INTRODUCTION

This paper is directed to certain theoretical considerations related to the promotion of leadership and imagination in complex service organizations. It is not directed to policies and practices in the Veterans Administration specifically. It would be fair to say, however, from the standpoint of an outside observer, that one cannot fail to be impressed by the climate of innovation in the social service division of the Veterans Administration, its vigorous forward thrust in setting objectives, determining quality of service, engaging in research and in training. When an organization as large as this sets these kinds of standards for its social work program, there is bound to be a constructive impact on all of social work.

My emphasis in this paper will be on three broad aspects of the subject: bureaucracy and service, personality and organization, and the environment of organizational planing and decision-making.

BUREAUCRACY AND SERVICE

There was a story in the newspapers not so long ago[1] of the visit to the United States of a British expert in playground design, who described school and other public playgrounds in the United States as "an administrator's heaven and a child's hell." The playgrounds had clearly been built primarily for the ease and economy of their maintenance, and to forestall insurance claims for accidents. They had not been built for the true needs of the children who were supposed to use them. Whether the criticism is fair or not for playgrounds, the vulnerability of complex service organizations to the ailment of turning administrative simplicity into a goal in its own right, whatever the results for consumers, is omnipresent.

Most of us in social work accept the fact that our activities in the service agencies *are* to be primarily directed to service — whether in the form of patient care in hospitals, treatment of children in child guidance clinics, or help to the economically disadvantaged in the public assistance agency. We are not always as mindful of the fact that as we evolve our administrative structure and patterns, some of this evolution can tend to be in the direction of making it easier for ourselves administratively, to the detriment of our presumed service function.

---

[1] *New York Times* (May 16, 1965), p. 46.

This paper was originally presented at the 92nd Annual Forum of the National Conference on Social Welfare, May, 1965. Reprinted with permission of the National Conference on Social Welfare.

It has been repeatedly observed[2] that as certain key features of bureaucratization set in, such as an impersonal social climate, proliferation of rules, and status barriers between professionals and clients and between different levels of staff themselves, the total administrative system tends to work more to the advantage of the experts than to its clients. The very features of bureaucracy that can give it the capacity to produce services economically and efficiently, that maintain stability, that provide role security for employees and objective criteria in the treatment of the consumers of its services, can develop a system related primarily to the interests of its staff, particularly its experts, rather than to the interests of its clientele. (A caricature of this phenomenon is the ironic statement sometimes heard in schools, including schools of social work, that "we could run a wonderful school here if it weren't for the students.")

The movement in hospital care for the mentally ill, from the custodial institution to the therapeutic milieu, provides one of the most vivid illustrations both of the need for loosening up, in the interests of patients, the rigidities of structure and process that emerge with overbureaucratization, and the strains that can develop when the loosening up goes so far that the essential structural requisites of complex formal organization are weakened. Two recent analyses of processes of debureaucratization in organizations designed for in-patient treatment provide valuable insights. One[3] deals with a specific treatment center for alcoholics, the others[4] with hospital treatment of mentally ill generally. In both, the meaning of debureaucratization consisted of reducing status differences between staff and clients, a general flattening of the hierarchical authority system, opening up new channels of communication between staff and patients, providing smaller, decentralized units for patient care, and promoting an informal, friendly social climate.

These are all moves reflecting the premise that the traditional custodial state hospital type of institution, one prototype of Goffman's profiles of "total institutions," essentially was designed for administrators and staff, not for patients. Both analysts agree that in the situations studied, debureaucratization results in a much greater orientation to patient care. The very words changed in the mental hospital from the formal, staff-oriented "going on ward rounds" to the informal, client-directed "chatting with patients."

The strains for patients ease, but in their place come strains for staff. The more personalized relationship of staff to patients, the greater personalization of relationships among staff themselves, the more amorphous systems of communications and control, and reduction in defined roles of authority, apparently create new pressures for staff. As one of these writers, William R. Rosengren, put it, the small non-bureaucratized total treatment milieu type of hospital becomes "total" for staff, instead of for patients.

While these analyses are directed primarily to consequences in changes of patient care systems, they indirectly reinforce certain other principles. One is that the way to prevent bureaucratic strains in the interests of better service to clients or patients is not to make the organization totally non-bureaucratic and loose in structure and process, but to modify existing and introduce new structure and process focused on patient interests. It is true that non-bureaucratic systems can provide greater latitude for innovation, individualization, professional self-fulfillment, and ready adaptability to change, than can more complex formal organizations. They also provide conditions that can make for instability,

---

[2] For example see: Earl Rubington, "Organizational Strains and Key Roles," *Administrative Science Quarterly*, IX, No. 4 (March, 1965), pp. 350-369; and Herman D. Stein, "Administrative Implications of Bureaucratic Theory," *Social Work*, VI, No. 3 (July, 1961), pp. 14-21.

[3] Rubington, *op. cit.*

[4] William R. Rosengren, "Communication, Organization and Conduct in the 'Therapeutic Milieu'," *Administrative Science Quarterly*, IX, No. 1 (June, 1964), pp. 70-90.

role confusion, and interpersonal tensions, which, if they become severe, can militate against the interests of clientele. The importance of demonstrating positive effect in interpersonal relationships in the non-bureaucratic structure is such that it may be said that "when it is good, it is very, very good, but when it is bad, it is horrid." There can be a price paid for drastic debureaucratization.

The directions for solutions in complex service organizations, one may suggest, are not in substituting role diffusion for role specificity, nor in minimizing hierarchical levels of responsibility, but rather in developing a balance between those elements of structure and process conducive to rational management of the organization, and those elements essential for optimum client service. Decentralization is a case in point. Decentralization may be necessary for service objectives in certain kinds of institutions. The smaller size, greater face-to-face relationships, permit more individualization and the kinds of treatment relationship that may be necessary. But rational administrative objectives, if the decentralized unit *is* a unit of a larger organization, would require consistency of policy and procedures in such units regarding such elements as staff roles and communication channels. One can avoid over-loading the decentralized unit with ritualistic procedures unnecessary to its proper functioning, but one does not remove role requirements, or hierarchical lines of responsibility. It is not easy to have one's bureaucratic cake and eat it too, but it is an attempt that should be constantly made.

The prime principle is to make sure that the service organization exists for service, not for ease of administration. The one is a goal, the other a means. Minimizing the strains inherent in bureaucratic structure requires approaches consistent with such rational formal organization – i.e., consistent with bureaucracy – and central to these approaches is defining responsibility within the structure for determining that all administrative means are related to the ends of service and do not become ends in themselves.

Where research and training are included with service systems, it is not easy to keep these three objectives in balance, under the best of circumstances. There are, however, certain preconditions for maximizing the reciprocal reinforcement of these systems, and reducing conflict and waste of effort. One is for the organization to have its priorities clear for each system. What is it *primarily* in business for, what secondly, and what comes third? The budgetary and non-budgetary investments should reflect these priorities. The systems should be differentiated, which is not to say that individuals may not be located in more than one system, but the service, teaching, and research systems, as such, should be differentiated, not only in such respects as personnel, space, and equipment allocation, but also in terms of administrative responsibilities, and most important, in terms of objectives and expectations.

Organizations geared primarily for service can develop far greater leadership potential with the addition of teaching and research functions, if such preconditions exist, and if there is a pattern of communication and influence among the three systems so that they are individually reinforced in function and effectiveness, and together create an increasingly potent and effective service operation.

PERSONALITY AND ORGANIZATION

The relationship between the needs of the individual and the needs of the organization has come into increasing prominence as a concern in the development of organizational policy as well as organizational analysis.

Thus, Argyris[5] stresses the basic impact of formal organization "to make employees

---

[5] Chris Argyris, *Personality and Organization* (New York: Harper & Brothers, 1957); and *Interpersonal Competence and Organizational Effectiveness* (Homewood, Illinois: The Dorsey Press, Inc., 1962), Ch. 2, pp. 38-54.

feel dependent, submissive and passive, and to require them to utilize only a few of their less important abilities," and calls for a better "mix" of individual needs and organizational demands. Marshall Dimock similarly stresses the incompatibility of bureaucratic structure and personality requirements.[6]

I do not feel that the conflict is inevitable, if thought is given to utilizing the capacities of people in organizations to the fullest, and individualizing them. Fundamental as the problem is for the mental health of our working population, it is equally significant for the welfare of the organization itself. The waste by organizations, in industry, government, and the voluntary sector, incurred by the failure to utilize the human potential, is prodigious.

The essence of the dilemma is that since bureaucratic organizations tend to enhance role specificity, definite and circumscribed job demands, and provide rewards for conformity alone, they may not tap the special abilities, imagination, or views of employees that can well serve the interests of the organizations themselves, as well as enhance the sense of individual worth and self-respect of employees.

Several approaches can be taken to reduce this potential conflict. One concerns the planned involvement of personnel in organizational decision-making. Some years ago the term "democratic administration" was popular, to connote the proper recognition of all individuals in administration. In this simplistic form, however, this concept is antithetical to hierarchical organization, placing an excessive egalitarian demand on policy involvement without appropriate responsibility and competence.

The concept of "relevant participation"[7] meets this problem by identifying which kinds of policy and operational problems require the participation of which kinds of personnel. In its fullest expression, this concept would invite the participation of every member of an organization, no matter how huge the organization is, in contributing to issues in which their special experience and competence are relevant. A management specialist put it as follows:

> The participative principle . . . gives recognition to people as human beings — individually and in their group relations — and it brings dignity and meaning to their jobs. It can tap the creative imagination and inventive ingenuity for which we Americans are justly famous. It can banish fear and dependence by giving the members of the organization an opportunity to exert control over their own destinies and to acquire genuine understanding of what are usually felt to be mysterious and arbitrary management actions. It offers, *par excellence*, a way to encourage the development of genuine personal responsibility among all members of the organization, and with it, the freedom which is always lacking when control is centralized.[8]

A second approach involves continuous assessment of special strengths as well as weaknesses of personnel, relevant to the organization's needs, irrespective of the specific occupational roles assigned.

Some years ago, when I was serving as consultant to a middle-sized manufacturing organization, we introduced a policy of having every formal employee evaluation by a

[6] Marshall E. Dimock, "Bureaucracy Self-Examined" in *Reader in Bureaucracy*, ed. by Robert K. Merton, Ailsa P. Gray, Barbara Hockey, and Hanan C. Selvin (Glencoe, Illinois: The Free Press, 1952), pp. 397-406.

[7] Stein, *op. cit.*

[8] Douglas McGregor, "Changing Patterns in Human Relations," an Address before the Society for the Advancement of Management, Cleveland Chapter (May 17, 1950) (mimeographed). Excerpt reprinted in *The Staff Role in Management: Its Creative Uses*, by Robert C. Sampson (New York: Harper & Brothers, 1955), p. 85.

superior of subordinates, include consideration of anything the employee was particularly good at or interested in, as well as what he seemed to do poorly. Supervisors were evaluated not only on the same basis, but on the basis of whether they did, indeed, present an assessment of positives and negatives in their subordinates. There is more to this approach than meets the eye, and it took over a year to be understood and take hold through all levels of the organization from the chief executive down. Permit me to give you one illustration of how it worked, at its best.

One twenty-four year old male employee had been hired as a supply clerk in the central office, where a variety of goods were received that were utilized by designers in fashioning and testing eventual design for mass production. The clerk's supervisor recommended his dismissal on the basis that his handwriting on shipping orders was often illegible, he was occasionally careless in filling out the form, and he was sometimes away from his desk, just "floating around." The supervisor was asked by *his* superior whether there was anything the clerk was good at, or interested in, and just why and where he was "floating around." This exploration, which was becoming routine in the organization, led to the information that the clerk spent most of his time, when he was not engaged in receiving and checking supplies, with the designers. When with the designers he asked a variety of technical questions, and inquiry with the designers in turn elicited their respect for his quick intelligence and capacity to see the relationship between a handmade design and the sequence and cost of steps in manufacturing. In this industry, few talents are more precious than the capacity to visualize production processes on the basis of a design. The clerk was reassigned as an assistant in the design section, and served as liaison with the factory. He became more technically qualified, developed his natural conceptual talent, and rapidly moved to important responsibilities. He became a precious asset to the company, and rose to an executive level within a few years. His handwriting, of course, remained poor.

This was a success story. Others were less dramatic, and some were not successes, but it was possible, in an organization of one thousand people, to individualize, on a recognition of assets and liabilities, and to keep the principle going of utilizing and building on strengths, building jobs around these strengths, wherever possible, and not insisting that employees only correct their weaknesses, particularly where these could not be altogether overcome. Both the organization and the individual benefited in ways both unexpected and expected.

The illustration is not from social work, but the concept is hardly less applicable.

A third approach involves flexibility of assignments and testing of capacities, such as the deliberate rotation of tasks within the organization. Such an approach can prevent monotony where the tasks are routine, increase flexibility in the utilization of personnel, and provide a broader perspective on their jobs by individuals seeing another aspect of the organization's effort, from the perspective of changed responsibility. Of course, this should not be overdone to the point where there is discontinuity, group instability or personal hardship.

Whether it is these or other approaches that are utilized, the essential concept is a deliberate attempt to maximize individual capacity and ideas. An innovative, forward-looking organization does not develop imaginative ideas at the top only, but in its administrative process, particularly through supervisory channels, helps make it possible for relevant ideas, perceptions, and information to flow freely through all channels of communication, up down, and sideways. Again, it should be borne in mind that the kinds of approaches referred to, for effective employee utilization in bureaucratic organizations, are themselves bureaucratic in character — they are stated policies, to be pursued throughout the organization, and not vague sentiments to be applied here and there on an individual, your-own-judgment basis.

THE ENVIRONMENT OF ORGANIZATIONAL PLANNING AND DECISION-MAKING

Herbert A. Simon has summarized[9] the developments in decision-making theory, research, and practice. He stressed the growth of quantitative decision-making tools in business, the growth of computer methods in decision-making, and the fact that laboratory experimentation in decision-making, following the computation schemes initiated by Bales and Bavelas, had become a thriving enterprise. From this growing body of tested assumptions will come increasing insights capable of translation into practical terms in our large service agencies. Indeed, some of these directions in the theory of rational choice, are finding their way into use now.

Both in the newer decision-making theory and in the older, traditional view of administrative planning, however, the emphasis has typically been on intra-organizational decision-making and planning, as if the organization were a closed system.

Of course, it is not, and least so with respect to organizational plans and decisions that are designed to shape its future. There is an external environment to every organization, with which it interacts. These interactions may be conceptualized into major systems for any one organization, affecting:

1. Support and maintenance of the organization.
2. Administrative policies.
3. Structure.
4. Operating function.

No organization operates in limbo, and the more an organization has become large, complex, and bureaucratized, the more does it have interdependent relationships not only with other organizations but with non-organizational forces. One of the reasons a large, bureaucratic organization tends to be stable and long-lived, is that by the time it gets to be large and complex, it is part of a network of other organizations and major groupings which have developed investments in the organization's survival. The consequence, however, as in all interdependent relationships, is some degree of loss of autonomy.

One of the most common illusions of personnel in large agencies, even in professional social work agencies, is that the executive, or the board, is really free to make decisions of any kind that affect the interests of the organization. The fact is that there are always a range of constraints on decision-making and agency planning, stemming from the extra-organizational environment as well as from the internal organizational considerations.

If the agency does not have a strong planning arm, projecting its aims for the short and long-range future, it can become simply the passive resultant of external forces shaping the nature of its financial support, its policies, structure, and operative function. Just as there is the illusion from staff below of the powers of the executive above, so there is often the illusion on the part of those in administrative authority that they are making genuine decisions guiding the destiny of their organization, when they are merely doing what has become unavoidable in the wake of prior decisions made by other organizations or groups.

Leadership within and by an organization requires the capacity of the organization to shape its own destiny. In turn, this necessitates a full understanding of the systems of interaction in which the organization is involved. The components in each of these

[9] Herbert A. Simon, "Administrative Decision Making," *Public Administration Review*, XXV, No. 1 (March, 1965), pp. 31-37.

systems may overlap, but their force will be different. A political special interest grouping may have considerable influence in the systems of financial support and policies, but have relatively little influence in systems affecting administrative structure or operating function. Agencies giving and receiving referrals may have considerable influence in operating function, but little in economic support.

In the case of large, national agencies with decentralized units, the same concepts apply, whether one is referring to the total agency, or treats each of its components as an organization in its own right. In the latter case the central headquarters and the other components of the national agency become part of the organization's significant external environment.

For an organization to have optimum control over its own destiny, and particularly where it is concerned with organizational innovation, anticipation of change, and adaptation to change, clear location of responsibility is needed to provide accurate assessments both of the internal organizational system and the extra-organizational systems.[10]

Should an organization such as the Veterans Administration move into different and closer relationships of service for out-patient clients with community agencies, a new system of interactions would develop. Not all such relationships may evolve the way decision-makers in the Veterans Administration or the other agencies concerned may have intended them to be to begin with. Different interests and organizational requirements will have to be negotiated. The direction of such relationships should ideally have been thought through by the initiating agency in advance, along with consequences that could be anticipated and ways of reacting to them. This is the kind of planning responsibility that, however much it draws on relevant participation of staff at all levels for ideas and information, in the last analysis has to be centralized.

CONCLUDING OBSERVATIONS

William Foote Whyte[11] observed that in the early history of human relations research in industry, with the fascination of the discovery of the "informal organization" and the fact that people were people even when they were working, little attention was given to formal organization, and to the impact of the environmental forces that shape systems of behavior within organizations. To this note may be added that the observation that those of us professionally reared in sciences and professions of human behavior, find it more congenial to attribute good and bad quality of administration to the personality and intellectual attributes of those in administrative authority. The news of human factors in organization was not exactly a revelation, although we could not perhaps have systematized our premises. We are, however, less inclined, by training, to concede to structure and process the force which they have, unless we make a special effort to do so.

In complex service organizations, the necessity to be highly cognizant of the repercussions of such structure and process, is great indeed. For leadership to be developed within and by such organizations, a perspective is needed which takes into account the

---

[10] In this general connection, one should note the increasing attention being paid to interorganizational analysis in the administrative literature. We are still at the level of guiding concepts, however, not of tested research. For example, see: Sol Levine and Pearl E. White, "Exchange As A Conceptual Framework for the Study of Interorganizational Relationships," *Administrative Science Quarterly* (March, 1961); Eugene Litwak and Lydia F. Hylton, "Interorganizational Analysis: A Hypothesis on Co-ordinating Agencies," *Administrative Science Quarterly*, VI, No. 4 (March, 1962), pp. 395-420.

[11] William Foote Whyte, *Man and Organization* (New York: Richard D. Irwin, Inc., 1959).

personality and group relationship dimensions on the one hand, and the structural, systemic factors on the other.

In this paper, stress has been placed on three dimensions of analysis, with deliberate compensatory emphasis on the structural attributes. All of this discussion is related, however, to one basic objective — how our service organizations, in an increasingly complex environment, can do the best job for those they serve and bring out the best in those they employ.

V. Environment

Goals, Environmental Pressures,
and Organizational Characteristics

RICHARD L. SIMPSON and WILLIAM H. GULLEY

Writers have often noted that the purposes for which an organization exists, and the environment in which it operates, will have effects on its internal structure and operating practices. Blau and others in the Weberian tradition, for example, have pointed out that a primarily "instrumental" organization designed to accomplish specific ends must place its main emphasis on efficiency, and hence is likely to be organized bureaucratically rather than democratically.[1] Lipset, Trow, and Coleman hypothesize that the most thoroughly centralized and undemocratic organizations will be those with narrowly defined instrumental goals; the broader the range of goals, the more likely the members are to desire some measure of control over policies.[2] Homans' concept of the "external system" emphasizes the shaping of the organization by its goals and environment.[3] These writings exemplify a growing recognition that the purposes and environmental situation of an

*This research was supported by a grant from Nationwide Insurance Companies to the Institute for Research in Social Science, University of North Carolina. Bert N. Adams did most of the IBM work and made many useful suggestions in connection with analysis methods. We are also indebted to W. Dwight Weed of Nationwide Insurance Companies for facilitating the research, to Donald M. Freeman and Donald D. Smith for work in data collection and preliminary analysis, and to Ruth E. Searles, Ida Harper Simpson, and Harry S. Upshaw for advice.

[1] See, for example, Peter M. Blau, *Bureaucracy in Modern Society* (New York: Random House, 1956), pp. 22-23.

[2] Seymour Martin Lipset, Martin Trow, and James S. Coleman, *Union Democracy* (Glencoe, Ill.: The Free Press, 1956), pp. 407, 415-416.

[3] George C. Homans, *The Human Group* (New York: Harcourt, Brace, 1950), pp. 90-94. For a treatment of a somewhat related problem, see also James D. Thompson and William D. McEwen, "Organizational Goals and Environment: Goal-Setting as an Interaction Process," *American Sociological Review*, 23 (February, 1958), pp. 23-31.

Reprinted from the American Sociological Review, *Vol. 27 (1962), pp. 344-351. Reprinted with permission of the American Sociological Association and the author.*

organization will influence its structure and behavior. However, little research except case studies of single organizations has been done to specify how these influences operate.[4]

In this paper we attempt to show some ways in which goals and environmental situations can influence the internal characteristics of one kind of organization, national voluntary associations. The general hypothesis is that organizations which must adapt to a wide range of pressures will differ in internal characteristics from those which face a narrower range of pressures. It is assumed that voluntary associations which pursue numerous goals, and which must satisfy demands made by the general community as well as by their own members, confront a more complex variety of pressures than associations which have few goals and little or no need to satisfy community expectations. Since they are exposed to pressures which are greater in number and different in kind, we would expect them to be organized differently. For example, we might expect that an association which has many goals and must satisfy an external constituency will be relatively decentralized, with initiation of activity concentrated at the local level and with a strong concern for grass-roots membership involvement and internal communication. With this kind of organization the leadership can respond to local community demands and to the changing desires of a membership which has diverse goals.

Following this kind of reasoning, we will present a typology of voluntary associations and a test of three specific hypotheses. Associations are classified as *focused* or *diffuse*, depending on the number of goals they pursue, and as *internal* or *external*, depending on whether they must satisfy their members alone, or both their members and the outside community. By these criteria, *focused internal associations* face the fewest pressures and *diffuse external associations* the most. The hypotheses are: (1) Focused internal associations· will tend to be centralized in authority structure and action-initiation, diffuse external associations decentralized, and the other two types of associations (focused external, diffuse internal) intermediate in degree of centralization. (2) Diffuse external associations will tend to stress loyal, active involvement of rank-and-file members in their activities, focused internal associations will tend not to stress membership involvement, and the other two types of associations will be intermediate in this respect. (3) Diffuse external associations will tend to emphasize internal communication, focused internal associations will tend not to emphasize internal communication, and other associations will be intermediate in this respect.

METHOD AND SAMPLE

The method used was the sample survey by mail questionnaire, with national voluntary associations as the units of analysis. Associations were chosen from the *Encyclopedia*

---

[4] Case studies showing relationships between goals and environmental circumstances and the internal features of single organizations are numerous. Examples include studies of government agencies, such as Philip Selznick, *TVA and the Grass Roots* (Berkeley and Los Angeles: University of California Press, 1949); studies of voluntary associations, such as David L. Sills, *The Volunteers* (Glencoe, Ill.: The Free Press, 1957); "industry and community" studies, such as W. Lloyd Warner and J. O. Low, *The Social System of the Modern Factory* (New Haven: Yale University Press, 1947); and studies of political machines, such as Harold F. Gosnell, *Machine Politics: Chicago Model* (Chicago: University of Chicago Press, 1937). Theoretical discussions of this topic are found in Selznick, *op. cit.*, pp. 250-259, reprinted in part as "A Theory of Organizational Commitments," in Robert K. Merton, Ailsa P. Gray, Barbara Hockey, and Hanan C. Selvin, ed., *Reader in Bureaucracy* (Glencoe, Ill.: The Free Press, 1952), pp. 194-202; and in Chester I. Barnard, *The Functions of the Executive* (Cambridge, Mass.: Harvard University Press, 1938), pp. 194-199.

of American Associations and *World Convention Dates.*[5] Coverage of a wide variety of types and sizes, rather than simple randomness, was the criterion for sampling. Even if randomness had been desired, it would have been impossible, since the available listings of voluntary associations are not complete. An original mailing asked officials of national associations to return questionnaires and to send us lists of local chapters, individual members, or both; these lists were used for subsequent mailing of questionnaires to local officials and rank-and-file members. In all, 1010 questionnaires were mailed out, and of these, 546 or 54 per cent were returned.[6] Of the 546 respondents, 485 representing 211 different organizations answered both questions used in establishing the typology of associations and were thus eligible for inclusion in the sample. So that no organization would appear more than once in the sample, one respondent was selected randomly from each organization having more than one respondent or, if respondents disagreed in answering the questions used to establish the typology, one was selected randomly from those giving the modal answer.[7]

TYPOLOGY OF ASSOCIATIONS

To form a typology of voluntary associations, we have classified them by two criteria.

[5] *Encyclopedia of American Associations*, second edition (Detroit: Gale Research Co., 1959). F. A. Duzette, ed., *World Convention Dates* (Hempstead, N. Y.: Hendrickson Publishing Co.), published monthly. Several 1959 issues were used.

[6] A more detailed description of the survey procedure appears in William H. Gulley, "Relative Effectiveness in Voluntary Associations," unpublished doctoral dissertation, University of North Carolina, 1961.

[7] An exception to this procedure was made in the case of 15 associations each represented by two respondents who disagreed as to typological classification. In these instances respondents were chosen purposively to equate the four types of associations as nearly as possible in the percentages of respondents in the sample who were national officials, local officials, and rank-and-file members. This departure from randomness seemed desirable since preliminary tabluations had shown that these three basic levels of respondents differed in their perception of organizational characteristics. These differential perceptions do not materially affect the findings of this paper since the proportional representation of the three levels is almost entirely controlled in the analysis sample, as is shown in Table 1. While the absolute scores on the three indexes differed, with officials assigning slightly higher scores than members on all three indexes, the comparative positions of the four types of organizations on the three indexes were generally the same when the associations whose respondents were national officials, local officials, and members were analyzed separately. Specifically, on the centralization index, all three levels of respondents placed the focused internal and diffuse external associations at the predicted extremes except that local officials placed diffuse external associations in the position next to the predicted extreme; the same was true of the membership involvement index except that national and local officials placed focused internal associations in the position next to the predicted extreme; and on internal communication, national officials and members placed both focused internal and diffuse external associations at the predicted extremes but local officials placed neither type at the predicted extreme. Thus out of nine tabulations controlling level of respondent, in only one (local officials' responses concerning internal communication) were the relationships not essentially as predicted, despite the fact that many of the categories of levels of respondents within associational types had very small frequencies ranging from six to ten respondents. The nine tabulations just discussed are not shown in this paper; they are similar in logic and format to the tabulations for organizational size classes shown in Table 2.

301

The first, *focused or diffuse*, refers to the number of goals an organization pursues. Associations are classified as focused or diffuse in goals on the basis of response to a question which asked, "How much better off do you feel that your members are then they would be if they did not belong to your organization, with respect to each of the following things?" (their income, financial condition, etc.; their prestige or status in the community; their feeling of contribution to society or community; their knowledge of world or community problems; their social lives, friends, etc.; their cultural or artistic lives; their ability to express points of view, have their ideas put into practice, etc.). With respect to each of these seven items representing organizational goals, respondents could indicate that membership led to a person's being "much better off," "somewhat better off," or "no better off," or that the item was "not relevant to the goals of our organization." If a respondent indicated that members were much better off or somewhat better off with respect to an item, this was taken to mean that he regarded the item as a goal of the organization.[8] The 112 associations whose sample respondents cited from one to four goals were defined as having focused goals; the 99 whose sample respondents cited from five to seven goals were defined as having diffuse goals.[9]

The second criterion by which associations are classified, *internal or external*, refers to the absence or presence of involvement with the community. An internally oriented association must satisfy its members but is not expected to satisfy any demands from the general community, while an externally oriented association faces demands from both the general community and its own members. To classify associations as internal or external in orientation, the following question is used: "Some organizations need more support from the general community than others need. Check the one statement below which comes closest to describing your situation." (1. "We could never accomplish anything without strong community support. 2. Community support is important to us but not absolutely essential for everything we do. 3. Community support is desirable, but not really a major factor in our success. 4. It does not really matter whether the community supports our program or not. 5. We hope to accomplish our goals despite opposition from a major element of the community.) The 93 associations whose respondents checked the first or second alternative, indicating need for community support, were classified as

---

[8] A critic has suggested that this method of ascertaining goals may have led us to classify associations as diffuse in goals, not because the organizations actually had numerous goals, but because these were associations which happened to be represented in our sample by enthusiastic respondents whose enthusiasm caused them to say that membership made a person "better off" in numerous ways. If this were so, it would point to a serious weakness in our method of classification, but there are three principal reasons for doubting that it is so. First, most respondents in all four associational types were officials, and one can probably assume that officials of all four types tended to be enthusiastic supporters of their organizations. Second, when we asked each respondent to rate his association on an eleven-point scale from full achievement of its goals (10) to no achievement at all (0), with 5 being "reasonable achievement," the ratings by respondents from focused and diffuse associations were very similar. The medians were 6.67 for focused and 6.77 for diffuse associations, and the means were 6.40 for focused and 6.53 for diffuse associations, suggesting that the two sets of respondents differed very little in enthusiasm. The third reason is the check on the reliability of the classification described in footnote 11.

[9] The 13 associations whose respondents cited no goals at all were eliminated along with four whose respondents did not answer, and these associations are not among the 211 in the sample used for analysis.

externally oriented; the remaining 118 were classified as internally oriented.[10]

By these procedures we arrived at the sample described in Table 1.[11] The representation of different organizational levels among the respondents is shown in order to indicate that this variable, which might have affected the results, has been largely controlled. When this typology is used to indicate the range of pressures to which voluntary associations are exposed, the polar types are the focused internal associations, facing the fewest pressures, and the diffuse external, subjected to the widest variety of pressures. (Note that "external" really means "external plus internal," since nothing in our data suggests that they face fewer internal pressures than the organizations we have called "internal"; the difference is that they additionally face external pressures.) For present purposes the focused external and diffuse internal associations may be regarded simply as intermediate

TABLE 1

SAMPLE OF ASSOCIATIONS BY TYPE AND LEVEL OF RESONDENT

Type of Association	Percent of Each Type's Respondents Who Were:		
	National Officials	Local Officials	Members
Focused internal (N=70)	60.0	20.0	20.0
Focused external (N=42)	64.3	19.0	16.7
Diffuse internal (N=48)	62.4	18.8	18.8
Diffuse external (N=51)	60.8	19.6	19.6

[10] No sample respondent checked the fifth alternative, indicating community opposition.

[11] It will be recalled that when an association had more than one respondent, one giving the modal responses was selected for inclusion in the sample, and that respondents from the same association sometimes disagreed in their answers to the questions used for classifying it. As a check on the reliability of the classification, we compared the classification each association would have been given if the classification had been based on the mean of all its respondents' answers to the two classification questions, with the classification it actually received on the basis of answers by its one respondent included in the sample. The means were based on the number of goals cited, for the focused-vs.-diffuse question, and on the code numbers used in the text of this paper to identify the five possible responses ranging from extreme community involvement to extreme lack of involvement, for the internal-vs.-external question. If we define the classification based on the means as the "proper" classification for the purpose of this reliability check, then 23 associations or 11 percent of the 211 were improperly classified in the sample used for analysis. When we regard the focused internal and diffuse external associations as extreme types in the range of pressures they face, only two of 211 associations were classified in the analysis sample at the wrong extreme.

303

types, although they are intermediate for different reasons and may very well differ from each other in ways not revealed by our data.[12]

FINDINGS

Table 2 tests the three hypotheses given earlier. It shows, for each associational type, the medians for three indexes composed of responses to questions in which respondents were asked to describe various characteristics of their organizations. Each index relates to one of the three hypotheses.

TABLE 2—MEDIAN CENTRALIZATION, MEMBERSHIP INVOLVEMENT, AND
INTERNAL COMMUNICATION SCORES BY SIZE AND
TYPE OF ASSOCIATION

Index and Size of Association	Focused Internal		Focused External		Diffuse Internal		Diffuse External	
	Median	(N)	Median	(N)	Median	(N)	Median	(N)
Centralization								
All associations	2.14	(55)	1.54	(39)	1.80	(45)	1.37	(44)
Small only	2.29	(23)	1.75	(9)	2.30	(14)	1.83	(8)
Medium only	2.00	(21)	1.63	(13)	1.70	(18)	1.58	(13)
Large only	1.75	(11)	1.43	(17)	1.33	(13)	1.00	(23)
Membership Involvement								
All associations	1.42	(56)	1.67	(39)	1.97	(46)	3.03	(46)
Small only	1.31	(25)	0.88	(9)	1.92	(13)	1.75	(9)
Medium only	1.75	(23)	2.00	(13)	1.79	(20)	3.00	(14)
Large only	0.50	(8)	1.87	(17)	2.38	(13)	3.27	(23)
Internal Communication								
All associations	1.80	(60)	2.33	(38)	2.27	(47)	2.67	(48)
Small only	1.88	(25)	2.33	(9)	2.10	(14)	1.83	(8)
Medium only	1.71	(23)	1.60	(13)	2.31	(19)	2.86	(14)
Large only	1.50	(12)	2.77	(16)	2.50	(14)	2.69	(26)

[12] Other typologies of voluntary associations are given in George A. Lundberg, Mirra Komarovsky, and Mary Alice McInerny, *Leisure: A Suburban Study* (New York: Columbia University Press, 1934), pp. 129-169; Arnold M. Rose, *Theory and Method in the Social Sciences* (Minneapolis: University of Minnesota Press, 1954), p. 52; and C. Wayne Gordon and Nicholas Babchuk, "A Typology of Voluntary Associations," *American Sociological Review*, 24 (February, 1959), pp. 22-29. Our typology is analytic and not based on the manifest functions of the organizations, and organizations of numerous kinds were classified in all four analytic types. Occupational organizations including academic, scientific, and professional societies, trade associations, and labor unions made up 43 of 70 focused internal, 12 of 42 focused external, 29 of 48 diffuse internal, and 25 of 51 diffuse external associations. Non-occupational organizations included recreational, social, and hobby associations, interest and pressure groups working to advance non-occupational goals (e.g., a veterans' organization) or benefit some non-occupational group (e.g., a religious pressure group), and charitable or philanthropic organizations. When we classified associations into eight types based on their principal manifest functions — four occupational and four non-occupational types — organizations of all eight functional types were found in all four of our analytic types, except that no recreational society or trade associaiton was classified as diffuse external.

Centralization. Hypothesis 1 was that focused internal associations would tend to be the most centralized in authority structure and action-initiation, and diffuse external associations the least. Three items went into the centralization index: (1) "Where would you say the main activity of your organization is carried out?" (National level is scored 1; regional, state, or local level is scored 0.) (2) "When changes have taken place in your . . . programs . . . from where has the initiative for the change usually come?" (National officials is scored 1; lesser officials or individual members is scored 0.) (3) "Please check the one statement below which most nearly describes the top leadership structure of your national organization." (Decisions made by national leaders alone is scored 1; decisions made by local officials or members, or by national leaders only after consultation with local officials or members, is scored 0.)

On this three-item index, median scores ranged from a high of 2.14 for the focused internal associations to a low of 1.37 for the diffuse external associations. The direction of relationships supports the hypothesis.[13]

Membership involvement. Hypothesis 2 was that diffuse external associations would show the greatest concern with involving rank-and-file members in their activities and maintaining membership loyalty, and focused internal associations the least. Membership involvement was measured with an index of four items. The responses which received scores of 1, paraphrased here to save space, were: (1) That members take an active part in the work of the organization is very important. (2) The members would feel a terrible loss if the organization did not exist. (3) Promoting cooperation among members is very important. (4) Recruiting members is very important.

As predicted, diffuse external associations scored highest in membership involvement, with a median of 3.03, and focused internal associations scored lowest, with a median of 1.42.

Internal communication. Hypothesis 3 was that diffuse external associations would place the greatest emphasis on maintaining channels of internal communication, and focused internal associations the least. Emphasis on internal communication was measured with a three-item index. Responses which received scores of 1, slightly paraphrased, were: (1) Educating members as to the objectives of the organization is very important. (2) Keeping members informed of the organization's activities is very important. (3) That members keep leaders informed of their opinions is absolutely essential or very important.

Again, the results are in the direction predicted by the hypothesis. Diffuse external associations showed the greatest emphasis on internal communication, with a median of 2.67, and focused internal associations showed the least, with a median of 1.80.

These findings thus tend to support all three hypotheses. Moreover, on all 10 separate items which went into the three indexes, the types of associations we have defined as lowest and highest in the range of pressures to which they are exposed — focused internal with diffuse external — were at the predicted extremes in the response distributions. In addition, if we compare the focused and diffuse associations within the internal and external categories considered separately, and the internal and external

---

[13] The findings were not tested for significance, since the sample was not a random one of any known universe, for the reason mentioned earlier. Writers on both sides of the recent controversy over the use of tests of significance seem to agree that such tests are hard to interpret, if not wholly meaningless, when random sampling procedures have not been followed. See Hanan C. Selvin, "A Critique of Tests of Significance in Survey Research," *American Sociological Review*, 22 (October, 1957), pp. 519-527; and James M. Beshers, "On 'A Critique of Tests of Significance in Survey Research,' " *American Sociological Review*, 23 (April, 1958), p. 199.

associations within the focused and diffuse categories considered separately, their relative scores on all three indexes are what we would predict: the associations facing more pressures scored lower in centralization, higher in membership involvement, and higher in internal communication.

Organizational size as a control variable. A number of studies have shown that the size of organizations is related to their organizational characteristics, as one would expect from bureaucratic theory.[14] Since the associations of our four types differed in average size, it seemed advisable to find out whether the differences we found in their organizational characteristics would hold up when the size of associations was controlled. To control size, we divided the associations into three size classes, from data on size of membership given in the *Encyclopedia of American Associations*.[15] Associations with 2499 or fewer members were defined as small, those with from 2500 to 24,999 members were defined as medium, and those with 25,000 or more members were defined as large.

Table 2 shows median centralization, membership involvement, and internal communication scores for small, medium, and large associations in each of the four typological categories. Most of the hypothesized relationships held up among the medium and large associations, especially those regarding centralization and membership involvement. For example, focused internal associations were always at the predicted extreme of the response distribution except that medium-sized associations of this type were next to the predicted extreme in internal communication. Similarly, diffuse external associations were at the predicted extreme except that large associations of this type were next to the predicted extreme in internal communication. The small associations, however, deviated from the general pattern. Among these, the focused internal associations were next to the predicted extreme on all three indexes, while the diffuse external associations were next to the predicted extreme twice and at the "wrong" extreme in internal communication.

These findings seem to support the conclusion that the range of pressures to which an organization is exposed, as indicated by our typology, is related to organizational characteristics in medium-sized and large associations, though perhaps not in small ones. One could feel safer in drawing this conclusion if the frequencies in the subcategories were larger, but by the same token it is noteworthy that the predicted relationships generally hold up despite the smallness of some frequencies.

DISCUSSION

In interpreting the findings one should bear in mind that they did not hold up within

[14] Some examples include William Foote Whyte, *Human Relations in the Restaurant Industry* (New York: McGraw-Hill, 1948), pp. 17-30; Frederic W. Terrien and Donald L. Mills, "The Effect of Changing Size upon the Internal Structure of Organizations," *American Sociological Review*, 20 (February, 1955), pp. 11-14; Lipset, Trow, and Coleman, *op. cit.*, pp. 150-154, 163-171; Theodore Caplow, "Organization Size," *Administrative Science Quarterly*, 1 (March, 1957), pp. 484-505; Edwin J. Thomas, "Role Conceptions and Organizational Size," *American Sociological Review*, 24 (February, 1959), pp. 30-38; Amitai Etzioni, "The Functional Differentiation of Elites in the Kibbutz," *American Journal of Sociology*, 64 (March, 1959), pp. 476-487; Sergio Talacchi, "Organization Size, Individual Attitudes and Behavior," *Administrative Science Quarterly*, 5 (December, 1960), pp. 398-420; R. W. Revans, "Industrial Morale and Size of Unit," in Walter Galenson and Seymour Martin Lipset, ed., *Labor and Trade Unionism* (New York: Wiley, 1960), pp. 295-300; and Theodore R. Anderson and Seymour Warkov, "Organizational Size and Functional Complexity: A Study of Administration in Hospitals," *American Sociological Review*, 26 (February, 1961), pp. 23-28.

[15] Encyclopedia of American Associations, op. cit.

organizations having fewer than 2500 members, that the differences were smaller and the relationships slightly less consistent with respect to internal communication than with respect to the other two indexes, and that the analysis assumes that officials and members can accurately perceive the characteristics of their organizations. However, the over-all consistency of the findings seems to lend support to the general hypothesis and the three sub-hypotheses.

It can be plausibly argued that the organizational features most frequently found in the different types of voluntary associations represent characteristically different modes of adaptation to their diverse situations. Consider the focused internal associations, with their tendencies toward minimal concern over membership involvement, lack of interest in maintaining internal communication channels, and centralized authority structure. In comparison with other associations, these are organizations which seek limited sets of goals and do not need the support of outsiders. Given this situation, it is understandable if their officials do not concern themselves deeply with recruiting, motivating, and keeping in touch with their members. The members do not need to act as ambassadors to the outside world, and therefore a high degree of membership loyalty and activity is not necessary. The members join for limited purposes, and as long as the officials stick to these purposes, the members do not have to be persuaded to support activity aimed at other goals. If the goals are limited, the chances are that the officials understand what the members want; therefore upward communication from members to officials need not be emphasized. Conversely, from the member's standpoint, neither frequent communication nor a democratic voice in policy-making would seem crucially important, so long as the officials deliver the rather well-defined goods they are expected to deliver.[16]

The situation of the diffuse external associations is somewhat the reverse. Nevertheless, the finding that these organizations, which must operate under a complicated set of pressures, tend to be relatively decentralized and democratic, might seem inconsistent with the ancient observation that "a tight situation makes for a tight authority structure." It has been said, for example, that the reason why military organizations must be authoritarian is that they need to move fast in exceedingly demanding situations.[17] The demands placed on organizations may differ, however, in nature as well as in complexity or urgency. In the case of diffuse external voluntary associations, the difficulty of their situation stems specifically from their need to satisfy both members and outsiders who have varied and possibly conflicting expectations. Therefore their mode of adaptation consists of trying to guarantee that the various pressures will be communicated to the leadership so that it can plan accordingly, and that the leadership's plans will be communicated to the members, on the local level, where the basic activities in these organizations tend to occur. The more decentralized authority structure, coupled with greater emphasis on membership involvement and communication, enables the leaders to keep in touch with local activities and the members to make their varied wishes known.

On a more general level, the findings seem to support the proposition that the characteristics of organizations will be systematically related to their goals and to the environmental circumstances in which they operate. It also seems clear that the relationships are amenable to statistical survey techniques using organizations as the units of analysis, along with other methods more commonly used in the past for studying com-

---

[16] Lipset has made this same point in his discussion of internal union politics: Seymour Martin Lipset, *Political Man: The Social Bases of Politics* (Garden City, N. Y.: Doubleday, 1960), p. 390. A similar statement also appears in Lipset, Trow, and Coleman, *op. cit.*, p. 407.

[17] See, for example, George C. Homans, *op. cit.*, p. 432; and Homans, "The Small Warship," *American Sociological Review*, 11 (June, 1946), p. 300.

plex organizations, such as individual case study.[18]

[18] Survey analysis with organizations as the statistical units is analogous to some of the research which uses cultures or societies as the units and examines relationships among their attributes; for example: Leonard T. Hobhouse, G. C. Wheeler, and Morris Ginsberg, *The Material Culture and Social Institutions of the Simpler Peoples* (London: Chapman and Hall, 1915); George Peter Murdock, *Social Structure* (New York: Macmillan, 1949); Linton C. Freeman and Robert F. Winch, "Societal Complexity: An Empirical Test of a Typology of Societies," *American Journal of Sociology*, 62 (March, 1957), pp. 461-466; Stanley H. Udy, Jr., *The Organization of Work* (New Haven: HRAF Press, 1959); and M. F. Nimkoff and Russell Middleton, "Types of Family and Types of Economy," *American Journal of Sociology*, 66 (November, 1960), pp. 215-225.

"Green Power" in the Government-Voluntary Partnership*

JACQUES COUSIN

We are here to discuss the single most important aspect of our nation's domestic policy — the poor or disenfranchised. Frequently, though not always, this means the Negro. We are here to discuss the problems of urban America. We are, in a sense, 20th century ancient Romans worrying about the Goths, Visigoths, and Vandals. Only instead of wild tribes beating against our frontiers, our potential Goths, Visigoths, and Vandals are American citizens. They live in the very centers of our culture, our seats of government where our industrial power and largest tax bases are concentrated. They live in the very places wherein one can find the vitality, imagination, intelligence, and earning power that have carried this country to its rich economy and generally good life.

Unfortunately, not enough Americans are in a position to earn this good life. While I am certain there never will be 100 percent of any population enjoying the "good life," we are faced with too large a group of disadvantaged people for whom there is nothing but frustration and a further sinking into despair.

Those of us in the larger cities must learn to work together to coordinate the private and public efforts. Neither the public trough nor the private purse has enough money to do it alone. Neither sector has a monopoly on the know-how to do it alone. Neither has enough manpower to do it alone. Lastly, and in some ways most important, problems of this nature cannot or should not be solved exclusively by government.

You cannot have a stable and successful economy, a happy society, unless you have productive, stable, law-abiding individual citizens. Government is not the answer to healthy productivity, and government alone does not teach citizenship in the true sense of the word. Government is, or should be, the servant of the people, and we cannot have the proper degree of government until we have a stable, educated citizenry.

The private sector must enable people to be productive and responsible citizens by offering each the same opportunity to succeed according to his mental and physical ability. This is more important than merely shelling out dollars.

It will take expenditures of funds, both governmental and private, to accomplish much of this at this time. But before these funds can be well spent, it is necessary for the private and governmental sectors to recognize some of the inherent differences and difficulties that arise when we attempt a joint attack on these serious problems. We must understand these before we can work together.

---

*This is a condensed version of the paper presented by Mr. Cousin at the "Big Cities" Institute of the UCFCA-OEO Leadership Training Project, which was held in Chicago in February, 1968.

Reprinted from Community, *November-December, 1968, pp. 3-6, by special permission of United Funds and Councils of America, Inc.*

How do you turn off poor programs?

Elected officials worry about reelection. Not only must they periodically undergo the physical trauma, mental turmoil and financial drain of seeking re-election, but they can't afford to alienate too many votes. They have to insulate themselves from criticism and satisfy as many people as possible.

A man in the private sector doesn't worry about re-election. As long as he or his product sells in the marketplace, he is safe. He can be much more objective because he isn't the servant of as many masters as the typical elected official. This means that in many ways the private sector is less afraid of criticism than government. If criticism is justified, the private sector can respond quickly and drastically.

For example, the Edsel was a flop – and Ford killed it fast. Can you imagine any level of government killing any public program or project it had conceived and brought forth with all the fanfare of the Edsel introduction? At best, there would be compromise. At worst, we would just add Edsels to our taxes.

This, I believe, is one reason the private sector is afraid of many governmental programs and services. How do you get them turned off, if and when they prove fruitless? In all honesty, it generally is equally difficult to kill programs in the United Fund movement and in social agencies. Some of these can't be measured qualitatively and each has a vocal band of supporters. But in his business context, the corporate official has no serious problem in killing a poor product and he is critical of government for not being able to do the same.

Another problem is communications. Governmental people at all levels listen to a great many persons who are wonderful problem staters, but many of whom are awfully short on problem solving. Successful executives are problem solvers. And while most problem staters can talk forever, problem solvers are short on patience. Throw in a bit of old-fashioned city hall politics, and many business executives say, "Life is too short to put up with this."

Another problem we face is the proclivity of elected officials for announcing programs that have not been fully financed or implemented. A screaming headline says, "X Million Dollars Awarded for Y Program." But the story under the headline shows it to be for the entire state, spread over several years, not funded beyond a year or sometimes not at all, especially if it is announced in a Saturday edition. Why such glowing publicity about what the program will do, when no one really knows how or even *if* it will perform?

Another point is credibility. One thing is firmly fixed in my memory as a result of two months with the New Detroit Committee. A great number of the disadvantaged, both black and white, asked us not to promise something we could not deliver. Time after time people told me that government, at all levels and of both political parties, made too many promises that were not kept.

For example, on a simple issue, it strains credulity to imagine that you can take an unemployed slaughterhouse porter and in six months teach him to be typist. You can teach him to finger the keys, but can he spell? Does he have the sense of responsibility or the office graces demanded of a typist as opposed to those of a slaughterhouse porter? I'm not saying that he should be doomed forever to unemployment, but you are doing this man a disfavor if you con him into thinking he can quickly gain a more responsible position than his previous one, or one significantly different. Things just don't work that way. Let us not promise something we cannot deliver, qualitatively or quantitatively.

WHAT WE MUST DO

We must do more for the poor, and we must do much more cooperatively – government and private sector working side by side. Speaking for the voluntary Fund in Detroit, in the past 18 months, we have invested about $1.75 million in the kinds of projects we never financed before. Six months *before* the riots, we took $400,000 out of reserves to help innovative agencies sponsor experimental programs; some of this for programs involving direct citizen participation and decision-making at the neighborhood or street level. Later in the year a separate capital fund we administer put $500,000 into a low-cost quasi-governmental housing corporation wherein it has the minority vote, though at the moment I believe it is the majority contributor. Uncle Sammy hasn't coughed up his share yet.

Apart from a couple of hundred thousand dollars for immediate post-riot relief we then invested $125,000 to help 100 deserving (and working) families devastated by the riots – help them buy homes, pay closing costs, buy furniture, etc. We took quite a beating on that from many people who felt we were rewarding rioters. We thought we were helping working men keep their families together and get started again to live with dignity. That money came out of reserves.

Earlier this year we set aside a half million dollars out of reserves to fund we know not what. We are in the process of approving $217,000 of it for two neighborhood units hiring indigenous aides and involving local citizens to help decide how to spend some of this money.

Having these reserve funds available gave the UF the flexibility to step into this area at this time. They also partially protect the UF from some very serious and costly fund-raising problems while the community reorients its thinking.

THE ANSWER – IN SURBURBIA

In my opinion, the plight of the cities will not be improved by concentrating our efforts on direct services to the ghetto alone. Problems are not limited to the poor. The quickest and the real answer to the problems we face lies in the suburbs – but it may be the toughest answer to get, because the suburbs are where the grass grows green and where "green power" is increasingly concentrated in 20th century America. Suburbia also has an increasing number of votes.

To solve the problems of the city's poor we need the dollars, the votes, the leadership and above all the understanding of white suburbia. Let us not forget this for one moment. We all face a tremendous educational job and one which I'm afraid will have many examples of failure before we get out of this impasse.

The United Foundation cannot spend $26,000,000 a year unless we collect it. And 70 percent of our pledged income is from individuals – individuals who have their private likes, dislikes, prejudices and problems. As our percentage of individual participation grows (and this is good because it indicates acceptance), our rate of poor risks and collection loss also grows. In 1967, while our corporate and retired wealth pledges increased, our individual broad-based citizen pledges either stood still or, in a few instances, decreased. (This is not all attributable to riots, but also to state income taxes, strikes, and other factors, as well.)

Though we are a heavily unionized city with a progressive UAW, one must recognize that the union rank and file is increasingly independent of union leadership these days. Union leadership endorsement of governmental or voluntary programs doesn't automatically mean cash support by the individual member.

All of us, in the private sector and in government, must recognize that the bulk of the money collected from individuals is from white and blue collar workers, many of whom live in suburbia. These people have needs in their communities. They want schools, sewers, hospitals, paved roads, Boy Scouts, YMCA's, child and family services, etc. It is ridiculous to ignore their needs, for many are legitimate. Many are for preventive medicine – as when suburban judges call for increased services to pre-delinquents.

311

Since it is in these suburbs where most individual earning power, "green power," resides and where votes are being increasinglyly concentrated — those of us who bear some responsibility for improving total urban life must find a way to make essentially white suburbia realize it holds the key to the ghetto.

BALANCING THE NEEDS

We must find a way to meet enough of the needs of suburbia. (At times I fear the day is not far off when suburbia will tell us all to go to the devil — inner-city resident, city official, or United Fund executive. They'll keep their voluntary "green power" where it is, and they'll send rock-ribbed conservatives to the state legislature. They will turn their backs on the cities. Some have started already.) But while we are meeting suburbia's minimum needs we must meet more than the minimum needs of the inner city. We must begin to gain on the situation — but this cannot be done without a broad and penetrating educational offensive in suburbia to permit diverting more than a "fair share" of dollars back into the cities. It won't be popular and there will be unpleasant repercussions. Obviously, such a cause is not politically attractive and it could have serious fund-raising implications.

Do you and your elected governmental bosses have the guts to risk losing elections? Do we on the voluntary side have the guts to risk taking a dunking now and then? And what happens if the "good guys" lose too many elections, bond issues, or fail to raise voluntary dollars?

We have a very fine line to tread. We must have more and more dollars, but dollars alone won't solve the problem because to spend dollars you have to raise them by means of voluntary contributions or taxes. And there are increasing signs indicating the bottoms of both barrels are about to be scraped.

I know for sure that voluntary contributions are becoming increasingly difficult to get, but that may be healthy. We must constantly improve our handling of them and our spending of them. People demand more accounting of how their gifts are spent, and people are so concerned about the failure of their city and their nation that they question whether they should not divert potential contributions to their own personal use or at best give them to a local charity; one whose function they can see and thoroughly understand.

We need to pour more money into the ghetto, but we must not lose sight of where this money comes from. In the battle to rescue the ghettos, we must not forget suburbia, lest once again we harvest disaster from the seeds of phony promises and false hopes.

Exchange as a Conceptual Framework for the Study of Interorganizational Relationships

SOL LEVINE and PAUL E. WHITE

Sociologists have devoted considerable attention to the study of formal organizations, particularly in industry, government, and the trade union field. Their chief focus, however, has been on patterns within rather than between organizations. Studies of interrelationships have largely been confined to units within the same organizational structure or between a pair of complementary organizations such as management and labor. Dimock's study of jurisdictional conflict between two federal agencies is a notable exception.[1] Another is a study of a community reaction to disaster by Form and Nosow in which the authors produce revealing data on the interaction pattern of local health organizations. The authors observe that "organizational cooperation was facilitated among organizations with similar internal structures."[2] March and Simon suggest that interorganizational conflict is very similar to intergroup conflict within organizations but present no supporting data.[3] Blau has commented on the general problems involved in studying multiple organizations.[4] In pointing up the need to study the organization in relation to its environment, Etzioni specifies the area of interorganizational relationships as one of the three meriting further intensive empirical study.[5]

Health and social welfare agencies within a given community offer an excellent opportunity for exploring patterns of relationship among organizations. There are an appreciable number of such organizations in any fairly large urban American community. Most of them are small so that relatively few individuals have to be interviewed to obtain information on their interaction. Within any community setting, varying kinds of relations exist between official and voluntary organizations concerned with health and welfare. Thus welfare agencies may use public health nursing services, or information on the status of families may be shared by such voluntary organizations as the Red Cross and the Tuberculosis and Health Association.

Facilitating communication between local organizations has been a major objective of

[1] Marshall E. Dimock, "Expanding Jurisdictions: A Case Study in Bureaucratic Conflict," in Robert K. Merton, Ailsa P. Gray, Barbara Hockey, Hanan C. Selvin, eds., *Reader in Bureaucracy* (Glencoe, 1952).

[2] William H. Form and Sigmund Nosow, *Community in Disaster* (New York, 1958), p. 236.

[3] James G. March and H. A. Simon, *Organizations* (New York, 1958).

[4] Peter M. Blau, "Formal Organization: Dimensions of Analysis," *American Journal of Sociology*, 63 (1957), p. 58.

[5] Amitai Etzioni, "New Directions in the Study of Organizations and Society," *Social Research*, 27 (1960), pp. 223-228.

Reprinted from Administrative Science Quarterly, *Vol. 5 (March, 1961) pp. 584-601, with permission of the* Administrative Science Quarterly.

public health administrators and community organizers. Their writings contain many assertions about the desirability of improving relationships in order to reduce gaps and overlaps of medical services to the citizens, but as yet little effort has been made to appraise objectively the interrelationships that actually exist within the community.

In the following pages we should like to present our theoretical interpretation of interorganizational relationships together with a discussion of our research approach and a few preliminary findings, pointing up some of the substantive areas in organizational sociology for which our study has relevance. Our present thinking is largely based on the results of an exploratory study of twenty-two health organizations in a New England community with a population of 200,000 and initial impressions of data on a more intensive study, as yet unanalyzed, of some fifty-five health organizations in another New England community of comparable size.[6]

The site of our initial investigation was selected because we found it fairly accessible for study and relatively independent of a large metropolis; moreover, it contained a range of organizations which were of interest — a full-time health department, a welfare department, autonomous local agencies, local chapters or affiliates of major voluntary health and social welfare organizations, and major community hospitals. Of the twenty-two health organizations or agencies studied, fourteen were voluntary agencies, five were hospitals (three with out-patient clinics and two without) and three others were official agencies — health, welfare, and school. Intensive semistructured interviews were conducted with executive directors and supervisory personnel of each organization, and information was obtained from members of the boards through brief semistructured questionnaires. In addition, we used an adaptation of an instrument developed by Irwin T. Sanders to locate the most influential leaders in the community for the purpose of determining their distribution on agency boards.[7] The prestige ratings that the influential leaders assigned to the organizations constituted one of the independent variables of our study.

EXCHANGE AS A CONCEPTUAL FRAMEWORK

The complex of community health organizations may be seen as a system with individual organizations or system parts varying in the kinds and frequency of their relationships with one another. This system is enmeshed in ever larger systems — the community, the state, and so on.

Prevention and cure of disease constitute the ideal orientation of the health agency system, and individual agencies derive their respective goals or objectives from this larger orientation. In order to achieve its specific objectives, however, an agency must possess or control certain elements. It must have clients to serve; it must have resources in the form of equipment, specialized knowledge, or the funds with which to procure them; and it must have the services of people who can direct these resources to the clients. Few, if any, organizations have enough access to all these elements to enable them to attain their objectives fully. Under realistic conditions of element scarcity, organizations must select, on the basis of expedience or efficiency, particular functions that permit them to achieve

[6] The project is sponsored by the Social Science Program at the Harvard School of Public Health and supported by Grant 8676-2 from the National Institutes of Health. Professor Sol Levine is the principal investigator of the project and Benjamin D. Paul, the director of the Social Science Program, is coinvestigator. We are grateful for the criticisms and suggestions given by Professors Paul, S. M. Miller, Irwin T. Sanders, and Howard E. Freeman.
[7] Irwin T. Sanders, "The Community Social Profile," *American Sociological Review*, 25 (1960), pp. 75-77.

their ends as fully as possible. By function is meant a set of interrelated services or activities that are instrumental, or believed to be instrumental, for the realization of an organization's objectives.

Although, because of scarcity, an organization limits itself to particular functions, it can seldom carry them out without establishing relationships with other organizations of the health system. The reasons for this are clear. To fulfill its functions without relating to other parts of the health system, an organization must be able to procure the necessary elements – cases, labor services, and other resources – directly from the community or outside it. Certain classes of hospitals treating a specific disease and serving an area larger than the local community probably most nearly approximate this condition. But even in this case other organizations within the system usually control some elements that are necessary or, at least, helpful to the carrying out of its functions. These may be money, equipment, or special personnel, which are conditionally lent or given. Usually agencies are unable to obtain all the elements they need from the community or through their individual efforts and, accordingly, have to turn to other agencies to obtain additional elements. The need for a sufficient number of clients, for example, is often more efficiently met through exchanges with other organizations than through independent case-finding procedures.

Theoretically, then, were all the essential elements in infinite supply there would be little need for organizational interaction and for subscription to co-operation as an ideal. Under actual conditions of scarcity, however, interorganizational exchanges are essential to goal attainment. In sum, organizational goals or objectives are derived from general health values. These goals or objectives may be viewed as defining the organization's ideal need for elements – consumers, labor services, and other resources. The scarcity of elements, however, impels the organization to restrict its activity to limited specific functions. The fulfillment of these limited functions, in turn, requires access to certain kinds of elements, which an organization seeks to obtain by entering into exchanges with other organizations.

Interaction among organizations can be viewed within the framework of an exchange model like that suggested by Homans.[8] However, the few available definitions of exchange are somewhat limited for our purposes because they tend to be bound by economics and because their referents are mainly individual or psychological phenomena and are not intended to encompass interaction between organizational entities or larger systems.[9]

We suggest the following definition of organizational exchange: *Organizational exchange is any voluntary activity between two organizations which has consequences, actual or anticipated, for the realization of their respective goals or objectives.* This

---

[8] George C. Homans, "Social Behavior as Exchange," *American Journal of Sociology*, 63 (1958), pp. 597-606.

[9] Weber states that "by 'exchange' in the broadest sense will be meant every case of a formally voluntary agreement involving the offer of any sort of present, continuing, or future utility in exchange for utilities of any sort offered in return." Weber employs the term "utility" in the economic sense. It is the "utility" of the "object of exchange" to the parties concerned that produces exchange. See Max Weber, *The Theory of Social and Economic Organization* (New York, 1947) p. 170. Homans, on the other hand, in characterizing interaction between persons as an exchange of goods, material and nonmaterial, sees the impulse to "exchange" in the psychological make-up of the parties to the exchange. He states, "the paradigm of elementary social behavior, and the problem of the elementary sociologist is to state propositions relating the variations in the values and costs of each man to his frequency distribution of behavior among alternatives, where the values (in the mathematical sense) taken by these variables for one man determine in part their values for the other." See Homans, *op. cit.*, p. 598.

definition has several advantages. First, it refers to activity in general and not exclusively to reciprocal activity. The action may be unidirectional and yet involve exchange. If an organization refers a patient to another organization which then treats him, an exchange has taken place if the respective objectives of the two organizations are furthered by the action. Pivoting the definition on goals or objectives provides for an obvious but crucial component of what constitutes an organization. The co-ordination of activities of a number of individuals toward some objective or goal has been designated as a distinguishing feature of organizations by students in the field.[10] Parsons, for example, has defined an organization as a "special type of social system organized about the primacy of interest in the attainment of a particular type of system goal."[11] That its goals or objectives may be transformed by a variety of factors and that, under some circumstances, mere survival may become primary does not deny that goals or objectives are universal characteristics of organizations.

Second, the definition widens the concept of exchange beyond the transfer of material goods and beyond gratifications in the immediate present. This broad definition of exchange permits us to consider a number of dimensions of organizational interaction that would otherwise be overlooked.

Finally, while the organizations may not be bargaining or interacting on equal terms and may even employ sanctions or pressures (by granting or withholding these elements), it is important to exclude from our definition, relationships involving physical coercion or domination; hence emphasis is on the word "voluntary" in our definition.

The elements that are exchanged by health organizations fall into three main categories: (1) referrals of cases, clients, or patients; (2) the giving or receiving of labor services, including the services of volunteer, clerical, and professional personnel, and (3) the sending or receiving of resources other than labor services, including funds, equipment, and information on cases and technical matters. Organizations have varying needs of these elements depending on their particular functions. Referrals, for example, may be seen as the delivery of the consumers of services to organizations, labor services as the human means by which the resources of the organization are made available to the consumers, and resources other than labor services as the necessary capital goods.

THE DETERMINANTS OF EXCHANGE

The interdependence of the parts of the exchange system is contingent upon three related factors: (1) the accessibility of each organization to necessary elements from sources outside the health system, (2) the objectives of the organization and particular functions to which it allocates the elements it controls, and (3) the degree to which domain consensus exists among the various organizations. An ideal theory of organizational exchange would describe the interrelationship and relative contribution of each of these factors. For the present, however, we will draw on some of our preliminary findings to suggest possible relationships among these factors and to indicate that each plays a part in affecting the exchange of elements among organizations.

Gouldner has emphasized the need to differentiate the various parts of a system in terms of their relative dependence upon other parts of the system.[12] In our terms, certain

[10] Talcott Parsons, "Suggestions for a Sociological Approach to the Theory of Organizations — I," *Administrative Science Quarterly*, 1 (1956), pp. 63-85.

[11] *Ibid.*, p. 64.

[12] Alvin W. Gouldner, "Reciprocity and Autonomy in Functional Theory," in Llewellyn Gross, ed., *Symposium on Sociological Theory* (Evanston, Ill., 1959); also, "The Norm of Reciprocity: A Preliminary Statement," *American Sociological Review*, 25 (1960), pp. 161-178.

Table 1—Weighted Rankings* of Organizations Classified by *Organizational Form* on Four Interaction Indices.

Interaction index	Sent by	N	Sent to					Total inter-action sent
			Voluntary		Hospitals		Official	
			Corporate	Federated	Without clinics	With clinics		
Referrals	Vol. corporate	4	4.5	5	3.7	4.5	5	5
	Vol. federated	10	3	4	3.7	3	4	3
	Hosps. w/o clinics	2	4.5	3	3.7	4.5	3	4
	Hosps. w. clinics	3	1	1	1.5	2	1	1
	Official	3	2	2	1.5	1	2	2
Resources	Vol. corporate	4	5	2	1	4	5	3.5
	Vol. federated	10	4	3	3	4	4	3.5
	Hosps. w/o clinics	2	2	4.5	4.5	5	3	5
	Hosps. w. clinics	3	1	1	2	1	2	1
	Official	3	3	4.5	4.5	2	1	2
Written and verbal communication	Vol. corporate	4	5	3	2	4	5	4
	Vol. federated	10	3	1	3	3	3	2.5
	Hosps. w/o clinics	2	2	5	4.5	5	4	5
	Hosps. w. clinics	3	4	4	4.5	1	1.5	2.5
	Official	3	1	2	1	2	1.5	1
Joint activities	Vol. corporate	4	4.5	4	3	5	3.5	5
	Vol. federated	10	3	3	5	3	1	3
	Hosps. w/o clinics	2	2	5	1	2	3.5	4
	Hosps. w. clinics	3	4.5	2	2	1	5	1.5
	Official	3	1	1	4	4	2	1.5

*Note: 1 indicates highest interaction; 5 indicates lowest interaction.

system parts are relatively dependent, not having access to elements outside the system, whereas others, which have access to such elements, possess a high degree of independence or functional autonomy. The voluntary organizations of our study (excluding hospitals) can be classified into what Sills calls either corporate or federated organizations.[13] Corporate organizations are those which delegate authority downward from the national or state level to the local level. They contrast with organizations of the federated type which delegate authority upwards — from the local to the state or national level.

It appears that local member units of corporate organizations, because they are less dependent on the local health system and can obtain the necessary elements from the community or their parent organizations, interact less with other local agencies than federated organizations. This is supported by preliminary data presented in Table 1. It is also suggested that by carrying out their activities without entering actively into exchange relationships with other organizations, corporate organizations apparently are able to maintain their essential structure and avoid consequences resulting in the displacement of state or national goals. It may be that corporate organizations deliberately choose functions that require minimal involvement with other organizations. An examination of the four corporate organizations in our preliminary study reveals that three of them give resources to other agencies to carry out their activities, and the fourth conducts broad educational programs. Such functions are less likely to involve relationships with other organizations than the more direct service organizations, those that render services to individual recipients.

An organization's relative independence from the rest of the local health agency system and greater dependence upon a system outside the community may, at times, produce specific types of disagreements with the other agencies within the local system. This is dramatically demonstrated in the criticisms expressed toward a local community branch of an official state rehabilitation organization. The state organization, to justify its existence, has to present a successful experience to the legislators — that a minimum number of persons have been successfully rehabilitated. This means that by virtue of the services the organization has offered, a certain percentage of its debilitated clients are again returned to self-supporting roles. The rehabilitative goal of the organization cannot be fulfilled unless it is selective in the persons it accepts as clients. Other community agencies dealing with seriously debilitated clients are unable to get the state to accept their clients for rehabilitation. In the eyes of these frustrated agencies the state organization is remiss in fulfilling its public goal. The state agency, on the other hand, cannot commit its limited personnel and resources to the time-consuming task of trying to rehabilitate what seem to be very poor risks. The state agency wants to be accepted and approved by the local community and its health agencies, but the state legislature and the governor, being the primary source of the agency's resources, constitute its significant reference group. Hence, given the existing definition of organizational goals and the state agency's relative independence of the local health system, its interaction with other community agencies is relatively low.

The marked difference in the interaction rank position of hospitals with out-patient clinics and those without suggests other differences between the two classes of hospitals. It may be that the two types of hospitals have different goals and that hospitals with clinics have a greater "community" orientation and are more committed to the concept of "comprehensive" care than are hospitals without clinics. However, whether or not the goals of the two types of hospitals do indeed differ, those with out-patient departments deal with population groups similar to those serviced by other agencies of the health

---

[13] David L. Sills, *The Volunteers: Means and Ends in a National Organization* (Glencoe, 1957).

system, that is, patients who are largely ambulatory and indigent; thus they serve patients whom other organizations may also be seeking to serve. Moreover, hospitals with out--patient clinics have greater control over their clinic patients than over those in-patients who are the charges of private physicians, and are thereby freer to refer patients to other agencies.

The functions of an organization not only represent the means by which it allocates its elements but, in accordance with our exchange formulation, also determine the degree of dependence on other organizations for specific kinds of elements, as well as its capacity to make certain kinds of elements available to other organizations. The exchange model leads us to explain the flow of elements between organizations largely in terms of the respective functions performed by the participating agencies. Indeed, it is doubtful whether any analysis of exchange of elements among organizations which ignores differences in organizational needs would have much theoretical or practical value.

In analyzing the data from our pilot community we classified agencies on the basis of their primary health functions: resource, education, prevention, treatment, or rehabilitation. Resource organizations attempt to achieve their objectives by providing other agencies with the means to carry out their functions. The four other agency types may be conceived as representing respective steps in the control of disease. We have suggested that the primary function determines an organization's need for exchange elements. Our preliminary data reveal, as expected, that treatment organizations rate highest on number of referrals and amount of resources received and that educational organizations, whose efforts are directed toward the general public, rate low on the number of referrals (see Table 2). This finding holds even when the larger organizations – official agencies and hospitals – are excluded and the analysis is based on the remaining voluntary agencies of our sample. As a case in point, let us consider a health organization whose function is to educate the public about a specific disease but which renders no direct service to individual clients. If it carries on an active educational program, it is possible that some people may come to it directly to obtain information and, mistakenly, in the hope of receiving treatment. If this occurs, the organization will temporarily be in possession of potential clients whom it may route or refer to other more appropriate agencies. That such referrals will be frequent is unlikely, however. It is even less likely that the organization will receive many referrals from other organizations. If an organization renders a direct service to a client, however, such as giving X-ray examinations, or polio immunizations, there is greater likelihood that it will send or receive referrals.

An organization is less limited in its function in such interagency activities as discussing general community health problems, attending agency council meetings or co-operating on some aspect of fund raising. Also, with sufficient initiative even a small educational agency can maintain communication with a large treatment organization (for example, a general hospital) through exchanges of periodic reports and telephone calls to obtain various types of information. But precisely because it is an educational agency offering services to the general public and not to individuals, it will be limited in its capacity to maintain other kinds of interaction with the treatment organization. It probably will not be able to lend or give space or equipment, and it is even doubtful that it can offer the kind of instruction that the treatment organization would seek for its staff. That the organization's function establishes the range of possibilites for exchange and that other variables exert influence within the framework established by function is suggested by some other early findings presented in Table 3. Organizations were classified as direct or indirect on the basis of whether or not they provided a direct service to the public. They were also classified according to their relative prestige as rated by influential leaders in the community. Organizations high in prestige lead in the number of joint activities, and prestige seems to exert some influence on the amount of verbal and written communication. Yet it is agencies offering direct services – regardless of prestige – which lead in

319

Table 2—Weighted Rankings* of Organizations, Classified by *Function* on Four Interaction Indices

Interaction index	Received by	N	Received from					Total interaction received
			Education	Resource	Prevention	Treatment	Rehabilitation	
Referrals	Education	3	4.5	5	5	5	5	5
	Resource	5	3	4	2	4	1	3
	Prevention	5	2	1	3	2	2.5	2
	Treatment	7	1	2	1	1	2.5	1
	Rehabilitation	2	4.5	3	4	3	4	4
Resources	Education	3	4.5	5	4	5	4.5	5
	Resource	5	1.5	3	3	4	3	3.5
	Prevention	5	1.5	4	2	3	4.5	3.5
	Treatment	7	3	2	1	2	2	1
	Rehabilitation	2	4.5	1	5	1	1	2
Written and verbal communication	Education	3	4	5	4.5	5	5	5
	Resource	5	3	2	2	3	2	2.5
	Prevention	5	2	4	3	4	4	3
	Treatment	7	1	1	1	2	3	1
	Rehabilitation	2	5	3	4.5	1	1	2.5
Joint activities	Education	3	4	4	1	3	4.5	4
	Resource	5	2	1	3	4	1	3
	Prevention	5	1	2	2	2	3	1
	Treatment	7	3	3	4	1	2	2
	Rehabilitation	2	5	5	5	5	4.5	5

*Note: 1 indicates highest interaction; 5 indicates lowest interaction.

Table 3—Weighted Rankings* of Organizations Classified by *Prestige of Organization* and by General *Type of Service Offered* on Four Interaction Indices

Interaction index	Received by	N	Received from				Total interaction received
			High Prestige		Low Prestige		
			Direct service	Indirect service	Direct service	Indirect service	
Referrals	High direct	9	1	1	1	1	1
	High indirect	3	3	3.5	3	3.5	3
	Low direct	6	2	2	2	2	2
	Low indirect	4	4	3.5	4	3.5	4
Resources	High direct	9	2	2	2	2	2
	High indirect	3	3	3	3	3.5	3
	Low direct	6	1	1	1	1	1
	Low indirect	4	4	4	4	3.5	4
Written and verbal communication	High direct	9	2	2	3	1	2
	High indirect	3	3	3	1	3	3
	Low direct	6	1	1	2	2	1
	Low indirect	4	4	4	4	4	4
Joint activities	High direct	9	1	1.5	2	2	2
	High indirect	3	2	1.5	1	1	1
	Low direct	6	4	3	3	4	3
	Low indirect	4	3	4	4	3	4

*Note: 1 indicates highest interaction; 5 indicates lowest interaction.

the number of referrals and resources received. In other words, prestige, leadership, and other organizational variables seem to affect interaction patterns within limits established by the function variable.

An obvious question is whether organizations with shared or common boards interact more with one another than do agencies with separate boards. Our preliminary data show that the interaction rate is not affected by shared board membership. We have not been able to ascertain if there is any variation in organizational interaction when the shared board positions are occupied by persons with high status or influence. In our pilot community, there was only one instance in which two organizations had the same top community leaders as board members. If boards play an active role in the activities of health organizations, they serve more to link the organization to the community and the elements it possesses than to link the organization to other health and welfare agencies. The board probably also exerts influence on internal organizational operations and on establishing or approving the primary objective of the organization. Once the objective and the implementing functions are established, these functions tend to exert their influence autonomously on organizational interaction.

ORGANIZATIONAL DOMAIN

As we have seen, the elements exchanged are cases, labor services, and other resources. All organizational relationships directly or indirectly involve the flow and control of these elements. Within the local health agency system, the flow of elements is not centrally co-ordinated, but rests upon voluntary agreements or understanding. Obviously, there will be no exchange of elements between two organizations that do not know of each other's existence or that are completely unaware of each other's functions. Even more, there can be no exchange of elements without some agreement or understanding, however implicit. These exchange agreements are contingent upon the organization's domain. The domain of an organization consists of the specific goals it wishes to pursue and the functions it undertakes in order to implement its goals. In operational terms, organizational domain in the health field refers to the claims that an organization stakes out for itself in terms of (1) disease covered, (2) population served, and (3) services rendered. The goals of the organization constitute in effect the organization's claim to future functions and to the elements requisite to these functions, whereas the present or actual functions carried out by the organization constitute de facto claims to these elements. Exchange agreements rest upon prior consensus regarding domain. Within the health agency system, consensus regarding an organization's domain must exist to the extent that parts of the system will provide each agency with the elements necessary to attain its ends.

Once an organization's goals are accepted, domain consensus continues as long as the organization fulfills the functions adjudged appropriate to its goals and adheres to certain standards of quality. Our data show that organizations find it more difficult to legitimate themselves before other organizations in the health system than before such outside systems as the community or state. An organization can sometimes obtain sufficient elements from outside the local health system, usually in the form of funds, to continue in operation long after other organizations within the system have challenged its domain. Conversely, if the goals of a specific organization are accepted within the local agency system, other organizations of the system may encourage it to expand its functions and to realize its goals more fully by offering it elements to implement them. Should an organization not respond to this encouragement, it may be forced to forfeit its claim to the unrealized aspect of its domain.

Within the system, delineation of organizational domains is highly desired.[14] For example, intense competition may occur occasionally between two agencies offering the same services, especially when other agencies have no specific criteria for referring patients to one rather than the other. If both services are operating near capacity, competition between the two tends to be less keen, the choice being governed by the availability of service. If the services are being operated at less than capacity, competition and conflict often occur. Personnel of referring agencies in this case frequently deplore the "duplication of services" in the community. In most cases the conflict situation is eventually resolved by agreement on the part of the competing agencies to specify the criteria for referring patients to them. The agreement may take the form of consecutive handling of the same patients. For example, age may be employed as a criterion. In one case three agencies were involved in giving rehabilitation services: one took preschool children, another school children, and the third adults. In another case, where preventive services were offered, one agency took preschool children and the other took children of school age. The relative accessibility of the agencies to the respective age groups was a partial basis for these divisions. Another criterion — disease stage — also permits consecutive treatment of patients. One agency provided physical therapy to bedridden patients; another handled them when they became ambulatory.

Several other considerations, such as priorities in allocation of elements, may impel an organization to delimit its functions even when no duplication of services exists. The phenomenon of delimiting one's role and consequently of restricting one's domain is well known. It can be seen, for instance, in the resistance of certain universities of high prestige to offer "practical" or vocational courses, or courses to meet the needs of any but high-status professionals, even to the extent of foregoing readily accessible federal grants. It is evidenced in the insistence of certain psychiatric clinics on handling only cases suitable for psychoanalytic treatment, of certain business organizations on selling only to wholesalers, of some retail stores on handling only expensive merchandise.

The flow of elements in the health system is contingent upon solving the problem of "who gets what for what purpose." The clarification of organizational domains and the development of greater domain consensus contributes to the solution of this problem. In short, domain consensus is a prerequisite to exchange. Achieving domain consensus may involve negotiation, orientation, or legitimation. When the functions of the interacting organizations are diffuse, achieving domain consensus becomes a matter of constant readjustment and compromise, a process which may be called negotiation or bargaining. The more specific the functions, however, the more domain consensus is attained merely by orientation (for example, an agency may call an X-ray unit to inquire about the specific procedures for implementing services). A third, less frequent but more formalized, means of attaining domain consensus is the empowering, licensing or "legitimating" of an organization to operate within the community by some other organization. Negotiation, as a means of attaining domain consensus seems to be related to diffuseness of function, whereas orientation, at the opposite extreme, relates to specificity of function.

These processes of achieving domain consensus constitute much of the interaction between organizations. While they may not involve the immediate flow of elements, they are often necessary preconditions for the exchange of elements, because without at least minimal domain consensus there can be no exchange among organizations. Moreover, to the extent that these processes involve proffering information about the availability of elements as well as about rights and obligations regarding the elements, they constitute a form of interorganizational exchange.

---

[14] In our research a large percentage of our respondents spontaneously referred to the undesirability of overlapping or duplicated services.

We have stated that all relationships among local health agencies may be conceptualized as involving exchange. There are four main dimensions to the actual exchange situation. They are:

1. *The parties to the exchange.* The characteristics we have thus far employed in classifying organizations or the parties to the exchange are: organizational form or affiliation, function, prestige, size, personnel characteristics, and numbers and types of clients served.

2. *The kinds and quantities exchanged.* These involve two main classes: the actual elements exchanged (consumers, labor services, and resources other than labor services), and information on the availability of these organizational elements and on rights and obligations regarding them.

3. *The agreement underlying the exchange.* Every exchange is contingent upon a prior agreement, which may be implicit and informal or fairly explicit and highly formalized. For example, a person may be informally routed or referred to another agency with the implicit awareness or expectation that the other organization will handle the case. On the other hand, the two agencies may enter into arrangements that stipulate the exact conditions and procedures by which patients are referred from one to another. Furthermore, both parties may be actively involved in arriving at the terms of the agreement, or these terms may be explicitly defined by one for all who may wish to conform to them. An example of the latter case is the decision of a single organization to establish a policy of a standard fee for service.

4. *The direction of the exchange.* This refers to the direction of the flow of organizational elements. We have differentiated three types:

(a) Unilateral: where elements flow from one organization to another and no elements are given in return.

(b) Reciprocal: where elements flow from one organization to another in return for other elements.

(c) Joint: where elements flow from two organizations acting in unison toward a third party. This type, although representing a high order of agreement and co-ordination of policy among agencies, does not involve the actual transfer of elements.

As we proceed with our study of relationships among health agencies, we will undoubtedly modify and expand our theoretical model. For example, we will attempt to describe how the larger systems are intertwined with the health agency system. Also, we will give more attention to the effect of interagency competition and conflict regarding the flow of elements among organizations. In this respect we will analyze differences among organizations with respect not only to domain but to fundamental goals as well. As part of this analysis we will examine the orientations of different categories of professionals (for example, nurses and social workers) as well as groups with varying experiences and training within categories of professionals (as nurses with or without graduate education).

In the meantime, we find the exchange framework useful in ordering our data, locating new areas for investigation, and developing designs for studying interorganizational relationships. We feel that the conceptual framework and findings of our study will be helpful in understanding not only health agency interaction but also relationships within other specific systems (such as military, industrial, governmental, educational, and other systems). As in our study of health agencies, organizations within any system may confidently be expected to have need for clients, labor, and other resources. We would also expect that the interaction pattern among organizations within each system will also be affected by (1) organizational function, (2) access to the necessary elements from outside the system, and (3) the degree of domain consensus existing among the organizations of the system. It appears that the framework also shows promise in explaining interaction among organizations belonging to different systems (for example, educational and business systems, educational and governmental, military and industrial, and so forth). Finally, we believe our framework has obvious value in explaining interaction among units or departments within a single large-scale organization.

The Volunteer and Social Change

NATHAN E. COHEN

The philosophy of the voluntary association and the role of the volunteer as developed in previous chapters emphasizes the volunteer's importance in furthering the democratic way of life. Volunteers serve as a connecting link between the personal and impersonal worlds within which most people live. "The personal world revolves about the individual's life, his family, and his friends. It is an immediate world and part of his consciousness. It is a local world, centering usually in his town or neighborhood. It is a world of sentiment and feeling, the individual being attached to it by emotional ties. . . . The impersonal world clearly has a tremendous impact on all the private worlds. One aspect of their relationships concerns a kind of continuous conflict. The motif of the external world is change, while the motif of the local world is stability and resistance to change. Intellectual understanding is necessary if the external world is to be meaningful, while such understanding is not as essential in the personal world — except perhaps in connection with the earnings of a livelihood."[1] The voluntary associations frequently have emerged in response to the changing external world of the individual, family, and friends. They can help immeasurably in bringing about essential and orderly social change or serve as channels for maintaining the status quo. They can help strengthen the individual's ties to the world as it has been, or help broaden his perceptions about the world as it might be.

Social change is dependent on individual as well as social institutional change. The individual, to be able to cope with a changing democratic society in which an important characteristic is its multigroup nature, must learn to be a team man as well as an individual. Part of the maturing of the individual is in learning to appreciate the value to society in being able to forego one's self-centered drives for the broader purposes and aims of the group. The development of a social consciousness involves the experience in practical democracy which group undertakings can provide. The very act of volunteering can be an expression of identification with broader purposes and aims. The experience, however, can be different for the "service volunteer" and the "policy volunteer."

The "service volunteer' may give time to a program within the context of "task" rather than "ego-involvement." To be ego-involving, the project must have meaning for the individual beyond just the act of doing certain things. There must be at least an intellectual understanding of the purposes and aims of the project so that doing is within the larger context of achieving the stated social goals. The service volunteer who remains

---

[1] Richard Carlton Snyder and H. Hubert Wilson, *Roots of Political Behavior: Introduction to Government and Politics* (New York: American Book Co., 1949), p. 155.

Reprinted from The Citizen Volunteer, *Nathan E. Cohen, ed., pp. 219-228, by permission of Harper & Row, Publishers.* © *1960 by The National Council of Jewish Women.*

only task-involved may be escaping into association work because of the feeling of hopelessness in coping with life in general. In the face of the growing bigness and complexity of society, unable to take responsibility on social issues, the volunteer may see the act of doing something within an organization with a social purpose as the way of discharging one's role as a responsible citizen. If the volunteer, however, even within this smaller segment of the society, cannot or is not helped to identify with the broader aims and goals of the organization or agency, the experience as a volunteer is again contributing to an approach where the individual has no control of the events around him and where the initiative and responsibility of social policy are left to others.

The problem is more sharply focused when one analyzes the programs in which volunteers are utilized. A large segment of the volunteer force provides its services to programs for the disadvantaged individuals in our society. This includes the poor, the sick, the uneducated, the unskilled workers, the immigrants of many nationalities, and racial minority groups. These are the very people who — despite the large number of groups representing the varied interests in our society — are, relatively speaking, without their own representative organizations. They need others to champion their cause, their fight for a share of the democratic way of life.

Educationally it should not be difficult to move from an interest in helping these disadvantaged people through specific services to an understanding of the larger environmental problems involved. For example, in working with economically disadvantaged children, it should become evident that to break the cycle of these families in trouble it is necessary to compensate for the inadequate resources provided by the family to their children. This means good schooling, adequate provisions for health and recreation, and nutrition services. Some of these programs are costly and may necessitate state and federal funds to supplement those of the local community.

Many volunteers are now working with the older citizens. Golden age clubs have become an integral part of community services. Leisure activities, however, are only one facet in the total program essential to meeting the needs of the older person in modern society. There is the matter of economic security, adequate health resources, and adequate housing which must be taken into account. The older citizen receiving public assistance as against social insurance approaches life with a great loss of dignity. The type of housing may determine the extent to which he can remain self-sufficient and ambulatory. Age brings an increase in illness and a corresponding increase in anxiety if adequate medical care is not available. To meet these growing needs the resources of government are necessary. The volunteer working with these individuals can be helped to understand the importance of these additional resources and the fact that their attainment depends on a legislative program on the local, state and federal levels.

Unfortunately, the agencies themselves do not always see the relationship of social policy and services. This dichotomy is deeply rooted in the historical development of social services in the nation. In the early years, the prevailing theory was that our society as conceived was perfect and provided the necessary opportunities for all who would seek them. Opportunity and success were for the asking. Any able-bodied individual who failed to achieve success needed punishment and moral preachments. Reform of the individual was the order of the day. As the problems became more intense and more extensive, better methods of organizing charity and better ways of helping the individual to change his way of life were sought. The pervading philosophy was to accept a simple, highly individualistic morality with little reference to environmental causes or to social responsibility.

With the impact of the industrial revolution and urbanization, the nation began to experience a series of recessions and depressions, creating great human suffering. It was no longer possible to think only in terms of individual inadequacy. One had to look for the conditions that were creating the problem and avoid confusing symptom with cause.

327

Under such circumstances they were reluctant to place the blame for failure and dependency on the individual alone. Reform of the environment through political and legislative means as well as reform of the individual had to be taken into account.

The reluctance to see the relationship between a program of services and broader social policy measures is at times attributed to the negative attitude of lay leadership in the community toward social change. The volunteer who has first-hand contact with the social problems is in an excellent position to serve as an interpreter. If adequately informed, he can help clarify the issues, remove some of the prejudices, and increase the total understanding of the community.

The policy volunteers, those serving on committees and boards, are a step closer to the responsibility of achieving the broader aims and goals of the association. If these policy workers have come through the ranks, beginning as service volunteers, they will be in a better position to understand the purpose and program of the association. Frequently, however, these steps are skipped and individuals are placed in important positions for status or economic reasons. If these individuals receive no orientation or understanding of the goals of the association, they may be more prone to seek policy decisions which are in line with their own personal philosophy.

I recall a study of a settlement house where the question of the role of the agency in social action was being discussed. A test issue was a low cost federal housing project which was being considered for the area served by the settlement house. One of the new members of the board, who had little previous contact with the agency, and was in the real estate business, was violently opposed to public housing. He stated that he would resign if the board took action in favor of the project. When it was pointed out to him that one of the stated functions of the agency was social action, and that one of the areas approved by previous board decision was public housing, he was shocked. He indicated that this type of information was never shared with him, and that the approach in recruiting his affiliation was helping deprived people through direct services. Furthermore, little had been said to him about how the board functioned in relation to such issues. When questioned whether he would have joined the board if he had known more about the total program in advance, he stated that he probably would have but that he would have had a better understanding of his role as a member of the board. Through the discussions he had formulated for himself the method of operation, namely, that he could express his personal opinions in the meetings, and that he could even try to have the functioning of the agency modified, but that others also had a right to their views. If decisions went against him, it was not a question of resigning — any more than he would think of giving up his American citizenship because his party had lost the election.

Voluntary associations vary in their purpose and, therefore, in their role in social change. A large number of these associations are concerned primarily with services to people. Examples of this category are the numerous social welfare agencies. Through experience, however, they have come to realize in varying degrees that social action may be an integral part of a program to help people in trouble, especially when the problem is effected largely by external conditions. As John Hill states the case: "When in recognition of such circumstances (problems due to external condittions beyond the ability of the agency or the client to modify) the social worker turns to the forces of community or government, he is still striving for the same objectives as he was formerly seeking through individual action. . . . Social action is not restricted to problems which will not yield to individual treatment. . . . There are many problems which could be handled more effectively, efficiently and economically within a mass or preventive way than through the slower and more expensive one-by-one method."[2]

---

[2] John G. Hill, "Social Action," in *Social Work Year Book* (New York: American Association of Social Workers, 1951), p. 456.

In these associations which have several functions, people may affiliate or volunteer their services for different reasons. In such cases the overall purpose of the association and the relationship of the various segments to the whole may not be clear. Several years ago I took part in a survey of an organization that has a threefold program — local community services, overseas projects, and a program of education and social action. The study revealed that the majority of members were interested in community services, a small group were mainly concerned with the overseas program, and about a fourth of the members were interested in education and social action. Only a small number were interested in all three aspects of the program. One of the problems in this type of situation is that the assumption is made that all of the members are interested and committed to the total program. This is especially true in the area of social action which necessitates the backing of a majority of the membership if the organization is to be able to go beyond the stage of a study of issues to a political action program. If members feel that they are being committed to a program which goes beyond their reason for joining the organization, conflict is likely to result over policies and goals. In such associations, education is essential to help the members understand the overall goals and the relationship of the various parts to them. It is also necessary to provide the type of structure through which policy decisions on social action reflect an opportunity for full participation of all members, and not only those committed to this aspect of the program. Freedom of action may seem cumbersome at times, but in the long run more members will be exposed to an educational process which will help them to understand the issues and to express their views in the many other circles in which they are involved.

There are other voluntary associations which are organized primarily for purposes of social change. Examples of this would be such organizations as the National Association for the Advancement of Colored People, The Citizen Committee for Children, the National Child Labor Committee, and the National Consumers League. In such associations the members are clear as to the primary purpose. There may be differences of views as to how to achieve the purpose, that is differences as to method, but agreement on goals is more definite than in the multi-functional associations.

Between these multi-functional and single-purpose associations are organizations like the League of Women Voters and the Foreign Policy Association. Their broad purpose is to create a sense of responsibility for government in as many American citizens as possible through continuing study of vital issues. For example, the League does not endorse or oppose candidates for public office, but studies their views and qualifications and makes this information known to the public. In the area of legislation, after full study of an issue, they will discuss the decisions which they have arrived at with the legislators and attempt to influence their thinking on the nature of the legislation. Their great strength is in the educational process and in the method of approaching a problem. They are not as free as the single-purpose associations committed to a particular area of social change, or even at times as the multi-functional associations where the area for action is clear to the membership, in pressing for specific legislation.

These various types of voluntary associations can provide channels not only for volunteer services but also for individuals to have their views aired and their voices heard. The democratic process is a complicated one. In a democracy there is no centralized authoritarian power. The power resides in the people, but for the individual person to be effective he must find a variety of channels through which his views can be tested and expressed to those who have the power of making policy. Thus, on the American scene an individual may belong to a variety of associations because of some particular area of interest even though these groups may have sharply contrasting viewpoints on matters of social change. Mrs. X, for example, may belong to the Women's Auxiliary of the American Legion, the health and welfare council, the women's auxiliary of the church, and the League of Women Voters. These varied groups can provide an important educational process for individuals and a good experience in citizenship responsibility if their involvement goes beyond the level of tasks to that of understanding and participating in the formulation of goals and purposes of the association. The more that the views which associations emerge with represent the give and take between the different viewpoints and the integration of these differences, the greater the probability of progress in terms of government by the people. If the membership, however, is not involved, the views expressed to government can become those of an active few and thus undermine the validity of this complicated process.

If the experience in the association is a constructive one, the individual will learn "to make social aims personally attractive and will learn to appreciate the values of submerging ego-drives for the broader purposes and aims of the whole group."[3] As the individual grows in knowledge and understanding, he may also learn to evaluate the conflict in views in the various associations to which he belongs and be able to see these associations within a new priority arrangement as related to his own philosophy and convictions. There is much growth and change in views of individuals which can emerge from these constructive experiences which have a bearing on social change in general. In a society made up of a proliferation of groups, many of which have special interests, strength out of diversity can come only through an educational process which helps the members of these groups see the importance of the broader public interest rather than just the narrow special interest. Richness out of difference can come only if there is sufficient concern for the fabric as a whole, out of which difference is possible.

It may be difficult to obtain agreement on substantive matters or even goals for the public interest. An important underpinning, however, is the means of obtaining the objectives. It is in the voluntary association, the everyday expression of the democratic way of life, that the democratic rules of the game can become internalized by the individual citizen. How much stronger the democratic process would be if through our large number of voluntary group experiences the following principles could be learned:

1. "...that good human experience cannot emanate from a relationship in which one person commands and the other obeys, from situations in which one person or one group chooses the ends and thereupon uses others as the means."[4]

2. That diversity is an essential part of the democratic process, and that "Democracy recognizes that richness and progress ensue from a process which permits individuals to express themselves, rather than forcing them to submerge their differences to a uniformity characteristic of totalitarian movements."[5]

3. That modern society is interdependent and it should be recognized, therefore, that the welfare of any individual, group, or community is inextricably woven with the welfare of the whole. This would mean that all individuals, groups, or communities, therefore, must be concerned with the development of material, human, and social resources to meet all the needs of all the people rather than the vested interest of any individual, any particular group or community.

America is passing through a crucial period of history. Her newly found role in world leadership demands that she be as clear about what she is for as what she is against. The seeking of common aims, however, cannot be at the expense of the multiplicity of different interest groups which have always been prominent in the pattern of American

---

[3] Snyder and Wilson, *op. cit.*, p. 158.
[4] Eduard C. Lindeman, "Functional Democracy in Human Relations," in Lloyd Allen Cook, ed., *Toward Better Human Relations* (Detroit: Wayne University Press, 1952), p. 33.
[5] *Ibid.*, p. 31.

political life. To do away with this pattern can result in the centralization of authority and the emergence of a totalitarian form of government. On the other hand, we must find ways of making the pattern work in a modern day society if we are to fulfill our responsibilities of leadership in a changing world. We have come to realize that although independence in the individual is a more mature development than dependence, independence without a sense of interdependence can also mean immaturity in our modern complicated society. In the same way, narrow special group interest without a sense of the public interest can retard progress toward a mature society.

It is in the voluntary associations which utilize volunteers that an important contribution to this problem can be made. Many of these voluntary associations in health, education, and social welfare have already taken a step away from narrow vested interest in that their programs are aimed at helping others. They have moved in the public interest. Furthermore, they deal in the main with the consequences of our way of life. They see all the blemishes in our system and the impact of our failures on human beings. What better laboratory is there for the citizen who is interested in the democratic way of life? What better way is there to help those of narrow special interest move toward greater public interest? The experience can have its greatest meaning not only in effecting the knowledge and attitudes of the individual volunteers but in the volunteers' desire to effect the knowledge and attitudes of others in the community. If this newfound knowledge and understanding can find its way into the numerous other groups with which the volunteer comes in contact, then a genuine contribution will be made in helping vested interest groups move toward a broader public interest.

The need for a better understanding of the broad public interest looms large today. We are rebounding from the impact of the "McCarthy era" when our basic values of individual dignity and liberty were almost snowed under. The test of our resiliency, however, is still before us, both in the way we handle the racial issue and our role of world leadership. There is a danger in our growing tendency to rely on a form of public relations which might best be characterized as "frictionless interpersonal relations." Vital issues involve an element of conflict which cannot be avoided if they are to be understood and dealt with through citizen action.

Part of our problem is the difficulty in perceiving the issues of the day. C. Wright Mills[6] describes four ways of reacting to changing situations. If the values are clear and we see no threat to them, the reaction is a feeling of well being. If the values are clear and we perceive a threat, the reaction is a feeling of crisis. If, however, the values are unclear and we see no threat, the reaction is a feeling of indifference or apathy. If the situation is one of both unclear values and no sense of something being wrong, the reaction is a feeling of anxiety. It is his contention that, unlike the thirties when both the values and the threat were clear, we are living in a period characterized by unclear values and a feeling of indifference, apathy, and anxiety.

The reason for this state of mind may well be that the changes which are taking place are not following the usual recognizable patterns. True the "McCarthy period" is over, but we are not free of a climate of conformity. We are not at war, but we are not at peace. We are not in a depression, but our economic stance is not a healthy one. We are not in the space age, but we are no longer completely in the earth age. The changes with which we are confronted are of a crisis nature, but the threat is not being fully perceived because we do not fully understand the changes and are not too knowledgeable about the methods essential for dealing with them.

If ever there was a time to seek ways of greater participation in our democratic way of life, that time is now. If ever there was a challenge to the efficacy of our voluntary

---

[6] C. Wright Mills, *The Sociological Imagination* (New York: Oxford University Press, 1959), pp. 11-13.

structure with its potential as a training ground for citizenship in a democracy, this is it. It should be possible to train volunteers to be skillful in services to individuals and groups, and also to be able to speak with knowledge and understanding of the wider social issues involved and with authority on possible courses of action and development for society as a whole. This will not happen by itself, but will be dependent both on the volunteer and the voluntary associations through which they express themselves, and give of themselves to a broader public interest.

Meaningful Consumer Participation –
A Challenge to the Social Agency Administrator

LOUIS E. CROWN

One resounding demand cuts across the many cataclysmic developments of the past decade in the political, economic and social arenas of our nation. That is the urgent insistence of the young, the poor, the black and others, alienated from the main stream of society, for more meaningful participation in the decision-making processes which affect their lives.

The response to this need has manifested itself in many ways. One is by recent requirements of federal law for "maximum feasible participation" of residents in O.E.O. programs[1]; for "widespread citizen participation" in the process of policy and program planning and program implementation and operation in Model City areas[2]; and by similar formulations by the Departments of HEW and Labor. A concomitant development is evident in legislative and administrative stipulations at state and local levels. But perhaps of even greater significance is the rising tide of demand for citizen and/or consumer involvement in, and in some cases control over, the administration of community agencies and institutions in the social welfare system – schools, hospitals, mental health centers, public welfare offices, etc.

Several years of implementation of the legislative mandates on participation have produced mixed results. These have led, in turn, to heated political controversy and some erosion of the belief in the positive value of such participation. The militancy with which community control of institutions has been pressed has also clouded the basic issue of its relevance and importance in affecting the quality of services emanating from those institutions.

The social work profession has had an historic commitment to citizen participation and client self-determination.[3] It has drawn its ideological rationale mainly from democratic theory which emphasizes the worth and dignity of the individual, through the active promotion of his individual growth, social opportunity and community development. It assumes man is entitled to the respect of others, to freedom and justice,

[1] Economic Opportunity Act of 1964, 88th Congress, 2nd Session, Sec. 202 (a) Subsection 3.
[2] "A Program Guide to Model Neighborhoods in Demonstration Cities," HUD-PG-47, Dec., 1947.
[3] Michael J. Austin and Brian W. Klepinger, eds. "Citizen Participation in Program Development and Implementation," Community Planning and Development Council, ed. (National Association of Social Workers – Northern Colorado Chapter, Denver, Colorado), 1968. (Extensive use was made of this work in securing ideas and some direct quotations.)

Excerpts from a working paper prepared for a sub-committee of the NASW Urban Crisis Task Force. Reprinted with permission of NASW and the author.

as a member of a rationally oriented society which is concerned with social problems and barriers to human well-being. This optimistic orientation provided the rationale for citizen involvement in community services beyond the in-group, beyond the religious society, and beyond the ethnic fraternity.

In our complex and troubled society, these democratic assumptions about man's ethical responsibility for himself and others are being severely tested. Society is critically suffering from a lack of community understanding of social problems and welfare services because of our neglect of community involvement in these activities.

Aside from the ideological rationale, however, there are other pragmatic reasons which militate toward greater consumer participation. In our vast impersonal bureaucratic institutions, both private and public, there is a need to monitor the system, to have those who receive the services have a voice in their evaluation. This can be accomplished best by having the consumer involved at all stages, from planning, through program development, to delivery of services. Furthermore, such involvement tends to legitimatize the activity, improve the chances of acceptance by the beneficiaries, and thus increase the likelihood of success of the program.

Failures of the social service delivery system in the past raise the question of whether we can adequately reach those who want and need services, without a significant input from those who are affected by them. The business community has long since recognized this concept and acceded to its validity through the extensive use of market research.

There is yet another important value in the involvement of citizens or consumers in planning and implementing programs designed for community service. That is the meeting of primary individual and group needs in the process itself. Self-help, self-fulfillment, and the general growth and maturation of individuals and community groups are significant and highly valued concomitant derivatives of such participation.

For both ideological and pragmatic reasons, therefore, the social work profession must assert its conviction about the importance of service to "different" others and to be identified with creative approaches to the involvement of all segments of our citizenry in the planning and delivery of services.

"Consumer participation" represents a wide range of concepts, as narrow as the ability of the individual to choose freely, and thus affect, the availability and quality of service (through "free" competition), and as all-encompassing as total community involvement toward ultimate control of their institutions (through the political or economic process).

Between these extremes and immediately relevant to the social service delivery system are the many forms of participation of "volunteers," community residents, clients and consumers on councils, boards, committees and advisory groups. These forms vary greatly as to level of influence on the decision-making process of those institutions. Agencies themselves vary greatly as to kind of service, clientele, financing and auspice. While patterns of participation are subject to these many constraints, some general principals may be formulated.

To be *meaningful, participation must:*

1. Be representative of the *consumer* and the *community* served.
2. Be *significant numerically*, not mere tokenism.
3. Be representative of the various *sectors of society* affected by the agency (racial, ethnic, economic, and, where appropriate, age-related).
4. Be included in the *decision-making* process from the early stages of *planning* through *program development, delivery of services* and *evaluation*.
5. Permit *ease of access and attendance* at meetings by those less able to participate conveniently (subsidization, appropriate scheduling, provision of transportation, day care, etc.).

6. Provide adequate orientation, information and *in-service training* as to the duties, rights, responsibilities, and options of the participant role at various levels.
7. Encourage *increased involvement* of those concerned, and afford the opportunity for growth to *higher levels of influence*.
8. Incorporate policies of *recruitment and rotation* to permit continual involvement of new participants.

While *meaningful* participation means greater consumer involvement and significantly increased influence over decision-making, this does not imply any abdication of the responsibility or ultimate authority of the administrator for the achievement of program goals and agency objectives.

Rather it implies the need for transforming "administration — to achieve support and involvement from consumers without losing the skill and decisiveness of administrators."[4] The task is to create competence on both sides and the development of a sense of sharing in the effort to achieve the agency's objectives.

In this process, the social work profession must play an increasing role in helping to:

1. define the complex nature of consumer participation;
2. suggest mechanisms for implementation;
3. assist in public and professional education towards an understanding and acceptance of the concept;
4. create a dialogue between agencies and institutions and their community and consumers toward mutual understanding of the need for consumer involvement and a definition of their respective roles in the decision-making process; and
5. prepare guidelines for and participate in the process of evaluation of consumer participation.

"There is a vital key to our new society. Without it we have no chance of survival for the next ten years, let alone the next fifty. Each man must be given power over his own life. We must cease to plan *for* people. We must begin to plan *with* people."[5]

---

[4] Bernice L. Bernstein, "Urban Crisis and the Delivery of Social Services," unpublished address, Association of Supervisors Dinner, New York City, Dept. of Social Services, May 2, 1968, New York City, p. 6.

[5] Robert Theobald, "Planning with People," *Environment and Change*, William R. Ewald, Jr., ed. (Indianapolis: Indiana University Press, 1968).

VI. Budget and Finance

Excerpts from The Impact of Budgets on People

CHRIS ARGYRIS

WHAT THIS STUDY TRIES TO DO

The purpose of the study is to examine problems and to raise questions concerning the possible human relations effects budgets have upon supervisors. Because of the nature of the problem this study cannot present final solutions to problems, nor answer questions in any definitive way. It can merely define a wider aspect of the budget problem and suggest possible solutions. Each controller must light up these approaches with his own experience. In short, this study, the first of its kind attempted by the Foundation, is primarily exploratory.

Because of the indefinable limits of the human problems in this area, the research team decided to focus its attention on how the supervisors feel about budgets and how the finance people feel about the same budgets. The group sought answers to questions such as these:

1. How do the finance people see their job?
2. What problems do the finance people see in relation to factory people? What problems don't they perceive?
3. Similarly, how do the factory supervisors see their job?
4. What problems do factory supervisors perceive in relation to the finance people and/or budgets? What problems don't they perceive?
5. What similarities and differences exist between factory people and finance people with regard to values, attitudes, and feelings toward budgets?

It should be pointed out that due to the exploratory nature of the study no recommendations could be made to the managements of the plants studied, which could then be observed in action, checked, and analyzed by the research team. Therefore, it is extremely difficult to present many recommendations based solely upon these findings. There is, however, a growing body of practical suggestions developed in other research work which is relevant to some of the problems unearthed by this report. In our recommendations we have drawn upon these suggestions because they are relevant and, we hope, useful to the controller.

HOW THE RESEARCH TASK WAS ACCOMPLISHED

The problem of human factors in the use of budgets is an extremely difficult one. Not only is the subject of budgets per se complicated, but, to make matters more difficult, budgets are so closely interrelated with the other parts and functions of organization that it would be an immense task to study carefully and thoroughly the problem as a whole.

The process of preparing manufacturing cost budgets is much the same in all four companies. In all cases the process starts with a meeting of the controller, the assistant controller and a top management group to determine over-all financial goals for the company in the forthcoming year. The controller's staff then translates the financial goals into the detailed cost breakdowns required for departmental budgets. This preliminary budget is sent to all superintendents who are asked to scrutinize the budget carefully and report any alterations they wish made.

Once the superintendents have their budget modifications clearly in mind, a meeting is held with the controller and his staff. Both parties come to the meeting "armed to the teeth" with ammunition to back their demands. After the disagreements are resolved, all parties sign the new budget proposal. The superintendents return to their offices, awaiting the new budget and the expected drive to "put it over."

SOME LIMITATIONS OF THE STUDY

Any study whose approach is purely exploratory must be conducted within the limits of fairly well-defined boundaries. These are some of the more important limitations imposed upon this study by its exploratory nature:

1. None of the plants studied has a supervisory incentive system as a part of its budget system. This seems a serious limitation and points to the need for further research.

2. The report does not include any material concerning the effects budgets have upon the workers in the plant. Casual interviews with workers suggested that they are definitely affected. How much they are affected, and through what channels, is not clear. This problem also deserves further study.

3. Budgets constitute only one of the evaluation processes management uses. As is commonly known, most evaluation processes tend to have "two strikes against them" simply because they tend to set goals for, and make evaluations of, the supervisors. As such, budgets do not escape the usual complaints. Moreover, it appears that many complaints are focused upon the budget because the budget is one of the few evaluation processes that is always in writing, and therefore concrete. Thus, some of the supervisors tend to use it as a "whipping post" in order to release their feelings about many other, and at times totally unrelated, problems.

THE USE OF BUDGETS

To the budget people, budgets have an extremely important function in the organization as the "eyes and the ears of the plant." They provide the answers to most questions and the budget people see themselves as the "answer men" of the organization. Consider the following examples:

First let me say that budgets are the watchdog of this company. What do I mean by that? Two things: First, if we have profit, there's no problem; Second, if we are losing money, what can we do about improvement — any kind of improvement?

We guard the fields. The budget department has to constantly strive to improve the goods and make the plant better. There is always room to make things better.

There is, therefore, an important emphasis made on budget people constantly finding things that are "sour," looking for weaknesses, and, in general, looking for things that are wrong, not right.

Another emphasis is equally important. All the budget people interviewed insisted that the errors found and the weaknesses uncovered should immediately be sent to top management.

> If I see an inconsistency, I'll go to top management and report it. No, I never go to the supervisor in charge. It is our job to report any inconsistencies to the top management.

Once the information is in top management's hands, it is up to it to take action. In other words, budget results are primarily top management control instruments.

Coupled with the task of finding weaknesses and reporting them to top management is a third emphasis on doing the reporting soon. Budget results can be effective only when they are "hot off the griddle." Whatever pressure budgets may generate to "motivate" a factory man to better his record would be lost if action was not taken immediately.

> It's our philosophy that we've got to get these figures to top management when they're hot. They're no good when the job is cold. As it is now, with our records, top management can get the factory supervisors together and do something right away.

A fourth emphasis is on using the budget as a means for putting pressure on operating supervisors.

> As soon as we examine the budget results and see a fellow is slipping, we immediately call the factory manager and point out, "Look Joe, you're behind on the budget. What do you expect to do about it?"
> True, he may be batting his brains out already on the problem but our phone call adds a little more pressure — er — well, you know, we let them know we're interested.

Finally, budget people believe that budgets present a goal, a challenge to factory people. They think that without budgets factory people would have nothing "to shoot for" — would lack the help of a great motivating instrument. For example:

> Production budgets set the goals. The budgets, yes, the budgets, set a challenge for those fellows (factory). It's something for them to shoot for. They need something to shoot for. All of us need a goal.

In summary, budget personnel see budgets as performing at least the following important functions:

1. They are a means to make things better. There is always room for improvement. Inconsistencies, errors, weaknesses are constantly being discovered, examined, and reported to top management.
2. Properly used, they are a means of instituting improvements quickly. Budgets are of most value when their results are in the hands of top management as soon as possible.
3. They are a means of putting pressure on factory supervisors.
4. They provide a goal, a motivating force for the factory people.

DIFFERENCES IN OUTLOOK

If the budget people see any important differences between the outlook of operating people and themselves, such information should be of value in ascertaining how "basic" are the causes of misunderstanding between the budget and production parts of the organization. The results indicate that budget people see some very basic differences. For example:

I would say that factory people have a different outlook on life. They tend to be more liberal toward others.

The financial people, on the other hand, look at life more coldly. To them, it's all figures. The only thing they look at is what amount of money is involved. It's the total figure that counts.

The factory supervisors' outlook on things is different. They emphasize today. Yes, they're looking at only the short run. We have to look at things in the long run. We have to see the whole unit. They worry about their individual departments.

I think you'd almost say there are personality differences between factory and finance. We (finance) tend to approach everything with figures. We have to. We've been retained that way. Factory people approach it without worrying about costs.

Yes, there are differences. We (finance) have been trained to see things as they are — to study them logically and systematically. We've been trained to look at a problem and say, "Well, this is it, one two, three, bang, that's it."

The differences described above may be clues for understanding the human problems that arise. For example, if the factory supervisors are, in fact, only interested in the short run and if the budget staff does not see the short run as being crucial, then trouble will arise. Similarly, if the budget staff has a basically different outlook on problems from the factory supervisors, this difference will tend to increase disagreements.

PROBLEMS WITH FACTORY SUPERVISORS

The budget people were asked to describe what they felt was the most difficult problem they faced in their relationships with factory supervisors. The majority of the replies fell into a very consistent pattern. The most pressing problem was "selling" budgets to factory supervisors. The budget people believed that the task was almost insurmountable. It was interesting to see that the three most often stated reasons for this problem with factory supervisors were (a) lack of education in the part of factory supervisors, (b) lack of interest, and (c) misunderstanding and/or mistrust of budgets.

SOLUTIONS TO THESE PROBLEMS

Most of the solutions suggested by budget people seem to revolve around educating, or training, factory people in the application and use of budgets.

These are some of the suggestions:

1. Supervisors should be taught the use and need for budgets in the company and specifically in their departments.

2. If possible, budgets should be explained so the supervisor would know exactly how and why budgets are constructed the way they are. (Most finance people were quick to caution against overwhelming the factory man with minute details of financial "buzz words." They all pointed out that the explanations should be kept as simple as possible.)

3. Closely connected with the above is the budget staffs' desire that factory people have more acquaintance with, and therefore respect for, the everyday problems of the finance staff in administering budgets.

4. Interestingly enough, most of the top controllers believed that the problems of administering the budget would not be alleviated until finance people, as well as factory people, changed. They felt that the budget people should be given a thorough course in self-understanding and in understanding and getting along with others — in other words, a course in human relations.

These, then, are the human problems involved in the administration of budgets and what can be done about them, as seen by the budget people.

WHAT FACTORY SUPERVISORS THINK IS THE USE OF BUDGETS

Just how important are budgets and budget departments to factory supervisors? Each factory supervisor was asked to name the department which affected him the most and then the second most important. Fifty-seven percent considered production control as number one and forty-five percent chose the budget department as number one. Of the fifty-seven percent who picked the production control department as number one, all but one supervisor chose the budget department as the second most important department.

It seems relatively safe, therefore, to say that budgets wield an important influence in the production supervisor's world. Here . . . [is a] typical comment:

> Well, if you want to study a department that has its clutches everywhere, go into the budget department. That's all over this plant.

In general, the supervisors close to the employees hardly ever used budgets. In fact, they suggested that the best way to cause trouble was to mention a budget directly or indirectly to the employees. The supervisors higher up in the line of authority did use them. Of course, their usage varied, but in general the budgets were used. We shall see subsequently that the amount of use by upper-level supervisors was closely related to the way they handled their subordinates.

Use by Front-Line Supervisors

In all the plants studied the research team obtained a definite impression that budgets were "taboo" with the employees who did the work. The writers could not help but sense an informal, but highly effective group norm of "no one speaks of or uses budgets seriously." This is, of course, merely an impression. No interviews were conducted with the employees to test the impression. Some idea of the validity of this observation may be obtained if one examines parts of the statements made below by the supervisors close to the people. These statements should also give the reader a vivid picture of the feelings and the human problems faced by these supervisors.

> You can't use budgets with the people. Just can't do anything like that. People have to be handled carefully and in our plant, carefully doesn't mean with budgets. Besides, I don't think my people are lazy.
> No, can't do it because some people see budgets as a target against a man. I'll have to admit that we cannot display the budget in front of our people. You have to be careful, you know. The first thing you know you'll have a grievance against you. We don't ask a man to look at a budget. Oh well, what we might do is put it under his nose so he can't help but see it. I should say, if we show the budget to any worker, it's only one out of every six.

No, no, I couldn't ever use a budget in front of my people. I just wouldn't dare. And, mind you, I don't think my top management would want us to. We wouldn't get any production out if we did.

Budgets, therefore, are far from being "cold pictures" of past production to the people. Rather they are symbols of something with may arouse fear, resentment, hostility, and aggression on the part of the employees toward the company and which may lead to decreased production.

The supervisor is, therefore, forced to refrain from mentioning budgets. He tries to accomplish what top management desires in distributing budget results, by translating these results into informal shop language and thereby calling these results to the attention of the employees. If he is not able to do this, he doesn't mention budgets at all.

The price for mentioning budgets is high. The supervisor who uses them explicitly is faced with a resentful work group which may express this resentment in many different ways, all of which lead to trouble for the supervisor.

It is not difficult, therefore, to see why a supervisor does not dare use budgets as some budget people want him to.

Use by Top-Factory Supervisors

We have seen that front-line supervisors are not able to use budgets freely with their employees. Top-factory supervisors, on the other hand, seem to use budgets quite frequently and strongly on the supervisors below them.

Clearly, the closer one is to the employees, the less one can use budgets to increase production or arouse interest in production. If such is the case, one begins to wonder about the supervisor who is in the position of receiving all the pressure from above, but cannot pass on the pressure to the people below him. Does all this pressure stay with the supervisor?

WHAT FACTORY SUPERVISORS THINK ARE BUDGET PROBLEMS

Although there may be some differences among levels of supervision in the use of budgets, all the supervisors, regardless of their rank, were pretty much agreed concerning the limitations of budgets. Some of the limitations mentioned were:

Budget Reports Only Include Results, Not Reasons

Perhaps one of the greatest criticisms of budgets was the fact that they never included the reasons why they were not achieved by a certain supervisor. There was considerable feeling about this problem. Supervisors disliked intensely the fact that their departments would look "sick" on the budget while the reasons for the "sickness" were never published along with the results.

> Budgets never show the reasons why they have not been met. They never take into account all variables that affect production.

The budget might contain the finance man's explanation: e.g., "The reason 'why' this budget has not been met is excess labor costs, or too much waste of time getting the job ready to be produced, etc.," but such reasons were not the real explanations as seen by the supervisors. They wanted the budget to state why they had excess labor costs, or why it took too long to get the job ready.

In other words, the supervisor's why was never included. Only the why of the budget man was included.

The following supervisor sheds additional light on the subject. It is interesting to note that he realizes why the budgets are not broken down further. But it is perhaps more interesting to note that even though he understands why budgets give only the total picture, he still feels quite strongly about them. Such data cannot help but lead one to wonder if a knowledge about budgets will really alleviate the feelings about them.

As I see it, budgets are for top management. Top management is only interested in the total picture. They just want to see the results. They're just interested in knowing if the goal has been met.

The deviations, the headaches are all ironed out for them at the end of the budget. But, you can bet your boots, they are not ironed out for me. They remain, to remind me of the many things that can go wrong in my department. It's like this: I'm in the forest. I see hundreds of different trees (problems) that go to make it up. Top management is up in the air looking down on the forest. They see a mass of green. Now the budget measures that mass of green, but they don't tell the top management anything about the different trees that make up the green. You might put it this way — my job is to worry about the feelings that go to make up these figures. Finance peoples' job is to worry about the figures without the emotions.

Emphasis on History

Another closely allied problem is that budgets emphasize past performance. Budgets are historical documents. As such, they are used primarily to project some predictions about the future based on the past.

Factory supervisors, on the other hand, place little emphasis on the past and hardly ever have time to think of the future. Their emphasis is on the present day-to-day situation.

Rigidity of Budgets

In addition to the emphasis on the past, supervisors felt there was an equally negative emphasis on rigidity of standards. Once established, budget people seemed to dislike changing standards. Most budget people, the factory supervisors stated, were inflexible.

This rigidity of the finance people, as seen by the factory supervisors, leads to some important feelings on the part of the latter. For example:

I'd say one of the biggest problems is that budgets are set up on past performance. Once they come up with a figure, they hate to leave it. Two years ago, my budget on errors was 100, now it's 150, but our production has increased a lot more.

Somehow the budget people freeze the figures in their minds and they just don't want to change.

Budgets Apply Pressure for an Ever-Changing Goal

One of the more important criticisms the factory people had was the feeling that the people who set the budgets were never satisfied. For example:

If I meet this budget, those guys up there will only raise it.

Or,

You can't let them know that you made the budget without too much trouble. If you do they'll up it as sure as hell.

These were typical remarks made by most of the factory supervisors. (In no case did the top-factory supervisor consider this to be a criticism.) It was quite obvious that the factory supervisors wondered when, if ever, the optimum level would be reached. For example:

They make a budget and then constantly increase it. There's too much of that constant raising and raising that thing. Pretty soon the boys catch on and figure out it's the same old stuff. So they don't respond.

The Implication That Budgets Motivate Supervisors To Do A Better Job

As we have seen earlier, the finance people perceive budgets as goal-setters for factory supervisors. They feel that the supervisors are "kept on the ball" because of budgets. Some finance people suggest that factory supervisors would be "lost" without budgets. On the other hand, factory supervisors resent quite strongly being thought of as people who would lose their motivation if it were not for budgets.

Some of them agreed that budgets had a function of helping them accomplish their work, but few if any saw budgets as the creator of their motivation. To accept budgets as motivators is to imply that supervisors do not have adequate interest in their jobs. This is seen as an insult to a man's integrity and the factory supervisors resent it strongly. For example:

I don't care much for budgets. I can use them, but I don't need them. My job is to get out the production, and I do the best I know how. What do I need budgets for? Now budgets can't help me in that.

Budget! Well, I know this is the way the other fellows feel about it. They don't want to be bothered with them. We do our job, and we do the best job we can. That's it. No matter what comes out, we know we've done our best.

Budgets Are Not Realistic

Another important criticism made by factory supervisors was that some budgets were purposely kept high so that they were almost impossible to meet. The supervisors definitely and sincerely resent this practice. They resent it primarily for two reasons.

Such a practice places a supervisor in a situation where he can never succeed. One supervisor expressed this when he said:

There's not much sense in setting a budget that's too high. What good is it? If a man doesn't meet it, he's going to say, "to hell with it." It's going to get him to think they're never satisfied. If you ever want to discourage a guy, just give him a budget you know he can't meet.

Such a practice implies that the company does not believe the supervisor's own desire to do a good job is sufficient to meet reasonable budgets. The unrealistic budget is used to spur supervisors on, but it does not work and is resented.

WHAT FACTORY SUPERVISORS THINK ARE THE DIFFERENCES BETWEEN THEIR OUTLOOK AND THAT OF THE BUDGET PEOPLE

[Earlier] . . . some differences in outlook between financial people and factory people as seen by the financial people were described. What are the differences in outlook as seen by the factory supervisors?

The first four basic differences as seen by the factory supervisors have already been discussed. They were:

1. Finance people are primarily interested in the past and the future. They don't think of the present.

2. Finance people tend to be too rigid once they have set up their figures.

3. Finance people see only the total picture. They never see the many problems that go to make up the total picture. They worry only about end results.

4. Finance people tend to see life only as a set of figures. They take the emotions out of life and deal only with the cold figures.

Some other differences have not been previously mentioned:

1. Finance people cannot see the other person's point of view. They know almost nothing about the problems a supervisor is faced with daily.

2. Finance people have a language of their own. It is completely different from the language of the shop.

3. The final difference is more in the area of attitudes. It was best expressed by one supervisor who said:

A big problem with budget people, and all finance people for that matter, is that basically they are — well — let's see — yes — sarcastic.

I think that they think they're the whole show. If you're asking for our opinions, we think they have an over-exalted opinion of their position.

WHAT FACTORY SUPERVISORS THINK ARE
SOLUTIONS TO SOME OF THESE PROBLEMS

1. By far the most frequent and most stressed recommendation made by factory supervisors was that the finance people should learn to see the other person's point of view. The supervisors recommended that the finance people be given a "taste" of factory problems. Some typical comments were:

They are not fully acquainted with our everyday production problems. They don't realize our troubles and our difficulties. The best thing to do is to bring them down and see our problems.

I'd tell you what I'd teach them: to know my job. See the problems I have. Bring them down here and see what really goes on.

2. The financial people should undergo some training to learn that budgets are not final. They are merely opinions. One supervisor stated:

Yes, I could recommend a good thing. I wish they could have their thinking about budgets changed. They are too rigid. Budgets are statements of opinions not facts. That's their big trouble. They think budgets are facts.

3. The financial people should change their belief that the employee is lazy and wants to do as little work as possible. For example:

I'd like to see them change their attitude that employees are out to get them (budget people) and do as little work as they can get away with.

4. Closely related to recommendation (3) above is one that recurred often: finance people should change their belief that the best way to raise production is through pressure.

5. Financial people should be taught that they are not superior to factory supervisors. Some typical comments:

> I'd deflate their ego — I'd give them something to take them down a peg.
> I'd like to teach them not to think their budgets are too important.

THE PROBLEM OF PRESSURE

One of the most common of the factory supervisors' attitudes about budgets was that budgets were used as a pressure device to increase production efficiency. Many cases were cited to support this point. Finance people also admitted that budgets helped "keep people on the ball" by raising their goals and increasing their motivation. The problem of the effects of pressure applied through budgets seems to be the core of the budget problem.

The Causes of Pressure

Employees and front-line supervisors believe that the cause for pressure from the top is due to top management's belief that most employees are basically or inherently lazy. Employees and front-line supervisors also feel that top management believes that employees do not have enough motivation of their own to do the best possible job.

The interviews with top management officials revealed that the employees' beliefs were not totally unfounded, as a few quotations from some of the top management (both line and finance) make clear:

> I'll tell you my honest opinion. Five percent of the people work, ten percent of the people think they work. And the other eighty-five percent would rather die than work.
> I think there is a need for more pressure. People need to be needled a bit. I think man is inherently lazy and if we could only increase the pressure, I think the budget system would be more effective.

Such feelings, even if they are never overtly expressed toward employees, filter through to the employees in very subtle ways. Budgets represent one of the more subtle ways. Once the employees sense these feelings exist in top management, they may become very resentful.

The Effects of Pressure

How do people react to pressure? In three of the plants studied factory supervisors felt they were working under pressure and that the budget was the principal instrument of pressure. Management exerts pressure on the work force in many ways, of which budgets is but one. Budgets, being concrete, seem to serve as a medium through which the total effects of management pressure are best expressed. As such they become an excellent point of focus for studying the effect of pressure on people in a working organization.

The Creation of Groups

An increase in tension, resentment, suspicion, fear and mistrust may not be the only result of ever stronger management pressures transmitted to supervisors, and in turn, to employees. We know, from psychological research, that people can stand a certain amount of pressure. After this point is passed, it becomes intolerable to an individual. We also know that one method people have to reduce the effect of the pressure (assuming that the employees cannot reduce the pressure itself) is to join groups. These groups then help absorb much of the pressure and the individual is personally relieved.

The process of individuals joining groups to relieve themselves of pressure is not an easy one. It does not occur overnight. The development of a group on such a basis seems to have the following general stages of growth.

First, the indivduals "feel" the pressure. They are not certain, but they sense an increase in pressure.

Second, they begin to see definite evidences of the pressure. They not only feel it, they can point to it.

Since they feel this pressure is on them personally, they begin to experience tension and general uneasiness.

Next, the people usually "feel out" their fellow workers to see if they sense the pressure.

Finding out that others have noted the pressure, the people begin to feel more at ease. It helps to be able to say, "I'm not the only one."

Finally, they realize that they can acquire emotional support from each other by becoming a group. Furthermore, they can "blow their top" about this pressure in front of their group. Gradually therefore, the individuals become a group because in becoming a group they are able to satisfy these needs:

1. A need to reduce the pressure on each individual.
2. A need to get rid of tension.
3. A need to feel more secure by belonging to a group which can counteract the pressure.

In short, a new, cohesive group has developed to combat management pressure. In a sense, the people have learned that they can be happier if they combine against this management pressure.

Suppose now that top management, aware of the tensions which have been generated and the groups which have been formed, seeks to reduce the pressure. The emphasis on budgets is relaxed. Perhaps even the standards are "loosened." Does this then destroy the group? After all, its primary reason for existence was to combat the pressure. Now, the pressure is gone. The group should eventually disintegrate.

The answer seems to be that the groups continue to exist!

The evidence for this is not as conclusive as it should be. Therefore, the following explanation should be considered primarily in the realm of inference and conjecture rather than scientific fact.

These factors seem to operate to keep the group in existence:

1. There is a "time lag" between the moment management announced the new policy and the time the workers put it into effect.

2. The individuals have made a new and satisfactory adjustment with each other. They have helped to satisfy each other's needs. They are, as the social scientist would say, "in equilibrium" with each other. Any attempt to destroy this balance will tend to be resisted even if the attempt represents an elimination of a "bad" or unhealthy set of conditions. People have created a stable pattern of life and they will resist a change in this pattern.

3. The individuals fear pressure will come again in the future. Because of this feeling, they will tend to create unreal conditions or to exaggerate existing conditions so that they can rationalize to themselves that pressure still exists and, therefore, the need for the group also exists.

349

But what about the foreman? Strong pressures converge upon him. How does he protect himself from these pressures?

He cannot join a group against management, as his work force does. For one reason, he probably has at least partially identified himself with management. For another reason, he may be trying to advance in the hierarchy. Naturally, he would not help his chances for advancement if he joined a group against management.

The evidence of the previous chapter seems to indicate that the line supervisor cannot pass all the pressure he receives to his employees. Time and time again the factory supervisors stated that passing the pressure down would only create conflict and trouble which would lead to a decrease in production.

The question arises, where does the pressure go? How do the supervisors relieve themselves of at least some of the pressure? There is evidence to suggest at least three ways in which pressure is handled by the supervisors:

1. Interdepartmental strife. The foremen release some of the pressure by continuously trying to blame fellow foremen for the troubles that exist. "They are," as one foreman expressed it, "trying to throw the dead cat in each other's backyard."

In three plants observed, much time was spent by certain factory supervisors in trying to lay the blame for errors and problems on some other department.

2. Staff versus factory strife. The foremen released much of the pressure by blaming the budget people, production control people and salesmen for their problems. The data already presented concerning factory supervisors' attitudes towards budget people substantiate this point.

3. "Internalizing" pressure. Many supervisors who do not express their feelings about the pressure have in reality "internalized" it and, in a sense, made it a part of themselves. Such damming up of pressure seemed to be expressed in the following ways:

(a) Supervisor *A* is quiet, relatively nonemotional, seldom expresses his negative feelings to anyone, but at the same time he works excessively. Supervisor *A* can be found working at his desk long after the others have gone home. As one supervisor expressed it, "That guy works himself to death."

(b) Supervisor *B* is nervous, always running around "checking up" on all his employees. He usually talks fast, gives one the impression that he is "selling" himself and his job when interviewed. He is forever picking up the phone, barking commands and requesting prompt action.

Both of these types (or a combination of these types) are expressions of much tension and pent up emotions that have been internalized. People working under such conditions finally are forced to "take it easy," or they find themselves with ulcers or a nervous breakdown.

But that is not the end of the problem. Constant tension leads to frustration. A frustrated person no longer operates as effectively as he was accustomed. He finds that he tends to forget things he used to remember. Work that he used to do with pleasure, he now delegates to someone else. He is no longer able to make decisions as fast as he did months ago. Now he finds he has to take a walk or get a cup of coffee — anything to get "away from it all."

Success for Budget Supervisors Means Failure for Factory Supervisors

Students of human relations agree that most people want to feel successful. We observe people constantly defining social and psychological goals, struggling to meet them, and as they are met, feeling successful.

Finance and factory supervisors are no exception. The typical finance supervisor does his work as best he can. He hopes and expects just praise of this work from his superior. Most of his success comes, therefore, from his superior's evaluation. It is the "boss" who will eventually say "well done," or commend a promotion. In other words, a finance supervisor measures his success on his job, to a substantial degree, by the reactions of his superior.

The situation is the same for the factory supervisor. He also desires success. Like the finance supervisor, much of his success also derives from the comments and behavior the "boss" exhibits. In short, the factory supervisor is also oriented toward the top for an evaluation of how well he is doing his job.

What is the task of a good and successful finance supervisor? The reader will recall that the finance people perceive their task as being the watchdog of the company. They are always trying to improve the situation in the plant. As one finance supervisor said, "Always, there is room to make it better." And finally, the reader will recall the statement that, "The budget man has made an excellent contribution to this plant. He's found a lot of things that were sour. You might say a good budget man . . . lets top management know if anything is wrong."

In other words, their success derives from finding errors, weaknesses, and faults that exist in the plant. But, when they discover these errors, weaknesses, and faults, they also single out a "guilty party" and implicitly, at least, accuse him of failure. This is true because in finding weaknesses, errors or faults in a certain department, one is at the same time telling the factory supervisors that "things aren't going along as well as they could be." This, naturally, gives many factory supervisors a feeling of failure.

To be sure, such an occurrence will not make every supervisor feel he has failed. Some supervisors do not worry much about their job. Therefore, we find that the supervisor who really feels the failure is the one who is highly interested in doing a good job.

Reporting Shortcomings of the Foreman

The way in which these shortcomings are reported is also important:

Assume that finance man *A* discovers an error in foreman *B*'s department. How is this error reported? Does the finance man go directly to the factory foreman? In the plants studied the answer, usually, is "no."

The finance man cannot take the "shortest" route between the foreman and himself. For one reason, it may be a violation of policy for a staff man to go directly to a line man. But, more important (from a human point of view), the staff man derives his success when his boss knows he is finding errors. Therefore, his boss would never know how good a job finance man *A* is doing unless it came to his attention. In short, perhaps because of organizational regulations but basically because much success in industry is derived from above, the finance person usually takes his findings to his own boss, who in turn gives it to his, and so on up the line and across and down into the factory line structure.

Taking the long way around has at least one more positive value for finance people. The middle and top management finance people also derive some success in being able to go to the plant manager and point to some newly discovered weaknesses in the factory. Therefore, not only one man obtains feelings of success, but all interested people up the entire finance structure obtain some feeling of satisfaction.

But, how about the factory people? The answer seems evident. They experience a certain sense of "being caught with their pants down."

Finally, to add insult to injury, the entire incident is made permanent and exhibited to the plant officials by being placed in some budget report which is to be, or has been, circulated through many top channels.

Effects of Failure on People

One might ask: What effects does this kind of failure have upon an individual? If they were insignificant, obviously we would not be concerned. Such is not the case. Feelings of failure can have devastating effects upon an individual, his work and his relationships with others.

Lippitt and Bradford, reporting on some ingenious scientific experiments conducted on the subject of success and failure, state that people who fail tend to:

1. Lose interest in their work.
2. Lower their standards of achievement.
3. Lose confidence in themselves.
4. Give up quickly.
5. Fear any new task and refuse to try new methods or accept new jobs.
6. Expect failure.
7. Escape from failure by daydreaming.
8. Increase their difficulty in working with others.
9. Develop a tendency to blame others, to be over-critical of others' work and to develop troubles with other employees.

On the other hand, people who succeed tend to:

1. Raise their goals.
2. Gain greater interest in the activity in which they are engaged.
3. Gain greater confidence in their ability in the activity.
4. Increase their persistence to future goals.
5. Increase their ability to cooperate and work.
6. Increase their ability to adapt readily to new situations.
7. Increase their emotional control.

In summary, we should point out that finance people aren't inherently "out to get them" as factory people in the plants described them. Rather, they are placed in a social organization where the only way in which they can receive success is to place someone else in failure.

The Wall Between Finance and Factory People

At least two more very interesting conditions are related to this peculiar position which the finance people hold:

First, since the budget people are always looking for weaknesses, errors, and faults, they begin to develop a philosophy of life in which their symbol for success is, not only the error discovered, but the very thought of the discovery of a possible new error. "Weaknesses," "discovery of errors made by others" — which are symbols of failure for others — are symbols of success for the budget people.

The realization and admission by budget people of the peculiar position in which they are placed, leads to the second interesting condition. The budget people tend to become defensive about their work. They don't like placing people in failure, but they have to. Being aware of this difficulty and the negative feelings it may create, they tend to become defensive about queries concerning "their books" or their methods. One has the feeling that, at times, they use their technical "know-how" and language to confuse the factory people. This confusion of the factory people serves, of course, as a defense for the budget man. As one man suggested, "After all, if they don't know anything about budgets, how can they criticize them?" In short, the ignorance of the factory people concerning budgets may become a wall behind which the finance people may work unmolested. It is interesting to note that one of the major causes of insecurity among factory supervisors concerning budgets (i.e., "we can't understand them") is one of the primary factors of security for the budget people.

The Problem of Department-Center Supervisors

We have already shown that supervisors are partially evaluated by budget records. The factory supervisor, who desires to be known as being an efficient, effective supervisor, must make certain that his daily, weekly, monthly, and quarterly results compare favorably with the predicted results defined by the budgets. In short, a factory supervisor will feel successful, other things being equal, when he "meets his budget."

The phrase "meets his budget" is crucial.

Such a philosophy overlooks an extremely important point, perhaps described by the statement, "An organization is something different from the sum of the individual parts." The difference of the whole from the sum of the parts lies in the fact that the parts of an organization exist in certain relationships with each other. It is these relationships which create the difference.

What Makes an Organization?

Parts, alone, do not make a whole organization. One cannot conceive of "adding" parts of an organization any more than adding together the hundreds of pieces that make up a watch in order to make the watch run. The crucial problem is to place the parts in correct relationship to each other.

Without laboring the point it seems clear that important relationships between departments are disregarded by an overemphasis on the individual departments. If everyone made certain his own department was functioning correctly, but at the same time, did not pay attention to the functioning of his department in relation to others, then trouble would still arise.

Controlling Conflicts Among Departments

It might be suggested that the control of the relationships between departments rests with the plant manager, or some higher authority. From his high position, he is best able to control the conflict between departments. The crux of the matter is that this is all the leader can do, i.e., control conflict. He is unable to eliminate it since the causes for the conflict are not within his reach. Since the top leader controls this conflict, the supervisors increasingly look to the leader to "break up a fight" or settle a dispute. This forces the supervisors to become increasingly dependent upon the leader. Furthermore, the more successful the top leader is, the less the supervisors need to worry about cooperation. They soon learn that the leader will solve any inter-departmental problems.

An example will illustrate the point.

In one of the plants studied a mistake was made on a customer order. The customer sent the material back to the plant. The error was corrected and the material sent back to the customer.

The cost of making the correction was nearly three thousand dollars. The error, especially since it was so large, had to be entered in the budget records. Some department had to be charged with the error. The problem was, who should be charged with the error?

For two months, supervisors of the departments most likely to be blamed waged a continuous campaign to prove their innocence. Each supervisor blamed the others. No one wanted the error on his record. The supervisors actually spent hundreds of man-hours arguing and debating among themselves. Emotions were aroused, people began calling each other names. Finally, two of the supervisors refused to talk to each other. Conflict reigned among the supervisors.

But, the supervisors were not the only persons in conflict. The division manager was also in conflict. He had to make the decision. To charge any supervisor with such an error would certainly invite hostility from that supervisor. This hostility might have further effects in the future. The division manager did not want to risk a weakening of his realtionship, especially with a supervisor. But, he had to make a decision.

A meeting was held with the interested supervisors. The problem was discussed until just about everybody and everything that could be blamed, were blamed for the error. The division manager finally "gave in." He decided to place the error under "general factory loss." No department would be affected. The plant, as a whole, would carry the stigma. The division manager expressed his thoughts behind his decision to the research worker as follows:

> Take that big three-thousand dollar error. We have to charge it up to someone. One man blames sales, another someone else. Everyone refuses to admit it might be their own fault. They each blame someone else.
>
> Well, I don't know. Perhaps, I thought it might be best to put the whole thing under general factory loss. Or else, they'd be hurt.

Note that the supervisors are willing to have the plant as a whole take the blame. But, they resist any attempts to place the blame on their individual departments.

In summary, budgets and budgeting tend to make the supervisor think of his, and essentially only his, department. Budget records, as administered, foster a narrow viewpoint on the part of the user. The budget records serve as a constant reminder that the important aspect to consider is one's own department and not one's own plant. As a result, supervisors become department centered rather than plant centered.[1]

Budgets as a Medium for Personality Expression

The final problem to be discussed became evident only after a series of interviews with different controllers and top factory officials. Then it became obvious that the way people expressed their interest in budgets, and the way in which they described and used them, were directly related to the pattern of leadership they used in their daily industrial life.

For example, if a rather domineering, aggressive, "go-getting" top executive was interviewed, his presentation of the problem would also be made in a domineering, aggressive, "go-getting" manner. Therefore, although it is accurate to state that budgets are composed of "cold, nonhuman symbols" (i.e., figures), it is equally valid to state that once human beings use these "nonhuman figures," they project onto these figures all the emotions and feelings at their command.

Because budgets become a medium of personality and leadership expression, and since people's personalities and leadership patterns are different, this research study found a number of methods with which top factory executives used budgets. A few of these methods are illustrated by the following comments made by top factory supervisors:

> I go to the office and check that budget every day. I can then see how we're

---

[1] One method to remedy this problem is to attempt to have the staff person report directly to the factory. For an interesting statement of this case see: Douglas MacGregor, "The Role of the Human Relations Consultant," *Journal for the Study of Social Issues,* Vol. IV (Summer 1948).

meeting the budget. If it's O.K., I don't say anything. But, if it's no good, then I come back here (smiles) and give the boys a little . . . Well, you know. I needle them a bit. I give them the old . . . hm . . . well . . . you know what . . . the old needle.

I make it a policy to have close contact, human contact, with all the people in my department.

If I see we're not hitting the budget, I go out and tell them I have $40,000 on the order.

Well, they don't know what that $40,000 means. They think it's a lot of money so they get to work.

Human factor, that's important. If you treat a human being like a human being, you can use them better and get more out of them.

You know, it's a funny thing. If I want my people to read the budget, I don't shove it under their nose. I just lay it on my desk and leave it alone. They'll pick it up without a doubt.

It is hoped that the above descriptions are adequate to convey the point that budgets furnish a means of expression. They serve to permit the user's pattern of leadership to blossom forth.

SUMMARY

This exploratory research has led to the tentative conclusion that budgets and budgeting can be related to at least four important human relations problems:

First, budget pressure tends to unite the employees against management, and tends to place the factory supervisor under tension. This tension may lead to inefficiency, aggression, and perhaps a complete breakdown on the part of the supervisor.

Second, the finance staff can obtain feelings of success only by finding fault with factory people. These feelings of failure among factory supervisors lead to many human relations problems.

Third, the use of budgets as "needlers" by top management tends to make the factory supervisors see only the problems of their own department. The supervisors are not concerned with the other people's problems. They are not "plant-centered" in outlook.

Finally, supervisors use budgets as a way of expressing their own pattern of leadership. When these patterns result in people getting hurt, the budget, in itself a neutral thing, often gets blamed.

In the preceding pages we have discussed our observations and findings in an extremely complex field — the impact of budgets upon people. Because problems are so complex and our research so obviously exploratory, we undertake the task of suggesting lines of action with considerable humility.

The Planning-Programming-Budgeting System: Rationale , Language, and Idea-Relationships

SAMUEL M. GREENHOUSE

An understanding of what the Planning-Programming-Budgeting System (PPBS) purports to be and to do for the U.S. Government rests, I believe, upon recognizing the primacy and interplay of two PPBS ingredients. These two "molecules" — as they stand individually, contribute proportionately, interact, and interdepend — compose the vital core of PPBS.

Let me begin by identifying the two ingredients, as a prelude to defining and discussing them.

- A single concept, dealing with the accountability of the Federal agency apparatus, forms the philosophic base of the PPBS structure.
- The main structural members of PPBS are eight terms with definitions so special that, in effect, PPBS has a "language all its own." True, none of the words and phrases in this language is really new. But each is used so very differently in the PPBS context that earlier-entrenched images (which our minds seem to conjure up whenever the terms are heard) may in some cases prevent comprehension. The eight terms are: objectives, programs, program alternatives, outputs, progress measurements, inputs, alternative ways to do a given job, and systems analysis. A true understanding of PPBS cannot derive from reliance upon the traditional definitions of these terms. Each has a particular meaning and significance in the *rearrangement of established ideas* which PPBS represents.

The fresh design which emerges from this rearrangement, rather than the individual ideas themselves, is what is new about PPBS.[1] But in rearranging, in linking and relating the ideas, a trimming and fitting had to take place. Through this tailoring process, the terms remained unchanged while the ideas (which the terms had so long and effectively stood for) took on subtle differences of flavor and shade. Given these new meanings, the terms have become coordinates with distinct functions, hierarchical placements, and highly significant relationships within the flow and overall framework of PPBS.

---

[1] In this regard, PPBS is not surprisingly like many conceptual "innovations." It is often said that there is "nothing new under the sun." That many discoveries consist in rearranging and regrouping ideas which are, individually, already known, does not diminish the usefulness of the results. The important question is whether and in what directions PPBS may prove useful.

Reprinted from Public Administration Review, *Vol. XXVI, No. 4 (December, 1966), pp. 271-277. Reprinted with permission of the American Society for Public Administration.*

PPBS is a multi-purpose system. If it is implemented and instrumented soundly, it should have a variety of uses. Only one of these – and perhaps not the most important one, although it is receiving predominant attention at this stage – is the improvement of individual Federal agency operations. Whether the regulation of Federal agency activities is a key purpose or not, the careful installation of PPBS in the individual agencies is of surpassing importance, because the agencies are indispensable building blocks in the overall system. That is to say, PPBS could not exist disembodied from the individual agencies, even if the main purpose of PPBS were, say, to accelerate the economic growth of the United States rather than to introduce a new technique of agency management. This may help to explain why the bedrock concept of PPBS concerns the matter of Federal agency accountability.

Now, what is the PPBS concept, and how is it different?

The PPBS concept is that each Federal agency is accountable to the President[2] for the production of goods and services, and more particularly, *for the distribution of these goods and services to the American people.*

This is a considerable departure indeed, for, until PPBS, the Federal agency apparatus, was considered to be held accountable by, and to, the President[2] for providing the Presidency with "administrative support." Application of this vague concept has become more difficult as the Federal apparatus has grown and diversified. Our Presidents have become too busy to locate, identify in specifics, and hold direct reins of responsibility.

The PPBS accountability concept focuses the attention of each agency on the question: What is our business? The PPBS concept provides a basis for particularizing the answers to the question: Accountable for specifically what products (goods or services), delivered to whom?

The PPBS concept matches the reality of today's Federal agency operations, demonstrating once again that "theory interprets established fact." The agencies *are* producing goods and services, and distributing them to the American people.[3] What PPBS *adds* to this reality is the assumption that product delivery to the American public is the *central* purpose of agency operation rather than merely a happenstance or a by-product of other, more characteristic purposes.

Of course, all Federal agencies perform other functions besides distributing goods and services to the public. For example, each agency generates goods and services for purely internal uses; for the use of other agencies; or for the President and Congress. However, an understanding of PPBS depends upon recognizing that all "inside-the-government" efforts and interchanges are considered subordinate to the central purpose. Inside-government activities are not pertinent for PPBS accountability. Unless this is recognized, the ideas which underlie the terms "objective," "program," "output," and "input" cannot be clearly discerned nor can the interplay of these terms be comprehended. The discussions of output and input allude in greater detail to this crucial matter.

If the agencies are to be held accountable for discharging the central purpose of distributing agency-produced goods and services to the American public, the public becomes, conceptually speaking, the market for the agencies' products and services. Thus, the explicit business of each Federal agency is to satisfy the public's actual and potential market demands for the agency's particular product/service lines. Accountability dis-

---

[2] And to the Congress.

[3] In some cases, the agencies contract for goods and services, and perform the distribution themselves. So long as the production is government financed, and performed under government auspices, it can be regarded the same way, for PPBS purposes, as in-government production.

charge becomes subject to evaluation in terms of each agency's success in (1) gauging the nature and proportions of the market demands, and (2) fulfilling these demands.

OBJECTIVES

With this background, it becomes clear that the apex-term of the PPBS idea-structure is "objectives." As the preceding discussion indicates, a more precise way to visualize the idea here denoted is to expand the term to "market objectives." Each agency is supposed to generate *explicit* market objectives, to make possible a genuine agency-wide under-standing and a common agency approach toward their achievement. Satisfactory market objectives would, one supposes, provide specific grounds upon which to base the answers to three questions[4] about *each* main class of items produced by a given agency:

- What class of goods or services is contemplated for production? (Each agency has at least one main class of items, or product line; most agencies have more than one.)
- What market group is each product line (good or service) intended to satisfy? (Some agencies have readily identifiable groups of customers, e.g., veterans; other agencies serve fluid and only temporarily associated groups, such as air travelers.)
- What specific needs, of the market group served, is the product designed to satisfy? (For example, if the American Indian, say, were assumed to need help in achieving economic well-being comparable to the "national average," what indications of this need might be cited in support of programmatic intentions?)

If this theme correctly interprets PPBS, customer-oriented market objectives are des-tined to become key standards for agency self-appraisal and accountability. Such stand-ards are quite common for private industry, except that total sales volume is a more readily obtainable index of market needs and satisfactions than will be available in government.

Allowing for the absence of various profit mechanisms in government, the effect of PPBS will be to bring governmental practice to a somewhat closer approximation of common industrial practice than has been possible before.

PROGRAMS

What idea underlies the term "program"? In PPBS language, a program is a package which encompasses each and every one of the agency's efforts to achieve a particular objective or set of allied objectives.[5] If the objective were to provide economic assistance to the American Indian, the program would be composed of all agency activities and expenditures put to that purpose.

Bear in mind that *this* idea of program is very different from the traditional govern-mental usage. Prior to PPBS, all agencies used the term to characterize functions and professional disciplines. Hence, "procurement," "data management," "engineering," and many other activities were called programs. The habit persists even now, because PPBS has not yet succeeded in making its point.

---

[4] These questions appear useful to the author to illustrate the concept of market demand which PPBS implies. They are not to be found in the available PPBS literature.
[5] Whenever the term 'objectives' is used hereafter, it should be read as 'customer-oriented market objectives.'

Those agencies which did not understand the new meaning of the term in advance of generating their initial PPBS "program structures," will certainly need to redo program structures if PPBS is ever to gain solid ground. Individual activities, functions, and professional disciplines are the very antitheses of programs in the PPBS sense. The whole PPBS idea is to facilitate the drawing together, the summation of all agency efforts to meet particular objectives, so that the validity of each program may be assessed in terms of overall approach, dimension, and costs and may be compared with other competing programs, potential or existing. It should be recognized, then, that in the future, a program which mirrors (corresponds with) a given agency's established organization structure will be a rarity, unless the agency happens to have only one program. An agency with a functional-type organization must break down functional efforts and apportion them among programs, in order to successfully sum each program.[6]

As the foregoing discussion may have indicated, there is a strong conceptual relationship between objective(s) and program. In "PPBS language," there are no objectives recognized except those which suggest a program designed specifically to fulfill them; and there can be no recognized entity describable as a program unless it is designed to accomplish explicit objectives (customer-oriented market objectives).

PROGRAM ALTERNATIVES

The term "program alternatives" is next in the PPBS hierarchy.[7] Within any one agency, his term means other possible programs besides those already decided upon. Consequently, it suggests a comparison of two or more programs (i.e., two or more possible approaches) toward fulfilling the *same market objective(s)*. For example, as in the hypothetical case mentioned earlier, suppose that an agency wanted to accomplish the objective of raising the economic well-being of the American Indian to some mythical level such as the national average. Presumably, any one of several programs, existing or new, might succeed in bringing this about. The agency would wish to choose the "best" program for the purpose, and to disregard other program alternatives.[8] Or, it might simply wish to evaluate a number of program alternatives so that, having selected one, it could demonstrate the wisdom of the selection by revealing the inadequacies (in the discarded programs) which the comparative evaluation had uncovered.[9]

OUTPUT

In PPBS language, an output must have, conceptually speaking, all of the following properties:

[6] However, it is not required that there be change in the established organization structure; merely a change in the accounting will do.

[7] Of course, these PPBS terms may be considered in any order, but the author finds the order of presentation given here easiest to work with for definition purposes.

[8] The term "systems analysis" will be defined later, at which point the mechanics for selecting a "best" program from among the possible program alternatives will be suggested.

[9] There are two other types of alternatives in PPBS language. One is "alternative ways to do a given job," to be defined later. At that time, the distinction between "program alternatives" and "alternative ways to do a given job" should become manifest. The other, which could be termed "comparison of all agencies' programs" is not discussed in this paper because it is not a prominent part of PPBS as applied in the individual agencies. It is applied, however, by the President and his executive staff.

- It is a product (either a good or a service).

- It is produced by a Federal agency, or is produced under the agency's auspices.

- It is a tangible outgrowth of a particular program (i.e., it is the result of a calculated program effort).

- It is the sort of product which can be appropriately singled-out as an indicator of program results. (Logically, therefore, it must be a program end-product, and an important one, at that.)

- It is considered by the agency as satisfying an explicit market objective (or related set of objectives).

The foregoing list of properties should serve to illustrate the connective tissue which runs all the way through PPBS. That is, the idea of output is inseparably linked to the earlier discussed ideas of market objectives and program(s). And this idea-connection is highly significant for interpreting the PPBS notion of output. It means that many types of products which the agencies have been accustomed to regard as outputs can no longer be so regarded. PPBS has preempted the word, so to speak, for a much narrower, sharper-focused usage than the traditional one. In order to be considered an output in PPBS language, the good or service produced must satisfy an explicit market objective *and* must be an indicator of program results.

Let us appraise a few items traditionally considered outputs, in light of these definitional criteria. Suppose that an agency decides upon a program to build schools. The agency's procurement division places a series of contracts with construction firms. One month later, the agency's statistical division prepares and forwards to the agency director a "construction progress report." Are the contractual documents properly countable as outputs? No! Is the statistical report an output? No! Why? Neither the documents nor the report satisfies a customer-oriented market objective, and neither represents an indicator of program achievement (although both of them do represent divisional, that is, internal, achievements).

They are intermediate, or contributory products, rather than outputs in the PPBS sense.

What would constitute *program* achievement, and thus be an output in the PPBS sense of the word, could in the example cited above be the number of schools built, number of new classrooms available, or number of new classroom seats set into place.

The distinction between intermediate or contributory products and output is a very critical matter, insofar as understanding PPBS is concerned. If we would follow the logic-structure of PPBS, we must reconstitute our thinking. We must consider many of the things we are accustomed to producing (and claiming output-credit for) as mere intermediates. This is not so illogical as it may at first appear to be. Coal is the output of a miner, but is only a contributing factor for the completion of industrial processes, rather than an output of any of those processes. In turn, the processes' outputs are, or may be, salable commodities. One man's output is, to another man, merely a contribution to *his* output. The logic of how to classify an item, such as coal, depends entirely upon the intent and purpose of the classification, rather than upon some immutable principle. For purposes of PPBS output, the government's many agencies may be regarded as analogous to the separate divisions of any large corporation. The corporate outputs, in any such enterprise, are only those items produced to reach the public. Neither those items consumed by and for the production processes themselves, nor those exchanged between the corporate divisions, are regarded by the corporation as outputs.

Given the realization that this is the output focus of PPBS, we can now get a clearer fix on the PPBS idea of progress measurement.

The notion that progress should be measured in some fashion is not likely to trouble many people. The question that may be vexing some students of PPBS is: What does PPBS want us to measure? Or, put in another way: What does PPBS regard as *progress* in a given program?

If output means only those programmatic end-products which satisfy explicit market objectives, then program *fulfillment* must imply that *both* of two conditions have occurred:

- The output which had been planned has materialized, *and*
- The output distribution which had been intended has been completed.[10]

If that is fulfillment, then progress must imply one of two questions, depending upon what stage the program happens to be in at the time when progress is measured:

- Either, how closely does the production progress match planned progress?
- Or, how well is the output distribution proceeding, as compared with the distribution plan?[11]

INPUT

Of all the words in the special language of PPBS, input is porbably the easiest to grasp, because the PPBS definition is fairly close to the traditional usage of the term. If all of the inputs to a given program were expressed in dollars, the sum would comprise the total costs incurred by the program (during the time-period that the program had been in effect). In other words, the total quantity of manpower, facilities, equipment, and materials applied to the program, expressed in either units or dollars, is the program input. Note, however, that the facilities, equipment, and materials applied may, in a given program, include some intermediate or contributory products.[12]

ALTERNATIVE WAYS TO DO A GIVEN JOB

The concept of "alternative ways to do a given job" is input-related, insofar as PPBS is concerned. The "given job" notion means that the output to be produced and the distribution pattern for that output have already been decided upon. The question, at any phase of the program subsequent to that decision-point, becomes: Can we alter the production of distribution *technique* and by so doing improve either:

---

[10] At this early stage in the evolution of PPBS, with the distribution aspect not yet generally recognized, few agencies' plans give distribution intentions any prominence. Where on-going programs are concerned, particularly, the agencies have tended to disregard distribution considerations altogether. If PPBS "makes it," this situation will change.
[11] The question of *how* to measure what PPBS wants measured is touched upon later, when systems analysis is discussed.
[12] In which case, we may be classifying as *inputs*, for PPBS purposes, some items which would have been classified, in pre-PPBS days, as *outputs*. But remember: don't duplicate inputs — that is, whether summarizing inupt units or input dollar costs, don't count both the intermediate/contributory products *and* the manpower, facilities, equipment, or materials that were used *in their production*. Count either one or the other as input, but not both.

- The timing of the production or delivery, or
- The quantity or quality of the item(s) being produced, or
- The unit or total cost of the production or delivery?

Every one of the three questions above is input-oriented. That is why defining the term program alternatives separately (as was done earlier) is advantageous. True, the word "alternatives" appears in both "program alternatives" and "alternative ways to do a given job." The first is output-related; it suggests substituting an entirely different program (and therefore a different output or outputs) for a program already planned or in progress. On the other hand, "alternative ways to do a given job" takes the program as given, and raises possibilities for changing the mix of inputs, and thereby redirecting the program.

Viewed in another way, the first involves policy questions, while the second involves operational matters. It is quite useful to distinguish between these two, as an aid in placing responsibility. That is to say, any single group of executives need not, sometimes should not, and often cannot answer both types of questions. However, the agency head, able in a given case to distinguish the PPBS situation as either policy or operations, is well on the way toward getting appropriate action taken, because he will know which group of his executives to contact.

SYSTEMS ANALYSIS

Of the eight terms characterized as important for understanding PPBS, only systems analysis remains to be discussed.

In the foregoing, the attempt has been to establish a distinct identity for PPBS. If this has succeeded, the reader already knows that systems analysis isn't PPBS, and that PPBS isn't systems analysis. The number of people who appear to regard these two things as one and the same is astounding.

Purely for purposes of differentiating the two, PPBS may be captioned as a bag of premises, concepts and relationships; whereas systems analysis may be captioned as a bag of techniques attached to a way of approaching problems. No disparagement of the latter is intended. To the contrary. The cause of technique is not advanced by confounding it with the very content to which it can be most profitably applied.

If systems analysis isn't synonymous with PPBS, what is it? More particularly, what is it insofar as PPBS is concerned?

A capsule definition would be: systems analysis is the application of "benefit-cost" analytical techniques to several areas of the PPBS anatomy.[13]

From the standpoint of the individual Federal agencies, two PPBS areas are especially amenable to benefit-cost techniques. One is the posing and evaluation of program alternatives, i.e., ascertaining the benefit-cost advantage (if any) of shifting to different outputs and/or distribution patterns so as to satisfy market objective(s) better. The other is the measurement of progress in a given program, i.e., ascertaining the benefit-cost advantage (if any) of changing the input mix so as to produce and/or distribute the output more efficiently.[14] In either case, the function of the systems analyst is to diagnose the benefit-cost situation as it exists, so that the agency head may have the opportunity to make his decision on a benefit-cost basis if the circumstances suggest to him that such is

---

[13] In the broader context represented by economic theory, benefit-cost techniques have been described for a century as "marginal utility" analysis.
[14] A special and very useful application of systems analysis, which overlaps both foregoing cases, is the benefit-cost evaluation of program expansion/contraction.

362

the appropriate basis. If other considerations suggest to the agency head that the decision should be predicated upon different or broader criteria than simply benefit and cost, that remains his prerogative. He should have the benefit-cost data in any case, so that he can know what sacrifice, if any, the exercise of the prerogative entails.

The preceding only skims the surface of systems analysis. A more complete treatment is beyond the scope of an essay on the nature of PPBS.

SUMMARY

What is PPBS? It is a structure with a base unusual for government, and with key structural members so interdependent that comprehension must extend to all, or true perception of the "building" is impeded. The base is accountability in the citizen market. Therefore, the objectives must be product supply and distribution. Accordingly, programs are conceived and executed as production/distribution entities. Consequently, program alternatives are different production/distribution entities which might offer better benefit-cost ratios than existing ones. End-products become the only items construed as outputs. And, progress is viewed and measured in terms of output/distribution timing and effectiveness vs. planned timing and effectiveness. Hence, the inputs are "whatever resources it takes to get the production-distribution job done." As a result, alternative input-mixes become important comparison bases within any given program. Finally, systems analysis contributes diagnosis and appraisal to the whole.

Those familiar with PPBS will have noted the omission of many details. The workaday requirements in planning, programming, and budgeting; the preparation and time-phasing of "program memoranda" and "program and financial plans;" the problems and reasoning associated with below-the-first-tier program structuring; the many different ways in which the cost-benefit approach and techniques (marginal utility theory) may be applied — all of these have been omitted or touched lightly, in large part because they have been treated thoroughly and in depth by many. Hopefully, the details will take on greater meaning within the framework of the "larger architecture" which this essay has sought to delineate.

Utilizing Cost and Efficiency Studies
in the Decision-Making
Progress in Health and Welfare

ROBERT ELKIN AND DELROY L. CORNICK

The need to improve the management of health and welfare services is increasingly recognized as a priority problem for the field. This concern parallels the development of new management concepts to meet the requirements of business and public administration.

Significant opportunities for the health and welfare field are suggested by such concepts as decision-theory, the systems approach, and management information systems. It is the purpose of this presentation to examine several pertinent management concepts within the framework of current developments and requirements of the health and welfare field.

This examination suggests an important role for welfare planning researchers in improving the management of health and welfare services.

THE DECISION-MAKING PROCESS

First, let us take a brief look at the elements of the decison-making process as they are viewed in contemporary management concepts. These elements are basic to any process of management whether it be in social welfare, or in public or business administration. The elements are:

1. Recognize the need to make a decision

2. Identify alternative actions

3. Secure the information required in the decision area

4. Recognize the limitations inherent in all decision-making

5. Build in the action to implement the decision

6. Evaluate the decision in terms of feedback resulting from the action taken.

INFORMATION – THE KEY TO SOUND DECISIONS

The most serious constraint on effective decision-making is information. Information is defined as data which has been received, evaluated, and organized. Information is the key to sound decision-making and therefore to sound management. In order for informa-

This paper was originally presented at the Community Welfare Research Workshop, United Community Funds and Councils of America, May 19, 1967, Dallas, Texas. Printed with permission of the authors.

tion to be effectively related to the decision area, an analysis of the informational requirements of the decision must be made. After the requirements are determined, we can then identify and organize the data flow.

There are essentially three classifications of data: (1) Data that are currently used in some decision process; (2) Data that are not currently used, but may be used in some predictable future decision process; and (3) Data that are not now used nor scheduled for future use in the decision-making process. This last category has been referred to as "noise".

Statistical and cost accounting departments turn out masses of reports, figures, and calculations. We have the capability through the computer of turning these reports out faster and at lower costs. However, much of the data gathered in the health and welfare field is descriptive and static; it does not contribute to decisions. It can be classified as "wouldn't it be nice to have" data.

The mass of data with which we innundate decision makers has many times confused and retarded sound decisions. What is needed is to develop concepts within which data can be organized for decision-making. We wish to illustrate how a concept may be developed for identifying decision areas and the requirements for information concerning efficiency, quality, and effectiveness of health and welfare services.

The terms efficiency, quality, and effectiveness have been and continue to be used without adequate or consistent definitions. Therefore before proceding further we must define what we mean by these terms.

EFFECTIVENESS DEFINED

Effectiveness may be defined as a measure of the degree to which a service reaches its objectives. The objectives may be stated in terms of outcome (i.e., impact of the service upon its target or goal) or in terms of output units (productivity).

In order to measure effectiveness we must recognize that the clarity with which our objectives are expressed will determine the extent to which effectiveness can be measured.

For the most part, welfare research literature on effectiveness directs our attention to changes occurring in personal or family functioning. We suggest that a more complete approach to assessment of effectiveness would recognize a series of levels; four are suggested below:

1. The first level is an objective, quantitative measure of productivity of the organization. An illustration of this would be in the Title V programs for job training where our objective might be to provide job training for a specified number of people. This kind of statistic is one which all agencies could develop. Effectiveness would be measured by the degree to which actual productivity approached the stated objective.

A more refined statement of objective at this level would be to place all persons who satisfactorily completed the training program in jobs for which they were trained. Effectiveness would be measured by how many trained people were actually placed.

2. At the second level, the objective is expressed in both quantitative and qualitative terms.

At this level, our objective is to prepare job trainees to perform their job adequately. Therefore, the objective must include an operational definition of quality of performance. For example, we might consider a placement successful if the person stayed at least six months and received a performance rating of more than 50 percent on a standard rating scale. Effectiveness would then be measured by the number of trainees performing adequately.

3. At the third level, we are concerned with assessing the outcome or impact of the

service on the individual in qualitative terms. At this level, our objective is concerned with the impact on the intra-psychic functioning of individuals. Therefore, the objectives may be expressed as operational measures of subjective states and effectiveness measured in these terms. Effectiveness would then be measured by what changes could be identified in how the job trainees functioned as citizens of the community, employees, parents, and how secure they were as individuals.

4. At the fourth level, we are concerned with assessing the impact of the service on the community. The measure of effectiveness is based upon the extent to which the number served by the agency relates to the total number in the target group who need the service. If, for example, the number in the community requiring job training is 10,000 and this agency is reaching 200, some perspective is gained on the impact of the service on the total community problem.

These levels of measuring effectiveness suggest a range of focus from organizational effectiveness at the first level to service effectiveness at the third and fourth levels.

QUALITY DEFINED

Quality is defined as the degree to which specific elements of input comply with standards. Quality has two aspects:

1. Standards related to the essential characteristics of the input. For example, social workers' training and experience.

2. Standards related to the ratio of input units to client units. For example, the number of qualified social workers required for a given child population in an institution.

Quality of a service may exist even though the service is inefficiently administered and ineffective in its outcome. In other words, a program may be administered in conformance with qualitative standards and still *not* meet the objectives of the service.

It is essential to emphasize the fact that quality cannot be assessed unless there are standards by which it can be measured.

EFFICIENCY DEFINED

Efficiency is defined as a ratio of the quantity of units produced from a system to the quantity of units put into the system. One illustration would be the number of interviews produced per caseworker per day. In other words, it is a ratio of what is produced to resources put into the service.

Although efficiency can be *measured* in quantitative terms, it can only be *assessed* if there is some standard of efficiency against which it may be measured. This is extremely significant because, for the most part, standards of efficiency do not exist in the health and welfare field. Conclusions about the number of interviews a day which a caseworker can produce are based upon actual performance data gathered in time studies. However, whether or not this performance is high or low in efficiency can only be satisfactorily assessed if there is an accepted standard of efficiency.

A MODEL OF EFFICIENCY, QUALITY, AND EFFECTIVENESS

Now that definitions have been presented, we can turn to a framework for relating efficiency, quality, and effectiveness to decision areas in health and welfare services.

A model is presented on the following page which is based on the systems approach.

The purpose of the model is to present visually major decision areas, their interrelationships, and typical information requirements. In each of the areas, decisions and information will be required relating to efficiency, quality, and effectiveness of the service. Each of the elements of the system is discussed below:

1. *Objectives.* Decisions about objectives must be made first. These decisions will determine the type of target group which will be accepted and the level of service to be rendered.

Typically, information will be required on the quantity, quality, and the cost of personnel, facilities, and other resources needed. Information on the need for the service and related community efforts will also be required.

A Conceptual Model of the Interrelationship of Efficiency, Quality, and Effectiveness as Applied to Decision-Making in Health and Welfare

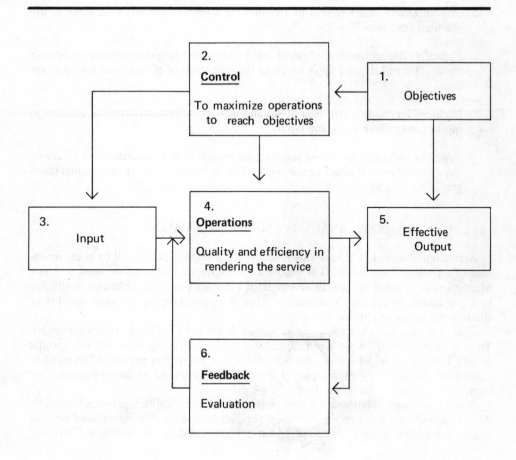

2. *Control.* Decisions must be made on the levels of efficiency, quality, and effectiveness to meet the specified objectives.

Typically, information will be required on the availability of funds, staff, and facilities. Information will also be required on the level of performance in terms of quality and productivity, costs, efficiency, and subsequent changes in objectives.

3. *Input.* Decisions must be made on the number and types of clients accepted. These decisions must be related to the objectives of the service. Decisions must also be made on the specific use of available resources in line with the standards established in control and the nature of the problems accepted.

Typically, information will be required relating to client needs, availability of resources of staff, funds, and facilities which meet quality standards and which match the needs of the client group.

4. *Operations.* Decisions are directed towards monitoring the level of quality and efficiency in rendering the service.

Typically, information will be required in the form of time, cost, and operations data – and data on client progress.

5. *Output.* Decisions are related to assessing the output of the service in terms of the specified objectives.

Typically, the information required will be expressed in quantitative or qualitative terms. This will depend upon which of the four levels of effectiveness measures are used.

Decisions are made which may affect and alter objectives, standards of efficiency, quality, and effectiveness, and inputs.

Typically, information will be required on effectiveness of operations in achieving the specified level of effectiveness, availability of resources and environmental changes.

COST ANALYSIS AND DECISION-MAKING

A concrete illustration of how this model may be applied might well be in the operation of a children's institution. The problem for consideration is that we want to know what is involved in the decison to change from a casework-oriented child care institution to a psychiatrically-oriented residential treatment center, keeping the same number of children and the same physical facilities.

First, we must learn what the quality standards are for a residential treatment center. Then we must convert these standards into specific quality objectives for our specific setting. By illustration, we convert the standard of one caseworker per ten children to five caseworkers for our fifty child capacity. We continue to determine our resource requirements for each quality factor involved.

Second, we must determine the cost of these resources (facilities, personnel, money). At this point, we require cost information for decison-making. The *operational analysis* system for analyzing time, cost, and operations developed by the American University

Project provides a significant source of such time and cost data. In this system it is possible to differentiate between fixed costs which will not change with the altered service and those costs which will vary directly with type and volume of service.

The American University System also provides for the use of time studies which identify the ways in which staff actually distribute their time to the various functions and services of the agency. The administrator can make judgments on the best use and distribution of staff time by first examining the way staff is actually using their time. This permits the agency to determine staff needs. The most efficient use of staff and the cost for professional and other staff can also be determined.

After determining our resource requirements in facilities, personnel, and money, we must then assess our ability to secure additional funds and other resources. Based on our decison as to the availability of resources, we must make other decisions from among a number of alternatives.

1. With adequate financing and availability of staff and facilities, we can proceed as proposed.

2. With inadequate financing, we have three alternatives:

   a. Maintain the proposed quality level and reduce our number of children (the quantity of service),

   b. Maintain the same quantity and reduce quality from the plan,

   c. Determine whether economies can be achieved through efficiency which would permit us to come closer to our desired objectives of both quality and quantity.

Once the decisions have been made as to the objectives, the measure of effectiveness will also be affected. For example, if the decision is to reduce the amount of psychiatric time from standard, we can no longer measure effectiveness on the basis of the original objective of furnishing a specified number of psychiatric hours per day.

In this illustration we have briefly explored decision-making as it may occur in a typical children's institution. The system of cost analysis outlined here is geared toward providing basic information required in a typical children's institution. It should be apparent that the specific nature of a problem will determine the requirements for information in a decision area.

There are other requirements for improved decision-making. When we look at our experience in improving the financial management of children's institutions, we are impressed with certain obstacles which have been encountered. We suggest four prerequisites to upgrading the level of decision-making related to the administration and organization of health and welfare activities: (1) Secure a commitment to improve decision-making, (2) Improve information for decision-making, (3) Recognize the limitations of decision-making, and (4) Upgrade the management capacity of executives in health and welfare.

1. *Secure a commitment to improve decision-making.* A commitment to improve the level of decision-making is necessary. It should be based upon an acceptance of the need to actively seek our decision areas. This calls for an analytical approach to many apparently routine and ongoing processes. First, there must be a recognition by the decision makers at all levels that a decision needs to be made.

Secondly, there should be willingness to invest time in the examination of the problem. Third, there should be a willingness and capacity to examine alternative solutions to a problem. These factors are many times overlooked by the decision makers.

2. *Improve information for decision-making.* It is obvious that improved information is required for improved decision-making. However, we suggest that a priority problem grows from the need to match data to the requirements of the decision-is not the lack of data. We have all types of statistics and cost information. Our problem grows from the need to match data to the requirements of the decision making process. We need to more carefully analyze problem situations in order to gain insights into the requirements for data. We must match data with the right questions. We must develop conceptual models which can be used to select and organize our mass of statistics into useful guides for decison-making.

3. *Recognize the limitations of decision-making.* A serious limitation in decision-making is the non-decisiveness which characterizes those who feel information is not sufficiently accurate, complete, and tested. These persons ignore the time constraints with which they are confronted. The lack of accurate information appears to be a long term liability of the decision-making process in all fields. Relevant information is almost never completely adequate and verifiable.

Implicit in any discussion of decision theory are the limitations of constraints of time and the state of the art. We must recognize that we will probably never have a perfect system. We will never have all the information that we would like to have and perhaps that we need. We should, however, be working to improve the state of the art.

In decision theory the term sub-optimization is used to characterize decisions that must be made with less than what might be considered optimum information.

4. *Upgrade the management capacity of executives in health and welfare.* A fourth prerequisite to improving decision-making in health and welfare is to improve the management ability of executives. There are currently several important attempts at the national level to upgrade the ability of managers of health and welfare organizations. The Family Service Association management development seminar at Arden House is one example; another is the University of Pennsylvania Institute of Administration for Child Welfare Adminstrators. These two institutes, however, are a "drop in the bucket" compared with the widespread need to reach the many persons who came up through the professional ranks to take on administrative jobs without appropriate preparation.

A SUGGESTED ROLE FOR WELFARE COUNCIL RESEARCHERS

Welfare planning researchers are in a unique position to give leadership to defining the significant decision areas which lead to improved social welfare. The following opportunities are suggested:

1. At the most basic level, there is a responsibility to question current practices of collecting static, descriptive statistics. Someone must assess the importance, relevancy, and utilization of the data collected to significant decision areas. This point must be taken seriously in this era of the computer in which we can produce data at amazing speeds and relatively low cost which may in fact be nothing more than "noise".

2. There is an opportunity to develop theories which can organize statistics into useful guides for decision-making. Theories give rise to experimentation, experimentation stimulates new theory. Use of models, theory statements, and experimentation are required to operationalize many of the variables encountered in decision-making — "quality", "efficiency", "effectiveness", and "productivity".

3. Finally, there is an opportunity for innovation. The opportunities lie not in the discovery of new tools and methods, but in the discovery of their applications to welfare needs.

In this innovative process we should gain the ability to apply definitions and terms used in other disciplines. This will enhance communications and avoid unnecessary obstacles to utilization of the professional resources available to us.

The opportunity for dynamic research and to serve as a vital and necessary link in improving the decision-making process in the administration of health and welfare services is available to health and welfare councils today.

The Management Function
in Planning Human Care Services

ARTHUR H. KRUSE

My focus is on the function of management in community planning to bring about more effective social services. This choice has been made for several reasons, the first of which is the under-emphasis which our field has given to the role of management in community social planning. This lack of attention is related to the disparagement of administration as a social work practice, and the failure of social work to make significant contributions to the practice of administration. This lack of interest in social work administration explains, in part, why social work has ignored its role in bringing about social change.

Public and business administration literature abounds with theory and experience dealing with planning for change. Much of the social work literature on community social planning talks about comprehensive, problem-focused community planning as if it were something which floats vaguely through the air and only occasionally comes down to earth in the social welfare marketplace, where answers are found to such questions as: How do we finance and staff what services to serve which objectives, and with what results? An even more important question is: How do we get existing social service programs to change, and in what way?

Let us turn to a second reason for the emphasis of this paper. In 1937 Porter R. Lee wrote a significant book with the title, *Social Work as Cause and Function*. For all of the years since Porter Lee's book, the duality of cause and function has been debated and has given more satisfaction to the advocates of either side than has any other pleasant social work controversy. As the dialogue goes, the answer is not to change the individual but to reform society; progress will be made not by advocacy but by service; change the world and people will take care of themselves. *Cause* in social work parlance has been identified with an end and not an accomplishment. Another word for *cause* is *purpose* or *goals*. It is interesting that *cause* is used most frequently when the ends are in the area of social reform, and *purpose* or *goals* are the terms used when applied to the aims of an organization performing a function. Actually, *cause* and *purpose* have the same meaning if treated as means and not ends, and if the final test applied to each is the test of accomplishment.

The preoccupation of our field with the duality of cause and function is equaled by its concern about the duality of saving the world and saving the individual. This duality is expressed in terms of expanding opportunity vs. expanding the capacity of the individual to take advantage of opportunity, or the objective of reforming society vs. changing the individual. These two dualities of cause and function, and society and the individual, are related to each other and both in turn are related to understanding the role

Reprinted from The Management Function in Planning Human Care Services, *1967, by special permission of the United Community Funds and Councils of America, Inc.*

of management in planning. The advocates of cause are identified with the reform of society, and an emphasis on function is associated with services and changing the individual. But is it not so, that the objective of managing an efficient and effective social service is a noble cause, and the objective of community reform, if properly carried out, requires a well-managed function?

In the case of the duality of society and the individual, William Gordon states a position to my satisfaction when he says,

> Social work has traditionally been concerned with the plight of those in whom the potential, as well as the opportunities, for growth was at such a minimum that survival was often the paramount concern. Survival is obviously a necessary but certainly not a sufficient end for us to seek for people; and here is where a different emphasis, if not a different explanation, could well open the door to science in social work. If our goal for people, the object of our effort and the criterion of our success, becomes self-realization for people, and the base of our expertise the part played in this by social functioning patterns, we open the largely undeveloped area of inquiry with unlimited and fascinating opportunities for research. Social functioning becomes the beginning of our social work concern, not the end. . . . [1]

A final observation about cause and function has to do with the fact that the test of accomplishment must be applied equally to cause and function. A significant function and a noble cause are equally lacking without this test; a cause remains a pious hope and a function a labor without meaning. Except for restating age-old moral principles and seeking their wider acceptance, a cause is tested in terms of creating a function, and this is not the final test because the function is tested in terms of outcomes. Civil Rights, our major social reform thrust, provides a good example to use in examining this thesis. It is concerned with moral issues and the acceptance of basic principles of decent human relationships. More important, Civil Rights and Equal Job Opportunity laws end up having to be administered and enforced. Non-segregated education has to be managed and practiced. Open housing requires the management of its goals. The gains will come not in terms of "How do you feel about me?" but, "What will you do for me?" The ultimate test of the guaranteed minimum income, as another example, is not the passage of the law but the administration of the program which the law creates and whether or not the actual accomplishments measure up to the theory of the projected outcomes. All social legislation, whether it is an Urban Renewal program or ADC, like many medicines, produces negative side outcomes which could not be foreseen and a totality of gains which fall far short of the dream.

The major problem in planning for change is not to achieve better cause statements but the examination and revision of goals and purpose in relation to existing service systems and programs. I recognize that persons are needed whose goals are so advanced that neither they nor their ideas can find acceptance from those who are responsible for the management of existing goals. Let us be reminded though, that Camelot remains beautiful as a legend but fades with the test of reality. Cause becomes tarnished by function because this is where the tire hits the road. Our cause investment should be directed more toward influencing the management of public and voluntary services which haven't yet begun to translate into reality the cause objectives of 20 years ago, or 100 years ago. Management must be held accountable for effecting change in cause as well as function, and the major social change forces should concentrate their efforts on social work management to this end. To ignore the existing management structures, as we have, may give a false illusion of progress, a sense of purity and idealism unadulterated by the smell of the marketplace, but this is only playing games in Camelot.

---

[1] William Gordon, "Toward a Social Work Frame of Reference," *Journal of Education for Social Work*, Fall, 1965.

Let us examine community planning as it is viewed in community organization literature. This will serve as a background to our discussion of the management function in relation to community planning. Community organization practice has been contaminated by its confusion about the relationship of community planning and administrative planning. This reflects the under-emphasis of social work education on administration and also the fact that most people in community organization practice have never administered a service of the kind for which they are planning. This may explain why much that is currently vital in social planning is associated with the operation of services and not central planning bodies. As an illustration of this fact, the growth of public social services has been accompanied by a substantial development of governmental planning as a part of agency administration.

Quite a shock was delivered to the voluntary sector in 1963, when Charles I. Schottland, once Commissioner of Social Security in the Department of Health, Education, and Welfare, delivered an address at the National Social Welfare Forum on "Federal Planning for Health and Welfare."[2] He stated that Federal agencies are spending millions of dollars on welfare planning which is significant and large, and is going to become more so. His main point was that this is the only way to plan the development of public programs, and the future will see the continued improvement of governmental planning at all levels. One key quote is useful, "One thing which the Federal programs are demanding is a plan. They cannot be content with coordination, or citizen participation, or social action alone. They require specific social plans."

Martin Rein and Frank Riessman furnish a perspective on the public agency challenge to voluntary planning in their discussion of the vitality of planning in the Community Action Program of O.E.O. in coordinating and delivering services. They observe, "Public planning is threatening voluntary planning, much as government responsibility for dispensing relief in the 1930's challenged the function of the family agencies and propelled them into new direction."[3] They explore public and voluntary relationships, and discuss the dilemma of social planning, traditional and new, in trying to increase the coherence of the community welfare system without decreasing the autonomy of social welfare agencies: One final quote bears on our discussion, "Social planning has not been able to reconcile its advocacy for directive policy with its faith in the vitality of an undirected, individualistic, market-oriented society."[4] Without further evidence, although much is available, we conclude that public social welfare, the dominant welfare sector, will continue to plan for its own future with its own technical planning resources, that influence on this planning will generate primarily within the political area, and that voluntary welfare councils as now constituted and operated will have a minimum future impact on these developments.

We consider now what some people are saying more specifically about current voluntary community planning. Robert H. MacRae, former Executive Director of the Welfare Council of Metropolitan Chicago and now Associate Executive Director of the Chicago Community Trust, has been a leader for many years in the voluntary planning sector. In a recent analysis of the state of voluntary planning councils, he summarizes as follows:

Looking ahead, I see the evolution of a social planning function within Government. I see the continuance of the voluntary social planning council in large communities, but with its functions more sharply defined. It will be concerning itself

---

[2] Charles I. Schottland, "Federal Planning for Health and Welfare," *Social Welfare Forum Proceedings*, 1963.

[3] Martin Rein and Frank Riessman, "A Strategy for Antipoverty Community Action Programs," *Social Work*, April, 1966.

[4] *Ibid.*

more fully in developing the effectiveness of the voluntary system of services. It will become engaged more actively in research and demonstration activities. It will struggle with the definition and development of public policy. It will serve as the constructive critic and watchdog of the public system of services.[5]

With most of this I would agree; my question concerns the feasibility of accomplishing these objectives in the light of past performance.

Several additional quick references to show how this scene is viewed and then we will proceed to the management function in planning. Franklin M. Zweig and Robert Morris, in the April, 1966, issue of *Social Work*, state, "One of the most salient features of social work practice at the community level is the virtual absence of capacity to formulate comprehensive social plans."[6]

At the 1965 Social Welfare Forum Alvin L. Schorr said, "If councils are to do the over-all job, they must diversify their income and leadership, following the service for which they plan. If it was ever possible for councils to succeed in doing this over-all job, it may now be too late."[7] This quotation properly refers to the need for a vital connection between the planning function and the management of the services which are involved in the planning. This observation bears on our contention that significant planning is going to take place in direct relation to service management.

Elmer J. Tropman, Executive Director, Health and Welfare Association of Allegheny County, Pennsylvania, is one of the strong leaders in the field of community planning. On September 29, 1966, he presented a lead-off paper on the *Future Role of the Council* at a national conference of executives from the 35 largest welfare councils in the United States. Mr. Tropman's conclusions are significant and enlightening:

The traditional Council is at a crossroad. It has three choices:

1. It can move in the direction of becoming more *service-oriented*. This would make it more a departmental operation of the United Fund, more of a Council of Social Agencies, or at least more concerned with agency problems. This is a perfectly respectable role but it is a limited one.

2. It can continue to remain as it is. This might be a trifle frustrating because its resources in money and manpower (both professional and lay) are insufficient to fill the role it has projected for itself. I doubt if we can long function on this basis.

3. It can move in the direction of a non-partisan problem-centered voluntary planning body.

   This will require a commitment to this objective on the part of our leadership and some changes in scope, program emphases, financing, staff and citizen support to make it a reality.[8]

With Mr. Tropman's second point I would agree completely; with his third point I would observe that this is a dream which has been discussed for years and few of the requirements which he sets forth as essential ingredients for carrying it out appear on the

---

[5] Robert H. MacRae, "Over-all Community Planning — How and By Whom?" Conference of the Council on Foundations, Inc. Printed speech, May 20, 1965.

[6] Franklin M. Zweig and Robert Morris, "The Social Planning Design Guide: Process and Proposal," *Social Work*, April, 1966.

[7] Alvin L. Schorr, "The Future Structure of Community Services," Social Welfare Forum, 1965 *Proceedings*.

[8] Elmer J. Tropman, "The Future Role of the Council." Mimeographed speech, 1966.

horizon. The question is whether or not they ever will. His first choice bears directly on the contention of this paper; i.e., that community planning which is service (management) oriented has never really been tried in the light of the present technology of social problems and services, organizational management competence, and the complexities of planning for change.

Our emphasis so far on what is wrong could give one an unbalanced view of the present strength and weakness of the voluntary planning program and, even more important, lead to a too discouraging picture of community organization practice as a vocation. Make no mistake, there is no more important social work practice than community organization and administration. It is on this level that social workers will influence the community and agency policy decisions which will determine the future course of social welfare. The issue of whether one practices community organization in a public or voluntary setting is academic.

Critical examinations of community social planning structure, function and method should serve as a challenge for those who wish to occupy future positions of great responsibility and reward. There will be more planning in the future rather than less, and more social workers would equip themselves for this demanding role.

Recently, United Community Funds and Councils of America has published a position statement of the current planning programs and directions which are being taken by the major voluntary welfare system of our country.[9] As we seek to change and improve our planning efforts, we should be reminded that there are in the United States 500 professionally staffed Welfare Councils, 2,100 United Funds, and some 3,000 professional community organization staff employed at an average annual salary of $12,000. Our objective is not to destroy but to improve the effectiveness of these programs and to bring about a new rationale for the relationship of community planning and administrative planning.

We come now to a discussion of why we believe community planning must relate to administration in a different fashion. Community planning should not ignore community social policy, problem solving planning and inter-agency coordination, but it must relate these to a primary focus on management's own planning responsibility. Only if voluntary community planning comes to terms with this idea, rather than going around it, will its accomplishment meet the ultimate test of planning — translation of plans into operations. Architects don't live by or get judged by fine drawins. Artists do, but not architects, and this may be a useful distinction. The test of an architect's plans has to do with what is built: how does it look? Whom does it serve? How efficiently does it operate? And what are the aesthetic and utilitarian consequences for human beings? Should social planning meet any lesser standards of judgment?

Some of the under-emphasis of social work on administration is being corrected as a result of the activation of the Council on Social Work Administration by NASW. Following a two-day meeting at the Columbia University Greystone Conference Center in September 1966, a steering committee prepared a draft statement under the title, "Social Work Administration: A Framework for Advancing Knowledge and Practice." The following quote from the first part of the document suggests some of the possibilities in the connection between administration and planning:

> The keystone for optimum efficiency and effectiveness in the achievement of social work goals in a changing society is the *administration* of social work programs. Such programs may be under public or voluntary auspices. Their scope may be broad or narrow. Their supporting or operating structures may be gigantic or

---

[9] "The Role of Community Health and Welfare Councils," pamphlet, United Community Funds and Councils of America: 1966.

376

small in scale. The quality and nature of their administration in large measure determine both the potential for, and the realization of their success.

Rapid acceleration of social work expansion and the unprecedented formation of a multiplicity of new social agencies and programs contribute to the growing concern about the extent to which traditional programs are effective instruments for the solution of social problems. It is therefore imperative for the social work profession to identify and assess the elements that contribute to successful social work administration.

In order further to appreciate the relation of administration to planning, a few comments are appropriate about the nature of administration. The content of administration – the responsibility of management – may be described as follows:

Planning – determination of what is to be done and what it takes to do it. Planning is a definite function which must be identified and organized if it is to be properly carried out. As a part of social administration, it is related to the concepts of research and development in private business. The execution of this function requires internal organization for this purpose and consideration of external forces which bear on change; i.e., knowledge developments, public and voluntary relationships, other agency operational developments, and changing community conditions and needs. Broad policy formulation should be organized so that future directions can be established in the face of internal staff resistance to change and external pressures to preserve the status quo.

Execution of organizational objectives. The necessary organizational structures and a framework of policy and administrative practice must be established to achieve the planned objectives. Resources of staff, money and property must be secured and administered. A climate should exist which stimulates staff to a high level of performance and involves their participation in not only doing the job but also planning for change.

Evaluation of accomplishment – accountability for efficiency and effectiveness. This completes the circle of administration. Plans are developed and executed, but the final step is to examine one's accomplishment, and the efficiency and effectiveness of execution. Were the program objectives the right ones, and, if not, how should they be changed? Were the resources of staff and money adequate and, if not, how can they be improved? In providing the answers to such questions as these, planning becomes a constant process of examining existing ends and means, and has a vital connection with the competence that is required to do the current job.

This gets at the crux of planning; i.e., who has the competence to do it? In business, the research and operating competence that have made the business successful in the past and present is the stuff out of which change comes for the future. The average community planning staff does not possess the expertness about social work content, research or management that is necessary to give strong leadership to planning. Maybe the past emphasis of the planning field on staff as enablers properly reflected its planning competence and properly rationalized it.

A dramatic example of a change breakthrough which illustrates the relatedness of operations, research and planning is the story of the evolution of the jet engine. The critical ratio that describes the efficiency of a motor is the amount of horsepower generated in relation to each pound of weight of the engine. With piston engines, the ratio started at .20, jumped quickly to .35, then gradually increased to .76 and flattened out at .99. All this took place over some 40 years. The development of a new approach, the jet engine, took off at a new ratio of 2.7 and has been climbing ever since. This is what happens when a major breakthrough in technique occurs. This is the kind of change breakthrough social work must achieve and hasn't. Social work is now a highly technical business and planning for its change has to be organized to mobilize existing competence in harness with substantially expanded research – all as a part of administrative operations geared to change.

377

The functions of administration are generic to any setting; business, government, and the voluntary agency. Business and public administration literature[10] emphasizes the role of change and planning; without this, business management would not survive. Such students of administration as Chris Argyris,[11] Peter Drucker,[12] Rensis Likert,[13] and others establish planning as a highly technical and complex function which is an integral part of the total administration of an enterprise. Time does not permit further documentation of this point of view, and I will add it up by saying that *planning is too important a matter for any organization responsible for administering a significant function to delegate its planning responsibilities to someone else.*

If social work administration is to carry out the major responsibility for planning, it must be organized and administered to do so. *In the light of this focus on management's responsibility for planning, the two major objectives of community planning agencies should be: (1) Bring about a system of large multifunction agencies whose structures and management enable them to deal properly with the complexity of modern social problems and to staff a program of planned change, and (2) Provide the central leadership and resources which supplement the planning resources of the agency structures and help relate their planning to each other, and to the larger community. This approach is different from the present platform of community planning councils, which is to substitute their planning responsibility for that of the agencies.*

An example of a community planning approach to encourage sound agency administration is one currently being taken by the Community Fund of Chicago to improve the package of voluntary services which it helps to finance. This approach grows out of a directive of the Chicago Community Fund Board of Directors which states that the Fund should take all necessary steps to improve the efficiency and effectiveness of its member agencies. During the past year, as one example of the results of this program, 15 agencies have merged with the consequence of stronger administrative structures and programs. A statement of the kind of thinking which guides this program is taken from the 1966 Annual Report of the Chicago Community Fund:

> There are some technical aspects of agency management which are often not identified or understood. These relate to executive responsibility for management leadership – stimulating and executing a program of planned change, expanding the agencies' resources of personnel and money, and administering the agencies' services within a framework of accountability. Even if a small agency has a good board and a good executive, does it possess the necessary tools to develop and maintain an effective program? If an executive is unable to delegate to his associates large portions of his responsibility for agency functioning, he is not going to be able to function as an executive. One might say that he ends up being a part-time everything – accountant, personnel director, program supervisor, group worker, case worker, fund raiser, public relations director, building superintendent, research expert, and executive. Our point of view holds that the executive can be an executive only if his position permits him to do those things which uniquely are the responsibility of an executive: Relating the organization to the external community, determining direction, formulating policy and developing and managing the agency's resources.

We come to the identification of the two areas within which one looks for the

[10] Wallace G. Lonergan, "The Management of Change" and "The Management Role in Community Development," *Public Management*, December, 1965, and January, 1966.

[11] Chris Argyris, *Organization and Innovation* (Richard D. Irwin, Inc., Homewood, Illinois, 1965).

[12] Peter Drucker, *The Practice of Management* (Harper & Row, New York, 1957).

[13] Rensis Likert, *New Patterns of Management* (McGraw-Hill, New York, 1961).

answers to the question, 'When is an agency large enough?' One of these areas has to do with having program staff of sufficient size and competence to provide effective services. The second area has to do with those supporting specialized skills and ancillary services which make possible the performance of the agency's functions. Regardless of variations in an agency's functions. Regardless of variations in an agency's functions. Regardless of variations in an agency's service demands, the following considerations are always present and cannot be ignored in determining the staffing patterns which are necessary for good agency functioning. In turn, any conclusions with respect to these considerations directly bear on the size of the organization.

1. Staff continuity to counteract the negative impacts of the tremendous turnover rate in our field. If there are only two positions and one person leaves, there is a 50 percent turnover, whereas if there are 10 positions and two people leave, there is only a 20 percent turnover.
2. Different levels of skill and experience. It is important for an agency to have a well-balanced program staff, some of whom are young in experience, others who are in a middle group, and those who are advanced in their skills.
3. Diversity in points of view. This can come about only as a number of staff are brought together in a team operation.
4. Professional stimulation for staff development and performance growing out of staff inter-action.
5. A variety of staff viewpoints which contribute to agency policy formulation and help to evaluate its accomplishments.
6. Staff of sufficient size to relieve the executive of performing direct program functions and from having to devote an undue amount of effort to internal program leadership.

There is reason to believe that the complexity of changing social problems is such that only an organization which possesses a high level of professional skills and management competence can produce effective services. In addition to sufficient program staff which meets the previous considerations, one may wonder how a voluntary welfare agency can be fully effective unless it possesses such management ingredients as:

1. Specilized competence in personnel management.
2. Specialized expert approaches to public relations and fund raising.
3. Proper management of financial and business affairs.
4. Expertness in fact finding and research, and an objective program seeking to measure the effectiveness of agency results.

This perspective on and approach to agency management's responsibility provides a new platform for any central planning effort as it seeks to influence planning for human care needs. Instead of starting with the global approach and ending up with little influence on existing services, one should start with the existing services and their planning responsibilities, and expand the perspective vertically (local, state, and national) and horizontally (area and problem scope) as this is appropriate.

This brings us to our second objective of community planning agencies, which is to provide central leadership and resources which supplement and influence the planning resources and efforts of agency operations. The major ingredients in such a comprehensive program directed toward strengthening the effectiveness and efficiency of agency operations and planning activities are as follows:

1. Functional financial accounting.
2. More precise service accounting.

3. Unit cost analysis.
4. Evaluation of program accomplishment.
5. Functional clarification of agency service goals and establishment of service priorities.
6. Use of job study methodology and effective personnel administration.
7. Management consultation directed toward the development of sound agency structures and their proper administration.

The central planning organization should adopt a framework of principles and policy incorporating these elements in its partnership relationships with participating member agencies. Allocations of funds should reward efficiency and effectiveness and every encouragement should be given to agencies to carry out this seven-point program. The central planning organization should be staffed to provide agencies with the specialized technical competence to help implement this program as well as provide general management consultation. Without these ingredients, it is not possible for an organization to evaluate properly its current accomplishments or to plan for change. The elaboration of these points would take several additional papers, one on each subject. These are highly technical subjects; most voluntary agencies are not beginning to staff and practice these approaches in an elementary fashion and most welfare planning organizations neither understand this approach nor are equipped to give leadership to agencies in carrying them out. To put it plainly, the welfare planning field and most welfare agency administrators are in kindergarten when it comes to having the management and research substance out of which planning for change can become meaningful.

Traditional community planning approach might well modify its existing programs by moving in the directions I have just indicated. Instead of dealing with agencies at arm's length, the community planning agency should join in a close partnership with them. It should develop its central resources of staff and functions with a primary goal of facilitating administrative change. It should provide central services which, when added to the ingredients present in the agency structures, add up to the total elements required for planning change. This means increasing tenfold our emphasis on research, with agencies and planning bodies joining in this endeavor with university research centers. Every agency cannot have skilled personnel management personnel, cost accounting expertness, program analysis specialists, qualitative research skills or all of the ingredients necessary for administering and planning the program effectively. I believe that a sensation would be created by the first community planning council that would staff itself in a way to help its member agencies develop an effective management of their existing programs and to implement a program of planned change.

This does not mean that the central planning organization settles just for what the agencies want, but it does mean that a framework of goals and objectives would be developed, the end product of which is not the glorification of the central planning organization and its planning activities, but rather a system of efficient and effective operating services with its own planning prowess.

In conclusion, we would observe that some of the flavor of present community planning appears to be related to the monolithic atmosphere of social work itself. Social work is not a monolithic force for good, even though some of its members act as if this is so. We should respect the values of a pluralistic social work community in a pluralistic society. Social work systems can compete with each other to their mutual advantage and the advantage of the community. Social work doesn't need more consensus but it does need more healthy differences. All social workers don't need to work to prove they are for the right things by simultaneously working to expand voluntary services, seeking better social welfare legislation, expanding public services or improving social work practice. Within social work there should be an opportunity for a vigorous vocational and professional pursuit of objectives which are not the total objectives of social work but a specific and more limited objective of human betterment.

I believe that voluntary planning is no substitute for the deficiencies of planning in the public sector. The magnitude of public social service is such that it must continue in the future, as it has already, to develop its own planning instrumentalities. Any deficiencies in resources for planning and interagency coordination must be corrected within the governmental structures themselves. Local, state and national voluntary planning organizations can act as outside consultants and critics. They will never have but a minor influence on public planning and surely will not be able to compensate for its weaknesses.

The significance of the voluntary community social planning program is to be found in terms of the importance of the voluntary social welfare sector itself and the vigor of the influence of voluntary planning efforts on the voluntary welfare system. I predict that the voluntary welfare sector will be more vigorous ten years from now than it is today. A proper objective for our society and for government is the elimination of poverty. For social work as a profession to identify its primary reason for existence with serving the poor is to eliminate it as a significant force in our community. One does not build a vocation or a profession on a cause. This point of view bears on the future importance of the voluntary welfare sector, which is expressed in the following two observations:

> The war on poverty is not just a war on economic poverty – it is a war on the poverty of ideas, ideals and incentive. The voluntary human care program must be in the forefront of this poverty war. The mass attack must be government's, but the voluntary agency has a major role to play in helping to develop the living skills of the economically disadvantaged, living skills which are essential for healthy family life and successful individual performance.
>
> Social problems are not related exclusively or even primarily to economic poverty. Social poverty – the poverty of total human functioning – exists in all income brackets.
>
> Healthy total human functioning without economic opportunity and achievement is almost impossible. The converse is not true. Economic achievement, unfortunately, is no guarantee of healthy total human functioning. Solving serious life adjustment problems is more normal than abnormal in all walks of life.[14]

If voluntary community planning organizations devote their major resources to advancing the objectives of the voluntary sector instead of charging windmills all over the landscape to no avail, they may have a purpose. This purpose could be further served if they joined in a partnership with voluntary agency management in a different fashion than in the past and staffed this relationship with new skills and new objectives.

One final statement on the relationships of social work education and community organization practice. Schools of social work have paid little or no attention to community organization as an area of knowledge and practice until the last few years. Even less attention has been paid to administration and management. This could explain in part the present state of social work leadership in the areas where public policy is shaped. A recent publication of the Council on Social Work Education states that, in 1955, there was not a single school of social work with a concentration in Community Organization; in 1960, there was one school and 85 students, or 1.5 percent of the total enrollment; in 1966, there were 20 schools and 789 students, or 7 percent of the total enrollment. This is progress, but only a small beginning.

Looking ahead over the next twenty years, we need to think of the qualifica-

---

[14] Arthur H. Kruse, "The Future of Voluntary Welfare Services," printed pamphlet (Community Fund of Chicago, 1965).

tions of individuals who occupy key Fund and Council positions in terms other than our current standards. As Funds and Councils emphasize the efficiency and effectiveness of those operating services on whose behalf they are raising funds and planning services, it becomes even more important to evaluate the efficiency and the effectiveness of our central services. As more demands are placed upon the voluntary field to justify its existence in competition with governmental welfare services and to maintain its leadership role, it becomes increasingly necessary that better educated people fill key positions in budgeting, planning and fund raising.[15]

---

[15] Arthur H. Kruse, "The Endless Demand for 'Social Statesmen' in the United Way," *Community*, UCFCA, September-October, 1966.

Bibliography

Additional readings from the literature of social work, business management, and public administration, and from the related fields of psychology, sociology, and political science have been selected for further reference and study. This extensive listing is selective rather than exhaustive in identifying the resources of the vast and rapidly growing literature on the many aspects of administration.

Two categories in the bibliography have been added to the groupings in the volume of Readings: "Classics and Landmarks" and "Compilations." Some of the earlier writings on administration are included in "Classics and Landmarks" which have served as foundations for the subsequent development of administrative literature. "Compilations" includes collections of readings that open still further the way to the available resources on administration.

Note is taken that inclusion of an item in a particular category does not preclude the contents of that item from dealing with additional topics that might be considered appropriate for another category. The arbitrary choice was the editor's difficult decision.

BIBLIOGRAPHY

Overview

Bennis, Warren G. *Organizational Development: Background and Prospects.* Reading, Mass.: Addison-Wesley, 1969.

Charlesworth, James C., ed. "Theory and Practice of Public Administration: Scope, Objectives, and Methods," Philadelphia: American Academy of Political and Social Science (October, 1968).

Council on Social Work Administration. *Social Work Administration: A Framework for Advancing Knowledge and Practice.* New York: National Association of Social Workers, 1968. Brochure.

Donnison, D.V. and Chapman, Valerie. "The Development of Social Administration," *Social Policy and Administration.* London: George Allen & Unwin Ltd., 1965, pp. 15-30.

Glover, E. Elizabeth. "Social Welfare Administration: A Social Work Method," *Child Welfare*, Vol. XLIV, No. 8 (October, 1965), pp. 431-441.

Greenwood, William T. *Managament and Organizational Behavior Theories: An Interdisciplinary Approach.* Cincinnati: South-Western Publishing Co., 1965.

Koontz, Harold. "The Management Theory Jungle," *Academy of Management Journal*, Vol. IV (December, 1961), pp. 174-188.

_____,ed. *Toward a Unified Theory of Management.* New York: McGraw-Hill, 1964.

Kruse, Arthur H. "Peculiarities in the Administration of Health and Welfare Agencies," 1962. Pamphlet.

Lippincott, Earle and Annestad, Elling. "Management of Voluntary Welfare Agencies," *Harvard Business Review* (November-December 1964).

Newland, Chester A. "Current Concepts and Characteristics of Administration," *Child Welfare*, Vol. XLII, 1963, pp. 276.

Pollard, Sidney. *The Genesis of Modern Management.* Cambridge, Mass.: Harvard University Press, 1966.

Presthus, Robert V. "Toward A Theory of Organizational Behavior," *Administrative Science Quarterly* (June, 1958).

Roethlisberger, Fritz J. "Contributions of the Behavioral Sciences to a General Theory of Management," *Toward a Unified Theory of Management.* Koontz, Harold (ed.),New York: McGraw-Hill, 1964, pp. 41-67.

385

Scott, William G. "Organization Theory: An Overview and an Appraisal," *Journal of the Academy of Management*, Vol. 4, No. 1 (April 1961), pp. 7-26.

Selznick, Philip. "Foundations of the Theory of Organization," *American Sociological Review*, Vol. 13 (February 1948), pp. 25-35.

Simon, Herbert A. "Comments on the Theory of Organizations," *American Political Science Review*, Vol. 46, No. 4 (December, 1952), pp. 1130-1139.

Spencer, Sue. "The Nature of Administration in Social Work," *The Administration Method in Social Work Education*. New York: Council on Social Work Education, 1959, pp. 8-32.

Stewart, Rosemary. *The Reality of Management*. London: Pan Books Ltd., 1963.

Strother, George B. "Problems in the Development of A Social Science of Organization," *The Social Science of Organization*, Harold J. Leavitt (ed.), Englewood Cliffs, N.J.: Prentice-Hall, 1963.

Warham, Joyce. *An Introduction to Administration for Social Workers*. New York: The Humanities Press, 1967.

Classics and Landmarks

Appleby, Paul L. *Policy and Administration*. University, Alabama: University of Alabama Press, 1949.

Barnard, Chester I. *The Functions of the Executive*. Cambridge, Mass.: Harvard University Press, 1938.

Fayol, Henri. "General Principles of Management," *General and Industrial Management*. London: Sir Isaac Pitman & Sons, Ltd., 1967, pp. 19-42.

Follett, Mary Parker. "Coordination," *Freedom and Co-ordination*. L. Urwick (ed.), London: Management Publications Trust, Ltd., 1949.

Gulick, Luther and Urwick, Lyndall, eds. *Papers on the Science of Administration*. New York: Institute of Public Administration, 1937.

Learned, Edmund P., Ulrich, David N. and Booz, Donald R. *Executive Action*. Boston: Graduate School of Business Administration, Harvard University, 1951.

Mayo, Elton. "Hawthorne and the Western Electric Co.," *The Social Problems of an Industrial Civilization*. Boston: Graduate School of Business Administration, Harvard University, 1945.

Merrill, Harwood F. *Classics in Management*. New York: American Management Association, 1960.

Metcalf, H. C. and Urwick, Lyndall, eds. *Dynamic Administration: Collected Papers of Mary Parker Follett*. New York: Harper and Bros., 1942.

Mooney, James. *Principles of Organization*. New York: Harper and Row, 1947.

Rathe, Alex W. *Gantt on Management*. New York: American Management Association, 1961.

Roethlisberger, F. J. and Dickson, William. *Management and Worker*. Cambridge, Mass.: Harvard University Press, 1939.

Selznick, Philip. *TVA and the Grassroots*. Berkeley: University of California Press, 1949.

Simon, Herbert A. *Administrative Behavior*. New York: Macmillan, 1945.

Street, Elwood. *Social Agency Administration*. New York: Harper and Bros., 1948.

Taylor, Frederick W. *Scientific Management*. New York: Harper and Row, 1947.

Weber, Max. "Bureaucracy," from *Max Weber: Essays in Sociology*, H. H. Gerth and C. Wright Mills, eds. Oxford University Press, 1946, pp. 196-244.

Wilson, Woodrow. "The Study of Administration," *Political Science Quarterly*, June 1887, Vol. 2, pp. 209-213. Reprinted December 1941, Vol. 56, pp. 481-506.

Organizational Structure

Aiken, Michael and Hage, Jerald. "Organizational Alienation," *American Sociological Review*, Vol. 31, No. 4 (August 11, 1966), pp. 497-507.

Blau, Peter M., Wolf, V., and Stauffer, Robert E. "The Structure of Small Bureaucracies," *American Sociological Review*, Vol. XXXI (April, 1966), pp. 179-191.

Delany, William. "The Development and Decline of Patrimonial and Bureaucratic Administrations," *Administrative Science Quarterly*, Vol. VII, 1963, pp. 476.

Etzioni, Amitai. "Two Approaches to Organizational Analysis," *Administrative Science Quarterly*, September, 1960.

Fisch, Gerald G. "Line Staff Is Obsolete," *Harvard Business Review* (September-October 1961), pp. 67-69.

Gouldner, Alvin W. "The Secrets of Organization," *Social Welfare Forum*, 1963.

Hall, Richard H. "Bureaucracy and Small Organizations," *Sociology and Social Research*, Vol. XLVII (October, 1963), pp. 38-46.

Hall, Richard, Haas, J. E. and Johnson, N.J. "An Examination of the Blau-Scott and Etzioni Typologies," *Administrative Science Quarterly*, Vol. 12 (June, 1967), pp. 118-139.

Lefton, Mark and Rosengren, William R. "Organizations and Clients: Lateral and Longitudinal Dimensions," *Administrative Science Quarterly*, Vol. XXXI (December, 1966), pp. 802-810.

Likert, Rensis. *New Patterns of Management*. New York: McGraw-Hill, 1961.

Lippert, Gordon, L. "Emerging Criteria for Organization Development," *Personnel Administration*, Vol. 29, No. 3 (May-June, 1966), pp. 6-11.

Litterer, Joseph A. *The Analysis of Organizations*, New York: Wiley, 1966.

Litwak, Eugene. "Models of Bureaucracy Which Permit Conflict," *American Journal of Sociology* (September, 1961), pp. 177-184.

March, James G. and Simon, Herbert A. *Organizations*. New York: John Wiley and Sons, 1958, especially Chapter 5, pp. 112-135.

Marcus, Philip M. and Cafagna, Dora. "Control in Modern Organizations," *Public Administration Review*, XXV, No. 2 (June, 1965).

Mouzelis, Nikos. *Organization and Bureaucracy*. Chicago: Aldine, 1967.

Newman, William H. "Common Ways of Grouping Activities," *Administrative Action: The Techniques of Organization and Management*. Englewood Cliffs, N.J.: Prentice-Hall, Inc., 1953, pp. 125-144.

Palola, Ernest G. "Organizational Types and Role Strains: An Experimental Study of Complex Organizations," *Sociology and Social Research*, Vol. XLI (January, 1967), pp. 171-174.

Presthus, Robert. *The Organizational Society*. New York: Random House, 1962.

Rein, Martin. "Organization for Social Change," *Social Work*, Vol. IX (April, 1964), pp. 32-41.

Rubenstein, Albert H. and Haberstroh, Chadwick J. *Some Theories of Organization*. Homewood, Illinois: Dorsey Press, 1960.

Shipman, George A. "Complexities of Goal Attainment," *Public Administration Review*, Vol. XXIX, No. 2 (March-April, 1969), pp. 210-213.

Smith, Dorothy E. "Front-Line Organization of the State Mental Hospital," *Administrative Science Quarterly*, Vol. 10, No. 4 (December, 1965).

Stein, Herman D. "Administrative Implications of Bureaucratic Theory," *Social Work*, Vol. 6, No. 3 (July, 1961), pp. 14-21.

Thompson, James D., ed. *Approaches to Organizational Design*. Pittsburgh: University of Pittsburgh Press, 1966.

_____. *Organizations in Action*. New York: McGraw-Hill, 1967.

Urwick, Lyndall. *Notes on the Theory of Organization*. New York: American Management Association, 1952.

White, Orion F., Jr. "The Dialectical Organization: An Alternative to Bureaucracy," *Public Administration Review*, Vol. XXIX, No. 1 (January-February, 1969), pp. 32-42.

Whyte, William F. "Models for Building and Changing Organizations," *Human Organization* (Spring/Summer, 1967).

Wilensky, Harold L., and Lebeaux, Charles N. "Agency Structure and Social Welfare Policy," *Industrial Society and Social Welfare*, Section X. New York: Russell Sage Foundation, 1958, pp. 233-282.

Young, Stanley, "Organization as a Total System," *California Management Review*, Vol. X, No. 3 (Spring, 1968.)

Administration Processes

Beck, Bertram M. "Knowledge and Skills in Administration of an Anti-Poverty Program," *Social Work*, Vol. XI (July, 1966), pp. 102-106.

Brown, David S. "POSDCORB Revisited and Revised," *Personnel Administration*, Vol. 29, No. 3 (May-June, 1966), pp. 33-38.

Drucker, Peter F. *The Effective Executive*. New York: Harper and Row, 1967.

Etzioni, Amitai. "Administrative and Professional Authority," *Modern Organizations*. Englewood Cliffs, N.J.: Prentice-Hall, Inc. 1964, pp. 75-93.

Evans, William M. "Organizational Lag," *Human Organization,* Vol. XXV (Spring, 1966) pp. 51-53.

Granger, Charles H. "The Hierarchy of Objectives," *Harvard Business Review*, Vol. 42, No. 3 (May-June, 1964), pp. 63-74.

Hanlan, Archie. "Counteracting Problems of Bureaucracy in Public Welfare," *Social Work*, Vol. 12, No. 3 (July, 1967), pp. 88-94.

Heany, Donald. "Introducing New Management Techniques Into Your Organization," *Stanford Graduate School of Business Bulletin*, Vol. 34, No. 2 (Autumn, 1965), pp. 18-23.

Marrow, Alfred J. *Management by Participation*. New York: Harper and Row, 1967.

Miller, David and Starr, Martin. *The Structure of Human Decisions*. New York: Prentice-Hall, 1967.

Newman, William H. *Administrative Action*. Englewood Cliffs, N.J.: Prentice-Hall, 1963.

Newman, William, Summer, Charles E., and Kirby, Warren E. "The Management Process," *The Process of Management*. Englewood Cliffs, N.J.: Prentice-Hall, 1967, pp. 9-14.

_____ . "PERT" (Program Review and Evaluation Technique), *The Process of Management*. Englewood Cliffs, N.J.: Prentice-Hall, 1967, pp. 713-717.

Odiorne, George S. *Management By Objectives*. New York: Pitman, 1965.

O'Donnell, Cyril. "Ground Rules for Using Committees," *Management Review*, Vol. 50, No. 10 (October, 1961), pp. 63-67.

Owen, Joseph K. and Eislenben, Robert K. *Modern Concepts of Hospital Administration*. Philadelphia: W. B. Saunders Co., 1962.

Pierrel, Gren O., ed. *The Executive Role in YMCA Administration*. New York: Association Press, 1951.

Redfield, Charles E. *Communication in Management*. Chicago: University of Chicago Press, 1958.

Roy, Robert Hall. *The Administrative Process*. Baltimore: Johns Hopkins Press, 1958.

Simon, Herbert A. "Administrative Decision-Making," *Public Administration Review*, Volume XXV, 1965, pp. 31-37.

Spencer, Sue W. "The Administrative Process in a Social Welfare Agency," *Social Welfare Administration*, Ella W. Reed, ed. New York: Columbia University Press, 1961, pp. 30-49.

Thompson, James. "The Administrative Process," *Organizations in Action*. New York: McGraw-Hill, 1967, pp. 144-158.

Trecker, Harleigh B. *New Understandings of Administration*. New York: Association Press, 1961.

Wilensky, Harold L. *Organizational Intelligence*. New York: Basic Books, 1967.

Man in Administration

Argyris, Chris. "Introduction to Individual and Organizational Effectiveness," *Integrating the Individual and the Organization*. New York: John Wiley and Sons, Inc., 1964, pp. 3-19.

_____. *Organization and Innovation*. Homewood, Ill.: Richard D. Irwin, Inc., 1965.

_____. *Personality and Organization*. New York: Harper and Bros., 1957.

_____. *Understanding Organizational Behavior*. Homewood, Ill.: Dorsey Press, 1960.

Aronson, Albert H. "Human Dynamics in Administration," *Social Work Journal*, July, 1950.

Bernthal, Wilmar F. "Contributions of the Behavioral Science Approach," *Academy of Management: Proceedings of the Annual Meeting*, 1963, pp. 21-28.

Cartwright, Dorwin. "Achieving Change in People," *The Planning of Change*, Bennis, Warren G., et al., eds. New York: Holt, Rinehart and Winston, 1964, pp. 698-705.

Davis, Keith. *Human Relations at Work*. New York: McGraw-Hill, 1967.

Dubin, Robert. *Human Relations in Administration*. Englewood Cliffs, N.J.: Prentice-Hall, 1951.

Epstein, Laura. "Differential Use of Staff: A Method to Expand Social Services," *Social Work*, Vol. 7, No. 4 (October, 1962), pp. 66-72.

Etzioni, Amitai. "Modern Organization and the Client," *Modern Organizations*. Englewood Cliffs, N.J.: Prentice-Hall, Inc. 1964, pp. 94-104.

French, David G., et al. "Homans' Theory of the Human Group: Applications to Problems in Administration, Policy and Staff Training in Group Service Agencies," *Journal of Jewish Communal Service*, Vol. 40, No. 4 (Summer, 1964), pp. 46-62.

Gardner, Burleigh and Moore, David G. "Status and Status Hierarchies," *Organizations: Structure and Behavior*, Joseph A. Litterer, ed. New York: Wiley, 1963, pp. 171-178.

Golembiewski, Robert T. "Authority as a Problem in Overlays," *Administrative Science Quarterly*, Vol. IX, No. 1, June, 1964.

Gouldner, Alvin W. "Cosmopolitans and Locals," *Administrative Science Quarterly*, Vol. 2, No. 3 (December, 1957), pp. 282-292.

Homans, George C. *The Human Group*. New York: Harcourt, Brace & Co., 1950.

Katz, Daniel. "Human Interrelationships and Organizational Behavior," *Concepts and Issues in Administrative Behavior*, Sidney Mailick and Edward H. Van Ness, eds. Englewood Cliffs, N.J.: Prentice-Hall, 1962, pp. 166-186.

Katz, Daniel and Robert L. Kahn. *The Social Psychology of Organizations*. New York: John Wiley, 1966.

Kruse, Arthur H. "Psychodynamics of Administration," *Social Welfare Forum 1958, Proceedings of National Conference of Social Welfare*. New York: Columbia University Press, 1958, pp. 166-176.

Lawrence, Paul R. and Seiler, John A. *Organizational Behavior and Administration*. Homewood, Ill.: Irwin Dorsey Press, 1965.

Learned, E. P., Ulrich, D. N., and Booz, D.R. "The Role of An Executive," *Executive Action*. Boston: Harvard Graduate School of Business Administration, 1951, pp. 53-63.

Leavitt, Harold J. *Managerial Psychology*. Chicago: University of Chicago Press, 1958.

Levy, Charles S. "The Executive and the Agency Board," *Journal of Jewish Communal Service*, Vol. XXXVIII, No. 1 (Spring, 1962), pp. 234-248.

Litterer, Joseph A. "The Informal Organization," *Organizations: Structure and Behavior*. New York: Wiley, 1963, pp. 138-145.

McGregor, Douglas. "Leadership and the Conditions of Organizational Effectiveness," *Public Health Reports*, LXVII, No. 1 (January, 1952).

McMurry, Robert N. "Conflicts in Human Values," *Harvard Business Review*, Vol. 41, No. 3 (May-June, 1963), pp. 130-145.

Montgomery, H. "Practice of Administration: The Role of the Executive," *Child Welfare* (February, 1962).

Morgan, Ralph W. "Completed Staff Work in Social Service Administration," *Social Work*, Vol. 3, No. 4 (October, 1958), pp. 52-57.

_____. "Role Performance by Social Workers in A Bureaucracy," *Social Work Practice*. New York and London: National Conference on Social Welfare by Columbia University Press, 1962, pp. 111-126.

Olmsted, C. B. "Some Management Principles of Staffing Social Welfare Organizations," *Social Work* (July, 1961), pp. 22-28.

Osborn, Phyllis R. "Meeting the Needs of People: An Administrative Responsibility," *Social Work*, Vol. 3, No. 3 (July, 1958), pp. 70-75.

Parkinson, C. Northcote. *Parkinson's Law*. Boston: Houghton Mifflin Co., 1957, pp. 2-7.

Piven, Herman and Pappenfort, Donnell M. "Strain Between Administrator and Worker: A View From the Field of Corrections," *Social Work*, Vol. 5, No. 4 (October, 1960), pp. 37-45.

Presthus, Robert V. "Authority in Organizations," *Concepts and Issues in Administrative Behavior*, Sidney Mailick and Edward H. Van Ness, eds. Englewood Cliffs, N.J.: Prentice-Hall, 1962, pp. 122-136.

Rubington, Earl. "Organizational Strains and Key Roles," *Administrative Science Quarterly*, Vol. IX, No. 4 (March, 1965), pp. 350-369.

Schatz, Harry A. *Staff Involvement in Agency Administration*. New York: National Association of Social Workers, 1965.

Schmidt, William D. "The Function of the Executive," *The Executive and the Board in Social Welfare*. Cleveland: Howard Allen, 1959, pp. 25-37.

Sherman, Harvey. *It All Depends*. University of Alabama Press, 1966.

Smith, Michael P. "Self-fulfillment in a Bureaucratic Society: A Commentary on the Thought of Gabriel Marcel," *Public Administration Review*, Vol. XXIX, No. 1 (January-February, 1969), pp. 25-31.

Stahl, O. Glenn. "Liberating the Will to Work," *Public Personnel Administration*. New York: Harper and Row, 1962, pp. 197-222.

Stein, Herman D. "Board, Executive and Staff," *Social Welfare Forum, Proceedings of 1962 National Conference on Social Welfare*. New York: Columbia University Press, 1962, pp. 215-230.

_____. "Administrative Leadership in Complex Service Organizations," *National Conference on Social Welfare*, 92nd Annual Forum, May, 1965.

Tannenbaum, Robert and Massarik, Fred. "Leadership: A Frame of Reference," *Management Science*, Vol. 4, No. 1 (October, 1957), pp. 1-19.

Trecker, Harleigh B. "Work With Staff," *New Understandings of Administration*. New York: Association Press, 1961, pp. 181-201.

Wilcox, Herbert G. "Hierarchy, Human Nature and the Participative Panacea," *Public Administration Review*, Vol. XXIX, No. 1 (January-February 1969), pp. 53-64.

Zaleznik, Abraham. "Conflicts in Work, Authority and Self-Esteem," *Human Dilemmas of Leadership*. New York: Harper and Row, 1966, pp. 5-29.

Financial Administration

Bauling, Henry. "The Budgeting Process," *Jewish Social Service Quarterly*, Vol. XXXI, No. 1 (Fall, 1954), pp. 90-95.

Brundage, Percival F. "A Critical Look at the Budget Process," *Public Administration Review*, Vol. XIV (Autumn, 1954).

Community Fund of Chicago, Inc. "Priorities, Part 1: Recommended Criteria for Agency Performance and Priorities of Community Fund Support of Agency Services," 1967.

_____. "Letter to Community Fund Agency Executives." (September 27, 1967). Mimeographed.

Dimock, Marshall E., Dimock, Gladys O., and Koenig, Louis W. "Budget Administration," *Administration*, New York: Rinehart, 1958, pp. 246-260.

Gross, Bertram M. "The New Systems Budgeting," *Public Administration Review*, Vol. XXIX, No. 2 (March-April, 1969), pp. 113-132.

Hathaway, Frank A. "Securing and Controlling Adequate Funds for Current and Capital Fund Financing," *The Executive Role in Y.M.C.A. Administration*, Gren O. Pierrel, ed. New York: Association Press, 1951, pp. 250-282.

Henderson, Louise. *Business Administration Manual for Community YWCAs*. New York: National Board of YWCA, 1962.

Hill, John G., Ormsby, Ralph, and McCurdy, William B. *Time Analysis Manual*. New York: Family Service of America, 1962.

Levine, A. S. "Cost-benefit Analysis and Social Welfare Program Evaluation," *Social Service Review*, Vol. 42, No. 2, pp. 173-183, 1968.

Lewis, Verne B. "Toward A Theory of Budgeting," *Public Administration Review*, Vol. XII (Winter, 1952).

McGilvery, Francis. "Program and Responsibility Cost Accounting," *Public Administration Review*, Vol. XXVIII (March-April, 1968), pp. 148-154.

Mosher, Frederick C. *Program Budgeting*. Chicago: Public Administration Service, 1954.

National Health Council and National Social Welfare Assembly. *Standards of Accounting and Financial Reporting for Voluntary Health and Welfare Organizations*. New York, 1964.

Novick, David, ed. *Program Budgeting*. Cambridge: Harvard University Press, 1965.

Ormsby, Ralph. "Cost Analysis in the Family Field," *Planning Social Services for Urban Needs*. New York: Columbia University Press, 1957, pp. 102-111.

Schick, Allen. *PPB's First Years: Premature and Maturing*. Washington, D.C.: U.S. Bureau of the Budget (September, 1968). Mimeo.

_____. "The Road to PPB: The Stages of Reform," *Public Administration Review*, Vol. XXVI, No. 4, 1966, pp. 243-258.

_____. "Systems Politics and Systems Budgeting," *Public Administration Review*, Vol. XXIX, No. 2 (March-April, 1969), pp. 137-150.

Smithies, Arthur. "The Budgetary Process in the United States," *Public Administration Review*, Vol. X (Winter, 1950).

Therkildsen, Paul and Reno, Philip. "Cost-Benefit Evaluation of a Work Experience and Training Project," *Welfare in Review* (March-April, 1968), pp.1-12.

Thompkins, Leslie, ed. *Association Accounting*. New York: Association Press, 1967.

United Community Funds and Councils of America, Inc. "Projection for the Seventies." New York, 1967.

United Community Funds and Councils of America. *United Fund Budgeting: A Manual of Policies and Procedures*. New York, 1967.

United Fund of the Philadelphia Area. "Voluntary Financing Policy," 1967. Pamphlet.

Wildavsky, Aaron. "The Political Economy of Efficiency: Cost-Benefit Analysis, Systems Analysis and Program Budgeting," *Public Administration Review*, Vol. XXVI, No. 4 (1966), pp. 292-310.

_____. *The Politics of the Budgetary Process*. Boston: Little, Brown & Co., 1964.

_____. "Rescuing Policy Analysis from PPBS," *Public Administration Review*, Vol. XXIX, No. 2 (March-April, 1969), pp. 189-200.

Blau, Peter and Scott, W. Richard. "The Social Context of Organizational Life," *Formal Organizations: A Comparative Approach*. San Francisco: Chandler Publishing Co., 1962.

Cohen, Nathan E. *The Citizen Volunteer*. New York: Harper and Bros., 1960.

Community Funds and Councils of Canada. "Statement on United Fund-Agency Relationships." Ottawa: The Canadian Welfare Council, 1966.

Dill, William R. "The Impact of Environment on Organizational Development," *Concepts and Issues in Administrative Behavior*. Sidney Mailick and Edward H. Van Ness, eds. New York: Prentice-Hall, 1962.

Etzioni, Amitai. "Organization and the Social Environment," *Modern Organizations*. Englewood Cliffs, N.J.: Prentice-Hall, Inc., 1964, pp. 105-116.

_____."Toward a Theory of Societal Guidance,"*American Journal of Sociology*, Vol. 73 (September, 1967), pp. 173-187.

Evan, William M. "The Organization-Set: Toward a Theory of Interorganizational Relations," *Approaches to Organizational Design*, J. D. Thompson, ed. Pittsburgh: University of Pittsburgh Press, 1966, pp. 173-192.

Friedman, Robert S., Klein, Bernard W., and Romani, John H. "Administrative Agencies and the Publics They Serve," *Public Administration Review*, Vol. 24 (September, 1966), pp. 192-204.

Kruse, Arthur H. "The Future of Voluntary Welfare Services," *New Dimensions-The Challange for 1965-70*. Pamphlet, 1965.

Lawrence, Paul R. and Forsch, Jay W. *Organization and Environment*. Boston: Division of Research, Harvard Business School, 1967.

Levin, Herman. "The Essential Voluntary Agency," *Social Work*, Vol. XI (January, 1966), pp. 98-106.

Maniha, J. and Perrow C. "The Reluctant Organization and the Aggressive Environment," *Administrative Science Quarterly,* Vol. 10 (September, 1965), pp. 238-257.

Mencher, Samuel. "Current Priority Planning," *Social Work* (July, 1964), pp. 27-35.

Miller, S. M. and Rein, Martin. "Participation, Poverty and Administration," *Public Administration Review*, Vol. XXIX, No. 1 (January-February, 1969), pp. 15-24.

Nagle, Paul. "The Significance of United Funds and Community Health and Welfare Councils in Urban Affairs." New York: United Community Funds and Councils of America, Inc., 1966.

Pennock, J. Roland and Chapman, John W., eds. *Voluntary Associations*. New York: Atherton Press, 1969.

Pusic, Eugene. "Territorial and Functional Administration in Yugoslavia," *Administrative Science Quarterly*, Vol. 14, No. 1 (March, 1969), pp. 62-72

Schwartz, Jerome L. and Cherin, Milton. "Participation of Recipients in Public Welfare Planning and Administration," *The Social Service Review,* Vol. XLI (March,1967), pp. 10-22.

Simpson, Richard L. and Gulley, William H. "Goals, Enviornmental Pressures, and Organizational Characteristics," *American Sociological Review,* Vol. 27 (1962).

Terreberry, Shirley. "The Evolution of Organizational Environments," *Administrative Science Quarterly*, Vol. 12, No. 4 (March, 1968), pp. 590-613.

Thompson, James D. and McEwen, William J. "Organizational Goals and Environment: Goal-Setting as an Interaction Process," *American Sociological* Review, Vol. 23 (February, 1958), pp.23-31.

Compilations

Bennis, Warren G., et al., eds. *The Planning of Change*. New York: Holt, Rinehart and Winston, 1964.

Cleland, David I. and King, William R., eds. *Systems, Organizations, Analysis Management: A Book of Readings*. New York: McGraw-Hill, 1969.

Fanshell, David, ed. *Research in Social Welfare Administration*. New York: National Association of Social Workers, 1962.

Golembiewski, Robert T., Gibson, Frank K., and Cornog, Geoffrey Y., eds. *Public Administration: Readings in Institutions, Processes, Behavior.* Chicago: Rand McNally & Co., 1968.

Gore, William J. and Dyson, J. W. *The Making of Decisions: A Reader in Administrative Behavior*. New York: Macmillan, 1964.

Koontz, Harold and O'Donnel, Cyril, eds. *Management: A Book of Readings*. New York: McGraw-Hill, 1968.

Lazarus, Harold and Warren, E. Kirby, eds. *The Progress of Management: A Book of Readings*. Englewood Cliffs, N.J.: Prentice-Hall, 1968.

Lepawsky, Albert. *Administration: The Art and Science of Organization*. New York: Alfred A. Knopf, 1949.

Mailick, Sidney and Van Ness, Edward H., eds. *Concepts and Issues in Administrative Behavior.* Englewood Cliffs, N.J.: Prentice-Hall, 1962.

March, James G., ed. *Handbook of Organizations*. Chicago: Rand McNally & Co., 1965.

Merton, Robert K., ed. *Reader in Bureaucracy*. Glencoe, Ill.: The Free Press, 1952.

Moore, Franklin G., ed. *A Management Source Book*. New York: Harper and Row, 1964.

O'Donnell, Maurice E., ed. *Readings in Public Administration*. Boston: Houghton Mifflin, 1966.

Reed, Ella W., ed: *Social Welfare Administration*. New York: Columbia University Press, 1961.

Sisk, Henry L., ed. *Principles of Management*. Cincinnati: South-Western Publishing Co., 1969.

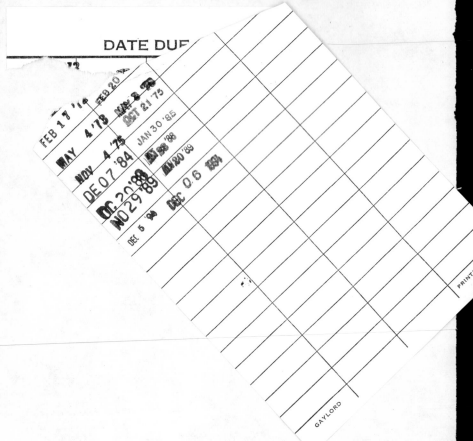